WITNESS

P9-DFF-542

HORATIO: *If thou art privy*

to thy country's fate,

which, happily,

foreknowing may avoid,

O speak—

HAMLET, *Act One, Scene I*

RANDOM HOUSE

NEW YORK

Witness

Whittaker Chambers

First Printing

Published in New York by Random House, Inc.,
and simultaneously in Toronto, Canada, by
Random House of Canada, Limited
Library of Congress Catalog Card Number: 52–5149

Manufactured in the United States of America
by H. Wolff, New York
Designed by Jerome Kuhl

To my wife,

infinitely loving

and infinitely beloved.

CONTENTS

WITNESS

FOREWORD IN THE FORM OF A LETTER TO MY CHILDREN

Beloved Children,

I am sitting in the kitchen of the little house at Medfield, our second farm which is cut off by the ridge and a quarter-mile across the fields from our home place, where you are. I am writing a book. In it I am speaking to you. But I am also speaking to the world. To both I owe an accounting.

It is a terrible book. It is terrible in what it tells about men. If anything, it is more terrible in what it tells about the world in which you live. It is about what the world calls the Hiss-Chambers Case, or even more simply, the Hiss Case. It is about a spy case. All the props of an espionage case are there—foreign agents, household traitors, stolen documents, microfilm, furtive meetings, secret hideaways, phony names, an informer, investigations, trials, official justice.

But if the Hiss Case were only this, it would not be worth my writing about or your reading about. It would be another fat folder in the sad files of the police, another crime drama in which the props would be mistaken for the play (as many people have consistently mistaken them). It would not be what alone gave it meaning, what the mass of men and women instinctively sensed it to be, often without quite knowing why. It would not be what, at the very beginning, I was moved to call it: "a tragedy of history."

For it was more than human tragedy. Much more than Alger

Hiss or Whittaker Chambers was on trial in the trials of Alger Hiss. Two faiths were on trial. Human societies, like human beings, live by faith and die when faith dies. At issue in the Hiss Case was the question whether this sick society, which we call Western civilization, could in its extremity still cast up a man whose faith in it was so great that he would voluntarily abandon those things which men hold good, including life, to defend it. At issue was the question whether this man's faith could prevail against a man whose equal faith it was that this society is sick beyond saving, and that mercy itself pleads for its swift extinction and replacement by another. At issue was the question whether, in the desperately divided society, there still remained the will to recognize the issues in time to offset the immense rally of public power to distort and pervert the facts.

At heart, the Great Case was this critical conflict of faiths; that is why it was a great case. On a scale personal enough to be felt by all, but big enough to be symbolic, the two irreconcilable faiths of our time—Communism and Freedom—came to grips in the persons of two conscious and resolute men. Indeed, it would have been hard, in a world still only dimly aware of what the conflict is about, to find two other men who knew so clearly. Both had been schooled in the same view of history (the Marxist view). Both were trained by the same party in the same selfless, semisoldierly discipline. Neither would nor could yield without betraying, not himself, but his faith; and the different character of these faiths was shown by the different conduct of the two men toward each other throughout the struggle. For, with dark certitude, both knew, almost from the beginning, that the Great Case could end only in the destruction of one or both of the contending figures, just as the history of our times (both men had been taught) can end only in the destruction of one or both of the contending forces.

But this destruction is not the tragedy. The nature of tragedy is itself misunderstood. Part of the world supposes that the tragedy in the Hiss Case lies in the acts of disloyalty revealed. Part believes that the tragedy lies in the fact that an able, intelligent man, Alger Hiss, was cut short in the course of a brilliant public career. Some find it tragic that Whittaker Chambers, of his own will, gave up a $30,000-a-year job and a secure future to haunt for the rest of his days the ruins of his life. These are shocking facts, criminal facts, disturbing facts: they are not tragic.

Crime, violence, infamy are not tragedy. Tragedy occurs when a human soul awakes and seeks, in suffering and pain, to free itself from crime, violence, infamy, even at the cost of life. The struggle is the tragedy—not defeat or death. That is why the spectacle of tragedy has always filled men, not with despair, but with a sense of hope and exaltation. That is why this terrible book is also a book of hope. For it is about the struggle of the human soul—of more than one human soul. It is in this sense that the Hiss Case is a tragedy. This is its meaning beyond the headlines, the revelations, the shame and suffering of the people involved. But this tragedy will have been for nothing unless men understand it rightly, and from it the world takes hope and heart to begin its own tragic struggle with the evil that besets it from within and from without, unless it faces the fact that the world, the whole world, is sick unto death and that, among other things, this Case has turned a finger of fierce light into the suddenly opened and reeking body of our time.

My children, as long as you live, the shadow of the Hiss Case will brush you. In every pair of eyes that rests on you, you will see pass, like a cloud passing behind a woods in winter, the memory of your father—dissembled in friendly eyes, lurking in unfriendly eyes. Sometimes you will wonder which is harder to bear: friendly forgiveness or forthright hate. In time, therefore, when the sum of your experience of life gives you authority, you will ask yourselves the question: What was my father?

I will give you an answer: I was a witness. I do not mean a witness for the Government or against Alger Hiss and the others. Nor do I mean the short, squat, solitary figure, trudging through the impersonal halls of public buildings to testify before Congressional committees, grand juries, loyalty boards, courts of law. A man is not primarily a witness *against* something. That is only incidental to the fact that he is a witness *for* something. A witness, in the sense that I am using the word, is a man whose life and faith are so completely one that when the challenge comes to step out and testify for his faith, he does so, disregarding all risks, accepting all consequences.

One day in the great jury room of the Grand Jury of the Southern District of New York, a juror leaned forward slightly and asked me: "Mr. Chambers, what does it mean to be a Communist?" I hesitated for a moment, trying to find the simplest, most direct way to convey the heart of this complex experience to men and women to whom the very fact of the experience was all but incomprehensible. Then I said:

"When I was a Communist, I had three heroes. One was a Russian. One was a Pole. One was a German Jew.

"The Pole was Felix Djerjinsky. He was ascetic, highly sensitive, intelligent. He was a Communist. After the Russian Revolution, he became head of the Tcheka and organizer of the Red Terror. As a young man, Djerjinsky had been a political prisoner in the Paviak Prison in Warsaw. There he insisted on being given the task of cleaning the latrines of the other prisoners. For he held that the most developed member of any community must take upon himself the lowliest tasks as an example to those who are less developed. That is one thing that it meant to be a Communist.

"The German Jew was Eugen Leviné. He was a Communist. During the Bavarian Soviet Republic in 1919, Leviné was the organizer of the Workers and Soldiers Soviets. When the Bavarian Soviet Republic was crushed, Leviné was captured and court-martialed. The court-martial told him: 'You are under sentence of death.' Leviné answered: 'We Communists are always under sentence of death.' That is another thing that it meant to be a Communist.

"The Russian was not a Communist. He was a pre-Communist revolutionist named Kalyaev. (I should have said Sazonov.) He was arrested for a minor part in the assassination of the Tsarist prime minister, von Plehve. He was sent into Siberian exile to one of the worst prison camps, where the political prisoners were flogged. Kalyaev sought some way to protest this outrage to the world. The means were few, but at last he found a way. In protest against the flogging of other men, Kalyaev drenched himself in kerosene, set himself on fire and burned himself to death. That also is what it meant to be a Communist."

That also is what it means to be a witness.

But a man may also be an involuntary witness. I do not know any way to explain why God's grace touches a man who seems unworthy of it. But neither do I know any other way to explain how a man like myself—tarnished by life, unprepossessing, not brave—could prevail so far against the powers of the world arrayed almost solidly against him, to destroy him and defeat his truth. In this sense, I am an involuntary witness to God's grace and to the fortifying power of faith.

It was my fate to be in turn a witness to each of the two great faiths of our time. And so we come to the terrible word, Communism. My very dear children, nothing in all these pages will be written so much for you, though it is so unlike anything you would want to read. In nothing shall I be so much a witness, in no way am I so much called upon to fulfill my task, as in trying to make clear to you (and to the world) the true nature of Communism and the source of its power, which was the cause of my ordeal as a man, and remains the historic ordeal of the world in the 20th century. For in this century, within the next decades, will be decided for generations whether all mankind is to become Communist, whether the whole world is to become free, or whether, in the struggle, civilization as we know it is to be completely destroyed or completely changed. It is our fate to live upon that turning point in history.

The world has reached that turning point by the steep stages of a crisis mounting for generations. The turning point is the next to the last step. It was reached in blood, sweat, tears, havoc and death in World War II. The chief fruit of the First World War was the Russian Revolution and the rise of Communism as a national power. The chief fruit of the Second World War was our arrival at the next to the last step of the crisis with the rise of Communism as a world power. History is likely to say that these were the only decisive results of the world wars.

The last war simplified the balance of political forces in the world by reducing them to two. For the first time, it made the power of the Communist sector of mankind (embodied in the Soviet Union) roughly equal to the power of the free sector of mankind (embodied in the United States). It made the collision of these powers all but inevitable. For the world wars did not end the crisis. They raised its tensions to a new pitch. They raised the crisis to a new stage. All the politics of our time, including the politics of war, will be the politics of this crisis.

Few men are so dull that they do not know that the crisis exists and that it threatens their lives at every point. It is popular to call it a social crisis. It is in fact a total crisis—religious, moral, intellectual, social, political, economic. It is popular to call it a crisis of the Western world. It is in fact a crisis of the whole world. Communism, which claims to be a solution of the crisis, is itself a symptom and an irritant of the crisis.

In part, the crisis results from the impact of science and technology upon mankind which, neither socially nor morally, has caught up with the problems posed by that impact. In part, it is caused by men's efforts to solve those problems. World wars are the military expression of the crisis. World-wide depressions are its economic expression. Universal desperation is its spiritual climate. This is the climate of Communism. Communism in our time can no more be considered apart from the crisis than a fever can be acted upon apart from an infected body.

I see in Communism the focus of the concentrated evil of our time. You will ask: Why, then, do men become Communists? How did it happen that you, our gentle and loved father, were once a Communist? Were you simply stupid? No, I was not stupid. Were you morally depraved? No, I was not morally depraved. Indeed, educated men become Communists chiefly for moral reasons. Did you not know that the crimes and horrors of Communism are inherent in Communism? Yes, I knew that fact. Then why did you become a Communist? It would help more to ask: How did it happen that this movement, once a mere muttering of political outcasts, became this immense force that now contests the mastery of mankind? Even when all the chances and mistakes of history are allowed for, the answer must be: Communism makes some profound appeal to the human mind. You will not find out what it is by calling Communism names. That will not help much to explain why Communism whose horrors, on a scale unparalleled in history, are now public knowledge, still recruits its thousands and holds its millions—among them some of the best minds alive. Look at Klaus Fuchs, standing in the London dock, quiet, doomed, destroyed, and say whether it is possible to answer in that way the simple question: Why?

First, let me try to say what Communism is not. It is not simply a vicious plot hatched by wicked men in a sub-cellar. It is not just the writings of Marx and Lenin, dialectical materialism, the Politburo, the labor theory of value, the theory of the general strike, the Red Army, secret police, labor camps, underground conspiracy, the dictatorship of the proletariat, the technique of the coup d'état. It is not even those chanting, bannered millions that stream periodically, like disorganized armies, through the heart of the world's capitals: Moscow, New York, Tokyo, Paris, Rome. These are expressions of Communism, but they are not what Communism is about.

In the Hiss trials, where Communism was a haunting specter, but which did little or nothing to explain Communism, Communists were assumed to be criminals, pariahs, clandestine men who lead double lives under false names, travel on false passports, deny traditional religion, morality, the sánctity of oaths, preach violence and practice treason. These things are true about Communists, but they are not what Communism is about.

The revolutionary heart of Communism is not the theatrical appeal: "Workers of the world, unite. You have nothing to lose but your chains. You have a world to gain." It is a simple statement of Karl Marx, further simplified for handy use: "Philosophers have explained the world; it is necessary to change the world." Communists are bound together by no secret oath. The tie that binds them across the frontiers of nations, across barriers of language and differences of class and education, in defiance of religion, morality, truth, law, honor, the weaknesses of the body and the irresolutions of the mind, even unto death, is a simple conviction: It is necessary to change the world. Their power, whose nature baffles the rest of the world, because in a large measure the rest of the world has lost that power, is the power to hold convictions and to act on them. It is the same power that moves mountains; it is also an unfailing power to move men. Communists are that part of mankind which has recovered the power to live or die —to bear witness—for its faith. And it is a simple, rational faith that inspires men to live or die for it.

It is not new. It is, in fact, man's second oldest faith. Its promise was whispered in the first days of the Creation under the Tree of the Knowledge of Good and Evil: "Ye shall be as gods." It is the great alternative faith of mankind. Like all great faiths, its force derives from a simple vision. Other ages have had great visions. They have always been different versions of the same vision: the vision of God and man's relationship to God. The Communist vision is the vision of Man without God.

It is the vision of man's mind displacing God as the creative intelligence of the world. It is the vision of man's liberated mind, by the sole force of its rational intelligence, redirecting man's destiny and reorganizing man's life and the world. It is the vision of man, once more the central figure of the Creation, not because God made man in His image, but because man's mind makes him the most intelligent of the animals. Copernicus and his successors displaced man as the central fact of the universe by proving that the earth was not the central star of the universe, Communism restores man to his sovereignty by the simple method of denying God.

The vision is a challenge and implies a threat. It challenges man to prove by his acts that he is the masterwork of the Creation—by making thought and act one. It challenges him to prove it by using the force of his rational mind to end the bloody meaninglessness of man's history—by giving it purpose and a plan. It challenges him to prove it by reducing the meaningless chaos of nature, by imposing on it his rational will to order, abundance, security, peace. It is the vision of materialism. But it threatens, if man's mind is unequal to the problems of man's progress, that he will sink back into savagery (the A and the H bombs have raised the issue in explosive forms), until nature replaces him with a more intelligent form of life.

It is an intensely practical vision. The tools to turn it into reality are at hand—science and technology, whose traditional method, the rigorous exclusion of all supernatural factors in solving problems, has contributed to the intellectual climate in which the vision flourishes, just as they have contributed to the crisis in which Communism thrives. For the vision is shared by millions who are not Communists (they are part of Communism's secret strength). Its first commandment is found, not in the *Communist Manifesto*, but in the first sentence of the physics primer: "All of the progress of mankind to date results from the making of careful measurements." But Communism, for the first time in history, has made this vision the faith of a great modern political movement.

Hence the Communist Party is quite justified in calling itself the most revolutionary party in history. It has posed in practical form the most revolutionary question in history: God or Man? It has taken the logical next step which three hundred years of rationalism hesitated to take, and said what millions of modern minds think, but do not dare or care to say: If man's mind is the decisive force in the world, what need is there for God? Henceforth man's mind is man's fate.

This vision *is* the Communist revolution, which, like all great revolutions, occurs in man's mind before it takes form in man's acts. Insurrection and conspiracy are merely methods of realizing the vision; they are merely part of the politics of Communism. Without its vision, they, like Communism, would have no meaning and could not rally a parcel of pickpockets. Communism does not summon men to crime or to utopia, as its easy critics like to think. On the plane of faith, it summons mankind to turn its vision into practical reality. On the plane of action, it summons men to struggle against the inertia of the past which, embodied in social, political and economic forms, Communism claims, is blocking the will of mankind to make its next great forward stride. It summons men to overcome the crisis, which, Communism claims, is in effect a crisis of rending frustration, with the world, unable to stand still, but unwilling to go forward along the road that the logic of a technological civilization points out—Communism.

This is Communism's moral sanction, which is twofold. Its vision points the way to the future; its faith labors to turn the future into present reality. It says to every man who joins it: the vision is a practical problem of history; the way to achieve it is a practical problem of politics, which is the present tense of history. Have you the moral strength to take upon yourself the crimes of history so that man at last may close his chronicle of age-old, senseless suffering, and replace it with purpose and a plan? The answer a man makes to this question is the difference between the Communist and those miscellaneous socialists, liberals, fellow travelers, unclassified progressives and men of good will, all of whom share a similar vision, but do not share the faith because they will not take upon themselves the penalties of the faith. The answer is the root of that sense of moral superiority which makes Communists, though caught in crime, berate their opponents with withering self-righteousness.

The Communist vision has a mighty agitator and a mighty propagandist. They are the crisis. The agitator needs no soap box. It speaks insistently to the human mind at the point where desperation lurks. The propagandist writes no Communist gibberish. It speaks insistently to the human mind at the point where man's hope and man's energy fuse to fierceness.

The vision inspires. The crisis impels. The workingman is chiefly moved by the crisis. The educated man is chiefly moved by the vision. The workingman, living upon a mean margin of life, can afford few visions—even practical visions. An educated man, peering from the Harvard Yard, or any college campus, upon a world in chaos, finds in the vision the two certainties for which the mind of man tirelessly seeks: a reason to live and a reason to die. No other faith of our time presents them with the same practical intensity. That is why Communism is the central experience of the first half of the 20th century, and may be its final experience—will be, unless the free world, in the agony of its struggle with Communism, overcomes its crisis by discovering, in suffering and pain, a power of faith which will provide man's mind, at the same intensity, with the same two certainties: a reason to live and a reason to die. If it fails, this will be the century of the great social wars. If it succeeds, this will be the century of the great wars of faith.

You will ask: Why, then, do men cease to be Communists? One answer is: Very few do. Thirty years after the Russian Revolution, after the known atrocities, the purges, the revelations, the jolting zigzags of Communist politics, there is only a handful of ex-Communists in the whole world. By ex-Communists I do not mean those who break with Communism over differences of strategy and tactics (like Trotsky) or organization (like Tito). Those are merely quarrels over a road map by people all of whom are in a hurry to get to the same place.

Nor, by ex-Communists, do I mean those thousands who continually drift into the Communist Party and out again. The turnover is vast. These are the spiritual vagrants of our time whose traditional faith has been leached out in the bland climate of rationalism. They are looking for an intellectual night's lodging. They lack the character for Communist faith because they lack the character for any faith. So they drop away, though Communism keeps its hold on them.

By an ex-Communist, I mean a man who knew clearly why he became a Communist, who served Communism devotedly and knew why he served it, who broke with Communism unconditionally and knew why he broke with it. Of these there are very few—an index to the power of the vision and the power of the crisis.

History very largely fixes the patterns of force that make men Communists. Hence one Communist conversion sounds much like another—rather impersonal and repetitious, awesome and tiresome, like long lines of similar people all stolidly waiting to get in to see the same movie. A man's break with Communism is intensely personal. Hence the account of no two breaks is likely to be the same. The reasons that made one Communist break may seem without force to another ex-Communist.

It is a fact that a man can join the Communist Party, can be very active in it for years, without completely understanding the nature of Communism or the political methods that follow inevitably from its vision. One day such incomplete Communists discover that the Communist Party is not what they thought it was. They break with it and turn on it with the rage of an honest dupe, a dupe who has given a part of his life to a swindle. Often they forget that it takes two to make a swindle.

Others remain Communists for years, warmed by the light of its vision, firmly closing their eyes to the crimes and horrors inseparable from its practical politics. One day they have to face the facts. They are appalled at what they have abetted. They spend the rest of their days trying to explain, usually without great success, the dark clue to their complicity. As their understanding of Communism was incomplete and led them to a dead end, their understanding of breaking with it is incomplete and leads them to a dead end. It leads to less than Communism, which was a vision and a faith. The world outside Communism, the world in crisis, lacks a vision and a faith. There is before these ex-Communists absolutely nothing. Behind them is a threat. For they have, in fact, broken not with the vision, but with the politics of the vision. In the name of reason and intelligence, the vision keeps them firmly in its grip—self-divided, paralyzed, powerless to act against it.

Hence the most secret fold of their minds is haunted by a terrifying thought: What if we were wrong? What if our inconstancy is our guilt? That is the fate of those who break without knowing clearly that Communism is wrong because something else is right, because to the challenge: *God or Man?*, they continue to give the answer: *Man.* Their pathos is that not even the Communist ordeal could teach them that man without God is just what Communism said he was: the most intelligent of the animals, that man without God is a beast, never more beastly than when he is most intelligent about his beastliness. *"Er nennt's Vernunft,"* says the Devil in Goethe's *Faust, "und braucht's allein, nur tierischer als jedes Tier zu sein"*—Man calls it reason and uses it simply to be more beastly than any beast. Not grasping the source of the evil they sincerely hate, such ex-Communists in general make ineffectual witnesses against it. They are witnesses against something; they have ceased to be witnesses for anything.

Yet there is one experience which most sincere ex-Communists share, whether or not they go only part way to the end of the question it poses. The daughter of a former German diplomat in Moscow was trying to explain to me why her father, who, as an enlightened modern man, had been extremely pro-Communist, had become an implacable anti-Communist. It was hard for her because, as an enlightened modern girl, she shared the Communist vision without being a Communist. But she loved her father and the irrationality of his defection embarrassed her. "He was immensely pro-Soviet," she said, "and then—you will laugh at me—but you must not laugh at my father—and then—one night—in Moscow—he heard screams. That's all. Simply one night he heard screams."

A child of Reason and the 20th century, she knew that there is a logic of the mind. She did not know that the soul has a logic that may be more compelling than the mind's. She did not know at all that she had swept away the logic of the mind, the logic of history, the logic of politics, the myth of the 20th century, with five annihilating words: one night he heard screams.

What Communist has not heard those screams? They come from husbands torn forever from their wives in midnight arrests. They come, muffled, from the execution cellars of the secret police, from the torture chambers of the Lubianka, from all the citadels of terror now stretching from Berlin to Canton. They come from those freight cars loaded with men, women and children, the enemies of the Communist State, locked in, packed in, left on remote sidings to freeze to death at night in the Russian winter. They come from minds driven mad by the horrors of mass starvation ordered and enforced as a policy of the Communist State. They come from the starved skeletons, worked to death, or flogged to death (as an example to others) in the freezing filth of sub-arctic labor camps. They come from children whose parents are suddenly, inexplicably, taken away from them—parents they will never see again.

What Communist has not heard those screams? Execution, says the Communist code, is the highest measure of social protection. What man can call himself a Communist who has not accepted the fact that Terror is an instrument of policy, right if the vision is right, justified by history, enjoined by the balance of forces in the social wars of this century? Those screams have reached every Communist's mind. Usually they stop there. What judge willingly dwells upon the man the laws compel him to condemn to death—the laws of nations or the laws of history?

But one day the Communist really hears those screams. He is going about his routine party tasks. He is lifting a dripping reel of microfilm from a developing tank. He is justifying to a Communist fraction in a trade union an extremely unwelcome directive of the Central Committee. He is receiving from a trusted superior an order to go to another country and, in a designated hotel, at a designated hour, meet a man whose name he will never know, but who will give him a package whose contents he will never learn. Suddenly, there closes around that Communist a separating silence, and in that silence he hears screams. He hears them for the first time. For they do not merely reach his mind. They pierce beyond. They pierce to his soul. He says to himself: "Those are not the screams of man in agony. Those are the screams of a soul in agony." He hears them for the first time because a soul in extremity has communicated with that which alone can hear it—another human soul.

Why does the Communist ever hear them? Because in the end there persists in every man, however he may deny it, a scrap of soul. The Communist who suffers this singular experience then says to himself: "What is happening to me? I must be sick." If he does not instantly stifle that scrap of soul, he is lost. If he admits it for a moment, he has admitted that there is something greater than Reason, greater than the logic of mind, of politics, of history, of economics, which alone justifies the vision. If the party senses his weakness, and the party is peculiarly cunning at sensing such weakness, it will humiliate him, degrade him, condemn him, expel him. If it can, it will destroy him. And the party will be right. For he has betrayed that which alone justifies its faith—the vision of Almighty Man. He has brushed the only vision that has force against the vision of Almighty Mind. He stands before the fact of God.

The Communist Party is familiar with this experience to which its members are sometimes liable in prison, in illness, in indecision. It is recognized frankly as a sickness. There are ways of treating it —if it is confessed. It is when it is not confessed that the party, sensing a subtle crisis, turns upon it savagely. What ex-Communist has not suffered this experience in one form or another, to one degree or another? What he does about it depends on the individual man. That is why no ex-Communist dare answer for his sad fraternity the question: Why do men break with Communism? He can only answer the question: How did you break with Communism? My answer is: Slowly, reluctantly, in agony.

Yet my break began long before I heard those screams. Perhaps it does for everyone. I do not know how far back it began. Avalanches gather force and crash, unheard, in men as in the mountains. But I date my break from a very casual happening. I was sitting in our apartment on St. Paul Street in Baltimore. It was shortly before we moved to Alger Hiss's apartment in Washington. My daughter was in her high chair. I was watching her eat. She was the most miraculous thing that had ever happened in my life. I liked to watch her even when she smeared porridge on her face or dropped it meditatively on the floor. My eye came to rest on the delicate convolutions of her ear—those intricate, perfect ears. The thought passed through my mind: "No, those ears were not created by any chance coming together of atoms in nature (the Communist view). They could have been created only by immense design." The thought was involuntary and unwanted. I crowded it out of my mind. But I never wholly forgot it or the occasion. I had to crowd it out of my mind. If I had completed it, I should have had to say: Design presupposes God. I did not then know that, at that moment, the finger of God was first laid upon my forehead.

One thing most ex-Communists could agree upon: they broke because they wanted to be free. They do not all mean the same thing by "free." Freedom is a need of the soul, and nothing else. It is in striving toward God that the soul strives continually after a condition of freedom. God alone is the inciter and guarantor of freedom. He is the only guarantor. External freedom is only an aspect of interior freedom. Political freedom, as the Western world has known it, is only a political reading of the Bible. Religion and freedom are indivisible. Without freedom the soul dies. Without the soul there is no justification for freedom. Necessity is the only ultimate justification known to the mind. Hence every sincere break with Communism is a religious experience, though the Communist fail to identify its true nature, though he fail to go to the end of the experience. His break is the political expression of the perpetual need of the soul whose first faint stirring he has felt within him, years, months or days before he breaks. A Communist breaks because he must choose at last between irreconcilable opposites—God or Man, Soul or Mind, Freedom or Communism.

Communism is what happens when, in the name of Mind, men free themselves from God. But its view of God, its knowledge of God, its experience of God, is what alone gives character to a society or a nation, and meaning to its destiny. Its culture, the voice of this character, is merely that view, knowledge, experience, of God, fixed by its most intense spirits in terms intelligible to the mass of men. There has never been a society or a nation without God. But history is cluttered with the wreckage of nations that became indifferent to God, and died.

The crisis of Communism exists to the degree in which it has failed to free the peoples that it rules from God. Nobody knows this better than the Communist Party of the Soviet Union. The crisis of the Western world exists to the degree in which it is indifferent to God. It exists to the degree in which the Western world actually shares Communism's materialist vision, is so dazzled by the logic of the materialist interpretation of history, politics and economics, that it fails to grasp that, for it, the only possible answer to the Communist challenge: Faith in God or Faith in Man? is the challenge: Faith in God.

Economics is not the central problem of this century. It is a relative problem which can be solved in relative ways. Faith is the central problem of this age. The Western world does not know it, but it already possesses the answer to this problem—but only provided that its faith in God and the freedom He enjoins is as great as Communism's faith in Man.

My dear children, before I close this foreword, I want to recall to you briefly the life that we led in the ten years between the time when I broke with Communism and the time when I began to testify—the things we did, worked for, loved, believed in. For it was that happy life, which, on the human side, in part made it possible for me to do later on the things I had to do, or endure the things that happened to me.

Those were the days of the happy little worries, which then seemed so big. We know now that they were the golden days. They will not come again. In those days, our greatest worry was how to meet the payments on the mortgage, how to get the ploughing done in time, how to get health accreditation for our herd, how to get the hay in before the rain. I sometimes took my vacation in hay harvest so that I could help work the load. You two little children used to trample the load, drive the hay truck in the fields when you could barely reach the foot pedals, or drive the tractor that pulled up the loaded harpoons to the mow. At evening, you would break off to help Mother milk while I went on haying. For we came of age on the farm when we decided not to hire barn help, but to run the herd ourselves as a family.

Often the ovenlike heat in the comb of the barn and the sweet smell of alfalfa made us sick. Sometimes we fell asleep at the supper table from fatigue. But the hard work was good for us; and you knew only the peace of a home governed by a father and mother whose marriage the years (and an earlier suffering which you could not remember) had deepened into the perfect love that enveloped you.

Mother was a slight, overalled figure forever working for you in the house or beside you in the barns and gardens. Papa was a squat, overalled figure, fat but forceful, who taught John, at nine, the man-size glory of driving the tractor; or sat beside Ellen, at the wheel of the truck, an embodiment of security and power, as we drove loads of cattle through the night. On summer Sundays, you sat between Papa and Mama in the Quaker meeting house. Through the open doors, as you tried not to twist and turn in the long silence, you could see the far, blue Maryland hills and hear the redbirds and ground robins in the graveyard behind.

Only Ellen had a vague, troubled recollection of another time and another image of Papa. Then (it was during the years 1938 and 1939), if for any reason she pattered down the hall at night, she would find Papa, with the light on, writing, with a revolver on the table or a gun against the chair. She knew that there were people who wanted to kill Papa and who might try to kidnap her. But a wide sea of sunlight and of time lay between that puzzling recollection and the farm.

The farm was your kingdom, and the world lay far beyond the protecting walls thrown up by work and love. It is true that comic strips were not encouraged, comic books were banned, the radio could be turned on only by permission which was seldom given (or asked), and you saw few movies. But you grew in the presence of eternal wonders. There was the birth of lambs and calves. You remember how once, when I was away and the veterinarian could not come, you saw Mother reach in and turn the calf inside the cow so that it could be born. There was also the death of animals, sometimes violent, sometimes slow and painful—nothing is more constant on a farm than death.

Sometimes, of a spring evening, Papa would hear that distant honking that always makes his scalp tingle, and we would all rush out to see the wild geese, in lines of hundreds, steer up from the southwest, turn over the barn as over a landmark, and head into the north. Or on autumn nights of sudden cold that set the ewes breeding in the orchard, Papa would call you out of the house to stand with him in the now celebrated pumpkin patch and watch the northern lights flicker in electric clouds on the horizon, mount, die down, fade and mount again till they filled the whole northern sky with ghostly light in motion.

Thus, as children, you experienced two of the most important things men ever know—the wonder of life and the wonder of the universe, the wonder of life within the wonder of the universe. More important, you knew them not from books, not from lectures, but simply from living among them. Most important, you knew them with reverence and awe—that reverence and awe that has died out of the modern world and been replaced by man's monkeylike amazement at the cleverness of his own inventive brain.

I have watched greatness touch you in another way. I have seen you sit, uninvited and unforced, listening in complete silence to the third movement of the Ninth Symphony. I thought you understood, as much as children can, when I told you that that music was the moment at which Beethoven finally passed beyond the suffering of his life on earth and reached for the hand of God, as God reaches for the hand of Adam in Michelangelo's vision of the Creation.

And once, in place of a bedtime story, I was reading Shakespeare to John—at his own request, for I never forced such things on you. I came to that passage in which Macbeth, having murdered Duncan, realizes what he has done to his own soul, and asks if all the water in the world can ever wash the blood from his hand, or will it not rather

The multitudinous seas incarnadine?

At that line, John's whole body twitched. I gave great silent thanks to God. For I knew that if, as children, you could thus feel in your souls the reverence and awe for life and the world, which is the ultimate meaning of Beethoven and Shakespeare, as man and woman you could never be satisfied with less. I felt a great faith that sooner or later you would understand what I once told you, not because I expected you to understand it then, but because I hoped that you would remember it later: "True wisdom comes from the overcoming of suffering and sin. All true wisdom is therefore touched with sadness."

If all this sounds unduly solemn, you know that our lives were not; that all of us suffer from an incurable itch to puncture false solemnity. In our daily lives, we were fun-loving and gay. For those who have solemnity in their souls generally have enough of it there, and do not need to force it into their faces.

Then, on August 3, 1948, you learned for the first time that your father had once been a Communist, that he had worked in something called "the underground," that it was shameful, and that for some reason he was in Washington telling the world about it. While he was in the underground, he testified, he had worked with a number of other Communists. One of them was a man with the odd name of Alger Hiss. Later, Alger Hiss denied the allegation. Thus the Great Case began, and with it our lives were changed forever.

Dear children, one autumn twilight, when you were much smaller, I slipped away from you in play and stood for a moment alone in the apple orchard near the barn. Then I heard your two voices, piping together anxiously, calling to me: "Papa! Papa!" from the harvested cornfield. In the years when I was away five days a week in New York, working to pay for the farm, I used to think of you both before I fell asleep at night. And that is how you almost always came to me—voices of beloved children, calling to me from the gathered fields at dusk.

You called to me once again at night in the same orchard. That was a good many years later. A shadow deeper and more chilling than the autumn evening had closed upon us—I mean the Hiss Case. It was the first year of the Case. We had been doing the evening milking together. For us, one of the few happy results of the Case was that at last I could be home with you most of the time (in life these good things usually come too little or too late). I was washing and disinfecting the cows, and putting on and taking off the milkers. You were stripping after me.

In the quiet, there suddenly swept over my mind a clear realization of our true position—obscure, all but friendless people (some of my great friends had already taken refuge in aloofness; the others I had withdrawn from so as not to involve them in my affairs). Against me was an almost solid line-up of the most powerful groups and men in the country, the bitterly hostile reaction of much of the press, the smiling skepticism of much of the public, the venomous calumnies of the Hiss forces, the all but universal failure to understand the real meaning of the Case or my real purpose. A sense of the enormous futility of my effort, and my own inadequacy, drowned me. I felt a physical cold creep through me, settle around my heart and freeze any pulse of hope. The sight of you children, guiltless and defenseless, was more than I could bear. I was alone against the world; my longing was to be left completely alone, or not to be at all. It was that death of the will which Communism, with great cunning, always tries to induce in its victims.

I waited until the last cow was stripped and the last can lifted into the cooler. Then I stole into the upper barn and out into the apple orchard. It was a very dark night. The stars were large and cold. This cold was one with the coldness in myself. The lights of the barn, the house and the neighbors' houses were warm in the windows and on the ground; they were not for me. Then I heard Ellen call me in the barn and John called: "Papa!" Still calling, Ellen went down to the house to see if I were there. I heard John opening gates as he went to the calf barn, and he called me there. With all the longing of my love for you, I wanted to answer. But if I answered, I must come back to the living world. I could not do that.

John began to call me in the cow stable, in the milk house. He went into the dark side of the barn (I heard him slide the door back), into the upper barn, where at night he used to be afraid. He stepped outside in the dark, calling: "Papa! Papa!"—then, frantically, on the verge of tears: "Papa!" I walked over to him. I felt that I was making the most terrible surrender I should have to make on earth. "Papa," he cried and threw his arms around me, "don't ever go away." "No," I said, "no, I won't ever go away." Both of us knew that the words "go away" stood for something else, and that I had given him my promise not to kill myself. Later on, as you will see, I was tempted, in my wretchedness, to break that promise.

My children, when you were little, we used sometimes to go for walks in our pine woods. In the open fields, you would run along by yourselves. But you used instinctively to give me your hands as we entered those woods, where it was darker, lonelier, and in the stillness our voices sounded loud and frightening. In this book I am again giving you my hands. I am leading you, not through cool pine woods, but up and up a narrow defile between bare and steep rocks from which in shadow things uncoil and slither away. It will be dark. But, in the end, if I have led you aright, you will make out three crosses, from two of which hang thieves. I will have brought you to Golgotha—the place of skulls. This is the meaning of the journey. Before you understand, I may not be there, my hands may have slipped from yours. It will not matter. For when you understand what you see, you will no longer be children. You will know that life is pain, that each of us hangs always upon the cross of himself. And when you know that this is true of every man, woman and child on earth, you will be wise.

Your Father

1

FLIGHT

I

In 1937, I began, like Lazarus, the impossible return. I began to break away from Communism and to climb from deep within its underground, where for six years I had been buried, back into the world of free men. "When we dead awaken. . . ." I used sometimes to say in those days to my wife, who, though never a Communist, had shared my revolutionary hopes and was now to share my ordeals: "When we dead awaken. . . ." For this title of an Ibsen play I have never read somehow caught and summed up for me feelings that I could not find any other words to express—fears, uncertainties, self-doubts, cowardices, flinchings of the will—natural to any man who undertakes to reverse in mid-course the journey of his life. At the same time, I felt a surging release and a sense of freedom, like a man who bursts at last gasp out of a drowning sea.

This elation was not caused by any comparison of the world I was leaving and the world I was returning to. By any hard-headed estimate, the world I was leaving looked like the world of life and of the future. The world I was returning to seemed, by contrast, a graveyard. It was, in fact, the same world I had abandoned as hopeless when I joined the Communist Party in 1925. Only, now, its crisis, which a few men could diagnose thirteen years before, had reached the visible brink of catastrophe. And still that stricken world did not know the nature of the catastrophe. It still did not know, or even want to know, two facts that it must know to survive: the meaning of Communism, the meaning of that new breed of man, the Communist.

I wanted my wife to realize clearly one long-term penalty, for herself and for the children, of the step I was taking. I said: "You know, we are leaving the winning world for the losing world." I meant that, in the revolutionary conflict of the 20th century, I knowingly chose the side of probable defeat. Almost nothing that I have observed, or that has happened to me since, has made me think that I was wrong about that forecast. But nothing has changed my determination to act as if I were wrong—if only because, in the last instance, men must act on what they believe right, not on what they believe probable.

Then in 1938, with the clearest understanding of the consequences, we freely made the choice which history is slowly bringing all men to see is the only possible choice—the decision to die, if necessary, rather than to live under Communism. Nothing has made us regret that decision.

I I

There is a difference between the act of breaking with Communism, which is personal, intellectual, religious, and the act of breaking with the Communist Party, which is organizational. I began to break with Communism in 1937. I deserted from the Communist Party about the middle of April, 1938.

At that time, I was living with my family in one of the somber old double brick houses that stand above Mount Royal Terrace, in Baltimore, and are reached from the street level by flights of dark stone steps. It was then a somewhat faded street, but we loved it for its spaciousness and its overarching elms. When I deserted from the Communist Party, I took into hiding with me my wife, my five-year-old daughter and my son, who was about two years old.

I use the word "deserted" deliberately. The members of the Communist Party are bound by a semimilitary discipline which each man and woman agrees to submit to when he joins the party. It is a mistake to suppose that this discipline is an arbitrary strait jacket. This discipline is a Communist's pride. It means that each of his acts is a contribution to the total action of an army. It means that a small group of disciplined men and women, acting as one, can accomplish feats impossible to undisciplined groups many times their numerical strength. Every Communist shares this organic sense of functional solidarity and effectiveness, which is the emotional root of the slogan: "There is no fortress that the Bolsheviks cannot take." It is misleading, too, to call this discipline the action of a flock of sheep following a leader. The discipline is effective because, in the first instance, it is self-imposed.

I also use the term "deserted" in its simple military sense. At the time I broke with the Communist Party, I was the contact man between a powerful Soviet espionage apparatus in Washington and my superior in New York City. Each of us was a link of unequal size in the invisible chain of Communist command that laces the world.

My superior was Colonel Boris Bykov, a Russian officer of the Fourth Section (military intelligence) of the Red Army. At that time, and for some time after I broke, I did not know whether I was working in the Fourth Section or the Foreign Section of the G.P.U.* (the Soviet secret police). During the six years that I

* Later the N.K.V.D. Later still the M.V.B. Throughout this book I use the term G.P.U., the term most familiar to me.

worked underground, nobody ever told me what service I had been recruited into, and, as a disciplined Communist, I never asked. From the work, I assumed that I must be in one or the other of the two secret services I have mentioned. When it was necessary to refer directly to the underground apparatus, it was simply called "the apparatus" or sometimes "this institution." Its personnel were called *apparatchiks,* a Russian word meaning just what it sounds like: apparatus workers. Sometimes the apparatchiks were called "*Illegale*" (illegals) and their work "*illegale Arbeit*" (illegal work). These terms were used from habit or nostalgia, chiefly by older foreign Communists whose memories and activities went back to times before the Russian Revolution. They were proud terms, uttered proudly by the men and women who used them and who held that the Communist Party could call its members to few higher (because few more hazardous) activities.

I did not know the identity of the apparatus I was working in. Nor, during all the time that I worked with him, did I know Colonel Bykov by that name. I first learned it from General Walter Krivitsky, the former head of the Fourth Section in Western Europe, when we later met in New York as fugitives from the Communist Party, from which each of us had deserted independently. Krivitsky had worked underground with Bykov in Italy.

In 1937 and 1938, I knew Colonel Bykov as "Peter"—Peter, nothing more. Wherever possible, underground Communists are known to each other by such simple first-name pseudonyms. This practice, which puzzled many Americans when the Hiss Case first highlighted it, has been a commonplace of Europe's revolutionary movement for almost a hundred years. The purpose is security. Usually, the underground worker has several pseudonyms. In higher underground circles, I was called "Bob." In Washington, I was called "Carl." Men and women may work together in the underground for years, may become close friends, without ever knowing (or asking) one another's real names.

By 1938, the Soviet espionage apparatus in Washington had penetrated the State Department, the Treasury Department, the Bureau of Standards and the Aberdeen Proving Ground in Maryland. In the State Department, it had two active sources and two contacts that had not yet become active sources. In the Treasury Department, it had one active source and a contact who was used for a short time to watch and report on the active source. This contact later became a member of one of the underground apparatuses headed by

Elizabeth Bentley. In the Bureau of Standards, the apparatus had one active source and one inactive contact. In the Aberdeen Proving Ground, it had one active source.

By active source, I mean a man who supplied the Soviet espionage apparatus with secret or confidential information, usually in the form of official United States Government documents for microfilming. By an inactive contact, I mean a man who had been recruited into the Soviet apparatus for espionage purposes, but who, for one reason or another, was not transmitting information.

Seven of these Soviet apparatus workers were members of the American Communist Party. Two were fellow travelers. These two were so deeply engaged in Communist espionage that the organizational differences between them and their Communist co-workers were largely metaphysical. One of them was so indistinguishable that I always supposed him to be a Communist, and did not learn that he was not until he testified to that effect during the Hiss Case.

All these men knew that the chief purpose of the apparatus they served was espionage. The seven Communists were members of the apparatus in obedience to the discipline of the Communist Party. Five accepted this discipline eagerly. One obeyed it reluctantly, not from a scruple about espionage (I know because I discussed his transfer with him at the time), but because he was active in an underground cell of the American Communist Party and preferred to continue its activities for which he was strategically placed in the Government.

Thus, the number of productive sources in the Soviet apparatus was small. But their activities were supported by a larger number of apparatus people—photographers, couriers, contact men and people who gave the use of their homes for secret photographic workshops. The sources did not know that most of these people existed and very few of the non-sources knew the identity of the sources. None of the active sources knew of one another's identity. I was the only man in the Washington apparatus who knew all of them and met them regularly or irregularly as the work required. Colonel Bykov knew the identity of all of them and had met all but two of the sources.

But the productive sources, though few in number, occupied unusually high (or strategic) positions in the Government. The No. 1 source in the State Department was Alger Hiss, who was then an assistant to the Assistant Secretary of State, Francis Sayre, the son-in-law of Woodrow Wilson. The No. 2 source in the same

Department was Henry Julian Wadleigh, an expert in the Trade Agreements Division, to which he had managed to have himself transferred from the Agriculture Department. He had done so at the *request* of the Communist Party (Wadleigh was one of the fellow travelers) for the purpose of espionage. The source in the Treasury Department was the late Harry Dexter White. White was then an assistant to the Secretary of the Treasury, Henry Morgenthau. Later White became an assistant secretary of the Treasury, at which time he was known to Elizabeth Bentley. The source in the Aberdeen Proving Ground was Vincent Reno, an able mathematician who was living at the Proving Ground while he worked on a top-secret bombsight. Under the name Lance Clark, Reno had been a Communist organizer in Montana shortly before he went to work on the bombsight. The active source in the Bureau of Standards I shall call Abel Gross.

Thus, the group of active sources included: one assistant to the Assistant Secretary of State; one assistant to the Secretary of the Treasury; a mathematician working on one of the top-secret military projects of that time; an expert in the Trade Agreements Division of the State Department; an employe in the Bureau of Standards. The contacts included: two employes in the State Department and a second man in the Bureau of Standards.

In addition, the apparatus claimed the services of the Research Director of the Railroad Retirement Board, Mr. Abraham George Silverman, whose chief business, and a very exacting and unthankful one too, was to keep Harry Dexter White in a buoyant and co-operative frame of mind. Silverman also passed on as "economic adviser and chief of analysis and plans, assistant chief of air staff, material and services, air forces," into Miss Bentley's apparatuses. I did not recruit any of these men into the Communist Party or its work. With one possible exception (the mathematician), all of them had been engaged in underground Communist activity before I went to Washington or met any of them.

The espionage production of these men was so great that two (and, at one time, three) apparatus photographers operated in Washington and Baltimore to microfilm the confidential Government documents, summaries of documents or original memoranda, that they turned over. Two permanent photographic workshops were set up, one in Washington and one in Baltimore. Furthermore, the apparatus was constantly seeking to expand its operation. One of the Communists in the State Department and Vincent

Reno, the man in the Aberdeen Proving Ground, were late recruits to the apparatus. Most of the sources were career men. In Government they could expect to go as far as their abilities would take them, and their abilities were considerable.

It is hard to believe that a more highly placed, devoted and dangerous espionage group existed anywhere. Yet they had rivals even in the Soviet service. While trying to expand the secret apparatus, Alger Hiss, quite by chance, ran across the trail of another Soviet espionage apparatus. This was the group headed (in Washington) by Hede Massing, the former wife of Gerhardt Eisler, the Communist International's representative to the Communist Party, U.S.A. In this second apparatus was Noel Field, a highly placed employe of the West European Division of the State Department. Field, his wife, brother and adopted daughter all disappeared into Russian-controlled Europe during the Hiss Case, in which he was involved. Among the Massing apparatus' contacts was Noel Field's close friend, the late Laurence Duggan, who later became chief of the Latin-American Division of the State Department.

Moreover, the Washington apparatus to which I was assigned was only one wing of a larger apparatus. Another wing, also headed by Colonel Bykov, operated out of New York City, and was concerned chiefly with technical intelligence. It numbered among its active sources: the head of the experimental laboratory of a big steel company; a man strategically connected with a well-known arms company; and a former ballistics expert in the War Department. Presumably there were others. I learned the identities of these sources from an underground Communist known by the pseudonyms of "Keith" and "Pete." Keith had been Colonel Bykov's contact man with them. Later he became one of the photographers for the Washington apparatus. Incidentally, he has on all material points corroborated my testimony about him, about our joint activities, and the technical sources.

There were no doubt other apparatuses of the G.P.U. and the Fourth Section in Washington, of which I knew nothing. Behind this multiplying of organizations is what Communists call "the principle of parallel apparatuses." This is a swollen way of saying that a variety of self-contained underground apparatuses, ignorant of one another's existence, operate side by side for more or less the same purpose. For the Russians are great believers in bulk. They are not highly selective, and they mass their apparatuses in about the same way that they mass their artillery.

The Washington apparatus to which I was attached led its own secret existence. But through me, and through others, it maintained direct and helpful connections with two underground apparatuses of the American Communist Party in Washington. One of these was the so-called "Ware group," which takes its name from Harold Ware, the American Communist who was active in organizing it. In addition to the four members of this group (including himself) whom Lee Pressman has named under oath, there must have been some sixty or seventy others, though Pressman did not necessarily know them all; neither did I. All were dues-paying members of the Communist Party. Nearly all were employed in the United States Government, some in rather high positions, notably in the Department of Agriculture, the Department of Justice, the Department of the Interior, the National Labor Relations Board, the Agricultural Adjustment Administration, the Railroad Retirement Board, the National Research Project—and others.

A number of these men I knew personally as Communists. The treasurer of the Ware apparatus, Henry H. Collins Jr., Princeton and Harvard, and a scion of a Philadelphia manufacturing family, was my personal friend. He also served, voluntarily and, in fact, irrepressibly, as a recruiting agent for the Soviet apparatus among members of the State Department. It was he who recruited one of the Bykov apparatus' State Department sources, a man of much more glittery social background than Alger Hiss.

I knew much less about the other underground apparatus of the American Communist Party. Apparently, it included somewhat less exalted Government employes. I met only two of its members personally. One of these was a Government employe. The other, the head of the apparatus, was Eleanor Nelson, who later became a national official of the C.I.O.'s union of federal employes. At that time, she was a close friend of my immediate assistant in Washington (David Carpenter, now a staff member of the *Daily Worker*). She was then divorcing her husband, a former Socialist and a former well-known Government official.

At the very end of my activity in Washington, as a result of preparations I was secretly making to break with the Communist Party, I came across what appeared to be a third underground apparatus of the American Communist Party. Its members, too, were Government employes (I knew three of them), chiefly in the W.P.A.

There may also have been another type of apparatus which I then learned of with surprise, and which in this country's present crisis assumes a special importance. This is the so-called "sleeper apparatus." Very shortly before I broke, Colonel Bykov told me one day that I was being considered for a job of "the greatest importance." I was to organize and head an entirely new apparatus within the American Government. It was to be made up of men as highly placed as I could recruit. But it was to be wholly a reserve apparatus. Its members were not to engage in active espionage. They were to become active only in event of war (Bykov did not say war between the Soviet Union and the United States), when the other apparatuses might be disabled or destroyed.

The Soviet espionage apparatus in Washington also maintained constant contact with the national underground of the American Communist Party in the person of its chief. He was a Hungarian Communist who had been a minor official in the Hungarian Soviet Government of Bela Kun. He was in the United States illegally and was known variously as J. Peters, Alexander Stevens, Isidore Boorstein, Mr. Silver, etc. His real name was Alexander Goldberger and he had studied law at the university of Debrecen in Hungary. In addition, I had myself, during my entire six years in the Soviet underground, been the official secret contact man between a succession of Soviet apparatuses and the Communist Party, U.S.A. Both the open and the underground sections of the party were under orders to carry out, so far as they were able, any instructions I might give them in the name of the Soviet apparatuses.

It is sometimes said that the Communist penetration of the United States Government, while sensational, was after all comparatively small. The comparison is with the thousands of loyal Government employes. I think this a poor yardstick. Effectiveness, not numbers, is a more accurate measure of the infiltration. But even if numbers are the yardstick, I am inclined to believe, from what I saw of the operation through my relatively small peephole, that the Communist penetration was numerically great. J. Peters found perhaps the best standard of comparison.

The first time I met Peters in Washington, we walked from the Union Station to a downtown restaurant. In New York, Peters' manner had always been that of a minor commissar—a little more human than the breed, for he had a sense of humor—but reserved, innately distrustful, secretive. In Washington, he was like a king returned to his kingdom—suddenly gay and expansive. He enlarged on the party's organizational and human resources in Washington, mentioning, among others, the man whose name he always pronounced "Awl-jur"—with a kind of drawling pleasure, for he took an almost parental pride in Alger Hiss. Then, with a little inclusive wave of his pudgy hand, he summed up. "Even in Germany under the Weimar Republic," said Peters, "the party did not have what we have here."

III

The first impact of this blueprint of Communist penetration is likely to be shock at the espionage revealed. That is not the important point. Espionage is always intolerable, just as it is indispensable. No government in sound political health, no government which was not subtly infected with the revolutionary virus of the age, could tolerate in its service any employe against whom there was a suspicion of Communist espionage or even of indiscretion that might serve an espionage purpose.

The important point about the Washington apparatuses is that, in the 1930's, the revolutionary mood had become so acute throughout the whole world that the Communist Party could recruit its agents, not here and there, but by scores within the Government of the United States. And they were precisely among the most literate, intellectually eager and energetic young men in a nation which by all its traditions of freedom, initiative and opportunity, its institutions and the circumstances of its geography and history, was farthest removed from the revolutionary struggles of Europe.

The deeper meaning of the Soviet underground apparatus, and all the apparatuses that clustered hidden beside it, was not so much their espionage activity. It was the fact that they were a true Fifth Column, the living evidence that henceforth in the 20th century, all wars are revolutionary wars, and are fought not only between nations, but within them.

The men and women Communists and fellow travelers who staffed this Fifth Column were dedicated revolutionists whose primary allegiance was no longer to any country—nor to those factors which give a country its binding force: tradition, family, community, soil, religious faith. Their primary allegiance was to a revolutionary faith and a vision of man and his material destiny which was given political force by international Communism, of which the American Communist Party and the Russian Communist Party (and hence the Soviet Government, which is only an administrative apparatus of the Russian Communist Party) are component sections.

No other government in the world but that of the Soviet Union could possibly have corrupted these people from their original allegiance. They were not venal. They performed their espionage services without compensation, as a party obligation. The very repugnance of the task was a witness and a sacrifice to their faith. With few exceptions, offers of money would have outraged them. With few exceptions, they cared little or nothing for money as money. It is also absurd to say, as I have often heard it said, that they were moved by a desire for power. A few may have been, and these, like their kind the world over, would have sought power in terms of any situation they were in. The plain fact is that most of them held tangible power of some kind in the Government they were betraying, with every assurance that simply by not endangering their routine rise that power would grow. Neither power nor money moved them. Nor was adventure a factor. An incurably romantic Communist is a contradiction in terms. A romantic underground worker endangers himself and his whole apparatus. Faith moved them, as, in the final conflict, only equal faith can overcome them.

The terrible meaning of the Washington apparatus is that, even in the United States, that stage of the revolution of our times has been reached, "that decisive hour," which Karl Marx acutely forecast a hundred years before: when "the process of dissolution going on within . . . the whole range of the old society" becomes so violent "that a small section of the ruling class . . . joins the revolutionary class." This "small section," says Marx, is "in particular," the middle-class intellectuals.

When this happens, it is very late in the night of history, and in the life of nations. What is irreparable is that faith between man and man which is the arterial pulse of community; for henceforth the conspirator is indistinguishable from the man beside you. Security shatters, not because there are no more locks, but because the men naturally trusted with the keys and combinations are themselves the conspirators.

IV

When a man deserts from such a concentration of hidden power as I have described, and the much greater power that lurks behind it, he challenges the underground in the one condition without which it cannot exist: its secrecy. The mere fact that the deserter, by an act of his own will, stands outside the control of the Communist Party is a threat. He must therefore expect that the party will act to remove the threat. All revolutionary experience shows that there is only one guarantee of a deserter's silence: his death. Both the Communist Party and the deserter know, too, that if he goes to the police and informs against it, it will scarcely be worth the party's while to kill him. Thus, a race often develops in which the party's killers try to reach the fugitive before he can reach the police.

The party's problem is a practical one: 1) to protect the threatened apparatuses; 2) to reassure the loyal underground workers whose morale is bound to be shaken by a defection. It is necessary to demonstrate that the apparatus moves swiftly to safeguard them, and that no one can defy it with impunity.

I never doubted that the party's first reaction to my break would be an attempt against my life. I assumed that sooner or later the G.P.U. would be given the assignment. I did not know whether they would elect the "wet" or "dry" method—whether they would try simply to kill me or whether they would prefer to trap me, smuggle me aboard a Soviet ship (there is often one lying in Baltimore harbor) for a later settling of accounts in Russia. "*Das wird auch abgerechnet,*" I once heard Colonel Bykov say in a voice taut with rage when he realized that an earlier fugitive had given him the slip and suspected (quite rightly) that it had happened with my help—"That account will also be settled." I knew that he, or some other Bykov, would phrase a similar epitaph for me.

Moreover, I deserted in the year of the long knives. In the twelvemonth in which my flight took place, more revolutionists deserted from the Communist Party, and the G.P.U. cut down more fugitives in their flight than in any other period of the party's history. For "political differences were being settled"; Stalin was consolidating his power.

In the Soviet apparatus there was a saying that sounds merely brutal, but whose cynicism betrays the wrenching effort of the soul to seek relief from the death in which it lives. It was: "Any fool can commit a murder, but it takes an artist to commit a good natural death." In those months, the G.P.U. had no time to commit "good natural deaths"; it killed without artistry. The secret police padded like ferrets through the undergrounds. From the buried darkness came sounds of struggle and cries, all the more chilling because it was impossible to know just what was happening. Then, suddenly, revolutionists with a lifetime of devoted activity would pop out, like rabbits from a burrow, with the G.P.U. close on their heels—Barmine from the Soviet legation in Athens, Raskolnikoff from the Soviet legation in Sofia, Krivitsky from Amsterdam, Reiss in Switzerland. Not that Reiss fled. Instead, a brave and a lonely man, he sent his single-handed defiance to Stalin: Murderer of the Kremlin cellars, I herewith return my decorations and resume my freedom of action. But defiance is not enough; cunning is needed to fight cunning. It was foredoomed that sooner or later the door of a G.P.U. limousine would swing open and Reiss's body with the bullets in the defiant brain would tumble out—as happened shortly after he deserted. Of the four I have named, only Barmine outran the hunters.

Reiss's death moved me deeply. But another murder touched me closely—that of Juliet Stuart Poyntz, Barnard College graduate, Midwestern American, former member of the Central Committee of the Communist Party, U.S.A., long an underground worker in a Soviet apparatus whose existence (until her death revealed it) I had not suspected. I had known Juliet Poyntz. She had been a member of the first unit of the Communist Party which I joined in 1925. A heavy-set, dark, softly feminine woman, she was also a little absurdly imperious and mysterious as Communist bureaucrats often become, sagging self-consciously under the weight of so much secret authority and knowledge.

In 1937, Juliet Poyntz deserted from the Communist Party. She was living in a New York hotel. One evening she left her room with the light burning and a page of unfinished handwriting on the table. She was never seen again. It is known that she went to meet a Communist friend in Central Park and that he had decoyed her there as part of a G.P.U. trap. She was pushed into an automobile and two men drove her off. The thought of this intensely feminine woman, coldly murdered by two men, sickened me in a physical way, because I could always see her in my mind's eye.

I was not a quarry of those twilight manhunts. I was too small a figure, compared to those great ones in the underworld of Communism. I was affected but not endangered. Moreover, I had never been a Trotskyist. But these episodes from our daily life served me as profuse examples of what I could expect when I broke. I studied the mistakes by which the deserters were trapped as a man might study the chart of a minefield. I determined to fight the Communist Party as a Communist would fight, to prepare my break carefully, using against the conspiracy all the conspiratorial method it had taught me, and especially to guard against premature, impulsive actions caused by tensions more or less natural in the circumstances.

Those months, when I was preparing my flight under the eyes of my acute, observant and habitually distrustful co-workers, were possibly the most dangerous, certainly the most nerve-wearing. I met my comrades regularly, often at night, in lonely places, in their houses, in automobiles—all ideal traps if I had become suspect. When I was with Colonel Bykov, I was not master of my movements. Most of our meetings took place in New York City. We always prearranged them a week or ten days ahead. As a rule, we first met in a movie house. I would go in and stand at the back. Bykov, who nearly always had arrived first, would get up from the audience at the agreed time and join me. We would go out together. Bykov, not I, would decide what route we should then take in our ramblings (we usually walked several miles about the city). We would wander at night, far out in Brooklyn or the Bronx, in lonely stretches of park or on streets where we were the only people. As we walked and talked, I would think: "Does he know anything? Is there anything in my manner that could make him suspicious? Where is he taking me?"

I always assumed that one member of the Washington underground acted for Bykov as a pair of eyes and ears to observe and report my conduct. This is routine Communist practice. I never knew to whom those eyes and ears belonged. I also had reason to believe that the Soviet counter-intelligence had me under routine surveillance.

Thus, my practical problem was to organize my flight and the safe removal of my family under eyes which could see me but which I could not see, while I took the calculated risk of nightly meetings with men and women who seemed perfectly unsuspicious. On the other hand, they might be suspicious and therefore operating against me with the same calculation with which I was operating against them.

I decided that five main points were essential to my break: 1) a weapon; 2) a hiding place; 3) an automobile for swift movement; 4) an identity, an official record of the fact that a man named Chambers had worked in Washington in the years 1937 and 1938;

5) a life preserver, in the form of copies of official documents stolen by the apparatus, which, should the party move against my life, I might have an outside chance of using as a dissuader.

Set down in this way, with numbered points, for the sake of clearness, my plan of action may give a misleading impression of neatness and firmness. Actually, it was much more stumbling, improvised and random, for it must be remembered that I was troubled and confused. I had the general plan of my break in mind. I worked on the details as opportunity and new ideas occurred. Nor can I any longer, after so many years, be positive of the order or the exact way in which I did certain things. Thus, I have the impression that my secreting of microfilm and copies of documents was a late decision, hastily carried out; I was conscious of a general, but not of a specific purpose, for which I might need them.

For defense, I bought a long sheath knife. I bought it chiefly with my lonely walks with Bykov and my automobile rides with other Communists in mind. It was a poor weapon, but the most easily procured and concealed, and therefore the only equalizer I risked carrying at that time. I wore it belted around my undershirt, and kept the strap across the handle and the shirt under my vest unbuttoned so that I could reach it more easily in a fight. About the time I began to carry a knife, Colonel Bykov developed a curious habit. He would crowd close to me when we sat together in a street car or subway train and repeatedly lurched against me when we walked on the street. He had never done this before. I instantly suspected that he was trying to feel if I was armed. I still think this must have been his purpose, not because he suspected that I was breaking, but because, by coincidence, it occurred to him at that time to find out if I was armed. And, by coincidence, he was right, though he did not find out.

The problem of a car I considered of first importance. Both the Soviet apparatuses and the American underground used automobiles constantly in their operations. But Bykov was against automobiles. He could not drive and, perhaps for that reason, considered cars a hazard to underground work second only to the "American secret police"—one of his obsessions. Above all, I think he did not want the expense.

I owned a Ford sedan which J. Peters had provided for me a year or two before Bykov's arrival. Because of his prejudice, I had not at once told Bykov about this car. I am no longer certain whether I ever told him. In any case, the car was old and ailing; the Communist Party, having paid for it, knew of its existence and might easily trace it. For purposes of flight it seemed a serious handicap. I began a systematic campaign to get Bykov to finance a new car. I urged its importance in the work and, what I thought a telling point, the loss of prestige to the Soviet apparatus when I, its face in Washington, had to go on foot or accept rides from the sources and even the photographers, two of whom had their own automobiles.

I had told Alger Hiss about Bykov's automotive prejudice. I also told him about my campaign to get a car. We laughed about it. In this I had no double purpose. I did not foresee Hiss's reaction. Alger, however, quickly grew serious and agreed that a car was a necessity of the work (after all, he had a stake in efficient operations). He offered to lend me four hundred dollars to use as part payment on a car. I declined. But I used Alger's offer in my campaign with Bykov, who, to my surprise, one night suddenly capitulated. He explained that he did not have the necessary money on him at the time (he frequently carried hundreds of dollars in currency), but he authorized me to accept the money from Hiss, add it to whatever apparatus funds I might have on hand, and buy a car. He said he would give me the money for Hiss the next time I saw him. He always managed to forget it. When I broke, the repayment had not been made. I knew, of course, that if Alger claimed the loan, the apparatus would be bound to repay him.

Since the Communist Party might later try to trace the new car, I decided not to buy it in Baltimore. With the loan from Hiss, I had my wife go to the Schmitt Motor Company in Randallstown, a village northwest of Baltimore. There she traded in our old car and bought a 1937 Ford. We had wings.

The problem of a hiding place was equally important. I was sure that the Communist Party, once it learned of my desertion, would expect me to go as far away as possible from Baltimore. I decided that the unexpected tactic was to remain close to it. My wife and I began to look for quarters in a wide arc north and west of the city. Since we had little money, our hideaway had to be inexpensive. It had to have a commanding situation so that we could see around us in all directions. It could not be in a thickly populated neighborhood. We wanted only one or two rooms which had to be away from the street. We looked at many places before we found one that suited our peculiar needs. It was a big house, near the city, but in the country. It stood well back from the Old

Court Road, near Pikesville, Md. The house was on a gentle rise with wide lawns around it. The road was visible for a distance in both directions. Best of all, there was a police dog. We rented two rooms at the back of the house.

If the Communist Party did not succeed in taking my life, I assumed that it would try to act against me in other ways. I could not foresee what they might be, but I could see that I might need weapons with which to fight back. If I should ever have to tell my story (and the problem of becoming an informer confronted me, as it does every ex-Communist, from the moment I began to break with Communism), it would also be important to have some proof that I had worked with the Communist Party in Washington. There could be no more official proof, it seemed to me, than to let the Communist Party get me a job under my own name in the United States Government. This would serve two other purposes: by working under my own name, I would help to restore my identity, which for five or six years had been all but lost. And a job would bring in a little money which we badly needed for the break.

For this purpose, and without at first taking Colonel Bykov into my confidence, I instructed one of the apparatus men in Washington (George Silverman) to get me a job in the United States Government, where I knew he had placed other Communists. I gave as a pretext my need for a "cover." Almost overnight, I found myself employed by the National Research Project. I used the name Chambers. It had been a simple matter for the party to place me in the Government, since one of the national heads of the Research Project, George Silverman, the research director of the Railroad Retirement Board, for whom the project was making a study, and my immediate boss on the job were all members of the Communist Party.

I told Alger Hiss and others that I had taken a job in the Government, for I thought that the knowledge might give them pause, if, after I broke, they were moved by zeal (or by others) to attempt reprisals against me. Hiss laughed when I told him: it was the capstone of the legend of "Carl's" Bolshevik daring. "I suppose you will turn up in the State Department next," he said. I kept the job only long enough to establish the fact that I had it, three or four months.

Shortly before my break, I began to organize my life preserver. I secreted copies of Government documents copied in the Hiss household, memos in the handwriting of Alger Hiss and Harry Dexter White, microfilm of documents transmitted by Alger

Hiss and the source in the Bureau of Standards. This selection was not aimed at any individual. There was much of the Hiss material because he was the most productive source. There may actually have been more of the material from the Bureau of Standards, but by the time it was developed in 1948, the film from which it was copied had deteriorated so that much of it could not be read. There was no material from Julian Wadleigh because, in the spring of 1938, he was out of the country on a diplomatic mission to Turkey, though I believe that he had returned by the time I broke.

I was now ready to desert.

It seemed to me that the deserters from Communism whom the party had killed had nearly all made one mistake. They had shared in advance with other Communists their doubts, fears and plans to break. Out of friendship, or pity, or loneliness, they had tried to move those others to break with them. Their comrades had then betrayed them. I resolved to say nothing to anyone. Yet, like the others who had broken before me, I found that I could not leave these people whom I had known intimately for years, with some of whom I had formed close attachments, for all of whom I must answer the question asked of Cain, without trying to tell them something.

One night, as Felix Inslerman, one of the photographers for the apparatus, drove me around Baltimore, I found myself brushing the dangerous subject. I did not particularly like Felix. He looked like an average young fellow, seemingly simple, not overbright. Actually he had been a Communist from boyhood. But I knew that he had recently been married. I felt pity for him. I asked him if he never thought of leading a more ordinary life, if he never thought of settling down quietly and having children. The complete blankness with which he listened warned me that it was probably no use, and certainly dangerous.

In a very different way, I also worked around the subject with Alger Hiss. I made a point of criticizing Bykov, carefully feeling out how far I could safely go. Plainly, Hiss thought that my attitude was the usual subaltern's grudge against his superior. He was sympathetic, but he smiled off my remarks and tried to justify Bykov without wounding me. Later I ventured into the much more perilous field of Communist politics, criticizing the Russian purges and especially the character of Stalin. For the first time, I saw Alger glance at me out of the side of his eye. "Yes, Stalin plays for keeps, doesn't he?" he said. I had not heard the expression used before except in marbles. I thought that it was a neat summing up. I also thought that I had gone too far, and stopped.

In April of 1938, on the morning of a day when I was to have met Colonel Bykov in New York, my wife drove the children away from the Mount Royal Terrace house to our hiding place on the Old Court Road. I followed with the moving men. For the move, we had hired a Negro with a truck and helper. We had little furniture and it fitted easily into the small van. This move was the only direct link between Mount Royal Terrace and our hideaway. It could not be avoided. The best solution seemed to be a Negro mover, who was least likely to be traced if a hunt began and most likely to play dumb with inquisitive white men.

As usual on moving day, we left something indispensable behind—something of the children's, though I no longer remember just what. I decided to drive back later to retrieve this treasure. It was dusk when I reached Mount Royal Terrace, an hour or so after I should have met Colonel Bykov in New York. I could imagine that unhappy little man becoming more frantic when I failed to appear. Not to be punctual is one of the underground's cardinal sins.

I parked the car several blocks from the house and reconnoitered the back. I saw no sign of prowlers. I let myself in through the kitchen. I found whatever I had come for, and was peering out the front windows to see if there might be any watchers on the street, when, in the bare, darkening rooms, the telephone rang shrilly. I froze perfectly still at the window. "Dear comrades," I thought, "it is you," for we had a telephone by order of the apparatus and almost no one but Bykov ever called us.

While the telephone rang and rang, I picked my way across the resounding floors. I caught myself closing the kitchen door over-quietly, and smiled as I hurried down the brick path, beside which, in autumn, the spoon chrysanthemums bloomed. In neighboring houses, the windows were lighted. The quiet people of Baltimore, where life is so uneventful, were sitting down to their suppers. As I opened the gate upon the alley in back, I could still faintly hear the telephone, exploding regularly in the empty house, like an alarm clock in a bucket.

V

Pursuing feet are not less disturbing because they are not seen or heard. Of an evening, when the children were in bed, my wife and I would sit in our small room, where we were so packed in that our goods were stacked against the walls and we had somewhat the feeling of sitting in a sandbagged dugout. The blinds were drawn. It should have been rather snug. But that time remains in my memory as a smudge of feeling, a bad time from which the details have been rubbed out by a merciful erasure. Two things I remember. Whatever we were doing, we were really always listening; and I remember my wife's rising from time to time during the night to see if I was all right and the children were in their beds.

We were absolutely alone. In the whole world, no one, friend or (we hoped) enemy, knew where we were. For we had followed the basic underground rule: what a man does not know, he cannot tell, inadvertently or otherwise. So we had not told even the few people we trusted where we were hiding. That was our safety. But I soon found out that it worked two ways. If the Communist Party did not know where we were, we could not know what the Communist Party was up to. So we waited and listened. We had joined the millionfold households of fear over each of which the revolutionary century has closed its individual night. They were less common in the American spring of 1938 than they have since become.

In the small city of Westminster, Md., near which we now live, there is a little German girl. She and her mother and father had lived in the Russian sector of Berlin. One night the knock came on the door. The secret police took her father away. Now she knows only two things: he died in Siberia; she will never see him again. That knock, in another form, was what we were listening for on the Old Court Road.

Our listening was made stranger by the fact that we listened in the midst of people leading simple, open, busy American lives. Outwardly, we were composed enough. But inwardly, we cried out to those around us. Our cries were paralyzed by the knowledge that no one could hear us, or if he heard us, he could not understand because he could never believe us; so that we were like a trapped man in a nightmare who summons up his last strength to cry: "Help!" and then realizes that he has lost his voice, no sound comes at all, and he strangles on the cry he cannot utter.

In those weeks on the Old Court Road we began a routine which we kept up, except for my infrequent absences, until I went to work for *Time* magazine in 1939. All night I would sit up watching while my family slept. I would sleep for a few hours in the daytime. Fortunately, I had found work—translation—that I could best do in the still nights.

V I

The party moved at once to find out what had become of me. The day after my disappearance, Colonel Bykov, the head of the Soviet apparatus, and J. Peters, the head of the underground Communist Party, U.S.A., paid a somewhat awesome visit to "Paul." The mood of both chiefs was glum and that of Bykov rather desperate. This information, and what follows, was given me by Paul himself on a later occasion.

"Paul" was the pseudonym of a secret Communist who had been turned over to the Soviet apparatus by the American Communist Party for the specific purpose of using his business to provide legal "cover" for a Soviet underground apparatus to be set up in England. For various reasons, that apparatus was never set up. Instead, Paul provided legal "cover" for a Soviet apparatus operating in Japan.

The world knew Paul better as Maxim Lieber, an authors' agent who handled, among others, the profitable marketing problems of Erskine Caldwell, author of *Tobacco Road, God's Little Acre* and other best-selling fiction. Paul also handled *Tobacco Road* when it was made into a play which, lacing social consciousness with a dash of pornography, ran so long on Broadway that it closed at last chiefly because there was scarcely a literate American of playgoing age who had not seen it. This enabled Paul to buy a farm in Bucks County, Pa., which also played its small part in the underground. In 1938 Paul's office was on Fifth Avenue in New York City.

Paul knew J. Peters from earlier days in the American Communist Party. He was seeing Colonel Bykov for the first time. Paul was then a short, slight, nervous man with a shoebrush mustache. He affected tweeds and a bulldog pipe, and his eyes behind his horn-rims were those of a frightened rabbit. Paul is timid, but he is not a coward. Colonel Bykov, on the other hand, who was menacing by force of habit, was a pathological coward—the only cowardly Communist I ever knew. Like most cowards, he was a bully. He set out to bully Paul. Where, he demanded, is Chambers? It was a question that Paul could not possibly have answered. Bykov made it plain that he did not believe him.

In Paul's presence, the head of the Soviet underground apparatus and the head of the American underground apparatus then exchanged theories about my disappearance. As so often happens in life, each was discovered to hold exactly the view that the other might have been expected to hold. Bykov, the astute and experienced Russian, nursed the hope that I had merely been killed outright in an automobile accident, perhaps with my wife and children. Peters, the representative of the provincial American Communist Party, shook his head. "He has deserted," he said quietly. Perhaps some trifling change in my manner, which I always feared might betray me in the days when I was preparing to break, had registered on Peters' mind, and he had dismissed it, but now it hardened into certainty.

Both chiefs agreed on one point: Paul must go to Baltimore at once and trace me. Paul had no choice. He had to go. But he made the trip reluctantly. Among the world's mistaken ideas about Communists is the notion that they are never swayed by simple human feelings. Because a man submits himself to a rigorous discipline, because, in the last instance, he will act on that discipline and against his natural feelings, it does not follow that he lacks such feelings. In the first place, life, even among Communists, is not in general made up of last instances. And while Communists are more self-consciously consistent than the run of men, they cannot escape the inconsistency that is life's most consistent pattern. Hence, on the human side, the terrifying conflicts that come to light in the party's purges, in its expulsions, in its defections.

Paul now suffered such a conflict. He did not want to find me. After the Alger Hisses, Paul, of all the people in the underground, had been closest to me. In many ways our relationship was freer than mine with the Hisses. Paul was engaged in less hazardous activities than Hiss. He had a lively sense of humor which Hiss lacked. We shared a common intense love of music and books. And Paul knew my real name and had known and respected me as a Communist writer before either of us went underground. Paul sensed that Peters was right: I had deserted. It sickened and frightened him, as the defection of a close friend usually sickens a Communist, because it strikes at the root of his own faith. It also endangered him, because we had been closely associated. If there were to be reprisals, he was in the line of fire. The burden of proof of his loyalty to the party was on Paul. He understood quite well the expression in the eyes of the other two men when they ordered him to go to Baltimore.

Paul went. He climbed the stone steps to the Mount Royal Terrace house. He peered through the windows and saw the bare front room. He asked the neighbors: "Where did the Chamberses go?" "We don't know," they said. Paul deliberately made no further effort to trace me.

He went back to New York and reported to Bykov and Peters: the Mount Royal Terrace house is empty. Now Bykov knew that I was not dead, that Peters was right, that I had deserted. He had his tantrum. He cursed me (quite justifiably) and shouted at Paul (also quite justifiably) that he had not tried to trace me. Bykov and Peters ordered Paul back to Baltimore the next morning. Dutifully, he made the second trip.

He checked, if I remember correctly, with the post office. There was, of course, no forwarding address. He went to the agent who had rented us the Mount Royal Terrace house. "They paid their rent," said the agent. "That's all I know or care."

Paul reported back to New York again. He was a very worried Paul. But by then, Bykov was more frightened of Paul than Paul was of Bykov. He suspected him of having a hand in my disappearance. Bykov vanished. This glimpse through Paul's eyes is the last I have of Bykov. No doubt, the G.P.U. came in at the point where Bykov went out.

I know these details because Paul told them to me. I called him up unexpectedly one day some time after I broke, and asked him to meet me in the Automat in the basement of his building. I met him there because I wished to give him as little time as possible between my call and our meeting. He was surprised and pleased, in a perfectly human way, to see me alive. We sat laughing and talking as if I were not a fugitive from the Communist Party, as if his sitting there with me were not grounds for very serious party action.

I think I can hear someone ask: "If you were afraid for your life, why did you get in touch with Paul?" For two reasons. I will discuss the less important one first. It is loneliness. No one who has not known it can readily grasp the annihilating loneliness of the ex-Communist who, after the tight associations of the underground, finds himself not only a fugitive from violence, but absolutely alone in a world which has become alien to him, to which he is an alien, to which a few moments before he was an enemy. His simple longing not to be entirely alone pleads with his sense of caution, and he is drawn back toward the very force that must seek to destroy him for its own security. This almost universal behavior of the ex-Communist, the Communist Party understands quite well and uses it to trap him. Thus Juliet Poyntz, Walter Krivitsky, Ignatz Reiss were trapped. I saw Paul in part because we had been friends. But if this had been all, I would not have seen Paul.

In my case, the decisive reason was practical. The Communist is a new type of man in history—the thinking commando. His rule for action is: caution, careful preparation, swiftness and surprise in striking. In my little war with the Communist Party, I needed to find out what the enemy was doing. I struck unexpectedly at the point where I was most likely to find out what I needed to know.

I saw Paul three times. The last time I took a friend with me for security. On each occasion, I sensed that Paul was becoming more and more worried about seeing me. I suspected that he had told the party that he was seeing me and that he had been instructed to continue meeting me with a view to preparing a trap at a suitable time and place. The last time we met, Paul told me, with a sad embarrassment, that his loyalty to the party outweighed his friendship for me. I respected him deeply for that. I sensed that it was his way of saying that, if we met again, he would not be responsible for the consequences. He could have betrayed me into the party's hands. He chose not to do so.

There is much good in this man—so much good that I want to speak directly to him as I cannot otherwise do across the barrier of fear and conflict that divides us. Since there was much humor in our friendship, and it is the instinct of both of us to treat very serious things with a saving lightness, I would like to say the serious thing I have to say in the least serious way. I should like simply to quote (commandolike) from the least expected text—I mean that other pirate story, *Treasure Island.*

I have in mind the moment when the small loyal party is abandoning the *Hispaniola* to fight its forlorn hope against the mutineers ashore. As the last boat is ready to push off from the ship, Captain Smollett calls out to the one decent man whom the pirates have somehow won over. " 'Now, men,' said he, 'do you hear me?' There was no answer from the forecastle. 'It's to you, Abraham Gray—it's to you I am speaking.' Still no reply. 'Gray,' resumed Mr. Smollett a little louder, 'I am leaving this ship. . . . I know you are a good man at bottom, and I dare say not one of the lot of you's as bad as he makes out. . . . Come, my fine fellow, don't hang so long in stays.' . . . There was a sudden scuffle, a sound of blows and out burst Abraham Gray with a knife cut on the side of his cheek. . . . 'I'm with you, sir,' said he."

While it is possible to hold it, I will not give up the faith that Paul is the man I believe him to be and that one day the world will hear that scuffle and that sound of blows and see the slash of honor on his face.

VII

My second glimpse of the Communist Party's interest in me was somewhat more sinister. I glimpsed it at all because the party, using somewhat the same tactic I had used in approaching Paul, tried to reach me through my brother-in-law. He is an attorney in New York City.

A few days after Paul had made his fruitless trips to Baltimore, there strode into my brother-in-law's office one morning a rather striking-looking white-haired woman, about fifty years old. She told the receptionist that Miss Grace Hutchins wished to see Mr. Shemitz. Mr. Shemitz was in court. So Miss Hutchins scribbled a note which she left for him. This note which my brother-in-law, with a lawyer's squirreling instinct, hoarded, unknown to me, over the years, is now in the custody of the F.B.I., and the handwriting has been officially certified as that of Miss Hutchins. In fact, I have never seen the note. My brother-in-law prudently never showed it to me. He turned it over to the F.B.I. during the Hiss Case.

But I know that the note said something very close to this: "Tell Esther's husband to contact Steve at once. Very urgent." Esther is my wife. Steve is Alexander Stevens, alias J. Peters, the head of the underground section of the American Communist Party. My brother-in-law could not possibly have told me to contact "Steve," because he did not know, and had not known for years, where his sister and I were living. This had been true from the time I went underground.

Nothing having happened, Miss Hutchins appeared again several mornings later. Again Mr. Shemitz was in court. Miss Hutchins said that she would wait. Perhaps she suspected that Mr. Shemitz was really skulking in his private office. She waited through the morning. She waited austerely through the lunch hour. She waited through the afternoon. As the day passed, the other people in the office became, first vaguely aware, then vaguely uneasy, at the silent presence in their midst. They did not recognize the woman with the magnificent white hair upswept from the high forehead.

My wife and I would have recognized her, for she had been my wife's close friend for years and one of the witnesses of our marriage.

Her classmates at Bryn Mawr would have recognized her, for, like Mrs. Alger Hiss and her friend, Mrs. Carl Binger, the wife of the psychoanalyst in the Hiss trials, Miss Hutchins is a Bryn Mawr alumna.

Certain social circles in Boston and elsewhere would have recognized her, for she came of an old Back Bay family.

Certain Christian pacifist circles would have recognized her, for she had once worked for *The World Tomorrow,* a pacifist magazine, together with my wife and Nevin Sayre, the brother of Francis Sayre, who, as Assistant Secretary of State, had hired Alger Hiss as his assistant.

Scotland Yard would have recognized her, for when the British police raided the Arcos, the London counterpart of the Amtorg, *circa* 1927, they found a Russian employe frantically trying to burn documents. Among the names listed in the documents, as a trusted Communist contact in the United States, was Grace Hutchins.

The Central Committee of the American Communist Party would have recognized her, for she had publicly announced her conversion to Communism, had since served the party loyally, and had been its official candidate in various election campaigns.

In fact, Grace Hutchins, of Back Bay and Bryn Mawr, had been for years a fanatical Communist, and was, to my personal knowledge, in touch with more than one underground operation. It was she who first told me of a Japanese underground apparatus which was working out of the United States, screening, among other activities, Japanese students in America for Communist work in Japan. I can still see Miss Hutchins, sitting among the handsome old pieces in her Greenwich Village apartment, describing in her cultivated voice how difficult the work was made by the untrustworthiness of the students. "You can't trust one of them. The only safe way is to regard everyone in advance as a Japanese police spy." ("Due to Zhitomirsky's treachery," says Lenin's wife indignantly in one of her letters, "Comrade Kamo was arrested with a suitcase full of dynamite.")

Later in my experience, I met Miss Hutchins on other underground business. When Robert Gordon Switz, also a member of a good American family, but a Soviet agent (later an anti-Communist), was arrested with other members of his Soviet apparatus in Paris, it was Miss Hutchins who brought me together with Switz's brother so that I could turn over to him several hundred dollars for Switz's defense.

When my brother-in-law finally returned from court after four o'clock, Miss Hutchins was still waiting for him. In his private office, she came to the point at once: "If you will agree to turn Chambers over to us," she said, "the party will guarantee the safety of your sister and the children." My startled brother-in-law, who, like most Americans, was completely unaware of what Communism is really like (we had never discussed the subject), tried to explain that he did not know even the whereabouts of his sister, her husband or their children. The grand manner is second nature to Miss Hutchins, a fact which has long made her a butt among the more self-consciously proletarian levels of the Communist Party. But it also serves the revolution. She stared at my brother-in-law as if he were engaged in trade. "If he does not show up by (such and such a day)," she said briskly, "he will be killed." With that she left.

This interview has always had a special fascination for me. It is almost classically Communist; first, in its simple audacity; second, because, as usual with Communists, the party offers something it has no intention of giving ("the safety of your sister and the children," who were obviously much safer in any other hands) for something which it wants but cannot get (the custody of Whittaker Chambers). And its bad melodrama is saved by a comedy, at once low and touching, because the emissary, Miss Hutchins, even in the moment of trying to make a deal, cannot quite throw off the traditions of a gentle past which have become a part of her.

My brother-in-law, as a participant, took a different view. Terrified by the visit and unable to warn us, he was frantic. He rushed to the only two people he could think of who might know where we were: my mother and Miss Grace Lumpkin, the author of *To Make My Bread*, winner of the Maxim Gorki prize for literature, and long a friend of my wife's. Neither of them could help him. But I first learned of Grace Hutchins' mission from Grace Lumpkin when I called on her one day some time later. For Grace Lumpkin, now a devout woman whose days are filled with good works, had been a close fellow-traveler who broke from the Communist movement after me. A member of one of the South's oldest families, she was the sister of the late Senator Lumpkin of South Carolina, close friend for many years of James F. Byrnes, former Supreme Court Justice, Secretary of State and now Governor of South Carolina. I mention these origins deliberately, as I have dwelt on Grace Hutchins' antecedents, for the consideration of those people who still say: "But how could a man with Alger Hiss's background ever have been a Communist?"

VIII

I had another curious, and, at the time, much more disturbing brush with the Communist Party. It occurred somewhat later, but it had its beginnings from the very moment that I broke. In those days I kept all my associations carefully sketchy. My rule was to trust no one, even those whom perforce I must trust; for there are always some who must be trusted. Out of this necessity, I dealt with one man with increasing confidence. He was an executive. It lay in his power to give me work. Therefore, he gave me hope.

Let me call him Noel. Noel was a big, fair, effete, rubbery man, who lolled in his chair or over his desk, collapsed in a kind of hereditary fatigue, or as if he had recently been boned. With me he was so grossly upper class that I suspected him of doing a caricature of the type, and doing it rather amusingly, for he had a catlike grace and craft. He was casually kind and covertly cruel. I think he liked to blend the two. I think that this was one of his chief pleasures in life, in which he felt justified because his kindness usually outweighed his cruelty. A hundred such patrician Noels must have toddled out of the public baths in the warm dusks of dying Rome, with nothing more real on their minds than supper and the vomitorium.

He drove a glittery convertible. One night, after he had taken me to a thirty-dollar supper at the Chambord (at home my wife and I were eating breakfast food for all meals to conserve our money so that the children could have nourishing food), Noel found his car parked so tightly between two others that there seemed no way to get out. I watched him free himself by driving the beautiful machine, forward and backward, with a crash of fenders and denting of mudguards (including his own), that could be heard for a block, until he had rammed the obstructing cars away. I watched this splendid destruction with a slightly sick feeling. I felt as if I were caught between the crashing cars, as if Noel were challenging me each time they collided: "You see, the Communists are right about us playboys."

For he knew that I was an ex-Communist and liked to twit me about it. I took this twitting to be part of the price a workingman pays for his job, and merely endured or parried it. I recognized that in Noel's circles Communism was an amusing foible. The friend who had introduced me to Noel had assured me that he was a political blank. There was only one disturbing fact about him. One of his close friends was a man whom I suspected of being a Communist.

But Noel was so far from anything that resembled Communism that at last even I was almost completely off guard. To simplify our business relations, I gave Noel my address, and, when I acquired a telephone, my number.

One day he called me up long distance. He said he must see me at once. He would not tell me why. I had five dollars, which, with the gas that was in the car, was just enough to enable me to drive to New York from Baltimore, provided nothing untoward happened. I hoped, somewhat breathlessly, that his call meant a job.

I walked into Noel's office. It was a long room, thick-carpeted, with paneled ceiling or walls. Noel's desk was at the far end. As usual he was lolling half across it. He first glanced up when I was directly in front of the desk. He stared at me a moment, and then, without greeting me, said, "Ulrich is looking for you." Ulrich was the pseudonym of a Russian in the Soviet underground apparatus into which I was first recruited.

"Who is Ulrich?" I asked.

"O-o-o-h, you know," he answered, "Ulrich from Berlin."

Ulrich had worked underground in Berlin.

"How do you know Ulrich?" I asked.

"Because," said Noel, "when I was in Berlin, I joined the Communist Party."

"Then why are you warning me?" I asked.

"Because," he said, "I admire what you have done, but I do not have the courage to do it myself."

He then pulled out the right-hand top drawer of his desk and took from it a number of his commercial products which he piled in front of him. He ripped them open and out slid little heaps of Communist Party propaganda in a foreign language, some of which he handed silently to me. He explained that he was smuggling the leaflets abroad, in which operation he was working with V. J. Jerome. I had known Jerome in the open Communist Party in which he was the Agit-Prop (director of agitation and propaganda).

Noel told me that, a night or two before, he had had supper with Ulrich, who was hunting me and had asked Noel to bring him together with me.

Then Noel began to reminisce. He told me that he had made two trips into Nazi Germany at the Communist Party's orders. On the first trip, he was carrying "material," which in Communist language may mean anything from secret communications to microfilm. While he was passing through Belgium, an underground Communist agent had boarded the train at a way station and warned Noel that the Germans suspected him and were waiting to search him at the frontier. The agent took away the material. Noel went on to Aachen, the first German passport and customs post, where he was taken off the train, stripped and searched thoroughly.

On the second later trip, Noel was sent to contact two men: a Communist Party member who was working secretly in the top grouping of the Gestapo, and Ernst Torgler, a former member of the Central Committee of the German Communist Party, one of the defendants at the Reichstag fire trial, then in a concentration camp.

The day Noel arrived in Berlin, he found red placards posted on the walls, announcing that the Communists in the Gestapo had been beheaded. Noel described to me how the shock of this news was followed by a feeling of hopelessness and lassitude, so that all his strength seemed to be draining out of him. He went down to a little restaurant on one of the lakes, which he had frequented in earlier times, and simply sat there all day, staring at the water and drinking. He told me this quietly, without any histrionics, in a tone which I find it incredible that any man could have counterfeited who had not suffered the experience. Noel was not able to contact Torgler, either. But he managed to catch a glimpse of him, from a distance, walking with some other prisoners, and thus learned that Torgler was still alive.

I saw Noel only a few times afterwards, and only at his office. I would never again have gone to a restaurant with him, or to his house, as I had previously done, for despite his good intentions, Communists are subject to compulsions that he might not have been able to withstand. I heard about Noel from time to time from mutual acquaintances, whose various accounts, when their differences are duly allowed for, seem to add up to this: in 1939 Noel himself broke with the Communist Party.

Our mutual acquaintances always laugh at Noel's tale of Communist Party membership and his experiences as an underground courier. They insist that he is an incurable romantic. It is possible that Noel may have colored some of his exploits. But three things I find it impossible to believe. I find it impossible to believe that any man, romantic or merely cruel, or both, would bring another troubled man two hundred miles for the purpose of watching his reaction to a hoax. I find it impossible to believe that any man could have told me, so quietly and circumstantially, the story of Noel's trip to Berlin without its having happened. And I find it impossible to believe that one man would say to another: "I admire what you have done, but I do not have the courage to do it myself" unless he means it. For it is my experience that men's invention does not take that turn.

Moreover, some hard facts are involved. One, Ulrich was a pseudonym known only to a few members of the Soviet underground; few even of Ulrich's American Communist connections knew him by that name; they knew him as "Walter." Noel could not have known that name unless he knew Ulrich well or had deep underground connections. Two, an official (repeat official) record exists in which, while Noel fails to remember our conversation about his other underground activities, he remembers quite clearly that he pulled out his desk drawer, and showed me the concealed propaganda.

Regardless of the truth or falsity of Noel's warning about Ulrich, its impact on me was brutal. Even if it was intended merely as a move in the Communist war of nerves against me, it backfired badly. It failed to terrify me, but it did give me a feeling of desperation. It made me feel with fresh acuteness that I was at grips with an implacable enemy at which I must strike before it struck at me. It stirred in me a slow and deep anger whose roots lay at the point where the threat against me touched my wife and children. It faced me clearly with a question that I had been brooding on since my break: what must I do against the Communist Party? It hardened my purpose to take the offensive and attack the underground myself—as I shall presently describe—using my own methods and means. "*Denn wir haben eine Krise der Verzweiflung erreicht*—for we have reached a crisis of desperation," I wrote a friend at the time. This sentence from a letter which still exists (in the custody of the United States Government) suggests better than any effort of memory to recapture it the mood of those days and nights.

IX

This was not my only mood or my dominant mood. It was an undertone in our lives, like surf heard, continuously but unconsciously, far off at night, which only an episode such as that with Noel brought into full play.

I had prepared my break from the Communist Party with careful guile. But through Noel the shadow of the party and its secret apparatuses had fallen on me. It had been lifted from me by no talent of mine, no conspiratorial skill or alertness. Noel, like Paul, had not chosen to do me harm. Something in me which he called courage, something insubstantial, a mere quality, without material form, having nothing to do with intelligence or shrewdness, had touched something in him to which he gave no name; had fortified his weakness and moved his natural goodness.

In short, all my precautions had not saved me. I had been saved. It occurred to me: "How silly to suppose that any man by his own efforts can ever save himself."

I have one of those curious minds in which strong feeling almost always summons up involuntarily some passage of music or verse that has the same emotional quality. And since my memory for rhythm is better than my memory for words or notes, the rhythm of such passages sometimes pulsates for days at the back of my mind before I can recall what goes with it. That happened now. As I went over and over in my mind the meaning of the strange experience with Noel, I felt a premonitory rhythm, but I could not recapture the words. One day they burst the surface of my mind:

There is a Power whose care
Teaches thy path along that coast—
The desert and illimitable air—
Lone, wandering, but not lost.

I had memorized the stanza as a boy, and for more than twenty years I had not thought of it.

X

There was one comparatively bright month for us in this somewhat overcast period. During the 20's and 30's I had translated a dozen books from German and French, including the best-selling *Bambi,* but none had ever meant so much to me as the translation by which I was now earning my way to freedom. In our crowded quarters, it was difficult to work on the book even in the quiet nights. Our rooms were uncomfortable, our nerves were so raw that the sense of freedom, like a rebirth, that had possessed us when I broke with the Communist Party was wearing thin in furtive isolation. All of us needed a complete change. Tactically, too, perhaps, this was the moment to leave Baltimore and emerge somewhere else. It must be some miscellaneous place, where new arrivals make no stir. The only place of the kind I could think of was Florida. "Why not go there?" I thought. It was between the seasons and would probably be inexpensive. If I could find a library nearby, I could do whatever research was necessary for the translation. I told my wife: "We are going to Florida," and explained why. She smiled for the first time in weeks and the children caught her excitement.

We kept our rooms on the Old Court Road, but started south at once. We traveled lightly and I drove as fast as possible. I knew that the Communist Party had undergrounds in the South. I knew that it had members in the least expected places (filling stations and tourist camps worried me most). I did not know how widely it had alerted its members to be on the lookout for me. I still had no weapon but a knife.

Four days after we started, we crossed the upper bridge over the Halifax River and rolled into Daytona Beach between gardens of hibiscus and oleander that made my wife gasp with delight. We had told the children simply that we were going to a beach and all day each day my daughter had badgered me as I drove by asking: "Are we at the beach yet?" So I drove at once along the hard sand speedway at the surf's edge about a mile below the city. My family tumbled out on the sand. My daughter announced: "I'm not going in the car again." The boy had been sick for the last day.

Behind us on the high dune were two white bungalows, with blue shutters, facing the sea. They were the only houses anywhere around. They stood side by side in a little clearing. Around them was dense palmetto scrub. A dirt track, wide enough for one car, ran behind them. Cars constantly drove up and down the beach in front of them. A sign said that one of the bungalows was for rent.

It would have been hard to find a location more dangerous for us. But my wife begged me to rent the house. She said that the boy could not travel any farther. I made one of those foolish decisions people make under pressure. In addition, the rent was more than I could afford. But with my family in mind I rented the bungalow.

We resumed our security routine at once. While my wife and the children slept, I sat up all night, translating. The very first night, I heard a sound of footsteps under the window. I told myself that it was nothing, but I knew that I had not been mistaken. I heard the footsteps go around the house. My wife appeared in the bedroom door and said: "Are you all right? I think I heard footsteps outside." I stopped work, put out the light and spent the rest of the night watching in the dark. This happened several nights in succession. I did not even know how to go about procuring a gun. I was desperate for one.

On the third or fourth day, my neighbor in the next bungalow knocked at the door. He was holding a revolver. "There are people prowling around these bungalows at night," he said. "Would you mind keeping this gun, and if you hear anybody, come out shooting and I'll come out shooting?" He was a Government employe, a direct sort of man, who had once killed a rattlesnake by crushing its head with his Ford crank. As a result, the venom spurted in his eyes; he had nearly died. His hospital expenses were paid by the Government which, with a flash of unbureaucratic admiration, ruled that any man rugged enough to tackle a rattlesnake with a Ford crank deserved to have his expenses paid.

I took the revolver with something more than gratitude to my neighbor. Thereafter, I worked with the heavy gun lying on the table beside my typewriter.

The second night I had the weapon, I distinctly heard a hand fumbling with the back door. My neighbor ran out, firing his own gun. I followed. A car was parked, lights out, on the dirt track behind the houses. We heard someone crash through the palmetto and leap on the running board. The car started and tore, blind, down the road.

That was the end of our peace for some time. But the prowlers were not the G.P.U. Many transients go to Florida with large sums of money in cash. A gang had been looting the houses near Daytona Beach. Several hundred dollars had been stolen from the tenants before us. But this we did not learn until later, and the awareness of people lurking in the scrub at night was part of our nerve pattern at the time. Yet the sense of security in having a revolver was worth the anxiety.

Amidst these foolish alarms, the translation moved along. In nearby De Land, I found the library of Stetson College a friendly and helpful haven. The fugitive from the Communist Party often sat, of a sweltering afternoon, among the spooning coeds, doing his quiet research into the blood-and-iron policies of Bismarck and the gaudy follies of the man whom he called "the Sphinx without a secret"—Napoleon III.

In Florida, I finished the translation. It was published as *Dunant, The Story of the Red Cross.* The author of the book was Dr. Martin Gumpert. I met him again years later when he was the medical adviser to *Time's* medicine section and I was its editor.

We were in Florida exactly a month. We returned north through a cold, delayed spring, and, with the bleak weather, the fears that we had briefly fled closed in on us again. One thing I had made up my mind about: when I returned my neighbor his revolver, I resolved that I would not again be without the comfort of a gun. As we entered Baltimore, I stopped at Montgomery Ward's and bought a shotgun. It looked big enough to fell an elephant and the clerk warned me that the kick might knock me down. "Just what do you want it for?" he asked me. What I wanted it for was so much in the front of my brain that I felt as if I had been caught with my thoughts down and fumbled: "Well, I think there are prowlers around the house and a gun might come in handy." His reaction was completely different from what I expected. He was a Southerner with the fine abandon some Southerners have about firearms and related matters. "Well, sir," he said with immense pleasure, "you've bought the right gun. Just hold it in front of you, squeeze the trigger, and, brother, it will be *fay-ya*-you-well."

I have sometimes thought of him since. I have thought that while there are a few such uncomplicated souls around perhaps the battle is not quite lost yet.

X I

We settled back into our crowded rooms on the Old Court Road (in view of the future, a rather prophetic name) and resumed our furtive life. If that had been all we had to look forward to, it would have been intolerable. But in Florida I had made more than the decision to buy a gun. I had decided to come out of hiding.

In their concern for us, our few friends strongly opposed this move. They saw in it an unnecessary doubling of our risks. One or two freely predicted that, if I came out of hiding, I would not survive a month. Those were the days when the G.P.U. dared to stage a daylight attack on Walter Krivitsky and his wife and small son as they stepped off the boat train in France to take ship for the United States. It was a time of tenseness. My friends were quite right in supposing that by coming out of hiding I would double the risks. They were quite wrong in thinking that the move was unnecessary. The logic of my position was that I must come out of hiding. Hiding had been a temporary tactic. Its purpose was to baffle the party in its first automatic lunge to capture or destroy me. That period had passed.

Now, so long as I remained in hiding, I stood, in relation to the Communist Party, like a Communist Party that has been outlawed, driven completely underground and can no longer operate because it is severed from the normal life around it. Like the outlawed party, I was deprived of any base from which I could maneuver because I was cut off from the multitude of contacts through which a man (or a movement) uses his personal or social resources to go forward in life. While I was in hiding, I could not go forward, I could only go slowly backward. I could only become more and more depressed by my foredoomed position. Until I came out of hiding, I could not get a regular job. Until I had a regular job, I could not begin to reintegrate myself in life. Once I had a foothold in life, once I was in the open, the party would weigh much more carefully the risks involved in attacking me. Until then, I was a lone man fighting a war in the dark against a vastly superior force —a war whose secret nature worked in favor of the Communist Party and against me. Until I came out of hiding, the party could terminate this war whenever it might discover or trap me, leaving no more trace than a shot, a scamper of feet and the slam of a car door.

Coming out of hiding meant much more than walking freely on the streets of Baltimore, receiving letters through the United States mails or openly looking for a job. It meant ceasing merely to survive and beginning to live as other people live. It meant sinking roots and fostering growth. This was the problem which my wife and I, with the children in our minds, had discussed in Florida. In this sense, the question of coming out of hiding and the question of establishing a permanent home were one.

It seemed an impossible project. But I had gone to school to Lenin, who had taught me: "There are no absolutely hopeless situations." The whole aggressive mood of Communism, which had been mine for years, now came to my aid against the Communist Party. Its mood had been: there is almost nothing that is impossible if the imagination is bold enough to block it out and the will resolute enough to carry it through. I had not lost the Communist imagination and will by ceasing to be a Communist.

With little else but faith and this will to back us, my wife and I decided that if we could possibly manage it, we must buy a house. We decided that we would buy it in Baltimore. From a purely practical point of view, there were strong reasons against this. Washington with its heavy Communist concentration, and the Soviet embassy, which must harbor secret police, was only an hour away. In Baltimore itself the Communist Party was active and there were underground Communists in the city, some of whom I knew and who would have a special interest in getting rid of me. Yet where, in the eastern United States, and within easy reach of New York City, were there not Communists?

Besides, the problem from our standpoint was not purely practical. My wife and I had come to love Baltimore above all cities. We were at home in it, finding in its kindly people and their quiet lives a tranquillity contrasting with our distress. We loved the physical city, its old brick houses in whose grave and fine proportions, we sensed the proportions of a soul as well as an architecture. We loved its moods of morning and of evening light, its long gardens, sometimes brick-walled, its gas-lit streets at night. We loved the touch of the continuing past and the present sense that, while the city's commerce tapped the mainland, its harbor looked seaward. And under its traditional and easy order, we sensed a sultriness that spiked it with a special character, of people as well as of climate, and saved it from monotony—a sultriness that stirred the city and its people less in the dog days than in the bursts of hot spring nights. There was thus a propriety of the spirit in our choice that went beyond any practical reason, and determined us to make in this gracious and loved city our stand against death and for life. For that is how my wife and I regarded our next step.

With my mother's help, we bought, not long after our return

from the South, a small brick house in the 2700 block of St. Paul Street. We made a down payment, $500, I believe—the balance to be paid monthly as rent. The difficulty was how, from month to month, we were going to pay the rent.

In the months when I was carefully preparing my break with the Communist Party, and my friends, with whom I had shared some of my thoughts, became more and more impatient, thinking that I lacked courage, I used to ask half-jestingly: "What is a man to do with a wife and two small children?" One of them answered: "If you will break, I give you my word that I will help you until you can take care of yourself." Give my word is easily said, I thought. The fact is harder, not because the generous will is lacking, but because all men have needs and obligations of their own which must come first. I never really expected help from our friends. Nevertheless, they stood by us loyally. We could not have pulled through without them. It is no disparagement of the rest to say that the friend who had least helped most. Grace Lumpkin, whom I have mentioned, lent us all her savings, the first debt that I repaid when I went to work for *Time*.

Still, for us, the months on St. Paul Street were months of the shadows, the months that we do not often or willingly recall. We now received mail in our own name. We installed a telephone as a business necessity. We went openly about the streets. The old routine of vigilance continued. I still wrote or translated (for I presently got another book to translate) all night, now with the shotgun beside me. But the house had taken all our money. Want and the blank future had moved into the house with us, and were actually more real than fear of reprisals, which merely impended.

In the back of our Bible, I keep a letter from my wife. It is undated but it seems to have been written to me at *Time* a day or two after I was made a senior editor. It says:

"Dearest Loved One,

I want to tell you how very proud we are of you and how much we love you. You have achieved so much in such a short time. It probably doesn't seem so short to you, but when I remember that only so short a time ago you made your little trips to Center Street that we might eat, I am filled with the marvel of you and the tremendous urge that kept you at your job which has often been too humiliating and difficult. I naturally cannot see the entire picture as you have gone through it, but I could guess at agonies you have never expressed. Through it all, you have been the kindest, sweetest of husbands and most loving and thoughtful parent."

The little trips to Center Street that we might eat. . . . Center Street means the pawnshop. There were one or two such shops on that street, and the little trips were to pawn our only valuables —the watch I had been given at graduation, my wife's wrist watch —so that the children could have food. This was the period when, for the same reason, my wife and I had decided to go on a diet of breakfast food. What father out of work has not felt like a man trying to scale a bare cliff at night, with his wife and children roped to him for safety though his least misstep may send them all below?

We tried to spare the children this mood. We thought we had succeeded. But one day, when I was driving my daughter somewhere, a rather shabby man flagged us for a lift. As a precaution, I took no riders in those days. My daughter wanted to know who he was. I said that he was probably a poor man, hitching around the country looking for work. I said that when she was older I would tell her about such things; now it was too hard to explain. "And too sad?" she asked quietly. She was five.

I think of that period in terms of two or three days that seemed catastrophic to me then, but have a comedy quality now. The rent was about to fall due and we did not have it. The thermometer suddenly fell steeply. We had a low fire burning and did not notice how cold it had become outside. When I went out, I found that the car had frozen (we kept it in the yard to save garage rent); the ice had forced the hoses from the pipes. I thought that the radiator was surely ruined. I had no way of replacing it. It was a psychological, as well as a mechanical, disaster. The car was our means of flight. We hoped never to have to use it, but the fact that it was there to use gave us peace of mind. Without it we were crippled.

I went into the house in a fairly desperate mood to find that something was wrong with the furnace. It was an old one and had probably been cracked when we bought the house. The crack had opened and the water was putting out the fire in clouds of steam. In the chilling house we felt that we had been wiped out. It was all the more humiliating because the blows had not come from an enemy but from our own failure to meet ordinary life on its own terms.

Somewhere we found a repairman. Most of the next day, he and his helpers spent tearing down the furnace. My wife kept the children in bed under blankets and coats. Late in the afternoon, the repairman gave it up. He said there was just one possibility of sealing the crack: to pour a mending liquid in the tank. It might work, it might not.

While the men worked, I saw them eyeing me as I helped them, eyeing my wife on their trips through the house, trying to figure us out. The poor can smell poverty as a doctor can smell sickness. No doubt, they noted, those plain, untalkative men, that I was a jobless man with two small children. No doubt, they had children of their own. No doubt, they remembered months without work. Once again, I learned that the kindness of the poor to the poor is overpowering, given greatly out of little, without expectation or thought of return. When I finally asked the question that had been devouring my peace: "How much do I owe you?" the answer came: "The price of the mend-it, because we couldn't do nothing with the furnace." It was ridiculously little.

By a small miracle the crack in the furnace sealed and the mend-it filled the house for weeks with a smell like simmering library paste. By another small miracle, the car suffered no damage from its freeze. So my wife and I found ourselves using, about this and similar experiences, the word that had come into my mind when my neighbor handed me the revolver in Florida—the word: "providential."

XII

I left the Communist Party to fight it. I was already fighting it when I left it, as the manner of my break implies. There were other, less hazardous ways of disengaging myself from the Communist Party. I knew them. I could, possibly, have had myself transferred, on one pretext or another, from the underground to the open Communist Party—such transfers are not uncommon. Once back in the open party, after a suitable period of shuffling, I could gradually have lapsed from it. It would have been unpleasant. There might have been petty annoyances. It is unlikely that I would have been physically molested. But such a course would have meant some agreement, some kind of hobbling terms, between the Communist Party and me. I wanted no terms. I deliberately deserted from the Communist Party in a way that could leave no doubt in its mind, or anybody else's, that I was at war with it and everything it stood for.

There are men and women who break from the Communist Party and then have just one need: peace. Escape was all they had strength for; they have none left over to fight with. They are like shipwrecked men who can only slump down on the saving beach to which they have brought nothing from their experience but exhaustion. Let those who have never struggled with the sea blame them. If they ask only to be left alone, I should never disturb them. If they expressly refuse to help in the fight against the common enemy, I must respect their decision though it cause me hardship. During the Hiss Case, I learned that a former Communist had met Alger Hiss, in the 30's, at a Washington party to which only Communists or their close sympathizers were invited. He remembered his introduction to Alger Hiss clearly because, when he heard that name, he thought: "What ridiculous phony names our party people sometimes take." But the ex-Communist begged that he be spared from giving this information. He had suffered all that he could take, he said; he could not stand any more. His information had some value at that time. I never mentioned it, or his name, of course, to anyone.

In my own case, it would not have occurred to me that, if I survived the ordeal of deserting, I would then settle down with my family, wash my hands of the past and live entirely for myself. It is practically impossible for a man who knows there is a murderer at large, quietly to cultivate his garden while ignoring the screams of the victims in the next yard. It is practically impossible for a man who joins the Communist Party for the purpose of correcting an evil condition of the world not to turn against the party the force of the same purpose when experience convinces him that Communism is a greater evil. And there was something else that I shall come to presently.

By fighting the Communist Party, I do not mean that, day and night, I had no other thought. I do not much enjoy fighting. And my mind has a dozen active interests the least of which is more pleasant, fruitful, and engrossing than fighting Communism, which, by its very nature, is, of all the activities I know, the most sterilely wasteful of mind and spirit. But this fight happens to be a necessity of the 20th century, and I, by an accident of individuality and history, and hence by my special experience, happened to be one man who could make it.

There are many ways of fighting and I had hoped to use means and weapons best suited to my temperament and abilities. History soon proved to me that the enemy, and the conditions of the struggle, not I, would choose the weapons. Therefore, I carried on the fight against the Communist Party on more than one level. I carried it on for ten years before the world at large ever noted the name of Alger Hiss. I carried it on, in Marx's phrase, by "now open, now hidden means." For most of those ten years, the files of *Time* magazine reflect my fight week by week. The secret files of more than one security agent would reflect it more explicitly.

I began my active fight a few months after I broke from the Communist Party, some time in the fall of 1938, amidst the minor distresses of our life on St. Paul Street.

XIII

To a friend who, in 1938, was urging me, with some eloquence, to break with the Communist Party, I said at last: "You know that the day I walk out of the Communist Party, I walk into a police station." I meant, as he well knew, for he was an ex-Communist himself, that the question which first faces every man and woman who breaks with the Communist Party is: "Shall I become an informer against it?" My answer stopped that conversation, for to my friend, as to me, "informer" is a word so hateful that when, years later, in testifying before a grand jury, I came to that word and my decision to become an informer, I could not at once go on.

In the months after my break, I faced this word daily. For I faced daily the question: "What must I do about the underground apparatus in Washington?" I did not mean simply to let it go on operating. I was determined to immobilize it, and, if possible, to smash it. But I was not then prepared to do this by informing. Informing involves individual human beings, and neither then, nor at any subsequent time, were my actions directed against individual Communists, even when, perforce, I had to strike at the Communist Party through them. My actions were directed against the Communist Party as a political organization. I therefore decided to try first of all to smash the secret apparatus by myself.

The Communist Party, despite occasional pious statements to the contrary, is a terrorist organization. Its disclaimers are for the record. But its record of kidnappings, assassinations, and murders makes the actions of the old Terror Brigade of the Socialist Revolutionary Party[*] look merely romantic. No argument can reach the Communist Party unless it sees in it some self-serving advantage. It respects only force. Only terror terrifies it. I knew that if I merely returned to Washington and got in touch with the members of the underground, my reappearance would send a tremor through the apparatuses that would paralyze, if it did not stop, their work. I knew, too, that regardless of the party's reaction, if I returned to Washington and threatened the individual underground Communists, the party would be all but powerless to keep them active, and must, at the very least, declare a holiday. I knew that if I merely tried to argue the underground Communists out of their activity, most of them would laugh in my face and then demand that the party take steps to get rid of me.

It was a dangerous task to attempt. The party could not have overlooked the possibility that I might turn up again. Past friendship and loneliness both made it likely. I had no way of knowing whether my former underground comrades had been alerted against me or what measures had been taken to trap me if I should reappear. For safety I could count only on surprise and the fact that the conspirators were kept apart from one another by the form of the organization, and thus probably could not warn one another. I did not know whether, assuming that the party had not already sounded an alarm, it would act swiftly to warn all of them after my attack on the first ones, or whether it would try to avoid a panic by keeping the news from the rest and taking other special precautions. It might, for example, set a guard in the house of Alger Hiss, where I might be expected sooner or later to show up. My margin of safety lay in one chance: the party did not know whether I was working alone or together with an American security agency. If the latter, the guard might itself be endangered, and I did not think that the party would take that risk.

Nevertheless, the undertaking was so formidable that I kept put-

[*] The Terror Brigade, the underground section of the Socialist Revolutionary Party, made no secret of its purpose and methods. It organized and carried out the assassinations of the Russian Prime Minister von Plehve, the Grand Duke Sergei, and others. The Brigade was headed at one time by Yevno Asiev, the classic type of the double agent. As head of the Terror Brigade, Asiev planned and executed political murders. As a lifelong police agent, he constantly betrayed the terrorists to the police. Among those he betrayed was the young Lettish terrorist, Karl Trauberg, who had organized a highly mobile and effective unit of the Terror Brigade known as "Karl's Flying Detachment of the Northern Area." It was as a gesture of revolutionary respect to Karl Trauberg that I took the underground pseudonym "Carl."

ting it off. But one day, without telling my family where I was going, I drove to Washington.

I first called on Julian Wadleigh. In a series of syndicated articles which appeared during the Hiss Case, Wadleigh has described how I telephoned him at the State Department, how he met me somewhere outside, how I frightened him. From Wadleigh's account, I gather that my first attempt, though effective, was somewhat bungling and embarrassed. I say "I gather" because, over the years, this meeting with Wadleigh has faded from my mind; I have no independent recollection of it. But I remember clearly my meetings with Harry Dexter White and George Silverman.

I had intended simply to walk into Harry White's office in the United States Treasury. I had never met any of the sources at their offices and I thought that my sudden appearance in White's office would in itself be alarming. It would also be practically impossible for White to trap me in the swarming Treasury building.

But there was a uniformed guard at the Treasury door. I thought that I would be asked my business and my name. My business I could scarcely disclose and any name I might give would be meaningless to White, who would probably refuse to see me, for he had known me only as "Carl." So I called White from a drug or cigar store near the Treasury. White was not at all surprised that I should tell him over the telephone where to meet me, though I would never have done this in the old days. He said he would be right down. He was delighted to see me. "Back on a little trip to inspect the posts?" he asked cheerily. White, I concluded, had not been told about my break.

We started walking. I set the course and he came along just as in the past. We went to a candy and soda shop, sat down at the back and ordered coffee. White, with whom my relations had never been particularly friendly, was never so communicative. He talked, as usual, about "the Secretary" (Henry Morgenthau), about George Silverman, but not about the apparatus. I did not ask him about it. But at some point, he asked me: "Are you coming back to Washington to work?" I answered to this effect though I no longer remember my exact words: "No, I am not coming back to Washington to work. I am not here 'to inspect the posts.' The fact is that I have broken with the Communist Party and I am here to break you away from the apparatus. If you do not break, I will denounce you."

Harry White was a nervous man. At first he merely bent

over his coffee and said nothing. Then he tried the "you don't really mean that" rejoinder. I left him in no doubt that I meant that. I do not remember the rest of the conversation. I doubt that we said much more. I remember only that we were both embarrassed and that that made me stiff and probably grim.

As we left the shop in this mood, a street photographer pointed his camera at us. I spun White around and we walked in the opposite direction. Over his shoulder White glimpsed the camera. The action had been a reflex on my part, a hangover from the past. But White was abjectly grateful. I never saw him again. For some time, I thought that I had surely frightened White out of the underground. Certainly the flow of documents from the United States Treasury must have dried up temporarily. But, according to Elizabeth Bentley, White was active again in her apparatus a few years later.

From my meeting with White, I went directly to the Railroad Retirement Board, where George Silverman was director of research, and walked unannounced into his office. He was much more surprised than White had been to see me, and, as I had expected, he was startled that I should come to his office. He hurried me down to the street and we walked along Florida Avenue, through the Negro section, where I could easily keep track of the white faces around me.

Silverman also knew nothing about my break. He was in no way suspicious of me. He told me that the espionage operation was still in full swing, only there were new faces. George was frankly happy to see me again and in the warm glow of his welcome, I felt my purpose go soft. Nothing could have hardened it so quickly as his news about the apparatus. He told me, further, that in a day or two, he was meeting his new contact man, a Russian with a pseudonym that Silverman mentioned (one of the innumerable Tom, Dick or Harrys), but which I have forgotten. He was meeting the Russian in a drug store near Thomas Circle. I said: "Tell him without fail that you have seen me and say that Bob sends his greetings."

A week or so later, I again walked unannounced into George Silverman's office at the Railroad Retirement Board. This time he looked terrified. Again he hurried me downstairs. "What has happened?" he asked in a frightened voice. "What has happened? When I gave (Tom, Dick or Harry) your message, he jumped up from the table and grabbed his hat. He said: 'Don't ever try to contact me again unless you hear from me first.' Then he rushed out of the drug store."

Then I told George. I told him just as grimly as I had told Harry White. (Since, on my second visit, Silverman still knew nothing about my visit to White, I can only assume that under the new management of the apparatus, White and Silverman, who had formerly worked together, had been separated like the other workers.)

Like White, Silverman was a slight, nervous little man. But he lacked a pushing quality that I disliked in White. He aroused a protective feeling. For, in fact, he was a child, and the effort that it cost him to be a man was apparent in the permanently worried expression of his eyes. You cannot strike a child whom life costs such an effort. I told Silverman that I would surely denounce him if he continued in the apparatus which, I assured him, I meant to wreck. But we talked quietly. We wandered in the back streets beyond Florida Avenue. He confessed that he sometimes had his own doubts about the Communist Party. We parted gently.

And yet, when Elizabeth Bentley took over the Soviet espionage apparatuses in Washington, she found George Silverman still busily at work. He had gone ahead in the American Government service. He had become economic adviser and chief of analysis and plans to the Assistant Chief of the Air Staff (the unhappy General Bennett Meyers), in the Materiel and Services Division of the Air Force. Silverman had advanced in the Soviet service too. He no longer had to play underground nursemaid to Harry Dexter White. He had, according to Miss Bentley, become a full-fledged productive source himself.

My last call on George Silverman ended my private offensive against the underground in Washington. One part of that offensive I did not go through with. There was a photographic workshop in Washington to which I had a key. Part of my plan had been to go there and wreck the equipment. This was the most dangerous venture possible. The workshop was one place where the G.P.U. could easily prepare a trap for me and even "commit a good natural death." I found that I lacked the courage for this attempt.

XIV

I made one other visit to a former underground comrade. I made it, as nearly as I can reconstruct the pattern of that troubled time, between my visit to Julian Wadleigh and my visit to Harry Dexter White. It was my visit to Alger Hiss. It is the only one of the visits that I can date with certainty. It took place shortly before Christmas, 1938. I have taken it out of its chronological order because it differed in quality from the others.

I had never liked Harry White. I had no particular feeling, one way or the other, about Wadleigh. Silverman was merely a curious co-worker. But Alger Hiss and his wife I had come to regard as friends as close as a man ever makes in life. By unnumbered little acts of kindness and affection, by the pleasure, freely expressed, which they took simply in being together with my wife and me, they had given us every reason to believe that their feeling for us was of the same kind as our feeling for them. Therefore, I had some grounds to suppose that my break must disturb Alger Hiss deeply. But because it is my habit to think in terms of people first, and their function in life only secondly, I failed to measure accurately how much Hiss's regard for me had been regard for me as a Communist organizer. Perhaps he did not realize it himself. Thus my personal feeling for Hiss got in the way of my sober judgment, and, as Colonel Bykov had once fondly hoped against all probability that I had not deserted, but merely been killed, I, in my wishfulness, nursed the unlikely hope that my break might have shaken Alger Hiss. Nothing could have been less realistic.

But, with this hope at the bottom of my mind, I thought that simply by seeing Alger again, by talking quietly with him, I might pry him loose from the party. In any case, I could never have acted with him as I had with White and the others; our friendship made it unthinkable.

It was early evening when I reached the Hisses' house, probably between six and seven o'clock. They were then living on Volta Place in Georgetown, in a house whose narrow end faced the street. It was, in fact, flush with the sidewalk. I went in through the little gate, at the right side of the house. A colored maid, probably Claudia Catlett, who was a witness for Hiss at his trials, came to the door. She said that neither Mr. nor Mrs. Hiss was at home. I left. But as I stood for a moment in indecision on the sidewalk, Priscilla Hiss drove up. She headed in to the curb on a slant to park. The headlights swept the sidewalk and I stepped into the beam so that Priscilla could see me clearly and would not be frightened by a loitering figure.

Her greeting was pleasant but not effusive, and I decided at once that Alger Hiss had been warned of my break. We went into the house together. Yet there was nothing in Priscilla's manner, as we sat chatting in the living room, that enabled me to tell what Alger really did know. Then Timmie joined us. Timmie is Timothy Hobson, Priscilla Hiss's son by her first marriage. Timmie was delighted to see me.

I had to go to the bathroom. Priscilla followed me upstairs. The bathroom was at the front of the house, facing the street. Directly to the right of the bathroom door, there was a bedroom door. A telephone was on a little table near the door. As I went into the bathroom, Priscilla went into the bedroom. I closed the bathroom door and thought: "This situation is tight." Before I washed my hands, I opened the bathroom door halfway. Priscilla was speaking in a very low voice into the telephone. I walked directly up to her. She hung up. We went downstairs in silence.

At that nerve-tingling moment, Alger Hiss came home. We were in the living room and he saw me the moment he came into the house. He was surprised, of course, and his surprise showed in his eyes. But he smiled pleasantly, said: "How do you do," and made me the little bow with his head and shoulders that he sometimes made when he was being restrained. It was both whimsical and grave.

We went in almost at once to supper. The dining room was also at the front of the house. The light supper, which had been intended for three, and was stretched for four, was quickly over. With Timmie present and the maid serving, we again made the kind of random talk that Priscilla and I had had before Alger arrived. Again, I do not remember just what we talked about, but I seem to recall that Timmie, who had never taken much interest in athletics, was trying out for the wrestling team at his school, and wanted for Christmas, or had just bought, some wrestling shoes.

Timmie left the table while we had our coffee and I said good night to him—in effect good-bye, for I have never seen him since. Once Timmie was gone some question was asked which I answered in the faintly foreign tone that I had always used in the underground. The reaction was electric: "You don't have to put on any longer. We have been told who you are." To understand what was meant, it is necessary for me to explain that Alger Hiss, like everybody else in the Washington underground, supposed that I was some kind of European. I do not want to interrupt the narrative to explain how this was possible. But during the Grand Jury hearings in 1948, one of the former underground people was brought into the witness waiting room so that he could hear me speak because, while I looked like the man he knew as Carl, I spoke like an American, and the man he knew as Carl spoke like a European.

The angry answer at the dinner table meant that two facts were known: I was an American; I had broken with the Communist Party. Alger, who was sitting at the head of the table, to my right, tried to dispel the awkwardness. He said something to this effect: "It is a pity that you broke. I am told that you were about to be given a very important post. Perhaps if you went to the party and made your peace, it could still be arranged." I thought: "Alger has been told to say that to me." The "important post" was perhaps Bykov's old project of the sleeper apparatus now doing service as bait. I smiled and said that I did not think I would go to the party.

I began a long recital of the political mistakes and crimes of the Communist Party: the Soviet Government's deliberate murder by mass starvation of millions of peasants in the Ukraine and the Kuban; the deliberate betrayal of the German working class to Hitler by the Communist Party's refusal to co-operate with the Social Democrats against the Nazis; the ugly fact that the German Communist Party had voted in the Reichstag with the Nazis against the Social Democrats; the deliberate betrayal of the Spanish Republican Government, which the Soviet Government was only pretending to aid while the Communists massacred their political enemies in the Spanish prisons. This gigantic ulcer of corruption and deceit had burst, I said, in the great Russian purge when Stalin had consolidated his power by massacring thousands of the best men and minds in the Communist Party on lying charges.

I may have spoken for five or ten minutes. I spoke in political terms because no others would have made the slightest impression on my host. I spoke with feeling, and sometimes with slow anger as the monstrous picture built up. Sometimes Alger said a few objecting words, soberly and a little sorrowfully. Then I begged him to break with the Communist Party.

Suddenly, there was another angry flare-up: "What you have been saying is just mental masturbation."

I was shocked by the rawness of the anger revealed and deeply hurt. We drifted from the dining room into the living room, most unhappy people. Again, I asked Alger if he would break with the Communist Party. He shook his head without answering. There was nothing more to say. I asked for my hat and coat. Alger walked to the door with me. He opened the door and I stepped out. As Alger stood with his hand on the half-open door, he suddenly asked: "What kind of a Christmas will you have?" I said: "Rather bleak, I expect." He turned and said something into the room: "Isn't there . . . ?" I did not catch the rest. I heard Priscilla move. Alger went into the room after her. When he came back, he handed me a small cylindrical package, three or four inches long, wrapped in Christmas paper. "For Puggie," he said. Puggie is my daughter's nickname. That Alger should have thought of the child after the conversation we had just had touched me in a way that I can only describe by saying: I felt hushed.

We looked at each other steadily for a moment, believing that we were seeing each other for the last time and knowing that between us lay, meaningless to most of mankind but final for us, a molten torrent—the revolution and the Communist Party. When we turned to walk in different directions from that torrent, it would be as men whom history left no choice but to be enemies.

As we hesitated, tears came into Alger Hiss's eyes—the only time I ever saw him so moved. He has denied this publicly and derisively. He does himself an injustice—by the tone rather than by the denial, which has its practical purpose in the pattern of his whole denial. He should not regret those few tears, for as long as men are human, and remember our story, they will plead for his humanity.

XV

What lonely rides men take. That night ride from Washington back to Baltimore was one of the loneliest I shall ever make. It is not good to lose good friends for less than human reasons.

In the house on St. Paul Street, I opened the Hisses' gift to my daughter. I do not know why I opened it instead of keeping it and putting it under the Christmas tree—probably some precautionary sense. The package contained a little wooden rolling pin such as could be bought at the dime store for a nickel. The Hisses had loved my daughter, played with her, cared for her. If the gift had been intended as an insult, I should have smiled regretfully and reflected on the ways of men. It was because it had been given in spontaneous kindness, the last thought at the final parting, that it seemed to me to betray completely the mind of the giver and what I had become to it; and through me, it struck at the child.

"This," I thought, "is the gift that you think fit for the child of a renegade from the Communist Party. The father is irredeemable, but the child must not be wholly included in the father's guilt—not wholly. So you condescend to conscience and send her a five-cent toy."

I am not saying that I was necessarily right in my feeling or that I drew the right inferences. I have, in fact, since come to think that I was deeply wrong. I am reporting what I felt as an instance of the curiously taut emotions almost inseparable from the turmoil of such a break with the past as mine. I took the little rolling pin and its wrappings down to the cellar and threw it in the furnace. It was years before I could bring myself to tell my wife about it.

XVI

When I told Alger Hiss that our Christmas would probably be bleak, it was the children, of course, that I was thinking of. It was a Christmas bleak for the children that troubled me. But Christmas, 1938, was not bleak.

My mother came to spend the holidays with us and with her the spirit of Christmas entered the house. Our friends, everybody who knew about us, and by then such people were more numerous, seemed to have had the children in mind too. Presents for them began to arrive by mail. On Christmas Eve, we heaped them under the tree, which glittered with the ornaments of my childhood Christmases, fragile birds, spikes, horns, bunches of grapes, now practically unobtainable because the only people who really know how to blow them, the Germans, have been blown by the century into chaos. My mother had kept boxes of those delicate toys through all the years when they had lost their meaning for me. She had given them back to my children.

It was my son's first Christmas—the first in which he was old enough to take a conscious part. He padded downstairs early on Christmas morning and stopped short before the tree. But it was not the tree that had stopped him. His grandmother had given him a gaily painted wagon filled with big, bright-colored wooden blocks. It stood unwrapped under the tree. He simply stared at it. We smiled encouragement to him. "For *me*?" he asked incredulous.

For, in the presence of such benefaction, the act of belief was too much for him.

In a sense, different, but perhaps not so much different, it was my first Christmas too. For the first time in our lives, I tried to tell my children the Christmas story. I tried to tell it in such a way that each of its elements, the sheep, the hills, the sky, Bethlehem, would remind them of something they knew that would be real to them. I told them that on Christmas Eve sheep were being pastured on bare hills, like the hills in the poorer parts of Maryland. Men were watching them, poor men, the kind of men who tend sheep. As they listened to the sound of the sheep moving and tried to follow them in the dark, they became aware of an unusually bright star, burning in the sky in the direction of Bethlehem, a village beyond the hills. There was a sudden brightness and they heard voices saying: "Glory to God in the highest. On earth peace. Good will to men." Years later, men still felt that moment so strongly that they had caught it in the song which my daughter was just learning:

Noel! Noel!
Noel! Noel!
Christ is born in Bethlehem.

Bethlehem, I told them, is our hearts.

XVII

I have described how I broke with the Communist Party. I have not told why I broke with Communism. It would have been all but meaningless to try to describe a crisis of the mind and spirit before I had given some idea of the organization and atmosphere in which that crisis occurred.

In 1935 or 1936, I chanced to read in the press a little item of some nine or ten lines, perhaps less. The story said that Dmitri Schmidt, a general in the Red Army, had been sentenced and shot in Russia. I have forgotten whether it said "for treason." I had never heard of Dmitri Schmidt before. I still do not know anything more about him. He is a ghost who appeared to my mind a few hours after his death, evoked by a few lines of type.

I do not know why I read and reread this brief obituary or why there came over me a foreboding, an absolute conviction: Something terrible is happening. I felt this so strongly that I mentioned the item to J. Peters, the head of the underground section of the American Communist Party. He did not answer me at once. Then he said fiercely: "A comrade who has just come back from Moscow is going around saying that there is a terror going on there and that they are arresting and shooting everybody. He should be taken care of." This was Peters' way of saying that I should shut up. Then I knew that my foreboding was right.

The little item about Dmitri Schmidt meant, of course, that the Great Purge had reached the Red Army. Like a single, absurd revolver shot far off on the sidelines, it announced the opening of an immense and bloody engagement. The Communist Party of the Soviet Union had begun to condition itself for the final revolutionary struggle with the rest of the world by cutting out of its own body all that could weaken or hamper it in that conflict. It was literally sweating blood.

More nonsense, if possible, has been written about the Purge than about any of the great events of our age. It has been described as a drama of the Russian mind and soul which a non-Russian can hope to understand only by reading the novels of Feodor Dostoyevsky. It has been cited (for example, in *Mission to Moscow*) as an act of high patriotism whereby the wise Stalin rid his country of those traitors who were trying to negotiate an agreement with the Nazis. The fact that Stalin and his group shortly thereafter negotiated such an agreement with the Nazis is tactfully overlooked. The great public trials, by which the Purge was dramatized in the person of former high Communists, who sometimes abjectly, sometimes with apparent delight, confessed to the most fantastic lies, had just the effect they were intended to have abroad. They distracted attention from the main purpose of the Purge, while the wise men of the West wrote with brilliant inconclusiveness on "Why They Confess." (They confess, of course, because, if a man's family is completely at the mercy of his captors, and if he is systematically tortured by experts, he will, unless he is exceptionally strong or already more than half-dead, confess to almost anything. If he does not confess, he will not be tried publicly; he will be shot secretly.)

The Great Purge was in the most literal sense a massacre. It was like one of those Western jack-rabbit hunts in which a whole countryside forms a vast circle that finally closes in on its victims and clubs them to death. The purgees, like the rabbits, had no possible chance to escape; they were trapped, arrested, shot or sent to one of those Russian slave-labor camps on which the Nazis modeled their concentration camps, substituting the gas oven for death by enforced starvation, hard labor and undoctored disease.

This great massacre, probably the greatest in history, was deliberately planned and executed. In the interest of the Revolution (and, as always in politics, this higher interest can also be translated into terms of personal interest without at all challenging its sincerity), the group of Communists headed by Stalin decided that the historical situation through which the world and the Communist Party was passing, justified them in killing off those Communists who opposed their indispensable strategy and tactics. Those killed have been estimated from several hundred thousand to several million men and women. The process took about three years, 1935 through 1938. Its immediate purpose was to give the Stalinists absolute control of the Communist Party and the Soviet Government, then of the Red Army, then of the secret police (G.P.U.). This seizure of power in the party and the state, which the Stalinists carried out with the same careful craft that the Communists had used in seizing power in Russia, took place in three well-marked waves and several subsidiary waves. In the first wave, aimed at consolidating their power in the party, the government and the army, the Stalinists used the secret police to massacre their opponents in the party and the general staff. In the second wave, the Stalinists turned on the secret police and replaced the head of the G.P.U. (Yagoda) with his second in command (Yezhov). Yezhov then liquidated Yagoda and his friends (on charges of murder). In the third wave, the Stalinists killed Yezhov, who had been their tool in killing Yagoda, and secured absolute control of the secret police. This act, which was the crest of the Purge, gave them complete control of the party and the government.

The principle is the old Oriental one whereby a great king commanded a group of slaves to dig and construct a treasure vault. When the treasure was moved in, the king commanded a second group of slaves to massacre the first group, so that the secret of the vault and its location died with them. To make doubly sure, he then commanded a third group of slaves to massacre the second group, so that even the knowledge that the second group had massacred the first group was buried with them. Colonel Bykov never had the slightest doubt as to what was happening in the Purge. As each new list of executed men was published, he would quote Lenin to me gleefully: "Loochye menshe, no loochye—Better less, but better."

Since the Purge, millions of men, women and children in the world have died violently. The 20th century has put out of its mind, because it can no longer cope with the enormity of the statistic, the millions it has exterminated in its first fifty years. Even among those millions the number killed in the Purge makes a formidable figure. But, on a Communist, not only the numbers, but the revolutionary stature of the purgees, had a shattering impact. To the Western world, those strange names—Rykov, Bukharin, Kamenev, Zinoviev, Piatakov, Rakovsky, Krylenko, Latsis, Tuchachevky, Muralov, Smirnov, Karakhan, Mrachkovsky—were merely tongue twisters. To a Communist, they were the men who had made one of the great transformations in human history—the Russian Revolution. The charge, on which they were one and all destroyed, the charge that they had betrayed their handiwork, was incredible. They *were* the Communist Party. If the charge was true, then every other Communist had given his life for a fraud. If the charge was false, then every other Communist was giving his life for a fraud. This was a torturing thought. No Communist could escape it.

The Purge struck me in a personal way too. Like every Communist in the world, I felt its backlash, for the Purge also swept through the Soviet secret apparatuses. I underwent long hours of grilling by Colonel Bykov in which he tried, without the flamboyance, but with much of the insinuating skill of Lloyd Paul Stryker, the defense lawyer in the first Hiss trial, to prove that I had been guilty of Communist heresies in the past, that I was secretly a Trotskyist, that I was not loyal to Comrade Stalin. I emerged unharmed from those interrogations, in part because I was guiltless, but more importantly, because Colonel Bykov had begun to regard me as indispensable to his underground career, so that toward the end of his grillings he would sometimes squeeze my arm in his demonstrative Russian way and repeat a line from a popular song that had caught his fancy: *"Bei mir bist du schön."*

Actually, Bykov's cynicism was harder to bear than his grillings. He was much too acute to suppose that I was sound about the Purge, and he took a special delight in letting me know it. Sometimes, after the purgees had been sentenced to be shot, there would be no official announcement of their execution, as if to emphasize playfully that this official silence was part of the silence of death. "Where is Bukharin?" Bykov asked me slyly some weeks after the Communist Party's leading theoretician had been sentenced to death for high treason, while his death had not been announced.

"Dead," I answered rudely. "You are right," said Bykov in a cooing voice, "you are right. You can be absolutely sure that our Bukharin is dead."

The human horror of the Purge was too close for me to grasp clearly its historical meaning. I could not have said then, what I knew shortly afterwards, that, as Communists, Stalin and the Stalinists were absolutely justified in making the Purge. From the Communist viewpoint, Stalin could have taken no other course, so long as he believed he was right. The Purge, like the Communist-Nazi pact later on, was the true measure of Stalin as a revolutionary statesman. That was the horror of the Purge—that acting as a Communist, Stalin had acted rightly. In that fact lay the evidence that Communism is absolutely evil. The human horror was not evil, it was the sad consequence of evil. It was Communism that was evil, and the more truly a man acted in its spirit and interest, the more certainly he perpetuated evil.

But, at the time, I saw the Purge as the expression of a crisis within the group—the Communist Party—which I served in the belief that it alone could solve the crisis of the modern world. The Purge caused me to re-examine the meaning of Communism and the nature of the world's crisis.

I had always known, of course, that there were books critical of Communism and of the Soviet Union. There were surprisingly few of them (publishers did not publish them because readers did not read them). But they did exist. I had never read them because I knew that the party did not want me to read them. I was then entirely in agreement with the European Communist who said recently, about the same subject: "A man does not sip a bottle of cyanide just to find out what it tastes like." I was a man of average intelligence who had read much of what is great in human thought. But even if I had read such books, I should not have believed them. I should probably have put them down without finishing them. I would have known that, in the war between capitalism and Communism, books are weapons, and, like all serviceable weapons, loaded. I should have considered them as more or less artfully contrived propaganda.

It will be impossible for a non-Communist to conceive the fever with which I decided to read my first anti-Communist book. I mean fever quite literally; and furtiveness as if I were committing an unpardonable sin, as I was. For the fact that I voluntarily opened such a book could mean only one thing: I had begun to doubt. By chance, and I will let that evasive word stand for something which I do not hold to be chance at all, the first book I read was the book best calculated to shake me to the depths. It was called *I Speak for the Silent.* Its author was Professor Vladimir Tchernavin.

Professor Tchernavin was not a Communist. He was a Russian technician of some kind. He was a little man in the Communist world, gentle, humane, good. He went about his routine chores, finding what happiness he could in his love for his wife and small son. Suddenly, for no reason at all, he was arrested and carried away by the secret police. He began that long transit of the Soviet prisons, like a gummed fly slipping from strand to strand in the web of a spider that was always waiting to pounce. At last he was sent to a sub-arctic prison camp (from which together with his wife and son he later made a sensational escape to Finland). In freedom, he wrote of the horrors of that slave labor camp, simply, factually; it was their monstrousness, not his pathos that sickened the soul. Some years before, a British trade-union delegation had toured Russia and reported that there were no slave labor camps, and that had been good enough for me. I wrote off the recurring rumors as propaganda. Now for the first time, I believed that slave labor camps existed.

A year before, that would not have mattered much to me. I would have put down Tchernavin's book and would not have reopened it. I would have known that, even if some of it were true, it was the price of social progress. I would have known, as what Communist does not know, that terror is an instrument of policy, right if the Communist vision is right, justified by history, enjoined by the balance of forces in the social wars of this century. Now, too, I put down *I Speak for the Silent.* But for a different reason; because I could not go on, because I could not endure the question that it raised. I was that Communist whom I have described in the foreword to this book. About me had closed a separating silence—the deathly silence of those for whom Tchernavin spoke—and in that silence I heard their screams. "He hears them for the first time. For they do not merely reach his mind. They pierce beyond. They pierce to his soul. He hears them for the first time because a soul in extremity has communicated with that which alone can hear it—another human soul."

I did not know what had happened to me. I denied the very existence of a soul. But I said: "This is evil, absolute evil. Of this evil I am a part."

I can no longer retrace with certainty the stages of my inner earthquake or distinguish its successive shocks. The structure of my Communist thought was firmly and logically built. It was not the structure but the ground it stood on that was in convulsion. I knew confusion and despair long before I knew what to do about it. I knew that my faith, long held and devoutly served, was destroyed long before I knew exactly what my error was, or what the right way might be, or even if there were a right way. For my mind and the logic of history had told me that Communism was the only way out for the 20th century. If Communism were evil, what was left but moral chaos?

One thing I knew: I was no longer a Communist. I had broken involuntarily with Communism at the moment when I first said to myself: "It is just as evil to kill the Tsar and his family and throw their bodies down a mine shaft as it is to starve two million peasants or slave laborers to death. More bodies are involved in one case than the other. But one is just as evil as the other, not more evil, not less evil." I do not know at just what point I said this. I did not even know that with that thought I had rejected the right of the mind to justify evil in the name of history, reason or progress, because I had asserted that there is something greater than the mind, history or progress. I did not know that this Something is God.

Obviously, no book, however moving, could have overthrown the faith and viewpoint of an adult lifetime if that faith and viewpoint had not been secretly and deeply sapped. I do not know how long there had existed, side by side with my militant acceptance of the implications of Communism, an uneasiness, an anxiety, which I would now call spiritual, but which in the past I would never willingly have admitted to my mind. If ever it slipped out, I would have crushed it back as a weakness, a base token of my inadequacy as a Communist, of my immaturity as a revolutionist—for, of course, Communists are not born fully developed Marxists.

I do not know, either, by what subtle stages this conflict of the spirit of man gained on the doctrine and practice of Communism in me. I do know that over the years the unwanted thought sometimes crossed my mind: What is lacking in Communism? What lack is it that keeps the human level of Communism so low, that makes the party a rat's nest of intrigue and faction? What is the source of its corroding cynicism, that makes the workers, in contrast to the Communists, seem like heroes of simple honesty, that makes us waste human life and effort without scruple and turns our greatest victories into sordid waste? Why is it that thirty years after the greatest revolution in history, the Communists have not produced one single inspired work of the mind? What is our lack?

Now in my despair, I asked at last: can it be God? I asked it first as an acknowledged absurdity which the mind is reduced to after rejecting every other possibility. I asked it, astounded that I could ask it at all, and with aversion as if something old, cunning and fetid from the past had reached out unfairly to possess my mind in its moment of greatest weakness. I associated God with ill-ventilated vestries and ill-ventilated minds.

How could it be God? Yet if it was just as evil to kill the Tsar as to kill two million peasants, it was evil because a violence had been committed against the soul—the soul of the murderer as well as of the murdered. It was not evil for any lesser reason. By the logic of history it was expedient, and in its directness merciful. "How long are you going to keep on killing people?" Lady Astor would ask Stalin brightly. "As long as it is necessary," he answered and asked in turn: "How many people were killed in the First World War? You killed that many people for nothing," he had added, "and you blame us for killing a handful for the most promising social experiment in history?" In terms of the modern mind, which excludes from its reasoning the undemonstrable fact of God, Stalin's answer was unanswerable. It could only be answered by another question: "And man's soul?"

At some point, I sought relief from my distress by trying to pray. I had tried to pray a few times before, in my boyhood and my youth. I had not been successful. My whole life as a man lay between those failures and my present need. Now, as I tried to pray, it was as if that spirit from my boyhood and youth took my hand and knelt and prayed beside me, so that in the act of seeking oneness with God, I became one with myself. The secret springs of my life, which had been lost so long in the desert of modernity, joined their impulses, broke free and flowed unchecked. At the same time, I began to sense that the two mirages that had beckoned me into the desert—the mirage of Almighty Mind and its power to plan human salvation—were illusions.

As I continued to pray raggedly, prayer ceased to be an awkward and self-conscious act. It became a daily need to which I looked forward. If, for any reason, I were deprived of it, I was distressed as if I had been deprived of some life necessity, like water. I cannot say I changed. There tore through me a transformation with the force of a river, which, dammed up and diverted for a lifetime, bursts its way back to its true channel. I became what I was. I ceased to be what I was not.

What I had been fell from me like dirty rags. The rags that fell from me were not only Communism. What fell was the whole web of the materialist modern mind—the luminous shroud which it has spun about the spirit of man, paralyzing in the name of rationalism the instinct of his soul for God, denying in the name of knowledge the reality of the soul and its birthright in that mystery on which mere knowledge falters and shatters at every step. If I had rejected only Communism, I would have rejected only one political expression of the modern mind, the most logical because the most brutal in enforcing the myth of man's material perfectibility, the most persuasive because the least hypocritical in announcing its purpose and forcibly removing the obstacles to it. If I had rejected only Communism, I should have changed my faith; I would not have changed the force that made it possible. I should have remained within that modern intellectual mood which gives birth to Communism, and denies the soul in the name of the mind, and the soul's salvation in suffering in the name of man's salvation here and now. What I sensed without being able to phrase it was what has since been phrased with the simplicity of an axiom: "Man cannot organize the world for himself without God; without God man can only organize the world *against man.*" The gas ovens of Buchenwald and the Communist execution cellars exist first within our minds.

But the torrent that swept through me in 1937 and the first months of 1938 swept my spirit clear to discern one truth: "Man without mysticism is a monster." I do not mean, of course, that I denied the usefulness of reason and knowledge. What I grasped was that religion begins at the point where reason and knowledge are powerless and forever fail—the point at which man senses the mystery of his good and evil, his suffering and his destiny as a soul in search of God. Thus, in pain, I learned the distinction between wisdom and knowledge—knowledge, which however exalted, is seldom more than the making of careful measurements, and wisdom, which includes knowledge, but also includes man's mystery.

I cannot say that I then believed in God. I sought God. I sought Him with the hopeless sense that by finding Him I must at once lose what I had scarcely found. For though in finding prayer, I had found myself, I did not see how I, or any other man like me, could at so late an hour retrace the steps of his life and make what I have called in the first line of this book "the impossible return." I asked myself if I must not kill myself. And even when I answered: "No," not from force of reason, but from force of life, I felt that the answer should be: "Yes."

Then there came a moment so personal, so singular and final, that I have attempted to relate it to only one other human being, a priest, and had thought to reveal it to my children only at the end of my life.

In those days, I often moved about or performed tasks more or less blindly from habit, while my mind was occupied with its mortal debate. One day as I came down the stairs in the Mount Royal Terrace house, the question of the impossible return struck me with sudden sharpness. I thought: "You cannot do it. No one can go back." As I stepped down into the dark hall, I found myself stopped, not by a constraint, but by a hush of my whole being. In this organic hush, a voice said with perfect distinctness: "If you will fight for freedom, all will be well with you." The words are nothing. Perhaps there were no words, only an uttered meaning to which my mind supplied the words. What was there was the sense that, like me, time and the world stood still, an awareness of God as an envelopment, holding me in silent assurance and untroubled peace. There was a sense that in that moment I gave my promise, not with the mind, but with my whole being, and that this was a covenant that I might not break.

On one side of that moment were nearly forty years of human waste on all the paths and goat paths of 20th-century error and action. On the other side was humility and liberation, the sense that the strength would be given me to do whatever I must do, go wherever I must go. The moment itself was something which to deny would be a blasphemy. It was decisive for the rest of my life, and incomparable in that I never knew it again. I have sat in a Quaker meeting, in which I shared with the others a spiritual experience so intense that the leader of the group, the late Arthur Burke, had no choice but to say in the silence: "This meeting has had a divine covering." But even that was not the same.

If I were asked to say, in terms of the modern mind: "What is the meaning of this experience?" I should answer: "I do not know. Something happened in the hall at Mount Royal Terrace. I experienced something." From that hall, I walked into life as if for the first time. I do not mean that I was exalted or conspicuously changed. I was still an erring, inadequate man, capable of folly, sin and fear. Like other men, I still must walk through damp pockets of desperation. But those were surface vicissitudes, as the surface of water is torn up while the depth below remains unchanged. Henceforth, in the depth of my being there was peace and a strength that nothing could shake. It was the strength that carried me out of the Communist Party, that carried me back into the life of men. It was the strength that carried me at last through the ordeal of the Hiss Case. It never left me* because I no longer groped for God; I felt God. The experience was absolute.

I did not seek to know God's will. I did not suppose that anyone could know God's will. For, as I was to tell a grand jury ten years later: "Between man's purpose in time and God's purpose in eternity, there is an infinite difference in quality." The words are Kierkegaard's; the experience that gave them life for me is mine. Nor did I ever regard myself as an instrument of God. I only sought prayerfully to know and to do God's purpose with me. And I did not suppose that those words, "All will be well with you," implied my happiness, for I never supposed that what man means by well-being and what well-being means to God could possibly be the same. They might be as different as joy and suffering. I only knew that I had promised God my life, even, if it were His will, to death.

This is my ultimate witness.

XVIII

One night, in the spring of 1939, my wife opened her purse and showed me that it contained less than fifty cents. It was all the money that we had. The rent was due or overdue. I had borrowed all that I could borrow. There was really nowhere to turn. I thought: "Well, we are beaten at last." I went to bed.

The morning mail brought a letter from my friend, Robert Cantwell, the author of *Laugh and Lie Down,* and later, the biographer of Hawthorne. Cantwell was then one of the editors of *Time* magazine. Some time before, Cantwell had asked me whether he should take the job that *Time* had offered him. I had urged him to, in part because I thought that the experience and the salary would do him good; in part, because, at the back of my mind, was

* Except for one moment, which I shall relate, when I felt that God had left me.

the thought that my having a friend at *Time* might some time be useful to the underground. The Communist mind works in that thrifty way. Cantwell, of course, was not a Communist, and knew nothing about what was in my mind. He was one of the people who urged me to break away from the Communist Party. He helped me with money and part-time work after I broke. One day I said to him that I thought that I should like to work for *Time*. "You are not really serious?" he asked, a little aghast; and quickly added that there were no jobs then. I thought that that was his way of saying no.

But his letter, on that rather desperate morning, urged me to go to New York at once. As sometimes happens at *Time*, several jobs were suddenly open. Cantwell thought that I might get one of them.

I did not have the train fare to New York. Without telling me what she was about to do, my wife went to our next-door neighbors, explained the situation and asked them to lend her ten dollars. Those generous people, the Eubanks and Chesneys, who over the years have become our friends, were then practically strangers. Without question, they lent my wife the money.

I went to New York. I rode, for the first of several thousand times, in the swiftly purring elevator to the twenty-ninth floor of the Time and Life Building in Rockefeller Center. I had wanted to write foreign news. Cantwell thought I should try for a book reviewer's job. I wrote several trial reviews. A few days later, *Time* hired me at $100 a week. I have always insisted that I was hired because I began a review of a war book with the line: "One bomby day in June. . . ."

Thus, we crossed that bridge from death to life which faith said: "Try," but cold reason said: "Even to think of trying is hopeless."

XIX

I was thirty-eight years old when I went to work for *Time*. It was the first real job that I had ever held. I held it for nine years. I went to *Time* in April, 1939, almost exactly a year after I had deserted from the Communist Party. I resigned from *Time*, at my own suggestion (the Hiss Case had reached a crisis), in December, 1948, almost a decade after I broke with the Communist Party.

In those nine years, I rose from third-string book reviewer to senior editor (there are seven of them). I became at last the editor who could do almost anything and was moved at need from one section of the magazine to another. For in time I had edited or written all the departments except Business. I also became *Time's* most controversial foreign news editor; in the middle of World War II, I reversed the magazine's news policy toward Russia, making it clear on the basis of the weekly news that Russia was not a friend, but an enemy, who was actively using World War II to prepare World War III. With the same weekly insistence, I pointed out that China was the key to world politics, and that to lose China to Communism was to risk losing World War III. In later years, when *Time* wished to point out how prophetically right its interpretation of foreign news had been in the past, it saw fit to reprint *The Ghosts on the Roof,* the sad satire I had written on the Yalta Conference the week that it took place (I did not then know that Alger Hiss was a member of the American delegation).

In my last years at *Time,* I organized, edited and wrote a good deal of the section known as Special Projects. It dealt chiefly with religious, literary and philosophic subjects.

I began writing for *Time* at a salary of about $5,000 a year. At the time I resigned, *Time* had just multiplied that figure about six times—on its own initiative, for at no time during my nine-year service, did I ever ask for a raise, or know exactly, or particularly care what I was earning.

Nine years is a large part of an adult man's life to invest in any experience. It was time enough in which to accumulate a body of work faithfully and carefully done, and to develop habits of working and thinking, a way of life and of the mind, very difficult to dismiss when it was abruptly broken off. It was time enough, too, to form close working relationships, some of which developed into strong personal attachments for my colleagues, all the stronger because they were made at a time of life when men make friends slowly, judiciously and even reluctantly. These friends on all levels of the corporation never wavered in their loyalty to me—they knew me better than any other group of people in the world. If anything, they are closer to me today than in the past. I can write about them and about *Time* freely, without any imputation of self-serving, for I do not expect ever to work for *Time* again.

My debt and my gratitude to *Time* cannot be measured. At a critical moment, *Time* gave me back my life. It gave me my voice. It gave me sanctuary, professional respect, peace and time in which to mature my changed view of the world and man's destiny, and mine, in it. I went to *Time* a fugitive; I left it a citizen. In my years with it, I became a Quaker and took my wife and children with me into the spiritual peace of the meeting. I returned to the land and undertook that second life, which was not only an experience in creative labor, but first and foremost a way of bringing up my children in close touch with the soil and hard work, and apart from what I consider the false standards and vitiating influence of the cities.

Time gave me more than time and peace in which to measure the meaning of my total defeat as a Communist. It made it possible for me to redress the journey of my whole life—and such a life and such a journey. It would be hard to tell how hard it was.

2

THE STORY OF A MIDDLE-CLASS FAMILY

My brother lies in the cold earth,
A cold rain is overhead.
My brother lies in the cold earth,
A sheet of ice is over his head.

The cold earth holds him round;
A sheet of ice is over his face.
My brother has no more
The cold rain to face.

(Written in the Sand Hill graveyard,
the first winter of my brother's death.)

I

I was born in Philadelphia, on April 1, 1901. When my father, Jay Chambers, who was then a young staff artist on the New York *World*, received the startling news, he crumpled the telegram and threw it into a waste basket. He did not believe it and he did not think that April Fool jokes were in good taste.

I was born in the house of my grandfather, James S. Chambers. I began to come into the world very early in the morning. Snow was falling and soon turned into a blizzard. From her high bed, my mother could look into the whitening world outside the window and see the cemetery across the street. She wondered if, in a day or two, she would be lying under the snow.

The doctor had not been told that I was arriving. He lived several miles away and my grandmother Chambers was waiting for my grandfather to return from his office so that he could go for the doctor. My grandfather, one of the crack political reporters of his day, was then with the Philadelphia *Bulletin* or the *Record*. He reached home, tired from a day's editorial work, some time after one o'clock in the morning. He took one look at my mother, jumped on his bicycle and returned through the snow with the doctor. His prompt action probably saved my mother's life.

Mine was a dry birth and I weighed twelve pounds and measured fourteen inches across the shoulders. I had to be taken with instruments. After this frightful delivery, Dr. Dunning sat for several hours beside my mother, holding together the edges of a torn artery. At one point, he thought that she was certainly dying and asked: "Are you afraid?" My mother said: "Doctor, the Power that brought me here will take me away again." She said "Power" because she belonged to a generation of intellectuals for whom the word God was already a little embarrassing. But the calm with which she accepted the possibility of death was a quality that she transmitted to me; it is part of my heritage from my mother.

Other women seem to forget the sharpest agonies of childbirth. My mother overcame her memory sufficiently to bear a second son, my brother, Richard Godfrey. But my terrible birth was fixed indelibly in her mind. Throughout my boyhood and my youth, she repeated to me the circumstances of that ordeal until they were vivid to me. They made me acutely unhappy, and her repetition of them made me even unhappier (for it seemed to imply a reproach). But I never told her so.

My mother's maiden name had been Whittaker and her parents called her Laha, explaining that it was a Malay word for "princess."

However exalted it may have sounded in Sumatra, the unusual name caused my mother acute discomfort all her life. But she promptly contrived an even more distressing name for me. She named me Jay (for my father), Vivian (for the surname of the English branch of the family of one of her childhood schoolmates and lifelong friends). It would have been hard to go farther afield for a more unsuitable name. As soon as I knew anything I knew that I loathed that name. I determined that as soon as I was able, I would take any other name in preference to it.

II

The world I first became aware of was not Philadelphia, but the south shore of Long Island. When I was two or three, my parents bought a big frame house (my mother still lives in it) in Lynbrook, about eighteen miles from New York City and seven miles from the Atlantic Ocean. Lynbrook was then a village of some two hundred souls. They were chiefly workingmen, shopkeepers, farmers and "baymen"—men who owned or worked oyster beds in the tidal creeks and salt marshes between the ocean and the firm land. The villagers regarded newcomers with great curiosity (and probably with aversion). Since my father was dark and an artist, and my mother had been an actress who was possessed of a soulful beauty uncommon anywhere, the village promptly summed them up by dubbing them "the French family."

My first view of the world was largely vertical—the chair and table legs in our kitchen. I spent several years of my life on its floor, for, like most country people, then and now, we lived chiefly in the kitchen. In summer, we moved partly out of doors. But the kitchen remained the beachhead. Each of the other rooms in the house had its own stove. In winter, by an economy of fuel and labor, these stoves were kept banked when they were used at all. Since there was no central heat and no running water (a force pump raised the water), there were no pipes to freeze.

The kitchen was the only really warm room in the house. It was heated by a big, black, nickel-trimmed coal range in which the steady warmth could be seen as well as felt through the cracks of the draught doors and the glow beneath the grate. I have never overcome the feeling that central heat is a poor substitute for the parlor stove and the kitchen range.

The twilights of my early childhood, which gathered among the chair and table legs before they darkened the room at window level, were lifted by a daily ritual when the oil lamps were lit and shed that soft glow which is still my preferred light. My parents did not put in gas light until the First World War and electricity after it, though other houses had them.

Yet our old kitchen in Lynbrook was only the anteroom of my world. It was from its two back windows that I received the most intense of my earliest impressions—the enfolding beauty of the external world. Imagine a view, unimpeded by house or tree for as many miles as a child's eye could gaze, in which there was almost nothing but a sea of goldenrod and a foam of the small, white, starlike asters called Michaelmas daisies. I would stand at the window for half an hour, staring out in a kind of breathless stupor. Sometimes, my brother Richard also stood at the window beside me. But he was not looking at the asters. He was looking out because I was looking out. He tagged after me everywhere to my great annoyance.

There was another view, almost as good, through the pickets of our front gate, which I was forbidden to open, for my parents feared that I might be run over by a horse and buggy (automobiles were still unknown in that village). The street in front of our house was overarched by old silver maples, and farther up by elms. Like most of the other streets, it was of unpaved sand, and the wagons, by passing to the right or the left, had left here and there, in the middle of the street, tapering islands of turf, which in spring were starred with dandelions. Just beyond our house ran the Merrick Road, then Long Island's great southern highway. It was paved with pegs and for a long time existed for me only as the slow clop clop of horses' hooves, the creak of axles under heavy loads and the grind of wagon wheels on the hard surface. Near us, the Merrick Road was flanked by a double line of forty-year-old cherry trees which in spring became domes of whiteness whose fragrance reached our windows. People who drive down the Merrick Road today, through the incredible ugliness of its neon age, will wonder if I am not merely nostalgic. I am not.

In the first decade of this century, the south shore of Long Island was a landscape of unself-conscious, miniature beauty. Everything was small—little farms, little orchards, little unplanned villages, little white houses master-built in exquisite, functional proportions, little birch and swamp-maple woods following the course of little streams that slid silently over glinting sand. It was all saved from paltriness by the tremendous presence at its edge of the ocean, with its separating miles of salt marsh and sweeps of sky across which fleets of cloud rode continually to and from the sea.

Inland, too, the sea was always around us. Sometimes it came as fog, rolling in suddenly, heavy with the smell of tidal water, softly blotting out the houses and the streets. Sometimes it came as sound —the terrible sound of the surf pouring without pause on the beaches seven miles away. As a boy, I used to hear it while I tried to fall asleep. I would sit up in my bed to listen to it, on winter nights when the cold air brought it in clearly. I was frightened, for it seemed about to pound away the land. It was the sound of inhuman force—the first I knew.

The tides, too, moved through my earliest childhood consciousness. On Sundays, my father always went to sketch or paint in the open. When I was too small to walk, he used to take me with him in my carriage, packing his paint box at my feet. It was he who first introduced me to the tides which fascinated him. The immense silent flooding of the sea into the land filled me with wonder and anxiety. I remember distinctly the moment when I first realized that this secret power of the sea moved no farther away than the foot of our street, in the little tidal Mill River that flowed sluggishly through acres of cattails. It brought the sea home to me directly in its gentlest but most resistless form. It did more. It first carried my child's mind beyond the horizon of the world. I can remember my father explaining to me more than once, when I was very small, that this regular rise and fall of the tides was in response to a pull from beyond our world in unimaginable space. My father did a good deal of quiet questing in unimaginable space. Years later, when I came to read Walt Whitman, through whose verse the same tides flood and the same surf pounds the same beaches, it was not like reading any other verse. It was as if, by plugging my ears, I were listening to my own blood pound. No land ever again has such power over him as that in which a man was once a child.

Next to the sea and skies, I loved the cedar trees. This, too, I caught from my father, for he spent endless sunny days sketching them. At that time, Long Island was dotted with cedars. The young trees were light green columns to the ground. The old, pyramidal trees were almost black. The young trees grew in groves. The old ones often stood alone, dominating a single field. They had the dignity that merely being very old confers. I did not think this as a child, but I sensed something of it. I listened carefully when my father once told me that the Indians had looked at the same cedar we were looking at. After that, I liked to stand under an old cedar and listen to the wind pour through it while I thought that those other shadowy people, about whom I began to wonder a good deal, had also stood there and listened to the same sound.

My father had many curious preoccupations which, at rare intervals, and by a kind of wrench, he would shyly disclose to me. Indians was one of them. It was from him that I caught that sense of living on Indian land that goes back into my earliest childhood. The past haunted my mind in the Indian. I sought eagerly for some print of those former feet.

One day, near a brook, when I was somewhat older, I came upon a stone knife. It was roughly chipped from one reddish brown stone. A bit of quartz embedded in the top had been rudely shaped into a little knob. When I first noticed it, I could not stoop to pick it up. I stood staring at it as if I had suddenly seen a snake —in fact, the long serpent of the past. I felt wildly excited. Some coppery hand had chipped the knife and dropped it and my finding of it carried my boy's mind backward to a point where it was lost. I think that then, without at all realizing it, I first became conscious of history.

I never told anybody about the knife. I kept it to handle and to wonder at. In my mind it was connected with the cedars. Now, like the man who made it, I have lost it.

Two impressions sum up my earliest childhood world. I am lying in bed. I have been told sternly to go to sleep. I do not want to. Then I become conscious of an extreme silence which the fog always folds over the land. On the branches of the trees the mist has turned to moisture, and, as I listen to its irregular drip drip pause drip pause, I pass into the mist of sleep.

The other memory is of my brother. He is standing on our front porch, dressed in one of those shapeless wraps children used to be disfigured with. It is raining softly. I am in the house. He wants me to come out to him. I do not want to go. In a voice whose only reproach is a plaintiveness so gentle that it has sounded in the cells of my mind through all the years, he calls: "Bro (for brother), it's mainin (raining), Bro." He calls it over and over without ever raising his voice. He needs me because he knows what no child should know: that the soft rain is sad. I will not understand this knowledge in him until too late, when it has ended his life. And so I do not go out onto the porch.

III

Shortly before my parents moved to Long Island, my father fell victim to what people would later call "technological unemployment." The news camera and the newsphoto began to replace the staff artist on the newspapers. Soon there were few such jobs as staff artist, and my father was no longer with the New York *World*. I used to hear conversations about the way a machine could take away a man's job. They cut a tiny but definite groove in my mind. So did a certain clammy anxiety called "your father is looking for work." With that uneasiness went something much more frightening that people were always mentioning in taut voices: "a panic." Panics, I gradually learned, were what happened when the banks failed and nobody could get any money. This was brought home to me when the Knickerbocker Trust failed and grandmother Whittaker, who lived entirely on her income, found herself without it for a while.

I early learned that the root cause of panics was Democrats. I knew about "Democrats and hard times" long before I knew what a Democrat was. For my parents were Republicans the way an Englishman is for the king; it was not a matter that required any thought. Even my father, who never had the slightest interest in politics and never mentioned the subject, always went off dutifully to the polls when the party buggy called for him on election day, and voted the straight Republican ticket. In the 1912 election, though all the family were intense admirers of Theodore Roosevelt, and my grandfather Chambers considered himself his friend, both my father and grandfather voted for William Howard Taft against Roosevelt and Woodrow Wilson.

I think my father viewed the news camera as a liberator. He disliked newspapers as much as his father loved them (in part, perhaps, for that reason). Without much jolting, he slipped into a field that suited him much better—book and magazine illustrating. Talk about unemployment faded and my father continued to make a very good salary almost without interruption for the rest of his life.

During most of those early years, he worked with a group of illustrators known as the D.D. (Decorative Designers). They were headed by Emma Lee Thayer who, long after the D.D. was forgotten, made a reputation as a detective story writer. This group somehow impinged on the circle of Stanford White. When Harry Thaw shot him, our home was deliciously abuzz with the scandal for weeks.

My father was a short, mild man whom good eating presently made rather soft-looking. He had a taste for high sauces and cheeses, lobsters, oysters and hot curries, which my mother, who was a really remarkable cook, spent hours preparing for him. Actually, my father was a powerful man, even late in life, as I discovered in my one desperate fight with him. But he was almost wholly sedentary. Not once in our whole lives did he ever play with me. He was uncommunicative to the point of seeming mute. Occasionally, he took me to New York to his studio or the art museum. On the train we rode side by side in complete silence. In the studio, he would seat me in a corner and go silently to work. Hours later, we might go out for a silent supper. When he was sketching in the open, he would sit silently, almost motionless, for hours, rising only to squint one eye and hold up a finger to gauge perspective (a gesture that I came to detest). Once in a long while, he would utter one word: "Don't"—when my brother and I were doing something that he did not like. This habit of silence, which was less like silence than an atrophy of ordinary feelings, made his rare disclosures, his thoughts about tides, trees and Indians, impressive and almost shocking.

My mother wanted me to call him Papa. But he insisted that my brother and I call him Jay—his given name. For years, that single, colorless syllable was like an insulation between us, as, no doubt, it was intended to be. For me, my father early invented a nickname —"Beadle"—which I found even more distressing than my given name. He never called me anything else, and he would utter the ugly word with four or five different intonations each of which was charged with quiet derision, aimed not at me, but at my mother. For this nickname, I presently came to see, was his revenge for her having named me Vivian. Thus, I was caught between them, as my brother and I were to be caught all our lives.

All this was done very quietly, almost in pantomime. The voices around me in my early childhood were all gentle voices. Outright rudeness or meanness were unthinkable. Ours was a highly decorous life. Every evening, when my father came home from his office, my brother and I had to meet him at the door and kiss him. He would stoop to receive each kiss with a smile that was less affectionate than baffling. In the morning, we would repeat this ceremony and kiss him good-bye. Then, with my mother, we would go to the window and watch him down the street. As he reached the corner, he would wave once and be gone.

I loved my father dearly in those days. If he "had to work," and did not get home until late, I would often lie awake listening until I heard him turn the knob of the front door. Only then, sometimes after midnight, would I fall asleep.

Yet when he left home in the morning, it was as if the sun had come out, and the image of my mother, which, when my father was home, seemed rather quiet and withdrawn, took over and dominated the house.

IV

In my earliest recollections of her, my mother is sitting in the lamplight, in a Windsor rocking chair, in front of the parlor stove. She is holding my brother on her lap. It is bed time and, in a thin sweet voice, she is singing him into drowsiness. I am on the floor, as usual among the chair legs, and I crawl behind my mother's chair because I do not like the song she is singing and do not want her to see what it does to me. She sings:

Au clair de la lune,
Mon ami, Pierrot,
Prête-moi ta plume,
Pour écrire un mot.

Then the vowels darken ominously. My mother's voice deepens dramatically, as if she were singing in a theater. This was the part of the song I disliked most, not only because I knew that it was sad, but because my mother was deliberately (and rather unfairly, I thought) making it sadder:

Ma chandelle est morte,
Je n'ai plus de feu;
Ouvre-moi la porte,
Pour l'amour de Dieu.

I knew, from an earlier explanation, that the song was about somebody (a little girl, I thought) who was cold because her candle and fire had gone out. She went to somebody else (a little boy, I thought) and asked him to help her for God's sake. He said no. It seemed a perfectly pointless cruelty to me. The song continued to its sorry end while I crept farther into the shadows beyond the lamplight and thought how much I disliked my mother's dramatic singing and how happy I would be when my brother fell asleep and she put him to bed.

Those earliest days of my childhood were probably among the happiest of my mother's married life. But it seems to me that, even then, she always sang sad songs. She sang them in English, French and German—songs that I have seldom heard anyone else sing, and most of whose titles I did not know. Some of them I have come on unexpectedly over the years. The melody of one of them, a Southern song, of which I recall only a few bars that went with the words:

All those little colored girls,
Way down Mobile,

I suddenly recognized, as a grown man, in the stately, uncoiling theme of *Khovantchina.*

Another was a simple German song. Its melody is a theme in the first movement of Mahler's First Symphony, of which somebody gave me a recording during the Hiss Case. Hearing that mournful phrase for the first time since I was a boy, and remembering the words that went with it:

Allein, und doch nicht ganz allein,
Bin ich in meiner Einsamkeit.

(*Alone, and yet not quite alone,*
Am I in my great loneliness),

I felt my morale dissolve. For, like Lenin, who gave up listening to music because of the emotional havoc it played with him, I have always been extremely susceptible to it.

There was another song which I thought was about some poor soul trying to get into heaven and having rather a bad time of it. I later discovered it as the little maid's song in Tennyson's *Guinevere*:

Late, late, so late,
And dark the night, and chill,
Late, late, too late,
Ye cannot enter now.

I am not sure that this is the way Tennyson wrote it, but that is how my mother sang it. My dislike of my mother's dramatic singing went so deep that even today I cannot bear to have anyone sing around me.

For that unstaunchable undertone of sadness, my mother had reasons that lay far back in her own childhood and young womanhood. She told me about them so often, and in such detail, that I seem to have lived through her life with her.

Most of her stories began with her father, my grandfather Charles Whittaker, who had died a year or two before I was born. He was the heroic presence of my childhood, and, though I did not then know what he looked like, he seemed more alive to me than many of the people whom I knew. He was born in Scotland. When he was a small boy, his father, a revolutionist of some kind, apparently a Scottish nationalist, took him in his arms, walked into the Glasgow garrison, and invited the soldiers to revolt. They declined. For this act, my great-grandfather was to have been transported to Tasmania. But friends in the government arranged to have him slip away to the United States. The Whittakers settled in Wisconsin, about 1849.

In his early teens, my grandfather Whittaker ran away from private school to fight the Civil War for the North. He was little more than a boy, and the only regiment that would accept him was a convict regiment. With this group of jailbirds, he was stationed at Harper's Ferry, not very far from where I now live. From there, tired of the inaction, and probably of the company, my grandfather slipped off to Canada to visit a distant relative, who, to make matters worse, was also a relative of Jefferson Davis. Somehow he learned, or inferred, that active fighting was about to begin. He rejoined his regiment and was pardoned, for bravery on the battlefield. Throughout his campaigns, he carried on his back and studied the massive Greek and Latin lexicon which I now have. For, like me, he was a student of languages all his life. Like me, he spoke German fluently. Like me, he read French, Spanish and Italian. And it was from his old Ollendorff grammars that I began to study those languages.

One incident of his soldiering made a lasting impression on me. In a little engagement at Snicker's Gap, in Virginia, my grandfather and the others found themselves advancing without cover across a line of Confederate fire. One man became so nervous that he jumped from behind my grandfather, whose body was protecting him, in front of my grandfather, and was instantly shot dead. That was in my mind when I used to say sometimes to nervous friends, during the Hiss Case: "Let's not jump out of line"—for the past reaches out incalculably to touch the present.

After the war, my grandfather married Mary Blanchard, of a refugee Huguenot family that had reached the United States after several generations in Ireland. Even in her ravaged old age, my grandmother Whittaker was one of the most majestic women I have ever seen. Later, my grandfather published the first literary magazine in the Northwest, became superintendent of schools in Milwaukee, was a successful inventor (the hat rack under theater seats, the hot and cold water faucet, which, for some time, he manufactured himself). He also owned a brass factory in Chicago. The workers were German radicals and he had trouble with them. My mother sometimes told me how my grandfather borrowed from them several German pamphlets by Marx and Engels (two German "anarchists," she explained), which he studied in an effort to find out what was stirring up his men. In that way, I first heard the names of the founders of Communism.

My grandfather, like most Whittakers and most Chamberses, had no sense at all about money. He made and lost several small fortunes. But in their prosperous days, my grandparents' social life was so crowded with spanking teams, smart carriages and smart parties, that they had little time for their only child. So, at the age of five, my mother was packed off, a lost and lonely little girl, to a private school in Racine, which happened to be an extremely good one. There she remained most of her girlhood, learning the proper manners, reading the proper books. There she grew up with the scions of other rising middle-class Western families—"the Case girls" (farm machinery), the Horlicks (malted milk) and others whose patents of business nobility have slipped my mind. Even as a child, I used to wonder why, if all these great people were such dear friends, they never came to visit us.

Those golden girlhood days in Racine, with its beautiful old homes, were my mother's land of lost content. For she turned from that loved life just when she should have entered upon it most fully. Just when she should have gone to college in the East, as she planned, my grandfather Whittaker lost his last fortune. He was too old, too tired and beaten, ever to make another. To support herself and her parents, my mother, untrained for any useful work, did the most sensible and profitable thing a beautiful girl could do. She went on the stage. In those days, the 1890's, it was an almost scandalous course, and by taking it my mother shut the door to the only world she loved and longed for quietly behind her.

She was desperately out of place on the stage for whose atmosphere her whole past unfitted her. She deplored what she called its "moral laxness." Even Isadora Duncan, probably the most gifted of her theatrical friends (after the Russian Revolution she was to dance the *Marseillaise* barefoot down the streets of astonished Moscow), seemed to my mother "to lack refinement."

Then my mother met my father, who, if scarcely refined in the sense she meant, was gentle and quiet. He could talk about books, pictures and plays. They married. But she never quite accepted my father as a social or intellectual equal. In her heart of hearts, my mother always felt, or at least she made me feel, that she had married the cook.

So she buried herself in the little Long Island village and resolved "to live," as she said, "entirely for her children." Some day, she hoped, the children would find their way back, translating her with them, to that upper-middle-class world which was, for her, the earthly paradise. But I think that something told her—perhaps by then she knew too much about chance and time—that this would not happen. And that is why she sang in the sad voice from which, as a child, I recoiled:

Late, late, too late,
Ye cannot enter now.

V

My father had never wanted to buy the house on Long Island, in the first place. It was big, built like a nest of boxes and painted a faded yellow. Over the years, the paint faded still more and peeled off in an incurable acne. The shutters, that had once been green, weathered to a washed-out blue. Some became unhinged and had to be taken down. That made some of the windows look like lashless eyes. My father would never give my mother money to repaint the house. I believe that I was in college before my mother somehow saved or earned enough money to have the house repainted—at least fifteen years after we moved into it.

The kitchen was an addition to the original house. It had been made by moving an outbuilding against the main structure. The joining at the room was never tight, and in spring when the snows melted, or during rains, water would flood in through the joining until the kitchen floor was awash. We used to rush up pots, pans and floor rags, but whoever passed from the kitchen to the next room, which was known as "the dog room," had to step through a little Niagara. My father refused to have this leak repaired or even to notice that it was leaking. We lived with it for ten or twelve years until my brother, who early showed unusual skill with tools and for practical jobs, built himself a ladder, begged some pitch from a road gang and got tin from somewhere else. Then he climbed up to the roof and mended the leak.

"The dog room" was completely bare and was used as a spacious kennel for our part-bull dog whom my father named "Taurus." This was considered very clever, and I sometimes heard my mother explaining to people that *taurus* is Latin for bull. There was never enough furniture in the other rooms, either, and what there was was hodge-podge and nondescript, though I believe that both my parents were under the impression that some of the older pieces were rarities. But they had a habit of coming unglued.

The paper on most of the walls was faded and browned and sometimes bubbled and peeled off. Where a new partition had been run up, the walls were rough, unpapered plaster. At one end of the living room, which was also the dining room (in those days we still ate at the table; later we gave up the constraining practice), a sizable piece of ceiling fell down one day, exposing the laths. My mother endured this for some time. Then, she donned overalls (rather a daring act in those days) and stretched and glued cheesecloth over the hole. My brother and I admired her skill. We were even more interested by the fact that mice soon nested behind the cheesecloth. It sagged where their feet made little twinkling bulges. This fascinated our cat which would sit for hours on the floor below, watching the cheesecloth with drooling bafflement. My father had named the cat Claude (i.e., "clawed") because it had been altered. This, too, was considered very clever and was told to people in whispers, which were unnecessary, for Claude was dead before I grasped the point.

My mother often begged my father to give her the money to repaper the house. He always refused. She had overridden him in buying the house, and he was determined that he would do nothing to improve it. As long as he lived, he never did.

At last my mother made a little parcel of her jewelry—a fairly pathetic hoard, which included a brooch watch her father had given her and some rings and pins, chiefly of sentimental value. These she took to New York and pawned—an act that made her skin crawl, as she told me. With the money she obtained, she had the walls repapered. She expected my father to be pleased. Instead, he studiedly ignored the papering while it was going on and made no comment at all when it was finished. My mother wept and her sobs were dreadful to hear.

My father also refused to give her the money to redeem her jewelry and she lost all of it.

V I

In justice to my father, it must be said that he regarded himself first and foremost as an artist. How he lived meant little or nothing to him and he had no intention of surrendering to middle-class standards of comfort. He would not have said middle class. He would have said "other people's" standards; for, in matters of art and culture, he felt himself divided by a deep gulf from all but a very tiny circle of mankind. He was withering in his comments on those who could not make the small talk he loved about art shows and plays, and having discovered that there were few fellow spirits around him on Long Island, he rode the commuter trains a solitary recluse, never having, for over twenty years, more than a nodding acquaintance with one or two others in that swarming fellowship.

Just what his own standards were, it is difficult to say. When I became old enough to wonder and observe, it seemed to me that he had no general view of the world at all, no coherent system of ideas, not even a suspicion that ideas have a history, a force, an interaction, and that art is one expression of them. This lack, which would have been perfectly natural in somebody else, I found rather strange in a man who was so self-consciously artistic. At last, to my astonishment, I was forced to conclude that for art in its great forms—painting, sculpture, architecture—my father had no real liking at all. I first suspected this when, in our occasional dreary tours of the Metropolitan Museum, he would rush me through the great paintings down to the medieval armor or textiles. I had the feeling that greatness annoyed him in a personal way, like a challenge to which he felt unequal, and that he endured it only as a backdrop to his real interest, which was in ornament, costume, scenery—the minutiae and surfaces of things.

Later on, he developed a passion for grand opera. (E. B. White, in the *New Yorker*, has caught a blurred glimpse of him in that phase.) His interest was not in the music, for which he cared little, but in the spectacle, for which he cared a great deal. He rarely, if ever, listened to symphonic or chamber music. In his later years, he became an omnivorous reader of the moderns—Ibsen, Shaw, Strindberg, Hauptmann, Tolstoy, Nietzsche—men who had struck the chords to which man's spirit was to reverberate for a century—all lay on his table from time to time. They were always library books. He never cared to own them. Curiously enough, he did own three volumes of Dostoyevsky—*The House of the Dead, The Idiot, Crime and Punishment*—which stood in his bookcase between D. G. Rossetti's poems, Schnitzler's *The Green Cockatoo* and a half-dozen King Arthur books in which my father prized the Howard Pyle illustrations (Pyle had been one of his art teachers). My father and I were reading the great Europeans at about the same time. But I never discovered what they meant to him, or what, if anything, he made of them, for we were scarcely speaking to each other at that time.

Nevertheless, our house was a peeling outpost of what both my father and mother would have summed up as "culture." Culture was visible in the overflowing bookcases and bookshelves, which were everywhere, and culture was visible in the pictures that covered the walls. Both provided curious clues to the character of my parents' tastes and minds. On one wall of the living room was a big India print against which was hung a big, round, flat Spanish wool basket. Nearby, was a line of framed color prints—illustrations for (if I remember rightly) *Goblin Market*. As a child, I did not like these, just as, later on, I was never able to share my parents' enthusiasm for Arthur Rackham. There were other framed prints: a Holbein, a Velasquez, Van Dyke's Charles I, Dürer's *Melancholia* and a *Ritter, Tod und Teufel*. And there was, of course, a Mona Lisa and a sizable plaster cast of the Venus de Milo. At one end of an old couch, hung a print of a 19th century Italian painter which showed a hooded skeleton, beckoning to its embrace a line of proletarian figures with bundles—rather like a scene in an Ellis Island waiting room. During the frightful toothaches that often tormented my brother and me (nobody paid much attention to our teeth), this couch was our refuge, and we would lie for agonized hours, gloomily studying that print, which was titled: *Il Conforto—Death, the Comforter*.

Among this medley of masters (I never discovered how or why they were chosen), my father was heavily represented. There were framed originals of his Christmas cards, which became an institution among his artist friends; he would spend months, sketching, designing, selecting special papers for them and coloring them, individually, by hand. There were framed originals of his bookplate designs (as a bookplate artist, my father had an international reputation and the elaborate plate he made for me while I was still in diapers is well known). There were also many of his imaginary landscapes—piles of Oriental minarets with the sun flashing from their golden bulbs (my father pasted on gold paper for that effect) and somber vistas of cypresses in whose purple shadows barely discernible human figures merged mysteriously.

For the yearning of my father's mind was for far horizons in time and space—a yearning, which, in a very different way, my mother shared with him, just as she shared his enthusiasm for Omar Khayyam. The gorgeous East held my father's spirit very much in fee. He was always sketching the Bosporus waterside (in fancy) or describing the Oriental restaurants he frequented in New York, one of which (he once took me there as a great treat) was run by a Hindu woman named Miss Little Bird and boasted a snake charmer with a basket of cobras. Around the house, in those early days, my father sometimes wore a flowing linen samurai robe on which was stenciled a magnificent Japanese dragon that harmonized with the mood of the ferocious Japanese masks and windbells, the Chinese lanterns, parasols, and the Hindu elephant god, Ganassa, that stood on his desk. There were five illustrated editions of the *Arabian Nights* in my father's room, and both Scheherazade and Omar Khayyam were to play an important part in our lives, as I shall presently describe.

But the subtle spirit that informed our culture, and the only point of intellectual unity that I can detect in it, was pre-Raphaelitism. Either at Drexel Institute, where he had studied art in Philadelphia, or later, my father fell under the spell of the serpentine neck, the elegant anemia and flowing robes, the flight from the actual and ugly into the arabesque and the exotic. I suspect that my father's artistic sense came to birth in that brief spasm of the dying 19th century, and there it rested. He never outgrew it. It was the names of the pre-Raphaelites, and others oddly associated with them, that I first heard as a child, in awed conversations between my parents or with my father's artist friends, who occasionally visited us in those days: Rossetti and his sister, Holman Hunt, Aubrey Beardsley, Oscar Wilde, Walter Pater, Botticelli (whom Pater had helped to revive), Whistler, William Morris, Hokusai, Du Maurier and his Trilby. I memorized the exciting names as naturally as a boy memorizes a bird call and with no more understanding of what they meant.

Even my mother would sometimes suddenly announce that:

> *The blesséd damozel leaned out*
> *From the gold bar of heaven,*

or ask dramatically:

> *What is he doing, the great god Pan,*
> *Down in the reeds by the river?*

I early learned to be extremely proud of the fact that my father was an artist and that ours was a "cultured" home, though as I had scarcely seen any other at that time, I supposed that the rest were much like ours. I had no way of knowing that there is a difference between the words "art" and "arty," that it is the difference between reality and unreality, and that our home was arty.

As a child, I could scarcely have surmised from anything I saw or heard that, in the world around me, realities were taking shape that would affect my whole life—that a new economic form had appeared (the trust) which would provide the logic of all totalitarian organization; that the great war, which would first reveal that the world was in mortal crisis, was less than a decade away; that in Russia (nobody ever mentioned Russia), the 1905 revolution had brought to life a new political form—the soviet—and, at its head, a new political figure—Leon Trotsky. Nor would I have understood what he meant if I had heard his warning that anybody who wanted to lead a peaceful life had picked the wrong century to be born in.

VII

My parents believed that children should also be taken to the theater, and as early as possible. My brother wailed when he was left home and I went off to see *Peter Pan.* But my early exposure to Sir James M. Barrie was not a success. The pirates terrified me and so did the crocodile (or whatever it was) with the ticking clock inside it. Maude Adams' flittings and dartings about the stage left me only a little less uneasy. At last, my howls became so shameless that I had to be taken home in disgrace.

It was a blow to my parents. They discussed the episode with the uneasiness born of an awful suspicion that they had given birth to a cultural defective. But they persevered. Cautiously, my father conditioned me by taking me to a number of adult plays, which were in general less hair-raising than plays for children. I had no idea what they were about and have forgotten what they were. Then, with grave misgivings, and many warnings that I was to behave myself, they tried me out on another "child's play."

It was Maeterlinck's *Bluebird.* I was gripped in silence from the start. I had only the vaguest idea why the children, Tyl Tyl and Mytyl, had to go to such lengths to find a bird that was at home all the time. But two scenes I never afterward forgot. One was the land of the dead, which rose with a sizzling rush out of the flower-grown graveyard. Grandfather and grandmother Tyl were sleeping beside their cottage. I somehow grasped the idea that the dead wake from their sleep only when a living person thinks of them, and that they do not wake often. That thought I stowed carefully away to reflect on later.

The other scene that impressed me was the land of the unborn children. One side of the stage was space from which came a deep, resonant humming. "That," my mother whispered to me, "is the mothers, singing to the babies that are coming to them." On the other side of the stage was a landing platform, where Father Time was shooing into a little boat the unborn children that were going down to earth. Each child hugged a box that contained the deed that he would do during his life. At the back of the platform were two great doors. One child was almost in the boat, when he broke away from Father Time and ran back through the doors. Father Time scolded him.

That puzzled me and afterwards I questioned my mother about it: "Why did the little boy run back?" She glanced at me with that look of amused pride with which we glance at our children when we think they are asking something too old for their age. "Why," she said, "he had forgotten his crime. He had to go back to get the box with the crime that he would commit on earth."

VIII

In winter, my mother dressed my brother and me in blue serge jackets and knee breeches, Eton collars and floppy red or blue bow ties. In summer, we wore V-neck sailor suits with a whistle on a braided cord, or little white linen Norfolk jackets and knee breeches. These struck the authentic middle-class note, and, as might be inferred from such attire, we were in close touch with Little Lord Fauntleroy and were cover-to-cover readers of *St. Nicholas* magazine, which was read to us long before we could read.

My parents took *St. Nicholas* for us just as they took the New York *Evening Sun* for themselves, though we were forbidden to read the *Sun* or any other newspaper. We were especially forbidden to read the comics—a rule that I carried over to my own children until Little Abner proved too strong for me. *St. Nicholas* was intended to be the formative literature of my childhood. Certainly, my brother and I wore out our files. Yet, for me at least, the magazine's chief charm was exotic; it dealt with people and a way of life completely different from anything I saw around me. Of the scores of stories I read in it, the one that made the strongest impression on me was *Rackety Packety House* (like Little Lord Fauntleroy, another of Mrs. Burnett's fancies). In it a family of wooden dolls (if I remember rightly) lived a genteel life in a shabby house. It impressed me because their doggedly cheerful existence in tattered surroundings seemed to me to bear a faintly distressing resemblance to our own.

We had in the house a French book on child etiquette with the charming color illustrations of Maurice Boutet de Monvel. (When his son, Bernard Boutet de Monvel, also a painter, was killed in an Air France crash in the Azores, about the time of the second Hiss trial, his name meant little to most Americans, but it brought back my childhood to me.) This book my mother would translate for us, and so my brother and I learned in the most painless way that nice little boys do not yank off the tablecloth and all the dishes when they do not like their supper, or scratch their heads with a fork at table. In later days, Colonel Bykov sometimes complimented me on my table manners, which he considered an asset in an underground Communist.

But for me my mother had in mind a sterner code than Boutet de Monvel's. She did so thorough a job of impressing it on me that, even as a Communist, I was never quite able to shake off its rigors. She began by explaining to me that a gentleman, or, as she would say, "a man of breeding," is known not so much by what he does as by what he will not do. First and foremost, he never imputes a base motive to anyone else. If someone is rude to him, he assumes that the rudeness is unintentional. If he knows that it is intentional, he acts as if it were not. He never insulted anyone himself except by intention. He never met anger with anger. He never patronized anyone because he never assumed that he knew more than anyone else or that uneducated people are unintelligent. He never corrected (or smiled at) other people's slips. "Always," my mother would say, "allow other people the luxury of being mistaken. They will find out for themselves soon enough. If they don't, they are the kind of people in whom it does not matter."

Never, under any circumstances, did a man of breeding eat in public in front of people who were not eating (to this day, I have to be pretty famished before I will order a sandwich in a day coach). There were many similar don'ts. But there were three things, which if all else failed, a man of breeding never did. He never discussed food (which is vulgar). He never discussed money (which is even more vulgar). He never discussed religion (which is the most vulgar of all). For it is equally impossible to prove or disprove the existence of God, my mother pointed out, and the subject is not one that could possibly interest intelligent people. "Nobody," she said, "is more vulgar than an atheist, except the people who try to force religion on one."

I have always been extremely grateful to my mother for impressing upon me these rules, which, in the main, when toned down and adjusted to life, I hold to be sound. But in the circumstances, there was almost nothing (except the artistic altitude at which we lived) better calculated to unfit me for the simple realism of the Lynbrook grammar-school yard, into which I was about to be thrust with results startling to it and stunning to me.

I X

"And what is *your* name?" the first-grade teacher asked me in my turn. She was taking the class pupil by pupil to get acquainted.

"Vivian," I said.

There was a sudden silence in the room, and all eyes swiveled toward me in astonishment. The teacher mastered her own start by asking: "What did you say?"

"Vivian," I repeated.

A ripple of laughter swept the other children, like a shower of rain that you hear coming before it reaches you, and hear passing on after it has drenched you. The teacher tapped her desk lightly with a piece of chalk, struggled to restrain her own laughter, failed and joined in frankly with the children.

"Vivian," she repeated, like an editorial comment. Then she hurried on to the child behind me, who was happily named Jack. It had begun—the torment of the name that was to last for some ten years, until I dreaded to have anyone ask me what my name was. I was seven. It was my first day at school.

Next, the teacher tried sorting us out according to our fathers' occupations. Again, she went around the class, child by child. One girl's father was a butcher. One boy's father was a tailor. Another's was a shoemaker. There were children of plumbers, carpenters, farmers, bakers, clerks. One boy said: "My father is dead." "What does your mother do?" the teacher asked pleasantly. "Washing," he blurted. His clothes were all too tight for him. When he moved, it looked as if they would split at the seams.

There were several Italian boys in the class and one ferociously beautiful Italian girl. They did not speak English very well. The question reached the first Italian boy: "What does your father do?" He stared at his desk. The teacher repeated the question. He glanced up with a sheepish grin. "Junk," he said with fierce shame. Most of the Italians were the children of junkmen.

"And what does *your* father do?" the teacher asked me.

"He is a painter," I said.

"Does he paint houses or barns?" she asked helpfully.

I was confused. "He paints pictures," I said. "He is an artist."

"An artist?" she said, but decided to drop that one quickly. Again, all the eyes in the room swung to me, but this time not with amusement, with the distrust of one species for another.

On the blackboard was a chalk drawing of a cat with arched back and swollen tail. Opposite was the letter F. Below, was an apple drawn in colored chalk. Opposite was the sentence: "It is an apple." The teacher now informed us that the letter F is the sound made by an angry cat. We made this noise in chorus. After that, we chorused: "It is an apple." In time, we went through the alphabet in that way—"oo" is the noise of an owl, S is the sound of a snake. It proved to be an unforgettable method. But since I knew my letters before I went to school, it did not take me long to learn, "It is an apple." I found time to study my classmates. They were the first children I had ever met close at hand or in the mass. They were just as surprising to me as I was to them. Most of them were Americans of English or Irish stock. But, in addition to the Italians, there were Germans, a German Pole, several Jews, two Danes, a Swede and a Greek who rejoiced in the name of Constantinopoulis. Some of them were the children of fairly recent immigrants.

One of my classmates fascinated me, as he did most of the boys. Most of the little girls looked steadily away from him. He was much bigger and older than the rest of us with a huge head and enormous hands. He wore baggy, dirty clothes and smelled foully. He was an idiot. If he caught your eye, he would fix it with a challenging leer that hovered over his pasty face while his enormous hands made obscene gestures. Soon most of the boys could imitate him. I did not understand what was implied, but I knew that it was somehow sickening. He had been in first grade several years before I arrived and remained there several years after I moved on.

He came of an inbred family that lived in shacks beyond the woods in a settlement with the terrifying name of "Tigertown." Most people avoided it. But my father once took me there to sketch, and what I remember of Tigertown is that around the patched and pitiful shacks, the moist, low-lying ground was covered with acres of white violets.

To get to school, I had to cross a main road and the railroad tracks. This my mother would not let me do alone. She arranged with the undertaker's daughter to take me to school and bring me back. But this girl's class let out one hour later than mine, so that I had to wait in the schoolyard for her.

On my first day at school, I watched my class swarm home while I waited at the gate with that feeling of being left that even older people dislike. Presently, I became aware that three of my classmates, boys, were still in the yard. One of them was sucking on a lollypop. They were in a huddle near the school house. They were whispering and, from time to time, they cast a furtive glance at me. Then I saw the boy take the lollypop out of his mouth and hold it down. As I watched with great interest, they formed a little circle, and, with giggling and some pushing to keep their aim true, all three of them wet on the lollypop.

Soon a fourth boy, for whom they had evidently been waiting, came out of the school. They welcomed him and crowded around him. Their faces were masks of earnest and innocent friendliness.

There was not a single telltale tone or expression. Then the boy with the lollypop offered it to the newcomer. He smiled, a little taken aback by the generous gesture, but he accepted the lollypop. They watched him with birdlike intentness while he held it in his hand. As he put it to his mouth, they burst into shrieks of derision, doubled up with laughter, slapped their knees and whooped around him like Indians. I felt that I was going to be sick.

I think it was at that point that I developed a deep distrust of the human race. It was not only the filthy act that disgusted me. Something else shocked me much more deeply: the thought that inspired the act, its absolutely unmotivated malice, and the complete boyish guilelessness of the faces watching their victim. From that moment I hated school and everything about it. I was always expecting somebody to offer me a lollypop in one form or another.

"What did you learn at school today?" my mother asked brightly when I was once more among the *Goblin Market* prints, the bookplates and the landscapes.

"To make a noise like an angry cat," I said, "and 'It is an apple.' "

It is only fair to point out that the character of Long Island has changed greatly since those days. Lynbrook is now in effect a thriving suburb of New York. Its grammar school is thoroughly up to date. Even when I went there, the rudiments of knowledge were taught simply and thoroughly. I was given a grounding that served me well throughout life.

X

I ran away from my first fight. In those days I did not know that courage is the indispensable virtue. Life had not yet taught me that, without courage, kindness and compassion remain merely fatuous postures.

I have never been able to fight without a reason, and in that trifling corner of the world of force in which I suddenly found myself, I could see no reason for fighting and felt a desperate, personal violation that I should be forced to. I have never been afraid of pain or being beaten. In this case, my small opponent was flailing just as ineffectually as I was. But the crowding faces of my schoolmates suddenly transformed into those of animals, and their howling for a kill, filled me with overpowering disgust.

At that point, when my opponent, who was just as reluctant as

I was, was also flagging, two bigger boys stepped in and set us on again, like dogs. A little girl, whom I had thought of as being especially pretty, screamed: "Give him a bloody nose." I stopped and walked away. A howling gaggle of children trailed me, like crows over a maimed rabbit, yelping "Sissy" and less printable words. I did not know what the words meant but I knew what they were intended to mean. I could not say to those who were shouting at me that they filled me with a loathing so deep that I could not resist it even by fighting it.

I could fight when I had a reason, and what I would not do for myself, I could do for something else. We had an old, wet-eyed female dog that used to follow me on errands to the village. One day, the dog and I, going home, met one of my schoolmates, going to the store. By way of making himself agreeable, he kicked the dog in the stomach. Then he went on.

My first reaction was stunned astonishment that anybody would do such a thing to an animal. My next was anger, which, as usual with me, mounted very slowly until there was little else in me but anger. I sat down on a stump (the beautiful old trees that once shaded the village streets were already falling to progress) and waited for the boy to come back. I waited some time. When he reached me, I got up and slapped his face. Then I waited until he put down his mother's groceries. Then we fought. The battle ended when I punched his vulnerable nose. The blood ran down very satisfactorily and he began to blubber. My anger was gone. I felt only regret. I helped him pick up his bundles and tried to comfort him. He shrugged me off. As I watched him walk away, still bleeding and crying, I learned the valuable lesson that you may not comfort a man whom necessity forces you to defeat. We never fought again and we never became friends. I used to catch him watching me sometimes with a rather puzzled look, for I was the butt of the school.

I never had any real friends. From time to time, this made me unhappy, or at least it gave me an unpleasant feeling of being out of step. But I was not a child who could go to anybody with his troubles. Besides, there was nobody to go to (my father was unapproachable and it would never have occurred to me to talk to my mother about such things).

I do not mean that I never played with other boys. I played a good deal. I was active and strong. In time, I became a tireless basketball player, a tireless canoeist on the tidal creeks, a poor skater and swimmer, a good wrestler, and when I discovered that I could ride horses free by exercising them for a riding stable, I spent as much time as I could on horseback.

But I felt that there was a wall between me and other children. I used to think it was of their making. I realized by degrees that it was of mine. If I had really wanted the fellowship that lay on the other side of the wall, I would have battered my way or scrambled over. The real wall was my own indifference and my liking for solitude. No matter how much I played or mixed, I never gave myself whole-heartedly. I was always making my own peculiar observations. In the end, I always withdrew to my own chief interests—books and nature.

In some ways, I was more of a child than any child I knew, and remained a child longer. For one thing, I was incurably innocent. I had heard a good many things spelled out in frank detail and franker Saxon. They took no hold of my mind. In other ways, I was an adult, used to discussing the problems of adults as a grown-up with grown-ups. I knew what children should not know: that children are childish. I knew it better about others than I knew it about myself. I was not self-conscious. I did not realize, although I early began to write stories and poems, that what I was passing through, was my special version of the fumbling, painful, comical fore-life of the artist. I did not know that what seemed the special handicaps of my boyhood—extreme sensitivity, imaginativeness, gentleness, a need for quiet and seclusion—was the real difference between me and my fellows, a difference in the whole pitch and purpose of our lives, that is to say, a difference in the soul's angle of vision.

XI

In fact, I did not know for some time that I was supposed to have a soul. I do not know where I first found out—possibly at Sunday school. For some months, my brother and I attended the Episcopal Sunday school (my parents were nominal Episcopalians). This brief exposure to formal religion ended abruptly when one of our small co-religionists developed whooping cough and it was suggested that the Chambers boys spread the germs.

This was no hardship to my brother and me. There were kind and good people in that church, but I do not remember ever seeing any face transfigured by the awareness of God or of salvation. I do not even remember our Sunday-school teacher, what she looked like, or who was in the class with us. I do not remember anything we were taught. I remember only that each Sunday we were given a little colored card with a Biblical text encircled with forget-me-nots or some other flowers. We were also given two books (for perfect attendance, if I remember rightly). The cover of my book showed Christ standing in a field of lilies. My brother liked to tease me by joking about this picture. For he had discovered that I felt about it an unreasoning awe which I was ashamed to admit, but which his teasing exposed. At last I hid the books where he could not find them. From time to time, I would look at them surreptitiously.

If there was any religion in our home, I do not remember it. We never prayed or said grace at table. I never heard my father mention religion in his life. My mother mentioned religion from time to time, but scarcely in a religious way. It was absurd, my mother sometimes said, for people to call themselves Christians when they did not practice Christianity. This does not mean that my parents were atheists. Each of them, I suspect, had a personal belief of some kind, which, in my mother's case, later became active. But they shared the view (still current) that it is wrong to influence children's minds in religious matters, and that they should be left to develop their own religious beliefs, or to have none at all, if they chose.

What I knew, as a child, about religion I did not know as the result of any instruction. I knew it as a result of something I heard by chance, or that happened to me, and that touched something that was already in me.

There were three such experiences. The first was a conversation with my mother, which had on me almost exactly the opposite effect to what was intended. In summer, my mother was a great pie maker and she had a way of holding up a pie on the fingertips of one hand while she trimmed the loose edges of crust with the other. She was doing this one day, when, in some rambling child's conversation, I said something about "when God made the world." I think I was trying it out on her. If so, the result was much better than I could have expected.

She froze with the pie in one hand and the trimming knife suspended in the other. "Somebody told you that," she said with a severity she seldom used to me. "You picked that up somewhere. You must learn to think for yourself. You must keep an open mind and not accept other people's opinions. The world was formed by gases cooling in space."

I thought about this many times. But it was not the gaseous theory of creation that impressed me, though I did not reject it. What impressed me was that it was an opinion, too, since other people believed something else. Then, why had my mother told me what to think? Clearly, if the open mind was open (as I would say to myself later on, still turning over this conversation in my mind years afterwards), truth was simply a question of which opening you preferred. In effect, the open mind was always closed at one end.

The other experience also occurred in my early childhood. One day I wandered off alone and found myself before a high hedge that I had never seen before. It was so tall that I could not see over it and so thick that I could not see through it. But by lying flat against the ground, I wriggled between the privet stems.

I stood up, on the other side, in a field covered from end to end, as high as my head, with thistles in full bloom. Clinging to the purple flowers, hovering over them, or twittering and dipping in flight, were dozens of goldfinches—little golden yellow birds with black, contrasting wings and caps. They did not pay the slightest attention to me, as if they had never seen a boy before.

The sight was so unexpected, the beauty was so absolute, that I thought I could not stand it and held to the hedge for support. Out loud, I said: "God." It was a simple statement, not an exclamation, of which I would then have been incapable. At that moment, which I remembered through all the years of my life as one of its highest moments, I was closer than I would be again for almost forty years to the intuition that alone could give meaning to my life—the intuition that God and beauty are one.

The third experience occurred at school. There was a big girl at school who seemed much older than I; she may have been fifteen or sixteen. Her family was extremely poor; I had heard that her father was a drunkard. I thought that she was dreadful to look at. Her head was rather large. Her face was red-skinned, bony and hard, and there was an expression on it that I did not understand, but which I now realize was hunted and knowing.

The other children called the unhappy girl "Stewguts." As she walked home from school, they would form a pack around her, yelping "Stewguts! Stewguts!" until she went berserk. They were careful to keep out of her reach, for she was quick and strong. I never took part in these baitings. My mother warned me never to have anything to do with that girl, never to speak to her.

Stewguts had a younger sister in my class—a pasty-faced child who looked a little like a sheep. She always kept her eyes down, as if she were keeping a secret. She was also very stupid.

One day, during recess, I found myself alone in the classroom with this younger sister. Nobody else was in the room. The door to the cloakroom, which was beside the blackboard at the front of the classroom, opened cautiously. Stewguts peered in warily, and, seeing only the two of us, slipped in.

She had come for a purpose. To impress the meaning of words on us, the teacher used to draw a column of flowers on the board with colored chalk—a different color for each flower. Opposite each flower was a word. The teacher would point to the word. If you knew it, you were privileged to go to the blackboard and erase the word and the flower. This was called "picking flowers."

Stewguts drew a column of colored daisies on the blackboard. Then she beckoned her sister to come up. Patiently, she went down the column of words, asking her sister each one. The younger girl got most of them wrong. Gently, they went over and over them again. Stewguts never showed impatience. Sometimes, she let her sister "pick a flower." I watched fascinated, listening to the girls' voices, rising and falling, in question and answer, with the greatest softness, until, with Stewguts' help, almost all the flowers had been "picked."

Then there was a tramp of feet in the hall outside the room. Stewguts slapped down the pointer and hurriedly erased the last of the flowers. Suddenly she took her sister's face in both of her hands, and, bending, gently kissed the top of her head. As the hall door opened with a burst of voices, Stewguts silently closed the cloakroom door behind her and fled.

I knew that I had witnessed something wonderful and terrible, though I did not know what it was. I knew that it was a parable, though I did not know what parable meant, because I knew that in some simple way what I had seen summed up something very important, something more important than anything I had ever seen before. It is not strange that I should not have understood what I saw. What is strange, and humbling, is that I knew I had seen something which I never could forget. What I had seen was the point at which from corruption issues incorruption.

After that, I knew that Stewguts, who was bad, was not bad.

XII

While I was taking my first insecure steps in the outside world, the one secure world that I knew—my home—collapsed. I had noticed that my father was "having to work" more and more often and was getting home from the office later and later. I remember the strange feeling of anxiety and curiosity when one morning I found that his bed had not been slept in and realized that he had not been home all night.

We began to have an uneasy feeling about supper. Supper would be waiting. My brother and I would be hungry. We would listen to the trains steam into the station, which was only a few blocks away. "Perhaps Jay will be on that one," my mother would say. By eight o'clock, my brother and I would be hungry. "Let's wait one more train," my mother would say. By half-past eight, we would be ferociously hungry. By nine o'clock, my mother would say: "I guess Jay had to work late again tonight." Our supper would have to be warmed over, but by then we were no longer very hungry, anyway.

Once or twice, at this time, I was awakened in the night by angry voices—voices such as I had seldom heard anywhere. In terror, I realized that they were my parents' voices. They were quarreling. Sometimes, in the morning, my mother would be crying. She took to shutting us out in the kitchen while she paced up and down the long living room, holding desperate monologues with the walls, her voice soaring dramatically in charge or devastating rejoinder. Sometimes a woman's name was mentioned, a woman my father knew. The fact that our mother was alone in the room filled us with an anxiety that I could scarcely control. Once I opened the door and asked with the innocent guile of childhood: "Are you talking to somebody, Mother?" She turned on me fiercely and I never tried that again.

At last, in her distress, my mother began to tell me expurgated snatches of what she was going through—and not very expurgated at that. I knew what frantic jealousy looked like long before I knew what jealousy was. From that time, I became my mother's confidant, and I think that there is very little about her life with my father that she did not tell me.

One night my mother served supper early. My father had long been disturbed by the way we children behaved (despite Boutet de Monvel) at table. I had a habit of resting my head on my fist that especially annoyed him. Twenty times in the course of a meal, he would say with conspicuous patience: "Beadle, take your elbow off the table." At last, he bought us a child's table and chairs (the only new furniture I ever remember his buying). Henceforth, my brother and I ate in resentful exile.

It was at that table that my mother served us that night. There was juicy steak and mashed potato (I can see it clearly in my mind's eye). But I must have sensed something, for, before I touched the food, I asked: "When is Jay coming home?"

"Jay is never coming home again," said my mother.

I pushed away my plate. I was no longer hungry, but sick. I could not eat. Neither could my brother.

XIII

"Why did Jay go away?" I asked my mother.

"I sent him away," she said. He had taken a large room in Brooklyn. A family of his artist friends lived near by.

I am not competent to discuss the immediate grounds for the separation of my parents, whom, moreover, I may not judge or judge between. I can only note their incompatibilities.

No doubt, in his own way, my father loved his wife and children. Like other people, he must have craved affection himself, at least at times. Yet the slightest display of spontaneous affection toward him caused him an almost organic embarrassment. It challenged a similar response from him, and that he was unable to make. At the least loving gesture or word, he would freeze physically. His whole nature seemed to withdraw in a slow, visible motion that I can compare only to the creepy contraction of a snake into its coils—and, as in a snake, it was physically disturbing to watch. Then, from a cold fastness, he would strike deliberately at the very impulse of affection, by waiting silently with a cuttingly tolerant smile, for the impulse to pass; or he would simply disregard it with a bitingly irrelevant remark.

The effect was inhuman insult. Two or three such treatments were enough to poison a lifetime. There was almost no defense, since it is in the nature of a family to show its father affection, and spontaneous affection, by its nature, always lays itself open to such repulse. My father never failed to take advantage of this whenever we forgot ourselves. Or so it seemed. Yet sometimes, when the irreparable damage had been done, and the wincing victim was turning angrily away, my father's face would reveal a baffled loneliness, in which his inability to give and take simple affection encased him, like a mute in a coat of mail. Only to those who made no real claim on his affection, did my father seem able to step out of his armor. Then, to his friends, and he had many of them, he would appear as a being singularly simple, gentle, warm, fun-loving, rather childlike, rather happy.

I do not know to what degree this reaction was natural to my father's character, and how much it was a result of his struggle with my mother. Certainly, it grew more noticeable as their relations grew more bitter. It also helps to explain those relations. For my mother was a woman the central need of whose life was affection. She needed, moreover, to be the unique center of affection. Not that she was conscious of this herself. For she never asserted her will, only the fullness of her nature, which was spirited, self-reliant, courageous, proud and capable of an intensity of devotion that required her to deny herself in all ways so that she could give herself more fully to the objects of her love. In return, she hoped only for a similar dedication from them. Sometimes, it used to seem to me as if the real meaning of affection for her lay in her continuous self-sacrifice. If, for any reason, the object of her affection drew away, or failed to respond in kind, it seemed to her like a betrayal, and in her hurt, she could react instinctively and fiercely. But her natural sweetness and sense of justice always asserted themselves, and she would deny her hurt, or that she had any reason to be hurt, with a gallantry made all the more eloquent by the quiet tears that she could not quite keep from filling her eyes.

Obviously, my father was not a man who could sustain the force of such affection. When he was gone, my mother prepared to live wholly, as she said, for the only beings life left to her, my brother and me.

XIV

The first night that my father was gone, my mother moved my brother's cot and mine into her bedroom, which was at the back of the house. For the first time, we locked the front door. Until then, it had always been open all night. My mother also locked our bedroom door and we helped her move a heavy bureau against it. I do not know just why my mother felt that my father's departure might be a signal for marauders to swarm in. Nor do I see that his permanent absence (after all, he had often been away a good part of the night) greatly changed the balance of forces in event of an invasion. But I was naturally impressed by these precautions. I found it more difficult to fall asleep and I woke up more easily.

Sometimes, in the dark, my mother would suddenly ask: "Are you awake?" Often it turned out that we were. Then she would say: "Listen!" We would listen tensely, more alarmed by my mother than by anything we heard, though the old house was full of noises. Soon my mother took to keeping an axe in the closet. "A woman with an axe," she said, "is a match for any man." In that somewhat uneasy atmosphere, I began to take a knife to bed with me. Sometimes, in the middle of the night, I would feel to make sure that it was still under my pillow. I always put it away carefully in the morning. My mother never knew that I had it.

There were no streetlights in those days. One night, we heard a woman's terrified screams quivering in the dark, almost under our windows. My mother sat up in bed and screamed in sympathy. "Scream!" she shouted to us and screamed again herself. It was a hold-up, the only one I recall in that community.

After that, my mother moved the axe under her bed.

X V

Every week, my father sent us eight dollars for living expenses. At the time and place, it was possible to manage on eight dollars, and my mother was a good manager. But, as a child, I knew that we were poor. I knew it by direct experience. Perhaps my mother felt that she was stared at in the village, for I did most of the family shopping.

One of my mother's ways of managing was to charge things at the stores. "Charge it," I would say as casually as possible, with increasing embarrassment when I knew that the unpaid bill was big. Sometimes, the baker's wife would whisper with him before letting me have a loaf of bread. Sometimes, a storekeeper would say: "Tell your mother, no more credit till the bill is paid." Once an angry woman leaned over the counter and sneered at me: "Your mother is a broken-down stagecoach." In times the bills were always paid, but I knew a good deal about the relations of the poor man and the shopkeeper before I read about them in Karl Marx. Of course, the shopkeepers had bills to pay too.

We were never hungry. Rutabagas were very cheap then and a big one would last us several meals. We also ate a good deal of pea soup and a great deal of spaghetti and rice. I grew husky on a diet that would scandalize a dietitian.

Fuel was sometimes a problem. We used to keep a sharp eye out for new houses building. After the carpenters had gone home at night, we would fill burlap bags with beam and board ends. My brother and I could each manage one bag. I have seen my beautiful and slender mother, plodding through the dark, with a heavy bag of kindling slung over each shoulder. Sometimes we picked up coal along the railroad tracks.

To eke out our living, my mother began to bake cakes for sale. I would go out and hustle orders. The next day I would deliver the cakes. In summer I peddled vegetables. I also developed a regular route for eggs. My mother had an incubator in the attic. Through the glass door, at hatching time, we could watch the wonder of chicks breaking the shell. Sometimes my mother had to take a hairpin and help the chick chip the egg.

When the first of these chicks grew big enough, I went out and got orders for dressed broilers. Then my mother told me to go and kill the first chickens. The thought of hurting anything so helpless and foolish was too much for me. I said: "I can't." My mother did not even answer me. She took a sharp knife and pressed the handle into my hand. "I will not have any man in this house," she said fiercely, "who is afraid of blood." I knew that she was thinking of my father.

I caught a chicken. I sat down with it in the coop, stroked its feathers and tried to quiet its alarm. It was a sunny day. It was the thought that from the bird's bright eye that world of light must now fade that unnerved me. Why must I darken it? So that the live, free creature could pass through the bowels of a gross person? It made no sense.

I tied the chicken's legs and hung it, head down, from a nail, and as quickly and as mercifully as I could, severed its head. The knife fell as if gravity had jerked it from my hand. Then I hid.

In hiding I had these thoughts, in other words or phrases, but substantially these thoughts. Something in me, the deepest thing that makes me what I am, knows that it is wrong to kill anything. But there is something else—a necessity—that forces me to kill. I have the strength to overcome the feeling in myself against killing, and I am proud that I have it for it is part of what makes me a man. All right. As a man, I will kill. But I will kill always under duress, by an act of will, in knowing violation of myself, and always in rebellion against that necessity which I do not understand or agree to. Let me never kill unless I suffer that agony, for if I do not suffer it, I will be merely a murderer. This was one of the decisive moments of my boyhood.

I came out of hiding, cleansed the knife in the ground, took it in the house and laid it down in front of my mother. I have always been grateful to her for handing it to me in the first place. For years, I was the family butcher. My brother never killed anything. I never killed anything, and never kill anything today, without suffering the same ordeal.

XVI

Those years when my father lived away from us were happy years for my mother. Perhaps they were happy for my brother and me too. Without my father, our home, though divided, was tranquil, and we experienced a new sense of freedom, which made us realize for the first time how heavily my father's chilling presence had weighed upon us.

We were poor, and there was something humiliating in the knowledge that it was an unnecessary poverty—that my father was earning a good salary, which he did not share with us. But there was exhilaration in the knowledge that our own efforts could make our poverty comfortable and even enjoyable. My mother, my brother and I were a tightly knit unit. Completely engrossed in our own lives, we shut out the world. My mother enjoyed the proud sense of being equal to any challenge life made of her.

Our simple life never dragged, for my mother's energy and imagination were continually passing from one absorbing interest to another. There was the time that my mother began to suspect the presence of petroleum under our backyard. We promptly wrote to the Interior Department, asking for advice as to how best to tap this subsoil wealth. We waited impatiently for the reply, which rather dashed us, for it said that oil could not possibly exist under the soil formation of Long Island. I do not believe that my mother ever quite regained her confidence in the Interior Department.

Often these interests developed as a result of something my mother had read. From time to time, she would read an article about ranching in Montana or Idaho, states that she knew and loved. On such occasions, she would decide that our manifest destiny lay in homesteading (there were still free lands in those days). She would describe our future life in vivid detail. My brother and I would be wildly excited by the prospect of living in primitive health among coyotes and range cattle, and the promise that simply by working a tract of land for a few years, it would be ours. We would write to the Government (again the unfortunate Interior Department, I believe) for details. Then the land fever would subside or take a new turn.

Once we were going to buy one of the Thousand Islands. The shadow of pines fell across our fancy and we could hear the St. Lawrence sliding past our island. That time we wrote to the Canadian Government and learned that the Thousand Islands were of all shapes and sizes and some of them were, indeed, for sale. Nothing could have been more jarring than that prosaic fact. We hastily dropped the Thousand Islands.

From time to time, my mother would decide to go back on the stage, and my brother and I would begin to prepare for a future of all-night train trouping and sleeping in wardrobe trunks. Once she even went so far as to have a set of theatrical photographs made (rather shocking to my brother and me, since they showed our mother with much more shoulder than we were accustomed to around the house). For a short time, my mother made the rounds of producers and theatrical agents. During that flurry, we met some of her stage acquaintances. On the whole, we were rather pleased when nothing came of it.

Once, in mid-winter, our mother concluded that our musical education was neglected. She decided to buy a phonograph. Since there was no other way to do this, she used the winter's coal money for that purchase. We had central heat by then, so that it was necessary to drain the pipes and radiators, shut off the rest of the big house and sleep (and otherwise live) in the kitchen. We placed the phonograph in the kitchen too, where, clumped around the coal range, we could listen to Alma Gluck singing "Musetta's Waltz," Caruso singing *Ridi, Pagliaccio* and Clarence Whitehill singing Wotan's *Abschied.* Unfortunately, not all the radiators had been completely drained, and those burst.

The saddest of such excitements, and the most persistent, was the one about buying a farm. It came up nearly every year. It was the one that touched me closest and it always ended in disappointment. But while the back-to-the-land mood was on us, we would send for Strout's farm catalog and make active plans to take advantage of the remarkable bargains it offered. It was always just a matter of "come spring" until my brother and I would be milking our own cows and slopping our own pigs. But when spring came, we never went.

By degrees, I sensed, as a boy, that behind my mother's enthusiasms there was a restlessness, and behind that, a strain of that unhappiness that I recoiled from as a small child. Unlike my brother, who all his life confided in his mother, and had few secrets from her, I was always aware of an intangible point beyond which I could not confide, not because I wished to be secretive, but because I wished to be myself. It was precisely my deepest and most personal thoughts that I withheld and it was precisely these that my mother needed as a pledge of affection. This implicit reserve, which became more pronounced as I grew older, and in adolescence began to lunge tactlessly against the tender mesh in which her affection sought to hold me, wounded her deeply. It was one reason why she abruptly shifted the weight of her affection and her hopes for the future from me to my brother.

XVII

In those years, certain miscellaneous people faded in and out of my days with no apparent meaning, like strangers we see walking down a road, and scarcely glance at, because there is nothing to tell us that they will come back to spread their shadows on our lives. In those years, too, I heard or observed certain things that seemed irrelevant in themselves, as a child growing up in a war listens to his parents talk about it, not knowing that it is the war in which, when he is old enough, he will lose his life. I first heard of the revolution in those days.

Peddlers marked our calendar. Like the birds, each had his season for arriving. The broom man came in the early spring; he had spent the winter tying his straws. The honey man always came in the fall, with a heavy tub of clammy comb balanced on a thick pad on his head. The flower man came in May; my mother always bought from him a flat of bellis daisies, of which she was very fond and which always died.

There was one peddler who came in midsummer. He was short, Jewish and had a cast in one eye. This gave me the uneasy feeling that he could watch me while he looked directly at my mother. But his smile was warm and simple. He traded enamel saucepans, which he carried strung on a cord over one shoulder, for old boots and rubbers, which he carried strung on a cord over the other shoulder. The saucepans usually turned out to have a small chip in the enamel which my mother always discovered after he had gone. But the idea of exchanging old lamps for new was irresistible.

One day, the peddler was standing outside our picket fence and my mother and a neighbor were gossiping with him over the gate. Talk got around to "hard times," an expression which, like the word "panic," had a scary sound.

The peddler said: "There is a terrible war coming between the rich and the poor. When it is over, there will not be any more rich people. Everybody will have the same." Thus the tidings of the proletarian revolution came to Lynbrook. After he had gone, my mother and the neighbor continued to gossip over the gate about this grim prospect.

Years later, after I had joined the Communist Party, I saw the "rubber man" one day on an elevated train. He was sitting with his head down, as though lost in thought, with his pans and rubbers on the seat beside him. He looked much older and very tired. I recognized him with a start of nostalgia and the recollection that he had dropped the first tiny seed that had taken root in me. I went up to him and asked him if he remembered me from my boyhood. He shook his head and glanced away uneasily, as if he thought that I were a provocative agent. So I left him to his historic thoughts.

XVIII

About the only "family" we had, or even knew the names of, was my grandparents. I did not like either of my grandmothers, but my grandmother Whittaker was the one I admired. She happened in on us only at long intervals and always unannounced. She was always in transit, as if in perpetual flight from something. She had run in to New York from Chicago to shop for clothes. She was on her way across the continent or across the ocean (she sometimes spent a year or two in Paris). California was one of her more permanent addresses, and I knew her in those days as "the grandmother from San Jose" (as distinguished from "the grandmother from Philadelphia"). She had just lived through a California earthquake, and from her early descriptions I got my first impression of what happens when the underpinnings of a world give way, walls fall out in clouds of suffocating dust, chasms open in familiar streets through which the buried pipes writhe up like snakes.

She was a magnificent woman with a lofty forehead, wide-apart, commanding eyes, a crown of white hair and an imperial presence. Her speech was a flowing texture of precise and graphic English. Sometimes she would break into rippling French, in which she thought almost as easily as in English. It was she who first began to teach me to read French, using an old convent primer in which the mute letters were in hairline type.

The first time I remember my grandmother Whittaker, my mother was recounting to her in bitter detail the part which she believed my grandmother Chambers and her daughter (my Aunt Helen) had played in wrecking her marriage. Whenever my mother paused for breath, my grandmother would clinch each passage with one line of lilting disdain: "Oh, Mama, what people!"

She was a little formidable. I do not believe that I ever felt the slightest affection for her nor did she ever show the slightest affection for my brother or me. She never brought us anything from her travels, and, except for starting me on French, seldom took any notice of us. When we came in on anything she did not want us to hear (and that was a great deal), she would stop and say to my mother: "*Les enfants.*" We quickly learned that that meant "the children," and that we were in the way.

Of course, this sketchy recollection is overcast by my later, more vivid image of her as a grizzled head, the woman with the knife, a gratuitous fury in the last years of our house.

X I X

"The grandmother from Philadelphia" was an entirely different character. No sooner had my father left us than my grandmother Chambers left my grandfather to fend for himself in Philadelphia and rushed to Brooklyn to rent an apartment and "make a home for Jay"—to make more trouble, according to my mother. From this Brooklyn apartment, she made frequent descents on our house.

I early had grounds for disliking my grandmother Chambers. I discovered that she was given to tantrums, hours of sobbing and weeping, which were obviously fraudulent, but by which she managed to get her own way. Sometimes, when we were alone, she would urge me "just for fun" to say to my mother: "I love Grandma more than you." I used to look at her silently at such times, but she was a tireless, surreptitious troublemaker and nothing feazed her. I had also learned (from my mother) that, when my father was a boy, she had made him sit all day in a chair, embroidering, until my grandfather discovered what was going on and smashed the embroidery frames in a storm of curses. I liked that scene, but I resented the indignity to my father.

An excellent dressmaker, she was obsessed with clothes, and seldom talked about anything else. She would spend an hour, describing down to the last buttonhole stitch what the woman wore who sat opposite her on the train. No interruption, no hint however broad, could stop her.

For years, I thought of my grandmother Chambers as the one absolutely brainless person I had ever known. And yet I have two curious memories of her.

I once discovered from something she said that my grandmother could remember the Civil War. Though she was a little girl, she had sat with a hundred older women, making bandages after the Battle of Gettysburg. Once or twice, I plagued her to tell me what those times were like, for I was already absorbed in history. She tried. She would begin. Then she would burst into tears (these tears were real). "I can't," she would say, "I can't talk about the War."

Though she spent most of her time in our house rustling patterns, cutting cloth, pinning, basting and sewing, she would never do any of those things on Sunday. This self-imposed idleness made her extremely irritable, and Sundays, as a result, were the days when she was most mischievous.

One Sunday, when she was complaining peevishly that she could do nothing and that nobody paid any attention to her, I asked, to annoy her: "Why don't you sew, Grandma?"

"Because it's Sunday," she snapped.

"Why can't you sew on Sunday?"

"Because my mother was a Quaker."

"What are Quakers?" I asked.

I saw come over her face, on which the flesh was prematurely translucent, an expression of gentleness and reflection that I had never seen there before. She began to talk, more to herself, I felt, than to me, about the Quakers—how they were quiet, how they sat in meeting without saying anything. She began to describe the "plain dress" with her usual thoroughness about clothes. With a chuckle, she mentioned the "thee" and "thy." She talked about the meeting houses—how they were usually built on hilltops, were built of stone, with little white porches and green shutters.

"What was inside?" I asked.

She paused for a moment. Then she said: "Peace."

X X

My grandfather Chambers was a bully and a blusterer. He also had a keen political brain. In my early days he was, I believe, the city editor or news editor of the Philadelphia *Public Ledger*. He was a short man, with a bald head (about which he was acutely sensitive), a Foxy Grandpa expression behind his gold-rimmed glasses and a corporation that preceded him through doors. He was a gross eater and a heavy drinker. Every year, with the panting of the hart for the water brooks, he made straight for our house. My mother looked forward with dread to this annual visitation. For our house was only a kind of landing strip for my grandfather's great circle swing around the Long Island bars.

My brother and I, while tactfully sympathizing with my mother, secretly looked forward to his coming. He was the only member of the family who blanketed us in a completely natural, warm, animal affection. No sooner was he inside the house than he would sit down and invite us to commit mayhem on his kneecaps, grunting in a voice that grew louder and more anguished with each of our ineffectual efforts: "Ouch! Ouch! Ouch!" Then he would rumple our hair and say in a tone of lingering love: "Grandpa surely does love his little jack rabbits." It was unqualified: Grandpa simply did love his little jack rabbits. Nobody else ever treated us like that.

My grandfather's habitual tone of voice to his wife, his daughter and my father was a snarl. At times, it was a blast like a buccina. I can remember standing on the ground floor of my grandparents' house in Germantown while my grandfather's voice floated down from the third floor in a hog call that rattled the decorative plates in the rack that ran around the dining room walls: "Ma-a-a! Where in hell are my lightweight dra-a-awers?" This was mild; often he cursed like a pirate. Around his grandsons, he was strictly blasphemous (rather than foul). His cursing, it seems to me, had become almost wholly a reflex. He cursed, by ear, for euphony. The frightful imprecations in the frightening voice were his flowers of rhetoric.

He never turned his blistering broadsides on my mother, my brother or me. He saved them for my father, his wife, his daughter, and the world. Throughout my father's boyhood that voice had struck terror into him. And much that was agonizingly mute in my father's nature may be laid as much to his father's bullying as to his mother's coddling.

Grandfather approached Falstaff in girth, and equaled him in capacity for liquid intake—chiefly beer. His father, a doctor, had died when my grandfather was about twelve years old, and the boy went to work as a printer's devil to support his mother and sisters. He had grown up in print shops and graduated into a rough-house school of journalism, where hard drinking was a professional talent.

During his working year, he kept this talent fairly well in check. But he had scarcely arrived at our house when he would announce a little sheepishly (for everybody knew what he really meant): "I must go downtown and get shaved and cleaned up." Off he would toddle, returning at nightfall, somewhat unsteady, but happily primed "to take the boys out for some root beer tomorrow." It was our root-beer binges with Grandpa that made his visits a nightmare to our mother. But my grandmother, who always accompanied her husband, would plead tearfully: "Oh, Laha, let him take them or he will be brutal to me." So, in the morning, we would set off, each clinging to one of Grandfather's hands, perfectly delighted to go.

Our course seldom varied. My grandfather's memory was good. He remembered from year to year just where his favorite haunts were and he disliked to slight one of them. We always made at once for Freeport, Long Island, where there was a cool and spacious waterside taproom. There, while we filled up on unstinted schooners of root beer and heapings of free lunch, Grandfather would fill up in his own fashion, going occasionally to the rail of the porch, which overlooked the tide where, with no trace of self-consciousness or discomfort, he would disgorge like an antique Roman—and be ready for more.

Presently, we would take a motor launch for Point Lookout or Long Beach, where he would slap his chest and draw in great lungfuls of sea breeze, extolling the health-giving virtues of salt air as we made a beeline for the lager fumes. Later, we would cross Long Island by trolley to the North Shore, where other taverns beckoned from the hills around Hempstead and Manhasset Bays. Sundown would find us in the taprooms of Brooklyn or Jamaica. Long after dark, we would venture home, we children so tired by then that we could scarcely keep awake, each of us still clinging to one of Grandfather's hands. This was somewhat more necessary on the return than at the departure, since, by that time, he was no longer quite sure of his footing and depended on us to help him across streets and on and off conveyances. We felt especially proud to be able to help him. He never disgusted or frightened us. However loud or rude he might be with others, he was always supremely gentle with us. We always felt perfectly safe with him.

From observing my grandfather carefully, I presently concluded that his air of public fierceness was almost wholly a fraud, that he was no fiercer than I was. But the world, which had taught him a good many unpleasant things, had taught him that it was a good deal of a fraud itself, and he meant to take it on its own terms.

By the time I was nine or ten, my grandfather had dragged me through most of the saloons in eastern Long Island. An atmosphere of alcoholism is admittedly not the best for two small boys. Apart from that, my mother need never have worried about us. Saloons, I early discovered, were singularly tranquil places. As a rule, my brother and I would be seated at a table as far from the bar as possible. From time to time, my grandfather would bustle over to make sure that our plates were heaped with free lunch, which, in the quantity we made away with, should have made both of us violently sick. I do not remember that it ever did.

Nor do I ever remember anything but a kind of buzzing order in those intemperate havens. Occasionally, the drone of conversation at the bar would flare up into loud words. This would be followed by some cautionary remark and a general over-the-shoulder glance at my brother and me. Then the conversation would lapse again into its easy, somnolent drone. The chief effect of my precocious pub crawl seemed to be that, having seen the inside of so many saloons, I never had the slightest curiosity about them. I neither liked nor disliked them, never went into one alone and seldom went in with anybody else, except for a later period in my brother's life. But I do not believe that my brother's drinking was in any way inspired by his early exposure to the swoosh of taps. I myself am one of those untempted people who dislike the taste and smell of liquor.

This old reprobate was the first man who sat down with me and explained to me the world in terms of politics and history. He first made me aware that politics is history in the making. His chief interest was national politics, in which his knowledge and experience seemed to me vast. My chief interest, from the beginning, was foreign affairs in which he seemed much less at home, though he had a realistic grasp of the main lines of political force. He never tried to switch my interest to his. Instead, he urged me to keep up those clipping books in which I used to paste the heads (so that I could memorize the faces) of leading European statesmen and dynasts (a practice that paid off years later when I was foreign news editor of *Time*). Almost every week, I wrote him a letter with my boy's thoughts about current history. Almost every week, tired or ill, he wrote me back, guiding, correcting and directing. It was he who taught me that the Italo-Turkish War and the Balkan Wars were the first tremors of world war, and that the dismemberment of the Ottoman Empire meant the downfall of Europe. And though in all other ways I was always his "little jack rabbit," in our political talks and letters, he invariably treated me as one political intelligence speaking to another. This was his temperance, and for it and for his mind, I respected him deeply.

He was a selfish, gross and in many ways, I suppose, a vicious old man. I loved him dearly because he loved me without reserve in the simplest human terms. My affection for him never diminished or changed.

XXI

About two hundred of my grandfather Whittaker's books lay in barrels in our attic, just beyond the incubator where we hatched our chicks. One day, when I was eight or nine, my reading curiosity took me up there. I lifted from the top of one barrel a big book whose pages were dog-eared, evidently from much turning by my grandfather. It was an old-fashioned book. The text was set in parallel columns, two columns to a page. There were more than a thousand pages. The type was small. I took the book to the little diamond-shaped attic window to read the small type in the light. I opened to the first page and read the brief foreword:

"So long as there shall exist, by reason of law and custom, a social damnation, which, in the face of civilization, creates hells on earth, and complicates a destiny which is divine with human fatality—

"So long as the three problems of the age—the degradation of man by poverty, the ruin of woman by hunger, and the stunting of childhood by physical and spiritual night—are not solved;—

"So long as, in certain areas, social asphyxia shall be possible—

"So long as ignorance and misery remain on earth, books like this cannot be useless."

I did not understand half the words. How should I know what "human fatality" meant, or "social asphyxia"? But when I read those lines, there moved through my mind a solemn music that is the overtone of justice and compassion. A spirit moved upon the page and through my ignorance I sensed that spirit.

The book, of course, was Victor Hugo's *Les Misérables—The Wretched of the Earth.* In its pages can be found the play of forces that carried me into the Communist Party, and in the same pages can be found the play of forces that carried me out of the Communist Party. The roots of both influences are in the same book, which I read devotedly for almost a decade before I ever opened a Bible, and which was, in many respects, the Bible of my boyhood. I think I can hear a derisive question: "How can anyone take seriously a man who says flatly that his life has been influenced by Victor Hugo's *Les Misérables?*" I understand. I can only answer that, behind its colossal failings, its melodrama, its windy philosophizing, its clots of useless knowledge, its overblown rhetoric and repellent posturings, which offend me, like everybody else, on almost every page, *Les Misérables* is a great act of the human spirit. And it is a fact that books which fall short of greatness sometimes have a power to move us greatly, especially in childhood when we are least critical and most forgiving, for their very failures confess their humanity. As a boy, I did not know that *Les Misérables* is a *Summa* of the revolt of the mind and soul of modern man against the materialism that was closing over them with the close of the Middle Ages and the rise of industrial civilization—or, as Karl Marx would later teach me to call it: capitalism.

I took the book downstairs and read for the first time the first line of its story: "In 1815, Charles Francois Bienvenu Myriel was Bishop of Digne." I do not know how many times I have since read that simplest of leads, which has for me, like many greater first lines, the quality of throwing open a door upon man's fate.

I read and reread *Les Misérables* many times in its entirety. It taught me two seemingly irreconcilable things—Christianity and revolution. It taught me first of all that the basic virtue of life is humility, that before humility, ambition, arrogance, pride and power are seen for what they are, the stigmata of littleness, the betrayal by the mind of the soul, a betrayal which continually fails against a humility that is authentic and consistent. It taught me justice and compassion, not a justice of the law, or, as we say, human justice, but a justice that transcends human justice whenever humanity transcends itself to reach that summit where justice and compassion are one. It taught me that, in a world of force, the least act of humility and compassion requires the utmost exertion of all the powers of mind and soul, that nothing is so difficult, that there can be no true humility and no true compassion where there is no courage. That was the gist of its Christian teaching. It taught me revolution, not as others were to teach me—as a political or historical fact—but as a reflex of human suffering and desperation, a perpetual insurgence of that instinct for justice and truth that lay within the human soul, from which a new vision of truth and justice was continually issuing to meet the new needs of the soul in new ages of the world.

I scarcely knew that *Les Misérables* was teaching me Christianity, and never thought of it that way, for it showed it to me, not as a doctrine of the mind, but in action in the world, in prisons, in slums, among the poor, the sick, the dying, thieves, murderers, harlots and outcast, lonely children, in the sewers of Paris and on the barricades of revolution. Its operation did not correspond to anything I knew as Christian in the world about me. But it corresponded exactly to a need I felt within myself.

Les Misérables gave me my first full-length picture of the modern world—a vast, complex, scarcely human structure, built over a social abyss of which the sewers of Paris was the symbol, and resting with crushing weight upon the wretched of the earth. Dickens' novels showed me much the same thing, in a series of glimpses rather than in one appalling view of the human pit. But Dickens' novels, when they did not merely bore me, left me completely unmoved. His tear-jerking scenes jerked no tears from me, though I sometimes resented their efforts to. I knew that the unfortunate hero would always come into a legacy, or a kindly eccentric would intervene to snatch the good outcast or the lost child from the engulfing evil which was, after all, rather quaint. And though I did not know that there was such a thing as a problem of evil, I recognized that Dickens' way was too easy a way out, and no more an answer to the problem that he had raised than life insurance is an answer to the problem of death. Moreover, Dickens was entirely secular. Again, while I did not know the difference between secular and spiritual, I felt it. I brushed Dickens aside and plunged into Hugo.

It was, above all, the character of the Bishop of Digne and the stories about him that I cherished in *Les Misérables*. As a boy I read them somewhat as other people read the legends of the saints. Perhaps it is necessary to have read them as a child to be able to feel the full force of those stories, which are in many ways childish, and appeal instantly to the child mind, just as today they appeal to what is most childlike in me as a man.

That first day, when I sat in our living room and read how the Bishop came to Digne, I knew that I had found a book that had been written for me. I read how the Bishop moved into his palace with its vast salons and noticed next door a tiny hospital with its sick crowded into a few small rooms. The Bishop called in the director of the hospital and questioned him: How many rooms are there in the hospital; how many sick; how many beds in each room? "Look," he said at last, "there is evidently some mistake here. You have my house and I have yours. Give me back my house and move into yours." The next day the Bishop was in the hospital and the patients were in the palace. "He is showing off," said the solid citizens.

The Bishop's views on human fallibility fixed mine and made it impossible for me ever to be a puritan. "To be a saint," he sometimes preached to the "ferociously virtuous," "is the exception; to be upright is the rule. Err, falter, sin, but be upright. To commit the least possible sin is the law for man. . . . Sin is a gravitation."

He first raised in my mind the question of relative human guilt. Everybody was praising the cleverness of a public prosecutor. A man and woman had been arrested for some mischief. There was no evidence against the man. By a trick, the prosecutor convinced the woman falsely that the man had been unfaithful to her. She testified against him. "Where are the man and woman to be tried?" asked the Bishop. "At the assizes." "And where," asked the Bishop, "is the prosecutor to be tried?"

The Bishop lodged in my mind a permanent suspicion of worldly success and pride of place that never changed in all the changes of my life. He was not one of the "rich mitres." In Paris he did not "catch on." He was not considered "to have any future." For, said Hugo, "We live in a sad society. Succeed—that is the advice that falls, drop by drop, from the overhanging corruption."

The story about the Bishop that I liked best also involved the question of worldly appearances. One day the Bishop had to visit a parish in the steep mountains, where no horse could go. Few bishops would have gone there, either. The Bishop of Digne went, riding on a sure-footed donkey. The solid citizens of the town turned out to greet him. When they saw the Bishop climbing down from his donkey, some of them could not hide their smiles. "My bourgeois friends," said the Bishop pleasantly, "I know why you are smiling. You think that it is pretty presumptuous of a poor priest to use the same conveyance that was used by Jesus Christ." Thus I first learned the meaning of the word bourgeois, so that, unlike most Americans, I was quite familiar with it when I came across it later in the writings of Marx and Lenin.

Finally, the Bishop's view of the world left a permanent, indelible impress on me: "He inclined toward the distressed and the repentant. The universe appeared to him like a vast disease; he perceived fever everywhere; he auscultated suffering everywhere. And without trying to solve the enigma, he sought to staunch the wound. The formidable spectacle of created things developed a tenderness in him. . . ."

My life failed at the moment when I began to try to "solve the enigma" and "staunch the wound," for Marx and Lenin did little more for me than give me a modern diagnosis and a clinical ways and means to deal with that "vast disease" which the Bishop of Digne felt and that "social damnation" which his author first made me conscious of. Even as a Communist, I never quite escaped the Bishop. I put him out of my mind, but I could not put him out of my life.

One night, in the Union Station, in Washington, I stood in line with J. Peters, the head of the underground section of the American Communist Party, to buy a ticket for New York. I noticed a man watching me closely. As I left the line, he came up to me and explained that he had some kind of special ticket to New York. It was good only for the week-end. It was Sunday night. He wanted to stay over in Washington. Would I exchange my regular ticket for his special ticket? His ticket seemed to be in order. I gave him mine. Peters, who had walked away so as not to be observed, asked me what had happened. I told him. "Bob," he said, "you're a fool." He must have been pondering on the matter, for as we walked out to the train, he suddenly put his hand on my arm and said gently: "The party needs more fools." I would have been surprised if someone had then suggested to me that the Bishop of Digne had handed my ticket to the stranger. J. Peters would have been horrified to think that it was still the invisible Bishop who made him touch my arm and say: "The party needs more fools."

No doubt, the Bishop was invisibly present still when I broke from the Communist Party, though by then I had strayed so far from him that I could no longer hear him saying: "Jean Valjean, my brother, you belong no longer to evil, but to good. It is your soul that I am buying for you. I withdraw it from dark thoughts and the spirit of perdition, and I give it to God."

XXII

One passage of *Les Misérables* I knew almost by heart.

Jean Valjean, whom the Bishop had reclaimed, had told the police that he, the prosperous factory owner and philanthropist, was in fact the convict they were looking for. They had jailed him. He had escaped. Nevertheless, he risked returning to the city hospital to tell a dying streetwalker that he would take care of her child. The police, with Inspector Javert at their head, closed in. Jean Valjean retreated to a little room, where he stood motionless in a corner, out of sight of the door. In the room with him was a nun, Sister Simplice, who loved him for his goodness and pitied him for his suffering.

One fact distinguished Sister Simplice from the rest of the human race. In all her life, she had never told a lie. Sister Simplice heard Javert coming and fell upon her knees. The police inspector opened the door, but seeing her in prayer, stopped abashed. "This was Sister Simplice, who had never lied in her life. Javert knew this and venerated her especially because of it."

"Sister," he said, "are you alone in this room?"

Sister Simplice looked up and answered: "Yes."

Javert continued: "Excuse me, if I persist. It is my duty—you have not seen this evening a person, a man—he has escaped and we are searching for him—Jean Valjean—you have not seen him?"

Sister Simplice answered: "No."

"She lied. Two lies in succession, one upon another, without hesitation, quickly, as if she were an adept in it."

"Your pardon," said Javert and withdrew.

Then followed the words that became a part of my mind: "Oh, holy maiden . . . may this falsehood be remembered to thee in Paradise."

XXIII

One day my mother told my brother and me that my father was coming home to live. For some time he had been spending his Sundays with us. Once more the Sunday sketching trips were revived.

Once more my mother would brush and brighten us up to accompany my father wherever his fancy led us. These outings, which we had once enjoyed, and later endured, we now openly detested. There was little fun in them for us and they broke up our free day. They were only one of our causes of resentment toward our father.

In his absence, we had been half a family, but that half had been a happy, active unit. With his return, the chill of his presence spread through the house. Before, we had been able to forget that we were divided. Now the division had been closed, but not healed. Its infection no longer drained away; it festered inwardly and poisoned all our relations. On one side were my mother, my brother and I. On the other side was my father. Between the two sides was a pocket of hostility. My mother had told us that she had let my father come back because "it is better for you children to have a father at home." I scarcely regarded him as my father. My mother, in sharing the too heavy burden of her unhappiness, had disclosed to me that my father had never wanted children in the first place; specifically, he had never wanted me. This information was like a poisoned knife. It cut the last ties that bound us. Yet if my father had tried to win us back, he might even yet have succeeded. It would never have been an easy task, and my father did not even know how to begin.

He moved into the big front bedroom (the best room in the house, my mother pointed out). Soon he was surrounded by the artistic clutter without which he seemed unable to live—his big boxes of paintings, drawings, sketches and all kinds of drawing papers; his collection of bookplates; his miniature theater for which he used to spend hours painting scenery and cutting little figures out of pasteboard; the puppets which he was continually contriving out of glued strips of cloth and cardboard; his collection of toys, jumping-jack bears, wooden dolls, little carts and horses, be-babos that we were forbidden to touch. Once installed, he retired into this den and closed the door upon us.

For years, all my father's meals were served to him on a tray in his room. The rest of us ate downstairs in the kitchen, in part because that was the room farthest away from him. We were no longer a family in the usual sense of the word. We were four people, living in emotional and physical anarchy.

For years, my brother and I had scarcely more than a nodding acquaintance with my father. But my brother was a cheerful, active boy and his terse acquaintanceship was probably easier to bear than the sullenness which I developed as a defense against my father's chilling rebuffs.

As soon as he entered the house, my father would go to his room and shut the door. Before we sat down to eat, I would take his tray of food upstairs. I would knock at his door. In a voice deliberately pitched so low that sometimes I could not hear him, he would say: "Come in." When I entered, he would usually glance up with a smile. It was not an open or a pleasant smile. It was a faintly derisive smile, I thought then. Now I know that it was the smile of the defeated. It used to shrivel me night after night for years, like a bug on a hot stove lid. Sometimes, if he were feeling humorous (as I thought), my father would make a great show of clearing the heap of artist's materials from his table so that the messenger from afar could set down the tray of food. There is almost nothing that a boy can take less easily than sarcasm. This pathetic by-play of my father's put off for years my understanding of his loneliness.

In the kitchen, we spoke in carefully lowered voices. We knew that my father had a habit of opening his door quietly and padding halfway downstairs so softly that we often did not hear him. When we thought we did, my mother would say to my brother or me in a voice that carried clearly: "I think I hear your father. Will one of you go and see?" Sometimes, as we reached the hall stairs, we would see his door close noiselessly.

Sometimes, the tension among us broke out in strange ways. In the back of our yard, my mother had had a pergola built. It was somewhat in the Italian style with arches supporting the upper struts. But the side posts were unbarked, so that there was also a touch of American rustic. Against this structure my mother, my brother and I had lovingly planted a grapevine and a clematis. In time, the clematis developed a trunk as thick as a small tree. Its vine covered half the pergola and masked its oddity. In the autumn, when the grapes were ripening, the little white clematis flowers filled the air with a fragrance like crushed cherry pits.

One Sunday we heard my father quietly leave his room, pad downstairs and out the front door. He was carrying a sickle (one of the few tools I ever saw him use). With it he began to slash down some rank grass and weeds along the fence. This was sufficiently unusual so that each of us watched him furtively from behind separate curtains. But we lost interest and, presently, we heard him pad softly upstairs again. Nobody had said anything to him and he had said nothing to any of us.

Later in the day, my mother came in from the yard and, in a voice in which there was a touch of horror, and, what was worse, a touch of fear, asked which of us had cut down the clematis. Neither of us had. Then she led us out to the pergola. The clematis had been hacked in two at the root, evidently by sickle strokes. Along one side of the pergola, the massive vine hung dying. My mother said: "Jay must have done this." We all felt a little sick. We all realized that it was an outrage deliberately committed by him against us. I do not think that we ever mentioned it again, certainly not to him. But I think I understand now why he did it—because he had to perpetrate some violence on us or the tensions of his hostile home would have driven him mad.

XXIV

While our family life festered incurably at the heart of our home, my father and mother began to lead a rather active, and outwardly rather uncomplicated, public life. My mother claimed to loathe the stage. My father was stage-struck. Shortly after he came back to live with us, he got together, under circumstances that I have forgotten, a group of young people from Lynbrook and neighboring villages for the purpose of giving amateur theatricals. They called themselves "The Larks."

There must have been eight or nine Larks. Two or three of them, like my father, were stage-struck. The rest were along for the fun. Somewhat against her will, I believe, my mother was also a Lark. Sometimes, the troupe met at the homes of individual players. More often, they met at our house, and I would sometimes waken in the night to hear a young male Lark, moaning, in simulated agony: "A-oh, my laig! A-oh, my laig!" Whereat a young woman player would answer with inspired flatness: "Darling, I did not mean to shoot you."

The Larks presented a number of plays. I must have heard them rehearsed in part or at length scores of times. I must have seen them acted publicly. I cannot remember what they were about or a single scene from one of them. But I remember quite well that I disliked seeing my father and mother act on a public stage. I remember how our house became a property room with rose-grown trellises standing against one wall, finished or half-finished scenery leaning against another wall, chairs draped with costumes or the iridescent silk fabrics for which my father gloatingly rummaged the East Side pushcarts.

I remember much more vividly certain scenes that were enacted between my parents in private. To make costumes for *Nance Oldfield,* my father bought some rather sleazy seersucker for my mother and some bright, rosebud stuff for a younger member of the cast. All day my mother brooded. When my father came home that night, there occurred the first scene that I had actually witnessed between my parents. It was the first time I had seen their faces as they raised their voices against each other. I do not know what years of hoarded bitterness then found release to swell my mother's surges of anger or my father's white-faced, stolid rage. The scene ended when my brother and I hid weeping in one of the unlighted rooms. A tense quiet settled over the house. When I took the tray of food to my father's room, he smiled at me impishly. It was like a wink, and if I had been big enough, I think that I would have knocked him down.

I sided completely with my mother, not because I knew or cared whether my father was a poor actor or a good one. I sided with her because my father obviously made her suffer and because, in his acting and his theatrical posturings, I felt a failure of dignity that struck me at the point where a boy is most vulnerable—his need to respect his father as a man.

The Larks were long-lived birds. They did not fold, if I remember rightly, until after the First World War when the leading man (the player with the "laig") went into the Navy, and perhaps the others had lost interest. Long before, my father's interest had shifted to another art form.

This was tableaux. In tableaux, a whole book or drama was presented as a series of living pictures—static scenes in which nobody acted, nobody said anything, everybody stood still. The curtain rose and simply showed a group of people posed rigidly. After a few minutes, the curtain went down and then went up on a second scene. The art lay in the organization of the groups and poses and the sumptuousness of the sets. Tableaux exactly suited my father's talent. It also gave my mother full scope since, before the curtain went up and while the actors were posing, she read dramatically a text which explained the scene.

Sometimes, the tableaux were Biblical (Joseph and his brethren). More often, *Ali Baba and the Forty Thieves* was the subject. Most often, the *Rubaiyat* of Omar Khayyam was given. I hesitate to think how many times that great atheist and alcoholic tract was given under pious auspices, for my father usually presented his tableaux for the benefit of libraries, schools and churches, in neighboring villages, Brooklyn and New York.

The tableaux called for much bigger casts than the plays. Even my brother and I were drafted under protest. In *Ali Baba,* we were the arms of the dead thieves sticking out of the jars in which we had been killed with hot oil. In the *Rubaiyat,* I was for years "I sent my soul through the invisible." The curtain would rise. I would be discovered seated, very insecurely, on a globe made of cheesecloth and hoops. My right arm was thrust straight up. My hand was held as still as I could hold it and I wore nothing at all but a scrap of gauze laid across my middle—rather an accent than a concealment.

"I sent my Soul through the Invisible (my mother's voice would announce with soaring resonance)

> *One letter of that After-life to spell,*
> *And by and by my Soul returned to me,*
> *And answer'd 'I Myself am Heaven and Hell.'*

This tableau always called forth a number of audible ahs and brought a great hand. I long fought helplessly against the indignity of this public exposure. An unexpected ally came to my aid —nature. For at last it became inescapable, even to my father, that his oldest son was on the way to manhood. To my great relief, some younger rival supplanted me as "I sent my Soul through the Invisible."

XXV

The close of my stage career was a tiny turning point in our lives, though none of us knew it. It had happened because I had entered adolescence. Henceforth, I was to be a new disruptive force in our disrupted house. For with the other changes in me, I began to undergo a change of disposition. From being even-tempered, cheerful, active, I became lethargic, moody, irritable. I had only a vague idea of the reasons for this change, for nobody had ever told me the simplest facts that are now taught schoolchildren as a matter of course.

My change was first noticeable in connection with our after-school walks. My mother loved to walk and long afternoon rambles with my brother and me had become one of our rituals. I no longer wanted to go. Sometimes, I would go to the window and watch my mother and brother walk off a little forlornly without me. I felt a little forlorn, too, but I wanted to be by myself, to think my own thoughts, which were beginning to be a little harsh. They became a little harsher as my mother and brother began to form a new separate unit of our family whose interests and intimacy I no longer shared.

A change of schools played its unlucky part in my greater change. I had never been happy at the Lynbrook school, but, in time, I had grown used to my schoolmates and they had grown used to me. They were no longer a strange breed to me, and as we all grew older, I began to sense in them a simple humanity, spontaneous and unpretentious, with which I felt at one. I began to make friends. At that point, it was decided that I should go to high school in a neighboring village, where my parents had made connections in the course of their theatrical ventures.

The impact of this new experience caught me in the midst of my organic turmoil, complicated by my ignorance and our family peculiarities. I had always been docile and obedient. I became impudent and rebellious, and one of the school mischief-makers. (I was by no means alone.) I had never cursed, but, with an effort, I acquired the knack and found that there was nothing easier. I loathed foul language, but I forced myself to use it. It was almost harder for me not to learn than to learn, but I made a brave effort and soon my marks tumbled to just above failing. Only in English and Latin, when the spell of Vergil overtook me, did my marks hold up despite myself.

I had become conscious of girls and felt that I was not attractive to them. With that went a new self-consciousness about appearance and a new sense of difference. My attitude was: if I am to be outcast, I will be outcast to the hilt. It amused me to be shock-headed and untidy among my barbered and tidy schoolmates. I wore short pants some time after most of my generation had let theirs down, for my father would not buy me long pants. When it became impossible to avoid long pants any longer, my father still refused to invest in a new suit for me. I was given his old suits to wear and I wore them as a badge of shame.

I was afflicted, too, with that yearning for horizons which is so strong in some adolescents. Sometimes, on warm spring days, the drowsy tinkle of a junkman's bells, the clop of his horse's hoofs, or the cackle of a hen, would drift lazily into the study hall. I would suffer a longing to be free so acute that it seemed as if the heart would burst out of my body.

While I was desperately trying not to learn at school, I was doggedly studying by myself. My mother had urged me to study Gaelic, since that was the language of our forebears. I worked away zealously at the rather inadequate grammars of that nearly dead language. In this connection, I had begun a correspondence with an eminent philologist, George Frazier Black, who was then with the New York Public Library. With patient understanding, Dr. Black encouraged me, sending me a number of grammars from his own philological library. With his help, I began to study Arabic, Persian, Hindustani and the Assyrian of the cuneiform inscriptions. Dr. Black was the outstanding authority in the United States on gypsy dialects, and one of the leading authorities in the world. He encouraged me to visit a Rumanian gypsy encampment near us. I presently picked up a rough smattering of the dialect* and began collecting vocabularies for Dr. Black. When he retired, he made me a present of the manuscripts of his Welsh and Rumanian gypsy studies. I still have most of Dr. Black's grammars and dictionaries, long unused.

For one day it occurred to me that, instead of studying languages that at best I could only hope to talk to myself, I might much better be learning German and mastering French. I got out my grandfather Whittaker's old self-taught grammars. After that, I woke myself early enough each morning to study two lessons of each language before I got up. At night, I used to work on a translation of that least comic of comedies, Lessing's *Minna von Barnhelm*, and of Goethe's *Iphigenia in Tauris*, parts of which I still know by heart. I also began to study Spanish and Italian.

These studies proved more useful than anything I ever learned in high school. As a German and French translator, I was later able to earn my living. In the underground, I was to speak German almost as much as English. Spanish was to be useful to me sooner than I knew.

* Enough, however, so that when a *Time* researcher in later years called up Columbia University to check my translation of a paragraph of gypsy, she was asked: "Why do you call me? One of your editors knows more about gypsy languages than any man in the United States." This is wild exaggeration. I never knew that much, and I have forgotten most of what I knew.

Sometimes, as I sat translating *Minna von Barnhelm,* I would hear in the distance the shuffling feet of the Home Guard and fifes playing "Little Shaver." For the World War that my grandfather had predicted had come, and added a new element of turmoil to my mind. The First World War was in my thoughts day and night; I felt it with an intensity with which I never felt World War II. My family was traditionally Francophile. I was brought up to believe that Paris was less the capital of a country than the capital of Light. The German advance through Belgium filled us almost with as much consternation as if we had been invaded ourselves. I can still remember the Sunday morning when I picked up the newspaper and saw the headlines about the Battle of the Marne. I felt that I was experiencing an authentic miracle. After that, I lived day by day through the deadlock of the trench war on the Western Front. My grandfather had sent me a big military map of Europe, showing forts and naval bases. It covered almost one wall of my room. I had marked out the fronts with rubber bands. Every night before I went to bed, I moved the bands to correspond with the day's communiqués.

The war was the direct cause of my Russian studies. After the Russian Revolution (which interested me only as it affected Allied strategy), my mother decided that we might be fighting the Russians soon. She urged me to prepare for a career in the military intelligence by studying Russian. I had only Thimm's *Russian Self-Taught,* which consisted chiefly of vocabularies. These my mother patiently heard me repeat day after day until I had learned two or three thousand Russian words. I never learned Russian grammar, though I learned to read Russian type and to write Russian script.

I planned to get into the war as soon as I finished high school—a plan that I did not share with my mother. The false armistice was a tremendous blow. But as soon as it was denied, I saw that there was no time to lose. In New York City, one day, I had passed the British recruiting office and made a careful note of its address. The day after the false armistice, I left a note for my family, saying that I had gone to enlist. I walked into the British recruiting office and offered my services to the Empire. A stiff English officer looked me up and down. "Hell, boy," he said, "the war's over." I slunk home. My family was amused. It should have been handwriting on the wall.

As nobody seemed able to help me, I strove to help myself. I sought refuge in those places where I had always found it. I became a haunter of the woods and fields. I would set out by myself before the family was stirring in the morning and spend whole days in the woods, which required of me only that I be silent, patient and harmless. In return, nature gave me the peace that it gives to anyone who comes to see and hear and not to change.

Those woods, and their lakes and streams, were then a part of the Brooklyn waterworks system. They have become a part of the New York State park system, and thousands pass through them in a day. In those days, I had them almost entirely to myself. I seldom met another person. I could soon find my way about them even at night, as I sometimes used to do. For I never found the loneliness of the woods at night as disturbing as people by daylight. I soon knew their birds, plants and insects as well as I knew my way along their trails. Only those who really live close to nature can understand the elation I felt when I first discovered where the seagulls roosted seven miles from the sea, or the shallow stream in the dense woods where all the robins in the area bathed just at sunrise, or the one brook where a cardinal flower grew, or my first pinxter bush in bloom.

I presently discovered that the life below the surface of shallow ponds was as absorbing as the life on their shores. It reached a climax in the fore-spring when the alder catkins were bursting with pollen and the ice was still rotting on the pools. Through the ice I used to watch the watery world below coming back to life after winter, while the toads came down to the lowlands to deposit their masses of jellied eggs or the frogs unwound their slimy ribbons in the shallows. In these pursuits, I could not always take off my shoes in time to follow an exciting specimen. I learned simply to wade in with my shoes on. This habit so impressed one of my schoolmates that he remembered it through the years, and was able to testify to it, as an example of my bizarre behavior, during the first Hiss trial.

In time, my ear became so sensitive that, sitting silently, I could sometimes hear the tiny tearing sound that a caterpillar makes in gnawing a leaf, and by following it, locate him. My eye, too, became sensitized, so that the slightest movement, the waving of grass stems, the way a leaf hung when the others were blowing, or the way a twig vibrated, always meant something and often something terrible, since nature, under the leaves, is a vast concealment and pursuit. I still retain this power to pick out minute movements in nature. But I have lost the power to sit silent for an hour, mentally alert, but physically lulled by the sun and the smell of plants each of which has a distinct odor. It was not necessary to sit motionless, but only to make those slow and explicit motions which said that I was not in hiding and did not mean attack. I never had to move much to observe the life of fields and woods, for its inquisitiveness is equal to its fear, and the woods and fields sooner or later drew near to observe me. I was a part of nature myself. In that habit of identification with nature is a healing peace more medicinal than herbs. Undoubtedly it carried me through the worst of my adolescence.

During those quiet sessions, I was not only observing the life of the woods. I was making inner and outer observations of another kind, trying to sort out my thoughts about myself, my family and our dislocation within ourselves and within the life around us—dislocations both of which made me a fugitive in the woods. I sensed that one dislocation was connected with the other. I felt that the failure of my family was in part a failure of the life in which it found itself. But since I had no grasp of why these things were so, I was chiefly engaged in adding up the ways in which they were so. By degrees I told myself:

I am an outcast. My family is outcast. We have no friends, no social ties, no church, no organization that we claim and that claims us, no community. We could scarcely be more foreign in China than in our alienation from the life around us. If we tried to share with it our thoughts, it would draw away, uncomprehending. If it tried to share its hopes with us, we would draw away, uncomprehending. It does not want what we want. We do not want what it wants. It puts the things of the world first. We put the things of the mind first. It knows what it wants better than we know what we want. They are simple things. It measures happiness and success in terms of money, comfort, appearances and what it calls pleasure. I, for one, would not want to live a life in which money, comfort, appearances and pleasure mean success. There is something wrong with a people that measures its happiness and success in those terms. It has lost its mind. It has no mind; it has only activity. "What shall be said," I had written, for I was writing more and more, "of those who have destroyed the mind of a nation?"

But if there was something wrong with the life around us, there was also something wrong with us. Compared to us, the life around us was orderly and happy. We were not happy. Beneath our quiet, we were wretchedly unhappy. We were not a family. Our home was not a home. My father was not a father. My mother was not a mother. He was nothing. She was trying to be both father and mother. She dominated through her love, which was genuine, tender and sacrificing, but was dangerous. I felt it around me like coils, interposing between me and reality, coddling my natural weaknesses, to keep the world away from me, but also to keep me away from the world. "My mother does not want me to grow up," I thought, "because she does not want me to go away from her." As the life around me had no mind, only activity, my mother had no plans, a few hopes—not many of them.

That left me absolutely alone. My family could give me no support against the alien world, from which the whole influence of our life divided me. And I felt about our family, a foreboding, an indefinable sense of doom, which I would also share unless I found the strength to free myself from it. I doubted that I had that strength. I decided to find out.

I did not understand that the malady of the life around me from which I retreated into the woods, and the malady of the life of my family, from which I was about to retreat into the world, were different manifestations of the same malady—the disorder that overtakes societies and families when a world has lost its soul. For it was not its mind that the life around me had lost, though I thought so as a boy and was to continue to think so for almost twenty years, but its way, because it had lost its soul. I was about to set out from those quiet woods (to which I would return only at the decisive moment of the Hiss Case) on a lifelong quest for that lost way, first in personal, then in revolutionary, then in religious terms.

XXVI

It was the summer I graduated from high school. My mother wanted me to go on to college. My father was opposed. So was I, but for different reasons. I had had enough of school. I needed a job, but I was peculiarly helpless in finding one in the white-collar world where it was taken for granted that I should look, but where we had no roots. My father refused to interest himself in the problem.

I decided to solve it for myself, to leave home, to make my own way, to turn my back on that middle-class world of white collars in which our claim to belong seemed to me a pretense unjustified by any reality. I knew that this announcement would cause wild emotional scenes, tearful charges of ingratitude and lack of love. Because I was a boy, I slipped away secretly, and, because I was a boy, and because even a wanderer likes to have a destination, I headed for Mexico.

XXVII

Few boys run away from happy homes. The world is too wide; it is easier to stay put. I left my unhappy home with a wrench that I could barely master. Once or twice, I was on the point of turning back. I kept on chiefly because I knew more about the unhappiness behind me than about the loneliness of the world ahead. I had a little money of my own—ten dollars possibly. I bought a ticket to Baltimore. It seems prophetic, but I was simply heading south, and Baltimore was about as far as I could go on the money I had.

I reached Baltimore for the first time on a singeing Saturday afternoon. I was wearing my graduation suit—the first suit of my own I had had. I wandered in the stunning heat until I found an old flea-bag opposite the Calvert Station. There I took a room. There I met my first bedbugs and learned that there are worse things than a shabby house: there are filthy rooms.

On Monday morning, after I had paid my bill, I had just enough money left for a newspaper, rolls and a cup of coffee. The coffee was a declaration of independence. I had never been allowed to drink coffee. In the newspaper, among the help wanted ads, I found that Engel & Hevenor, contractors, were hiring on laborers for a street railway job in Washington. Their address was on Eutaw Street. Seventeen years later, in underground days, I would live on its upper extension, Eutaw Place, where Alger Hiss, who was a younger boy in that same city on that morning of my first job hunt, would sometimes visit me.

Engel & Hevenor's headquarters was an empty store. Outside, on the sidewalk, a hard-faced young man in shirtsleeves was doing the hiring. A long line of men of all nationalities and all styles of rough faces and rough clothes, stretched away for a block. These had passed the hiring test; they already had jobs.

The test was simple. When a man asked for a job, the hiring boss said: "Stick out your hands." If the hands were callused, the man was sent to fall in at the end of the line. I was wearing a hat, my trim graduation suit with jacket (although it was hot), and my tie was neatly tied. The hiring boss took one startled look at me (one way or another, my appearance always seems to work against me). "Stick out your hands," he said. They were soft, of course. "Can't use you."

I turned away, with crushing defeat in my eyes, and walked down the line of life's successes, trying to look invisible. Every man in the line knew what had happened. As I neared the end, hands reached out and pulled me through the line to the far side, where I was largely out of sight of the hiring boss, who was busy with others. Somebody said: "Give me your hat." Somebody else grabbed the hat from my hand, folded it and stuffed it in his pocket. "Mess up your hair." "Take off that tie." "Take off your coat." Somebody snatched my jacket and passed it down the line. Somebody else scooped muck out of the gutter and made me rub it on my hands. Then they made room for me in the line.

It was moving. A boss, standing at the head, was handing out transportation to Washington. The man behind me said: "Keep moving. Take a ticket. He won't know you." I shuffled along with the rest. I stood before the transportation boss. I reached out my grimy hand for a ticket. He slapped one into the palm. I walked past him. The line followed. The faces remained expressionless.

In a rough group, an insurgence from the netherworld that made respectable Baltimoreans turn to stare, we marched to the Washington, Baltimore and Annapolis railroad station. We crowded together in a special coach—special in the sense that it was old and shabby. On the train, somebody handed me back my hat and jacket.

The proletariat and I had met. The wretched of the earth had stretched out their hands and claimed me for their own because they understood my need. In four minutes, they had done for me what others failed to do in a lifetime. They had taught me that there is a level of humanity where compassion is a reflex of distress, and, in that sense, they humanized my soul for the rest of my life.

XXVIII

We piled off the W. B. & A. train on New York Avenue in Washington. The job lay just beyond. For a mile or so, the Engel & Hevenor company was tearing up street railway tracks or laying new ones. It was a little like a daylight scene from Hell. In places, big fires were burning and asphalt pots were belching blackly. For several blocks, the asphalt of the street and the concrete around the tracks had been cut out by pneumatic drills and picks and shoveled away. Elsewhere, picks and drills were clattering, air compressors were throbbing, the noise was deafening. In places, the earth had been scooped out around the tracks and the excavation shored up with timbers. Men, shoveling, picking, hammering, drilling, swarmed over the construction and destruction.

I gave an assumed name, Charles Adams, to a straw boss, who handed me a badge with a number. Then I was attached to a gang whose boss wore a sweat-drenched silk shirt with peppermint candy stripes (post-war prosperity had not faded yet). He was a big, reserved, pleasant-looking man with a walrus moustache, who moved slowly among the men, giving a quiet order here, a quiet suggestion there, sometimes gently taking a tool from a laborer's hand and showing him how to do the same job with less effort and more effect. He never raised his voice. The men respected him deeply—in part, because he had been a construction boss on a New York subway job and knew every detail of the work, in part, because he was fearless about what they most feared—the third rail.

Sometimes, in cutting up concrete between the tracks, the stuttering, unwieldy pneumatic drills would go through the surface. The blade of the drill would touch the third rail below and the drill would stick there, burning with a brilliant blue electric light. The drillers wore heavy gloves and the shock of contact seemed to hurl them off the drills, so that I never saw anyone hurt in this way. Calmly, the boss would walk over to the blazing drill. Deliberately, he would take off his battered felt hat, punched with holes. He would fold it, wrap it around the drill handle and lug out the heavy tool.

When I was turned over to him, he had stared at me a moment a little curiously. Then he went and got a short cold chisel and a short-handled sledge and set me to cracking the nuts on the bolts that tied the rail plates together. I worked doggedly in the killing sun. Once in a while I caught the boss watching me. Once he came over and told me not to grip the sledge and the chisel so tight. He did not mention my hands though he glanced at them. Ten minutes after I started working there was scarcely any skin left on palms or fingers. In that condition, I worked with them through the afternoon.

At quitting time, we piled into a street car on our way to a boarding house, not far from the Capitol, where we all ate around trestle tables in a long bleak room. There was nothing in it but those tables, the folding chairs and a mantelpiece on which stood two small plaster busts. Across the flattened base of each was printed a name: Mozart.

The food was prison fare; meat that was unidentifiable, and lapped in a greasy suspect stew. Potatoes were the filler. Dessert was nearly always the same—bread, the refuse from the last meal, glued into a pudding and concealed in a glutinous sauce that reminded me of masses of toad eggs in my boyhood (not far in the past—though one day made it seem like a decade). We were always ravenously hungry, and, while we sometimes grumbled at the food, we always wolfed it, washing out the more questionable tastes with unlimited coffee.

By a selective seniority system, some of the men slept upstairs in the boarding house. Most of them, perhaps a hundred or more, drifted after supper to a barracks a few blocks away. There in a big hall, dingy and bare, and reeking of disinfectant, were a hundred or so beds, most of them double-deckers. Each man had his bed under which he kept his few belongings.

I slumped down on my bed with my clothes on. My skinless hands were burning. A tall, lean, middle-aged man with an elusive face in which dissipation lurked, walked over to my bed. "Let me see your hands," he said. He examined them as if he had been a doctor. "I'm an old soldier," he said, "and I know what to do for these."

He rummaged among his things and brought up two bottles of iodine. "I am going to hold your wrist tight," he said, "because when I pour this on your hand, it's going to burn like hell, and you're going to jump." A crowd of men had slipped over and stood quietly watching.

My doctor uncorked the first iodine bottle, and, like a doctor, he talked to distract me. "My name's York," he said, and unruffled by the listening gallery, added, "I had a good upbringing. You know what's the matter with me? Women. Keep away from them." (How often I was to hear that one.) While he talked, he emptied the whole bottle of iodine over the palm and fingers of my hand. I managed not to wince and even to smile. Then York grasped my other hand and emptied the other bottle over that.

The men drifted away as quietly as they had drifted up. I knew that I had passed a test. In a short time, my hands healed with calluses that should have got me a job anywhere.

XXIX

Learning to do my different jobs kept me busy; the heavy physical work kept me exhausted. At first, in the evening, I would collapse on my bed at once and fall into a deep sleep. Gradually, I hardened. Then I began to look at the men around me.

They were my first International. Practically every European nationality was represented. Yet they had no nationality, just as they had no homes. That was the difference between them and other men: they were the men who had no homes at all. They had reached that bleak barracks in the unheroic course of a workingman's everlasting search for work which, as Tolstoy has noted, beggars the wanderings of Odysseus. The job was the nearest thing to home they felt. Few of them spoke English and I found that my scrappy knowledge of half a dozen languages was one way I could get to know them.

I worked day after day beside a silent, sour, potato-faced Russian. One day I got tired of this mute companionship. I pointed to the rails and said: "Zheleznaya daroga" (railroad). The Russian froze, leaning on his pick, and repeated after me in a rapt voice, as if the words were a phrase of music: "Zheleznaya daroga." Thereafter, when we got bored with the work and our silence, we would hold that kind of one-word conversation. He would point to something and I would give the Russian word for it, if I knew it. If I didn't, he would tell me the word. We never progressed beyond that. But he seemed perfectly satisfied.

There was a burly, surly Pole who ran the cement mixer near me on the job. In the barracks, he had the bed next to mine. Sometimes, as I fell asleep, I would hear him coughing his lungs out. Sometimes, his coughing woke me at night. After speaking to him once or twice and getting no response, I decided that he was ill-tempered, and gave it up. One day I asked somebody about him. I was told: "Paul's got T.B. The cement dust is killing him." So I took to greeting him again. Usually, he merely grunted and kept on shoveling cement and sand. One day I found him sitting on a pile of blocks beside the cement mixer. "How are you, Paul?" I asked. He looked up, not at me, but at the blistering blue Washington sky. "I die soon," he said, "some day I die soon."

There was a Belgian, a Fleming, a wiry, sallow, hawk-faced young man, who sometimes spoke French to me. I think he doubted how much I understood, for one day he dove into his suitcase and brought up a copy of *Madame Bovary.* He opened it at random and said: "Translate." I translated a page, haltingly. "If you can read Flaubert," he said, "you can read anything." Thereafter, he spent much time with me. Our conversations, on the sweating job or in the disinfected barracks, were persistently literary, though on a somewhat narrow range. For, outside of *Madame Bovary,* he seemed to have read nothing but the novels of Emile Zola, whose massive social tracts he admired tremendously and talked about continually. " 'E 'ave written many books," he said to me one day as if that were the first time we had touched the subject, "many books, beautiful books, and so filthy. But 'e 'ave written one book—listen, *La Rêve*—so piure that it can be read by the piurest virgin." I have never read this immaculate book, but in his anonymous memory (for I cannot recollect his name), I hope to do so before I die.

The Belgian said that he had been the boss of several gangs of native rubber gatherers in Malaya. He had fabulous stories of slave driving with whips, of monumental heat in which the workers sometimes dropped dead and were simply left to rot or be gnawed by beasts or insects. He was sincerely puzzled that I should find that a little horrible, for he was completely without pity or mercy, as if his reactions were on a different range from the human, more like a bird of prey's.

He brought the jungle creepily alive, with slow muddy rivers, a nocturnal pulsation of men, beasts and bugs and tales of king cobras stalking rubber gatherers in lonely huts. He insisted that men could make a fortune in a short time, gathering rubber (he had made a fortune himself, but lost it, according to the usual tale, on women). He begged me to go back to the East with him, and he began to teach me Flemish, for he planned that we should go to the Dutch East Indies. For a while I was strongly tempted, thinking that I heard my future coming up like thunder out of China cross the bay. But I did not like or trust him. I thought that he would not hesitate to kill me, and would scarcely know that he had done it, if I were in the way. And there was something about his yellowish complexion, his taut gestures and the way the pupil of his eye would contract to a fine point that made me guess at madness, drugs or less mentionable things. I gradually detached myself from him.

My real cronies were the Latin Americans. They outnumbered

any other language group on the job, and they all clumped together in one corner of the barracks. There was Manuel, who was close to being a friend. Manuel was a Venezuelan, short and doll-like, with a loose, ugly mouth topped by a black, hairline mustache, but with gentle and very intelligent eyes. He told me that in Venezuela, he had been studying for the law, but he had got a girl in trouble, and had left the country a skip ahead of her pursuing kinsmen. (I never quite believed this story.) But Manuel was an educated man, and, in my long talks with him, I became fluent in a kind of pidgin Spanish (for Manuel could not speak any English). We used to stroll, on Saturday nights, up Pennsylvania Avenue, among the monuments of government, and the honky-tonk shop windows full of workingmen's clothes or trays of rhinestones, and the phrenologist's chart of a human head that hung outside a doorway where gypsies beckoned us in to learn our fates.

Washingtonians who glanced at the two young workingmen gesturing and jabbering in Spanish could scarcely have guessed what the discussion was about. It was usually about *la Liga de Naciones*—the League of Nations. Manuel was an impassioned admirer of Woodrow Wilson (and I was not). But from him I first sensed what Wilson had meant to the masses of Europe. Manuel also believed that the League of Nations was the hope of mankind while I thought that it was foredoomed to failure. We argued endlessly about it.

Manuel was one of the casualties of the job. Sometimes, between three and four o'clock in the morning, when the street-car traffic was least, we would tear up the old rails and lay new ones. The work had to be done very quickly. Everybody was tired out with the previous day's work and almost no sleep, and bad tempered and high strung, for the work was dangerous. In the speed-up, rails sometimes fell on men's feet and crushed them. Manuel was anything but quick, even in the day time, and I often heard him bawled out for dawdling. On one of those frantic early morning jobs, he was working with a long-handled shovel. The handle was damp. Manuel was tired, slow and was being cursed at. He touched an exposed third rail with the shovel and the current flowed up the damp handle. They took him to the hospital. When he came out several days later, the skin below his eyes was drawn down exposing the dull and bloodshot eyeballs. He could barely walk and he seemed to have trouble thinking and speaking.

At the very end, I lost track of Manuel. When the job was finally finished and we all burst out like boys when school's over, I somehow missed him. Perhaps he went back to Venezuela, where life is less frantic, if not more tranquil, and there are fewer third rails.

We had been separated for some time. For seniority at last entitled me to move to the boarding house. It was more comfortable, but the atmosphere was much more relaxed. The barracks had been rather ascetic. In the boarding house, there was a good deal of drinking, and I could not help but overhear, and hear about, things that cannot be mentioned. But nobody ever molested me.

In time, my soft hands outlasted almost every man who had come down from Baltimore with me that first day. One by one, they tired of the heat, the work, the food, the boss—something—and drifted on their aimless way. I stuck to become a veteran.

There was one job that every man dreaded. The two third rails hung, just below the surface of the street, in a shallow tunnel. It could not have been more than four feet deep. The concrete in the tunnel had to be chipped out by hand with a cold chisel. I saw men refuse to go into the shallow tunnel and work with the live rails just above them. One day the boss ordered me down. I went. I thought: "I wonder if I will be killed." I had to lie prone on a heap of rubble. The third rails, with the full power of the Capital Transit System flowing through them, were about two inches above my sweat-soaked shoulders. In that cramping position, I had to break concrete. A sudden turn of my head, a slip of the hammer or chisel would have brought me in contact with the rail. It was an invaluable experience.

After several days of it, my boss moved me out of the tunnel. He began moving me from one job to another until there was practically nothing that I had not done. I was there when the last rail was laid and the last concrete poured. I had saved every cent that I earned. I was lean, hard and browned dark by the sun.

During the two or three months on that job, I had written weekly to my mother, long boy's letters, telling her not to worry, that I was well, and describing the job and the men. I did not send her my address. I did not want to hear from home. And I had another reason. As I feared, my grandfather Chambers used the facilities of the *Public Ledger* to set the Washington police hunting for me. They did not find me.

The day the job ended, I invested a good deal of my capital in a ticket to New Orleans on the Southern railroad (later I was to work at *Time* with the son of its president). That night, when I took the train, detectives were looking for me in the Union Station.

X X X

My first room in New Orleans was spacious, clean and airy. Even the inner doors were screened against mosquitoes. My second room was narrow and dark, with filthy unpapered walls. Between these two rooms lay two first-hand discoveries: 1) that the important day in a workingman's life is never a work day, but the day when he finds himself without work; 2) what a crisis at the top of the economic system means to the man at the bottom. Unknown to me while I chipped concrete, the graph of the national economy had dipped sharply. The post-war slump had set in. For some time to come, there would be no more silk shirts with peppermint candy stripes. For many men there would be no more jobs. Of these men I was one. In addition, I found myself a Yankee stranger in a Southern city where most of the rough work was not done by white men. If I had been a wiser boy, I might have caught on in a few days and left the South. But I was not wise. I believed that if I just stuck it, something would turn up. I read the help-wanted ads in the *Times Picayune* and *Item*. I do not remember that there were very many of them, and whenever I applied for a job, I was waved along. My money was going fast. I saw that things would soon be desperate.

My first step was to find myself a cheaper room. I drifted into the old French Quarter, past shops with tourist displays, their windows filled with trays of pralines and the works of Lafcadio Hearn and George Washington Cable (my mother was a great admirer of *The Grandissimes* and I had read *Madame Delphine*). The little houses of the old Quarter, with their long galleries and graceful grillework charmed me as they charm almost everyone else. I had not known that it was possible for a city to be so beautiful. It seemed to me the perfect place to live.

Walking up Bienville Street, I came to a high board fence, plastered with posters for a nearby burlesque house. In the fence was a board gate which was open. A brick path ran back two or three hundred feet, under a house, which it divided into two parts on the ground level. Beyond the house I could see into a sunlit court. Along one side of the brick wall, a tiny stream flowed. There must have been a sign that said: Room to rent. I went in. A disheveled, waspish, little woman, whom I shall call Mrs. Papyros, offered to show me the room. We climbed a circular staircase to the second floor. From the bridge that crossed the alley, we could look into the sunny courtyard behind. Then we went on to the long, iron-grilled gallery that ran across the front of the house. At the far end of the gallery, Mrs. Papyros flung open two full-length shutters and let the daylight into the dark room. It was foul. It was cheap. I rented it.

As we reached the bridge over the alley, we heard a woman scream. In the courtyard, a dark man in a black and white checked suit was swinging a revolver. Another shorter, darker man was grappling with him, trying to hold the arm with the revolver straight up in the air. A slatternly young woman, with a cataract over one eye, was trying to force herself between the men. It was her screams we had heard. This was my first glimpse of One-Eyed Annie.

The fight ended with the taller man sulkily pushing the revolver into a pocket of the checked jacket and stalking stiffly away. Then Annie tenderly took the hand of the victor, whom I shall call Ben Santi. By way of making me feel one of the family, as if I were the bringer of great good luck, Ben and Annie used sometimes to remind me, later on, that I had arrived on a momentous occasion—the day when Ben Santi took One-Eyed Annie away from the man with the revolver.

XXXI

My graduation suit, once more cleaned and neatly pressed, seemed a little bizarre for Bienville Street, and, besides, I needed money. Before I moved, I went to a second-hand clothing store and sold it. In exchange, I took the khaki trousers and jacket of an Army uniform. It was not a bad fit. The country was flooded with ex-servicemen back from World War I. Like me, many of them were looking for jobs dressed in just such uniforms as I wore.

I put myself at once on a strict regimen. Every morning, I bought a loaf of bread of which I then ate half. In the evening, I ate the other half. That was all I ate. I was proud of my ability to keep to this diet of bread and water, and my will to withstand temptation and not eat the second half of the loaf for lunch.

With my economic affairs in order, I continued my fruitless

search for work. After a time, I reached that point that every workingman knows, when the hunt for a non-existent job is no longer worth the effort. There was a wharf at the foot of Canal Street, where I used to sit and brood and stare at the green levees across the Mississippi, in Algiers. Once a banana boat unloaded there and I asked the white boss for a job. "Nigger work, boy," he said sternly. I envied the Negroes who had the work to do.

I tried to ship out. I was willing to ship to any port. But unless I was twenty-one, I had to have my parents' consent, and I was obviously not twenty-one. I might have managed it, anyway, if I had had a union card (New Orleans was a union port), but I did not have a fee for one or union dues.

One day I heard that a shipbuilding yard, on the Mississippi several miles below New Orleans, was hiring men. Ben Santi, his great friend, Jules Radon, and I got up before dawn and went down to see. By the time we got there, the lines of men looking for work were so long that we did not even bother to fall in. Since we did not have carfare back to town, we walked—through one of the most beautiful, sun-filled mornings I can remember, past little, whitewashed Negro houses, with banana palms whose big leaves just stirred in the heat, and hibiscus burning by the little fences.

The proletariat that had befriended me in Baltimore, and that I had lived among and worked with in Washington, was not the proletariat that Marx and Lenin talk about. It was not the factory proletariat. It was the lowest level of the laboring class. The poor that were around me in Bienville Street were a lower layer still. They were what Marx had called the *Lumpenproletariat*—the slum proletariat, "that passively rotting mass." But I had yet to learn of those distinctions, and to me these people too were simply the wretched of the earth. I observed them with interest and with pity. They taught me, once for all, what life swims in the dead deeps in which our society is moored, and which we try not to look into.

On one side of the alley lived Mrs. Papyros, her husband and her sister. Mrs. Papyros drank whenever she could afford to. She was sometimes reeking by midday, and by nightfall she was roaring. Sometimes, she would erupt into the upper house, and, at the top of her lungs, proclaim the vices and professions of her tenants. Some of her charges were imaginary; many were all too real. All were shocking.

Her husband was a Greek. He pushed a little peanut stand about the streets. He was quiet, well-behaved, and I almost never saw him. Her sister I never saw. To me, she was only a dry cough, somewhere in the dark downstairs room. She was dying of tuberculosis, near the open window, to which rose the mists that sometimes floated over the little stream, rippling along the alley.

On the other side of the alley lived a heavy-set man, with a completely bald head and pouchy eyes that gave him an expression of wrinkled watchfulness, like a buzzard's. He was always very polite and neatly dressed, which made him seem a little out of place. He seldom went out except at night. On one of the few occasions that I ever talked to him, he told me that he was a retired secret service agent.

Next to me, on the gallery, lived an impoverished widow, whom I never heard called anything but Alice. She was plump and very pleasant, and very kind to me in an unobtrusive way. Once in a while, she would ask me in and give me a cup of coffee. She never offered me anything else, and I understood that even the cup of coffee was, for her poverty, munificent generosity. Alice had a shelf of books, perhaps from better days. One day, I borrowed a volume of Shakespeare from her. Except for *The Merchant of Venice* and *Macbeth,* which had been ruined for me at school, I had never read any Shakespeare. I opened by chance to *Antony and Cleopatra,* expecting not to like it. I read it most of the day, lying on my filthy bed, stunned by the opulence of violence and of language. Then, I first read the line: "I have immortal longings in me." In that slum, I found Shakespeare.

On the third floor lived Ben Santi and One-Eyed Annie. They used to ask me up sometimes, together with Jules Radon. Often they received us in bed, and I could not help observing that, stripped of Shakespeare's splendor, their grotesque passion was the raw stuff of Antony and Cleopatra. They were quite shameless, so that sometimes I left the room quickly on one excuse or another. Their laughter would float downstairs after me. It was not mean or mocking, but indolent and a little wistful, as if to say that innocence is indeed a worthy thing, but, in the world as it is, such a burden.

One-Eyed Annie was as ugly a woman as I have ever seen. Ben doted on her. Whenever she was out of the house, he would prowl around restlessly, always in his undershirt. His shoulders were massive and he was tattooed like a head hunter. He walked noiselessly and he had a caressing softness of voice and an extreme gentleness of gesture that seemed less natural than the result of some conscious constraint that had settled into a habit. If I had known more about the world, I would have placed Ben Santi more quickly. He was a pimp.

Sometimes he would drift down to my room and ply me with the wisdom of the deep slums—a jungle theory of individualism, in which a man was merely a phallic symbol, as strong as his power to attract women, or pull a knife or a gun on the rest of life which was his natural prey. Ben liked to talk to me because I never interrupted him. It seemed to me at last that behind Ben Santi's compulsion to talk was a deep fear, a foreknowledge, like a touch of frost, that the powers he worshipped cannot last long, and that when they failed, he would be dead, although he must go on living.

Once I stood with Ben Santi, just at twilight, in a third-floor dormer and we looked out across the jumbled roofs of the Old Quarter. I did not know just why we were waiting there. Then a steamboat whistled on the Mississippi River. "Annie's comin' home," Ben said with sudden brightness and I realized that it was she we were waiting for in the dusk. "That's the steamer *Sidney* comin' in," said Ben. The steamer *Sidney* was an excursion boat. "Every day, I send Annie to hustle on the steamer *Sidney*. And I'm tellin' you, boy, when Annie gets home I'm goin' to beat the livin' hell out of her." "What for?" I asked. I saw from his eyes that he considered me hopeless. "For hustlin'," he said fiercely and walked away.

Jules Radon did not live in the house, but he spent a good part of his days there. He sometimes came in very early in the morning and slept on the bare floors. Like me, he wore a uniform. He had seen service in France. He was all but nondescript, except that his chin was a flat plane from his lip to his chin point. Like Ben Santi, he had a catlike walk. I never knew just how he lived, and he never told me, though I made several guesses. But I knew that, like me, he seldom had enough to eat.

From him I learned what kindness there was in the lower depths. My money had run so low that I now made a loaf of bread last for two days, instead of one. The diet began to tell. I was tired and weak, and sometimes in the great heat I found it too much trouble to get up or move around. I felt trapped too. Early one evening, as I lay with my face to the wall, I heard the shutters of my door open. Jules Radon said: "Let's go eat." I was too listless to turn and look at him. I said: "Thanks, I've eaten." I felt him stand there a moment, looking down at me. Then, without saying anything, he went out. When I finally turned over, I found that he had left a fifty-cent piece on my bed.

I had written to my mother several times from New Orleans, concealing my condition. Now it was clear that I must do one of two things: I must try to beat my way back north or I must ask my family to send me money to return with. I did not feel up to jumping freights or riding rods, especially in the South. I wrote for money.

My father wired me the price of a ticket to New York and a few dollars more.

XXXII

In New York, I missed my mother and brother who had waited for the train from the South in the Pennsylvania Station. By chance, I overtook them outside. For a moment, they did not recognize the gaunt youth in the uniform.

My father, when we met, had the good sense to ask me nothing at all. He was gracious. He seemed to recognize that something had happened. I felt a warmth toward him, as of son to father, that I had not felt before. Two things were quickly agreed: I was to enter college the following fall (1920); meanwhile, he was to get me a job at once at the Frank Seaman Company, the New York advertising firm, where he was manager of the art department.

The day he was to take me to Frank Seaman's, we rode together on the train to New York, as usual, in complete silence. As we neared the City, my father leaned over and said that it might be embarrassing for him if I worked at Frank Seaman's as his son. People might talk about favoritism. The new warmth I felt for him froze. I knew that my father's real reason was not talk about favoritism. That was nonsense. I knew that he was afraid that I might not do a good job. But since he wanted it that way, I said that I would take my grandfather's name: Charles Whittaker.

Under that name, I went to work and soon earned myself a couple of raises. I had the difficult task of dealing all day with my father without seeming to know him. He did not make this any easier by holding occasional unguarded conversations with me in the halls, conversations that were quickly noticed. Rumors spread. Soon the story was out. Everybody knew that I was Jay Chambers' son, and a very curious situation it must have seemed.

Incidentally, those were the days when E. B. White was seeing my father, and that curious situation is perhaps one reason why he never heard my father mention my name—as White hastened to inform the world in *The New Yorker*, soon after the Hiss Case broke.

XXXIII

In the fall of 1920, I entered Williams College. A room was assigned to me and my furniture had been shipped. But one or two days on that beautiful and expensive campus told me that Williams was not the place for me, that my parents could never stand the costs of that little Harvard. I saw that I had a quick and difficult decision to make. I took a night train for New York. The next morning, before going home, I entered Columbia University. There I could live at home and all expenses would be less. Since I lacked certain requirements for entrance, I took a general intelligence test and passed without difficulty. I also used the occasion to rid myself at last of the name, Vivian. In its place, I took my mother's family name: Whittaker.

I remained at Columbia until my junior year. When I entered, I was a conservative in my view of life and politics, and I was undergoing a religious experience. By the time I left, entirely by my own choice, I was no longer a conservative and I had no religion. I had published in a campus literary magazine an atheist playlet, of which the Hiss defense was to make large use twenty-six years later. The same year, I went to Europe and saw Germany in the manic throes of defeat. I returned to Columbia, this time paying my own way. In 1925, I voluntarily withdrew for the express purpose of joining the Communist Party. For I had come to believe that the world we live in was dying, that only surgery could now save the wreckage of mankind, and that the Communist Party was history's surgeon.

At Columbia, like all freshmen, I was at once assigned a faculty adviser. In my case, he was Mark Van Doren, then a young instructor in the English department. Like all really first-rate teachers, Mark Van Doren's personal influence on his students was great—in my case, powerful and long-lasting. We quickly passed to a first-name basis and developed a friendship of respect and common interests, which, no doubt, was stronger on my side than on his. Mark was not then a nationally known literary critic and poet. He was working on his first book of poems, *Spring Thunder*, of which he sent me a copy as soon as it was published. All problems of writing, but especially of poetry, touched him profoundly, and he brought to them incisive judgment, humor and exceptional common sense.

I soon began to bombard him with the poems I was writing, very bad poems, most of which he rejected out of hand, but with such understanding that he never left any wound, only a disappointment that I could not measure up to his standard, and a determination to do so.

Mark Van Doren (and certain of my fellow students) first developed in me the belief that writing poetry is not, as my mother and many other people supposed, a somewhat disreputable pursuit, but a way of life—one of the highest to which a man can be called. I thought that I was called. Mark Van Doren agreed with me, or led me to suppose so.

When I returned from Europe in 1923, I began to arrange my life so that I could devote most of my time to writing verse. I took a part-time job at the New York Public Library, where I worked at the desk in the newspaper room at night. The rest of my time was my own. I was living at home. I set about a definite poetic project. Its purpose was twofold. I wished to preserve through the medium of poetry the beautiful Long Island of my boyhood before it was destroyed forever by the advancing City. I wished to dramatize the continual defeat of the human spirit in our time, by itself and by the environment in which it finds itself. With my deep attachment to the earth I grew up on, the spread of the tentacular towns across it, felling the little woods, piping the shallow brooks through culverts, burying the little farms under rows of identical suburban houses, struck me an almost physical blow. Those sprawling developments, without character or form, destroying the beauty that had been for an ugliness that had no purpose but function and profit, seemed to epitomize all that I dreaded in the life around me. By defacing the one part of itself that had been intimately mine, it cut my roots and left me more than an alien, a man without soil, and, therefore, without nation. I called the book: *Defeat in the Village.* It was to be an autobiography of mood, but not of factual reality. Each of the poems in it bore some relationship of tone or feeling to the next poem, and all were intended to build up to a climax of despair. Few of the poems were autobiographical in any other sense. Few were based on real occurrences, though some were touched off by them. Many of them were inspired by places, and in the years when I was composing them, I took to wandering a great deal at night, especially around the little Long Island harbor of East Rockaway, where the tides of my childhood still exerted a strong pull, and the mists and the darkness blotted out the ugliness of the present and helped me to recall the Long Island of the past.

In time, I had written a fair-sized book. I submitted it to a national poetry contest where *Defeat in the Village* was just "nosed out" of first place (I was duly informed) by *Chinese White,* a book of poems by the wife of the *Daily Worker* cartoonist, William Gropper.

I concluded, after several years of trying, that I never could write poetry good enough to be worth writing. My natural development had, in fact, settled the matter for me. For as soon as I began to shake off the influence of authentic poets, I found myself writing prose. I used to think, sometimes, that those versifying years were a complete and stunning waste. But I came to see that I was mistaken. Those were the years of apprenticeship, during which, by trial and error, I was beginning to learn the difficult, humbling, exacting art of writing.

They were more. They were the years in which my mind first awakened to one of the languages of the soul. It filled me with a strange elation. I realized at last that I had been listening to it all my life without knowing what it was, and that its unheard logic blended in a consistent tone all that was most personal in my experience. I was like an adult who first learns to speak. Awkwardly, I fumbled, in my early manhood, to give expression to the strongest impression of my earliest childhood—the enfolding beauty of the external world. It was the flooding and ebbing tides, the sense of the ocean, beating on its beaches as on the edge of the world, or of its mists, folding the houses and streets of my childhood under silence, that I groped to express in verse. I remained a babbler, in part because I grasped the outward effects of that language, but not its inward principle. I continued to hear it in the highest moments of my life long before I recognized what voice spoke it to me.

XXXIV

When I first withdrew from Columbia College, I felt a renewed sense of life, and a great desire to go somewhere and do something entirely new. I spoke to Mark Van Doren about it. "Why don't you go to Soviet Russia?" he asked. "The Russian Revolution is like Elizabethan England. All the walls are falling down. You should go and see it." He suggested that I might go as a relief worker for the Friends Service Committee which was then administering Quaker relief in the Russian famine areas. He offered to write, recommending me to certain "weighty Friends."

The first Friend I saw was J. Barnard Walton, a pleasant, businesslike Quaker who was then, I believe, the head of the Service Committee. I stayed in Philadelphia several days, meeting other Friends and canvassing the possibilities of my going to the Soviet Union. A new and enormously tranquilizing spirit enveloped me. It emanated from those quiet presences whom I met, from the chaste Quaker rooms with their plain and fine proportions, or simply from the sound of the plain language, as voices asked me: "How is thee, Whittaker Chambers?" The 17th century form was still touched with the sweetness of the Middle Ages. This is my natural home, I thought. I wanted nothing so much as to remain in it.

Then the story of my atheist play reached Friends. There was a horrified reaction. I received one of those letters, such as only Quakers can write, which, in the most restrained language, said in effect: "You are outcast."

It was an invisible turning point in my life. If, at that moment, one Friend had said: "Sit down with me and tell me, what have you in your heart," this book need never have been written. As it was, it took me seventeen years to find my way, unaided, back to that peace.

I thought of this incident when, later on, I translated from the German a number of little parables and stories about the Arj. The Arj was a Jewish religious leader, who, like Christ, used to walk about the hills of Palestine, teaching and talking with his disciples. One day, the Arj suddenly said: "Let us all go down to Jerusalem." The disciples began to murmur. Some thought of their wives at home. Some thought of their suppers. They said that they would not go. They walked on in silence. Then one of the disciples asked: "Why did you want us to go down to Jerusalem?" The Arj answered sadly: "That was a moment in eternity. If, at that moment, we had all been of one mind to go down to Jerusalem, the people would have been saved."

At the time, I felt only a stinging sense of rejection. I asked myself bitterly: "Where in Christendom is the Christian?"

XXXV

One misty midnight, as I wandered home from one of my lonely ramblings around East Rockaway Harbor, I made out the figure of a woman, waiting for the trolley to Brooklyn. The tracks were two blocks from our house. When I came up to her, I saw that it was my grandmother Whittaker. "Grandma!" I said. I had not seen her for several years.

She smiled sweetly without answering, as if we had just parted or there was nothing strange in our meeting unexpectedly at that lonely place and hour. I supposed that she had been at our house during my absence (she had not).

"Aren't you going to stay overnight with us?" I asked.

She raised her hand for quiet. "Ssshh," she said, "he's calling me."

"Who is?" I asked. I listened and heard only night sounds. "Nobody is calling, Grandmother," I said.

"Oh, yes, he is," she said. "Listen. He's saying: 'Mary! Mary!' Don't you hear him?"

I realized that my grandmother Whittaker was insane.

XXXVI

My grandmother would not come home with me that night. I waited with her, and, with many misgivings, put her aboard the late trolley. I did not know what else to do. I told my mother what had happened and she told me a bit of family lore quite new to me. Grandmother Whittaker had been in love with the president of one of the big railroads. She understood that he meant to marry her. But they broke up. One day, she tried to see him at his office. He would not see her. After that, she told my mother, she had found detectives trailing her. My mother thought that the part about the visit and the detectives might be true, that the gentleman had taken that means to rid himself of my grandmother, and that the shock, remembered over the years, had unsettled her mind in old age. She hoped that it would pass. It did not, of course.

One evening I came home to find my mother sitting ready in her coat and hat, waiting for me to go to Jersey City with her. Grandmother Whittaker had been picked up. It was late when we reached the city hospital of which I retain only an impression of dim lights burning and rather shadowy people moving about quietly and speaking in low voices. We were ushered into the insane ward. It was a vast room filled with cots. On each cot lay, or sat, women in all stages of dementia. Their clothes had been taken away. They wore shapeless hospital wraps. The hair of some was hanging in wisps about their cheeks. Others stared into space with dull eyes from deadened faces. At the sight of a man (myself), all the women sat up and fastened their empty eyes on me.

Grandmother's cot was in a far corner. She was perfectly composed and never more charming. "I am delighted to see you both," she said. We did what we could to reassure her. What had happened was commonplace enough in such cases. My grandmother had been staying at a Y.W.C.A. About two o'clock in the morning, "they" (there is always a "they") had driven a spike through the ceiling and began to pump gas into the room. In her terror, my grandmother had run down to the street in her nightdress and tried to board a street car.

We took Grandmother home and gave her a room. "You will have to stay up tonight," my mother said to me. "She may try to kill us all." The family settled into sleep. I sat downstairs, reading. Presently, I heard bare feet patter down the stairs. Grandmother began to throw open windows and doors. I closed them. She threw them open again. "They're pumping gas in here," she said, "the house is full of gas." I tried to explain to her that, if there were any gas, I would notice it too. Finally, I got her back to bed. I went back to reading. Ten minutes later, she was throwing open the doors and windows again. This kept up all night. For years, in addition to our old tensions, this dark, demoniac presence sat at the heart of our home.

Usually, her movements were almost soundless and she seemed to be able to move with abnormal swiftness. She would be standing beside you before you knew she was there. Winter and summer, she wore a long sealskin coat in the house. For long periods, she would be quiescent. Then a spell would come. She would float downstairs, take a knife from the kitchen and sit by the window in my mother's bedroom, where she knew that she should not go. There, muttering and growling, an ominous figure in her sealskin coat, she would rock back and forth, the knife clutched defiantly in front of her. "You will have to take the knife away from her again," my mother would say. My grandmother was quite powerful and there was usually a sharp scuffle before I got the knife. I suppose nobody ever sleeps quite peacefully in a house where a woman sometimes wanders around with a knife.

Except for these sallies, and her shopping trips to the village, Grandmother spent most of her time in her room. She always kept her door locked. Behind that locked door she cooked. How she cooked was long a mystery. We learned to disregard the smell of burning wood, and the more frightful culinary smells, that drifted through the house. But once the smell of burning was so strong that my mother knocked on Grandmother's door and asked if anything was on fire. There was complete silence. My mother was afraid that something had happened to Grandmother. "You will have to break down her door," she said. I put my shoulder to the door and burst the lock. As I plunged into the room, Grandmother was waiting for me just on the other side. In her most gracious voice, she asked: "Did you want to see the little contrivance, dear?"

The little contrivance was a tiny oven made of a tomato can with the top cut out. A small stoking door had been neatly cut in one side. Through it, Grandmother fed a little fire with old match sticks, splinters of wood and scraps of paper. On top a pan of water was bubbling. The can rested on a hearth of two bricks which she had carried unnoticed to her room. Before the pathos of such ingenuity, I withdrew abashed.

All day long, and often much of the night (for she slept very little), my grandmother talked to herself. Much of what she said could not be made out, but the sound was insistent, like the sound of a sewing machine that never stops, and it had the same disturbing effect on the nerves. When her monologues were intelligible, they were uttered in the same beautifully modulated voice, with the same precise eloquence as in the past. Often she relived the years of her social life, interrupting the flow of reminiscence to touch off with a few blistering words some character, whom she did not like. One of her favorite targets was John D. Rockefeller, Senior. In a voice of withering pity, she would dilate on the havoc of his personal appearance, his diet, his general decrepitude, his religious interests. She would mimic his singing of a hymn, squeaking in an intentionally cracked and quavering voice:

"Ro-o-o-ck of A-a-ages cle-eft for me-e-e."

Then would come a swooping laugh, intended to annihilate Mr. Rockefeller and his world, and her favorite lilting clincher: "Oh, Mama, what people!"

My father was an even better target than John D. Rockefeller, and handier. My grandmother developed several artful ways of tormenting him. Sometimes, when he got home tired from work, she would be waiting for him just inside the front door—a startling enough experience in itself. She would stand perfectly still, gaze intently at him, and say in a tone of abysmal pity: "Oh, that *depraved* face!" I have seen a look of something like murder pass across my father's face, which was of all faces the mildest and least depraved.

My grandmother's door was almost opposite my father's. Both doors were kept constantly shut. When my father was resting of an evening, my grandmother would stand just behind her door, and in those withering tones that had an almost toxic effect on a normal mind, would take derisive inventory of his appearance, his habit of walking or standing, or various other failings, and what she imagined, or pretended to imagine, were his depravities. My father would stand this for long periods. But sometimes it would get too much for him. He would fling himself out of his own room in a berserk rage, and hurl himself against her locked door. From the other side, she would shout mocking defiance. There would be a sound of splintering wood, a crack as the lock snapped, then cries. For Grandmother was a courageous woman, and she was always waiting to defend her stronghold with the scissors which she kept handy for such occasions. I would rush in and throw, or wedge, myself between them. The small scars on my hands are where the scissors missed my father and caught me.

For years, such scenes were a regular part of our life and they took place in an appropriate setting. My mother had begun to remodel our house and her plans were on a fairly heroic scale. My brother, working steadily and with great skill in his spare time, was never able to complete them. The house in which my grandmother became a brooding presence was itself rather spectral. Part of the back was torn out for two stories and rigged with scaffolding. For years it stood open to the wind, rain and snow. Even the habitable part of the house was sometimes piled with bags of cement, lumber, pipes and tools, which crowded the worn furniture in such a way that access to the kitchen, the one relatively clear room downstairs, was often by runways through these stores.

When my brother went to college, he left that unresolved chaos.

XXXVII

My brother was eighteen or nineteen when he left for Colgate University. He set out gayly, for he went with a group of his fellow high-school students who were his close friends. Unlike me, he had been very popular, for he was a smiling, candid, uncomplicated boy. He had been on the baseball and track teams.

Throughout our early boyhood, my brother had been a shadow that, in the way of older brothers, I tried to shake off. "He worships you," my mother would say, "how can you be so mean to him?" For a long time I was not aware of any particular feeling for him. He was simply someone who belonged, someone in the order of nature, like my mother. Actually, the tie between us was close and tender, woven of all the hours and days of quiet, intimate, unquestioning association. The most observable tie between us was that we thought the same things were funny. Neither I, nor anyone else, knew how close we were until, when I was about eight years old, I came down suddenly with scarlet fever. My brother was whisked away to Philadelphia. That night, as I became delirious, I repeated over and over: "Where is my brother? I want my brother." "You would never think," I heard my mother saying to the doctor the next morning, "that he ever noticed him."

I did not notice him when he came back, either. We spent long hours over the years playing a game we never tired of—drawing plans for the farms we would have when we were men. They were to be in the South, on a river so that we could irrigate. We used to lay off fields of yams, peanuts and cotton. Aside from that, we had little in common. At school, he moved with a crowd of younger boys whose names I scarcely knew. He took part in most sports from an early age. From the time he could read, and unlike me, he learned to read slowly, he studied books of carpentry, plumbing or physics. He seldom read anything else. My mind was entirely closed to him, and his to me.

In character, too, he was wholly unlike me—not so good-natured, but much livelier, much more active but not nearly so strong, in all ways more alert, likable, and without that reserve, reflective and observant, that made people react from me. In appearance we were so unlike that people often refused to believe that we were brothers. By the time he left for Colgate we were almost strangers.

From college, he wrote my mother regularly. He had not been

there long when she told me that she was worried about him. He had failed to make a fraternity which his close friend and roommate had made. My mother thought that this had hurt and shocked him in some very deep way. I laughed. It seemed to me incredible that anybody should be upset about a fraternity. But I am now convinced that my mother was right and that I was wrong, that this social rejection to which his sociable nature made him vulnerable, for which nothing in his past prepared him, and which he lacked the human resources to resist, was the starting point of his disaster.

To my surprise, for we never corresponded, I received a letter from him. He was not at the college. He had taken to the road and had got as far as Buffalo. He was rather pleased with himself and his adventures on the way. With a pang, I grasped that he felt that we had much in common. He went back to college and I wrote at once, urging him to stay there and not to think of leaving, for I was not so sure of my own course that I wanted to see anybody else follow it, and I was completely sure that what might be right for me was not right for my brother.

When my brother got home for the Christmas holidays, I came in one night to find him sitting in the kitchen with my mother—an almost unrecognizably white-faced, taut-lipped boy, arguing desperately, but, with the natural courtesy that almost never failed him, that life is worthless and meaningless, that to be intelligent is to know this and to have courage to end it. His appearance and a few minutes of conversation was enough to tell me that this was not a schoolboy pose, that this crisis was real and terrifying. My mother was frantic. As soon as she could get me alone, she said: "You must talk to him and find out what is wrong. You're the only one who can."

I took him for a long walk. My brother, who never discussed anything with me, was bursting with talk. My brother, who never read anything, had been reading voraciously—Rabelais, Montaigne, Voltaire, Diderot. Of the moderns, he seemed to have read only Anatole France and Thomas Hardy. All his reading, more jumbled and more immature than mine had ever been, added up to one certainty: the folly of life, the need to end it. He did not yet talk about ending his own life.

"Look around you," he said, "look at people. Every one of them is a hypocrite. Look at the world. It is hopeless. Look at religion. Nobody really believes in that stuff, even the people who pretend to.

Look at marriage. Look at Mother and Jay. What a fraud! Look at the family. Look at ours! And children! It's a crime to have children."

I tried to argue with him that the answer to the wretchedness of life was not death, that life itself was not evil, but that what men had made of life was evil, that struggle was the answer to evil, and that all strength and all virtue lay in struggle. I was speaking as a Communist.

"What for, what virtue?" he wanted to know. "It's stacked against you from the start. What's the use of struggling when everybody has to die, anyway?—good and bad, in a grave where you rot, simply rot." (I am not quoting him exactly, of course, but piecing out things that I remember with a paraphrase of his violence.)

I said: "The Communists have found a way out."

He simply laughed at me. "What way?" he asked. "What are they going to do that the others don't do? What do they want that the others don't want? They're just like the others, only they have invented a new way. There is only one decent way."

In my desperation, I heard myself saying a surprising thing. I said: "The kingdom of God is within you." The phrase came back from my own struggle.

"That's junk," he said and laughed the flat, unhappy laugh with which he had punctuated the whole conversation. I was trying to face the world with the mind and will. He was facing it with loathing. It was an organic loathing. Between the two attitudes was a difference in kind. There was no way for them to meet or for us to communicate. I saw that the one person on whom he had counted for understanding was failing him. We were back in that morning of our childhood when he had stood on the porch in the soft rain, calling me, and I did not go.

"We're hopeless people," he said by way of ending the conversation. "We can't cope with the world. We're too gentle. We're too gentle to face the world." He was to say it many times.

By the time his vacation was over, he had withdrawn from me, and I, feeling the baffled hopelessness of helping him, had withdrawn from him. He went back to college, not gayly this time.

XXXVIII

I do not remember exactly when my brother came home to stay. I do not believe that he completed his freshman year. For a time, I scarcely saw him. He slept most of the day and was gone most of the night. When I did see him, he was pleasant, but uncommunicative. He had nothing more to say to me. But he was no longer excited. He was very quiet.

One day I came in and found him lying on the old couch, where we had suffered the toothaches of our childhood. His eyes were open and he was staring at something ahead of him. His face was pinched and white. After a while, he raised his arm and pointed to the old print that still hung at the end of the couch: *Il Conforto—Death, the Comforter.*

Then he asked slowly without looking at me: "If I kill myself, will you kill yourself with me?"

I said: "No."

"Why not?" he asked.

"You are not going to kill yourself," I said.

He laughed meanly. "You're a coward, Bro," he said.

XXXIX

My brother went back to remodeling the house. All day he worked steadily, apparently cheerfully. He finished the long, tedious job of moulding the baronial ceilings. He put in a new bathroom, laid the tiles and did the plumbing. He finished building the fireplaces, framing oblong panels on them, which my father, with an unusual burst of homemaking, filled, in one case, with a droop of autumn leaves against a turquoise sky, and in the other, with a swirl of pink roses or peonies in an archaic vase.

My brother also built himself a workshop behind the house. It was a little house in itself with a gabled roof and a fireplace of its own. He piped in gas from the main house so that he could use his workshop after dark. He moved in a couch and sometimes slept there, surrounded by his tools, his pipe wrenches, vises and dies. My mother was paying him regular wages, which he certainly earned, for he was a first-rate workman.

One day my mother said to me: "Your brother is drinking." I said: "I don't think so." "I know," she said. She told me that he had been drinking for some time, that now it was becoming a habit. She knew how and where he spent his nights, the names of his friends and that girls were involved. She knew the details of his most intimate life. I was horrified that she should have to hear such things and shocked that he should dream of telling them to her. I saw that he was a man in his actions, but a child in his relations with his mother.

"You must go with him," she said, "and watch over him. I do not know what he is going to do next. But I am afraid that he is going to try to kill himself." She wept. "What have I done that was so wrong?" she said. "Oh, God, what have I done? I only tried to love you both."

X L

I was still working in the New York Public Library. I took to going home directly after work. My brother would meet me at the Lynbrook station. One of his friends had an old car in which the whole crowd—there were five or six young fellows about my brother's age—would make a circuit of the Long Island speakeasies. Prohibition was in force, but clandestine bars were everywhere, and I sometimes stood at them beside most substantial citizens.

My brother's evenings usually began at a little store with the lower half of the show windows painted or blinded. Behind the store was a backroom. Here a mousy Greek, with graying hair, served a home-brewed wine. It was red, watery, sour, rasping and very heady. The backroom was dense with tobacco smoke, warm, and, on cold nights, cozy. It was filled with the murmur of voices talking Greek and sometimes a rough French—a lingua franca of the Levant. The talkers, who sat around the walls, like the proprietor, were chiefly Greeks. They were very quiet and never spoke to any of us or paid the slightest attention to us.

I quickly came to understand why my brother liked Nick's place (I never heard the proprietor called anything but Nick). It was peaceful—a retreat from life so retired that the world seemed to have fallen completely away. It was friendly and the wine was cheap and not nearly so harmful as the villainous whiskey sold at the bars.

My brother and his friends almost always sat at the big center table, laughing and joking. I used to be amazed at the endless inane conversation that kept them amused. I sat, a silent presence, enjoying the peace and my own thoughts. Nobody seemed to mind my just sitting there. My brother was delighted to have me.

One night, when the wine was having its effect, my brother and his friends began to sing songs in turn—chiefly the song of the year: "If You Knew Susie, Like I Knew Susie." When my turn came, I sang the first verse of the "*Internationale*:"

Arise, ye prisoners of starvation,
Arise, ye wretched of the earth,
For justice thunders condemnation,
A better world's in birth.

When I reached the refrain, from a darker corner of the room, a clear, deep voice suddenly joined mine, singing the original French words:

C'est la lutte finale,
Groupons-nous et demain,
L'Internationale
Sera le genre humain.

Tis the final conflict,
Let each stand in his place,
The International
Shall be the human race.

The dream of human brotherhood, lifted in two languages, rose through the eddying smoke and wine fumes. A fair-haired, middle-aged workingman detached himself from his darker friends, wove over to our table, and asked in French if he might sit down. "*Vous êtes bolchévique?*" he asked me— "You are a Bolshevik?" I said: "Yes." "*Moi aussi,*" he said and grasped my hand. He told me that he was a Rumanian from Bessarabia, that he had been through the Russian Revolution and the civil war in Odessa. He had been a sailor around the Mediterranean and later on the ocean. Now he was a tinsmith. He was not a member of the Communist Party and never had been. He was one of the drifting thousands in whose dark lives the vision is a nameless hope. He was only semi-literate, but he spoke Greek, Russian and Rumanian as well as French. He would sit slumped over his wine, singing the slow, mournful Communist "Funeral Hymn"—one of the most moving songs in the world—which became slower and more mournful as he got more drunk.

Thereafter, while my brother and his friends laughed and canvassed their sexual exploits at their table, I would sit discussing world politics with the Rumanian and the Greeks, who also spoke French and most of whom were sympathetic to Communism.

XLI

Often Nick's place was only the evening's starting point. From there, the crowd would pile into the car and visit other speakeasies near the village. Sometimes they drove to East Rockaway where there was a very comfortable blind tiger beside the harbor. Sometimes we drove eastward on Long Island, to the North Shore or to New York where there was a speakeasy at the Manhattan end of the Queensboro Bridge. There was exhilaration in the wild rides in the open car through the brisk nights. I began to sense a pleasure of fellowship and mindless, animal activity that I had missed in my own youth, for these lapses take unexpected revenges.

Not all of those occasions were pleasant. When my brother drank the poisonous Prohibition whiskey, he inclined to be fighty. Once standing at the bar in East Rockaway, he began to tell me, for everyone to hear, what he thought about our family. He shouted that our mother and father had ruined their own lives and both of ours, and then dismissed them with a foul expression. I picked up a tumbler of whiskey and threw it in his face. It was an involuntary action. He sprang at me and we fought. Others pulled us apart and hustled him, cursing and struggling, to the back of the room. The woman who ran the place screamed: "Your brother did right to throw the whiskey in your face."

The bad blood seethed between us for the rest of the night. It boiled up again in a service station where one of my brother's cronies was on night duty. My brother baited me and again shouted his filthy remark. Again, we grappled and this time crashed to the concrete floor, he underneath. As I tried to extricate myself, he reached up, and, taking careful aim, struck me in the face with the stone set in his ring. The little scar on the bridge of my nose is one of the things he left me to carry permanently through the rest of my life.

My pleasure in those aimless and besotted rovings faded. I could not prevent my brother's drinking. He laughed at me savagely whenever I tried. I could not prevent his drunken night drives. In time, I thought, he must tire of them as I was tired of them. Until then, I could not see what good my supervision did. I began to go my own ways again.

XLII

Late one night I came home and, as I opened the door, the smell of gas struck me. I rushed into the kitchen. All the jets and the oven were turned on in the gas stove. The room was filled with gas. My brother was slumped across a chair. I picked him up and dragged and carried him into another room. I worked his arms across his chest and slapped his cheeks. Very quickly he revived. He sat up. Presently, I made black coffee and gave him some.

"Why did you stop me?" he asked in a voice so pitiful that I wondered if I had not, in fact, committed a sin. Then, as he sipped his coffee, he said: "You're a bastard, Bro. You stopped me this time, but I'll do it yet."

XLIII

My father had watched all this helplessly. But one night I heard a shout in the kitchen. I hurried down to find my father and my brother fighting furiously. My brother was drunk and could not see what he was doing. My father was blind with rage and no longer knew what he was doing. He was pummeling my brother's face which was streaming with blood. My mother was screaming: "He'll kill him!"

I tried to pry my father off and failed. At that, the ulcer of years of anger burst within me—as if my father had not done his part to make my brother what he was. I struck at my father. My brother slid to the floor and lay there prone. Above him, my father and I wrestled and fought. Finally, I flung him against a cabinet. The ferocious strength drained out of him. His face was ashen and twitching. He was an old man, fighting for breath and panting: "He—has been taking girls—into that little house—at night. Your mother—I won't stand for it."

I walked over to my father and put my arms around him. We wept.

XLIV

Now my brother was seldom sober even in the daytime. He used to wear a vivid plaid pullover, violent checked knickerbockers and green or red golf stockings. Above this atrocious outfit, which seemed to me to symbolize the whole failure of our judgment, peered my brother's pale, drawn face from which all joy had gone.

One cold night, with the snow lying hard on the ground, I reached home about midnight. Before I went to bed, some instinct, some prescience, something, made me decide to look in the little house in the yard. I had never done so before.

When I opened the door, gas rushed out at me. My brother was lying on the couch. His hands were cold. I dragged him frantically into the yard. I could scarcely manage his dead weight, his heels hit the snow lifelessly as I lugged him into the big house. His face was rigid, and from the fixed, open mouth came the smell of gas and alcohol. He was almost gone but his heart was still beating.

I laid him on the floor, and endlessly raised and lowered his arms as we do to resuscitate a drowning person. I must have worked over him half an hour. Slowly, life came back. It came in a hideous form. He did not regain normal consciousness. Instead, he pulled himself up on all fours and began to drag himself across the floor. He would hook his leg around a chair or table leg, and his muscles were set in such an iron clamp that it took all my strength simply to pry him loose. Then he would drag himself around again and bark like a coyote—a thin, inhuman yelp repeated four or five times. That kept up all night.

When my mother came down in the morning, I went to bed.

X L V

After that, it was decided that I should again sit up and watch through the nights. Sometimes my mother watched part of the night with me. More often, I sat in the kitchen alone. Sometimes, in the dead of night, the door from the living room would open noiselessly. My grandmother's face would appear in the opening, and stare fixedly at me. "Do you want something, Grandmother?" I would ask. The face would silently withdraw and the door close noiselessly again. I used to wish that the house would burn down with all its horrors.

My brother knew that I was watching and laughed at me for it. He simply took to staying away all night, though sometimes I would hear him crunching the snow in the yard outside as if he were stalking us. Then I would go out and inspect the little house in back, from which my mother had had the gas disconnected.

XLVI

My brother had introduced me to a girl. He told me that he intended to marry her. I urged him not to, supposing that marriage could only lead to unhappiness for both of them. He said, with a touch of his old grace, that he had promised and he thought he should. I saw that both what was best and worst in him was driving him on.

He was married. My brother's friends attended the wedding. My brother and his wife went to live in a little apartment in a neighboring village. For a time, I did not see my brother at all. After some months, he began to appear at our house again. He said very little, but I gathered from my mother, to whom he still told a great deal, that his wife had gone back to her parents. It was summer. They were living at one of the ocean beaches.

One night, my brother drove to the station in Lynbrook with a friend from whom I learned the details that follow. They waited for the train I usually came home on. I was not on it. I had stayed in New York, chatting with a Communist college friend. They waited for another train and another. I was not on them. I had failed my brother for the last time.

My brother and his friend drove to a pier from which they could see across a tidal inlet to the lights of the beach where his wife was staying. He sat there for an hour or more, saying nothing, smoking cigarettes and staring across the black water. Then he drove his friend home and went to his own apartment where he now lived alone.

XLVII

In the morning, I was awakened by the telephone ringing. I heard my mother hurry to answer it. The instrument fell from her hand. I heard it strike the floor. One single, terrible scream swelled through the house. I knew, even before I reached my mother's side, that my brother had at last killed himself.

XLVIII

We drove to the next village and climbed the stairs to the little apartment. The kitchen was crowded with police and people I had never seen before. My brother was lying with his head in the gas oven, his body partly supported by the open door. He had made himself as comfortable as he could. There was a pillow in the oven under his head. His feet were resting on a pile of books set on a kitchen chair. One of his arms hung down rigid. Just below the fingers, on the floor, stood an empty quart whiskey bottle.

I picked it up and put it out of sight. "Put that back. Don't touch anything," an officer snapped at me. I pointed to my mother who was sobbing, with her face buried in my brother's chest. Nobody put back the empty bottle.

XLIX

They took my brother's body to be embalmed.

My parents had collapsed. They lay, as I had never seen them before, side by side across my father's bed, eyes open, not even weeping. At last, my father tottered out and said: "You will have to take charge. Do what you think best."

I supervised the barbaric rites of a modern funeral. I told the men where to place the casket and the flowers. I arranged for a preacher. I had known the young funeral director all my life. As we stood looking at my brother together, he said: "When I look at the stars at night, I sometimes wonder."

My mother wanted to spend the last night in the room with my brother's body. I set up a cot for her. She asked me to stay with her. I lay down on the floor with my clothes on beside my brother's casket. I did not sleep. Sometimes my mother made a little gurgling sound. She had been weeping in her sleep and awakened when the tears choked her. I prayed: "Evil that drifts through the world, pass by this house tonight."

We buried my brother in the Sand Hill graveyard. It was a sunny autumn day, shortly before his birthday. As I stood by the open grave, I could see one of the lakes where I had wandered as a boy. We tossed in the handfuls of earth. I took my mother and father home.

L

Only when my brother was dead did I know how much I had loved him. Death had never really touched me before. I had to fight an all-pervading listlessness of the will. I would lie for hours and watch the leaves, heaving gently in the wind. To do anything else seemed, in the face of death, gross and revolting, seemed a betrayal of my brother because any activity implied that life had meaning. Life that could destroy so gentle a nature as my brother's was meaningless. I wanted to talk to nobody, see nobody.

I forced myself to go to work every evening. I sometimes forced myself to go on long rambles during the day. On one of them I composed that dirge that later appeared in *Poetry* magazine, and which was read in court by the Hiss defense to prove something about me that I never quite understood. Its first verse went:

> *The moving masses of clouds, and the standing*
> *Freights on the siding in the sun, alike induce in us*
> *That despair, which, we, brother, know there is no*
> *withstanding.*

Every day, before going to work, I walked to the graveyard, sometimes with my mother. Every night, when I came back from work, I went to the graveyard alone. I went in rain and in snow. I never missed a night.

The thought that tortured me was whether my brother had not been right in that repeated insight: "We are hopeless. We are gentle people. We are too gentle to face the world." My instinct told me that he was right. I thought that he had acted quickly and bravely to destroy his life before the world could destroy it. But I questioned whether I was not wrong to have let him make the lonely journey alone. That was the question I was seeking an answer to.

One night, after returning from the graveyard, I went to look inside the little house, where I had once narrowly saved my brother. There I made my decision: "No. I will live. There is something in me, there is some purpose in my life which I feel but do not understand. I must go on living until it is fulfilled." I added to myself: "I shall be sorry that I did not go with my brother."

LI

Not long after my brother's death, I was living in a cottage on one of the Long Island tidal inlets. I was living with a Communist girl in what was called a "party marriage"—the kind of union that the Communist Party sanctioned and, in fact, favored. My mother knew where I was living, but, of course, never visited us.

One morning, she drove up to my house, breathless and distraught. "Your father is dead," she said. "You will have to come and move his body." He had dropped dead in the bathroom as he prepared to shave.

My father lay huddled in his bathrobe on the sea-blue tiles my brother had laid. His body was still warm. Of the bodies I had lifted in the last years, his was the most inert. I could move him only inch by inch. My mother had to help me raise him to his bed.

Later, the undertakers carried my father downstairs. Without my knowledge, they began the preliminary stages of embalming, in our living room. Unsuspectingly, I walked into the room. My father lay naked on a stretcher. One of his arms was dangling. From this arm, near the shoulder, his blood, the blood that had given my brother and me life, was pouring, in a thin, dark arc, into a battered mop bucket.

We buried my father beside my brother.

Our line seemed to be at an end. Our family was like a burnt-over woods, which nothing can revive and only new growth can replace. The promise of new growth lay wholly within me—in my having children. No need was so strong in me as the need to have children. But by then I agreed with my brother that to repeat the misery of such lives as ours would be a crime against life.

L I I

My relations with my father softened after my brother's death. His loneliness, his sense of the failure of his whole life, was inescapable, and he began to show me as much affection as it lay in his nature to show anyone. His hand fumbled for mine and my hand fumbled for his. I thought: "Under so great a damnation, how can any one of us feel anything but pity for any other?"

We took to meeting in New York for lunch or supper. Then we would ramble aimlessly around the insensible city. We were still almost as silent with each other as in the past, but now my need for silence had become almost as great as my father's. Sometimes his old sardonic coldness would betray him and rebuff me. But I felt a will to ignore it. He, too, struggled against it, and this struggle was visible and absolving. From things he let drop, or ventured almost furtively, I began to grasp that, in the long drama of our house, he, too, had a human case.

One night, not long after my brother's death, we met by chance on the Long Island train and walked home from the station together. It was a very starry night. As usual, we walked in silence. Both of us were watching the sky. Both of us saw a shooting star streak across it and flash out as it hit the earth's atmosphere. "Strange," said my father (who knew even less about science than I did), "to think that a world has ended."

LIII

I never questioned that my brother's death was due to great weaknesses in himself. But it was also due to strength and clarity—his undeflected vision of his own weaknesses and of the world in which they had come to light and to grief. That world was dying of its own vulgarity, stupidity, complacency, inhumanity, power and materialism—a death of the spirit. The toxins of its slow decay poisoned all life within it—but first of all that life which was most gentle and most decent because its sensitivity (that is to say, in part, its weakness), made it most susceptible and most incurable.

That this world was dying both brothers knew. We differed as to how to face the fact. My brother's way had the grace of disdain and simple subtraction. He removed himself from what he found unsolvable or unworthy to be solved, and which he refused to encumber. Such fortitude and such finality are like a smile before a firing squad. When a man makes himself his own firing squad, he is beyond pity or judgment, since it is difficult to pity or to judge those who are merciless first of all with themselves.

This view I understood. In part, I shared it. In so far as I was gentle, I shared it. But I was not only gentle. Deep within me there was a saving fierceness that my brother lacked. If you kick my dog in the stomach, though I have refused to fight one hundred times, and will refuse again, that time I will wait and fight to destroy you. I cannot help myself. Within me there is a force. It says that that gentleness, which is not prepared to kill or be killed to destroy the evil that assails life, is not gentleness. It is weakness. It is the weakness of the merely well-meaning. It is the suspended goodness of the men of mere good will whose passivity in the face of evil first of all raises the question whether they are men. It is the permanent temptation of the Christian who, in a world of force, flinches the crucifixion which alone can give kindness and compassion force.

That dying world, which, in the death throe of the First World

War, had just destroyed eleven million lives, and was visibly preparing to destroy as many more in its next convulsion, that dying world, of which my family was a tiny image, and whose poisons had also killed my brother, inspired in me only a passing mood to flinch it. Much more, it stirred a grimness in me, a will to end it, not so that kindness and compassion might reign on earth—we are not children—but that the possibility of kindness and compassion might survive at all, that human life might survive the death that fed on it.

The New Year's Eve following my brother's death, I reached the Sand Hill graveyard a little before midnight. It was a very silent night. A wet snow was falling. The raw earth over my brother's grave had begun to settle. A pool of rain and thaw water had collected. A sheet of ice covered it. As I stood looking at it, the year ended. In an instant, in all the Long Island villages around the horizon, the sirens wailed; bells rang from the firehouses. From a road house beyond the graveyard, a crowd burst, shouting. Someone snapped a clacker. Cars hurtled down the Merrick Road, filled with hooting, singing people. A bottle, tossed from one car, shattered against the cemetery wall.

I listened, leaning against a gravestone. There, as the hubbub died away, I began to compose a poem—one of the last few poems, it turned out, that I would ever write. It was scarcely a poem at all. It was the cry with which I surmounted the spiritual exhaustion of my long struggle to keep my brother alive, and of his death, and a statement of what that experience meant to me in terms of my own life and all life. It was long, and, like my other poems I later destroyed it, so that I can remember only snatches. It began:

Blow, whistles, blow,
Ring out, joyful bells,
Shout and caper, happy people,
You have killed him.
Reel, shouting, into your cars.
Where your clotted brains and ugly hands cannot be on him,
He gives you dirt for dirt.
The gentle of heart, the firm of will, is dead.
The fools, the cowards, the evil, the cunning, the low, live on.
His life is well withdrawn from such.

The peace of the graveyard, the night, the snow, took hold of me again. I wrote:

This is the silence of the sky
Thrown over us in congelation by the snow;
A clacker in the hands of a fool
Has shattered snow's silence.

I wrote more about the meaning of my brother's death, the rightness of the act for him, his courage in retiring from the hubbub of the world to that silence which the world abhorred because it betrayed the world's inconsequence. I spoke of the quiet of the graveyard and its stones at night, which the world feared, but which I had learned not to fear. (The gentle dead harm no one.) I spoke of my brother's grave, which I had faithfully visited, but which I would not visit again. For he had made his choice. I had made mine, and mine was not for death. I wrote:

Ring out, glad bells,
I shall not die.
By this stone of death I lean against
I hold myself upright for life,
For as long as I seem to serve.
This order must go.
I hold no brief for any other,
But this must go.
Help me, God (if there were God),
Before I die,
In my good time or under the hands of the police,
To make of myself one tiny cell, a bacterium,
To serve the organization of love as hate,
The union of the weak to kill the evil in power,
The outrage and the hope of the world.

And, as I left the graveyard for the last time (I never went back), I ended:

Fall on me, snow,
Cover me up;
Cover the houses and the streets.
Let me see only in the light of another year
The roofs and the minds that killed him,
And the earth that holds him,
Forever dead.

I was already a member of the Communist Party. I now first became a Communist. I became irreconcilable.

Lies scattered among silence.

For as long as I am to live,

3

THE OUTRAGE AND THE HOPE OF THE WORLD

I

Sooner or later, one of my good friends is sure to ask me: How did it happen that a man like you became a Communist? Each time I wince, not at the personal question, but at the failure to grasp the fact that a man does not, as a rule, become a Communist because he is attracted to Communism, but because he is driven to despair by the crisis of history through which the world is passing.

I force myself to answer: In the West, all intellectuals become Communists because they are seeking the answer to one of two problems: the problem of war or the problem of economic crises.

This is not to say that personal factors play no part in making a man a Communist. Obviously, they do, if only because every man's character and experience, and therefore his biography, are different from every other man's. No two are ever the same. Hence some men will always be more susceptible to Communism than other men, just as some are less resistant to disease than other men. But whatever factors make one man more susceptible than another to Communism once he is driven to entertain it at all, it will be found that, almost without exception, the intellectuals of the West are driven to entertain it in terms of just two challenges: the problem of war and the problem of economic crisis. This is equally true, even for men of untrained minds or without the habit of reflection; men who find it difficult to explain to themselves or to others the forces that move them to Communism. For while the susceptibility to Communism varies among men, the problem of war and economic crisis do not vary. In this period of history, they are constant, and must be until, in one way or another, they are solved.

Some intellectuals are primarily moved by the problem of war. Others are first moved by the economic problem. Both crises are aspects of a greater crisis of history for which Communism offers a plausible explanation and which it promises to end. When an intellectual joins the Communist Party, he does so primarily because he sees no other way of ending the crisis of history. In effect, his act is an act of despair, regardless of whether or not that is how he thinks of it. And to the degree that it is an act of despair, he will desire the party to use him in overcoming that crisis of history which is at the root of his despair.

There is a widespread notion that men become Communists for reasons of material gain. There are always a certain number of "rice Christians" in any movement that has anything at all to offer them. Of all movements in the world, the Communist Party has the least to offer a man bent on personal advantage. For the intellectual of any ability, it has nothing whatever to offer in the way of gain. In the days when I joined the Communist Party, it could offer those who joined it only the certainty of being poor and pariahs. During the 1930's and 1940's, when Communism became intellectually fashionable, there was a time when Communist Party patronage could dispose of jobs or careers in a number of fields. But the jobs that the Communist Party could give, or the careers it could further, presupposed that the men and women in them must have some ability to hold them at all. Almost without exception such men and women could have made their careers much more profitably and comfortably outside the Communist Party. For the party must always demand more than it gives. What material advantage, for example, could the Communist Party possibly offer an Alger Hiss, a Noel Field, a Dr. Klaus Fuchs, equal to the demands it made on him? This persistent notion that men become or remain Communists from motives of personal advantage constantly baffles those who hold it with the fact that Communist parties everywhere are filled with talented men and women, often of good family, and that these people are precisely among the most fanatical Communists, those most likely to be found in the party's most hazardous and criminal activities.

Nor do Marxist dialectics or Marxian economic theories have much to do with the reason why men become and remain Communists. I have met few Communists who were more than fiddlers with the dialectic (the intellectual tool whereby Marxist theoreticians probe and gauge history's laws of motion). I have met few Communists whom I thought knew more than the bare rudiments of Marxian economics, or cared to. But I have never known a Communist who was not acutely aware of the crisis of history whose solution he found in Communism's practical program, its vision and its faith.

Few Communists have ever been made simply by reading the works of Marx or Lenin. The crisis of history makes Communists; Marx and Lenin merely offer them an explanation of the crisis and what to do about it. Thus a graph of Communist growth would show that its numbers and its power increased in waves roughly equivalent to each new crest of crisis. The same horror and havoc of the First World War, which made the Russian Revolution possible, recruited the ranks of the first Communist parties of the West. Secondary manifestations of crisis augmented them—the rise of fascism in Italy, Nazism in Germany and the Spanish Civil War. The economic crisis which reached the United States in 1929 swept thousands into the Communist Party or under its influence. The military crisis of World War II swept in millions more; for example, a third of the voting population of France and of Italy. The crisis of the Third World War is no doubt holding those millions in place and adding to them. For whatever else the rest of the world may choose to believe, it can be said without reservation that Communists believe World War III inevitable.

Under pressure of the crisis, his decision to become a Communist seems to the man who makes it as a choice between a world that is dying and a world that is coming to birth, as an effort to save by political surgery whatever is sound in the foredoomed body of a civilization which nothing less drastic can save—a civilization foredoomed first of all by its reluctance to face the fact that the crisis exists or to face it with the force and clarity necessary to overcome it.

Thus, the Communist Party presents itself as the one organization of the will to survive the crisis in a civilization where that will is elsewhere divided, wavering or absent. It is in the name of that will to survive the crisis, which is not theoretical but closes in from all sides, that the Communist first justifies the use of terror and tyranny, which are repugnant to most men by nature and which the whole tradition of the West specifically repudiates.

It is in the name of that will to survive that Communism turns to the working class as a source of unspoiled energy which may salvage the crumbling of the West. For the revolution is never stronger than the failure of civilization. Communism is never stronger than the failure of other faiths.

It is the crisis that makes men Communists and it is the crisis that keeps men Communists. For the Communist who breaks with Communism must break not only with the power of its vision and its faith. He must break in the full knowledge that he will find himself facing the crisis of history, but this time without even that solution which Communism presents, and crushed by the knowledge that the solution which he sought through Communism is evil against God and man.

I was one of those drawn to Communism by the problem of war. For me that problem began in 1923. In that year, I went to Europe with Meyer Schapiro who had been my classmate at Columbia College. He had already begun those studies that were later to make him a professor of Fine Arts at Columbia and one of the outstanding art critics in the country. We planned to spend the summer in Europe's galleries and museums.

I saw the galleries and museums. But I also saw something else. I saw for the first time the crisis of history and its dimension. It was not only that Germany was in a state of manic desperation, reeling from inflation, readying for revolution while three Allied armies occupied the Rhineland and refugees flooded back from the occupied area into the shattered country. It was not only the aftermath of the World War, the ruins of northern France or what Bernanos would presently call "those vast cemeteries in the moonlight." What moved me was the evidence that World War II was predictably certain and that it was extremely improbable that civilization could survive it. (In this I was mistaken, though, by the end of the Second World War, civilized Europe would shrink to little more than it had been in the Dark Ages.) It seemed to me that the world had reached a crisis on a scale and of a depth such as had been known only once or twice before in history. (And in that I was not mistaken at all.)

During my years at Columbia College, I had known a number of socialists, including two or three extreme left-wingers. They had devoted a great deal of time, tact and patience to winning me to their views. They had no effect on me whatever. What their theories could not do, the crisis did. For, in searching for the answer to the crisis, I found none but socialism.

I returned to the United States and plunged into Fabian Socialism, studying as I seldom had before in my life. I abstracted and made mountainous notes on the dull dry works of the Webbs, R. H. Tawney, Hobhouse and the endless volumes in which G.D.H. Cole urged Guild socialism. There was no life in those books. There were statistics and theories. The reek of life was missing.

I brushed them aside. Socialism was not the answer. It was perfectly clear, too, that if socialism was to stem the crisis and remake the world, socialism involved a violent struggle to get and keep political power. At some point, socialism would have to consolidate its power by force. The Webbs made no provision for getting or keeping power. Moreover, I had a profound antipathy to force. I was glad to shelve the problem.

In that disenchanted period I returned to Columbia College to major in history, attending classes by day and working at night to pay my way. History was medieval history and I rehearsed in the collapse of Rome the crisis of history in our own time.

One day, by sheer chance, there came into my hands a little pamphlet of Lenin's. It was called *A Soviet At Work.* In a simple strong prose, it described a day in the life of a local soviet. The reek of life was on it. This was not theory or statistics. This was socialism in practice. This was the thing itself. This was how it worked.

I quickly passed on to *Lenin's State and Revolution* and the *ABC of Communism* (its three authors were all shot during the Great Purge). Here was no dodging of the problem of getting and keeping power. Here was the simple statement that terror and dictatorship are justified to defend the socialist revolution if socialism is justified. Terror is an instrument of socialist policy if the crisis was to be overcome. It was months before I could accept even in principle the idea of terror.

Once I had done so, I faced the necessity to act.

II

One day, early in 1925, I sat down on a concrete bench on the Columbia campus, facing a little Greek shrine and the statue of my old political hero, Alexander Hamilton. The sun was shining, but it was chilly, and I sat huddled in my overcoat. I was there to answer once for all two questions: Can a man go on living in a world that is dying? If he can, what should he do in the crisis of the 20th century?

There ran through my mind the only lines I remember from the history textbook of my second go at college—two lines of Savinus', written in the fifth century when the Goths had been in Rome and the Vandals were in Carthage: "The Roman Empire is filled with misery, but it is luxurious. It is dying, but it laughs."

The dying world of 1925 was without faith, hope, character, understanding of its malady or will to overcome it. It was dying but it laughed. And this laughter was not the defiance of a vigor that refuses to know when it is whipped. It was the loss, by the mind of a whole civilization, of the power to distinguish between reality and unreality, because, ultimately, though I did not know it, it had lost the power to distinguish between good and evil. This failure I, too, shared with the world of which I was a part.

The dying world had no answer at all to the crisis of the 20th century, and, when it was mentioned, and every moral voice in the Western world was shrilling crisis, it cocked an ear of complacent deafness and smiled a smile of blank senility—throughout history, the smile of those for whom the executioner waits.

Only in Communism had I found any practical answer at all to the crisis, and the will to make that answer work. It was not an attractive answer, just as the Communist Party was not an attractive party. Neither was the problem which had called it forth, and which it proposed to solve, attractive. But it had one ultimate appeal. In place of desperation, it set the word: hope. If it was the outrage, it was also the hope of the world. In the 20th century, it seemed impossible to have hope on any other terms.

When I rose from the bench, I had decided to leave college for good, and change the whole direction of my life. I had decided to join the Communist Party. The choice was not so much for a program that promised to end war, economic chaos and the moral enervation of the West. I had already said to myself what Lenin had already said better: "We do not presume to maintain that Marx or the Marxists can show us the way to socialism in perfectly concrete terms. That would be absurd. We know the direction of this road: we know which class forces lead to it. But in actual practice, only the experience of millions of men and women can show it when they begin the actual work."

The ultimate choice I made was not for a theory or a party. It was—and I submit that this is true for almost every man and woman who has made it—a choice against death and for life. I asked only the privilege of serving humbly and selflessly that force which from death could evoke life, that might save, as I then supposed, what was savable in a society that had lost the will to save itself. I was willing to accept Communism in whatever terms it presented itself, to follow the logic of its course wherever it might lead me, and to suffer the penalties without which nothing in life can be achieved. For it offered me what nothing else in the dying world had power to offer at the same intensity—faith and a vision, something for which to live and something for which to die. It demanded of me those things which have always stirred what is best in men—courage, poverty, self-sacrifice, discipline, intelligence, my life, and, at need, my death.

I went to my campus friends who had so long and patiently worked to convert me to Communism and said that at last I was ready. I asked them where the Communist Party could be found. To my great surprise, they did not know. For I was then unfamiliar with that type of fellow traveler who also serves Communism, but chiefly by sitting and talking.

I remembered that there had once passed across the Columbia campus a high-strung, red-headed boy from an upstate college. He had slept overnight on the bare floor of a friend's room in one of the residence halls. He talked incessantly in a voice like a teletype machine; and what he talked about was the Soviet Union and Communism. His name was Sender Garlin. I thought that Sender Garlin would probably know where to find the Communist Party. Presently I located him.

Garlin said that, in fact, there was no Communist Party. For reasons of expediency, the Communist Party which had just come up from underground, now called itself the Workers Party. He was not sure that he knew how to contact it or that he knew anyone in it. But if it turned out that he did, he would mention my name, and a man might presently come to see me.

I decided that Garlin knew exactly where to find the Communist Party and was telling me that he would put me in touch with it.

THE COMMUNIST PARTY

I

A stocky young man in a shabby overcoat walked past my desk in the Public Library and studied me. Then he walked back and studied me from another angle. He did this several times. I thought: "He is the man. He is the contact with the Communist Party."

Then the first American Communist I had ever seen edged up to the desk, looked at me out of distrustful, rather glassy eyes, and asked: "Are you Chambers?"

I looked at his dead-fish eyes and said that I was.

"I am the man you were told about," he said. "You want to join?"

"Yes," I said, "I want to join."

"Why?"

I said that I believed that Communism was the answer to the social crisis and that I wanted to do something about it.

"Do you read the *Daily Worker*?" he asked.

"Sometimes," I said. "Usually I read the *Volkszeitung*." The *Volkszeitung* was the best of the American Communist newspapers. It was published in German in New York City. Its editor was Ludwig Lore, who was expelled from the Communist Party (for "incurable Loreism") shortly after I joined it and whom I was later to know in the Communist underground. The *Daily Worker* was written in a heavy-handed gibberish that was almost unreadable.

"Have you read Marx's *Capital*?"

I said: "No," but that I had read *The Communist Manifesto* and Lenin's *State and Revolution*.

"You ought to read *Capital*," said my man pedantically. "They all think it's smart nowadays to read Lenin. Nobody knows anything any more about Marx or economics."

Evidently, he had made up his mind to take a chance on me, for he confided that he would take me to a meeting, and named a night when he would return for me. Then he left, blending easily with the stream of shabby or derelict people that flowed in and out of the newspaper room, where many of them came for warmth on bitter nights.

II

A few nights later, the Communist with the glassy eyes came back. It was the early spring of 1925, and cold. He steered me toward the Hudson River, and we worked our way on foot, against the wind, toward 59th Street. While we walked, he told me that his name was Sam Krieger. "But my name in the party," he said, "is Clarence Miller. Did you ever hear of the Clarence Miller case?" I said no. "You never heard of the Clarence Miller case?" he asked with what I took to be a touch of contempt. I said no.

He explained that he had once been a Wobbly (from him I first learned that a Wobbly is a member of the I.W.W.). He had been arrested somewhere in the West for some radical activity. The Civil Liberties Union had come to his rescue, and Krieger had at last gone free. For Roger Baldwin, the head of the Civil Liberties Union, he had a respect quite unusual among Communists. For while Communists make full use of liberals and their solicitudes, and sometimes flatter them to their faces, in private they treat them with that sneering contempt that the strong and predatory almost invariably feel for victims who volunteer to help in their own victimization.

Not far from the Hudson River, somewhere on or near 59th Street, Krieger drew me into a dark doorway. We went up a dirty stairway to a big lighted loft. At the door two or three short, dark men looked us over silently, nodded to Krieger and let us pass.

The ceilings and walls of the loft were festooned with faded red crepe paper put up for some past proletarian fête and never taken down. Two banks of folding chairs with an aisle between faced a plain table and some chairs, where I supposed that the leaders of the meeting sat. It was chilly in the loft. Most people wore their coats. At one side of the room, a group of Greeks were making hot tea, which they peddled for a few cents. It was served, in the Russian style, in glasses. My first impression was one of cold, dirt and drab disorder. I would presently learn that bleakness and disorder were the mark of all Communist Party offices, that this expressed a reaction, sometimes conscious, sometimes unconscious, against middle-class preoccupation with tidiness. I never got used to it.

I had expected to find a small group of Communists. I had hoped that they would be staid and serious working people, whose faces would reflect a sincerity and a purpose equal to the task of carrying through the greatest revolution in history. There were forty or fifty men and women in the loft. They were of several nationalities, but broken English, Greek and Yiddish seemed to be the prevailing languages: everybody was talking at once. There was a continuous buzz through which, now and again, a strident argumentative voice would slice. As I looked at my future comrades, they seemed to me less like the praetorian guard of the world revolution than a rather undisciplined group of small delicatessen keepers. (How unflatteringly they looked at me I would soon learn.)

Krieger began to identify various comrades out of the side of his mouth. "That's Gand. He's a Russian." I looked at a tall, pale man who was chain-smoking cigarettes. He was not talking to anyone, but staring intently at various individuals, shifting his gaze when they looked at him. "That's Ben Gitlow. He just got out of jail. You must have heard of Gitlow." Gitlow had been a Socialist member of the New York state legislature who had spent several years in prison for advocating the overthrow of the Government. He was a big, rather soft-looking, very pallid man with a pleasant, brooding, somewhat sad face. "That's Ma Gitlow next to him. The man is his father."

Everybody had taken a sidelong glance at me. But several comrades came up boldly and Krieger introduced them. "This is Comrade Bosse." Comrade Bosse was a neatly dressed man about thirty-two years old. I believe that he was an economics teacher. He stood so loosely that he seemed to be double-jointed. He was bald, which helped to give him the look of a baby that is prematurely aged.

"This," said Krieger, "is Eve Chambers." Eve Chambers (her real name was Eve Dorf) was a brisk, dark girl who needed only a bandolier of cartridges to look like a partisan. "And this is her husband, David Benjamin." David Benjamin was another pale-faced man with dark, quick eyes. Both Benjamin and his wife were schoolteachers. Both were conspicuously friendly. I thought then that they regarded me as a kindred intellectual. Presently I learned from Krieger that they regarded me as a potential recruit in the factional fight which was dividing the minds, and engrossing most of the time, of that small, anomalous band.

Eve Chambers and her husband have long been out of the Communist Party. They were expelled as "incurable right-wing deviationists and Lovestoneites" when the Stalinists took over the party in 1929. Today, David Benjamin is better known by his real name, Ben Davidson, and as an active lieutenant of the chief of the Liberal Party in New York—Adolf A. Berle, with whom, fourteen years later, when Berle was security officer of the State Department, I was to have a momentous conversation about Communist espionage.

This group of Communists was called the English-speaking branch of the Communist Party. It was called "English-speaking" to distinguish it from the more numerous Communist units where English was not spoken, and to indicate that the business of the meeting would be conducted in English, however broken.

What the business of my first meeting was I have forgotten. Much of it, in fact, I could not understand. For the Communists, even when speaking English, spoke a dialect most of whose terms—Polburo (political bureau), Ekki (Executive Committee of the Communist International)—I had never heard before. I soon grasped that Communist forensics had its own style. No matter what message a speaker had to deliver, it seemed to be etiquette for him to deliver it as ferociously and rudely as possible. At one point a heavy-set handsome woman rose from her seat and announced calmly: "The comrade is a liar." That was my first glimpse of Juliet Stuart Poyntz, a Midwestern American and Barnard graduate whose murder by the Russian secret police, thirteen years later, made a deep impression on me about the time of my break with the Soviet underground.

One incident at that meeting I never forgot. "Mother" Gitlow demanded the floor. She was the first of the American Communist Party's "mothers." After her expulsion from the party (*circa* 1929, for "incurable right-wing deviationism"), she was replaced by the late "Mother" Bloor whose son, Harold Ware, organized that Washington underground in which I was later to meet Alger Hiss.

Most of the speakers had merely leaped to their feet and stood by their chairs—all that was necessary in view of the fact that many of them had only a brief invective to deliver. Mother Gitlow left her seat, walked to the front of the room and turned to glare at the meeting. She was a short, sturdy Jewish woman, with shrewd eyes behind her glasses, suggesting a touch of earthy horse sense. She stood silent for a moment, waiting for the meeting to become quiet—an interval that she used to roll up or draw back her sleeves as if for a brawl. Then she said in a tone of challenge: "Cumreds! The potato crop has failed in Ireland and thousands of peasants are starving to death. Cumreds! What are we doing to help the starving workers and peasants of Ireland?"

There was a good deal more. I recognized the comic overtones. They did not seem funny to me. Mother Gitlow was Communism in action. That short, squat, belligerent woman, pleading in a thick Yiddish accent for food for hungry Irish peasants, personified the brotherhood of all the wretched of the earth. It made no difference that most Irish peasants would have hooted her out of town. She knew that too. But she was the Communist. In her worked the revolutionary will to overcome ignorance and prejudice in the name of militant compassion and intelligent human unity. In the light of her appeal, it made little difference that that small mob of Communists was torn by dissension. So long as there existed within the party one such woman to act, and men and women who understood her, the pulse of Communism pumped life, however feebly, into the veins of the future.

I do not mean that, on hearing her, I broke into a sweat of enthusiasm. I was more like a new recruit in the awkward squad, who looks around him, notes one or two others, and thinks: "If we can ever be licked into shape, we may some day make a company in the army of the future. At least, there are others."

I thought, as I left the meeting: "I did not expect much. I see that we shall have to begin even farther back than I expected." I was not disturbed or dejected. A Communist knows that a given situation, in a given period of history, will produce certain human materials, and that those, and only those, are what history gives him to work with. The point is to work with them right. Then the situation and history will change, and, with it, the human material.

III

I was not admitted to the Communist Party at my first meeting. First I was looked over. Looking over consisted chiefly of being invited several times to visit Sam Krieger and his wife. Sam Krieger was then the circulation manager of the Yonkers (New York) *Statesman*, which, of course, did not know that he was a Communist. Krieger pushed sales by giving bicycles to enterprising newsboys who, on competitive principles that would later be known as Stakhanovite, sold the most copies of that capitalist newspaper.

I used to meet Krieger at the *Statesman* office. He would drive me in a rather rattly car to the outskirts of Yonkers, where he and his wife had a small apartment and a large (and fierce) police dog. Carol Krieger was the daughter of the owner of a well-known chain of aseptic cafeterias on whose windows his name appeared in big, embossed, white enamel letters. She was a pretty girl, rather insipid, and ailing—one of her arms was nerveless or partially paralyzed. The Kriegers belonged to the extreme left wing of the Communist Party. They regarded marriage as a "bourgeois convention" and loathed it with the same intensity with which many middle-class persons loathe sin. Theirs was the first "party marriage" that I observed. I was also to observe, when it broke up, that "party marriages" sometimes led Communists to emotional upsets as shattering as any suffered by the bourgeoisie.

From Krieger I began to learn my way around the Communist Party. I learned that there were in it two factions (or fractions, as Krieger and many other Communists called them). One faction was headed, in some kind of uneasy fellowship, by William Z. Foster, Alexander Bittelman, William F. Dunne and James Cannon. This was the group that Sam Krieger belonged to. The other group was headed by the secretary of the party, Charles Ruthenberg, and Jay Lovestone. This was the group that Comrade Bosse, David Benjamin, Eve Chambers and the Gitlows belonged to.

For under the fiction of unity, the factions fought fiercely and shamelessly. Each sought to gain control by any means of the party press and all the units of the party organization. Each circulated secret mimeographed attacks on the other or promoted scandalous whispering campaigns, in which embezzlement of party money, homosexuality and stool pigeon were the preferred whispers.

This seemed to me a distressing and wasteful way for a party, poor in human and all other resources, to organize against the most powerful capitalism in the world. But again, I realized that no political organization can rise above its human and historical level and that these were the growing pains unavoidable in an immature party, recruited necessarily from a low level of the population, at an early period of its history. As the party developed, it would outgrow its dissensions.

After a few meetings, Krieger proposed me for membership in the Communist Party. I cannot report that the "general staff of the world revolution" gathered me in by acclaim. Some members abstained from voting, and there was a flurry of hands against me. There was nothing personal in this, Sam Krieger explained, after I had been inducted. The comrades who voted against me were members of the Lovestone faction. They had simply feared that, since Krieger was my sponsor, I would add one more vote to the strength of the Foster group.

After the voting, Ben Davidson and others took me aside and suggested that I was making a mistake to join the Communist Party under my own name. "Why?" I said. "I am not ashamed to be a Communist." I thought that they looked at me a little pityingly.

Later on, I went to the Manhattan headquarters of the Workers Party on 14th Street. There I met a fidgety, kindly man who duly issued me, in the name of Whittaker Chambers, a red party book, listing my party number, stamped with the party's rubber seal (a hammer and sickle) and signed by the nervous man's name: Bert Miller. I knew Bert Miller for many years and even worked closely with him in the Communist Party until his expulsion (another "incurable right-wing deviationist") in 1929. In all that time I never knew his real name. It was General Walter Krivitsky who first told me, one day, shortly before his strange death in Washington, that Bert Miller was really Ben Mandel. And it was almost a decade after that before I would resume my close acquaintance with Ben Mandel. By then he was the research director of the House Committee on Un-American Activities, and I was a witness before it.

IV

I hurried up to Columbia University to inform my friends on the campus that I had located the Communist Party, had made contact with it, and was, in fact, a registered member. By chance, the first man I met as I crossed the campus was one of my literary friends. I told him the news. As usual, he squinted one eye and lifted the eyebrow of the other, so that he looked as if he were peering through a monocle. "Do you drill in a cellar with machine guns?" he asked airily. It was he who, when I was first seeking enlightenment about Communism, had given me *The Communist Manifesto* to read. Now I saw that Communism as an idea was diverting. Communism as an idea to do something about was amusing. I turned away.

I looked up another great friend who was later with the Theater Guild. More than any other individual, he had been directly responsible for swinging me toward Marxism. Now that I was a Communist, I explained, I would be able to bring him into the party at once. There were some moments of painful embarrassment. He was delighted at my political enterprise, but he had no intention of joining the Communist Party himself. Nevertheless, his position was awkward and he felt obliged to put me off without actually saying no. The same pattern was repeated with others.

For the first time, I understood the contempt with which Communists pronounced the word "intellectuals." I thought: "That miscellaneous mob in the English-speaking branch may not know the English language, but they know a good deal about history. They are not as intelligent as my college friends, but they do not think that ideas are ping-pong balls. They believe that ideas are important as a guide to coherent action. They have purpose and they have courage. They are grown men and women, and these are children."

I felt a sudden warmth for my shabby, quarrelsome comrades, and a readiness to overlook their failings in the name of their faith and purpose. I began to see less and less of my college friends. There was a period when I scarcely saw them at all. But they had not forgotten me.

One night one of them showed up inexplicably at the *Daily Worker* office, and stood chatting with me even in the clatter of the composing room. Soon others appeared. I was not yet aware of it, but the great leftward swing of the American intellectuals had begun. I suddenly found myself in the role of a pioneer. But the hands of the clock of history had bumped a long way ahead. The year was 1929, and I was preparing to break away for the first time from the party which they had, belatedly, caught up with.

V

The word "intellectual" was the most lethal in the invective vocabulary of Communism. No one who could read or speak fluently was entirely invulnerable to it. Even a high-school education laid a man open to attack. No matter how ably a Communist might argue a point, he could almost always be stopped by any illiterate who chose to fling the annihilating term. "Isn't he an intellectual?" one comrade would ask about another in a tone of one teetotaler asking about another: "Isn't he a drunkard?"

Several comrades tried out the word on me or in my hearing. I was, happily, fairly immune to its effects, in part because, while indubitably an intellectual, I seldom thought of myself as one and did not like most intellectuals who did; in part because I agreed that in the nature of the revolutionary struggle, an intellectual could never be quite as reliable a Communist as someone who had the good fortune to be born in a tenement. For every society has its standards of nobility, and I was, moreover, not yet experienced enough to observe that every Communist Party in the world is led and staffed chiefly by middle-class intellectuals.

Besides, I had entered the Communist Party with a proper sense of humility—with somewhat the same feeling with which another man might enter a religious order. After a rapid glance around, I had few illusions about the party. Its methods were slipshod and much of its personnel inadequate or absurd. But about its historical necessity and purpose I had no doubts. I wished to serve. I did not particularly care how.

One day, shortly after we had met, Sam Krieger proposed that I should do "Jimmie Higgins work." He explained to me patiently that Jimmie Higgins is a character in one of Upton Sinclair's novels or stories with a passion for lowly jobs. I shared no such passion, but I readily agreed, for I wanted to know the party from the ground up. I began with the *Daily Worker*, but not on its editorial staff.

The party's "central organ," the *Daily Worker*, was then published in Chicago. But the paper had a New York office, a bare room on 14th Street. There Louis Katterfeld, the *Worker's* New York representative, presided.

Katterfeld looked like the type of Communist I had hoped to find on my first visit to the English-speaking branch. He was a German-American, humorless, grave, with a lined, austere face. He had been an unsuccessful Kansas wheat farmer, graduating from a native school of agrarian radicalism. Poverty was a vocation with him. His frayed overcoat was the uniform of his faith, and, like everything else about him, it was of a piece with a revolutionary integrity that shone from him more purely than from almost any other American Communist I knew. He lived in a little house on Long Island in the same woods where I had wandered as a boy, for, like me, he did not like cities. He had a big family of boys and girls, and, when I had come to know him better, he once confided to me with wistful dismay that his children "regarded the Communist Party the way Communists regard capitalism—as a cause of poverty and exploitation." They wanted to live like other people and detested Communists and Communist meetings.

During the party's underground days Katterfeld had briefly been the party's acting secretary. But his revolutionary intelligence was not quite up to his revolutionary spirit. Both made him something of a butt for men who were less good and less devout, but brighter. He was an extreme leftist and held that the Communist Party should have remained permanently underground, sensing, I think, that the underground experience inevitably winnowed out men less dedicated than himself, and thus left a core of hardened professional revolutionists. He could not face the fact that Lenin had tirelessly taught that, when a whole Communist party is outlawed, it is almost wholly paralyzed because it can no longer send into the surrounding community the filaments whereby it spreads its toxins and from which it draws its strength and life. That a hard core of devoted men like himself existed was more important to Katterfeld than what they existed for.

When the Lovestoneites took power in the party, Katterfeld withdrew from it. He began to publish a magazine called *Evolution,* for his mind was in many ways a petrifact of 19th-century radicalism, and among its oddments of conviction was militant Darwinism. I remember *Evolution* chiefly for one of its covers in which a stroke of editorial imagination came magnificently to the aid of its chronic poverty. The cover was simply a block of black ink in the middle of which was a pinpoint of white. It was titled: The Human Egg Magnified Several Million Times.

This was the Communist to whom I first offered my unpaid services. He looked me over in much the same way as the hiring boss in Baltimore had done. Clearly, he did not believe that I would be around very long. He set me to doing the task that nobody else would do—newsstand collections for the *Daily Worker.* Paying my own fare, I traveled around New York City, settling with news dealers for the *Daily Workers* they had sold, collecting the unsold copies in an old suitcase. One day I would be far out in Brooklyn, the next day in the Bronx. Years later, in my remote rambles about New York with Colonel Bykov, I would suddenly realize that I had been in some outlying place before, and think: "Oh, yes, it was when I was making newsstand collections for the *Daily Worker.*"

At the time I took over that duty, collections had not been made for a long while. Most of the dealers had no records of their sales and their accounts were largely fanciful. No doubt, they cheated me, but there was no way of preventing that. They were wretchedly poor men and women, and surly. In winter, they sat, bundled in wads of clothing, whipped by the wind in draughty stands under elevated stairs or on exposed street corners. Some of them were members of the Communist Party. I could always tell these because they displayed the *Daily Worker* prominently.

In time, I was able to bring some order into the collections and my regularity won the co-operation of the news dealers and the grudging respect of Katterfeld. Once in a while, a dealer would ask me: "Are you really a Communist?" The sight of a literate man patiently going about a humble chore puzzled them. "It is worth more," I used to think, "than all the unreadable propaganda in the *Daily Worker*." For a propaganda of words that is not backed by a propaganda of deeds is worthless.

VI

It is an axiom of Communism that practical activity and theory go hand in hand. Theory guides practical activity. Practical activity roots theory in reality and prevents it from becoming merely abstract. Comrade Krieger was not only concerned that I should collect *Daily Workers*. He was equally concerned about my "ideological development." In those days, ideology was one of the indispensable words in the Communist quiver, yielding only to "oriented," or its commoner form, "orientated"—as in the question: "Is the comrade properly orientated on that issue?" Krieger felt (quite rightly) that there were many issues on which I was not properly "orientated."

He pressed me to join a study group to which he and his wife belonged, with some ten or fifteen others. The group was led by Scott Nearing. It met once a week, sometimes in the Rand School, the Socialist headquarters on East 15th Street, sometimes in a Communist office. Its members were trying to formulate (another favorite word) "the law of social revolution." The members of the group, singly, or in teams, were writing papers on each of the great modern revolutions. When the papers were completed, the group would ponder upon the result and from it deduce the unifying law that underlay all violent political change. Scott Nearing and some of the more "developed" students would then formulate this revolutionary law in a study which would form a preface to the book that was to be made of all the papers.

It was a good deal harder to enlist me in this project than in Jimmie Higgins work. I suspected that Marx, Engels, Lenin and others had already formulated history's laws of motion more effectively than most American Communists could do. I finally joined up, more to observe the mind of Scott Nearing at work than for the sake of anything it might work on.

For Nearing, unlike most others in the radical movement, was not a new name to me. When I was a boy, Scott Nearing had been a young, Socialist economics instructor at the University of Pennsylvania. In class, one day, he had made a slighting reference to the millionaire, Edward T. Stotesbury. An academic storm blew up. Nearing left the University of Pennsylvania, amidst shrill cries of "Perish freedom!" The hubbub fixed itself in my mind because my mother, who was in most ways intensely conservative, admired Nearing greatly and was one of his partisans. For Nearing's face was his fate. It combined intelligence with strength, was as native American as Gary Cooper and somewhat in the same style. Women always flocked around him and, even at the time I knew him, the devotion of his volunteer secretaries was a subject for smiles among Communists.

When I first began to explore the law of social revolution, Nearing was not a Communist. But he had made a trip to the Soviet Union and had come back, feeling, in the words with which the late Lincoln Steffens glowingly reported a similar experience to Woodrow Wilson: "I have seen the future and it works." Nearing had also attended the Pan-Asiatic congress, organized in Baku by the Communists shortly after the Russian Revolution, and had caught the first streaks of the revolutionary dawn roaring up from the East thirty years before it roared through China and into Korea. Presently he joined the American Communist Party. But he soon left it. He had a good, plain, uncomplicated mind; the theoretical subtleties of Marx and the tactical flexibilities of Lenin were foreign to it. He was an extreme individualist, with a stubborn streak and used to getting his own way; party discipline irked him. Moreover, he was simple and sincere, and the low-level factionalism of the Communist leaders revolted him. He was in fact his own species of Christian socialist, moved primarily by pacifism. He presently retired to a Vermont farm from which he issued to give lectures on the sad state of the world when not growing evergreens for the Christmas trade.

Nearing's students in social revolution were not predominantly Communist, either. There were two or three suburban spinsters and two or three unattached younger women. Most of them were engrossed less by the law of social revolution than by Nearing. There were two or three socialists or liberals. I can no longer remember even what those people looked like. But there was also an infiltration of Communists who really ran the class, steered the discussions and whose purpose it was to make the law of social revolution a Marxian law. Besides Sam and Carol Krieger, there were my old comrades Eve Chambers and her husband, David Benjamin, and one Jack Hardy whose real name was Dale Zysman.* He was a physical education instructor in the New York schools.

I never took the law of social revolution with a proper seriousness. The discussions were extremely dull and rambling, and nothing that I heard in the class has stayed in my mind as vividly as my memory of Scott Nearing conducting it. Like many American radicals, Nearing had very strong views about diet, leaning heavily towards small grains and berries, and holding, if I remember rightly, that meat was toxic. He would sit or stand in front of the social revolutionists, from time to time slapping into his mouth and chewing with audible energy handfuls of whole oats which he poured from a candy bottle that he always carried with him.

Most of the revolutions had been shared out before I joined the class. But the Hungarian Revolution of 1919 was still unclaimed, chiefly because most of the source material on it was in German. This revolution was assigned to me. I did a good deal of research in the subject and acquired a fairly firm grasp of the history of the Hungarian Soviet and the part played in it by Bela Kun and other Communists, and by the Socialists who had invited the Communists to take over the government which they shared with them. But I never wrote up my findings. The *Law of Social Revolution* appeared (in bright red paper covers) without benefit of the Hungarian Revolution. I made an effort to read the book, but decided at last that the world revolution would probably take place before I discovered what the law of social revolution was.

The class in social revolution led to two unexpected developments. One concerned the Kriegers. From the first, I had disliked Jack Hardy, who was both dull and bumptious. But I kept meeting him on my visits to Yonkers. For he and Carol Krieger were collaborating on one phase of the law of social revolution, and were so absorbed in their researches that he was constantly around the Krieger household.

One day, I found Sam Krieger fighting back his tears. Comrade Carol had run away with Comrade Hardy, taking the police dog,

* Circa 1941, Zysman's party membership was suspected or discovered. He was eased out of the schools in an incident that made a day's headlines. Later, he went to work for the Communist Labor Research Group, which included among others, Comrade Grace Hutchins, whom I have mentioned in the first section of this book.

too, I believe. I never saw Carol again. Sam also dropped from sight soon after. In the Communist Party, it would have been thought unseemly for Sam to express any disapproval of what had happened. For sex was held to be merely functional and of little importance except as it might help or harm the party.

But I had always felt that there were limits to Krieger's Marxism. He was a broken man. Perhaps he asked the party to find him an assignment in some area less memory-haunted than Yonkers. I had never felt very friendly toward my glassy-eyed sponsor in the Communist Party, and I never asked what had become of him. In any case, it would have done little good. For Communists, I was presently to note without paying much attention to the fact, were always dropping out of sight, and questions about them were usually answered with a shrugging: "Don't know."

The other development was of a very different kind.

VII

I did most of my reading about the Hungarian Revolution at my desk in the newspaper room of the New York Public Library. Among other books I read *Class Struggles and the Dictatorship of the Proletariat in Hungary.* Its author was Bela Szanto who had been assistant commissar for war in the Hungarian Soviet Government. Some years later, I was to see the commissar for war himself, Joseph Pogany, the brother of Willi Pogany, long a scene designer at the Metropolitan Opera House. Under the name John Pepper, Joseph Pogany was the Communist International's secret representative to the American Communist Party. But in those early days, I did not know that there were such things as secret representatives.

One night, when I was absorbed in Bela Szanto, I suddenly became aware that a little man had been standing beside me unnoticed for some moments. He was trying to read the title of my book, which was in German. He was short, dark, and dressed quietly with an air of extreme tidiness. His eyes were black, intelligent, friendly and fearless. But the expression of his face was odd; it was vigilant and yet it was withdrawn. He asked me in German what I was reading, and I told him. He asked me why, and I answered: "It interests me." He smiled and began to talk about the cast of characters in the Hungarian Soviet, which I knew fairly well by then, but which he discussed as if they were familiar friends.

He came back on other occasions to read the Budapest newspapers. We had several long talks, which were very helpful to me. It was the belief of my unknown friend that the Hungarian Soviet Government had fallen in large part because it had tried to keep the great landed estates intact, to turn them into collective farms, instead of dividing them among the peasants—a mistake that the Communist Party was careful never to make again. This, among other reasons, had caused peasant outbreaks—outbreaks which Tibor Szamuely, the half-demented head of the Hungarian secret police, had put down in person by stringing up the peasants to telephone poles. Their corpses were known as "Szamuely fruit."

One night my friend closed a conversation by saying: "*Sie sind ein Kommunist, natürlich?*—You are a Communist, of course?" "*Natürlich,*" I answered. He asked me if I would like to go home with him to continue our conversation. When we were on the street, he said: "You must not tell anyone that you know me or where I live." He said it simply, without any mystery or affectation. But now he addressed me with the familiar "*du,*" which European Communists use to one another in sign of fellowship.

Home was a very shabby building somewhere west of the Pennsylvania Station. It was a walk up through an unlighted hall to the top floor. The room itself was a monk's room. It was clean but almost completely bare. There was no rug on the floor. There were a table, two chairs, a bed. There was little or no heat. A monk's room—that is to say, in the 20th century, a Communist's room.

He did not offer me tea or coffee, which, in the case of a European Communist, means that there was none to offer. We sat down. "Now," he said, "we will discuss the organization and function of the Communist Party." He spoke quietly, in the carefully spaced and articulated German that many Hungarian Communists speak. He seldom paused, laying out his thoughts like a man turning the pages of a book. Sometimes, in summing up, he closed his eyes, as if that way he could better see the order of the propositions on the page. Much of what he taught me I would later find in Lenin's *What Is To Be Done*—the meaning of the professional revolutionist, the tasks, the discipline and duties of that modern secular secret order which has dedicated its life and its death to initiating a new phase of history for mankind.

I visited the room more than once. Sometimes my comrade returned to the subject of the Hungarian Revolution. For part of the reasons for the downfall of the Hungarian Soviet, he was inclined to credit the American Relief Administrator, Herbert Hoover, whom he blamed for withholding food from the Hungarians. Years later, on the occasion of the opening of the Hoover Library of War and Revolution at Palo Alto, I was to interview the former head of the American Relief Administration for *Time* magazine. While Herbert Hoover talked to me, I had the curious sensation of hearing the story that my Hungarian friend had told me run off in reverse. Hoover told me how, when the Soviet collapsed, he had rushed his food trucks up to the ministries and filled them with the invaluable archives that now rest in Palo Alto. It was the same story from the other side of two embattled lines between which there could be no communication or sympathy, between which I was by chance a human link.

Our conversations were less like conversations than instruction in the religious sense. There was an urgency behind my comrade's deliberate way of speaking. I felt that he had come upon me wholly unexpectedly, that he he was patiently sowing seeds, not knowing whether any would take root, but believing that they might.

One night he told me that we would not meet again, that he was going away. As we shook hands, he glanced at me shyly. "I am the representative of the West European Secretariat of the Communist International," he said. He never told me his name and I never saw him again.

This chance meeting was of the utmost importance to me as a Communist. It came at a critical moment when, despite my daily obeisance to the historical purpose of the party and my daily apologies for its inevitably low level, its human paltriness, alternating with spurts of low comedy, was becoming too much for me. Above all, I had to fight the sense that I was absolutely alone. In the Communist Party I found at first no one else remotely like me. I believed that my vision of the Communist was the right one, but when a man finds himself completely alone, he must always question if he can be right.

What my Hungarian comrade said to me, more impressively than any words he spoke, was that my vision of the Communists was not mistaken. He embodied it. He was it. He was a man simple but sinuous, warm but disciplined, ascetic but friendly, highly intelligent but completely unpretentious. He was a man with whom I could communicate with instant ease and understanding. Therefore, there were others. I was not alone. I had only to stand in my place, to be what I believed in being, and one day I would find that others were beside me. The example of the Hungarian representative kept me going as a Communist at the moment when I was first faltering, and the experience was reinforced by the fact that it coincided with the beginning of my brother's disaster. No contrast could have been greater.

VIII

In the Communist movement, I met two other intellectuals who were several cuts above the members of the Nearing study group. One of them was Sender Garlin, the nervous, red-headed young man who had arranged my first contact with the Communist Party. He was not yet a member of the Communist Party, though he soon became one. At that time he was working as a reporter for the *Bronx Home News*. He introduced me to someone of much greater specific gravity than himself—Harry Freeman, the younger brothei of Joseph Freeman, the writer.

I recently opened a copy of the *Saturday Evening Post* to a photograph that ran across the top of one page. It was a picture of a banquet for Vyacheslav Molotov. Beside the Soviet Foreign Minister, and turned toward him deferentially in conversation, was my old comrade, Harry Freeman. He was sleeker than he had been twenty-five years before, but, except for the fact that he wore a formal black tie, not otherwise much changed. He is now, and has been, in effect or in fact, for many years, the assistant chief in the United States of Tass, the Soviet Government's official news service.

When I first knew him, Harry Freeman was just out of Cornell University, where he had brilliantly majored in history. He was a very middle-class intellectual, extremely youthful-looking, but quietly self-assured and perfectly confident of himself. His face was slightly Mongoloid and suggested some of the pictures of Lenin as a youth. He spoke in a thin, whiny voice, but through that curiously inadequate voice functioned the best mind that I was to meet among the American Communist intellectuals. It was an entirely new type of mind to me. No matter how favorable his opinion had been to an individual or his political role, if that person fell from grace in the Communist Party, Harry Freeman changed his opinion about him instantly. That was not strange; that was a commonplace of Communist behavior. What was strange was that Harry seemed to change without any effort or embarrassment. There seemed to vanish from his mind any recollection that he had ever held any opinion other than the approved one. If you taxed him with his former views, he would show surprise, and that surprise would be authentic. He would then demonstrate to you, in a series of mental acrobatics so flexible that the shifts were all but untraceable, that he had never thought anything else. More adroitly and more completely than any other Communist I knew, Harry Freeman possessed the conviction that the party line is always right.

He had been an ardent admirer of Trotsky. "The three greatest minds of our times," he said to me more than once, "are Freud, Einstein and Trotsky." But the moment Trotsky fell from power, Harry Freeman became a Stalinist overnight, and so completely a Stalinist that he was outraged that I should suggest that he had ever been anything else. I dwell on this because he was a faultless example of the Stalinist mind—instantly manipulable, pragmatic, motivated by the instinctive knowledge that political position (contingent in the Communist Party on unfailingly correct official views) is indispensable to political power. And that power he desired, not for itself, but for revolutionary ends, for without political power, nothing can be achieved in history—certainly not a revolution. In personal relations, Harry Freeman was an extremely kind and even sensitive man. But his sensitivity never got in the way of his realism.

I remember that one day, when we were both working at the *Daily Worker* office on First Street, we walked up the Bowery together at noon. We were going to have lunch with Ruth Stout, the sister of Rex Stout, the detective story writer of Nero Wolfe fame. It was bitter cold and the wretched Bowery floaters, most of them without overcoats, were trying to find shelter in doorways or warmth beside pathetic fires. A shivering derelict came up to us and asked for a handout. Harry glanced past him, which was the proper Communist attitude. Communists hold that to give alms is to dull the revolutionary spirit of the masses, but I could never get out of my mind the fifty-cent piece that Jules Radon had left on my bed in New Orleans. I gave the wretched man what change I had in my pocket. He seized my hand and kissed it. The gesture was so shocking that I could not control my feelings. Harry drew me away. "You must not think about them," he said, very gently, for he, too, was deeply moved. "We can't save them. They are lost. We can only save our generation, perhaps, and the children." There spoke the Communist, and, from the Communist position, he was right and I was wrong.

I am convinced that Harry Freeman in his black tie, sitting next to Molotov behind the silver and the linen, still believes that he is saving the children. But his mind tells him that the way to save them is to exercise a certain kind of political power, and to have that power to exercise as a revolutionist, it is necessary to be adept in making instant adjustments to the official party line. Which is more important: the power or the adjustment? As a realist, Freeman would answer: the power.

That is the mind of the Communist bureaucrat. It is a kind of mind that, even as a Communist, I found alien to me. But it is a mind that I think I understand, and that I think most of its opponents do not understand, for they suppose that it is greedy only for power, and not the revolutionary ends which that power has in view. In that lies the danger of underestimating the force of faith that moves the enemy, and a failure also to grasp to what a degree the revolution has grown up and history has transformed the techniques of struggle. There are no more barricades. Communist power today rides in tank armies and conspires in black ties to overthrow its enemies. But the Stalinist has changed only his tie, not his mind.

IX

Harry Freeman kept urging me to write for the *Daily Worker*. He had joined its staff as soon as he joined the Communist Party. One day I went up with him to the crowded office on First Street; Harry introduced me as a likely volunteer writer (in those days about half of all the work done in the Communist Party was done by unpaid volunteers). Actually, I had never written a news story, had never thought about the problem and was as baffled by it as I would now feel if faced with assembling a hay baler.

Harvey O'Connor was then the effective editor of the *Daily Worker*. He was a former correspondent of the Federated Press, a labor news service that the Communist Party kept in one of its many pockets. Later, he was the author of *Mellon's Millions*, an unsympathetic account of Calvin Coolidge's secretary of the Treasury and the donor of the National Gallery. O'Connor was the first of several professional newsmen, Communists or sympathizers, who were drafted to make the unreadable *Daily Worker*, if not readable (Communist jargon made that practically impossible), at least more intelligible. After a brief, convulsive struggle, most of the pros threw up their hands and fled. O'Connor was not, I believe, a Communist.

He handed me a clipping from the New York *Times* and told me to write a snappy lead and "class-angle" the story. The story was about the activities of one General Sandino, a Nicaraguan officer, who had sharked up a parcel of bandits (known to the *Daily Worker* as "the anti-imperialist forces") and had taken to the hills, where he was standing off the national constabulary supported by the United States Marines. (The marines were presently to be recalled amidst pangs of "imperialist" bad conscience.) "Class-angling" meant to give the news a Communist interpretation. I felt quite equal to that, but, though I have written hundreds of them since, a snappy lead then seemed to me a feat beyond my powers.

I assume that I succeeded, for I was asked to write more and more for the *Worker,* still on an unpaid voluntary basis. I know now that I could scarcely have failed. No ability was needed on the *Daily Worker.* All that was needed was a dim notion of Communist theory and the audacity to face a typewriter. What resulted was then "edited"—a mysterious process for which nobody seemed responsible, least of all the nominal editor. It was quite a test of revolutionary devotion to read the *Daily Worker.*

With my brother's death, I stopped writing for the *Worker.* I stopped all party activities. I seldom saw my comrades. Once in a long while I met Harry Freeman. He was tactful; he gently raised the problem to the plane of reason. He was organically incapable of grasping it in any other way. He pointed out the illogicality of my brother's act, which he regarded as a purely individualist and negative solution to a struggle that demanded that men live for it, and die only when they had to. He pointed out the greater illogicality of my grief, which it was unseemly not to master, since, as a Communist, I should understand clearly the forces that caused such disasters as my brother's, and what to do about them.

I did not then know that reason and logic can be a blasphemy. Freeman's calm exasperated me. But, as my grief shrank, in hardening, into a core of unchanging anger, I decided to go back to the *Daily Worker,* as the most obvious thing I could see to do. Now I went as a full-time writer and was paid a starting salary of ten dollars a week, when I got it. Often nobody received any wages, for the *Worker* was always on the brink of bankruptcy.

X

The *Daily Worker* office was a long, narrow room with only two windows at the front. Desks were set end to end against the two long walls. There was so little space that the writers, facing the opposite walls, sat so close that the backs of their chairs almost touched. I have seldom seen an orderly editorial office, though I have known newsmen with a talent for dissembling disorder by filing it in their desk drawers, bookcases or against the wall. The *Daily Worker* writers disdained subterfuge. Each desk was a triumph of chaos. Editorial and human relations were much the same.

Harvey O'Connor had left some time before my return. No one was responsible for the orderly routing and flow of copy, and it sometimes happened that two or three writers were discovered to have written the same story. The paper's nominal editor was J. Louis Engdahl, a Communist in his late forties or fifties, who seldom paid any attention to what was going on, for, at the time, he was a prey to both political and emotional stresses of great intensity. He sat at the front of the office, at one of the two windows, usually staring fixedly out. At long intervals, he would beat out a page or two of copy, which was dull but at least intelligible. Engdahl himself was not. If you asked him a simple question, he would turn away and stare out the window. When you had about decided that he had forgotten you, he would turn around and fix you with his big round lenses that magnified his eyes to a slightly mad expression. Then he would grunt. Sometimes he mumbled a few words, scarcely audible. I do not remember hearing him utter five coherent sentences.

In his prime, he had been a Socialist in Wisconsin. He was now a follower of Jay Lovestone and had received the editorship of the *Daily Worker* as a prize in some factional deal. He felt that he was slipping. He also lived in terror of the telephone, for that seemed to be his wife's preferred way of reaching him, and he did not wish to be reached. When it rang, he would stare at it gloomily, then have someone else answer it. We always knew who was calling when we heard: "Comrade Engdahl is out of the office. No, I don't think he will be back."

Behind Editor Engdahl, at the other window, sat Comrade Vern Smith. Comrade Smith was a tall, folded-over man with a shock of white hair, startling because he had a youngish face that at first glance looked fatuous. It was only on closer inspection and closer acquaintance that you perceived that the face was also wary and shrewd, and that behind the averted blue eyes there was a wry humor. Vern seldom looked directly at anyone. He seldom glanced up from his typewriter. But now and again, without preface, he would suddenly read out a bit of news that struck him as funny, winding up with a wild chuckle. He was a prodigious producer of yard-long copy, a talent that was prized, for one of the horrors of make-up was that there would not be enough copy to fill the paper. His copy had a special merit, too. If by chance, there was too much copy, his could be cut at almost any point, and in almost any amount, without at all changing the sense, which was always in the first and last paragraphs.

Vern Smith was a stalwart of the Foster persuasion, a Westerner, who had once been a Wobbly. For some time, he edited the I.W.W. central organ, *Solidarity*. But his great friend, Harrison George, whom I shall presently come to, boasted one day at a labor congress in Moscow that the Communist Party was so successfully "boring from within" the I.W.W. that even the editor of *Solidarity* was secretly a Communist. The news shot back across the ocean and the enraged Wobblies promptly tossed out Brother Smith, who thereupon reappeared as Comrade Smith of the *Daily Worker*. Once Vern made some passing reference to his white hair and I asked him how he came by it. "Trucking dynamite across the Rocky Mountains in a broken-down Ford," he said dryly, and said no more.

I always suspected that Vern was a knife thrower of parts, but it was not until 1929 that I really saw him at work, gleefully expediting the purge of the Lovestoneites. In the 40's, he was purged himself for "incurable Browderism," and is now outside the official Communist Party.

Next to Vern Smith sat a woman comrade whom I shall call Angelica Ratoff. Comrade Ratoff was a good-looking woman in her upper thirties, very generously constructed, with graying hair and rather sultry brown eyes—something of a Carthaginian beauty. She was a rather sullen Bolshevik (women comrades are often more self-consciously ferocious than the men). But I noticed that she reacted in a very womanly way whenever Harry Freeman stroked her hair, called her "Angelica, darling," and asked a favor.

I cannot remember what Comrade Ratoff was supposed to do on the *Daily Worker*, though I remember that she was always shuffling papers. But, in any case, her presence there had less to do with the world revolution than with Comrade Engdahl.

Behind Comrade Angelica sat Comrade Tom O'Flaherty. He was

a big, unhappy Irishman, who lived sadly in the shadow of his celebrated brother, Liam, the author of *The Informer* and *The Assassin.* He drank heavily, and I have sometimes seen him lying, stiff and foul, in front of the Workers Center on Union Square. He was bad publicity. So he would be roughly lugged inside, amidst taunts and remarks of disgust, by men who were not worthy to touch him. For Tom O'Flaherty was a man of some gifts and a brisk sense of humor (always a heavy cross for a Communist). Secretly, he hated the bad journalism, the low gossip, base intrigues, the foolish and fetid factionalism around him. Secretly, and sometimes openly, he would gibe at them. The American party was aping the Russian style of abbreviating organizational names (the world had not yet been conditioned to alphabet soup). I once heard O'Flaherty solemnly propose to the humorless Engdahl that henceforth the *Daily Worker* should refer to the United Councils of Working Class Housewives as the Uncopwokwifs.

One day Tom O'Flaherty did not show up at the *Daily Worker* office. The revolution of the 20th century was over for him. He was dead, a pathetic exile from his country, his church and his world.

Next to Comrade O'Flaherty sat Comrade Chambers. Behind me sat a man who, for good and sufficient reasons, I shall call simply Comrade Fowler. He was a Lovestoneite, high in party circles and deep in party intrigue. He was later to be a delegate from the American Communist Party to one of the world congresses of the Communist International.

Unlike most of my colleagues, Comrade Fowler talked a great deal, and what he said was almost invariably venomous. From him I always learned the latest slanderous whispers in the party. But he was not simply a gossip monger. I had the impression that all life seemed to him clinically vile. I remember his reading me an obituary of some perfectly inoffensive public figure, and then snarling: "He probably died of a complication of foul diseases!" He was an epicure of social scandal and used to touch up what he read with details so solemnly and childishly obscene that it was difficult not to laugh at him.

But Comrade Fowler was himself the victim of malevolent gossip. There was a persistent rumor in the party that he was a stool pigeon. It would not down, and may perhaps account for some of his own maliciousness. At last, the Central Committee handed down a verbal "directive" (that word, borowed from the Russian Communists, had not yet mysteriously become a part of American bureaucratic patter) that the incident on which the rumor was based had taken place at the command of the party, and that anyone repeating the rumor was to be expelled forthwith. Comrade Fowler, I am told, has long ceased to be a member of the Communist Party.

Next to Comrade Fowler sat a young man whom I shall call Comrade Cecil Haddock. He was the *Daily Worker's* labor reporter, and extremely proud of the fact that he was a charter member of the Communist Party. But he left the party many years ago. I believe that he also turned out to be an "incurable right-wing deviationist."

What I chiefly remember about Comrade Haddock is that, late one night, he rushed into the big back room behind the editorial office. There the cartoonist, Fred Ellis, worked and party literature was stacked. Comrade Haddock was palpitant and his eyes were starting out of his head. His mouth hung open, his lips quivered and it was a moment before he could gasp: "Angelica . . . Angelica . . . And Louis (Comrade Engdahl). . . . In the office. . . ." After that he passed into babbling.

The comrades tiptoed to the editorial office door, for, in matters of sex, Communists, who deny that it has any importance, are invariably as prurient as gutter urchins. To their wild delight, all that Comrade Haddock had said was true. The story enlivened the party for months.

X I

I have drawn an ugly picture. It would scarcely be possible to exaggerate it. But this, too, must be said: However unpleasant the Communists on the *Daily Worker* might be as human beings, there was not one of them who did not hold his convictions with a fanatical faith; and there was scarcely one of them who was not prepared to die, at need, for them. That gave them a force.

Moreover, I have described the *Daily Worker* as I first knew it, when it was at its worst. A change was about to set in. It was embodied in men like Harry Freeman, who was writing foreign news, and Sender Garlin, who, after a period of sharing his services with the *Bronx Home News,* had joined the *Daily Worker* staff as a full-time writer just before I did. But like me, they were little more than cubs in those early days, and did not begin to play a part until a little later.

There were also certain figures whose relationship to the *Daily Worker* was rather erratic or mysterious, and who wandered in and out of that little universe, like comets, at unpredictable intervals. One of them passed through the office one day, trailing an air of self-conscious mystery. He was a slight, little man in a cap that did not go at all with his somewhat mournful face and small mustache. He tiptoed in and stood silently, looking over everyone's shoulder for a few moments, in the manner of an inspector general. He did not greet anyone. Later, I asked who he was and was told: "Earl Browder. He's just back from China." For, like Harrison George, who was then his brother-in-law, Browder had been a Comintern agent in the Far East. It was the first of my only two glimpses of the former typewriter repairman from Kansas and later secretary of the American Communist Party (now expelled).

Another native American also nested briefly in the *Worker* office. He was a lean, young fellow in his twenties, also self-consciously mysterious and self-important. He arrived amidst warnings that his presence was never to be mentioned. I cannot remember whether or not he ever had any name. He spent his days working with several file drawers of metal addressograph tags, which, I presently learned, were the names of men in the United States armed services. Just what he was doing with them I do not know. He soon went his unquiet ways.

Still another mysterious visitor was a man called Robert Mitchell. He was a sturdy, bald Communist with a plain, pleasant face, which had a disturbing way of hardening into an expression that seemed cunning and brutal. I soon learned that his real name was John Sherman, that he was then engaged in secretly organizing a strike of New York subway workers. He was in the *Daily Worker* office to write stories about them. His presence, too, was never to be mentioned.

I became very friendly with Sherman. Like me, he loathed the factional wrangle and felt that it was base and wasteful of energy, and he was unusually forthright in criticizing the august party leaders. He was the first man I had met in the party of whom I felt unqualifiedly: he is a revolutionist. After the subway strike, Sherman remained to write as a member of the *Daily Worker* staff, and I came to know him even better. For good or ill, he was to play a more important part in my life than almost any other human being I would ever know.

Two staff members of the *Daily Worker* managed to live a little apart from the editorial zoo. One was Bert Miller, the business manager. The other was Fred Ellis, the cartoonist. Fred Ellis was a plain, unpretentious man with very blue, childlike eyes and a quiet, unaccented American sense of humor—that is, it was dry, and dealt in the unexpected and absurd. Fred could spot any sham at a glance and skewer it at a thrust. He was a foundling and had never known who his parents were. He told me one day how moved he had been at the birth of his child, who was the first family of his own blood he had ever known, so that he no longer felt himself to be a man absolutely alone in the world.

Ellis had begun as a sign painter in Illinois (he was as Midwest as corn) and had become a very good cartoonist. But he was not particularly political, and, as a political cartoonist, he suffered from a serious handicap—a lack of political ideas. Quite by chance one day, we discovered that I, who could not draw at all, could think up cartoon ideas with little effort. As long as we were on the *Worker* together, I pinch hit as Fred's idea man.

In those days Bert Miller was a harassed soul. As business manager of the *Daily Worker*, the future research director of the House Committee on Un-American Activities had to meet a weekly payroll and find money to pay the paper, print and other bills. Money was very hard to find and his life was a weekly crisis. Thus, my chief recollection of Bert Miller from the past is less as a face than as a weary plaint: money.

Bert suffered other grievances too. In his business office, he presided over a number of young women Communists, one of whom was a remarkably pretty Hungarian girl. He often protested that his girls were terrified to walk through the *Daily Worker* office (as they sometimes had to do) because, while they wriggled their way past the crowded chairs, each of the editors in turn reached back and pinched them.

X I I

I had not joined the *Daily Worker* staff simply to become a news writer or even because I was particularly interested in writing news. I joined it because it offered me the most obvious base from which to work as a Communist.

In looking around for ways to do this, I found them in an unexpected place and one that did not interest my colleagues at all, so that I had a completely free hand in the matter. Somewhere, in the past, I had read that Lenin attached the greatest importance to "worker correspondence"—the letters which simple workers in the shops, or soldiers and sailors in the services, or peasants, voluntarily wrote to the party. Those letters were filled with grievances, specific accounts of working conditions and wage conditions, suggestions for elementary organization. This was the arterial flow between the working class and the Communist Party that could feed each with the purpose of the other.

In the *Daily Worker* office this flow was completely blocked. Scores of such letters reached the paper, and lay, unanswered, gathering dust in heaps until they were swept into a trash basket to make room for more. I first began to read them simply for their wonderfully fresh accounts of working-class conditions. Sometimes they were heartrending. A worker, unemployed and ill, after a lifetime of labor, would describe how it feels to lie unwanted and disabled on the human dump-heap of the modern world. Sometimes the writer would add: "I am sending you all I can spare, a dime." For the *Daily Worker*, bad as it was, had given him something he found nowhere else: hope.

I volunteered to answer these letters and to edit the best ones for publication in the *Worker*. My comrades knew what Lenin had said about worker correspondence. They readily agreed. I caught the smiles of wise amusement. It was an inglorious little chore that would keep me busy and keep me from writing news stories (Communist newsmen are competitive too), and the letters made useful boiler plate to plug those occasional gaps in the *Daily Worker* at make-up time.

With the publication of the first letters, a dike broke. Letters poured in. My surprised comrades suddenly found themselves in touch with the force they lacked the simple humanity and revolutionary imagination to contact, but which, nevertheless, was the force they had at heart. The worker correspondence was like a sensitive antenna catching the least stirrings among the otherwise soundless masses. Long before the New Bedford and Fall River textile strikes broke out, around 1927, the worker correspondence had picked up the groundswell. Sometimes it picked up other things too. One of the most tireless worker correspondents turned out to be a stool pigeon in the Nash plant at Kenosha, Wisconsin.

Every year, the Executive Committee of the Communist International sent from Moscow a critique of the successes and failures of the *Daily Worker*. There was seldom anything but failure to report, and the critiques were long, dull and depressing. The critique that arrived the year the worker correspondence began was read at a noon-hour staff conference. I cut it, characteristically, for, whether at the *Daily Worker* or at *Time,* staff conferences wearied me. When I returned to the office, I found my comrades united in a most unusual smile of welcome. Moscow had spoken. The Communist International had roundly damned all of the *Daily Worker* with a single exception. It saw in worker correspondence the first evidence that the paper had struck roots among the American working class. Suddenly, I had become the indispensable man. It was decided that I must have an assistant to help me with my immense task.

Lenin had said: "The role of the Bolsheviks is patiently to explain." I thought that the role of the Bolsheviks was also patiently to act. A man had only to act as a Communist, however humble, and the results, I then believed, would take care of themselves.

XIII

My assistant turned out to be Nathan Honig, who had slid into the *Worker* staff almost unnoticed. I first became aware of him when I found him arriving at the office before me in the morning. Sometimes we worked a half day together in the office before anybody else arrived. He was an odd-looking young man, with owlish, greenish eyes and a head that seemed to have been briefly pressed in a vise. His manner, too, was odd. He was given to deliberately irrelevant answers and rather staggering impudence, and he liked to play the idiot. Slowly, I perceived that, like many sporadically impudent people Honig was painfully shy. His idiocy was part of a defensive act. Actually, his judgment about problems and people was surprisingly shrewd and sound. Like Fred Ellis, he had a litmus reaction to sham, but unlike Fred, Honig was infuriated by it and instantly attacked it. He was honest, devoted and a tireless worker, and his sallies against the party bigwigs, factionalism and corruption made many of his colleagues wince. But they seldom ventured reprisals, for he had one great advantage. Unlike most of them, he was an authentic proletarian. He came of a working-class family in Bayonne, New Jersey, where his father was a cooper (a dying skill) at the Standard Oil Company's works.

This gave him a special license to criticize the party's blunders, usually in the form of funny stories of which he had a fund. I remember one about a strike of oil workers in Bayonne. The party learned of it belatedly, but decided to try to wedge into the leadership. To address the strikers, it sent down the only proletarian available, a nervous young Hungarian from New York City. He stared out across the mass of hulking men packed into one of the big yards. "Comrades," he said, "I bring you striking oil workers the support of twenty striking dental mechanics in New York." The roar of laughter that greeted his words effectively shut the party out of the strike.

In time, my original feeling about Honig changed into respect and then into esteem. When my responsibilities increased on the *Worker,* Honig was one man on whom I could rely and absolutely trust. I lost track of him after I went underground and never saw him again. But rumors reached me that Honig had been sent to Russia for special training, and that, as soon as he could return to the United States, he broke with the Communist Party and repudiated Communism.

The worker correspondence also resulted in two other experiences: my first party editorship and my first contact with a party underground cell. As a result of New Bedford and Fall River textile strikes, the Communist Party organized the National Textile Workers Union. I was chosen by the Central Committee to co-edit the union paper, *The Textile Worker,* together with Michael Intrator (accent on the In). Intrator had also been taken onto the *Daily Worker* staff to cover the needle trades and other labor news. Until then he had been a fur worker and a good mechanic at his trade. He had been brought up on the lower East Side. He had a mind largely untrained and unschooled, but direct, forceful and supple, with an unerring ability to drive to the heart of any discussion or problem. He also had an endless intellectual curiosity. He first opened up to me the violent life of the needle trades, which, until then, had seemed to me more like a national minority than a trade-union movement. From him I first learned that the Communist Party employed gangsters against the fur bosses in certain strikes. From him I first learned how Communist union members would lead their own gangs of strikers into scab shops and in a few moments slash to pieces with their sharp hooked fur knives thousands of dollars worth of mink skins. Sometimes the Communists and their opponents fought pitched battles in the fur market, in one of which Intrator himself was stabbed, though he paid no attention to the wound until he collapsed from it.

Intrator gave me a sense of the working class at its most intelligent and militant. He was, besides, simple, human, humorous. We became close friends. He was, in fact, the only close friend I ever had in the open Communist Party. Our friendship survived all the changes of our party lives and often important differences of political opinion and activity. In 1929, Intrator was expelled as a Lovestoneite. The party did everything to make it impossible for him to get or keep a job. At one time, the Communist terror in the fur market was such that he had to carry a revolver to defend himself. That was while I was in the underground. We still remained friends. No one pled with me more strongly than he to break with the Communist Party. No one supported me more loyally after I had broken with it. Distance and experience have separated us in the last decade, but we retain for each other the special friendship of those survivors who feel: we went through it together.

The underground cell to which I referred was in the Johnson and Johnson factory at New Brunswick, New Jersey. I do not know who organized it. But, at one point, the party decided that, as worker-correspondence editor, I should be attached to the cell and attend its meetings.

For that purpose, I was introduced to Comrade Gertrude Haessler, a brisk, red-headed, somewhat leathery young woman, the sister of Carl Haessler, who was then, I believe, the head of the Federated Press. Gertrude Haessler was the wife of William Weinstone, Communist organizer of the New York-New Jersey district of the party.

Comrade Haessler first drove me out to New Brunswick, past the J. and J. factory and the Rutgers campus, to the house of a workingman where the meeting was held. She seemed to have general supervision of its activities. There were seven or eight Communists in the secret cell. All worked for Johnson and Johnson. All were Hungarians. One of them had served in the Hungarian Red Army under Bela Kun.

Few of them spoke much English and the meetings were conducted in Hungarian of which I know only a few words. I could not have attended more than four or five meetings of this cell. For the secret comrades presently decided to have Communist leaflets distributed at the factory gates by their children and others. The police picked up one or two of the children. Their mothers protested to their fathers. One comrade's wife made him leave the party and the cell broke up.

Before that disaster, Bert Miller had one night accompanied Comrade Haessler and me to New Brunswick. As we drove through the almost continuous industrial plant that extends from Jersey City to the Raritan River, Comrade Miller's eyes began to glow. I had the impression that he had never been outside of New York City before. We passed one vast factory whose buildings stretched for blocks. Bert looked at it in awe and asked me what it was. "The Worthington Pump Company," I told him. "We must get in here," he said solemnly.

XIV

I made one other trip to New Jersey that was to be much more momentous to me in a personal way. Albert Weisbord, a studious young trade unionist, then or later a member of the Central Committee (subsequently expelled for some special political heresy), had organized a great strike of the textile workers at Passaic. It was a long, stubborn struggle with recurrent violence. The authorities had repeatedly forbidden the strikers to demonstrate. Many of the workers were women, and they defied the ban by marching through the police, pushing their babies in carriages while the demonstration followed them.

The *Daily Worker* sent Harry Freeman and me to cover one of those prohibited demonstrations. We were sent only to observe and were strictly forbidden to take part in the march or the fights. We blended with the crowds along the sidewalks.

The strikers were in one of the strike halls. The doors were shut and the police were massed in force to keep them shut and to keep the strikers from marching. Inside, the strikers were evidently buzzing like swarming bees. Now and again, the doors would be thrown partly open. The police would close in and slam them shut again. At last the doors were forced wide open, apparently by the weight of massed men and women strikers behind them.

A slender girl in a brown beret rushed out before the police could stop her. The demonstration surged after her. "Get that bitch in the brown beret," an officer shouted. Without flinching, she walked forward as the police closed in, swinging their clubs. But the demonstration poured over them and swept them back. "There," I thought, "is a Communist."

I was mistaken. After the demonstration, Harry Freeman and I rode back to New York by train with a little group that had taken part in the march. Opposite me sat the girl in the brown beret. With her black bobbed hair, she looked like a Russian. She was very forthright and militant. I noticed particularly that her dark brown eyes were of a candor and purity such as I had never seen in any other woman in the Communist movement.

I was told that her name was Esther Shemitz. She was not a Communist, but a pacifist. Like her friend, who sat beside her, a Southern girl named Grace Lumpkin, whom I have mentioned in the first part of this book, Esther Shemitz was on the staff of *The World Tomorrow*, a pacifist magazine. Like me, she had been sent to report the strike. I thought that I had seldom seen a less pacific pacifist. I did not then know that even the mention of the word blood sometimes makes her faint, but the slightest hint of injustice or cruelty enrages and makes her fearless. Neither of us could foresee that, twenty years later, under the brutal bullying of Lloyd Paul Stryker, the same force that made her walk toward the police clubs would make her cry out in the first Hiss trial: "My husband is a great man and a decent citizen."

Esther Shemitz is my wife.

X V

The Communist lives in permanent revolt and anger against the injustice of the world around him. But he will suffer almost any degree of injustice, stupidity and personal outrage from the party that he serves. He may fuss, whimper, harangue and even intrigue. But he will not act openly against the authority of the party. For to do so would be to breach discipline. And discipline is not only, to this great secular faith, what discipline is to an army. It is also what piety is to a church. To a Communist, a deliberate breach of discipline is an act of blasphemy. Only an intolerable situation can make it possible or even imaginable.

The situation at the *Daily Worker* had become intolerable. Engdahl's editorial incompetence had brought the paper close to anarchy, and his personal behavior was demoralizing the staff. Vern Smith (no doubt with factional motives in mind, too) drew up a petition to the Central Committee of the party, asking for Engdahl's immediate removal. He proposed that all staff members sign it. Harry Freeman, Sender Garlin, John Sherman, Vern himself and I signed.

In the Communist Party, it was equivalent to mutiny on the

high seas, for Engdahl had been appointed by the Central Committee. Vern Smith and one of the other signers took the petition to national headquarters on 125th Street. There was consternation. It was not entirely due to the breach of discipline. Another peculiarly Communist attitude entered in. Revolutionists have a respect, amounting to awe, for the signed document. They have broken, or are trying to break, the continuity of order in society. By that act, they repudiate tradition, and the chaos they thereby unloose also threatens them, for they can no longer count on the inertia or authority of tradition to act as a brake or a bond on chaos. Hence that fussy attention which revolutionists pay to mere legalistic forms that puzzles outsiders both in the case of the Nazis and the Communists—their meticulous regard for protocol and official papers. Hence the tiresome detail and massive fictions of their legal and constitutional procedures, and the formal pettifoggery, with all the i's dotted, of a secret police that works entirely beyond the law. For in breaking the continuity of tradition, the revolutionist, for his own sake, must seek a cementing substitute. All he has left to fall back on, the mark of his blighting touch upon life's tissues, are those dead papers, interminable procedures, formidable quiddities—and his incongruous regard for them.

The petition as a document frightened the party brass. Speaking, if I remember rightly, through its national chief of propaganda and agitation, Bertram D. Wolfe, the party sternly informed the insurgents that the petition was impermissible, that Engdahl must remain as editor. Secretly, in the way of politics and politicians the world over, it prepared to get rid of him as a liability.

Since he could not be kicked downstairs without reproach to his faction, the Lovestoneites, he had to be kicked upstairs. He was presently sent to fill a post where unusual intelligence, alertness, human understanding and organizational talent were required: chairman of the International Labor Defense, which had in its care all legal and human relations involving workers and Communists who have been arrested or imprisoned as a result of strikes, demonstrations or other "class war" activities.

This perpetuation of dead wood constantly presents the party with a bureaucratic problem. It solves it in part through its periodic purges. Then it savagely and inhumanly rids itself of the clogging weight, which political expediency has retained for a while, and which the party has never devised any more efficient method of casting off. Then the party arbitrarily destroys the individuals whom it arbitrarily inflated and kept afloat, usually by casting them into the darkness outside its pale, by expulsion from its ranks. For the party "housecleaning" (*chiska* in Russian) is a permanent feature of Communist life. Only the Great Purge employed the "wet method"—bloodshed.

X V I

"And *what* do *you* do, com-rade?"

I glanced up from my desk to find peering over my shoulder a face that I had never seen before. It was an arresting face. I thought then that it was a good face (later on, I was to find that, in the way of human faces, it could sometimes be a troubled and a foolish face). Under a workingman's cap, two small dark eyes, like an old bull elephant's, twinkled on either side of a pugnacious nose. The chin was strong, the cheekbones prominent, like an Indian's. But the face lacked height, as if the chin and scalp had been squeezed forcibly together. And the tufts of gray hair around the ears and the trace of benevolence in the eyes suggested, not a revolutionist so much as Santa Claus.

The face belonged to Robert Minor, the son of a Texas judge, who had given up a career as one of the great American cartoonists to devote his life to Communism, to neglect his great draughting talent for the sake of becoming a factional politician for which he had no talent at all, so that he was forever backing the wrong group and the wrong man, doomed to make humiliating, eleventh-hour switches and recantations, and to be the butt and pawn of little men who could comprehend neither his indivisible faith nor his ultimate profound humility.

Comrade Minor had just returned from Moscow. The Central Committee had just decided that he was to succeed Comrade Engdahl as editor of the *Daily Worker*. Minor was making his preliminary tour of inspection. But, as the fallen Engdahl was still sitting at his desk, Minor was treading softly, politically and physically.

I explained to him the nature of worker correspondence. He did not interrupt me. When I had finished, he answered in his drawling voice, punctuated with odd stresses and inflections, that sometimes made it seem as if he were translating everything he said from Russian, which he spoke fluently. "Whain I was in *Mos*—coww," he said, "*Com*-rade Boookhh-*har*-reen (Bukharin) sayed to me—he sayed: 'Workers correspondence *izz* one of our *most* important act-i-vi-ties.'" Then the bearer of the oracle laid a fatherly hand on my shoulder and passed on to the next revolutionist.

Minor was scarcely out of the office before Sender Garlin, who was a superb mimic, had out a handful of filing cards and was giving the staff an imitation of Comrade Minor making a soap box oration. It ended: "Whain I wazz in *Mos*-coww; *Com*-rade Boookhh-*har*-reen sayed to me, sayed to me—he sayed (business of searching frantically through the notes on the filing cards) Ah! Here it is! He sayed to me: 'Workers of *thee* worald, *yew*nite!'"

Minor at once set about raising staff morale (by the simple method of paying wages occasionally, for one thing) and by tightening up the editorial routine. He crowded the office with new talent. Fred Ellis (who all but reverenced Minor as a cartoonist, but deplored him as a politician) used to describe his new editor as standing on the Bowery, gathering in the air with welcoming arms while he called to the floaters: "Come *een!* Come *een!* There are jobs for e-ver-y-bo-dy."

Minor's first elementary reform was to set up a copy desk to originate stories and control the flow of copy. At its head, he first placed Sterling Bowen, a pale, horse-faced recruit with sad eyes, who had worked with one of the Detroit newspapers and was then on the *Wall Street Journal.* Bowen had been an I.W.W. and wrote poetry in his off-hours.

Like the other professionals, he soon vanished. He was presently replaced by another veteran newsman and a Communist—C. Marion Hatch. Comrade Hatch was a thin, sharp-featured man, with popping, reddish-brown hare's eyes, and a face that grew turkey red when he was having tantrums. He had them often as a matter of editorial procedure. He had been an editor of one of the Vanderbilt tabloids in Florida. He at once set about keeping elaborate copy and work charts and turning the central organ of the American Communist Party into a tabloid. As he was short on Communist experience and theory and long on city-desk techniques, he soon found himself faced by a stolid, revolutionary opposition. Hence his tantrums. The comrades resented his lack of ideology, but they resented even more his efficiency, and he was undeniably efficient. Patiently, they waited for his downfall. It came in the form of a baby.

The *Daily Worker,* as befitted the mouthpiece of the world revolution, was a densely solemn sheet, because that was exactly how the comrades wanted it. Hatch dreamed of "brightening it up," of introducing "human interest." Somehow, the staff editors usually managed to defeat him. But late one night, when most of his colleagues had gone home, Hatch ordered the front page of the *Worker* to be torn out. He inserted a news photo that had come in from one of the picture services, and sent the paper to press.

In the morning, when the "general staff of the world revolution" opened its central organ, a baby, a naked little foundling, lying on its stomach, stared cheerfully at them from the front page. A shudder of horror passed through the party. "A baby!" said Comrade Fowler in the same tone in which he had snarled "complication of foul diseases." "Deliberately making us ridiculous in the eyes of the masses!" Most of the *Daily Worker* staff merely thought the baby convulsively funny.

But the Central Committee was appalled. There was a rumble of thunder from 125th Street and a buzz of rumor about Hatch's summary dismissal. Minor blocked that. But the dictatorship of the city desk was broken, though Hatch adjusted himself very neatly to the change and still managed to force a minimum of efficiency on some of the least efficient men on earth. For he discovered that he had allies in Freeman, Garlin, Honig and Chambers. At that point, the younger men began to emerge and presently to manage the *Daily Worker*.

Hatch was not only a better newsman than any of us. He was to that degree a better revolutionist. The value of babies to the class war would soon be recognized wherever the Communist press had a mass circulation.

XVII

I managed to be an active Communist for several years without ever attending a unit meeting. About the time that I went to the *Daily Worker*, the old organization of the Communist Party in branches, which had been borrowed from the Socialist Party, was abolished. The party was "Bolshevized," as it was called. It was reorganized in smaller units, beginning with what is now called a cell, but was then awkwardly called a "nucleus." There were street nuclei and factory nuclei. The street nuclei comprised the Communists living in a small city area. The factory nuclei included the Communists in one shop. In those days, there were many street nuclei and, except in the needle trades, very few factory nuclei.

I was assigned to a street nucleus. But the confusion that resulted from the wholesale organizational change was wonderful to behold, and in the confusion the party lost track of a number of people, including me. Everyone assumed that I was in some unit, but nobody troubled to ask which one. Since most party meetings are at night, my night hours on the *Daily Worker* soon made party meetings practically impossible anyway. I am so made that I dislike any meeting. Party meetings, dull, quarrelsome and interminable, were unbearable. Still I would have borne them but for something else. It was impossible to attend party meetings and not be drawn into the factional struggle. This I was determined should not happen to me. So I dropped out of that dreary side of party life, which is almost a complete blank to me.

The party was then divided into two "caucuses"—Lovestoneite and Fosterite. But a third group had also emerged—the Trotskyists, the American followers of the former Soviet commissar for war, who, at the time I am writing about, was on the point of being expelled from the Communist Party of the Soviet Union. Their leaders were James Cannon, the brother-in-law of Dr. Philip Rosenbliett, a Soviet agent whom I was presently to know very well indeed, and Max Schachtman. Max Schachtman was a bright young intellectual, who, among other activities, was given to writing mischievous jingles about party leaders. It was by way of one such jingle that I first became aware of an inconspicuous member of the Central Committee whom I had never seen, and knew nothing about except that he had a good many children, but who was presently to play a brief, decisive role in my life. The jingle went:

There was an old man named Bedacht,
Who had kids to the number of acht, etc.

But it was not Comrade Bedacht, whom I may have seen a dozen times without knowing who he was, who then disturbed me. Nor was it Dr. Rosenbliett whose office I must have passed, like thousands of others, not knowing that a dozen threads of international conspiracy were knotted behind its ground-glass doors. What disturbed me was the expulsion of Comrade Trotsky from the Communist Party on grounds that I believed to be unjust if not wholly fraudulent, and two aftermaths of that expulsion—the expulsion of Trotsky's American followers and a brief cable from Moscow that came to the *Daily Worker* office.

I was not then and never have been a Trotskyist. Insofar as I understood the issues between Trotsky and Stalin (and it was all but impossible to dig them out of the rich coating of recrimination and deliberate double talk with which they were caked), I was for Stalin and against Trotsky. What disturbed me deeply was the spectacle of the calculated degradation by lies and slander of the man who, after Lenin, was undeniably the Communist Party's best brain, and one of the outstanding political minds of the age. I felt, too, that a party which could conclude a decisive debate on strategy and tactics only by physically expelling an intelligent and very big minority group, betrayed a weakness that might become fatal. It was not only the despotic action that outraged me. It was the sure sense that only from a meeting of its best minds, even in tension, could be evolved those policies which alone would enable the party to solve the immensely complicated problems of revolutionary struggle posed by history in our age. I was sickened rather than aroused by a struggle in which I had had no part, and I kept my thoughts largely to myself. But that struggle was to touch me personally in a tiny way that I was never to forget.

The Communist International maintained a news service called Inprecorr (International Press Correspondence). It was published in Moscow (and perhaps Berlin) in several languages, including English. It reported all the weekly news of the Communist world and the proceedings, often in full, of the great Communist congresses. This service was used, practically unedited, in the Communist press all over the world. On live news, the Inprecorr also sent cables direct from Moscow to the *Daily Worker* and other Communist papers.

The day after the Soviet secret police seized Trotsky and packed him off to exile in Southern Siberia, one of the Inprecorr cables reached the *Daily Worker*. It was given to me to transcribe and write up, perhaps to test me, perhaps because no one else wanted to touch so hazardous, or so shameless, an item.

The cable was brief. It said, as nearly as I can recall: "Trotsky left Moscow today for Alma Ata with six carloads of baggage and his hunting dogs. At the railroad stations, the peasants gathered and asked: 'What great lord is this passing through the land?'" I transcribed it almost as it was. I felt helpless and ashamed.

It was several years before I would hear of the terrible insight that came to Lenin as he lay dying, and babbled from one side of his half-paralyzed mouth: "The machine has got out of control."

At the time, I knew only that the party and its purposes were greater than any man in it, greater than Lenin, greater than

Comrade Trotsky, and certainly greater than Comrade Chambers.

But, like a hot ash, the cable left on my mind a tiny, ineradicable char.

XVIII

Wages on the *Daily Worker* were so intermittent and so small that I began to look around to see if I could not make a little money in my spare time. My college friend, Clifton Fadiman, was then a reader at Simon and Schuster, the New York book publishers. He offered to let me try my hand at translating a little German book. It was about a deer named Bambi and was written by an Austrian, of whom I had never heard, named Felix Salten.

I thought the story rather sentimental, but it brought back to me my boyhood days in the woods, when I was watching the flight and pursuit of creatures under the ponds or among the grass stems. I made the translation. *Bambi* was an instant success, and I suddenly found myself an established translator. But I did not have time for the generous offers that came to me from capitalist publishers. The *Daily Worker* kept me too busy. And the party, suddenly awakened to the fact that I could translate from several languages, put me to work.

I was given a pamphlet by one of the French Communist leaders, Jacques Doriot. It was a report of his experiences in the Chinese revolution, which he had recently observed as member of a delegation from the Communist International. I was told that the translation must be done in a few days. So, after his work at the *Daily Worker,* the translator of *Bambi* hammered out the translation of Doriot—not for pay, of course. It was done in time. But it was never published. Even before I had completed it, Doriot had fallen from political grace. During World War II, he was chief of the fascist militia under the Vichy Government until he was killed by Allied strafing.

XIX

Some time in 1927 or 1928, an own-your-home impulse struck the Central Committee of the Communist Party. No doubt, several of its members on their illegal travels about Europe had been struck by the splendid headquarters and other real estate owned by the prosperous and self-supporting German Communist Party, and wished at least the semblance of something like it.

It was decided to buy an old building on the east side of Union Square. How the party paid for it I do not know. I heard whispers about the needle trades, "angels" and a mortgage from the Amalgamated Bank, which was controlled by the needle trades and which stood just across Union Square from the new Communist property. This holding was named the Workers Center.

The ground floor was remodeled as a great cafeteria. Its walls were devoutly muraled by artists from the John Reed Club, a Communist-controlled cultural organization. The effect was a foretaste of the murals that, in W.P.A. days, were to astonish citizens on the walls of United States post offices; in fact, John Reed Club artists participated in both achievements. The murals depicted workers and peasants, usually with heads that looked as if they had been carelessly carved out of soap, and muscles bulging like the sinews of lions and bulls in Assyrian bas-reliefs.

Under this ordeal of labor, a vast swarm of idlers chatted and wrangled most of the day and night. The cafeteria was soon known as the "zoo" and for its patrons Sender Garlin changed the term "rank and file" to read "the rank and vile." The *Daily Worker* writers preferred a little Spanish restaurant around the corner, where they could get a platter of saffron rice for twenty cents and eat it among sedate and quietly talking Spanish workingmen, whose faces were sometimes solemn, sometimes vivacious, and who were so thin that they seemed to have no muscles at all.

For the *Daily Worker* had moved into the Workers Center too. It occupied, if I remember rightly, the third or fourth floor. Above it were mysterious regions which I was to penetrate only on one mysterious occasion. On the lower floors were the pressroom, the business office and the offices of *Uj Elöre,* the Hungarian Communist weekly. The *Daily Worker* office occupied a whole floor. It was dominated by a vast copy table, designed and built under the personal direction of Robert Minor. It stood at the front of the office under the windows that overlooked the Square. At one side, was Editor Minor's private office, which was usually empty, for Minor spent most of his time in the more tremendous political atmosphere of national headquarters, dropping down upon the *Worker* chiefly late at night. His appearances were as frantic as they were fleeting, for he was usually dashing to make the late train for

Croton-on-Hudson, where then, as now, a number of Communists and sympathizers maintained summer *dachas*.*

At the slot of the gigantic copy desk sat Harry Freeman. Like all the men who successively sat in that slot, he was in effect the editor of the *Daily Worker*. For Comrade Hatch, after doing as much as any man could to whip the recalcitrant *Worker* into shape, had whipped off to do the last thing so dry and unimaginative a man might be expected to do—write a novel.

When Harry Freeman took over the copy desk, I took over his old job as foreign-news writer, and Honig took over my old job as worker-correspondence editor.

X X

Harry Freeman did not sit at the copy desk very long. His journalistic talents could have made him a career anywhere. Those, together with certain other qualifications, were about to carry him into a post that any Communist newsman might covet. He also used his social talents, quietly and effectively.

Harry, his wife, and his brother Joseph Freeman shared a fairly sumptuous apartment on Henry Street in Brooklyn Heights. I sometimes found myself wondering how they could afford it, but I supposed that Joe's salary as an employe of Tass (the official Soviet news service) paid the rent. The apartment had been sublet from Eugene Lyons, a former Tass man himself; at that time a United Press correspondent in Russia, and a Soviet sympathizer. (In 1937, his fierce indictment of the Soviet Government and Communism in *Assignment in Utopia* was one of the books that influenced my break with Communism.)

I was one of several *Daily Worker* people who sometimes spent pleasant evenings at the Freemans'. Among the others were Sender Garlin and Abe Magill, a solemn young Philadelphian, known, for his humorless ponderosity, as the "rabbi Magill," and more recently as one of the party's profounder theoretical minds. There was also Sol Auerbach, better known by his party name of James Allen. Auer-

* Besides Minor and his wife, the affluent Lydia Gibson, William Gropper, the artist, and his family, Harry Freeman and his wife (Vera Schap, the sister of Al Schap, in my time an organizer of the Young Communist League); Joseph North, of the *Daily Worker* and the *New Masses*, and his family; Anna Rochester and Grace Hutchins. These two implacable revolutionists named their rural retreat "The Little Acorn."

bach succeeded me as foreign-news writer at the *Daily Worker.* Later, he became the chief editor for International Publishers, the official Communist book-publishing house, whose manager, Alexander Trachtenberg, was a member of the party's Central Control Commission.

At the Freemans', too, I met Nadya Pavlov and her husband who was employed by Amtorg, the Russian American Trading Corporation. The Pavlovs were Russian Communists, and frantic Trotskyists (before Trotsky's downfall). Nadya, a bright, alert, belligerent Bolshevik, who wore her black hair in the official bob, used to insist, especially in her cups, that I was not a Communist, but a peasant—"simply a Russian peasant." At the time, that used to annoy me. But perhaps she was more right than either of us knew, and, curiously, she was not the only Russian who would make the same observation.

The centerpiece of the Henry Street evenings was Kenneth Durant and his wife. Durant was a bony, dark, saturnine scion of a well-to-do Philadelphia family. He combined a razor-shap intelligence with executive inaccessibility (at that time, he was the head of Tass in the United States). I remember him best for the acrobatic contortions with which he would wrap himself around the Freemans' big billiard table, the icy precision of his shots and the equally icy (and flagrant) rudeness with which he would turn away from billiards to crush his ebullient wife with a few terse, depressing words.

His wife was a big, plump girl in her thirties. The short skirts of the period and a somewhat babyish expression made her look like a grown woman who, by a characteristic lapse of judgment, had got herself up as a tot for a fancy-dress ball. She used to suffer her husband's jolting rudeness with skin-crawling meekness. I used to pity her, but perhaps that was not necessary. During the Great Purge, it was feared for a while that she had been liquidated by the Russian secret police. But she had merely dipped out of sight in the course of a private itinerary that had taken her from England, through Scandinavia into Finland.

One day Harry Freeman informed me, in strictest secrecy, that he was leaving the *Daily Worker* and going to assist Kenneth Durant at Tass. Later, I used to visit him at the Tass office. Sometimes he returned the call at the *Daily Worker.* His old loyalties were strong, and, though Tass employes were strictly forbidden to engage in American Communist activities, Harry would now and again knock out a foreign-news story for the *Worker.* Those were my last glimpses of him. I do not recall seeing Harry Freeman after 1929.

Sender Garlin took over Freeman's old post at the copy desk.

XXI

Like Freeman, Garlin was an able newsman. But he was not a good editor. In his fussiness or excitement over detail, the main editorial threads snarled in his hands. No editor but Hatch had ever made the mail trains to the West. Garlin succeeded in missing them by wider margins than most. The linotypers, who could make or break the edition in the last hour before the deadline, disliked him and deliberately sabotaged his work. His inspired mimicry of everyone made the older comrades fear (with reason) that he also mimicked them behind their backs. They disliked him too.

Once, he was ill for a few days, and chiefly because there was no one else to slide into the copy-desk slot, I was slid in. I had never paid much attention to the copy-desk routines. To everyone's surprise, but chiefly to mine, it all went off quietly. A sense of time, order and personal relations, I found, was chiefly required. The staff co-operated eagerly. I belonged to neither faction in the party. Both despised my neutrality, but there was an advantage in having an impartial umpire at the desk (Freeman and Garlin had been Lovestoneites). The linotypers co-operated too. They were Americans, who hated Communism and all its works. But we shared that obsession, common to all Americans, for getting a specific job done. I took to editing the paper in the closing hours from the linotype room, walking around among the men (where, by union rules, I had no business to be), splitting up copy so that they could set it faster, urging them on until we were caught up unconsciously in one purpose, and, for the first time since Hatch, the paper began to make the mail trains.

By the time Garlin came back, the staff had made known to Minor that they no longer wanted him at the copy desk. His indispensability as a newsman was urged. He bowed obediently to discipline and made only random cabals against me.

Sometimes the rush for the mail trains was defeated by a factor that I could not control. The *Daily Worker* still suffered almost weekly financial crises. When the linotypers had been unpaid for a week they refused to set copy. They would simply sit at their machines, smoking cigarettes and sneering at Communists until their wages appeared. Where they appeared from was always a mystery to me. But, at one point, I became aware that part of the mystery was a bookkeeping transaction with the Hungarian Communist weekly, *Uj Elöre*. Sometimes, during these crises, I met and spoke with a short, dark, friendly Hungarian named J. Peters who was connected with the business office of *Uj Elöre*. Sometimes, he ventured a kind word about my industry and, especially, my public relations with the linotypers.

The future head of the underground section of the American Communist Party was not the only underground shadow that touched me in the print shop. Though I did not then suspect it, I was also in touch with the Soviet underground. The assistant foreman of the shop was a Communist Party member. His name was Sam Shoyet. His brother-in-law also worked in the print shop, quietly setting up ads and easing them gently into the frames. He was a slight, stooped young man in his late teens or early twenties. He wore very thick-lensed glasses and his face was as white as a mushroom. His name was Harry Tamer.

Sam Shoyet was the party's secret eye in the print shop. He warned me when trouble was blowing up among the linotypers and what the temper of the night's morale was. So far as he dared, he helped me with the speed up. But the men did not like him. Sometimes, in a pinch, he sat down at a machine and set a few lines of type himself. We became friendly.

He was a strange-looking man, with a Kalmuck's broad cheekbones and slightly slant, squint eyes. He told me that he had been born in Russia. Later, he had worked at his trade in Paris and in Tokyo. I remember thinking: "But how could he set Japanese type?" It was one of those pointless little discrepancies that lodge in the mind because something is not quite right about them. They are not thought about, but neither are they quite forgotten.

Several years later, when I was myself underground, I was to meet another of Sam Shoyet's brothers-in-law—one of Harry Tamer's older brothers. I met him in his apartment in Brooklyn, which was one of the secret headquarters of the Soviet underground. Joshua Tamer, though I did not then know it, was an employe of one of the big steel companies. One day United States security officers appeared at the steel company's offices in New Jersey. Tamer was at lunch. The officers informed the company that Tamer was suspected as a Russian agent. "That is impossible," they were told. "Tamer is a quiet man who has worked here for years." But "the quiet man" promptly fled to the Soviet Union, where he has remained ever since.

Later I was to meet another brother of Harry and Joshua Tamer's. He was an employe at a waterworks system in northern New Jersey. Still later, J. Peters was to introduce me to a Soviet agent, who under the pseudonyms of Robinson and Rubens, was the center of a celebrated international mystery. (He was also the subject of one of the little memos in Alger Hiss's acknowledged handwriting which figured in the Hiss trials.)

After that, I thought that I knew why Sam Shoyet, of the *Daily Worker* print shop, had been in Tokyo. I no longer supposed that he had been setting Japanese type.

The underground was not only peering at me through the slant eyes of Comrade Shoyet. It was even closer to me in the person of John Sherman, whom I could see, as I glanced from the copy desk down the lines of writers, holding his bald head in a stern pose, which, the comrades said, he thought made him look like Lenin. A situation was developing in the party, whereby, in unforeseeable ways, the future would soon close in on both of us; on Sherman first, and, through him, on me.

XXII

Stalin was about to take another step in his gradual conquest of absolute power. By a guileful alliance with the right wing of the Russian Communist Party, he had destroyed Trotsky. Now he felt strong enough to dispense with his allies. He set out to destroy the right opposition in the person of Nikolai Bukharin, who at that time seemed the most powerful figure in Russia.

The political destruction of Bukharin took about a year, beginning, roughly, with the Sixth World Congress of the Communist International in 1928. It was a somewhat complicated task, for the temper of Stalin's mind requires a strategy of multiple deceptions, which confuse his victims with the illusion of power, and soften them up with the illusion of hope, only to plunge them deeper into despair when the illusion fades, the trap is sprung, and the victims grasp with horror, as they hurtle into space, that the levers of control were always in Comrade Stalin's hands.

Even the American phase of this struggle took place on a plane beyond my sight (for, contrary to a widespread notion, I was always a comparatively obscure member of the Communist Party). But, as acting editor of the *Daily Worker,* I could not fail to be touched by some of its frenzies; and in the person of Robert Minor, who, during the climax of the fight, was acting secretary of the Communist Party, I was able to observe some of its more awkward antics. For, unlike the destruction of Trotsky, which merely ruffled American Communist circles, the destruction of Bukharin affected the American Communist Party down to the smallest cell.

That repercussion was due to the factional situation within the American Communist Party and a shrewd error on the part of the Lovestoneite leaders who supposed that Bukharin, and not Stalin, was going to be the winner of the Russian party conflict.

Over the years, the Lovestoneites had won their own fight in the United States. Their power in the American Communist Party was all but complete. They had cajoled or coerced a majority vote in all the units of the party. They controlled most, if not all, of the party organizations and the press. The Fosterites had shrunk to a sullen, intractable, greatly outnumbered minority. For the first time in its history, the Lovestoneites seemed on the point of enforcing unity on the distracted party. It had been done by the methods of any political machine, by corruption and by pressure. But, for a moment, many Communists were inclined to welcome the blessings of forced harmony.

For the first and only time, I attended a Lovestone caucus meeting. I was not a very sympathetic observer. Of all that was said and done, I remember only two things. I remember the long bulk of Robert Minor, informally sprawled on the floor before the speakers' tables at the front of the meeting—the image of relaxed assurance and victory. And I remember the short, arrogant figure of John Pepper, who, as Joseph Pogany, had been the commissar for war in the Hungarian Soviet Government, and who was now the official representative of the Communist International to the American Communist Party, and Lovestone's "gray eminence." *

* A "C. I. Rep" is attached by the Comintern to every Communist Party except the Russian. He is never a citizen of the country to whose Communist Party he is accredited. Therefore, he is usually, if not always, illegally resident in the country to which he has been sent. His purpose is to keep Moscow posted on developments within the party he is attached to, and to advise and guide its Central Committee. In fact, his authority is such that he can usually dictate policy. The first C. I. Rep to the American Communist Party was the Japanese Communist, Sen Katayama. He was presently followed by a Red Army officer named Gusev, known in the American Communist Party

A stumpy figure, Pepper strutted down the center aisle of the meeting, staring haughtily to the right and left, but seeing no one —a small man swollen with pride of place and power. The spectacle was unforgettable, for Pepper was actually strutting toward a downfall that would strip him, at a snap of Stalin's fingers, of all those powers that meant life to him. It would lead him at last, through torments that can only be guessed at, to an execution cellar and a revolver bullet in the base of his brain.

The enforced unity of the American party was based on raw power. That power, in turn, depended on the favor of the ruling faction in Moscow. Policy consisted chiefly in guessing the winner in the struggle between Stalin and Bukharin. John Pepper, who prided himself above all on his political astuteness, was a Bukharin man. The Lovestoneite leaders would have embraced any winning Russian faction to secure their power, but they were tied to Pepper by the fact that he was the C. I. Rep.

In the spring of 1929, Lovestone and several of his leading colleagues were invited to go to Moscow. They left, to all appearances, gayly. A special commission of the Communist International was going to settle "the American question," by which was meant the leadership of the American Communist Party. The Lovestoneites had gone to receive the orb and scepter. For was not Comrade Bukharin, the great Russian leader, the protector of the Lovestoneites?

In the absence of Lovestone and the other hierarchs, Robert Minor had been left in charge of the party. In those days, I saw even less than usual of my absentee editor. But from time to time he would tear into the office with a "must" news story written in the "national office" on 125th Street, favorable to "com-rade Boookh-har-reen." In those days, Minor was radiant.

One afternoon, he brought me, scrawled out in his handwriting, a big banner head to spread across the top of the *Daily Worker*. It said in effect: "Lovestone Backs Bukharin." With it came a long story to the same effect. Minor's instructions were meticulous. I was to let no one touch the story. I was personally to see it through the press. "Guard it like your life, Comrade Chambers," said Comrade Minor. Faithfully, I watched while the story was set and Sam Shoyet set up the head. I was just about to lock the form when a

by the pseudonym, P. Green. P. Green was succeeded by John Pepper. Pepper was succeeded by a member of the Central Committee of the British Communist Party, whom I was presently to meet rather mysteriously.

frantic Minor shot into the composing room. He was hatless, breathless and very pale. "Stop press!" he shouted, for he was curiously given to melodramatics. One of the Lovestoneites in Moscow had somehow managed to get out the awful truth. They had backed the wrong man, after all. Stalin had won. Bukharin had begun a long death march that would take him, like John Pepper, to an execution cellar.

Frantically, Minor tore out the banner head and substituted another. In effect it said: "Lovestone Denounces Bukharin." Then, standing at a composing table, doctoring and rewriting, Minor exactly reversed the sense of the earlier story.

It was too late. Stalin, as Alger Hiss was to observe to me admiringly some years later, always plays for keeps. He never forgives those who play against him. Appeasement moves him only to contempt. Stalin decided to transform the minority of the American Communist Party into the majority by a simple method. He would expel the majority as enemies of Communism. But since the art of politics consists not only in robbing an opponent of his power, but also of his following, those members of the majority who crawlingly confessed their political heresy and denounced their former leaders could remain within the party. This was a simple necessity. It was plainly impossible to expel all the Lovestoneites because there were not enough Fosterites to man a party. Moreover, the confessions of heresy would serve as handy political blackmail against the men who made them.

XXIII

I was now to witness something for which nothing in my Communist experience had prepared me and which would soon cause my first break with the Communist Party. I was about to witness the coming of fascism to the American Communist Party, and the American Communists were probably the first group on this continent to whom it came. At the time, and for a long time afterwards, I supposed that what I had witnessed was, to a large degree, simply the imprint of the peculiarly malevolent character of Joseph Stalin, his personal perversion of what in itself was good. Not until much later would I recognize that Stalin's personal character was not the point at all.

The point was not that Stalin is evil, but that Communism is more evil, and that, acting through his person, it found its supremely logical manifestation. The important point was not the character of Stalin, but the character of Communism, which, with an intuitive grasp that was at once the source of his strength and his mandate to power, Stalin was carrying to its inevitable development as the greatest of the fascist forms.

I recognized the effects and reacted from them violently, but I failed to identify them for what they were. As usual in such a failure of intelligence, the penalty was high, for if I could rightly have understood what then I saw, I should have ceased to be a Communist, and many people, including myself, would have been spared much suffering later on. As it was, my reaction was strong enough to drive me out of the Communist Party for a time. But since my break was not intelligent, since I broke with effects and not with their cause, with Stalin and not with Communism, I would presently return to the party, a more devout Communist than when I left it.

The reception of the Lovestoneites in Moscow had not been warming. They found themselves virtual prisoners. The hearings before the special commission were an inquisition. At one point, Comrade Stalin himself, through an interpreter, took a hand in interrogating Lovestone. Mimeographed transcripts of that hearing were soon circulated in the American Communist Party, and Comrade Vern Smith triumphantly let me peep at a copy.

One passage fixed itself in my mind. The ruined Lovestone had been trying to shift responsibility for his pro-Bukharin activities onto Comrade Pepper. "But did not Comrade Lovestone know," asked Comrade Stalin gently, "that he should not have been friendly with Comrade Pepper?" I never forgot the line in whose blood-chilling softness could be felt the constriction of a serpentine force. For Comrade Pepper was delegated by the Communist International precisely to advise and direct Comrade Lovestone, and there was no reason at all why Lovestone should not have been friendly with him, and every reason why he should. And that no one knew better than Comrade Stalin.

Lovestone and the others were held prisoner for several months. Meanwhile, the Fosterite leaders, who were also in Moscow, were sent home to shatter Lovestone's power in the American Communist Party by a reign of terror such as I had never beheld. There had been much that was politically corrupt and high-handed in the Lovestoneite control of the party. But there had still been two factions theoretically sharing equal rights. The Fosterites were harried and hampered, but they were recognized as a legitimate group. They were free to express their viewpoint in party meetings and in the party press. They held party offices; they had members on the Central Committee.

Now, for the first time, only one group (the Foster-Browder group, as it was called after its leaders), and one viewpoint (the Stalinist viewpoint, which Foster and Browder represented), was permitted in the party. All semblance of inner-party democracy had vanished. The slightest suspicion of dissent was punished by instant expulsion from the party. Until then, there had been one Central Control Commission, the party's court of first and last appeal and punishment. Now, central control commissions were set up in all the sections to handle the glut of heresy trials. For a purge was on. The defections from Lovestone had begun. Denunciations were pouring in. The great charge was "Lovestoneism and right-wing deviationism." Men settled many an old personal score under the dark, roomy folds of that charge. And, since the majority of the party had been Lovestoneites, there were few men and women who were not open to it.

Someone from Moscow had to direct so sweeping a purge. Who he was I cannot positively say. But I believe, for reasons that I shall presently relate, that Stalin's agent was a member of the Central Committee of the British Communist Party.

Among the first to defect from him were some of Lovestone's most trusted lieutenants—Robert Minor leading all the rest. He confessed his heinous errors and was generously permitted to continue as editor of the *Daily Worker*, while he zealously helped to prosecute the purge of his fellow factionalists or to bring the waverers over to the Foster-Browder side. Then in one big purge meeting, where the goatish Stalinists were publicly separated from the sheepish Lovestoneites, a dark, rough, slightly sinister figure rose and walked from the Lovestoneites toward the Foster benches. It was Jack Stachel, another leading Lovestoneite. William Z. Foster saw him rise. "My God," he muttered, "I believe that son of a bitch is coming over on our side." He was. And he was welcomed, for Stachel was an important figure in the party's trade-union work. He is better known to Americans now as one of the eleven Communist leaders convicted of conspiracy in New York in 1950.

Deals were freely made to win away key figures to the new regime. Some years later, J. Peters was to boast to me that, for a price, he had brought over the Hungarian section of the Communist

Party to the Stalinists. The price, he explained complacently, had been his appointment as chief of the whole underground section of the American Communist Party.

However clouded by personal motives, in the end the question which all such men had to answer in their own minds was simple: which were they loyal to—Lovestone or the Communist International? It is not surprising that they answered as they did. But not all Lovestoneites defected or recanted. Scores of die-hards were summarily expelled. Others, for policy reasons, were not attacked at once. Cat and mouse was first played with them. They were encircled by Fosterite spies, usually in the guise of unwanted assistants whose business it was to contrive a case againt them.

One of these slow sufferers was Mother Gitlow, then the head of the United Councils of Working Class Housewives (Comrade O'Flaherty's Uncopwokwifs). The old woman asserted her Lovestoneism as belligerently as she had pled for food for the starving Irish peasants at my first Communist meeting.

Her son, too, Benjamin Gitlow, refused to recant or confess political errors that he did not recognize and could not repent. A great purge meeting literally howled for his head. And Gitlow, who had gone to prison for his Communist beliefs, accepted expulsion from the party rather than bow to Stalin. His mother watched his public humiliation. It was more than she could bear (she died soon after). "Diamonds," she screamed above the uproar, "diamonds you are throwing out of the party!"

XXIV

I watched the purge with growing revulsion, but it did not touch me personally. There was no political case against me. I had almost no enemies, and, since I was not registered in any unit, I was overlooked in the wild proscription. I had always been neutral in the factional fight, and while I had no illusions about the fate of neutrals in a war, and I assumed that my editorial post was a plum that the Fosterites would sooner or later covet, unlike most party functionaries, I did not care. I was not looking for trouble and I hoped to ride out the storm in peace. But as it lashed up, I grew more and more restive. I spoke and acted with hazardous freedom.

One night I came upstairs, on one of my frequent trips between the composing room and the editorial desk. In the hall, I found some of my old comrades from the English-speaking branch—David

Benjamin, his wife, Eve Chambers, and one or two others. They had just been expelled from the party. Their faces were drawn and distressed. They could scarcely speak. I do not know what impulse drew them back to the center from which they had just been cast out—for good, it developed, for they never returned to the party. I shook hands with them to show that I understood and sympathized. As I did so, I saw Jack Parilla, a hunchback from the *Daily Worker* business office, widely known in the party as a professional snoop, watching me with the delighted expression of a cat that sees a bird within reach. For even fraternization with expelled persons was ground for expulsion.

Then the first member of the *Daily Worker* staff was purged. One night John Sherman was called before his unit meeting. John Sherman had always hated the factional dissension in the party, had deplored its waste and corruption. He had never admired Lovestone but he had let the tide sweep him into voting with that faction. Now he stubbornly refused to denounce Lovestone on command or to repent errors that he felt he had never committed. He was expelled at once.

He stumbled into the *Daily Worker* office and sat down at his desk—a solid, solemn, broken man. As he gathered together some papers, tears streamed down his face. No one in the office would speak to him or even glance at him. No one dared. But there were covert smiles among his colleagues. I was busy at the copy desk and did not at once realize what was going on. Then Honig whispered in my ear what had happened. "You must do something for him," he said.

I walked over and placed my hand on Sherman's shaking shoulders to steady him. I urged him to leave the office quickly so as not to prolong his distress. I stood beside him until he had collected his things. I walked out of the office and down the hall with him. I did not try to comfort him—what could I say?—but, as we parted, I embraced him.

I walked back to the copy desk through a hushed office. The Stalinists kept their eyes fixed on their typewriters. Everyone knew that I had made my personal demonstration against the purge.

Few acts of my life ever cost me so dear, for the simple reason that Sherman never forgot it. He was grateful and his gratitude was to be my fate. But there are few acts of my life that I regret less or which I should be so happy to perform again.

Unlike many expelled people, who hovered, poor, hang-dog ghosts, around the dingy haunts from which they had been banished, snubbed or sneered at by their former comrades, John Sherman disappeared without a trace. During the next few years I sometimes asked what had become of him. Nobody knew.

XXV

Still no action was taken against me. No doubt, they reasoned: "Chambers is a sentimentalist. He is harmless, foolish and useful, for he gets out the paper. There's always time to break a neck."

Minor spent most of his days at the *Daily Worker* now. He was banished from the higher intrigues of the national office and had to prove himself the indispensable editor. He instituted staff meetings, probably by command, for, through these meetings, the Stalinists now had a controlling voice in the management of the paper. Meekly, Minor would listen to Vern Smith and other Stalinists, whom in the past he had scarcely noticed. "Yes, Vern," he would say deferentially, "that is an *ex*-cel-lent i-dea, Vern."

One day Minor called me into his office, and, after making sure that the door was shut, explained to me in a voice, hushed as much by awe as by precaution, that he must introduce me to someone of "the great-est im-*port*-ance." There was someone on an upper floor of the building, who, from now on, would wish to read certain copy that went into the paper. Whatever he asked for I was to give him. No one but Minor and I were to know that the man was there. I was never to mention him to anybody.

Then Minor led me upstairs to a room at the front of the building and knocked three times on its door. There was a sound of light footsteps. A lock turned and the door opened. In the big, bare, rugless office stood a withered, gnomelike little man. "This," said Comrade Minor, as soon as the door was carefully bolted behind us, "is Comrade Chambers, and this is Comrade Cohen."

Comrade Cohen took my hand limply, looked at me suspiciously and with apparent distaste, and uttered, in a richly unintelligible Scottish burr, something that I took to mean: "How do you do?" Beside this little Scotch terrier, Minor bulked huge. But his manner was little short of terror and mental obeisance. I quickly concluded that I was in the presence of the representative of the Communist International, that this little Scotsman was Stalin's special agent in purging the American Communist Party, and that he had at last found time to turn his thoughts to its central organ. This view was presently confirmed by Harry Freeman, who, as an employe of Tass, had met the C. I. Rep socially.

After that, I spent a good deal of time running copy from the *Daily Worker* editorial office and knocking three times on Comrade Cohen's door. Comrade Cohen was a great reader of *Daily Worker* editorials and stories that dealt with internal Communist affairs. Just how much he edited them, I have forgotten. Sometimes he had original copy for me. For he spent part of his days, which must have been rather lonely in the big, bare room, writing occasional editorials for the *Worker*. I remember one about Ramsay MacDonald, Britain's Labor prime minister, who had just made some abating gesture in that permanent crisis which, between the world wars, was known as "peace." The editorial was a fairly crushing assault on the prime minister's honesty, and Comrade Cohen had headed it: *Who Are These Angels of Peace?* He was rather taken with the title and asked me, with shy complacence, as one practitioner to another, what I thought of it. I said I thought that it was really awfully good.

One day Comrade Cohen jellied me by asking unexpectedly: "Do we have any *feuilleton* today, Comrade Chambers?" After I had clawed through the Scottish brogue, I decided that the unfamiliar sound at its core was the French word, *feuilleton,* which is European journalese for light reading. I told Comrade Cohen that I would show him what we had on hand. I rummaged through my "dead basket" and gathered up an armful of boiler plate so leaden that I had hesitated to print it. Comrade Cohen said that some of it was very acceptable *feuilleton.*

But our acquaintanceship was destined to be brief. The formidable little Scotsman was still sitting alone in his big room, answering to three knocks on his locked door and terrifying Comrade Minor when I first broke with the Communist Party. I never saw him again.

XXVI

After several grinding months, the Fosterites had firm control of the party. Lovestone and his colleagues had been expelled. They had at last been permitted to leave Russia and return to the United States, where they promptly organized an opposition group and loudly proclaimed their dwindling minority to be the true majority of the American Communist Party.

Within the party, the uproar slowly simmered down. Confessions were still published in the *Daily Worker*, but it had become an offense, itself subject to denunciation to the Control Commission, to reproach a Lovestoneite with his political past. Despite my provocative behavior with John Sherman and others, I seemed to have survived the purge. But I found that it is not enough merely to survive such an experience. I was confused and troubled, and more and more I felt that I had no moral right to continue editing the *Daily Worker*, where I had daily to set forth a political line with which I found myself in deep disagreement, and which I held to be often absurd, always harmful and dangerous to those who followed it.

For the Stalinists had swept into power, proclaiming that this was "the third period"—an epoch that I never understood very well and soon gave up trying to understand. But I knew that, whereas in the past, we had lived in a period characterized by wars and revolutions, we now suddenly found ourselves in a period of revolutions and wars, which must, officially, occur in that order. The reverse order was heresy. That, I thought, is nonsense.

Socialists, who, in the past, had been taunted as "collaborators with capitalism" for reasons which, from a Communist position, made sound sense, had now become "social fascists," which to me made no sense at all. "Is it not clear, comrades," asked Comrade Stalin blandly, "that social democracy and fascism are twins? It seems to me that this is decidedly clear." It did not then seem clear to me.

In the past, the Communist Party had struggled to form united fronts with almost any group that would tolerate it. That was one method of spreading its influence, especially in the trade unions. Now, the united front had become heresy and anybody advocating it was subject to expulsion. The "united front from below" had become the catch-phrase. Insofar as this meant anything, it meant that henceforth Communists would make united fronts only with the rank and file of any group against its official leaders. That, too, seemed to me nonsense, and so, indeed, it proved to be.

Arab outrages were occurring in Palestine. The Communist International chose that moment to call for the formation of a "Soviet Arabistan," and to attack the Zionists. Day after day bludgeoning stories and editorials along this mad line appeared in the *Daily Worker*. Editing them seemed less like a peculiarly trying exercise in party discipline than horseplay in a mental home.

The whole party had embraced, to the point of hysteria, the conviction that a gigantic economic crisis was about to strike the United States (the boom was still on), to be followed at once by a violent social revolution. In anticipation, the Young Communist League suddenly acquired a uniform—sleazy khaki blouses and red scarves. They devoted their free hours to military drill (with sticks). Very often I had to climb through masses of these martial young men and women on my way in and out of the Workers Center. For they had turned the lower hall into a kind of bivouac, where they sprawled in picturesque attitudes, practicing a useful revolutionary skill—how to plait nooses. It seemed to me that the party, of which it had been said in Lenin's time that it peopled the jails of Europe with philosophers, had simply gone insane. I was sure of it when one of the members of the *Daily Worker* staff rushed breathlessly into the office one day, shouting: "It's begun. The masses are storming the Amalgamated Bank." The insurrection on the far side of Union Square turned out to be a large group of needle-trades workers engaged in one of their usual sidewalk congresses. I was even more sure of it when Robert Minor tore out to the copy desk one day and slapped his hand upon a small news item that reported a small riot somewhere in rural Minnesota. "It's the beginning of the American revolution," he cried, "we must play it up *big*."

Of course, the party had not gone insane at all, though some of its members were momentarily weaving along the brink. The inducement of that kind of hysteria is one of the techniques of fascism, but we knew less about fascism in those days than we do now—though perhaps not much less. It must also be pointed out that the party was quite right about the economic crisis, and just as wrong about the violence of the ensuing revolution.

My doubts and disagreements, swelling within me like an abscess, were brought to a head in an unexpected way. The *Daily Worker* had acquired a new writer in the person of Harrison George, the brother-in-law of Earl Browder, who, it was beginning to appear, would nose out William Z. Foster as leader of the party. Harrison George was a middle-aged, middle-class American revolutionist of many years of activity. He was a former I.W.W. It was he who had indiscreetly broadcast in Moscow that his friend, Vern Smith, while editing the I.W.W. central organ, was secretly a Communist. It was Harrison George, too, who had shouted that the masses were storming the Amalgamated Bank.

George and I had once briefly taken part in a strike at the Michelin tire factory, in Milltown, New Jersey. While we were waiting for the police to beat us up, he told me how, together with Earl Browder, he had been a Comintern agent in China. He had been in Canton during the abortive Communist uprising in 1927. From his hotel window, he had watched as the Nationalist troops nosed their machine guns through the windows of a bank opposite and mowed down the Communists inside.

Harrison was a mischievous man whom I at once spotted as a troublemaker. But we got along pleasantly, and he sometimes whispered information to me that was helpful in those dislocated days. He was a somewhat formidable figure in Stalinist circles. He was also the determined enemy of Robert Minor.

One day he sidled up to me confidentially and said: "We'd get that old fool Minor off this paper in a minute if it would not give ammunition to the Lovestoneites." Those few sneering words, and the malevolent chuckle that went with them, were the drops that overflowed my mind and filled me with a mixture of chilling anger and despair. I thought: "The pigmies have taken over." No doubt, Minor was, in some ways, an "old fool." He was, in other ways, a gifted man, and, in my book, gifted men have a right to be old fools at times, and usually avail themselves of it, for their minds run along slightly different tracks to the mass of men, and at the best must seem a little odd.

I walked into Minor's office and closed the door. "Bob," I said, "I'd like to go away for a while. For a long time, I've been upset about what has been happening in the party. I can't seem to find my way in the new policies. I want you to let me go off for a month by myself and try to think things through. Until I do, I can't really edit the *Daily Worker*."

Minor was hard of hearing but often pretended to be quite deaf. Whenever he heard anything he did not want to hear, he would invariably cup his ear with his hand, affect an expression of tortured attention, and ask: "What did you say, com-rade?" He tried this on me now. I repeated what I had said.

"Oh, you're just tired," he said. "You've been working too hard. We can't spare you, not now. (I knew he was thinking that Honig and I were the only two men he could trust not to knife him.)

There is nothing happening in the party. Everything is all right now. We are all comrades together."

"We are so much comrades together, Bob," I said, "that they're after your scalp this minute." Then I repeated what Harrison George had just said to me.

Minor jumped out of his chair, red in the face, as he often became, and frightened. "Who told you that?" he shouted. I said that I was sorry, but I could not tell him.

"You *must* tell me, com-rade," he said. "I *must* know." I absolutely refused to tell. He stared at me out of his little elephant's eyes, now filled with anger and fright. I got up and left him.

I knew exactly what "the old fool" was going to do. He was going to the Central Control Commission to force me to tell. I also knew that I would not tell.

XXVII

Nevertheless, I was not quite prepared, when I walked into the *Daily Worker* office early the next afternoon, to find a stranger sitting at my place in the slot. But I knew at a glance what had happened. I had become "a politically unreliable element." Grateful Bob Minor, to demonstrate his new-found loyalty to the new overlords, had decided to make a political offering of me. He had warned them that I had doubts, that I had said that I was no longer able to edit the *Daily Worker*. I was not angry with him. But I was sorry that he should have let himself be less than he was, especially in truckling to men who were so much less than he.

The stranger at the copy desk turned out to be Nat Kaplan, a young Communist, who, if I remember rightly, had just returned from the Soviet Union. (Under another name, he was later to be employed by the C.I.O. Auto Workers Union.) Minor instructed me coldly to teach Kaplan my job. "Because you are overworked and need assistance," said that childish hypocrite.

Kaplan was restrained, self-consciously pleasant and very alert, exactly in the manner of any detective who hopes to elicit all possible information from a man before he arrests him. We worked together quietly through the afternoon. I showed him just what to do. He was quick and bright. In the office there was the stiff silence that usually enveloped those unhappy occurrences. No one spoke to me if he could help it.

Presently, the telephone rang. It was the call I had been expecting. "This is Charles A. Dirba," said a deliberately chilling voice. "Comrade, I would like to talk to you. Tonight." Dirba was the chairman of the Central Control Commission.

When I went down to supper, I left Comrade Kaplan sitting at the copy desk. It was my last impression of the *Daily Worker* office. I ate alone, for I had certain decisions to make. About two things I was determined. I was not going to betray Harrison George to the Control Commission. I was all the more determined in view of the way that Minor had betrayed me. There had been enough denunciations in the Communist Party. I was not going to add one more to the heap. Neither was I going to be put through an act before the Central Control Commission. From me, there would be no obscene confessions of political error, no public prostration or phony repentance. I had never asked the party for anything but the right to serve it. Clearly, it no longer needed my services.

I knew that I was putting myself outside the Communist Party. But if a man could remain within the party only by abasing himself, he and the party were better off if he got out. "But all that will change," I thought. "For the moment, the party has ceased to be a Communist Party. It is only temporarily deranged. It will have to come to its senses, or it will cease to be party at all. Meanwhile, I will wait until it does."

There was no point in returning to the *Daily Worker* office. I never went back.

XXVIII

I was outside the Communist Party, but not out of it. For during the two years I remained outside it, the party never expelled me. I still considered myself a Communist. I had broken with the Communist Party not because of differences in theory, but over problems of political strategy and tactics and the problem of the conduct of Communists within the party, which was, ultimately, a problem of organization. I was an independent Communist oppositionist.

Communists were strictly forbidden to fraternize with oppositionists of any kind. Some Communists pointedly cut me when we met on the street or in restaurants. Others remained as friendly as before. Among these was Jacob Burck, an extremely able artist who had succeeded Fred Ellis as the *Daily Worker* cartoonist (Ellis had gone to Moscow to draw cartoons for the Russian trade-union paper, *Trud*). In those days I spent much time at Burck's big studio on West 14th Street.

Several times the party sent me letters, sternly summoning me to stand trial before the Central Control Commission. These summonses always came by registered mail. I always signed for the letters so the party would be in no doubt that I had received them.

Later on, the party took to sending around its agents to feel out my state of mind. Usually, they brought small pieces of bait. One said that the party wanted me to sit on a committee which the Central Committee was setting up to develop worker correspondence on a national scale. Another asked me to translate the two volumes of an important study of Chinese agrarian problems by Karl Wittvogel (now an anti-Communist). But the party's agent, a young Harvard or Yale man whose name I have forgotten, grew so angry discussing Communist problems with me that he lost control of his voice and his temper together and rushed off, taking the volumes of Wittvogel with him.

It would have been a privilege to translate Wittvogel. But, like all party translating, it would have been an unpaid pleasure. I could scarcely afford that any longer. I had gone back to translating for a livelihood. Soon I had all the work I could handle, and, for the first time in years, was making a living.

One of the books I translated at that time was Franz Werfel's novel, *Class Reunion*. It was less a novel than an elongated short story. It related how an Austrian attorney supposed that he saw in a prisoner coming up for examination a classmate who, out of jealousy, he had managed to ruin in their youth. Most of the book was a flashback which described the trivial stages of that ruin (one of them, if I remember rightly, consisted in the bad boy's leading on the good boy to stuff himself with tarts). At the time, the novel seemed to me tiresome and overcontrived. It was one of what I call "unnecessary books"—books, that, for any bearing they have on man's mind, man's fate, or even his entertainment, might as well never have been written. Apparently, readers thought so, too, for *Class Reunion* was not a great success. I soon forgot the details of its story, with which, in any case, I had nothing to do but the tiresome labor of translation. I should probably never have remembered them, but for the Hiss Case.

For in *Class Reunion,* Dr. Carl Binger, the psychologist in the Hiss trials, undertook to discover the psychological clue to Chambers' "mysterious motives" in charging that Alger Hiss had once been a Communist. Chambers was the bad boy and Hiss was the good boy of *Class Reunion,* and the novel, unread by me for some twenty years, had put the idea of ruining Hiss in my mind—why I never quite understood, since it always seemed to me that if I had been bent on ruining Alger Hiss from base motives, the idea might well have occurred to me without benefit of Franz Werfel. But to many enlightened minds *Class Reunion* became a book of revelation.

I have always held that anyone who takes the trouble to read *Class Reunion* without having made up his mind in advance, can scarcely fail to see that, if there are any similarities at all between the characters, it is Hiss who superficially resembles the bad boy and Chambers who superficially resembles his victim.

XXIX

I had failed as an organization Communist. For all the influence I could have on the actions of the Communist Party or its thinking, I might just as well never have worked on the *Daily Worker.* I had never sought to influence policy. But now Communist policy must be influenced. For the economic crisis had begun in the United States. The stock market had crashed. In the cities, the breadlines were forming. In the countryside, they were selling up the farms for debts. To masses of men and women stunned by this turn of history, as completely as elsewhere they would be later stunned by bomb blast, the Communist Party could only iterate "third period," while it tried to turn the economic psychosis into premature and irresponsible violence.

It occurred to me that there was another way than politics to influence policy. I might try writing, not political polemics, which few people ever wanted to read, but stories that anybody might want to read—stories in which the correct conduct of the Communist would be shown in action and without political comment. While I was brooding on this, a small group of Midwestern farmers raided some stores for food. I had been brought up in a country village close to the land. I thought that I knew exactly what had happened. All that I wanted to say fell into place at one stroke in my mind. I wrote through one night and by morning had completed a rather long short story. It was about a farmers' rising in the West and the part played in it by an intelligent Communist.

For the Communist, I drew on my memories of that old Kansas wheat farmer and former secretary of the Communist Party, Louis Katterfeld

I took the story to Walt Carmon, a former seaman turned Bohemian, who was editing the *New Masses,* the Communist controlled literary monthly. He was editing it for much the same reasons that I had edited the *Daily Worker*—because the nominal editors were seldom around. Carmon liked the story which he called: *Can You Hear Their Voices?* A Communist group, headed by William Gropper, the *Daily Worker* cartoonist, protested that I was a renegade, but the story appeared in the *New Masses.*

It had a success far beyond anything that it pretended to be. It was timely. The New York *World-Telegram* spotted it at once and wrote a piece about it. International Publishers, the official Communist publishing house, issued it as a pamphlet. Lincoln Steffens hailed it in an effusion that can be read in his collected letters. Hallie Flanagan, then head of Vassar's Experimental Theater, turned it into a play. In a few months, the little story had been translated even into Chinese and Japanese and was being played in workers' theaters all over the world.

Can You Hear Their Voices? dealt with Communism in action. I wanted to deal with other aspects of the problem. In quick succession, I wrote three more stories which the *New Masses* published as fast as I finished them. *You Have Seen the Heads* dealt with the problem of defeat. It was a story of the Chinese civil war, which the Communists had been losing for years. It ended: "We were defeated at Han-lo. We were defeated at Chen-chow. The last was our eleventh defeat without a victory. We are harried among mountains. The road to victory is up the sharp sides of mountains." A Chinese Communist later assured me that I could not possibly have written the story "because only Chinese think like that."

Our Comrade Munn dealt with the problem of the conduct of the Communist within the party. It merely reported the life and death of an obscure Communist, such a man as I had sought to be myself. It was almost as successful as *Can You Hear Their Voices?* and, like it, was translated, dramatized and played in Europe and Asia. *The Death of the Communists*, the last of the four little stories, dealt with the problem of the Communist in the presence of death. It described the last hours of a group of Communists in the prison where they had been taken to be shot. It was reported through the eyes of a cynical fellow prisoner who, only when the execution was over, sensed that he had been touched by something new in his experience—the moral force of men who were prepared to die for what they believed.

The four stories would scarcely be worth dwelling on were it not for the turn they were to give my whole future. For if they had not been written, I should never have entered the underground, since I should not have been back in the party where the underground could reach me.

Moscow reacted to the stories at once. In *International Literature,* Elistratova, the reigning Soviet woman critic, wrote of *Can You Hear Their Voices?*: "It gives a revolutionary exposition of the problem of the agricultural crisis and correctly raises the question of the leading role of the Communist Party in the revolutionary farmers' movement." She added: "For the first time (in American writing), it raises the image of the Bolshevik."

It was the voice of authority. It could scarcely have been more explicit if I had written the party's theses on the agricultural crisis. "So," I thought, "my quarrel is not with Moscow or with Comrade Stalin. Raise the line correctly, and Moscow instantly accepts it. My quarrel is with the invincible stupidity and pettiness of the American Communist Party." That half-truth was to cost me dear. But I have since come to think that Moscow was as mistaken in me as I was in Moscow.

In Washington, one day, J. Peters surprised me by mentioning that he had been in Moscow when the stories appeared. He had fought fiercely to keep the State Publishing House from translating and publishing them. I asked him why. "They are against the party," he said, and we both dropped the touchy subject. At the time, I thought that Comrade Peters' views were somewhat narrow.

I think now that anyone who has the patience to read those four stories will agree that I was wrong, and that Comrade Peters was right. For in retrospect, it is easy to see that the stories are scarcely about Communism at all. Communism is the context in which they are told. What they are really about is the spirit of man in four basic commitments—in suffering, under discipline, in defeat, in death. In each, it is not the political situation, but the spirit of man which is triumphant. The success of the stories was due to the fact that for the first time that spirit spoke to American Communists in a context and a language which it was permissible for them to hear. For the same reason, Peters feared the stories. For he rightly sensed that Communism may never make truce with the spirit of man. If it does, sooner or later, it is the spirit of man that will always triumph, for it draws its strength from a deeper fountain.

X X X

It was rather embarrassing. Moscow had spoken. But the American Communist who "for the first time had raised the image of the Bolshevik" was not in the American Communist Party. Something must be done quickly.

Two editors of the *New Masses* looked me up—Michael Gold and Joseph Freeman (who appeared in the magazine's masthead as Robert Evans). There had long been widespread dissatisfaction with Carmon's editing. The ambassadors proposed that I should become the editor of the *New Masses.*

First my misunderstanding with the party would have to be adjusted. But there would be no difficulty about that. There was a friendly visit to Alexander Trachtenberg who, as head of International Publishers, was the party's "cultural commissar" and had the *New Masses* and the John Reed Clubs under his wing, and, as an old Bolshevik (he was said to be a former Tsarist cavalry officer and a doctor of philosophy from Yale), was a member of the Central Control Commission. Trachtenberg arranged an equally friendly talk with Charles A. Dirba, the chairman of the Control Commission. In fifteen minutes I was back in the Communist Party without ever having, officially, been out of it. I was also the editor of the *New Masses* at a salary of fifteen dollars a week.

But before those great things happened, something else had happened that makes them seem as foolish and offensive as trash.

X X X I

There is always one spring that is our own. Its memory, once we have it, is among the few things that cannot be taken from a man. He has only to let its special light fill his mind, and he feels again the pang with which it is given every man, the dullest and least worthy, to glimpse once in his life, if only for a moment, beyond a beloved head the boughs heave and the petals break and spin along the earth. I was about to find that love whose force, once felt, makes all a man's other gross or merely tender gropings seem irrelevant and meaningless, as if they had happened in another lifetime or to someone else. I was about to experience that love which, not to have known, seems to the man and woman who have shared it, never to have lived, and entitles them to the small, smiling condescension toward death itself of those to whom, in this sense, life has given all that life has to give.

I was about to meet again the girl who was to become my wife. She was, of course, Esther Shemitz, the girl with black, bobbed hair, whom I had seen walk toward the police clubs in the Passaic strike.

The world's image of Esther Chambers has been gained chiefly from a few unflattering newsphotos taken at a time of more than human stress. The Esther Shemitz I met again in 1930 was a slender, gay, laughing, utterly artless and unaffected but deeply sensitive and serious young woman. The gentle candor of her eyes, and the strong and pure planes of her face had been refined from within outward by the action of that beauty which outlasts all changes of time because it is cut, not after the fashion of the flesh, but to the template of the soul.

Neither of us had much to do with the fact that we met again. Our meeting came about by what the world calls chance, but in which we now see the workings of a grace before which we feel reason to be reverent. My friend, Michael Intrator, the fur worker, trade unionist and *Daily Worker* writer (then expelled from the Communist Party for Lovestoneism), had courted and married Grace Lumpkin. And so I came into their circle.

Grace Lumpkin and Esther Shemitz had been friends for years. They were widely known in the Communist movement for their inviolable "prudery," which was, in fact, chiefly their way of living uncontaminated by that steaming emotional jungle in which the party had raised promiscuity to a Marxist principle. They had taken a little house together in New York's East Side, on 11th Street, three blocks from the East River and the gas tanks. It was one of those brick houses that stand at the back of a courtyard behind the cold-water tenements, which towered over it and cut off most of the light. Hence the popular name for such rear houses: tuberculosis traps. The girls were clever with their hands and had remodeled the interior of the little house so that, when the fire was burning in the living-room fireplace, it was like a cozy farmhouse in the heart of the slum. Their rent was eight dollars a month.

They had almost no money. But by eating as seldom as possible, and editing other irrelevancies out of their lives, they were able to dedicate themselves rather relentlessly to Art. Art, in Grace Lumpkin's case, took the form of a novel on which she had been working for some time, and which eventually appeared as *To Make My Bread.* It was awarded Moscow's Maxim Gorki prize for literature, was turned into a play and, some years later, had a successful run at the Civic Repertory's old theater on 14th Street.*

Art, for Esther Shemitz, took the form of painting. She had been studying at the Art Students' League, and was designing terrifying posters in which hatless proletarians with clenched fists were always storming somewhere—apparently toward the barricades. For both young women were by now (also rather relentlessly) dedicated to the Revolution, about which, when I really came to know them, it seemed to me that their lack of practical experience was equaled only by their lack of humor and their implacable ferocity. This was all the more odd, because neither of them was ever a member of the Communist Party. But they were, I presently discovered, strongly influenced by two of the party's most militant figures—Miss Grace Hutchins and Miss Anna Rochester, whom I have mentioned before. Both of these older revolutionaries had money in their own right. Very properly, they were patrons of proletarian art, and a loan apiece from them had made it possible for the younger women to devote themselves to art and austerity. (Both those loans were paid back later on, painfully and in full.) Meanwhile, the two patrons of the arts were gently winding their protégés into the Communist Party.

My irreverent views about the American Communist Party horrified and enraged Grace Lumpkin and Esther Shemitz. One afternoon, my future wife, in a flare-up of her Passaic strike spirit, was belaboring me with my "renegacy" and related charges. I sat studying her. As I watched her climbing around on the barricades, I was given one of those rare, total insights into another soul that, for good or ill, we sometimes know. I felt like a man on a hilltop, who bursts through a screen of obstructing undergrowth, and suddenly sees, spread beyond him, the most tranquil of sunlit countrysides with its pattern of blown, green and ripening fields, its hedgerows and cool trees, its winding roads and falling brooks. I thought:

* I went to see it one night, probably in 1935, with Maxim Lieber. I pointed out to my friend a young woman who was the center of a lively group in the audience. "That," he said, "is Hede Massing"—my one and only glimpse of that important witness until after the second Hiss trial.

"This is no revolutionist at all. This is the most gentle and tender spirit, a child except for its courage and firmness and its capacity for love, should someone understand and awaken that love." I said: "Why don't you stop drawing those mob scenes and clenched fists and paint the landscapes you were meant to paint?"

Few courtships can have been much stormier than ours. For the Communist Party, too, soon actively interfered. I called one evening to find Esther Shemitz very silent, grave and evidently distressed. Presently, she blurted through her tears that Comrade Hutchins had paid her an official visit and brought the party's awful command that she was never again to see the "anti-party element, Chambers." I was never quite sure how official Miss Hutchins' mission was, and how much was self-imposed. For I sensed, behind the political ban another force, serpentine and cold, that deeply hated life. Nevertheless, the command was repeated over the months.

One evening, I arrived at Esther Shemitz's for supper—a very special occasion in that house of bare cupboards. I knocked. No one answered. I was certain that my future wife was inside. I beat on the door with my fist. At last a small voice said through its tears: "Go away. The party says I cannot see you. We can never meet again."

I went away, very angry. I cooled off by walking around the city streets for hours. Then I climbed up to Jacob Burck's big studio and went to bed. I could not sleep. Between four or five o'clock in the morning, I dressed. I walked back across town through the absolutely empty streets of the sleeping city.

Again, I knocked on the door of the little house. There was no answer. The door stood at the head of a flight of stairs a story above a flagged court. Just beyond the landing stage was a window. It was open a little way because it was supposed that nobody could reach the window from the landing. Ordinarily, no one could. But I am not the first man who, in my mood, has done what he did not know he could do. I looked down at the flagstones (even small heights usually make me dizzy). I swung from the rail of the landing, reached the window ledge, pushed up the window and climbed in.

Sitting beside my astonished girl's bedside in the dawning light, I explained to her that she must make a choice, and that that choice was not between the Communist Party and renegacy, or between any political viewpoint and any other, but between life and death.

I do not think that the declaration impressed her at all, or that she was much interested in what I was saying. Like so many women, she has a strong, simple, practical sense, and I think that she had begun to realize that if a man was intent enough on marrying her to climb through her window at five o'clock in the morning, even putting a bolt on it was probably not much use.

We never quarreled again. In the twenty years that we have been married, we have had a few disagreements, but never again about politics and not very often about anything else.

My *New Masses* stories presently began to have their effect. Grudgingly, Miss Hutchins and Miss Rochester conceded my new standing in the party. When Esther Shemitz and I were married, in 1931, at New York's city hall, Comrades Hutchins and Rochester, at my wife's request, were our somewhat formidable witnesses, and gave us our only wedding gift—an electric toaster.

XXXII

The *New Masses* was on the second or third floor of an old house on 15th Street just off Sixth Avenue. I went over one day to enter upon my editorship. As usual in the party, no one in the office had been told that I was coming. But Walt Carmon had disappeared, and I do not recall that I ever saw him again. His assistant, a young woman who was intensely loyal to him, and correspondingly hostile to me, announced firmly that I could not use the editor's office at the front of the building. Instead, she led me to a small, dark office, well out of sight at the rear. I sat down quietly. I could tell by the look that I have seen on so many bureaucratic faces that she thought I was a fool to let myself be treated in that way and that she would have no trouble in managing me.

Actually, the little dark office suited my needs very well. I knew that I faced an entrenched opposition on the *New Masses* staff. I did not wish to waste my time fighting it. The little dark office fought for me. I threw open the editor's door at once to the writers and artists (one of the charges against Carmon was his brusque treatment of contributors). Soon my office was crowded, and everyone who had to walk the length of the building to reach it, and everyone who had to crowd into it, had his own thoughts about the opposition.

There was a new spirit in the magazine. Until then, the Communist control had been masked. I edited as a Communist. Nothing was surer to attract the non-Communist intellectuals who were looking for the Communist Party as I had looked for it in 1925, and did not want to be put off with tactful substitutes. Their world had crumbled in the depression, and they were now thronging toward the party. Every year the Communist National Students League was graduating its hundreds from the colleges. These were the first quotas of the great drift from Columbia, Harvard and elsewhere. These were the years that floated Alger Hiss into the party and made possible the big undergrounds, the infiltration of the Government, science, education and all branches of communications, but especially radio, motion pictures, book, magazine and newspaper publishing. An entirely new type of Communist made his appearance, not singly, but in clusters, whose members often already knew one another, influenced one another and shared the same Communist or leftist views. A surprising number came of excellent native American families. Nearly all were college trained from the top per cent of their classes. Those who lacked the hardihood or clarity to follow the logic of their position and become Communists clumped around the edges of the party, self-consciously hesitant, apologetic, easing their social consciences by doing whatever the party asked them to do so long as they did not have to know exactly what it was. From 1930 onward, a small intellectual army passed over to the Communist Party with scarcely any effort on its part. Within a decade, simply by pursuing the careers that ordinarily lay open to them, these newcomers would carry the weak and stumbling American Communist Party directly into the highest councils of the nation, would subtly (or sometimes boldly) help to shape the country's domestic and foreign policies. They would, at last, in a situation unparalleled in history, enable the Soviet Government to use the American State and Treasury Departments as a terrible engine of its revolutionary purposes, by the calculated destruction of powers vital to American survival (like China), or by creating power vacuums (like Germany), which breached the American political outworks abroad. Meanwhile, the party's agents, working in the communications field, tirelessly justified those catastrophic betrayals to the nation as necessary acts of good faith to an ally (the Soviet Union whose philosophy denied the principle of good faith), or as prerequisites of permanent peace, or, if momentarily threatened with detection, as simply the unhappy blunders of American diplomatic innocence.

On the *New Masses* I saw only the onset of this tide. But by chance I was touched for a moment by an odd experience. There walked into my office at the *New Masses* one day a young man who seemed surprised not to find Walt Carmon and talked to me at first a little reluctantly. He was, he said, a minor United States Government official in China. He told me his name and where he was going next in the United States. We sat talking for a while about the Hanyang Arsenal, which had once been in Communist hands, and then he went on his way.*

*When these lines were written some time in 1950, I had not intended to divulge the messenger's name. Since then it has been in the news. For, one day, in our local newspaper, I saw a picture of Oliver Edmund Clubb, a U. S. consular official in China who had recently returned to the United States after the Communists captured Peking. I said to my wife: "I know this man. He paid me a visit in the *New Masses* office in 1932. But they have his name wrong. It should be Chubb." I mentioned the fact because it amused me that my memory could retain an impression of someone of no particular importance (I then supposed) and details of a conversation held fleetingly almost two decades before. Out of the same sense of amusement, and for no other reason, I mentioned the incident in a casual conversation with two F.B.I. friends.

I was startled by their burst of interest in my memories of Oliver Edmund Clubb (for the newspaper had been right, and my recollection wrong about his last name). Presently, an investigator for the House Committee on Un-American Activities called and questioned me about Clubb. Presently, Clubb testified before that committee. He had no recollection of visiting Whittaker Chambers in the *New Masses* office in 1932.

The matter did not end there. The State Department's Loyalty Board requested me to testify before it about a month later in the Case of O. Edmund Clubb, sending me one of its customary letters with the somewhat deterrent ending which notes that the Board, of course, pays no transportation or witness fees. Testifying before Loyalty Boards is entirely a voluntary matter. I had already testified before the State Department's Board in the cases of two other employes. The Board had treated me with a formally faultless courtesy under which I thought I sensed an indomitable hostility sublimated into glances, smiles and intonations of complacent amusement.

Since I was busy writing this book, I had little time to spare. Before my belated answer, saying that I would testify, had reached the Board, one of the higher officials of the State Department telephoned me. Warmly, he reminded me that we had a great mutual friend. Generously, he offered to send a car to fetch me if I would testify at once at the Clubb hearing. I agreed to testify, though I preferred to drive myself. The sudden urgency surprised me as much as the sudden warmth which again enfolded me when I reached the State Department.

The hearing began. Usually in a hearing it is possible to detect a logic and purpose in the questions asked. The questions put to me that day mystified me completely. Among other questions, I was asked if Mike Gold had been present at my conversation with Clubb, if Mike Gold had been present at all at the *New Masses* that day in 1932. I was asked if Mike Gold on meeting a stranger would be likely to call him "Comrade," what the geography of the *New Masses* building was like, if there were revolutionary posters on the wall. Two points, in particular, puzzled me. I could not understand why I was asked if a Communist would keep a diary (my answer: no). I could not understand the degree

XXXIII

One hot June day in 1932, while I was preparing my third issue of the *New Masses*, I answered the telephone, and an unfamiliar voice said quietly: "This is Comrade Bedacht. I would like to see you right away."

Bedacht's office was on the ninth floor of the Workers Center, which, during my absence from the party, had moved from Union Square to 13th Street. I knew of Bedacht only as the fatherly Communist "who had kids to the number of acht," as a singularly self-effacing member of the Central Committee, and head of the International Workers Order, a Communist-controlled benefit and insurance society. I tried to think of any possible reason why Comrade Bedacht would want to see me. I had no idea that that quiet little man had been for years a permanent link between the Central Committee of the American Communist Party and the Soviet Military Intelligence in the United States.

It was seven years since Comrade Krieger had appeared at my desk in the Public Library to guide me into the Communist Party. Comrade Bedacht was about to summon me into crypts of Communism that I scarcely dreamed existed, into its deep underground, whose door was about to close noiselessly behind me almost as if I had never existed.

of importance which was obviously attached by the Loyalty Board to the case of a man whose rank in China had not been especially exalted.

For I did not know two facts that I was to learn shortly after. The first fact was that Clubb, on his return from China, had abruptly been upped to head the State Department's China desk. The second fact was that he had kept a diary. In the course of his hasty departure from China that diary had passed into the hands of the British authorities. Always great readers of diaries, the British read this one and found an entry to the effect that, in 1932, O. Edmund Clubb had had a conversation with Whittaker Chambers in the *New Masses* office. Other entries provided the basis for the mystifying questions at the hearing. This diary the British had turned over to the American authorities. Clubb's recollection was refreshed by it so that he subsequently was able to recall our meeting.

Recently, Clubb was completely cleared of any aspersion of disloyalty, but was deemed a "poor security risk." Secretary Acheson then had the case reviewed by his own deputy who not only cleared Clubb of any suggestion of disloyalty, but also of the imputation of "a security risk." Clubb at once resigned and was given a pension. In fairness to the State Department, it may be noted, too, that the two employes against whom I had testified earlier also subsequently resigned.

5

UNDERGROUND

The First Apparatus

I

Max Bedacht had somehow convinced himself that I was the son of Robert W. Chambers, the novelist. No doubt, the same surname and the fact that we both wrote (though for somewhat different markets) made kinship seem self-evident to him. When the novelist died, shortly after I came to know Bedacht, he congratulated me on coming into a fat legacy, which I believe he thought was about to be swept into the party's till. When I tried to undeceive him, his disappointment was so great that at first he insisted that I was covering up, and I had some trouble convincing him that Robert W. Chambers and Whittaker Chambers were really unrelated.

For Bedacht had the thrifty, bookkeeping mind. He was a little man, a Swiss, who had once been a barber, and, later on, a taxidermist. When I knew him better, the Communist Party's secret link with the Soviet Military Intelligence would sometimes pause at the show windows of stuffed animal shops and complain about the uncraftsmanly mounting and especially the unrealistic way the glass eyes were done.

The day he first commanded me to his office, he was not cordial. He looked like a shopkeeper who has been caught by a late customer just at closing time and is trying to hide behind his glasses. He also looked a little like Heinrich Himmler. (Like Himmler before he became chief of the Gestapo, Bedacht, after his expulsion from the party in the 40's, became a chicken farmer.) About both brief, tidy men there was a disturbing quality of secret power mantling insignificance—what might be called the ominousness of nonentity, which is peculiar to the terrible little figures of our time.

"What are you doing now, Comrade Chambers?" Bedacht asked me. I said that I was editing the *New Masses*. "You were out of the party for a while, weren't you?" he asked. I said that I had been out of the party. "For some reason," he said, as if he strongly disapproved of the whole business, "they want you to go into one of the party's 'special institutions.'" Bedacht always used that expression in referring to any of the Communist underground apparatuses. But it was a term new to me.

I asked what he meant. "It is a 'special institution,'" he repeated. As I still looked blank, he added: "They want you to do underground work."

I asked: "What does underground work mean?" "I don't know," he said. "*They* will tell you." I saw that, even if he did know, Bedacht would not tell me.

I asked if it meant that I would have to leave the *New Masses.* He said that I would and that I would also have to leave the open Communist Party. I pointed out that I had just returned to the party and had just begun to edit the *New Masses.* If I dropped out of sight, there would be a lot of gossip. "I told them that," said Bedacht.

I said that I must have some time to think it over. Bedacht looked annoyed (I now know that he was under pressure from the underground to hurry). "You can have until tomorrow morning," he said. Then he warned me not to mention our conversation to anyone but my wife. I left him.

In our time, a thousand similar conversations must have taken place under just such unarresting auspices. Every man to whom such a summons has come must have found it deeply unsettling. Just the implication of undefined power lurking behind a figure like Bedacht and suddenly giving him ambiguous meaning, is disturbing. The terms "special institution" and "underground" could only mean secret, possibly dangerous party work. They could only mean that, somewhere beside the open Communist Party, there existed a concealed party which functioned so smoothly that in seven years as a Communist I had not suspected it. At that time, I thought of the underground as an underground of the American Communist Party.

As a Communist, I felt a quiet elation at the knowledge that there was one efficient party organization and that it had selected me to work with it. There was also a little electric jab in the thought. In the nature of its work, such an organization could not pick its personnel at random. Therefore, for some time, it must have been watching me. Unknown to me, eyes must have been observing me. For the first time, I did something involuntary that would soon cease to be involuntary, and would become a technique —I glanced back to see if anybody were following me.

It was clear that, reaching out, from where I could not tell, something completely unforeseeable had happened to me, which could only mean a turning point in my life. But my life was no longer only my life. It was also my wife's life. I had intended to spend that night in New York. Instead, I took the train home to discuss the new challenge with her.

I I

Home was then a wild lonely farm, six miles from Glen Gardner, in Hunterdon County, in western New Jersey. My wife and I had moved there early in the cold spring of 1932. The move was more like a flight than a move. It was the first outcropping of a need that was to die down, but never again to die out of my life, and was finally to dominate it—my need to live close to the land as I had when a boy.

During my years in the open Communist Party, I had little by little put the countryside out of my mind. The intellectual change that I had to make in becoming a Communist had required all of my effort. My hours at the *Daily Worker* had taken most of my time. Communism is a faith of the cities, and can look upon the countryside only to organize, that is to say, to destroy it. And while simply to enter a city is for me always a little like entering a grave, in those years I forced myself to live in New York and learned to shut my mind and my eyes against it because to open either to it filled me with dislike and disgust. As a Communist, that is to say, a man dedicated to directing history, I had no choice. For it is clear that the history of the 20th century will be determined by the cities, not by the countryside.

But in my two years outside the Communist Party, my old need for the land asserted itself. In the spring of 1932, that craving seized me like an infection which I could not throw off, and which made me physically ill. The slum in which we lived became unendurable to me—not just because it was a slum. Every other part of the city affected me in the same way. I felt that life was not worth living if it had to be lived away from the land.

At that point, two friends, two left-wing intellectuals, who owned a farm near Glen Gardner, proposed that my wife and I should go out and remodel their barn as a house, where we could then live rent-free.

The barn had not been used for years. It was weathered, windowless, drafty, but its frame was solid. It stood between a dirt road, where few cars passed, and a little brook, which could not be seen under its ferns. Behind rose a densely wooded mountainside. My wife and I had almost no money. We did not care. We set to work to lay floors out of old lumber and to raise walls of field stone. In our spare time we planted gardens. Few periods of our life have been so happy. All around us, in the earliest spring, the benzoin bushes put out their little yellow flowers on bare branches and filled the air with searching sweetness. Behind us, the brook gurgled, and all day the thrushes filled the mountainside with their flutings.

Sometimes, at sundown, we would walk to the edge of a hill from which we could see out across a valley, its farms and a village. One evening we reached the rim of the lookout, and the village with its white-spired church lay toylike and sun-touched below us. It had rained. The air was a pure ocean. Suddenly, there floated up to us through it from far below, the voices of hundreds of robins chanting together. The sound, floating in the air, seemed to have no connection with the earth, so that we stood silently side by side, listening to it, until the sun set and even the height where we stood grew dark. My wife and I do not often talk about such things, but each of us knew that it was one of the peaks of our life together, when we understood how deeply we needed each other because we understood how deeply we loved the same things. Recently, I was describing the farm at Glen Gardner to my children, and when that moment came back to me I stopped and smiled unconsciously. "I know what you are thinking about," said my wife who was watching me, "you are remembering the robins in the valley."

Glen Gardner was too far from New York for me to commute every day, and commutation was too expensive. During the *New Masses* week, I usually stayed at the Jacob Burcks' or the Intrators', for, after the fashion of Communist friends, we all shared our lodgings, our food, our money, and even our clothes. This weekly separation was hard on both of us, especially on my wife. But she spent the days in endless activity and one of the joys of homecoming was to see how much she had accomplished in the barn and the gardens while I was gone. For fifteen dollars, we had bought an old Ford with which we sometimes drove to and from the station at Glen Gardner. Much of the time it did not work. Then I would take the short cut across the mountain and walk the six miles to the station. This walk appalled our friends. But like our other hardships, we regarded it as something that a Communist takes in his stride.

My wife used to walk part of the way with me. The short cut ran through a great apple orchard that in April was heavy with bloom and humming with bees. Sometimes, as we climbed through the woods, deer, that we had not seen until they broke before us, would swim across fallen trees, and blend with the shadows and the stillness. Halfway up the mountain, my wife would sit down on a tree trunk while I climbed higher, turning to look back at her until she was out of sight—a lonely little figure in the silence (the partings were the worst).

It was to this sanctuary I hurried after my talk with Max Bedacht. I told my wife what had happened. She listened without interrupting. Then, like me, she asked what underground work meant. I said that I did not know exactly, but that it must be secret and important party work. She sat so silent that I glanced at her and saw that her face was quivering and that she was trying not to cry. I took her hand.

"I do not want to stand in the way of anything that you think is right and that you must do," she said through her tears. "But, dear heart, don't do it."

"Why not?" I asked. "It is the most responsible work the party can offer me. I am a revolutionist."

"I don't know," she said sobbing, "I don't know why not. You must do what you think is right. But I am afraid. Please, dear heart, don't do it." I cannot stand my wife's tears. I promised not to go into the underground.

III

I did not say no to Comrade Bedacht at once. I simply urged again that my recent return to the party, and the fact that I had edited only two issues of the *New Masses,* would cause talk if I disappeared. Impatiently, Bedacht brushed aside my objections as something that had already been settled.

Then I said: "I am sorry, but I have decided not to do it." "You have no choice," said the little man. He meant, of course, that I was under the discipline of the party and that, if I did not go into the underground, I would go out of the party. "In fact," he added, "in a few minutes I am going to take you to someone from the 'special institution.'"

We waited. Now and again, Bedacht glanced at his watch. Evidently, he had a prearranged appointment with the man he was taking me to and was giving him time to arrive. Then we left Communist headquarters (I for the last time). We walked to Union Square and down a subway entrance. Under Union Square, the tunnels that connect the B.M.T. and the East Side subways form a small catacomb. "You know the man you are going to meet," Bedacht said. But he would not tell me who the man was. In a tunnel we came upon a loitering figure who stood staring at the ground. He glanced up, as we approached, and smiled. It was John Sherman whom I had last seen crying in the *Daily Worker* office.

Bedacht introduced him formally as if we were strangers. "This is Don," he said. To Don he added: "If you have no more jobs for me, I'll leave you." Sherman and I walked quickly in the opposite direction to that Bedacht had taken, and presently strolled through the West Side. Sherman was almost kittenish, as if he had played a particularly good joke on life. Clearly, he felt that, in drawing me into the underground, he was rescuing me from the open Communist Party toward which, since his expulsion, he felt personally vindictive. He brushed off all my questions as to where he had been since I last saw him (later I was to learn that he had been in touch with the underground in 1929, and had been absorbed by it as soon as he was expelled). "You're in the underground now," said Sherman exultantly, "where I ask questions, but don't answer them, and you answer questions, but don't ask them."

He asked me if I was married and, when I told him that I was, said: Good. He asked me if I had any children and, when I said no, said: Very good. Then he told me that at seven o'clock that night, I must meet him on the uptown subway platform at 116th Street —the subway stop of Columbia University. "Where are you going now?" he asked as we parted. I said that I was going to the *New Masses*. "Do you have to?" he asked. I said that I had to. "It had better be the last time," he said. "In our work, you will never go near the *New Masses*. You will never have anything to do with party people again. If you do, we will know it. You're a respectable bourgeois now."

I V

I left the *New Masses* office about six o'clock to keep my uptown appointment with Sherman. I walked to the 14th Street subway station, glancing behind me, in my new way, to see if I were being watched. I could not see anybody. But, as I waited on the subway platform, a hand dropped on my shoulder. It was Sherman, who had come up behind me. "How did you know I would be here?" I asked. He smiled knowingly and did not answer.

At 96th Street, we had to change trains. I started to get up as the train drew into the station. Sherman gripped my arm and pulled me down. "Always stay seated," he said, "until everybody else is leaving the car. Always be the last one off."

We did not go to 116th Street. Instead, we got off at 110th Street, sauntered up Broadway and wove our way over to Riverside Drive near Grant's Tomb. On the downtown side of the Drive, a big black car was parked. A big man—a Russian, I would soon learn—sat at the wheel. Sherman opened the rear door and told me to get in. Then he sat in the front seat beside the driver, who did not turn to greet or look at me. He and Sherman discussed matters which I have forgotten and which, in any case, I did not understand. We drove down Riverside Drive.

Presently, the Russian looked at me in the mirror. He was young, perhaps in his thirties, with a round, firm, commanding face and a trick of opening his eyes wide to express surprise or emphasis. He was very well-dressed and wore an expensive fedora hat. (I was hatless, tieless, and had on a khaki shirt and slacks.) Sherman addressed the driver with the slight deference natural in speaking to a superior and called him Otto or Carl—I have forgotten which. I was later to know of him also as Herbert. All these names were underground pseudonyms. Herbert was, as Dr. Philip Rosenbliett, who will appear later on in this narrative, would afterwards tell me, a tank officer in the Leningrad military district of the Red Army.

I no longer remember the order of the conversation that followed. It was held in a slightly bantering tone and consisted of questions, which Herbert asked and which I answered. I had the impression that he already knew most of the answers and asked the questions as a matter of form, and perhaps to see if my answers would differ from what he knew.

He asked me when I had joined the Communist Party, why I had left it, if I was a Lovestoneite and the circumstances of my return to the party. (Both Sherman and Herbert treated this grave subject as if they viewed it from a height from which political differences in the American Communist Party were like the games of children.) Herbert asked about my work at the *New Masses*. He asked me if I knew the nature of the apparatus (the first time I had met that party word for organization) with which I was in contact. He seemed very much amused when I said that I did not. He did not offer to tell me what its nature was. He asked me if I was married and if my wife was a party member. He did not seem at all disturbed that she was not. But the fact that we lived in the country made him frown. In an aside to Sherman, he said that I must at once find a suitable place to live in New York City.

He warned me that henceforth I must absolutely separate myself from all contacts with Communists and the Communist Party, and live as much as possible like a respectable bourgeois. I saw him glance at my tieless shirt and slacks. In another aside to Sherman, he said something about getting me properly dressed while both laughed at the careless costumes of Communists in the open party. He said that the apparatus would give me $100 a month to live on, that Sherman would pay me, be my boss and that I was to obey him unfailingly. I have forgotten in what words Herbert gave me to understand that discipline in the underground was strict and that disobedience brought stiff penalties. It scarcely mattered, for his voice, manner and presence suggested secret and seemingly limitless power.

Then Herbert said to Sherman, "We will have to give him a new name." To me he said: "I think we will call you Bob. You look like Bob to me." He repeated solemnly that I was never to return to the *New Masses* or any Communist office. "That is a military command," he said stiffly and his eyes flew open in their peculiar way.

We had reached Broadway in the upper 40's. Sherman arranged with me the time and place when I would next meet him. Then Herbert asked me to get out of the car and he and Sherman drove off together.

I walked about the streets, still watching to see if I were followed, brooding on that strange meeting and my gentle wife, sobbing: "Dear heart, don't do it." A force greater than myself had picked me up and was disposing of me—a force that, in the end, it would all but cost me my life to break away from, and may yet cost my life, for there is more than one way of killing a man, and the story, begun that night, is not ended.

V

When I met and shook hands with Sherman a day or so later, he left in the palm of my hand a roll of bills. "Why?" I asked him. He said: "For clothes. In our work, you can't go around the way you used to on the *Daily Worker*." Without question he was right. Yet there was something ugly in the fact and in the gesture. The fact violated the asceticism (or puritanism), the denial of the values of the world as it is, that lies close to the heart of Communism, as of all great faiths. The gesture violated something else. Several years later, Sherman would say to me: "Always give money to a new man. It obligates him to you." Then I realized that it was the fact that

Sherman had been waiting for me with the money rolled up in his hand that had made the calculated gesture ugly. He had given me fifty dollars. With that I outfitted myself.

I can no longer distinguish one of those early meetings with Sherman from another, tell just where in New York they took place or what was said at each. But on one or more of them, Sherman began to instruct me in underground organizational techniques, the only real instruction of the kind that I ever had. There was no particular order in the instruction. Sherman simply took up points as they occurred to him. I had begun to call Sherman by his underground name, Don, and shall call him that henceforth.

Point one, at least in importance, was discipline. Absolute obedience was the rule in the underground. Whatever I was told to do was a military order, and I must obey it as such. I was not to question anything; I could be questioned about anything.

I was never to write anything about my work (my *New Masses* writing worried the members of that apparatus to the very end). I might keep a little memo book, with the date, hour and place of my appointments suitably disguised in any way I liked. It had been found that attempts to memorize future appointments led to confusion. Don preferred a system in which the entry in the memo was two hours later, or two hours earlier than the time set for the meeting. All meetings were by prearrangement. For example, when I met Don, we would agree before we parted where and when we would next meet. Telephones were always assumed to be tapped. They were to be used only in exceptional cases or in emergencies. For unscheduled or emergency meetings, there was a "reserve meeting place." In Don's case, this was an apartment, which I shall soon describe, and which was referred to over the telephone simply as "The Gallery." If Don telephoned me and said: "How would you like to meet me at The Gallery at seven o'clock?" he meant: Meet me at the apartment on West 51st Street.

Separation. For one reason or another, members sometimes lost contact with their apparatus. Don had once lost touch in that way for several months. Later on, I knew of other cases. If I should ever be "lost," I was never under any circumstances to try to reconnect myself with the apparatus. There might be good reasons why the apparatus wanted "to lose" me. No matter how long it took, I was simply to sit at home and wait until someone contacted me.

Technique of meetings. There was a traditional technique of meetings. It was simple, but decades of underground work had proved that it was successful. Before any meeting, at least half an hour, and preferably one or two hours, should be spent wandering around town, changing conveyances and direction to make sure that there was no surveillance. Undue nervousness about surveillance, always possible when a man was tired or strained, must be carefully avoided. But if there were definite signs of surveillance, if an apparatus worker found himself persistently followed by some one, or by a series of observers who seemed to be relieving one another, he must not keep his appointment. He must lead the men watching him as far away from the place of appointment as possible, and then try to give them the slip. For that purpose, buildings with more than one entrance, crowds of all kinds and especially crowded subway trains were useful. If the apparatus man eluded his followers, he would then go home and wait. The apparatus would contact him.

Punctuality was the absolute rule of all meetings. Failure in this respect was considered a cardinal sin in the underground, and even a cause for serious suspicion. Thus, in Washington, several years later, I refused to have any further dealings with an underground Communist because he came an hour late to an important appointment. The man who reached the meeting place first would wait fifteen minutes, and no more than fifteen minutes, for the second man. Sometimes there was an agreement that if one meeting failed, a second meeting would be held the next day at the same time and place, or at another prearranged time and place. In New York meetings were usually held in restaurants or movie houses. Sometimes the initial contact was made at a movie, followed by a long ramble around the city, winding up at a restaurant. Variations on that pattern were used. In Baltimore and Washington, I later found that few of the New York techniques were suitable, and worked out new techniques for meeting which I shall describe in the proper place.

In any one day, meetings should be widely separated in time and space. If a man were meeting three people in one day, he might meet one man in the Bronx. Several hours later, he might meet a second man in Brooklyn. Several hours after that, he might meet a third man in midtown Manhattan. Meetings on successive days should never be in the same area.

Forgetting and not seeing. Every underground apparatus has certain fixed points, headquarters, workshops, hideaways, houses of contacts, where one or another member must go more or less regularly. Nearly always he is first taken to such places by another member or contact of the apparatus. Don impressed on me the necessity of learning the way to such places without observing the name of the street or the number of the house where they were situated. The underground worker, he pointed out, must make an effort to put out of his mind any features that will identify such addresses. I found that that effort at first resulted in the very opposite to what was intended. At first the mind found itself "peeking" and actually noted things more vividly than it would ordinarily do. But after a while a habit of not seeing was formed. I know my way to a number of places which I could not locate by street name or address. That is why, in my early public testimony, I sometimes used to say "the up and down street" or the "cross street." I had forced myself not to learn their names.

Non-recognition. Underground workers who chanced to meet in public or at any kind of gathering must never, under any circumstances, greet each other or give any sign of recognition. To greet another apparatus worker on the street was a first-rate breach of discipline and punishable as such.

The Chain of Command. Decentralization was the principle of underground organization. Originally, Don told me, all the members of his apparatus had met together to discuss their work. Thus everybody in the apparatus knew everybody else. Later, a reorganization had taken place. Thereafter, few members of the apparatus met or knew one another's identity.

At the head of the apparatus was a chief. He might know all the members of the apparatus and from time to time, often at long intervals, meet them. Working directly under him, would be one, or perhaps several men, none of whom (at least in theory) knew one another, but all of whom dealt with the chief. Under each of those lieutenants, there might again be one or several men who also did not know one another or the existence of the other parallel chains of command within their own apparatus. This principle of separation continued down to the lowest link in each chain.

The chief knew the identity of each of the men in the apparatus. In theory none of the others knew the identity of his coworkers. They knew one another only by underground pseudonyms —Bob, Don, Otto. Each man usually had more than one pseudonym. Don was also known as Mike. Otto was also known as Herbert and Carl. I was known as Bob, Carl, Eugene.

The second man in each chain of command knew how to reach the last man on the chain; he knew his name, address and telephone number. But the last man in the chain did not know how to reach the second man, his immediate superior. A third man from the end of the chain knew how to reach the second man in the chain, but the second man did not know how to reach the third man—and so on up to the top. Thus, in theory, no subordinate knew how to reach his immediate superior at any point in the chain. If he were arrested, or deserted, he could only reveal the identity of the men under him. The upper reaches of the chain were hidden from his sight; he simply did not know them.

As in most human relations, this system was not kept to rigorously. Sometimes circumstances made it necessary to breach the rules. Sometimes carelessness, short cuts, the development of personal friendships, the boredom of keeping to an arbitrary conspiratorial pattern which, in the United States, often seemed pointless, and was always a nuisance, caused some let-down in precaution. But, in general, the rules were observed.

Arrest. If an underground worker were arrested, he must assert his innocence. He must deny all charges against him. He must divulge nothing. Decades of underground experience had shown that any suspect who admits to one fact, however trifling he may believe it to be, will end by telling all. This is a principle that all Communists are taught. I had known it even in the open party. It is in this light that the conduct of Hiss and others who denied my charges must be viewed.

Money. Underground work made it necessary for apparatus people to live somewhat better than other Communists. This was not only essential to the work, said Don. It was proper, since underground activity was more hazardous than work in the open party, and the people engaged in it should not have to worry about ways and means. But no underground worker should receive more than the "party maximum" (the highest salary that the open party paid its top leaders; at that time, $45 a week, if I remember rightly). In the conditions of underground work, it was often impossible for an apparatus man to live on that salary. Therefore, each man was also permitted an expense account, which was roughly geared to the kind of work he was doing. The expense account covered such items as transportation, telephone, medical expenses, rent, etc. These were the party's, not the individual worker's, expenses.

Drinking. Underground workers were absolutely forbidden to drink. This did not mean that underground people never touched liquor. But in their meetings with contacts, at social gatherings or in restaurants, liquor was banned. Actually, few underground workers ever drank. In my experience, I knew only one drunkard (Valentine Markin). His drinking cost him his life.

Penalties. It was Don's way to suggest, rather than to describe, the penalties for the infraction of underground rules. He would say: "If you do something wrong, we will soon find out"—from which I gradually gathered that one section of the apparatus, or some other apparatus, was assigned to watch us. But only once was I able to spot this surveillance. Don also solemnly cited the case of a minor apparatus worker who in some way had displeased Herbert. Herbert shipped him off to Russia and sent a covering letter which said simply: "I hope I will never see this man again." "You know," said Don, "what that meant."

But an underground worker was not without rights in the apparatus. If he had grievances against his superior, he could write out a statement about them and forward it to Moscow. "But," said Don with a wide smile, "the statement must be in the form of an unsealed letter. And it must be forwarded by the superior who is being attacked."

During my first days in the underground, Don explained to me that the party was always referred to as "the Bank." My job was to be the contact between the underground and the Bank in the person of Max Bedacht. Such a liaison man was often referred to in the apparatus by the German term, *Verbindungsmensch,* for German, not Russian, was the international language of Communism in those days.

In the past, Don had been the *Verbindungsmensch.* He met weekly with Bedacht, sometimes to ask specific favors of the Bank, sometimes to receive information from it. Sometimes there was no business at all. Then Don just chatted with Bedacht. Don met Bedacht by calling him at the Workers Center or the I.W.O. office and summoning him to some prearranged place. Bedacht had no way of reaching Don. Since Bedacht might have important unexpected news to give, the contact was indispensable and must be kept up regularly.

"Bedacht," Don added, "is used to thinking of you as a rank and file party member while he is a big shot. Now you are his boss. You must make him understand that."

"Is meeting Bedacht all I have to do?" I asked.

"That's all for now," said Don. "In our work, the worst part is the waste of time. But that's the kind of work it is. It was all thought out years ago. Don't try to improve it."

I had no desire to improve it. I realized that I was not in an underground of the American Communist Party. I was either in a Soviet underground or in an underground of the Communist International. In practice, it made little difference which. Each is a different organizational form of the same political purpose. No Communist can be loyal to the Communist International, or any of its component parties, without being loyal to the Soviet Union. No Communist knows any higher loyalty or he could not be a Communist.

I was in the Fourth Section of the Soviet Military Intelligence, though no one in the apparatus ever told me that fact and it would be years before I was sure of it.

V I

Don went with me to see Bedacht the first time. We met in an Automat. Bedacht was plaintive. My disappearance from the *New Masses* had caused a scandal. There had been charge and countercharge on the floor of the John Reed Club. One "non-party element" had demanded to know if the party had "liquidated Chambers." A loyal Communist had shouted that Chambers had probably walked out of the *New Masses* as he had walked out of the *Daily Worker*.

"Browder is furious," said Bedacht. "He stamped his foot at me." Browder and I had met just twice; we disliked each other at sight. "Browder," said Comrade Bedacht, "says that Chambers must come back." Don laughed. "Tell Browder," he said in the tone of a pasha of four horses tails talking to a rug dealer, "that he is faced with an accomplished fact. There is nothing he can do about it."

"He threatens to take it higher up," said Bedacht.

"Are we mice or are we men?" asked Don—a question that he was fond of asking. In this case it meant that the action of the underground in my case was irreversible. "From now on," he added, "this gentleman will be Bob to you. He will take my place. He will tell you what we need. Give him all the help you can."

VII

Following Don's instructions, I rented an apartment in New York. It was in Greenwich Village. I was able to rent it furnished (among other oddments, with a rather startling piece of African sculpture) from a staff member of a New York liberal weekly. From an underground viewpoint, this arrangement was ideal. The telephone was in my landlord's name. I did not change it. I did not change his name on the mailbox (we did not receive mail). I had practically disappeared as a person.

Rather sadly, my wife and I prepared to abandon our barn. We took a last look at our gardens, which the weeds would now smother, and a last walk to the rim of the valley. We decided to leave such furniture as we owned in the barn. All our other possessions filled two or three shopping bags.

The only thing that worried me at all about our apartment was our landlord, and he soon convinced me that he was not a cause for concern. He was one of those valiantly and vaguely unhappy middle-aging intellectuals who had spent years not writing the book he had planned to write as a younger man. He was not a Communist, though his wife, who was in publishing, was sympathetic. But we had a number of friends in common and he knew that I was a Communist. He himself was making his first tremulous splashes in the great leftward intellectual undertow of the 30's, borne up, more cheerfully than most, by a buoyant displacement of Scotch and soda.

About four o'clock in the morning of our first night at the apartment, we were awakened by a persistent drumming on the door. I opened it to find my landlord, happily teetering back and forth, smiling shyly and a little vacantly. "I want to tell you something," he said. "I *must* tell you something. I, too, believe in a proletariat revolution, although"—he added apologetically after a solemn interval—"I am not myself a proletariat."

He repeated these tidings several times, and then, with the satisfaction of a man who has made clear his discriminating stand on a difficult question, groped his way downstairs. For several successive nights, I opened the door in the gray dawn to receive his revolutionary avowal, always in the same slightly scrambled terms, sometimes a little tearful. Then I stopped answering (somewhat guiltily, for after all it was his apartment), and he grew discouraged. I saw that the liberal intellectuals were indeed mounting the barricades. I felt reasonably sure that whatever suspicions my landlord might have about my activities, he would never report them where it mattered. Neither would a dozen other liberals who, in the great whispering gallery of New York City, soon knew that I was engaged in some kind of underground activity.

VIII

I cannot remember now whether Don first introduced me to "The Gallery," or whether he first introduced me to "Ulrich," who then took me to The Gallery. Ulrich was my superior in the underground.

The Gallery was a private apartment on the second or third floor of a brownstone building at 7 West 51st Street, just off Fifth Avenue. I have a somewhat blurred recollection of a vast living room furnished with rather massive furniture, of many long windows in the west wall and bookcases from floor to ceiling. There were always ten or twelve boxes of candy lying about, from which I concluded that the tenant of the apartment was a woman. Though I was in The Gallery a number of times, I never saw her.

I presently learned (from Dr. Philip Rosenbliett) that she was Paula Levine. When the French police rounded up a Soviet espionage ring in Paris, *circa* 1933, Paula Levine was the only American member of the group (the other Americans were Robert Gordon Switz and his wife) to escape. She had noticed the lurking figures of the French police surveillance, and without returning to her room, fled to Istanbul and thence to Russia. She has not been heard from since.

The Gallery may once have been one of the headquarters of the underground. When I visited it, it was merely a convenient meeting place for several of the apparatus workers. Since I was taken there so early in my underground experience, I assume that a decision had already been made to abandon it.

It was probably at The Gallery that I last saw Herbert. One day shortly after I went underground, Herbert, Ulrich and I were in The Gallery together. It was hot, but Ulrich was pacing the floor, a nervous habit. He had taken off his jacket. I thought that his expensively tailored, but many-pleated gray trousers, his sweat-soaked silk shirt, slight stoop, and gait made him look a good deal like a gangster.

Herbert was sitting on a wide couch behind a low coffee table.

He would not have dreamed of taking off his jacket. He sat, stiff and soldierly. Suddenly, he said: "Bob, stand up in front of me." I stood up. "Empty your pockets." This was "pocket inspection," to which Herbert subjected all underground workers at irregular intervals to see if they were violating the rule about not carrying notes or non-essential papers in their pockets. Since my suit was new, and I had not had time to turn my pockets into a filing case, I passed the inspection handily.

Pocket inspection is my last clear recollection of Herbert, whom I was to see only three or four times before he faded from my horizon. I never asked, of course, what had become of him. But I know that eventually he returned to Russia. For Don talked with him in Moscow, in 1936, at the time when Don was engaged in a life and death battle of wits with the Fourth Section in the person of Colonel Uritzky (the nephew of Moses Uritzky, the organizer of the Red Terror).

IX

Like Herbert, Don too soon disappeared. I did not see him again for two or three years, when I would learn that, during his absence, he had set up an underground organization in California.

When Don disappeared, Ulrich was, for a time, my only contact in the underground. He was a Russian who was also known as Walter. His real name, as I was to discover much later on (and as Scotland Yard and the F.B.I. have confirmed), was Alexander Ulanov.* Before the Russian Revolution, Ulrich had been in a dozen jails in Russia and outside of it. He had been a fellow prisoner of Stalin's in a sub-arctic Siberian prison camp, from which Ulrich made a sensational escape that briefly made him a hero of the revolutionary world. During the revolution and the civil war, he had been a partisan commander in southern Russia, where his exploits were legendary.

He was a monkeyish little man, short, tough and agile. There was something monkeylike in his loose posture, in the droop of his arms and the roll of his walk (for some years, he had been, among

* Circa 1946, *Time's* Moscow bureau employed a Russian woman as a part-time translator. One day she casually pointed to my name in the magazine's masthead, and asked Craig Thompson, *Time's* bureau chief: "Do you know that man?" Thompson said that he knew me very well. "So do I," she said. Her name was Nadya Ulanova. She was Ulrich's wife. In that way, I learned Ulrich's real name more than a decade after I last saw him.

other things, a sailor). There was something also monkeylike about his features, which were small, lined and alert. Sometimes, they seemed young for his age, which was about fifty (old for an underground worker). Sometimes, they seemed almost ageless. But it was his brown eyes that were most monkeylike, alternately mischievous and wistful. They had looked out on all life in four continents, from top to bottom, from stinking prison cells to diplomatic dinners, from violence in battle to conspiracy in peace. They had observed it all tranquilly, beyond the terms of any political theory or doctrine, with an instinctive charity that took the form of irony and pity, and the wisdom of a man who knows that amusement at the folly of life begins first of all with amusement at the folly of himself.

Ulrich was a humble man (which sometimes made lesser people take him for less than he was), well aware of his own limitations, and not at all troubled by them. But his experience of life was great, his reading of men acute, though often he acted directly against what his intelligence told him about them. For his humanity was greater than anything else. And he had the rare faculty of seeing most things from a viewpoint outside of himself.

I was once walking with him in Central Park when an eclipse of the sun began. He suggested that we sit on a bench and watch it. We sat perfectly silent while the light thickened into a brownish murk. In that strange obscurity, the man of violence suddenly said in a voice of tender concern: "The little birds and the animals, what can they possibly make of it?" Yet one of his favorite expressions was: "I'll have you shot." I never doubted that, in an ultimate sense, he meant what he said, that he would indeed shoot me if he felt that he must for the safety of the organization, or because he had been ordered to. He would merely recognize, as he had before in his experience, that there is a necessity under which all men live, and against which his natural impulse to mercy was powerless. I never doubted, either, that, if he could possibly do so, he would find a way to let me, or anybody else, escape, for he hated necessity's brutal grip.

He was a natural leader of men at the human level. "Bob," he said to me at once by way of settling what our relationship was to be: "I will never ask you to do anything that I am afraid to do myself." But as a kind of military man whom history has largely outmoded, he sometimes felt a twinge of childlike envy for those whom history had replaced him with. "Herbert," he once said to me, "is a real soldier. He marches up to a regiment on the parade ground and shouts: 'Salute!' I can't do that. If I know we have to take a dangerous position, I just say (with a forward jerk of his arm): 'Come on, boys, we have to go up and take it.'"

This curious man, the only Russian who was ever to become my close friend, was not a Communist. He had been a member of the left wing of the Socialist Revolutionary Party which, during the Russian Revolution, had gone over to the Bolsheviks. His wife (whom I was soon to meet in the underground as Elena and Maria) was a party member. She was the party's eye on Ulrich—a loving eye, for they had been happily married for years. The party trusted Ulrich, insofar as it ever trusts anyone, because of his revolutionary past. Moreover, his son was kept as a hostage at school in Russia (the boy was killed fighting against the Germans during the Nazi invasion). For the complexities of Communist theory and the loopings of policy, Ulrich had an amused tolerance. He observed with the same detached amusement the foibles of Communists, especially of Communist intellectuals. (Ulrich himself was a proletarian, a former steel worker—but a proletarian who had read Byron as a boy, as he once told me, drawing a volume of the English Romantic from Paula Levine's crowded bookshelves.)

He once humorously pointed up the difference between the intellectual and the man of action in one of the stories of which he had scores. It was before the Russian Revolution. Ulrich had been arrested for political activities and was being marched in a mixed convoy of political prisoners and criminals to exile in Siberia. Now and again, the whole convoy had to halt while the snows melted and the roads opened to the east. To while away the time, a group of prisoners decided that each one should write out and read the story of his life. "There was one young student," said Ulrich. "He was just a boy. He had simply been arrested for reading some Marxist book. That was all. In his whole life, nothing had ever happened to him. But he wrote a long story, and, do you know, it was very interesting.

"Then there was a criminal. He was a grown man. When his turn came, he said that he had no story. 'Why?' we asked. 'Didn't you agree to tell the story of your life?' 'There is nothing to tell,' he said. 'I killed a man. They sent me to Siberia. In prison, they beat me. With another convict, I escaped. We got lost in the *taiga*. We were starving. I killed my comrade and ate some of his flesh.

If I had not killed him, he would have killed me. I went on. I met a bear. He attacked me. I had no knife, so I choked him with my hands. I ate some of the meat. So at last I escaped. What is there to tell?' "

During the civil war, Ulrich had commanded an armored train that ran north out of Nikolaiev. "Bob," he used to say to me, "if there is ever a revolution in America, get yourself an armored train. It is the only comfortable way to go through a revolution." But Ulrich did not have great faith in an American revolution. "When the revolution comes here," he once said, "it will only mean that the pants pressers are on strike and everybody has to go around without pants."

Once, during the civil war, two members of Ulrich's partisan band were captured by the White Guards. They were to be executed on a square in Sebastopol. Troops were posted everywhere, but Ulrich had decided to save his men. Under a guard of soldiers, they were marched out on the square to be shot. Alone, armed only with two revolvers, Ulrich opened fire on the troops. In a scene of truly Russian confusion, Ulrich and his two friends (for whom he had brought a revolver apiece), shot their way out and escaped.

Ulrich's wife told me that story. Ulrich told me another. In one pitched battle, his partisan forces were wiped out. Ulrich escaped by riding a horse until it foundered. Then he went on on foot. At last, he dropped, exhausted by combat and flight, on the banks of a little river and fell asleep. He awoke just at sunset and found two peasant children watching him. One of them was crying. He asked her why. "Because," she said, "Ilyosha Ulanov has been killed." (He made up another name when he told me the story.)

"Do you know, Bob," he said to me, "it is the strangest feeling to hear from a child that you are dead."

I did not care whether or not Ulrich was a Communist (it was some time before I discovered the fact that he was not). In him I felt the continuity of the revolutionary generations. In him, the wretched of the earth were no longer wretched. They had climbed to their feet in the dignity of effort and purpose to proclaim that they were the future. My work in the underground was a part of that revolutionary purpose. That feeling did not at all blind me to the fact that Ulrich himself was a rather careless underground worker.

X

One day Bedacht told me that "somebody" had been waiting in New York for some time to see my superior, and he was getting a little restless. Ulrich would know what it was all about. Ulrich did know at once, leading me to wonder then (as I was to wonder later) if there were not other means of communication between the underground and the open party in a Communist stratosphere closed to me.

Ulrich explained to me that he himself did not wish to meet the man who was waiting to see him. The man was a possible recruit for underground work in "one of the most dangerous countries in Europe." Bearing that in mind, I must meet him, said Ulrich, and decide whether I thought that the man was a good underground prospect.

In a day or so, Bedacht introduced me to a young American of Finnish extraction. His name was Arvid Jacobson. He had been a schoolteacher in Michigan, but had given up his job and come to New York at the party's orders. "Mrs. Morton" had recommended Jacobson, Bedacht said, as if he expected the name to electrify me. At that time, I had never heard of Mrs. Morton.

Jacobson seemed to me a highly nervous young man, somewhat truculent and petulant—not unnaturally, perhaps, since he had been kept waiting and his money was running low. But temperament is as hazardous in the underground as in the crew of a submarine. Moreover, Jacobson had one or two fingers missing from one hand—too easy an identifying mark.* Therefore, I advised against his use in the underground, especially in Europe. Despite that, Ulrich decided to meet Jacobson after all. I brought them together one day in Bryant Park, directly behind the New York Public Library. There I left them together.

I did not hear of Arvid Jacobson again until 1935 when he was arrested in Finland in a roundup of a Soviet espionage network, one of whose members was Colonel Pentakainen, the photographer of the Finnish General Staff. Jacobson was imprisoned, but

* I described this episode to the F.B.I., in 1949, without at first mentioning Jacobson's name, for I knew that this was one point of my story that the F.B.I. could absolutely check; and, at a rather unpleasant time, it gave me a childish pleasure to defer the climax. Then I held up one hand to show how Jacobson's fingers were missing. "Arvid Jacobson!" exclaimed Special Agent F. X. Plant who is a walking archive of the identities, features and peculiarities of Soviet agents.

subsequently returned to the United States. Colonel Pentakainen escaped by dashing across the Russian frontier in a car which contained his last consignment of highly secret Finnish military documents. It was the break-up of this ring in Finland that led, shortly afterward, to the break-up of the Soviet ring in France to which belonged Paula Levine, the tenant of The Gallery.

I presently asked Bedacht who Mrs. Morton was. He told me that she was the wife of Otto Kuusinen and that she had been working for some time in Detroit. Otto Kuusinen was for years a member of the Executive Committee of the Communist International and chairman of its Anglo-American bureau. When Russia invaded Finland, in 1939, Kuusinen was head of the puppet government of Finland which issued proclamations from behind the Russian lines.

One day Ulrich told me that he wished to visit Bedacht at his home. I arranged the meeting with Bedacht and then first learned from him where he lived. On an agreed night, Ulrich and I drove to Bedacht's red-brick house which was far out in Brooklyn. Inside and out, it looked like the home of a prosperous storekeeper. The "kids to the number of acht" were present, but were soon sent upstairs or outdoors. Ulrich, Bedacht and I sat around the dining-room table. I had the impression that Ulrich and Bedacht had never met before. They presently fell into a rambling argument about modern warfare. The mousy member of the Central Committee was all for tanks and mechanization. Ulrich, the former commander of an armored train, thought that cavalry was by no means outmoded and that the horse still played an important part in the Red Army.

When Ulrich had had enough of this, he asked me to leave the room. I went into the front living room. What the real business of the two men was I do not know. But as Ulrich parted from Bedacht in the hall, he slipped into his hand a large roll of bills, which Bedacht glanced at pleasurably. It was poor underground technique to pass this money in front of me. But that was Ulrich's way.

XI

One day Max Bedacht handed me a slip of paper on which was written the name and address of a doctor or dentist. It was a Russian or Jewish name and the address, by a curious chance, was Lynbrook, two or three blocks from the house where I had passed most of my life. Bedacht was excited. The doctor was a Trotskyist, he said, and Ulrich would want to do something about him. "Something"—I supposed that that meant hidden pressures, threats or perhaps death.

The slip of paper was my first challenge in the underground. Here, in a worse form, was the same malevolent force that in 1929 had driven me out of the open Communist party, reaching back again from the open party into the underground. Should I tear up the note? If I did, by the same action, I tore up the discipline that bound me as a Communist, and especially as an underground Communist. Moreover, my action would be futile. It would do the hunted man no good. It would almost certainly be found out. There would be penalties, probably severe penalties. I had a perfectly healthy fear of them. But that fear by itself would never have been enough to deter me. The real penalty that I feared was destroying my usefulness as a Communist. I gave the slip of paper to Ulrich and reported what Bedacht had told me. He glanced at it and thrust it into his pocket without comment.

Weeks later, I was sitting with Ulrich one day, when he took the same slip of paper from his pocket and showed it to me. Looking at me steadily, he said: "I don't think Uncle Joe (Stalin) would be interested in this. He has more important things to worry about." Then he crumpled the slip of paper and tossed it away. At the same time, he smiled very faintly.

It was a turning point in my experience as an underground worker, for to me it meant that at last I was working with an organization that understood that the revolution was not served by vengefully pursuing a Trotskyist dentist in a suburban village. It was also a turning point in my relations with Ulrich, for by his act, which was the same breach of discipline that I had lacked the will to make, he had consciously put himself at my mercy. At that moment, the relation between us ceased to be merely that of subaltern and superior, and became friendship. His deliberate look, passing into that fine smile, meant that each risked recognizing what the other was. It meant that we were revolutionists, not headhunters.

XII

The Gallery was situated toward the outer edge of the underground's system of headquarters and workshops. Maria led me a little farther toward the center of the underground. She first took me to the house on Gay Street.

Maria was an underground pseudonym for Ulrich's wife. Ulrich first brought us together at an Automat on Sixth Avenue near 42nd Street. As I watched her weave her way toward us between the tables, I had a first impression of a rather plump Russian woman in her early thirties, dark, with black bobbed hair. She wore a bright silk or rayon street dress without a jacket, and was hatless so that the big expensive brown leather briefcase she carried looked peculiarly incongruous. Maria was not beautiful, but she was striking-looking. There was an indolence about her movements (due perhaps to the fact that she was naturally lazy and at that time pregnant), and an occasional expression of fixed fierceness about her black eyes (due perhaps to the fact that she was near-sighted and sometimes squinted).

It was also due to something else. As a girl, Maria, like Ulrich, had taken part in the civil war in Southern Russia. During the French occupation of Odessa, she had remained within the city to carry on underground work. With another young Communist, who was little more than a boy, she was captured just as the French were evacuating Odessa. The pair were held for a short time and then ordered to be shot.

Maria described the incident to me. "One day they stood us up against the wall of a building," she said. "The French soldiers were drawn up with their rifles ready. I tried not to look at my comrade, who was crying. I wanted to give him an example. I knew that I should feel like a Bolshevik and be happy to die gloriously for the revolution. But all I could think of was my mother."

Maria survived because the underground Communists in Odessa got out a message to the Red Army whose artillery was posted on high ground commanding the city. The Red Army warned the French that if Maria and her companion were shot, it would shell the evacuation boats. While Maria and her comrade waited to be shot, they were suddenly told that they were free. It is unlikely that anyone who has survived such an experience ever again sees the sunlight and the trees in quite the same way as before. I came to think that much of Maria's sloppiness, and occasional disregard for other people were less personal than a result of that ultimate experience—a kind of shrugging indifference toward the details of a life that can be terminated so tersely. For, like Ulrich, she understood what perhaps only those can understand who have lived close to the heart of the violence of our time—that it is "the strangest feeling to hear from a child that you are dead."

Gay Street is a little street in Greenwich Village. It is about a block long, curving and very quiet. I scarcely ever saw anyone on it. Maria unlocked a door in a brownstone house and let us into a small dark hall. Then she led the way up one or two flights of dark, narrow, creaking, carpeted stairs, and unlocked another door.

We entered a small room. There was no rug on the floor. The only furniture was three or four wicker porch chairs and a low couch with a soiled cover that stood against one wall. In the wall opposite the door was a fireplace with a black marble mantel. At the front of the room were two or three windows, overlooking Gay Street. Next the windows, was a door that led into a smaller room. In it were a big locked trunk and a sturdy deal table. At the back of the room was a door that led into a bathroom. It was scarcely more than a big closet and had no window or other outlet so that it was an ideal darkroom. One side of the room was filled with a short tub, over which a shelf had been built to hold a photographic enlarger. Against the opposite wall were crowded a basin and a toilet bowl. The apartment on Gay Street was one terminal of an international communications system whose other terminal was presumably Moscow, and which had way stations in Hamburg and probably other European cities.

Gay Street was a workshop of that system. The bathroom was the laboratory in which microfilmed messages were enlarged. In the basin other messages in invisible ink were developed. On the table in the little front room, messages from New York to Moscow were photographed. In the fireplace, messages that had been read and noted were burned. The cold ashes were collected in a paper bag and dumped somewhere far off in the city.

A human chain of couriers and contacts stretched across the ocean and the continent of Europe, speeding communications back and forth between Moscow and New York. The last link which tied that chain to the Gay Street workshop was an underground worker known as "Charlie."

XIII

I know now that Charlie's real name is Leon Minster.* For one day I unexpectedly came across his picture in a group of F.B.I. photographs of Soviet agents in the Far East. My identification of him has been confirmed, independently, by someone else who also knew him as Charlie.

Charlie was born in Russia but had grown up in the United States, and was an American citizen. He was the brother-in-law of Vyacheslaw Molotov. He spoke a fluent Russian curiously roughened by overtones of New Yorkese. He had been, intermittently, a cab driver.

As a man, Charlie knew that everybody was against him. And, in the end, that almost proved to be true, because sooner or later his sullen and distrustful manner alienated most of his co-workers. But as a proletarian, Charlie knew that he belonged to the aristocracy of the new age, and that made him contemptuous and sometimes overbearing. Ulrich once summed up Charlie's attitude in a German line: *"Von unsrem Gott besegnet ist das Proletariat"*—which, to preserve its laughing overtone, may perhaps best be translated: "By our God geblessed is the proletariat."

Charlie was a *Techniker,* a technical worker. In the underground, technical workers occupy the lowest, or proletarian, rank, not because any disrespect attaches to technical work, but because a technical worker who can do anything else seldom remains a technical worker. Charlie had always been a technical worker, and that further embittered his life. As a result, he was extremely jealous of his special skills, imparted them slowly and grudgingly and was especially conscious of his prerogative as custodian of the key to the big trunk.

In the trunk, Charlie kept a Leica camera and a collapsible copying stand, the basic tools of espionage work, and other photographic and chemical supplies.

Charlie, Maria explained after she had introduced me to him, would soon begin to teach me something. The nature of "something" was not explained. But I was presently ordered to appear at the Gay Street apartment one morning about eleven o'clock. Charlie was also the custodian of the door keys and had given me a

* For details of Leon Minster's later activities in China, see General Charles A. Willoughby's testimony before the McCarran Committee in 1951.

duplicate key to the house and to the apartment. I was ordered to go to Gay Street only when told to, and never to go there at any other time.

Maria was in the apartment when I arrived. Soon Charlie came in. He took from his jacket a small pocket mirror and an unaddressed envelope. Maria opened the envelope and took out a typed letter occupying less than one sheet of paper. The letter was written in German. Then she took a nail file and pried up the soft metal edges of the mirror so that the glass came out. Between the glass and the metal covering was a very small tissue paper package. Within it, piled one on another, were five or six frames of developed microfilm which had been cut apart and trimmed. On the film, typed in Russian characters, were the messages from Russia, or some intermediate Russian underground post, for the underground in New York.

Charlie told me to fill the basin in the bathroom with warm water. From the trunk he brought a bottle of potassium permanganate crystals and spilled a few into the water which turned violet. Then he showed me how to move the typed letter slowly back and forth in the permanganate bath. Soon marks appeared between the typed lines. Then a small sharp Russian handwriting rose out of the blank paper to form a rusty brown script. It was the first time that I had ever seen invisible ink. The letter, like all the others I later developed, was signed: "Akyt." I never knew who Akyt was. But I supposed that the word was probably the pseudonym of an underground worker and was perhaps a Russian or German form of the English word, acute. Communists are often given to such overemphatic names: *viz.*, Stalin, the man of steel, and Molotov, the hammer.

While Maria read the secret letter, Charlie brought from the trunk a box of enlarging paper. He replaced the electric bulb in the bathroom with a red bulb. In two enamel cake pans, he prepared a bath of hydroquinone and a bath of fixative. Into a glass slide in the enlarger he placed one by one the little frames of developed microfilm. Each was focused until the Russian typing stood out crisply. Then a sheet of enlarging paper was placed under the enlarger, the exposure was made and the sensitive paper developed in the hydroquinone and fixed in the other bath. One sheet of enlarging paper was used for each frame. When the job was completed, there was a developed message in Russian five or six pages long. Though I can read Russian type, I was seldom able to understand any of the words in the messages except the salutation. Each letter always began: *Dorogoi droog*—Dear Friend.

The wet sheets of enlarging paper were laid to dry on the marble mantel or on the wicker chairs. Later Ulrich arrived. He read the secret letter and the photographed messages carefully, and made a few notes in his memo book. Afterwards, the letter, the photographs and the microfilm were burned in the fireplace.

Charlie had indeed taught me something. When I left the Gay Street house after that first lesson, I walked over to Washington Square and sat down on a bench. I now had little doubt that I was in a Communist espionage group. As a Communist, I knew that the revolution is made by any and all means. Of necessity it is in part a military operation, and espionage is inevitably a military function. If the revolution is justified, espionage for its sake is justified. But it is one thing to know that in theory, or even to read or hear about such an experience as I had just been through. It is quite different to participate in it. I sat on the park bench for a long while.

XIV

I guessed, of course, that the mirrors were brought by couriers. I did not understand how the system worked. But I picked up one or two clues. I noticed that shortly before a mirror arrived, Ulrich would sometimes buy a newspaper and turn at once to the shipping news which he studied carefully. I noticed that, when Charlie brought a letter to Gay Street, he once or twice wore on his lapel a cheap brass pin in the form of a scorpion or lizard. Sometimes Maria made shopping trips to the dime stores where she bought a dozen mirrors and a few of the scorpion pins. With a cryptic smile she once told me where she got them, for dime stores are a 20th century bazaar that never ceased to amaze and delight Russians.

Then, one day, I met Max Bedacht. The staid little man was elated. "You people," he said, "really do very stupid things sometimes. Somebody should hear about this." He told me that "one of the sailors" had come ashore. "Your man" did not show up for the appointment. The sailor went to the meeting place several times, but nobody came. His ship was about to sail. He was desperate. But he was "a smart workingman" so he went to Mink* and turned

* George Mink, an American citizen and former Philadelphia cab driver, was then the head of the Communist Party's seamen's organization on the New

"the stuff" over to him. I guessed that "the stuff" would be a mirror and letter and asked Bedacht where it was now. He had it in his pocket and turned it over to me. "You fellows," he said again with evident pleasure, "are not as smart as you think you are."

As a result of this incident, Ulrich told me something about the system in which I was presently to become a link. The underground couriers were sailors and stewards on the Hamburg-American and North German Lloyd steamships. I assume that they were Communists or trusted sympathizers. In Germany, they were given the mirrors and letters. In New York, they turned "the stuff" over to an underground worker who later turned it over to Charlie. Sometimes, for reasons not known to me, Charlie met the courier himself. Apparently, his meetings were always with new couriers because Charlie wore the scorpion pin on his lapel as an identifying mark. The courier also wore a similar pin, which must previously have been sent to Germany for that purpose. At one time Charlie's meetings with the couriers took place in front of the Cameo movie theater on 42nd Street in New York City.

The return mail from New York to Europe followed the same route. The letters were first brought to Gay Street. They had been typed in Russian somewhere else. Charlie photographed them with the Leica camera. The film was placed in a mirror and passed along the courier chain. So far as I know, there was no letter in invisible ink sent from New York to Europe.

XV

Ulrich presently decided to separate Charlie and the contact with the German sailors. I do not know exactly why that was done, but I seem to remember dimly that there was some comment about

York waterfront. Mink was a nephew of George Lozovsky, formerly chairman of Moscow's Red International of Labor Unions (the Profintern), later a Soviet press chief. Subsequently, Mink was a member of a Soviet espionage group arrested, chiefly because of his carelessness, in Copenhagen. Ulrich, also a member of the group, was also arrested. During the Spanish Civil War, Mink was charged with personally supervising the murders of anti-Stalinists in the Spanish Republic's jails. Still later, he was reported to be in the United States, organizing the assassination of Leon Trotsky, who was then in Mexico. Shortly after my break with the Communist Party, Carlo Tresca, the editor of *Il Martello,* told me that Mink was in the country and warned me against him. In 1943, Tresca himself was shot and killed as he stepped out of a building on lower Fifth Avenue. Mink is wanted by the United States Government for a variety of interesting reasons.

Charlie's being too friendly with the contact. In general, the underground does not encourage close friendships between its members. There is a danger of their sharing information, the principle of separation of the members is impaired, and personal loyalties may take precedence over loyalty to the apparatus, at least in small ways.

It was decided to place me between Charlie and the contact, who turned out to be a young German Communist known as Henry. He was a gnomelike man with a flip-up nose who looked and spoke as if he might have come out of a Berlin slum district or Hamburg's Reeperbahn. He was a perpetually worried man. He had reason to be, for in dealing with the couriers, he was constantly exposed to a number of strange and miscellaneous people. In addition, he was probably in the United States illegally.

When I first began to work with Henry, he used to meet his seagoing contacts in the 42nd Street area of Manhattan. Later, he would meet me in the same section. Once I found him trembling. "I was followed," he said. He passed me his mirror and we separated at once. He had had to make a difficult decision: whether to risk being picked up with the mirror on him, or whether to get rid of the mirror but risk exposing me. I told him that I thought he had made the right decision.

I reported to Ulrich that Henry thought that he had been shadowed. Both of us believed that Henry's "shadow" was merely a city detective who had noticed Henry loitering in midtown Manhattan and decided to keep an eye on him. But I pointed out that 42nd Street and Broadway was full of plainclothesmen and was one of the worst possible meeting places in the city. The situation was even worse than I realized, for I did not then know that the office of Dr. Philip Rosenbliett, where underground people were constantly coming and going, was at Broadway and 40th Street.

Thereafter, I met Henry in more tranquil neighborhoods. But he seemed to feel at home only in the white-light district, and he never approved of the meeting places I chose.

Henry once found himself in a different kind of tight spot. One night, pale and making a visible effort not to tremble or babble, he came into the restaurant where I was waiting for him. The German courier in an ugly mood had met him earlier and without his transmission. "Those stupid fools," said Henry, with a string of German curses, had given him three mirrors and two letters (an instance of the slackness in all branches of the Communist movement in Germany just before Hitler came to power). The courier had refused to endanger himself by bringing the mirrors off the ship.

Henry had made another quick decision. He went aboard the ship with the courier and brought off the mirrors and the letters himself. The guards, supposing that he was a member of the crew, had let him pass.

Not all the stupidities were committed at the German end of the network. One of the periodical rituals at Gay Street was known as "filling the box." Every so often, Charlie would bring to the apartment a big empty box. In the apartment, Charlie, Maria and I would fill it with hundreds of thin leaflets in white paper covers. These were patents which anybody could then buy for a small fee from the United States Patent Office. They were collected in the bottom of the trunk until there were enough to make a shipment.

Other perfectly legal documents also went into the box—the *Infantry Journal*, the *Cavalry Journal, Iron Age*. When packed, the box was heavy. Charlie and I would lug it downstairs and rope it to the bumper of Charlie's car. What Charlie did with the box I do not know. I suppose that it eventually reached the Soviet Union.

One day, Charlie and Maria took special care to leave a space in the middle of the packed patents. Charlie then brought from the truck several wide-mouthed flasks, filled with what looked to me like bits of uncooked yellowish-gray or brownish-yellow macaroni. I was curious enough to ask what they were. After a moment's pause, Maria decided to tell me. "Flashless powder," she said.

Some weeks later, we heard about this shipment in the German letter which I was in the habit of reading while I was developing the invisible ink. As a rule, the letters always said the same things. One line kept recurring: "We live here as on a hot griddle" (the Nazis were about to take power). But the flashless powder shipment caused an explosive change in style. "Your present," said Akyt with Bolshevik sarcasm, "arrived safely, but it was so stupidly packed that it was only due to the goodness of God that it did not go skyhigh."

XVI

At Gay Street an effort was made to teach me photography. We used an old German Leica camera; the tables of calibration and instructions were also in German. Charlie was surly and did not want to teach me. He evidently supposed (mistakenly, as it turned out) that Ulrich meant to replace him with me. I was a poor pupil. I have never had the slightest interest in photography. I spoiled a great deal of film and the results I obtained were never really creditable. I was extremely grateful when Ulrich suddenly decided to abandon the Gay Street apartment and my photographic studies were interrupted. I never met Charlie again.

The abandonment of the Gay Street apartment probably had something to do with the collapse of the courier system. The Nazis had taken over the Third Reich. "Do you suppose that the couriers will be safe?" I asked Ulrich. He smiled grimly. "*We* would know how to find them out and destroy them," he said, "and so will the Nazis." Two weeks after Hitler came to power, there was no more courier system.

I learned many things at Gay Street. But nothing made a more lasting impression on me than an incident which in itself was completely unimportant. One day, when we were "filling the box," Charlie and Maria were talking together in Russian. I became aware of some hitch in the conversation, which, of course, I could not follow. Maria turned to me and said: "Isn't it stupid—it comes from being away from home (Russia) so long—but neither Charlie nor I can remember the Russian word for shovel." Without thinking, I asked, "Can it be *lopata?*" Charlie, bending over the box, froze in that position. Maria sat rigid with her hand on a heap of patents. Both fixed me in silence with expressions that were blank and deadly. I thought: "They are wondering whether to kill me now or later." "How do *you* know that word?" Maria asked in a slow, guttural voice. I said: "It is a Rumanian gypsy word. I once knew some Rumanian gypsies. There are a good many Russian words in their language." It was one of the most implausible of the many implausible truths I was to utter in my life. But Maria and Charlie very slowly relaxed and the murderous look faded from their eyes. "It is very strange," said Maria in the same throaty voice, "that you don't know Russian, but you know the Russian word for a shovel. You might know the word for a man or a woman, but not a shovel. Are you sure you don't know Russian?" I told them just how much Russian I knew.

I saw that I had given them a bad fright. Their thought, of course, was that if I were concealing the fact that I knew Russian, I must have a purpose in concealing it. If I were concealing that, what else was I concealing? Who was I, anyway? A police spy? The son of a Russian refugee? For Maria was one of the Russians who always insisted that I was simply a Russian peasant. It was a good many days before the distrust completely left Maria's eyes and we resumed our friendly relations.

How great a commotion my little slip had caused I realized when I presently met Dr. Philip Rosenbliett. "Well, Bob," he said during our first conversation, "I hear that you are the American who knows what a shovel is in Russian."

The tension and suspicion that that one word invoked, though deeply hidden, are scarcely even for a moment absent among people in Communist underground work.

XVII

Dr. Philip Rosenbliett, the quiet, crafty, sorrowful man, was sometimes called "Phil" in the underground, but was usually called "The Doctor." His office was high up in a building at Broadway and 40th Street. He was a dentist. But dentistry was not his chief business.

In his office The Doctor had no assistant. No sound of drilling ever came from beyond his ground-glass doors. Sometimes for half an hour there might be heard faintly the sound of voices within, rising and falling in Russian cadences. There was nothing odd about that since The Doctor himself was born in Russia, and spoke English with a soft Russian intonation.

I have often sat in The Doctor's office with half a dozen other patients while he tended an earlier arrival inside. The Doctor's patients were a miscellaneous lot, though all of them seemed to be Europeans. I noticed that most of them shared one peculiar habit. Most patients enter a waiting room, look a little dismayed at those ahead of them, pick up a magazine, sit down, riffle through it, put it down and take up another. The Doctor's patients almost always entered the waiting room without glancing at anybody. They went directly to the magazine pile, picked up a magazine and buried themselves so deeply in it that sometimes it was almost impossible to see their faces.

The Doctor, too, had a peculiar habit. When the door from his office opened, he always leaned out before the patient he had been treating. He would look around at the faces in the waiting room and only after he had done that would the patient emerge and walk straight out, glancing neither to right or left.

Sometimes, I saw Ulrich walk out after a long professional treatment. Sometimes, I saw Maria. I merely glanced at them without any sign of recognition, and they, of course, gave no sign that they recognized me. Once a hard-faced man walked rapidly out of The Doctor's office. I went in next. "Do you know who that was?" The Doctor asked me. Then he answered his own question: "That was Tim Buck." Tim Buck was the secretary of the Communist Party of Canada. For The Doctor had a failing, a little streak of vanity: he liked his friends to know that he played an important part in certain cryptic affairs. He did play an important part and he had played it for a long time. For in the operations of the Fourth Section of the Soviet Military Intelligence, The Doctor's office was an all but permanent *yafka.*

The word is one that he taught me himself, first asking me if I knew its meaning, for he liked to ask questions, especially if he thought that he, and not the person asked, knew the answer. He never asked or answered arrogantly, for he was a very soft-spoken man. *Yafka,* he told me, is the Russian word for roof. It is the underground term for the one absolutely safe place where underground people, especially strangers in a city, can go for aid, direction, contacts and comfort. I do not know how many people came to Dr. Rosenbliett's *yafka* for such treatment. But I suspect that if somebody who was not *nashe* (one of ours) could have sat undetected in The Doctor's waiting room between 1930 and 1935, he would have gained a startling and inclusive insight into the activities and personnel of the Soviet Military Intelligence in the United States—and even into such apparently unrelated organizations as the Irish Republican Army.

But when I first visited The Doctor, I supposed that he was simply another Communist dentist, who was sufficiently trusted so that underground workers could go to him to have their teeth tinkered. That was why Ulrich had sent me to The Doctor in the first place. One of my upper incisors was missing. It had been broken off when I was a boy. Three pivots had been put in its place and each had been broken off in turn. At last I gave it up. That gap-tooth effect worried Ulrich (as it was later to worry Alger Hiss). One day he gave me The Doctor's name and address. "I want you to go to see him today," he said. "That is a military command."

I had to sit a while in the waiting room. Then The Doctor peered out of his door and permitted a patient to slip past him. He beckoned to me. "Well, Bob," he said, studying me carefully. He seated me in the dentist chair and peered into my mouth with his very gentle, observant brown eyes. "You should have been dead years ago," he said. I asked why. "You have no bite," said The Doctor. "How do you eat?" He took from his assortment of instruments some tool that he held out of sight and stood staring at me for a while. "Do I know who you are going to have supper with tonight?" he asked quietly. I said that I did not know myself. In fact, I did not know. Ulrich had merely told me that he was taking me to dinner with someone. "I *do* know," said The Doctor. "You are going to have supper with Dr. Isaac Katz (not the man's real name). He is a chemist at the Picatinny Arsenal."

For ten or fifteen minutes, I sat in the dentist's chair and The Doctor stood, rocking back and forth gently on his feet, talking to me quietly chiefly about his daughter whom he dearly loved and who was dying of an incurable ailment.

At last he said that he must call in the next "patient." He showed me to the door, opened it, and made me wait until he had looked out. He guided me past him with one hand. Even then—though I was puzzled, I did not realize that the "dental work" for which I had come to The Doctor was merely a pretext—to give him a chance to look me over. Neither on that first occasion, or at any later time, did Dr. Rosenbliett ever do any work on my teeth.

XVIII

Vacations for party members were not well thought of among Communists. But Max Bedacht announced one day that he felt need of a rest and change of scene. He would introduce me to a substitute who would act as contact with the apparatus during Max's vacation. His replacement turned out to be my old acquaintance of *Daily Worker* days, J. Peters. Comrade Peters was no longer with the Hungarian Communist weekly. He had become head of the entire underground section of the American Communist Party. As such, he was one of the two or three most powerful men in the party. He was also a lurking figure of fate in the lives of millions of Americans who did not dream that he existed.

Peters, of course, never sat down and disclosed to me the exact dimensions or the complex detail of his invisible empire. But I could gain some idea of its scope from the practical questions that from time to time he raised with me. They ranged from personnel problems involving men who were highly placed in the State and

Treasury Departments to a problem of spontaneous sabotage by the Communist secret cell in the airplane propeller-casting room of an aluminum company.* He was in touch with Communists in the Naragansett Torpedo Base, in the Electric Boat Company (submarines for the U.S. Navy) in the Department of Justice and in Hollywood, whose thriving underground made him ecstatic. He was also in direct touch with a number of separate Soviet underground apparatuses. For he operated a special apparatus of his own for the wholesale procurement of birth certificates and naturalization papers, and for tampering with official records—all a part of the important business of securing fraudulent passports.

Unlike Bedacht, Peters was eager to co-operate with Ulrich's underground. For a time, I continued to deal separately with both men. Tactically, this was advantageous, for it tended to develop a "socialist competition" between them. Organizationally, it was undesirable because it doubled the risks of meeting, and all other risks. At last I gave Ulrich my opinion of Bedacht and Peters and asked him which I should retain as the contact. "There is a Turkish proverb," said Ulrich. "It says: if you must choose between two wolves, a wolf that has eaten and a wolf that is hungry, choose the wolf that has eaten." Bedacht was the wolf that had eaten. But he had eaten too well. In the end, I retained Peters. Bedacht was never officially dropped. I simply ceased to see him. Peters became the exclusive contact with the Soviet underground.

XIX

Periodically, the underground reshuffled its quarters. The Gallery had been abandoned. I was told not to go there again. If the handful of Communists who moved in and out of it infrequently had ever been noticed by the neighbors, they were soon forgotten. The group (minus Charlie), which had disappeared from Gay Street, re-emerged in The Office.

The Office was the big living room of an apartment on the

* According to Peters, the aluminum company had been plagued by microscopic flaws in its propellers, the cause of which a careful check failed to reveal. The flaws were caused by members of the cell making tiny spitballs from the cellophane wrapping of their cigarette packs, and spitting them into the molten flux. Peters' problem was whether to order this pointless sabotage to be stopped, and thereby risk dulling the revolutionary temper of the comrades, or whether to wink at it and thereby risk eventual detection. I have forgotten what he decided.

edge of Brooklyn's Brownsville section. I had taught myself the habit of "not seeing" so well that I visited The Office many times, but I never learned the name of the street or the number of the house where it was located.

I no longer did any technical work. No technical equipment was kept at The Office. It would be more than a decade before I would discover that, unsuspected by me, the apparatus had a photographic workshop a floor or two above The Office. The photographer who worked in it was no longer Charlie. Though the new photographer and I must have circled around each other in those days, I had no way of recognizing him or knowing that he worked in the same underground. Nor could he recognize me. He was Robert Gordon Switz, who, in 1935, was tried in Paris with the Soviet espionage group of which Paula Levine (of The Gallery) was a member. In 1949 he was able to corroborate important parts of my testimony.

The Office was chiefly a meeting place. Maria typed there on her Russian typewriter. If there was any other activity, it was out of my range of vision.

The apartment that included The Office was the home of a studious-looking young man and his pretty wife and baby. For some time, I knew them only as Yosha and Rose. I do not know why Yosha decided to tell me who he was. But, one night, he suddenly said to me: "You don't know me, Bob. But I know a lot about you. You used to work with my brother on the *Daily Worker*." Yosha was Joshua Tamer. His brother was Harry Tamer, the consumptive-looking young man who used to glance up from the ads he was setting and peer at me through thick-lensed glasses. Both were brothers-in-law of Sam Shoyet, the slant-eyed assistant foreman of the *Daily Worker* composing room, who had once told me about his work in Paris and Tokyo. The past had caught up with the present. The pieces fell into place, and I could see from the Tamers how the underground coiled in and out of the open Communist Party, like a snake in a tree.

In The Office, too, I sometimes met Yosha's mother, a merry old Jewish woman, who looked like hundreds of others who can be seen, shopping and gossiping, any morning in Brooklyn. I always called her Babushka. She had taken some small part in the 1905 revolution in Russia. It was in her apartment, upstairs, that the photographic workshop was located.

But I remember The Office chiefly for two other reasons in which certain special tensions of the underground came to light. In The

Office I really entered the heart of the underground. Until then, I had been on probation, never overt, but detectable in small ways. In The Office, I passed a test that sealed my place as a member of the group, though it unsettled my friendship with Maria.

I do not know just why Ulrich decided at that time to probe what, if anything, lay behind my natural quietness. Perhaps, without realizing it, I had dropped some unorthodox remark about the party line. During that period, I was often in disagreement with Communist policy, which had turned Germany over to Hitler and led to the physical extinction of the second most powerful party in the International. Perhaps I had merely smiled slightly at the wrong time, or my comrades had inferred from my silences that I held heretical views. For they were extremely acute observers. The slightest gesture, hesitation, emphasis, change of intonation seldom escaped them, though they sometimes took pains to conceal the fact that they had noticed anything. In the underground, all of us lived constantly under one another's minute surveillance.

Ulrich set out to probe my thoughts in the oldest, simplest way. We had just moved to The Office. Maria proposed that we should celebrate with a party. I do not like parties. I tried to make excuses and beg off. Ulrich insisted and at last told me that it was "a command."

We ate around a big table. Babushka was present. Her grinning face was one of the last things I remembered of that night. For Joshua Tamer had brought a bottle of 90 proof alcohol from his place of business. With it he filled my glass and tinctured the alcohol with slivovitz (plum brandy) or vishniak (cherry brandy). I had not drunk for years. By the third glass, I no longer knew what I was saying, and soon I did not know what I was doing. They began to question me about my views on the German crisis.

When I came to, it was morning. Maria, disheveled and haggard, was sitting on a couch. Ulrich had rolled himself up in a rug on the floor. Maria would not speak to me. Ulrich asked coldly: "Do you know what you did last night? You denounced the party, and, when Maria defended it, you knocked her down. You also knocked me down."

Everybody was silent. I had a ferocious hangover. I wondered what they would do with me next. Ulrich in the same grim voice then told me that he had purposely got me drunk to find out what I really thought. "You said," he said, "that the Soviet Government had betrayed the German Communist Party for the sake of its own foreign policy. You said: because of you Russians, they are murdering the German comrades in the Moabit (a Berlin prison). You kept repeating it. You cried. It was disgusting."

In the Communist Party, statements such as I had made were grounds for instant expulsion. In the underground, they were high treason. Through my splitting headache, I wondered, without caring very much, whether they would send me to prison in Russia or find ways of dealing with me on the spot.

Ulrich had got up. He walked over and dropped his hand on my shoulder. "Bob," he said: "You're all right. You're the real thing." He began to smile. I realized slowly that my heresies did not interest him. He was concerned only with the force with which I held them, for that showed him the force of my Communist faith. That was what he wanted to know.

Maria was more personal. I apologized for knocking her down. "No," she said. "I believe in the saying, *in vino veritas*. If you really liked me, you would not have knocked me down." I pointed out that I had also knocked Ulrich down. Maria never wholly trusted me again. Once or twice afterwards, she told me stories, in a carefully casual way, about Communists who secretly hated the party, and had betrayed their hatred in little ways that nobody noticed at the time, and which perhaps they were not even conscious of themselves. Later on, they had broken with the party. At that time, I thought how much wiser Ulrich was than Maria. I have been less sure since.

The other incident at The Office concerned "Herman."

X X

When Ulrich first introduced me to Herman, the little Russian studied me briefly and asked in German: "What nationality is he?" "He speaks German too," said Ulrich hastily. "He's Irish." "I've shot a lot of Irishmen," said Herman and turned his back on me. The introduction took place in The Office. When, by request, I had left the two men alone, I felt that I had met what is much more unusual in life than a thoroughly good man—a thoroughly bad one. I was not yet mature enough to detect that there was in Herman a pathos that lay between what was able and what was vicious in him. Nor could I foresee how soon both qualities would leave him beaten and dying in a New York gutter.

Imagine a short, sturdy figure confined in a tight-fitting, rumpled suit and elevated on high-heeled German shoes. That was Herman. Soft, brown, pitiless eyes stared out of a soft, chalky face that suggested corruption. Above that face, a stubble of hair stood up stiff and uneven as if it had been cut by a sickle. From that short figure came a bass voice of startling resonance. But what I remember best about Herman was his habit, wherever he might be, of taking from each trouser pocket a fat roll of bills which he weighed lovingly in each hand. Before the Russian Revolution, Maria told me, Herman had been a janitor's son in Petrograd.

This odd Communist had, among others, three particular passions—intrigue, the piano (which, others who knew him tell me, he took up late in life and learned to play quickly and brilliantly) and Germany. He was a professional Germanophile in the way that certain Americans are professional Anglophiles. From him I first learned to my surprise that there was a large group in the Nazi party to which Communists felt extremely close.

The next time I met Ulrich, he asked me: "Do you know what *sookin sin* is?" I said that it sounded like a province in China. "It means son of a dog," he said, "and if you repeat what I am going to tell you, I will shoot you." He told me that Herman had arrived without any credentials and simply announced that he had been sent to take charge of the whole underground. Ulrich had refused to recognize his authority or to take his orders. They were waiting for Moscow to decide the dispute. Ulrich did not explain how Herman had got in touch with the apparatus. Apparently, he had been in the United States some time before I met him.

Herman had at once begun making trouble. He had taken out Charlie and got him drunk. Charlie had an old grudge against Ulrich. He poured out to Herman a tale of personal grievance and conspiratorial mismanagement, some of it true. Herman had at once filed a report to Moscow. Among other things, he charged that the underground was so badly organized that its headquarters were in "a little village near New York, called Brooklyn."

"He can't speak English," said Ulrich, "but he insists on being given work to do. You speak German and you are the only man I can trust. You must work with him."

Herman scheduled his first meeting alone with me in Central Park at nine or ten o'clock at night. I suggested that that was a poor meeting place. *"Unsinn!"* he said. "Nonsense!" When we met, a light rain was falling. Again, I said that if we walked around in the rain at that hour the police might pick us up. Again, Herman brushed me aside.

This time Herman did not talk about shooting Irishmen. Instead, he took my arm cozily and asked: "What's doing in Washington?" I said that I had no idea. "Bob," he said, standing in front of me and grasping both my arms, "*du hast eine grosse Kariere vor dir*—you have a great career ahead of you." It was the first time that I had ever heard a Communist use the word "career." For a Communist, career does not exist. Historical necessity exists. I asked what the great career might be. Herman said that it was to go to Washington and build the apparatus there. In Washington, he said, there were "*kolossale Möglichkeiten*—colossal opportunities." "All this here," he added sweepingly, "is just childishness."

I did not know that he could see my face in the dark, for I did not yet appreciate how sensitive and animal-alert he was. "*Warum lächelst du?*—Why are you smiling?" he asked angrily. With that he broke off our meeting. I knew he thought that he was dealing with a fool. His conspiratorial experience, and, above all, his conspiratorial imagination, were years ahead of mine. Beside him, I was a child. It is an irony that in large part I was to carry out what Herman had imagined. But, in fact, I was not smiling in the dark at Herman's project. I was smiling at the incredible performance of one Communist trying to bribe another with the word "career." I did not know then that Ulrich was a type of the past, and that Herman was the Stalinist of the future. Nor was I mature enough to know that, under his talk of career, Herman's Communist faith was quite as firm as mine, and more realistic.

I next met Herman in an Automat. He was late. I waited the prescribed fifteen extra minutes, then fifteen more. He was a stranger; he might have lost his way. Presently, I saw him weaving between the tables. I thought: "How clumsily he walks." He sat down, spoke thickly and nervously and left almost at once. Not until he was gone did the perfectly obvious fact flash on me: Herman was drunk. I could not grasp it at once because I could not believe that an underground Communist would come drunk to an appointment.

My relations with Herman grew steadily worse. Each of us disliked and distrusted the other. Neither of us concealed his feelings. Herman thought that I was stupid. I thought that he was irresponsible and corrupt. Our meetings became mere brush-offs. After a few contemptuous words and impatient gestures, he would dismiss me. He would not give me any work to do. I was no longer in touch with Ulrich and Maria, and had no right to ask to get in touch with them. I was completely at Herman's mercy. It is practically impossible to convey to a non-Communist the subtle destructiveness of this relationship, not because it threatened my life (with a man like Herman that was always an ultimate possibility), but because it threatened my life's whole meaning. After a few weeks of that treatment, I began to be demoralized.

One morning I was moping in a cafeteria. I had passed a sleepless night and had not even taken the trouble to shave—a breach of underground rules. Suddenly, Ulrich sat down beside me. I never asked him how he knew I was there, or whether our meeting was chance. To me he looked much as he must have looked to the two condemned men he freed from the firing squad in Sebastopol.

Ulrich took one good look at me and said: "You are not going to work with Herman any more. You are coming back with me. I don't care what happens." "He's no good," I said. "You're wrong," said Ulrich angrily. "You always see things in black and white. Herman isn't black and white. He's a very clever rascal."

I did not see Herman again while I was connected with that apparatus. But I had a lurking feeling that the clever rascal had jotted down my name in his doomsday book. I was relieved when Maria told me that Ulrich had won his fight with Herman, who had been recalled in disgrace to Moscow. There, she said with a triumphant laugh at so complete a humiliation, Herman had been made a "Red Professor." Neither she nor I then knew that, with an initiative unheard of among Communists, Herman had gone directly to Molotov, had told him that he had highly important contacts in Washington, but that jealous cliques in the Fourth Section kept him from developing them. Molotov sent Herman back to the United States as an agent of the G.P.U., the Soviet secret police.

That is why, one night months later, as I was walking down Broadway, I suddenly saw Herman walking toward me—a transformed Herman. He was elegantly sheathed in an expensive, form-fitting overcoat. He wore an equally expensive hat, very dashingly flipped and angled. I thought: "It's against all the rules. But if I don't speak to him, I shall never believe that I really saw him." We exchanged a few uncomfortable words. Then I broke off and said: "Good luck." "Good luck to *you,*" said Herman with deliberate, blood-chilling emphasis. I know now that my sudden appearance, as if I had been shadowing him, may well have stirred immeasurable fears in his mind.

A few days later, I told The Doctor: "Herman is back." "I know that," he said. "And I know what you don't know. Herman is very sick. He is in a hospital." Soon he told me: "Herman is dead." "What happened?" I asked. "Pneumonia," said Dr. Rosenbliett. I was sure, from something in The Doctor's manner, that Herman had not died of pneumonia.

He had, in fact, been murdered.

XXI

I have heard four versions of Herman's death. I heard the first from Dr. Rosenbliett some time after he had told me that Herman died of pneumonia. I heard the second from Ludwig Lore, the former editor of the *Volkszeitung*. Later on, in my underground days, I met and dealt with Lore when he was writing "Behind the Cables" as a columnist on the New York *Evening Post*. It was Lore who first told me that Herman was also known as "Oskar."

Colonel Bykov also knew Herman as Oskar. He gave me a third version of his death. General Walter Krivitsky first told me that Herman's real name was Valentine Markin. He gave me the fourth version.

Dr. Rosenbliett's final version was this. Herman had been drinking heavily. Late at night, he went, alone, into a cheap bar somewhere in midtown Manhattan. He drank more and flashed a big roll of bills. Two toughs followed him out of the saloon, and, on the deserted street, beat him up, robbed him and left him lying in the gutter. Herman died in a hospital of a fractured skull complicated by pneumonia.

Ludwig Lore's version, richer in detail, was substantially the same as Dr. Rosenbliett's. Lore, a generous man, had been Herman's close friend. It had fallen to him to hush up the story, to cover up the curious discrepancies in Herman's identification papers and, finally, to see that he was quietly buried in a Brooklyn cemetery.

Colonel Bykov's version was very different. I had never discussed Herman with Bykov. But one night that nervous man suddenly asked me: "What happened to the Oskar?" I told him that he had been killed while drunk. "Who killed him?" he asked. "Two hoodlums," I said. "No," said Bykov slyly, "the Oskar was killed by the American secret police." At the time, I thought that this was merely another amusing example of Colonel Bykov's obsession. He believed that "the American secret police" were omnipresent and operated by the same methods as the Russian secret police. But Russians are masters of confusion and one favorite tactic is to shift the blame for something they have done to their opposite numbers elsewhere. I now believe that Colonel Bykov knew the story that General Krivitsky was later to tell me, and that he deliberately shifted the blame from the Russians to the American police.

Walter Krivitsky, too, denied, that Herman had been killed for his money. His version went back to the time when Herman appealed to Molotov against the Fourth Section. The supreme head of the Fourth Section, General Berzin, an old Bolshevik who had once saved Lenin's life, had been enraged. When Molotov sent Herman back to the United States, Berzin saw to it that he did not go alone. He sent two of his killers, who caught up with Herman in New York. They knew his habits. They waited for a favorable chance. They followed him into the little midtown bar and out of it. On the quiet street they broke his skull.

It is all but impossible not to be affected by a melodrama working itself out so close at hand, among half a dozen people intimately known, in familiar rooms and streets, in a shared darkness and secrecy.

I did not think often or actively about Herman's life and death. But, for several years, his memory floated just below the surface of my mind, like a corpse constantly ejected by a whirlpool. I could not quite dismiss the question he raised: Is this the new man that Communism is breeding? I managed not to answer it until Colonel Bykov, who in some ways resembled the dead man, answered it for me.

XXII

In reporting the thinness of my own activities with this particular Soviet underground, the collapse of the courier system, and Herman's insubordination and death I do not wish to leave an impression that the apparatus was a costly farce that no one need take seriously. In the nature of underground work, there must be roughly two failures to every moderate success. I have reason to believe that the apparatus was engaged in much successful activity which it kept me, as a newcomer, away from but which involved others. The flasks of flashless powder, the photographic workshop just above The Office which was so carefully kept secret from me, remarks dropped by Ulrich, Maria, and especially by The Doctor, point to activities which I had not grown up enough in a conspiratorial sense to have a part in. That I learned as much as I did was chiefly due to the fact that I became so friendly with Ulrich and Maria so quickly.

The Doctor was scarcely less friendly and much more talkative. He told me many things that a junior undergroundling would never ordinarily know. One story he told me sheds light on the more menacing operations of the underground. It was the story of how the Russians obtained data about the Chrystie tank. This tank, developed by the American inventor, Walter Chrystie, was of great interest to the Russians. They set on foot an elaborate "combination" (as Communists call it) to secure its plans.

Somehow, possibly through a connection of Dr. Rosenbliett, who seemed to have connections all over the world, the Soviet apparatus discovered that an American Army officer who had access to the secret tank material was also an Irish patriot. He was in touch with the I.R.A., the Irish Republican Army, which was then fighting the British. The Fourth Section decided to secure this officer as a source.

In London, representatives of the Soviet underground made contact with an underground group of the I.R.A. The Russians undertook to send two submarines loaded with machine guns and other arms for the I.R.A. to the west coast of Ireland. In repayment, the I.R.A. agreed that the American Army officer whom I shall call General O'Gordon would regularly turn over to Soviet agents in the United States material relating to Chrystie tanks.

In the United States, the deal was clinched by a politician in Queens, New York (whose name I know), and whom The Doctor claimed as his friend. General O'Gordon, a man in advanced middle age, was introduced to a Soviet underground contact. The general agreed to take to his home on week-ends the secret tank material. He would then turn it over to a Soviet agent who would have it microfilmed and return it in time for the general to replace it in the Army's files early Monday morning. What the general thought was going on I do not know. But Dr. Rosenbliett quoted a curious remark made by him at his first meeting with the Soviet agent: "I am glad to help the I.R.A., but I would not do a thing to help those God-damn Rooshians."

From The Doctor I gathered that the system had worked smoothly for some time. There was only one hitch. One afternoon, the Army called up the general and asked him to return at once a document which for some reason was needed. The general was momentarily embarrassed because none of the tank documents was at that time in his possession. They were being microfilmed and he did not know where they were. If Dr. Rosenbliett explained how the general got out of that one, I have forgotten the explanation. But, to avoid unwelcome phone calls in the future, the general, after turning over his material, would go on week-end fishing trips and would not return until the documents were to be given back to him.

This fruitful relationship bore within it the seed of its own defeat. The general was very fond of good liquor in quantity. Prohibition was in force. One of the most important duties of the German couriers in those days, said Dr. Rosenbliett, had been to smuggle in sufficient cognac to keep the general in a co-operative mood. (No doubt, this had been one of Charlie's and Henry's duties, one that was kept carefully from me.) The cognac was the undoing of the general. One day he drank too much. He suffered a heart attack and died.

"I never before heard of a source just dying," said Dr. Rosenbliett.

The Soviet Government never delivered the promised arms to the west coast of Ireland.

XXIII

Underground work is one test of a Communist. Few other party activities make such insistent demands upon his devotion, discipline, resourcefulness, and courage, because few others require him to demonstrate daily, in action, his revolutionary faith beyond all appeals of country, family, friendship, and personal interest. But few others give him the same sense of participating directly in the revolutionary transformation of our time, for which a Communist exists. It is this sense of revolutionary purpose that gives underground activity whatever appeal it has. Once its startling novelty has worn off, and in my case that happened within the first few months, that revolutionary purpose alone makes it bearable.

For conspiracy itself is dull work. Its mysteries quickly become a bore, its secrecy a burden and its involved way of doing things a nuisance. Its object is never to provide excitement, but to avoid it. Thrills mean that something has gone wrong. The mysterious character of underground work is merely a tedious daily labor to keep thrills from happening. I have never known a good conspirator who enjoyed conspiracy. I have never known one who did not feel: If only I could perform one simple act simply and directly, unhampered by conspiratorial techniques. I have seldom known one who did not think: when will my term of service be up so that I can get on to something less peculiar? It is seldom up for Communists with that practical approach to its mysteries, but there are reprieves.

One came for Ulrich in the early spring of 1934. He told me abruptly one day that he and Maria were going "home"—back to Russia. The apparatus was to be disbanded. It now seems perfectly clear that the apparatus was not disbanded. It was given an interim rest, a common practice, during a change of chiefs. Certainly, Dr. Rosenbliett remained just where he had always been.

I was turned back to work in the underground section of the American Communist Party, where J. Peters was delighted to have me. No doubt, he knew more about the shuffle in which I was a pawn than I did.

I said good-bye to Ulrich and Maria. I never expected to hear of them again. My writing habits had been one of Ulrich's gnawing worries and they were on his mind still. "No writing," he warned me. "You are never to write down anything you have seen." When we shook hands, Ulrich smiled to soften the harshness, but not the meaning, of his last words to me: "Remember, Bob, there are only two ways that you can really leave us: you can be shot by *them* or you can be shot by *us*."

THE CHILD

"For one of us to have a child," my brother had said in his agony, "would be a crime against nature." I longed for children. But I agreed with my brother. There had been enough misery in our line. What selfish right had I to perpetuate it? And what right had any man and woman to bring children into the 20th-century world? They could only suffer its inevitable revolutions or die in its inevitable wars.

One extreme group among the Communists held that it was morally wrong for a professional revolutionist to have children at all. They could only hamper or distract his work. That was one of the penalties of being a Communist. I did not belong to that group, but in general I shared its views. As an underground Communist, I took it for granted that children were out of the question.

Not only left-wing and underground Communists took such matters for granted. Abortion was a commonplace of party life. There were Communist doctors who rendered that service for a small fee. Communists who were more choosy knew liberal doctors who would render the same service for a larger fee. Abortion, which now fills me with physical horror, I then regarded, like all Communists, as a mere physical manipulation.

One day, early in 1933, my wife told me that she believed she had conceived. No man can hear from his wife, especially for the first time, that she is carrying his child, without a physical jolt of joy and pride. I felt it. But so sunk were we in that life that it was only a passing joy, and was succeeded by a merely momentary sadness that we would not have the child. We discussed the matter, and my wife said that she must go at once for a physical check and to arrange for the abortion.

When my wife came back (we were still living in Greenwich Village), she was quiet and noncommital. The doctor had said that there was a child. My wife went about preparing supper. "What else did she say?" I asked. "She said that I am in good physical shape to have a baby." My wife went on silently working. Very slowly, the truth dawned on me. "Do you mean," I asked, "that you want to have the child?"

My wife came over to me, took my hands and burst into tears. "Dear heart," she said in a pleading voice, "we couldn't do that awful thing to a little baby, not to a little baby, dear heart." A wild joy swept me. Reason, the agony of my family, the Communist Party and its theories, the wars and revolutions of the 20th century, crumbled at the touch of the child. Both of us simply wanted a child. If the points on the long course of my break with Communism could be retraced, that is probably one of them—not at the level of the conscious mind, but at the level of unconscious life.

I won Ulrich's reluctant consent to take my wife back to our barn in Hunterdon County, where the child could grow among the things its mother and I loved—close to the earth, the gardens, the thrushes and deer in the mountain woods and the robins in the valley.

Because it was inexpensive, we arranged to have the baby born at Booth Memorial, the Salvation Army hospital on 15th Street in New York City. By then, we were living at Fort Lee, New Jersey.

The night of October 16, 1933, I reached home late, around eleven o'clock. My wife was dressed, sitting at a table with a clock in front of her. She was waiting for me and quietly clocking the intervals between her first labor pains. We rode the long miles downtown while she gripped my hand during her pangs. When they took her away from me, a terrible despair seized me. I felt sure that my wife would die. I blamed myself and I knew that, without her, I did not wish to live.

All night I tramped the streets, as I had done the night when I climbed through my wife's window. From time to time, I telephoned the hospital. The answer was always the same: my wife was in the delivery room; the baby had not come. At seven o'clock in the morning, the baby still had not come.

I took the ferry to Staten Island. Then I tramped into the open country where I could find the earth that I felt I must be close to in that crisis.

At nine o'clock, I called again from the ferry house at St. George. "The baby has been born," a nurse said. "It is alive. It is a girl." "And my wife?" I asked. "She is all right," said the nurse. It seemed to me that she had hesitated. Again, I was seized with panic that my wife would die.

She was scarcely out of the anaesthetic, and reeking of ether, when I sat beside her bed. As I looked at her white, hollowed face and the deep, leaden circles under her eyes, and felt her feverish fingers, I thought: "What have I done to her?" At that moment, I cared only for my wife and nothing at all for the child.

My wife kept urging me feebly to go and look at it. She wanted me, of course, to approve and love what had so nearly cost her life (the birth had been terrible). I went into the hall. Through a glass panel, I peered into the antiseptic nursery where banks of babies lay in baskets. A nurse, with a wonderfully personal smile, considering the miscellaneous fathers to whom she pointed out their babies, pointed out mine. The child had been born long enough to have lost the puckered, red, natal look. Her face was pink, and peaceful. She was sleeping. Her long lashes lay against her cheeks. She was beautiful.

I went back to my wife who was no longer only my wife but the mother of our child—the child we all yearn for, who, even before her birth, had begun, invisibly, to lead us out of that darkness, which we could not even realize, toward that light, which we could not even see.

UNDERGROUND

The Second Apparatus

I

No one who has, even once, lived close to the making of history can ever again suppose that it is made the way the history books tell it. With rare exceptions, such books are like photographs. They catch a surface image. Often as not, they distort it. The secret forces working behind and below the historical surface they seldom catch.

It is certain that, between the years 1930 and 1948, a group of almost unknown men and women, Communists or close fellow travelers, or their dupes, working in the United States Government, or in some singular unofficial relationship to it, or working in the press, affected the future of every American now alive, and indirectly the fate of every man now going into uniform. Their names, with half a dozen exceptions, still mean little or nothing to the mass of Americans. But their activities, if only in promoting the triumph of Communism in China, have decisively changed the history of Asia, of the United States, and therefore, of the world. If mankind is about to suffer one of its decisive transformations, if it is about to close its 2000-year-old experience of Christian civilization, and enter upon another wholly new and diametrically different, then that group may claim a part in history such as it is seldom given any men to play, particularly so few and such obscure men.

One of them was Alger Hiss. Since 1948, the press and other opinion-shaping forces have fostered the impression that, in the past, Alger Hiss was a figure of national prominence. The fact is that until I began to testify about him, in August, 1948, you could have asked the first one thousand people you met in almost any American city: "Who is Alger Hiss?" and the chances are that most of them would have answered: "Never heard of him." He had been active at Dumbarton Oaks, at Yalta, at the San Francisco conference which set up the United Nations. He was the president of the Carnegie Endowment for World Peace. There had been news stories about some of those activities. His name was familiar to the F.B.I., to the Office of Naval Intelligence and to the State Department, including its security division. It had troubled the thoughts of the former Secretary of State, James F. Byrnes, and a mental note had been made of it by a sharp-eyed layman.* But on the American consciousness Alger Hiss had made no dent. Nevertheless, he was a figure of power.

* George F. Allen, writing about the San Francisco Conference in *Presidents Who Have Known Me:* "So I asked Stettinius if he could get some State Department attaché, who was familiar with the preliminary negotiations, to give

Nobody starts from nowhere, and seldom alone. Beside Alger Hiss, from his earliest days in Washington, stood another man whose name, and other facts about him, were also presently on file at the F.B.I., the Office of Naval Intelligence and the security division of the State Department. He also would affect in incalculable ways the lives of millions of Americans and others who had never heard of him. For he had organized in the United States Government one of the most formidable little fifth columns in history, whose influence for evil, widening outward long after he was dead, would also be felt in the crash of China and the Carthaginian mangling of Europe. His name was Harold Ware, and his friends all called him Hal.

It suited him exactly. He was as American as ham and eggs and as indistinguishable as everybody else. He stood about five feet nine, a trim, middle-aging man in 1934, with a plain face, masked by a quiet earnestness of expression wholly reassuring to people whom quickness of mind makes uncomfortable. Nevertheless, his mind was extremely quick. I suppose that he owned several suits and sometimes changed them, but in my memory of him, he is always wearing an off-color brown suit of some heavy fabric, carefully pressed, and a brown fedora hat, carefully brushed. From his rimless eyeglasses, a fine gold chain loops behind one ear.

He might have been a progressive county agent or a professor of ecology at an agricultural college. And yet, there was something unprofessorially jaunty about the flip of his hat brim and his springy stride—as if he might have a racing form in his pocket, and be off for the day to the track at Pimlico or Laurel. It is true that he liked to drive his car at breakneck speed almost as well as to talk about soils, tenant farmers and underground organization.

For one fact set off this reassuring man from the mass of Americans whom he so happily blended with. He was a birthright member of the Communist Party. His mother was Ella Reeve Bloor,

me a fill-in. That very day he sent around to my room a personable, bright, obviously well-informed young man to tell me about the UN organization, its origins at the Yalta Conference, and its probable setup. He briefed me for several hours, using simple language, and treating me quite properly as an eighth-grader in my knowledge of diplomacy. When he was through, he asked me whether I had a copy of the speech President Truman would deliver at the close of the San Francisco meeting. When I said I had, he asked whether he might borrow a copy to read at his leisure and return. He did return it in due course with the comment that he considered it excellent. He was extremely curious as to who had assisted in the preparation of the material. The young man's name was Alger Hiss."

who, after the expulsion of "Mother" Gitlow from the party, became the second of its official "mothers," and even a kind of dowager fertility goddess. For at sixty, she was as frolicsome as a schoolgirl, and her vitality provided the party's inner circles with unlimited droll stories.

Hal Ware was one of a Communist dynasty. His half-brother, Carl Reeve, was at one time a district organizer of the Communist Party, and, during my time, was once briefly attached to the *Daily Worker* staff. Hal's wife was Jessica Smith (now Mrs. John Abt and the sister-in-law of Marion Bachrach*). For many years, Comrade Smith has been editor of *Soviet Russia Today* (now called *New World Review*), a magazine of facts and figures (impartially taken from Soviet sources) and adding up to a paean of Soviet progress, beamed monthly toward the unthinkingly enlightened American middle class.

Hal's sister, Helen Ware, in 1934 operated a violin studio on Connecticut Avenue in Washington. It will play a brief obbligato later on in this narrative.

Harold Ware was a frustrated farmer. The soil was in his pores. Unlike most American Communists, who managed to pass from one big city to another without seeing anything in the intervening spaces, Ware was absorbed in the land and its problems. He held that, with the deepening of the agrarian crisis, which had preceded the world financial and industrial crisis, and with the rapid mechanization of agriculture, the time had come for revolutionary organization among farmers.

But first he decided to do a little farming himself. In the early 1920's he set out with a group of American radicals for the Soviet Union to develop a collective farm, the so-called Kuzbas colony. Later, Hal Ware returned to the United States. He did not return empty-handed. The Communist International was also convinced that the time was ripe for organizing the American farmer. Harold Ware himself told me that, for that purpose, he brought back from Moscow $25,000 in American money secreted in a money belt—such a belt as I was soon to wear to San Francisco for another purpose.

Around 1925, Ware hired himself to the Department of Agriculture as a dollar-a-year man. Later on, he set up in Washington a small fact-finding and information bureau called Farm Research. In that enterprise he associated with him two congenial young men. One was

* Currently out on bail after her arrest with other leaders of the Communist Party.

the brother of a man named by Elizabeth Bentley as one of her contacts, and a close friend of Harry Dexter White, then with the United States Treasury Department, and also one of Elizabeth Bentley's contacts. The other, later an expert on labor relations at a United States consulate in Australia, was, until rather recently, an employe of the State Department.

Seldom has $25,000 bought so much history. But Ware did not invest all (or perhaps even much of his nest egg) in Washington. To my knowledge, he maintained close ties with the Communist Party's underground sharecroppers' union at Camp Hill, Alabama, and no doubt with other undergrounds in the West and South.*

It was not necessary to invest heavily in Washington. Once the New Deal was in full swing, Hal Ware was like a man who has bought a farm sight unseen only to discover that the crops are all in and ready to harvest. All that he had to do was to hustle them into the barn. The barn in this case was the Communist Party. In the A.A.A., Hal found a bumper crop of incipient or registered Communists. On its legal staff were Lee Pressman, Alger Hiss and John Abt (later named by Elizabeth Bentley as one of her contacts). There was Charles Krivitsky, a former physicist at New York University, then or shortly afterwards to be known as Charles Kramer (also, later on, one of Elizabeth Bentley's contacts). Abraham George Silverman (another of Elizabeth Bentley's future contacts) was sitting with a little cluster of Communists over at the Railroad Retirement Board. In the Agriculture Department (after a flier in the N.R.A.) there was Henry H. Collins, Jr., now the head of the American-Russian Institute, cited as subversive by the Attorney General. Collins was the son of a Philadelphia manufacturer, a schoolboy friend of Alger Hiss, and a college friend of the late Laurence Duggan (who was later to be one of Hede Massing's underground contacts). There was Nathan Witt in the National Labor Relations Board. There was John Abt's sister, Marion Bachrach. In the N.R.A., then or later, was Victor Perlo (also one of Elizabeth Bentley's contacts). Widening vistas opened into the

* One of them, described to me by J. Peters, was headed by Clarina Michelson, a Communist trade-union organizer, who was said to come of a good Boston family, but who had developed the chummy habit of addressing everyone as "dearie." Posing as a woman of means on her organizing forays, Comrade Michelson stayed at the better hotels in the South. In her underground activities she was assisted by Otto Hall, who posed as her "chauffeur." Otto Hall was a high man among colored Communists and the brother, or half-brother, of James Ford, the Communist Party's perennial vice-presidential candidate in national elections.

United States Government. Somewhat breathlessly, Harold Ware reported to J. Peters, the head of the underground section of the American Communist Party, with whom Hal was in close touch, that the possibilities for Communist organization in Washington went far beyond farming.

I do not know how many of those young men and women were already Communists when Ware met them and how many joined the Communist Party because of him. His influence over them was personal and powerful. But about the time that Ulrich and Charlie were initiating me into The Gallery and invisible ink, Harold Ware and J. Peters were organizing the Washington prospects into the secret Communist group now known by Ware's name—the Ware Group.

Under oath, before the House Committee on Un-American Activities, Lee Pressman, in 1951, testified that he, Witt, Abt and Kramer had been Communists and members of this group. He also gave an account of its organization which may well bear a sketchy resemblance to its first formative stage. But, by 1934, the Ware Group had developed into a tightly organized underground, managed by a directory of seven men. In time it included a number of secret sub-cells whose total membership I can only estimate—probably about seventy-five Communists. Sometimes they were visited officially by J. Peters who lectured them on Communist organization and Leninist theory and advised them on general policy and specific problems. For several of them were so placed in the New Deal agencies (notably Alger Hiss, Nathan Witt, John Abt and Lee Pressman) that they were in a position to influence policy at several levels.

They were so well-placed that the thought had occurred to Comrade Peters, and no doubt to others, that such human material could be used more effectively, and, moreover, that it was poor organization to leave so many promising Communists in one large group where everybody knew everybody else. Peters proposed to separate the most likely ones (an almost invariable underground practice) and place them in another distinct underground—a parallel apparatus—much more rigorously segregated and subdivided. When advisable, other Communists would be added to this special apparatus from other undergrounds in Washington. For the Ware Group was not the only Communist underground in the capital. This task Peters assigned to me.

The immediate plan called for the moving of "career Communists" out of the New Deal agencies, which the party could penetrate almost at will, and their gradual infiltration of the old-line departments, with the State Department as the first objective. Actually, Peters was organizing what Herman had dreamed of, and, ultimately, for the same master—the Soviet Military Intelligence. It is possible, though he did not tell me about it, that he was well aware of that fact.

In pursuance of this plan, in the early spring of 1934, J. Peters introduced me, in New York City, to Harold Ware. He introduced me as Carl, for I had decided to take a new pseudonym for my new work.

Ware and I quickly discovered that we had the same unromantic approach to conspiracy, the same appreciation of the difficulties of organizing intellectuals, and a common interest in farm problems. Before we parted, we knew that we would work together easily, and we had arranged a time and place where I would meet Hal Ware in Washington, and begin looking over the underground landscape.

Peters, too, presently decided that he would join us in Washington on the same day. His trip was made necessary by a fact that he did not tell me in New York. An underground Communist whose name I had not yet heard, a lawyer named Alger Hiss, had been offered the opportunity to move from the A.A.A. and to become counsel for the Senate Committee investigating the munitions industry, sometimes known as the Nye Committee after its chairman, Gerald P. Nye. For the penetration of the United States Government by the Communist Party coincided with a mood in the nation which light-heartedly baited the men who manufactured the armaments indispensable to its defense as "Merchants of Death." It is not surprising that Alger Hiss should first have emerged to public view in the act of helping the Communist Party to abet that disastrous mood.

II

I had not been in Washington since I left it in the fall of 1919. Then I had been a day laborer. I came back to it, in 1934, as a secret agent of a revolutionary party which seemed consciously to embody in politics what, as a youth, I had unconsciously groped for in life. I felt the past and the present fuse.

On my first day of laying rails in Washington, as I stood waiting for a streetcar to crawl over the partially dismantled tracks, a laughing man had leaned out an open window and casually and deliberately aimed at me a squirt of tobacco juice that missed my face but soaked my shirt. I had been a day laborer, that is to say, a target for any grossness from above. I had that jet of tobacco juice well in mind when I wrote for the *New Masses* a decade later:

"What do you make
Of our bare and lonely lives,
Working together
In the section gang, early and late,
In the heat of the day, in the warm spring weather?
You say: It is our fate that we must take.
But we say: "A grim fate
That sets you free,
And makes us slaves forever for your sake.
And one we should be able to unmake.
And will. Wait."

I had returned to Washington to assist in unmaking that fate, still with the proletariat, but with a proletariat that throughout the world was rising in the consciousness of its mass strength and the faith, that only through its unflinching intelligence and will, could all of mankind emerge from the disaster of this age to a better (or even a bearable) life. I had no doubt at all, as I stepped out of the Union Station, thinking of those things, that whatever I might do on my return to Washington was inseparable from that purpose.

I found Hal Ware waiting for me at exactly the time and place that we had agreed on in New York a week or so before. The place, as if predestined, was a Childs restaurant near the Union Station, a few doors from the Hotel Bellevue, where, six years later, General Walter Krivitsky would lie murdered by that same party which he and I had both devotedly served, but from which we had both broken.

Harold Ware was delighted to see me, for there were not enough hours in the day and night for him to manage any longer without help his heavy load of conspiracy.

III

It is difficult to disentangle the events and their sequence on that day seventeen years ago. That is also true for much that happened during the next few months, when I was meeting many new people and trying to adjust myself in underground work to a new kind of Communist (the collegiate conspirator who had gone almost directly from the campus to the underground without any experience of the open Communist Party). At the same time, I was commuting between Washington and New York, where something was about to occur that would direct my main organizational interest away from Washington at the very moment I arrived there, and turn it first toward England, and then toward Japan.

Therefore, I must simply set down my impressions of that first day as best I can, in part as recollection, in part as reconstruction of what took place. There may be errors of detail, but the general outlines will be accurate. Anyone who tries to recollect by his unaided memory what happened to him in the course even of one eventful day seventeen years ago will realize how the years blur detail.

I met Hal Ware shortly before noon. He drove me around downtown Washington, somewhat in the manner of a man showing his estate to a guest. Then we headed across the Potomac to Arlington National Cemetery, where we parked while Ware talked a little about the organization of the Ware Group, some of the people in it and others I would meet. Hal talked about them like a father who is tremendously proud of his sons, but who is also aware that they have not quite outgrown their political pinfeathers.

Then I first learned that I would stay overnight at "the violin studio." At first I thought that "the violin studio" might be a cover name, like The Gallery. A little later, I separated from Ware and, by a prearrangement made in New York, met J. Peters at the Union Station. Together we walked downtown, to kill time and to make sure that we were not followed. It was then that Peters made that exultant comment that I have quoted in the first part of this book: "Even in Germany under the Weimar Republic, the party did not have what we have here." At the time, I thought that Peters was exaggerating. I was mistaken.

Somewhere downtown Peters and I picked up Hal Ware as I had arranged with him to do. We drove in his car to a basement cafeteria on Wisconsin Avenue in Georgetown. There we sat talking. Ware and Peters worked out certain appointments for Peters which were meaningless to me. But there I again heard the name that was to be fateful for the world and for me—the name of Alger Hiss. I learned that he was an American, a lawyer, an exceptional

Communist for whom Peters had an unusual regard, and that he was a member of the Ware Group. He was about to leave, or had just left, the A.A.A., where he had been assistant general counsel, for the Senate munitions investigating committee. This change made it important that he should be separated from the Ware Group at once. He would be the first man in the new apparatus which I was to organize. For that purpose, I would meet Alger Hiss that day.

Peters, Ware, Hiss and I met at a downtown cafeteria, which, as nearly as I can remember, was located (rather fittingly) a few doors from the Washington *Post*, on Pennsylvania Avenue. It was a brief meeting, for the sake of introducing Hiss and me, and it broke up almost as soon as the introduction had been made. I believe that Peters and Hiss left separately and that, a little later, Ware and I left together. For my next recollection of that afternoon is driving with Hal to some point where we picked up an underground Communist whom I shall call Egmont Gaines. Probably we had an early supper together and probably at a co-operative cafeteria near the Y.M.C.A. Either before or after that, we were at the violin studio, which was not a cover name, but was in fact a studio on Connecticut Avenue, near Dupont Circle. There, during the day, Hal Ware's sister, Helen Ware, taught music. But at night the studio served as an informal meeting place for certain of Ware's underground connections.

The studio was one flight above a florist's shop. It was a big room as bare as a dance floor. Toward the Dupont Circle end, at the right-hand side, was a smaller room where there were one or two cots. There, Hal said, I could pass the night. I gathered from something else he said that transients from his farm undergrounds often spent the night there. Hal or Egmont gave me a key.* What I particularly remember is Egmont Gaines sitting on one of the cots, chatting about the possibilities of underground organization and insisting that we must make contact with "Larry" Duggan, whom he called "very sympathetic." Thus, on my first day in Washington, I first heard the name of the late Laurence Duggan, who was then in the State Department, and later became chief of its Latin-American Division. Fourteen years later, during the Hiss Case, Duggan would be killed by a fall from his New York office window several days after he had been questioned by F.B.I. agents.

* Later in 1934, the lock on the studio door was twice broken. The underground suspected, quite mistakenly, that that had been the work of the F.B.I. So the violin studio was given up as an underground meeting place.

That night I returned alone to the violin studio and slept there. That was, in general, my first day and night in contact with the Washington underground.

IV

If I did not meet all the leaders of the Ware Group during my first day in Washington, I met them soon after.

The headquarters of the Group was then the apartment of its treasurer, Henry H. Collins, Jr., at St. Matthews Court. There the leading committee of the Group held its weekly or fortnightly meetings. Collins' St. Matthews Court apartment remained the Group's headquarters until some time in 1936 or 1937, when Collins moved to a house just across the District Line in Maryland. After that, the Ware Group met at the house of John Abt—an ideal arrangement since, at that time, Abt was not only the head of the Group, but a special assistant to the Attorney General of the United States.

St. Matthews Court was the only place in Washington with a touch of Greenwich Village. It was a mews that lay between M and N Streets, just off Connecticut Avenue. The court was flanked by two- or three-story brick houses with window boxes and gay shutters. The tenants seemed to desire and respect privacy. That was an advantage, but, in general, St. Matthews Court was a little too conspicuously picturesque for an ideal underground headquarters.

Henry Collins' apartment was on the second floor of a house whose first floor was occupied in part by a Negro family, in part by a garage or car-washing establishment. It was a big, sprawling, attractive apartment. The entrance, as nearly as I can remember, led into a small hall. To the left was a big living room. It was really two rooms, shaped roughly like a reverse L, but the upright stroke of the L was oblique. To the right of the vestibule was a dining room. Behind the dining room were one or two bedrooms.

I have no recollection of the furniture in the apartment. But there were many books and its memorable feature was the Ethiopian tapestries and paintings that hung on its walls. For Henry Collins, before going to Washington, had made a trip to Ethiopia and was, he once told me, the only member of the Travellers' Club who at that time had been there. Collins was also an ornithologist and a dendrologist—interests that were not merely hobbies with him, as they were with me, but in which he was learned. He also had a passion for figures and often plagued J. Peters to let him leave Government service and go to New York to manage the Communist Party's finances. They might have proved a revelation to the Philadelphia manufacturer's son and graduate of the Harvard School of Business.

Henry Collins was all that Princeton and Harvard can do for a personable and intelligent young American of good family. To some, he seemed a little chilly and diffident. And there was in him a core, not so much of reserve as of incapacity for spontaneous feeling. But he was persistent, very tenacious and held at least his political convictions, with a fierce faith. I was constantly in touch with Collins almost until I broke with the Communist Party. During that time, he made several voluntary efforts to enter the State Department for the purpose of serving the Communist Party, and twice sought to recruit Laurence Duggan, a college friend, into that Soviet espionage apparatus. Incidentally, one of those recruiting attempts has been described in detail—not by me—and exists as a Government record. For, even more than keeping the party's books, Collins longed to enter the Soviet underground—a dream that seemed about to be realized when, in 1937, I introduced him in New York City, to Colonel Boris Bykov.

At St. Matthews Court, Collins lived alone. He was separated from his wife (he has since married Susan B. Anthony III). He had a son about ten years old whom I met once when he was visiting his father (on some holiday from school) and I was staying overnight at St. Matthews Court, as I sometimes did. To tidy up and cook occasional suppers, Henry had a colored maid. The leading committee of the Ware Group met after she had gone home.

The Ware Group, in 1934 and 1935, when I knew it best, consisted of a leading committee of seven men. All were Communists and they met to discuss policy, organization, personnel and projects. Several of the leaders of the Group also headed secret cells. Of one cell, I caught a glimpse when I once happened in unexpectedly at the apartment of Charles Kramer. I attended a meeting of another cell (headed by Henry Collins) at the house of a future employe of the State Department who has since left its service. Each meeting included some twelve or fifteen members. There must have been four (and possibly more) such cells. Assuming that each contained about the same number of members, there must have been seventy-five underground Communists in the Ware Group. That, it seems to me, is a conservative figure. The overwhelming number of these Communists were employes of the United States Government.

The relationship of the leading committee to the secret cells was much like that of the Central Committee to the units of the open Communist Party. The Group was headed, when I first knew it, by Harold Ware himself. After Ware's death in 1935, Nathan Witt became the leader of the Group. Later, John Abt, for reasons not known to me, became its leader.

An effort has been made to describe the Ware Group as merely a "Marxist study group." That is not true. The Ware Group was an integral (and highly important) unit of the underground section of the American Communist Party. Until his death, it was under the constant direction of Harold Ware. It was always under the personal supervision of J. Peters, whose visits to it were at least monthly, and sometimes more frequent. On trade-union questions, and much of its activity had to do with trade-union and other labor problems, at least one of its members sometimes consulted in New York with Jack Stachel, one of the party's top men in trade-union work.

There was Marxist-Leninist political instruction and discussion in the Group. The *Daily Worker* was received in Washington at several drug stores* where packages of it carefully wrapped were sent by express from New York. One of the functions of Alger Hiss's 1929 Ford roadster, and especially what he was later to describe as "its sassy little trunk," had been to pick up and distribute to the Ware Group those clandestine shipments of the *Worker*. The members of the Group were forbidden to keep more than one or two Communist pamphlets in their homes at any one time. But such party literature was studied by them. J. Peters occasionally lectured the leading Committee (and probably the cells) on the theory of Leninism, and on another subject which was very close to his heart, the problems of Communist organization (he had written the Communist Party's official *Manual of Organization*).

But one point should be made clear: all the members of the Ware Group were dues-paying members of the Communist Party and Peters considered the Group, together with his Hollywood underground, as one of his major sources of income. I am quite sure that I am right in remembering that members of the Ware Group regularly paid ten per cent of their salaries to the Communist Party, and were subject to special assessments, besides. It was a point

* The owner of the drug stores was the brother of a New York Communist doctor who was married to one of the party's highly trusted stenographers.

with J. Peters, stressed by him to the Group, and frequently mentioned to me, that since its members were intellectuals without open party experience, it was extremely important to their feeling of Communist solidarity that they make exceptional money sacrifices for the Communist Party. Lenin himself had stressed the importance of dues as a test and a binder of party loyalty. Long after he was in the Soviet underground, Alger Hiss continued devoutly to pay exorbitant dues to the party.

But while the Ware Group was not primarily a Marxist study group, neither was it an espionage group, as is sometimes supposed. To my personal knowledge, at least eight members of the Group were sooner or later involved with a Soviet espionage apparatus as members or helpers. (Later on, several members graduated into Elizabeth Bentley's espionage apparatus.) It is also highly probable that some members of the Group transmitted to the Communist Party Government documents, not privileged, but not intended for the party. For it is axiomatic that any Communist anywhere will always steal for the party anything that can possibly be of interest or use to it. I know, too, that a kind of Communist Kiplinger letter was sent weekly to the Communist Party by a Communist once highly placed in the Treasury Department. Nevertheless, in the technical sense, the Ware Group was not primarily an espionage group.

Its functions, if less sensational, were scarcely less important. They were on several levels. They involved the recruiting of new members into the underground and the staffing of Government agencies with Communist Party members (the overnight ease with which the Communist Party later on placed me in the Government, as I have described in Part I of this book, shows how it had streamlined that operation).

Those were more or less routine functions. The real power of the Group lay at much higher levels. It was a power to influence, from the most strategic positions, the policies of the United States Government, especially in the labor and welfare fields. Moreover, since one member of the Group was secretary of the National Labor Relations Board, and another member of the Group was in the top council of the C.I.O., the Communist Party was in a position to exert a millstone effect, both *in favor* of policies and persons it supported, and *against* policies and persons it disliked.

I can imagine no better way to convey the secret power of the Communist Party in the domestic policies of the United States

Government from 1933 to 1943, and later, than to list the members of the leading committee of the Ware Group and the posts that mark their progress through the Federal Government. That excludes the contributing efforts of all other members of the Group whose names and activities, with three or four notable exceptions, are not known to me.

The leading committee of the Ware Group included:

Nathan Witt

August, 1933, through February, 1934—attorney on the staff of the A.A.A.

1934—One of the four members of the Legal Staff of the Labor Relations Board, established under the N.R.A.

July, 1935—Transferred to the Legal Staff of the National Labor Relations Board.

December, 1935, through November, 1937—Assistant General Counsel of the National Labor Relations Board.

November, 1937, through December, 1940—Secretary of the National Labor Relations Board.

Lee Pressman

1933—Assistant General Counsel of the A.A.A.

1935—General Counsel of the Works Progress Administration and of the Resettlement Administration.

1936 through 1948—General Counsel of the C.I.O.

John J. Abt

1933—Attorney for the A.A.A.

1935—Assistant General Counsel of the Works Progress Administration.

1936—Special counsel to the Securities and Exchange Commission (to prepare the case against the Electric Bond and Share Company).

1936—Chief counsel to the Subcommittee on Civil Liberties Violations of the Senate Committee on Education and Labor (the LaFollette Civil Liberties Committee).

1937—Department of Justice as a Special Assistant to the Attorney General of the United States in charge of the Trial Section.

Charles Kramer

1933—On the staff of the A.A.A.

1935—On the staff of the National Youth Administration.

1936 through 1937—On the staff of the LaFollette Subcommittee of the Senate on Civil Liberties.

1938 through 1942—On the staff of the National Labor Relations Board.

1942 through 1943—With the Office of Price Administration.

In 1943—Joined the staff of the Senate Committee on War Mobilization.

1945 through 1946—On the staff of the Senate Subcommittee on Wartime Health and Education.

Henry H. Collins, Jr.

1933—N.R.A.

1935—Soil Conservation Service of the Department of Agriculture.

1938—Wage and Hour Division, Department of Labor.

Subsequently, the House Committee on the Inter-State Migration of Destitute Citizens.

1941—The Senate Committee on Small Business.

1942—On the staff of the Kilgore Subcommittee of the Senate Military Affairs Committee.

Subsequently, attended School of Military Government at Charlottesville, Virginia. From there was sent overseas and spent two years in military government in England, France and Germany.

Entered the Army with the rank of captain and was separated with the rank of major.

Now a major in the United States Army Reserves. After separation from the service, spent five months with the State Department in connection with the Displaced Persons Program. Thereafter, spent six months with the Inter-Governmental Committee on Refugees to South American Countries; then did free-lance writing.

1948 Executive Director of the American Russian Institute in New York City, cited by the Attorney General as a Communist front organization.

Victor Perlo

1933 through 1935—N.R.A.

1935 through 1937—Home Owners Loan Corporation.

1937 through 1939—Brookings Institution.

1940 through 1941—With the Commerce Department as a special agent and senior economic analyst. Thereafter, joined

O.P.A. as Chief of the Statistical Analysis Branch of the Research Division.

February, 1943—Joined War Production Board and handled problems relating to military aircraft production.

December, 1945—Joined the Treasury Department, Monetary Branch, where he remained for 1½ years.

Alger Hiss was also a member of the leading committee before his separation from the Ware Group.

For a long time, the fact that I had ever been inside the Collins apartment rested only on my unsupported word. But at a late stage of the Hiss Case, perhaps in an unguarded moment, more probably with some idea of bolstering Hiss's identification of me as "George Crosley," Henry Collins one night admitted to special agents of the F.B.I. that he had known me (as George Crosley, which is not true), and that I had been at his apartment (which is true). In Collins' version, I had been there only "for cocktails."

The existence of the Ware Group itself also rested for a long time on my unsupported word. During the pre-trial examination in the libel suit which Alger Hiss brought against me in Baltimore, one of his attorneys, William L. Marbury, was hugely amused by my claim that such a group had ever existed. At one point, he asked me to name the seven men on its leading committee. After hours of questioning, I was fatigued and, for a moment, could remember only six. "You have forgotten your prize exhibit," said Marbury helpfully in the tone of breezy skepticism and heavy sarcasm that characterized the proceedings. My "prize exhibit," the forgotten man, was Lee Pressman.

But, two years later, my "prize exhibit" testified under oath, before the House Committee on Un-American Activities, that he had been a member of the Communist Party, that there had been a Ware Group of which, of course, he had been a member, and that Nathan Witt, John Abt and Charles Kramer had also been members. Pressman's memory failed (or confused) him on most other relevant points, so that his testimony fell far short of the full facts. He should know, for example, that Hiss and Collins were both Communists and both members of the Ware Group. He should know that Hiss was connected with me, when, and for what purpose, and should be able to clear up those matters. But Lee Pressman's testimony settled once for all the basic question of the existence of the Ware Group.

Even without his assistance, the facts may presently become clearer and fuller. For I have reason to believe that there is still another witness with first-hand knowledge of the Group. At least, like Hamlet. I see a cherub who sees one.*

V

The Ware Group was a background and a base for my activities, from the time I arrived in Washington, in 1934, until I broke with the Communist Party, in 1938. Until his death, I was constantly in touch with Harold Ware. As long as Henry Collins lived at St. Matthews Court, his apartment was one of my informal Washington headquarters. Through it, I maintained contact with the Group, which stood ready to help me in any way that I saw fit. Through it, I often maintained contact with J. Peters, whose comings and goings in Washington it was sometimes more convenient to keep track of through the Ware Group than by direct contact in New York City.

Though members of my special apparatus were officially separated from the Ware Group, they continued to meet their former comrades by chance, socially or in the course of Government work. Sometimes Alger Hiss, in particular, found his separation and inactivity in the special apparatus so wearing that he broke the rules and spent a few hours with his former cell mates. Now and again, Alger would confess that he had seen Henry Collins, usually on the pretext of giving him party dues. I winked at these irregularities.

Two members of the Ware Group became my unofficial helpers and continued to act as such almost until the time that I broke with the Communist Party. One was Henry Collins. The other was Lee Pressman.

But the historical importance of the Ware Group is as the root from which divided two sinister stems—the Soviet espionage apparatuses of Elizabeth Bentley, about which the world now knows a great deal, thanks to her remarkably detailed recollection; and whatever apparatus Alger Hiss continued with after my break. The second, and the more important, still lies in the shadows.

* Since this was written, another witness has appeared. In February of this year, Nathaniel Weyl testified before the McCarran Committee that, early in 1934, he had been a Communist and a member of the Ware Group. With one exception (a man who presumably entered the Group after Weyl had left), he named as his fellow members all those whom I had named, including Alger Hiss. Weyl, however, was not the witness referred to above.

VI

Harold Ware was a man without personal ambition. The whole purpose of his life lay in promoting Communism. Many Communists would have been disturbed to have a newcomer intrude into their province. Ware, once he had formed his opinion of me, welcomed me without reservation, inducted me into all (and more than all) that I needed to know of his work, and built me up for my own work by discreet words dropped about my special experience.

As a result, no sooner had I reached Washington than I found myself wrapped in the aura of a man who had worked with "them"—the Russians. So great is the revolutionary spell of that word "Russian," that American Communists, who might hesitate to do certain things for another American Communist, will all but beg to do the same things for a Russian or anyone directly connected with the Russians. This attitude, which must seem outrageous or incredible to non-Communists, was the tribute that hope paid to success. The Russian Revolution had succeeded. The Russians incarnated success and power. The heart of every revolution is a struggle for power and there was little that the bright young men of Washington worshipped more fervently than power, often without being at all aware of the fact.

I reflected power in one of its most fascinating forms—invisible power. I was introduced to all the underground Communists simply as Carl. The decades-old practice of underground pseudonyms was excitingly new to the Washington revolutionists. I presently realized (and Ware used to smile at) the fact that I had become a figure of awe, not because of anything I pretended to be—I was simple and friendly—but because that was what those young zealots wanted me to be and made me. Their wishful thinking, almost at once, took a turn that neither Ware, Peters nor I could possibly have foreseen.

After my introduction to Alger Hiss, and some of the others in the underground, there occurred an interval of a month or more which long puzzled me in trying to recollect those days, because I could not remember why I should have gone to Washington, and then abruptly left it, or what I had been doing in the meantime. I shall report what I now believe to be the reason for that gap in the next chapter. In any case, I did not see Alger Hiss, after my first meeting, until he had moved to an apartment in one of three almost identical apartment houses on 28th Street near Woodley Road.

I looked forward with some concern to my first meeting alone with Hiss. In a special underground apparatus, where an isolated Communist's contact with the body of the party is maintained, as a rule, solely or chiefly through one man or woman, the personal factor is all important (as Ulrich well knew). On it depends whether the relationship is to be one of confident co-operation or mere grudging association, which, in a Communist sense, is unproductive, and may lead to personal crises, like my relationship with Herman, or worse. On me, therefore, rather than on the party's disciplinary power, depended the future success of the new apparatus.

Clearly, Alger Hiss was no ordinary Communist. My own first impression of him had been brief, but his manner told me something, and from Peters and Ware, I had learned enough of his background to know that he was highly intelligent, but without real Communist experience. Like almost all the Washington Communists, he belonged to a new breed—middle-class intellectuals who had gone directly underground without passing through the open party. Hence we had no common experience that could float us along until we found some other common ground in activity. I had no immediate task for Hiss to perform, so that there was nothing specific that we could discuss and agree or disagree about. I had the task of presenting myself as a man with whom he would henceforth be almost exclusively connected, and in whom, in that singular relationship, he must have confidence and find some intellectual community.

I arrived at Hiss's apartment after supper, about nine o'clock at night. It was a hot, sticky Washington night. We sat in the stifling living room, which was also the dining room, and the first room entered from the hall. Priscilla Hiss took almost no part in a conversation which was rather pawing and aimless. She watched me intently. I wondered rather desperately how I could give the conversation some point. I knew that intellectual Communists, especially those who are most fastidious, are usually fascinated by the image of the proletarian, or by proletarian experience. I thought that I could convey to Hiss something of the kind of man I was, and what Communism does to the workingman, by telling him what had been teasing my mind ever since I had returned to

Washington. I told him how I had once laid rails on New York Avenue and tried to communicate to him the curious feeling of the man, who has once been on the bottom of society, when he returns to the same scene as an agent of the Communist Party.

There was a polite but complete short circuit. I left shortly after, feeling that it had been pretty awful. I thought that I should probably have to call upon Ware or J. Peters to help me. But I also thought that I must make one more try.

A night or two later, I visited the Hisses again. The change in climate was a little stupendous. There were welcoming smiles and Alger was gracious in the way which is his peculiar talent. Graciously, he ventured an explanation. He was sorry about the other evening. But at first he had not known what to make of me. I had talked about laying rails, but I was obviously not a proletarian. I had said that I was an American, but I was not like any American he had ever known. Then the truth had suddenly dawned. I was a European who had spent some years in the United States. My mastery of English was remarkable (later, when we drove together, he would also be struck by my remarkable knowledge of American roads). But, said Alger, with the knowing air of a man who cannot be deceived, there were certain turns of expression, certain tones of voice, that gave me away. It was true. I had been with Russians so much that, to make myself understood quickly, I had taken to simplifying my sentences along the lines of their thought processes, and to relying, like a European, on intonation rather than phrasing to express shades of meaning. Moreover, said Alger, by way of a clincher, my habit of mind was ironic, and Americans do not like irony. That was also true. The habit of my mind is ironic, and was much more so then.

I do not remember whether the word Russian was actually used. But, if not, that was the unspoken word that made possible this strange self-deception. Carl was one of "them"—if not actually a Great Russian, what was even more appealing in a revolutionary sense, a member of one of the old subject nationalities that had been liberated by the revolution. Much later on, I was once talking about the Volga Germans,* and I suddenly realized, from an intent

* Formerly, one of the Socialist Soviet Republics. After the German invasion of Russia in World War I, the Volga German Republic was erased. The whole population, men, women and children were marched into some nameless part of Siberia, probably as slave laborers.

expression on Hiss's face, that he felt that I had unwittingly disclosed myself: Carl was a Volga German.

On that second visit to 28th Street, I was merely astonished. I was delighted at the change of atmosphere, and I meant to do nothing at the moment to unsettle it. I also sensed two other things. A curious kind of snobbery was playing a part in the delusion. Alger Hiss wanted to be one of those who were in direct touch with the real revolution, with the Workers' Fatherland. I sensed, too, that he felt more confidence in dealing with a Russian than he would have in dealing with the most trusted American Communist. And so I merely smiled to indicate that I did not wish to pursue a subject that bore on my identity and my status in the country. At that, I saw that I had also become something else in his eyes: the heroic revolutionist who lives always one jump ahead of the police. We spent a very pleasant evening together.

But I was also disturbed. I knew that when the deception was discovered, and I supposed then that that must happen almost at once, Hiss would be embarrassed, and probably resentful, precisely because it was he who had deceived himself. J. Peters was in Washington. That night or the next day, I went to him for counsel. "He thinks I am a Russian," I said. "What shall I do?" Peters laughed. "Let him think so," he said. "It's all the better." Like any Communist, he did not care how something was done so long as it produced results. Actually, that strange delusion lasted for more than four years.

When I broke with the Communist Party, Hiss, as he then told me, had learned from the party my true identity or at least the fact that I was an American. I am sure that, at that time, the disclosure of the deception had on him exactly the effect that I feared it would have in the first place.

Word quickly spread through the underground that Carl was a Russian. I have a feeling that Peters also gave the story a discreet nod. I myself quickly began to play the part assigned me. At first, it was as amusing as any charade. Soon it became another of the underground nuisances. It was not difficult. The great thing was not to overdo it. I had only to appear, not as a man with an accent, but as a man who is trying to purge his voice of any trace of accent. In part, the illusion was possible because every language implies a special logic of thought. I had only, once in a while, to think out loud like a German, though in unaccented English, to create the effect. An occasional European intonation, perfectly natural to someone who speaks another language, and the trick of never saying Russia, or the Soviet Union, but always saying "home," completed the illusion. But, in fact, it was scarcely necessary for me to do anything at all. Once the idea had been fixed, it was less anything I did than what they wanted to believe that made the illusion possible. In any case, my stature shot up overnight. I no longer needed to call upon Ware or Peters for support. With two exceptions (Victor Perlo and, later on, David Carpenter, neither of whom I suspect was ever deceived), there was almost nothing that the underground Communists in Washington would not gladly do for me as a Russian.

This story will seem perfectly incredible to anyone who has had no experience of the underground and cannot imagine its strange atmosphere and emotions. But it has been confirmed by witnesses before the Grand Jury of the Southern District of New York. I have already described how one witness had to be brought into the witness waiting room to listen to me speak because I was an American, and the man he knew as Carl spoke like a European. Thereafter he identified me.

Much more striking are two other instances. Ludwig Lore also knew me in the underground as Carl. The former editor of the *Volkszeitung*, a man of wide experience, had been born in Silesia and spent his youth there before coming to the United States. He himself spoke with a pronounced German accent. Yet almost until the day of his death, he believed that I was a German or a Russian despite the fact that his three sons (all living witnesses to this fact) insisted that I was an American. So far had the illusion gone, that, although I always wore the most ordinary of American clothes, Lore described me in an official report as "dressed like a German businessman."

Nor was Lore the most surprising case. Dr. Alphonse Goldschmitt, the German economist, then a fugitive from Nazi Germany, not only identified me as a Russian (I have never been in Russia), but identified me by name. He once asked me in Lore's house, before a number of guests, one of whom was Max Nomad, the author of *Rebels and Renegades:* "Why do you call yourself Carl now? I met you in Moscow in 1932. You are Colonel Dietrich of the General Staff."

VII

One difficulty in trying to reconstruct this period of the underground past, chiefly by the action of my undocumented memory, has been in establishing the order of events and the time intervals between them. Originally, I supposed that I had been with J. Peters and out of touch with any Soviet apparatus for some time. As other facts have come into focus, I am forced to conclude that the interval was much shorter than I had at first supposed, and that it blended in my memory with a longer interval when Peters and I were alone together before the arrival of Colonel Boris Bykov. Several factors bear this out, among others the recollections of my fellow underground worker, Keith.

I am now as sure as I can be, in the absence of corroborating proof or testimony, that the event which occurred between my first meeting with Ware and others in Washington, and my first conversation with Hiss on 28th Street, was the arrival in the United States of a Soviet agent known as "Bill."

After Ulrich had gone, I remained in touch with Dr. Rosenbliett, dropping in from time to time to see him at his office. One day The Doctor told me that he must introduce me to "somebody important." A day or two later, I met, in the privacy of the inner dental office, a tall, lank, unsmiling Soviet agent, with a very wrinkled face which should have been imposing, but was chiefly forbidding. The Doctor introduced me to him as Bob and him to me as "Willi." After the introduction, Willi left The Doctor and me alone. I suggested to him that Willi was scarcely the name for a man six feet tall and that, if its owner wanted to maintain his unbending dignity, he had better change it to "Bill." Thus Willi became Bill.

Bill was an Esthonian or a Finn. He was, though this fact I did not learn until recently, a Red Army officer, an authority on the problems of India, about which he had written a book. We got along well in a rather formal way, not at all like my easy relationship with Ulrich. Of the Soviet agents I knew, Bill is the one about whom I recall least, though, after Ulrich, he was the one with whom I was friendliest. He was a very tight-lipped man, literally and figuratively. He never told me more of what was in his mind than was strictly necessary. In time, I came to believe that that was because there was not much to tell. At first, I had supposed that that wrinkled mask concealed special ranges of experience and knowledge. By degrees, I came to believe that Bill was a naturally kind and generous man, but also a very limited one, and sensitive enough to fear that he might be found out—hence the mask. Hence, too, his taciturnity and, in part, his sudden shifts in plan and uncertainty of judgment.

Bill quickly took me away from Peters, put me in his own Soviet underground apparatus and attached me to himself. I used to meet him once a week or so, sometimes in Automats, sometimes in tearooms where few people could have looked more out of place than Bill. Once more I was the liaison between the Soviet apparatus and the Bank.

I have no such picture of Bill at work as I have of Ulrich. I assume that Bill was no more talkative with The Doctor than with me, for during that period, Dr. Rosenbliett's gossip was thin. But I do know about Bill's chief project. It was to set up a Soviet apparatus in England. This use of the United States as a base for establishing Soviet apparatuses in other countries was then a common practice.

I had been selected to assist Bill in London. This project Bill outlined to me in the course of several conversations. He instructed me to provide myself at once with a business "cover"—an American firm that would send me to represent it in London. I must also provide myself with papers on which I could secure a fraudulent passport. I needed papers for my wife, too, and what was much more difficult, for my infant daughter, both of whom were to accompany me to England. Furthermore, I was to organize in the United States a courier system such as I had formerly known of on the German boats. But the couriers for the English apparatus were to travel between New York City and Southampton, Portsmouth, or, preferably, the port of London.

Bill's instructions called for immediate action. He gave me to understand that we would both leave for England just as soon as our "covers" and other practical details were taken care of. Whoever was ready first would leave first. But the organization of "covers" is at best a slow business.

I took this complicated problem at once to J. Peters. That resourceful man foresaw certain difficulties, but none that were insuperable.

Clearly, the first step was to find me the firm that I would represent in England. It was not long before Peters informed me that he had the perfect "cover" for me. One day, he brought me together at lunch with a short, tweedy, mustached man whom I had noticed lugging his briefcase into John Reed Club meetings during my last months in the open Communist Party. We had met at that time. The man was Maxim Lieber, who managed a small literary agency on Fifth Avenue. Peters formally separated Comrade Lieber from the American Communist Party and relinquished him to work exclusively with the Soviet apparatus. I gave Lieber the underground pseudonym of "Paul."

I no longer remember whether Peters or I first explained his role in the English apparatus to Paul, and he now declines to remember anything (before the Grand Jury he pled self-incrimination). But I remember that he was very much pleased with the prospect. He had long wanted to open a London office, but could not afford to. Now he was able happily to combine business and party duty. The Soviet apparatus would pay all expenses of the venture and my salary, which would be given to Paul in New York for regular transmission to me in London. Thus, Paul would get an office and an office manager at no cost to himself. From my Communist writing and editing, Lieber had confidence in my editorial judgment, a confidence that was strengthened as we quickly became friends. Lieber's apartment on West 47th Street became my unofficial headquarters in New York—soon a necessity, for I was about to move my family to Baltimore.

The establishment of a courier system proved the most difficult part of the problem. Peters was unable to help. The party had no reliable contacts at that time on boats plying between New York and British ports—at least none that it could dispense with. The problem was solved unexpectedly in other ways.

A friend introduced me to a young man who was then a college student in New York. Let me call him Joe. Joe was planning to spend his summer vacation working as a seaman in order to organize Communist cells among his fellow crew members. He promptly agreed to get a job on a boat going to England so that he could act as an underground courier. The arrangement was all the better since it kept J. Peters from knowing more about the organization of the English apparatus; he already knew too much.

Procuring fraudulent birth certificates was no problem at all for Peters. It was at this time that he told me with some complacency how he had systematized that work, which is one of the most important of underground activities. Peters' system was ghoulishly simple. The head of the underground section of the American Communist Party had organized two teams of researchers. They were Communists. In the Genealogical Division of the New York Public Library, both teams were engaged in studying vital statistics. One team studied the dates of the birth of infants. The other team concentrated on infants' deaths. The results were compared, and when it was discovered that a baby had died shortly after birth, the name of the dead child and its parents was listed. In the name of the dead child, Peters' underground apparatus would then write to the Board of Health (enclosing the regular fee) and request a photostat of a birth certificate. The address would be one of the secret letter "drops" that Peters maintained around New York City, and no doubt elsewhere. As a matter of routine, the Board of Health would promptly issue a birth certificate, perfectly in order except that the person it certified had been dead for three or four decades. Using this fraudulent birth certificate, a Communist could then apply for an American passport, which, also as a matter of routine, was promptly issued, for there was almost no way to detect the fraud unless someone with knowledge of it revealed it.

These birth certificates were one of Peters' sources of underground revenue. He sold them in bulk to the Soviet apparatuses. Hede Massing has described (in *This Deception*) how she obtained such papers from him. Peters himself told me that he was trafficking in birth certificates, naturalization papers and other identifying documents with a Soviet agent whom he presently introduced to me as "Richard." Richard was the Robinson-Rubens of the celebrated international mystery, and the Rubens of Alger Hiss's handwritten memo to which I have referred earlier.

For my use in the English operation, Peters procured a birth certificate for one David Breen whose birth coincided roughly with mine. It was not until the second Hiss trial that I learned that David Breen was not the name of a dead child, but that of a living man from whom permission to use his birth certificate had been bought in another of Peters' operations. The birth certificate and the passport I procured on it, I turned over to the F.B.I. before the first Hiss trial.

For my wife, Peters procured still another birth certificate, which was never used. But a certificate for my daughter was also necessary. It was a much more difficult problem to solve, since it must also be in the name of Breen. Peters had a little arrangement for just such contingencies. In the city hall at Atlantic City, he had a contact. For a fee, the amount of which I have forgotten, that useful man agreed to enter the name of Ursula Breen (my daughter) in the official register of births, and to issue a birth certificate in that name. One day Peters proudly handed me the birth certificate, now also in the custody of the F.B.I.

I have reported these details together for the sake of order. Actually, they required many months to complete and were presently interrupted and complicated by Bill's instructions to assist in organizing a much more difficult and hazardous project—a Soviet underground apparatus in Japan.

VIII

While the preparations for the English apparatus were being made, I was in and out of Washington. Bill never at any time showed much interest in my connections there. There the initiative came from J. Peters. But Bill was willing to have me pull together the rudiments of an apparatus, which, he said, I could later turn over to somebody else, or which might prove of use in the English venture. Above all, he wanted to get me out of New York City, while we were waiting for the English project to take shape. No doubt, he felt that too many people there knew me. With that in mind, too, he permitted me, in the summer of 1934, to move my family to Baltimore.

At first, I had thought of moving them to Washington. But that city was crowded (the New Deal was in full swing) and rents were high. Moreover, it was better organization to have my family in a city where I was not active as a Communist. I had noticed an apartment-to-rent sign in a window at 903 St. Paul Street—an old brick building with Baltimore's traditional white stone steps. It was the headquarters of the Women's Christian Temperance Union. That seemed to me a properly sober address for an underground worker. Under the name "Lloyd Cantwell" I rented the apartment. I bought just enough second-hand furniture to furnish it scantily. If the good woman who superintended the house for the W.C.T.U. looked somewhat askance, she said nothing.

The house superintendent urged my wife to hire a colored girl to help her with our child. Almost everybody in Baltimore had colored help. We had never faced such a problem before. For me, as a Communist, it raised several questions. The first question was whether or not it was right for anybody to employ servants at all. The answer was, of course, that a servant is a worker like any other, and workers live by working. Much more serious was another question: how could we in conscience pay the shockingly low wages paid in those days to such help as we had in mind? To pay more might cause comment and even trouble. I decided that we would pay a little more. Then, what should our conduct be toward Negroes whom I, as a Communist, insisted on treating in every way as equals? That was a point on which I could give no ground. Even at the risk of widespread gossip (for a tremendous grapevine exists among Negroes), I insisted that I must act as a Communist and that we would take our meals at the same table with the maid, and in all other ways treat her as someone who worked with us, rather than for us. I maintained that, while news of our peculiar conduct might spread quickly among Negroes, they would cover up for us, both for their own protection and for ours, and that no hint of what we were doing would be whispered outside colored circles.

To those who wonder what the appeal of Communism is, this episode may be worth pondering upon. At least, it is thought-provoking to note the impact of Communism wherever it coincides with humanity and compassion, especially when the outside world denies them. Note, too, the long-range effect of the refusal of a Communist (myself, in this case) to compromise a basic issue.

When Edith Murray first sat down to table with us—and we were the first white people who had ever asked her to sit at the same table with them—she showed fear, then embarrassment. I will not presume to say what her final feeling was. In any case, what we had to give her was not a place at our table. What we had to give her was something that belonged to her by right, but which had been taken from her, and which we were merely giving back. It was her human dignity. Thus, by insisting on acting as Communists must, we found ourselves unwittingly acting as Christians should. I submit that that cuts to the heart of one aspect of the Communist appeal.

And, to me, it bears on a meaning of Edith Murray's testimony in the second Hiss trial, which was lost on the world (the world saw only the legal meaning), but was not lost on me. Throughout those two long trials until then, few voices, except my wife's, had been raised publicly to say even once that Whittaker Chambers was not an inveterately evil man. Then, at the very end of the second Hiss trial, there was put on the stand that slight, simple and plain-spoken colored woman, who had sometimes sat at table with my wife and me. For the first time, she did what the whole world would not do—she gave me back my human dignity. "Oh, *no*," she said in answer to some derisive question by Hiss's lawyer, "Mr. Cantwell (myself) was a *good* man." It moved me deeply, few things in the Hiss Case moved me more, for Edith Murray is a good woman.

IX

With the arrival of my family in Baltimore, there began a development of a kind that is not favored in underground work. Alger Hiss became our personal friend in a way that made my relationship with him unlike my relationship with any others in the underground. Organizationally, this was made possible by the fact that I was expecting to go abroad at any moment. Therefore, I relaxed the underground procedures by bringing Hiss and his wife to visit us in Baltimore one night. Another factor entered in, too. His personal connection with us rescued Hiss from his underground isolation. There was a stimulation in driving to Baltimore to visit a hidden family whose address only he knew, in parking his old Ford roadster in the shadows of a side street and walking slowly (to make sure there were no observers) to the house behind whose completely ordinary front was an outpost of the international underground. No one was more amused than Alger by the thought of the W.C.T.U. as an underground "cover."

The Hisses took an instant liking to my wife. She was transparently sincere, forthright, gentle, warm. They knew that she was an American, but with her dark complexion and bobbed black hair, she looked enough like a Russian to carry out the illusion of Carl's foreignness and to give point to the name Lise (pronounced Leeza) which they always called her. Where Priscilla Hiss was brittle and tense, Lise was mature and calm. She knew the revolutionary answers, but she was more given to talking about the care of her child, so that Priscilla Hiss found in my wife someone to whom she could talk without self-consciousness about her own young son, to whom she was devoted, but who, as the child of her first marriage, was a little out of place in her second marriage. In that strange friendship, the fact that both couples were firmly and happily married drew us together. And our family life obviously centered about our child. The Hisses at that time had no child of their own, though they deeply desired one.

Up until the very end, it was a friendship that existed on two incongruous levels. One was the level of conspiracy, which made my friendship with Hiss possible in the first place by throwing us together and holding us together for more than four years in the tight, exclusive secrecy of the underground. The second level seemed to have nothing to do with the first. It was the easy, gay, carefree association of two literate, very happy, fun-loving middle-class families.

For it was much more a friendship of families than of individuals, and on the Hiss side entirely so. Alger and Priscilla Hiss could scarcely be thought of separately. In all the time that I knew them, I almost never met them except together. Alger and Pross was one name, and so was Hilly and Pross (as they called one another). On the level of conspiracy, Alger dealt exclusively with Carl. But on the human level, Carl and Lise were as much a bracket as Alger and Pross.

People have sometimes asked me: What did you talk about when you were together? I have to stop and think. What *did* we talk about? We talked about everything. We were never together without talking. But, except for our talk about underground activity, what we said was completely without forethought, particular meaning or importance—the spontaneous surface talk of people among whom there exist, not only fierce convictions taken for granted, but intangible compatibilities of temperament, an instinctive feeling as to what is serious and what is absurd about people, things and life. People are truly friends when they love even one another's foibles as a necessary part of the pattern of character. We knew one another's weaknesses and could laugh freely at them as something amusing because endearing.

For our friendship was almost entirely one of character and not of the mind. Despite his acknowledged ability in the legal field, which I was not competent to explore with him, Alger Hiss is not a highly mental man. Compared to the minds I had grown up with at Columbia, free-ranging, witty and deeply informed (one has only to think of Clifton Fadiman or Meyer Schapiro), Alger was a little on the stuffy side. Ideas for their own sake did not interest him at all. His mind had come to rest in the doctrines of Marx and Lenin, and even then applied itself wholly to current politics and seldom, that I can remember, to history or to theory.

I cannot remember Alger Hiss ever drawing my attention to a book except certain books about birds. At the time it appeared, I gave the Hisses a copy of Franz Werfel's *Forty Days of Musa Dagh.* They read it dutifully as a study in the conflict of an oppressed minority (the Armenians) with the Turks, which echoed the Nazi-

Jewish situation in Germany. *Man's Fate,* Malraux' novel about the Chinese revolution, excited me tremendously. The Hisses bore my enthusiasm with good-natured patience. But Alger showed interest chiefly in Malraux' treatment of the psychology of the terrorist. The only book I can ever recall their praising was, rather curiously, Helen Waddell's account of the Goliards, of which Priscilla gave me her copy. They liked it, I think, because the wandering scholars were a note of dissent in the conformity of the Middle Ages.

I particularly remember Alger's opinion of Shakespeare. In 1936 or 1937, Maurice Evans played *Richard II* in Baltimore. It was the first time that my wife or I had ever seen Shakespeare acted. We were deeply impressed, not only by the new life the play took on for us on the stage, and the new texture given the verse by Evans' elocutionary style, but by the aliveness of the politics of the play. During the opening scenes, my wife whispered to me with awe: "It's just like the Comintern!"

A day or so later, I was trying to convey some of that to Alger. "I'm sorry," he said at last, somewhat less graciously than usual, "I just don't like Shakespeare—platitudes in blank verse." He quoted some Polonius, and I realized, for the first time and with great interest, that he disliked Shakespeare because the platitudes were all that impinged on his mind.

So great a gap in the temper of minds might have been expected to set us apart. On the contrary. To me such blind spots as Alger's were another amusing foible, and, in any case, I do not particularly care to be surrounded by literary friends. The bond that cemented his friendship and mine went much deeper than any similarities or dissimilarities of mind. It was a profound, tacit esteem of character, increasing as our Communist activity tested us in common. It is only necessary to recall how, in the days when faith divided us, each of us, in his different way, bore himself in the ordeal of the Hiss Case, to understand why we should have been friends in the days when faith knit us. Each of us sensed in the other an unyielding purpose about those things which we held to be decisive, and a resourcefulness and play of imagination in action, which, among the Communists we knew, I sensed to the same degree only in Harold Ware. No other Communist but Alger Hiss understood so quietly, or accepted with so little fuss or question the fact that the revolutionist cannot change the course of history without taking upon himself the crimes of history. That is why I said of him in a broadcast, shortly after the second Hiss trial, "I cannot hate even an enemy who shares with me the conviction that that life is not worth living for which a man is not prepared to dare all and die at any moment." The recognition that, as Communists, we shared that same force of purpose was the deepest bond between us. On Hiss's part, that bond snapped the moment that I broke with the Communist Party and my political purpose changed. On my part, it persisted, despite that change, because I cannot feel solely in political terms. I feel also in human terms.

All of us shared another more elusive, but very real bond. That was the mutual simplicity of our tastes, which reflected not merely a point of view, like our political opinions, but was an almost organic reaction to the life around us. It was expressed in a profound sense that labor in itself is one of the highest goods, in a profound suspicion of the pursuit of pleasure as an end in life, amounting to an antipathy and merging with a deep distaste, and distrust of materialism in its commonest forms of success and comfort. It is not at all chance that both the Chamberses and the Hisses, arriving over very different routes, should at last have found their way into the community of Quakers. For the simplicity inherent in the Quaker way of life must make an authentic appeal to the Hisses.

That simplicity is inseparable from a gentleness of character, though life and history may wrench and pervert it almost past recognition. In the Hisses, it found one expression in an absorption in nature, especially in the life of birds. When I first knew them, the Hisses used to rise at dawn on Sunday and take long rambles out along the Potomac River, around Glen Echo and Great Falls. I remember vividly how Alger came in one morning and announced with an excitement that he almost never showed that for the first time he had seen a prothonotary warbler.

They gave up bird walking in 1934. But even in the days of his greatest underground activity, Alger Hiss talked constantly about birds with an enthusiasm that he showed for little else. It was an enthusiasm that I shared with the Hisses, though I had passed the point where identifying birds interested me very much.

No account of our friendship would be complete without mention of the continual kindnesses of the Hisses to us, their untiring solicitude for my wife and child, the inconvenience that they voluntarily put themselves to to help us. In late years, I have sometimes wondered how much of Hiss's solicitude was for ourselves (as we then supposed) and how much was for Carl as the representative of the Communist Party. No doubt, he would prefer to believe that it was the latter. But I remember the simple pleasure that all of us took simply in being together, and I prefer to believe still that it was the former.

The outstanding fact about Alger Hiss was an unvarying mildness, a deep considerateness and gracious patience that seemed proof against any of the ordinary exasperations of work and fatigue or the annoyances of family or personal relations. Only very rarely did a streak of wholly incongruous cruelty crop out. From the first, my wife and I had been charmed by Baltimore and sometimes said so. "Baltimore," Alger once answered, "is the only city in the country so backward that it still lights its streets by gas. It's a city of dying old men and women." He was so unnecessarily savage that, by way of easing matters, I said: "They seem to be pleasant and harmless old people." "Yes," he said, "the horrible old women of Baltimore!" It was the tone with which the words were uttered and the dry laugh that followed them that made me feel that I had touched depths which I had not suspected. The same strange savagery cropped out in a conversation about Franklin Roosevelt. Hiss's contempt for Franklin Roosevelt as a dabbler in revolution who understood neither revolution nor history was profound. It was the common view of Roosevelt among Communists, which I shared with the rest. But Alger expressed it not only in political terms. He startled me, and deeply shocked my wife, by the obvious pleasure he took in the most simple and brutal references to the President's physical condition as a symbol of the middle-class breakdown.

Only once, did that deeply hidden streak ever touch me. It came out in connection with the poor condition of my teeth. Several times Alger had urged me tactfully to visit a dentist. Then one night, during the last year that I knew him, he evidently decided to be firm with me. He gave me a little lecture, the burden of which was that my teeth were not a personal matter, but, as identifying marks, concerned everybody's safety. My missing incisor must be replaced. He was oddly waspish, mincing no words. It was completely unlike him. I saw that I had touched something very important—his fastidiousness. The tone surprised, but the action did not offend me. For, toward the Hisses, we felt a tenderness, spontaneous and unquestioning, that is felt for one another by members of an unusually happy family. Nothing in their manner led us to suppose that they did not share the same feeling about us.

X

The English project slowly lost its urgency. Such ups and downs are a regular part of underground projects. In time, most people learn to accept the pattern without seeking to know the cause. When I grasped the meaning of Bill's tapering interest in the English apparatus, conveyed in the grimaces and eloquent little noises that made up half his speech, I said, "So the English business is dead." Bill insisted that the English apparatus was not dead but hinted that there were factors that I did not understand. Meanwhile, the Washington operation drifted. I was then too inexperienced to know that Moscow wanted the Washington group to drift.

One day, Bill met me, bringing with him an old acquaintance—Don—John Sherman. Sherman had been on the West Coast, he presently told me, setting up a Soviet apparatus in Los Angeles. He had driven east with his wife and child and his assistant in the California apparatus, a young Communist to whom he had given the pseudonym of "Pete." The West Coast apparatus, for reasons that belonged to the order of things that I did not understand, and do not now understand, had been partially disbanded.

Don was being sent to head another apparatus, elsewhere. In that connection he had a problem for me to solve. Bill's orders to me were to do everything possible to help Don. For some time, that was my chief concern and I was still working on the debris of Don's problem, washed in by the underground tides, after Bill had gone out of my life and John Sherman had broken with the Soviet apparatus.

Don's problem was simple and formidable. His instructions from Moscow were to organize a Soviet espionage apparatus in Japan. He was to travel there as the representative of an American business firm. He needed the usual legitimizing luggage: papers for a fraudulent passport, a business "cover." Don did not ask me to set up a courier system on the Nippon Yusen Kaisha, though I know that he was considering that problem. But he asked me for something just as difficult. He asked me to secure for him an assistant to work with him in Japan.

The specifications were somewhat staggering. The assistant must be a Japanese who was an American citizen. He must be a Communist Party member. He must have connections in the top governing circles in Japan. Don also had two other chores for me. He wanted legitimate credentials that would enable him to travel without arousing suspicion in Manchukuo. He wanted a direct contact with the Chinese Communist forces, which were still restricted to the Soviet area of Kiangsi province, although about the very time that Don and I were discussing that point, Mao Tse-tung was in Moscow where he had been called so that Stalin in person could give the great "agrarian liberal" the order to move the entire Communist population of Kiangsi several thousand miles to Yenan.

As usual, the birth certificate was the simplest part of the problem. J. Peters quickly provided one in the name of Charles F. Chase. On this paper Don procured a passport.

Business "cover" for an American going to Japan was more difficult to provide, and had to be even more flawless than a "cover" for an American going to England. For a time we got nowhere. Then Bill suggested that, since the English project was merely rocking along at the moment, and in any case my problem in England was much easier to solve than Don's in Japan, perhaps I should relinquish Lieber to Don as a "cover."

For that purpose, I introduced Don and Paul. Lieber pointed out the obvious fact that his literary relations with Japan were practically non-existent and that for him to open an office in Tokyo would be, to say the least of it, odd. Lieber was much upset at the idea of losing his London office. Don was able to solve his problem and satisfy Lieber at one stroke. He proposed that we organize a news syndicate under Lieber's auspices. It would be financed by the underground. The correspondents would be Soviet agents, though for purposes of verisimilitude and confusion there should be some who were not Communists and did not, in fact, know what it was all about. The correspondents, instead of concentrating on spot news, would file feature stories from various of the world's trouble centers, reporting the background of the news. Lieber would be the head of the syndicate and handle the New York marketing and other business. His office would be the New York headquarters. Once the syndicate was a going concern there was no reason why I should not represent Lieber in London. Paul was assuaged.

In New York City, Lieber, Sherman (under the name of Charles F. Chase) and I (under the name of Lloyd Cantwell) formally filed papers establishing the American Feature Writers Syndicate. These papers are a matter of record. After I had testified to this and related matters before the Grand Jury, the record was checked and my testimony confirmed.

Lieber then hurried over to the New York *Evening Post* and sold its publisher, David Stern, the idea of part-financing a series of articles on Japan by the Syndicate's Tokyo correspondent, Charles F. Chase. One or two of these articles subsequently appeared in the *Post*. Meanwhile, the name of the Syndicate had been neatly lettered on Lieber's door and its stationery filled his desk. Several thousand dollars of apparatus money filled his safety-deposit box, to be fed piecemeal into the Syndicate's account, or for emergency expenses. The American Feature Writers Syndicate, one of the Tokyo branches of the Soviet Military Intelligence, was ready to operate.

Credentials for Manchukuo proved a simple matter. Among Lieber's friends was an editor of the *American Mercury* (not Eugene Lyons, who was still a U.P. correspondent in Moscow). He gladly furnished a letter telling all whom it might concern that Charles F. Chase was a news gatherer for the *Mercury*.

The contact with the Chinese Communists seemed on the point of splendid success. Just as we were seeking it, Agnes Smedley happened into New York on her way to Russia from the Kiangsi Communist area, Shanghai and other Chinese centers where she had been active as a member of the first Soviet espionage apparatus organized in the East by Richard Sorge. Sorge, a great friend, among others, of Hede Massing, was the Communist who used his post as press attaché of the German embassy in Tokyo to organize a remarkable Soviet espionage apparatus in Japan. He was arrested in Tokyo, confessed and was executed during World War II.

I knew of Miss Smedley as the author of *Daughter of Earth*, a novel about her western girlhood, and as a persistent spokesman for the Chinese Communists. I asked Peters to arrange a meeting for me with her so that I could introduce a friend (Don) to her. I said that it would be unnecessary for Peters to go along (I did not want him to see Don) since I would easily recognize Miss Smedley from her pictures. I met her in an Automat on 72nd Street in New York. Peters had not told her whom she was going to meet and she was extremely surprised and distrustful at meeting a stranger. She was equally distrustful of Don. We separated without agreeing to anything, and Don never got his contact with the Chinese Communists.

But I was able to solve what seemed the most insuperable problem—the Japanese-American Communist who was connected in the highest circles in Japan. Through a non-Communist friend, I met a young Japanese who had been born in the United States. He was a member of the American Communist Party. He was also a cousin or nephew of one of the Japanese premiers—Prince Konoye, if I remember rightly. He was a young painter of exceptional promise, and one of the favorite pupils of Diego Rivera, the celebrated mural painter, formerly secretary of the Mexican Communist Party. The young man's name was Hideo Noda. He was extremely intelligent, alert, personable and likable. I introduced him to Don, and, at a conversation in my presence, Noda readily agreed to go to Japan to work as a Soviet underground agent. Don gave Noda the underground name, "Ned." By the end of 1934, many of the pieces in the Japanese puzzle had been moved into place. Their assembling was a much more sporadic process and took a much longer time than I have indicated here.

Before Don left for Japan (from San Francisco), he spent a night with me at my apartment in Baltimore. I had told him about the underground apparatus in Washington, with which I was in contact all the while that the Japanese underground was being organized, and especially about Alger Hiss. Don was eager to meet him. It was not strictly according to underground rules. But since Don was leaving for the Far East, there seemed no real reason against it. Besides, I thought that it would do Alger Hiss good to meet someone other than me connected with the international apparatus.

Alger was eager, too. He spent an evening with Don and me at St. Paul Street. The meeting was not a success. Don is at his worst with strangers, with whom he almost invariably becomes wary, mysterious and arch. The evening was almost as bad as my first evening with Hiss.

It was to have a curious echo years later. I had introduced Don to Alger Hiss as "Adam" (the first man in my underground experience). Don has steadfastly refused to discuss his part in these affairs. To the F.B.I. he has refused to answer questions. To the House Committee on Un-American Activities, he pled self-incrimination. But he did venture to answer one question. Asked if he had ever known Alger Hiss, he said: No, and added: "I do not believe that Alger Hiss would know me from Adam."

XI

Before he left for Japan, Don also introduced me to someone—his West Coast assistant, Pete. Later on, Pete was for a short time my assistant in Washington, where I renamed him "Keith." To simplify matters, I shall call him Keith henceforth. Fourteen years later, Keith's corroboration of those parts of my experience about which he had direct personal knowledge were to be important during the Hiss Case.

Keith was a tall, young, native American of good family, rather inexperienced, but a devoted Communist. I saw no reason to meet him in the first place, and less reason after I had met him. But Don had his own cryptic reasons, connected no doubt with his Japanese plans. For though I knew a good deal about the Japanese apparatus, there was also a good deal that I did not know, and did not want to know. One thing I never knew about was Don's courier system with the United States—he must at least have attempted to organize one. Nor did I know how Don received in Tokyo the large sums of money necessary to finance such an apparatus as his.

But about that I was presently to draw some conclusions that are not necessarily correct, but are probably not far from the facts. For later in 1934 or early in 1935, Bill instructed me to get myself a money belt. I bought one at R. H. Macy and Company in New York—a rayon belt with many little snap pockets rubber-lined against sweat. I gave it to Bill who returned it to me neatly packaged. By then it contained money, probably about ten thousand dollars in American currency, though I have no recollection of counting the money. Bill's instructions were to put on the money belt and not to take it off until I had delivered it to Keith in San Francisco. Separately, Bill gave me money for first-class fare to and from San Francisco and New York, and for other expenses. I took the Twentieth Century from New York.

The rubber lining of the money belt acted as insulation. It was hot and stiff with the bills packed in its pockets, and, of course, I slept with it on. But the trip proved otherwise pleasant. For outside Chicago, I became aware that there was someone I knew on the train. In the club car with me was Comrade Charles Kramer of the Ware Group who was traveling (to Omaha, I believe) on Government business. As the snow-covered prairie drifted past, we discussed the Russian Revolution, Communism and related matters. He was much excited at the mysterious circumstances of our meeting. He was prepared to believe that the world revolution was at hand when we crossed the frozen Platte River, and I pointed out to him, carved in four-foot letters on the icy surface, a rousing slogan: "Long Live Socialism!" I think that for a moment he believed that I had arranged it on purpose, for part of a growing illusion among the Washington Communists was that Carl could arrange almost anything.

In San Francisco, I stopped at the Golden Gate Y.M.C.A. and waited in my room for Keith to contact me. He reached me about noon the next day. How he knew where to find me, I have forgotten. It is his recollection that he was informed through a cover address in San Francisco.

All afternoon, Keith drove me in his car around San Francisco. In the evening, he took me to the house of the "Old Man." The "Old Man" is a California businessman and lifelong Communist of Russian birth, very active in party affairs on the West Coast. At the time I met him, he was also connected with my old comrade from the *Daily Worker*, Harrison George, who was then heading the West Coast office of the Pan-Pacific Trade Union Secretariat, an international Communist organization, which among other activities, was running couriers on the ships to Australia, Japan and Asiatic mainland ports. The "Old Man" was almost certainly involved in Don's Japanese operation.

To him or Keith, I turned over the money belt. I have always assumed that the greater part of the money went by some secret route to Don in Japan, though I have no proof of this. Some of it, however, remained in Keith's hands, for he later brought me back the money belt with about two thousand dollars in it, which he returned to me in New York.

A few days after delivering the money belt in San Francisco, I was able to report to Bill that I had completed my assignment.

XII

J. Peters, whom I was seeing regularly, gave the Washington activity a sudden new turn. I have already mentioned his plans for financing the American Communist underground with the help of the Russians. One day, by way of broaching this idea, he observed that, until the first Five-Year Plan began in the Soviet Union (*circa* 1929), the Communist International had subsidized the American Communist Party. During the rigors of the Five-Year Plan, that subsidy had been stopped, and the American Communist Party had been ordered to support itself. "The beggars of the *Machavaya*," as Comrade Stalin sometimes graciously called the representatives of the foreign Communist parties (after the Moscow address of the

Communist International), would now have to beg elsewhere. This, said Peters, had worked great hardships. Therefore, he had contrived a plan whereby the Russian Communists might continue to finance the American Communist Party—for services rendered. Through the Ware Group and others, Peters had access to Government documents. He proposed to connect me with the right people who would turn such documents over to me. Peters would provide me with a Leica camera. I would copy the documents, return them to whomever gave them to me and turn the copies over to Bill. If he were interested, Bill would pay for them. Peters appealed to me, as an American Communist, to co-operate.

The immediate transaction he had in mind involved Harry Dexter White, the monetary expert of the Treasury Department. White, a fellow traveler, was a great friend of one of Harold Ware's contacts, whom I shall call Wilton Rugg. Rugg had assured Ware that White was willing to turn over to him certain official Treasury documents which could then be photographed. Ware introduced me to Rugg. Rugg made his arrangements with White, who gave him documents. Rugg gave them to me in Washington. I photographed them.

I am no longer sure whether I photographed them at Alger Hiss's house on P Street or at the Washington apartment of a Communist writer and member of the John Reed Club in New York, whom Harold Ware had brought to Washington to assist him when I was claimed by Bill. I am more and more inclined to believe that the White photography was done at the writer's apartment and that certain later photographic work was done at Hiss's P Street house.

I was supposed to return White's documents to Rugg the next day. The appointment was on a street corner. I waited for an hour before Rugg appeared. Thereafter, I refused to have any further connection with Rugg, since I held that any Communist who would endanger a man like Harry White by coming an hour late to an appointment was unfit for underground work.

From Peters' viewpoint, the transaction was not a success. Bill took the films to examine them at his leisure and presently announced that he was not interested in them, and did not wish me to continue with such work.

XIII

I live in Westminster, Md., today because of an incident which at that time seemed of no importance. In conversation with the Hisses, my wife or I had said something about the effect of the Baltimore heat on my daughter, and had spoken of renting a small place outside the city. One Sunday Alger appeared with a newspaper advertisement of two small properties at Westminster. On one there was a small house. They were unusually cheap—$500 for the house and fifteen acres of land.

Alger proposed that he and I drive to Westminster, of which at that time I had never heard, look at the little house, and, if it were at all livable, buy it. Then my family could spend the summer there, the Hisses could visit us, and both families could be together without the precautions that hampered us in Baltimore or Washington. There was never any question of underground work at Westminster. The place was simply to be an inexpensive summer residence.

Alger and I went to look at the house. It was one of those little country-built houses common in Maryland, constructed against the slope of a hill so that one side is three floors high, with the basement counting as a room. The house was neither beautiful nor ugly. It had never been painted, but it was weathered a rich gray. A great wistaria of the sweet native Maryland variety grew rankly over the front porch and coiled through the rotted shingles of the roof. Two tall cedars stood, sentinel-like, beside the small weathered barn which was in front of the house on the road. On one side of the house, was a small, uncared-for orchard of apples and sour cherries. Under one window grew a big apricot. At the back of the land was a grove of persimmons. The land looked out across a shallow valley. A wind blew continuously through the rank grass that had not been cut for years.

Alger left a small deposit on the property in his name. Later, he decided against buying the place. Priscilla had been to see it, and, used to the beautiful open valleys of Pennsylvania, she asked me: "Do you really like that nasty, narrow valley?"

I really did. "What a dump!" I once overheard someone say about that little house. The dump charmed me. In the way of shelter and seclusion, it was about all that I asked of life. It was neglected, but it was tight. The little rooms were cozy. On three sides, the land was surrounded by woods from which, on the day when I was first there, tanagers were calling—birds that carol like robins, but more ringingly. I stood beside the cedars and, for the first time since my boyhood, I listened consciously to the wind drift through their branches. For two years, I could not get out of my mind the memory of the land, the wind and the cedar trees.

Then, in the spring of 1936 or 1937, when the thawing roads were still all but impassable, without saying anything to anyone, not even to my wife, I drove one day to Westminster. That most beautiful countryside had drawn me back. I did not want the real-estate agent to suppose that I knew anything about the old house, so I asked him to show me his list. He took a route through the rutted back roads that brought us at last to the house that Alger and I had looked at. Even in the bare spring, always the test in the country, the old ruin had much charm for me. I had scarcely any good reason or right to buy it. I did not know how I was going to pay for it. But it was one of those occasions when a man feels: this I am meant to do. I left a deposit. No doubt, I could have borrowed enough to meet further payments, but by a curious turn of circumstance, I did not have to. Before I returned to Westminster, the owner and her next of kin died in quick succession. It became impossible to clear the title. I had been at *Time* magazine two years, and we had been living in the little house some time, before it became necessary for me to pay the purchase price.

I have another memory, too, connected with the old property. The day that Alger and I inspected it, we also looked at the other piece that had been advertised with it. It was a much bigger, adjoining tract. It had once been a farmstead, but the house had burned and the old barn was collapsing. Past the fallen timbers of the barn, a tiny stream ran the length of the land. The place had been abandoned so long that the wild life had taken over and seemed completely undisturbed as we clambered through the bushes and the bracken.

There were birds of all kinds, and Alger stood by the brook in front of the barn, identifying them. In a burst of gleaming black, white and chestnut, a ground robin flashed out of a shrub, and, standing on a fence post directly in front of us, sang. "Do you know what he says?" Alger asked me. I had not heard the old country translation of his song. The bird sang again. "Listen," Alger said, "he says: 'Sweet bird, sing!' " It did not seem silly to him, for he was completely caught up in the bird's song. I have no more vivid recollection of Alger Hiss.

And that is why, twelve years later, in a room in the Federal Building in New York, with a dozen intent men watching every expression of my face to see if I was lying, and three congressmen shooting questions at me, I could testify: "Alger Hiss is a man of great simplicity, and great gentleness and sweetness of character."

XIV

By April, 1935, I began to think we had been at St. Paul Street long enough; it was time to move. I toyed with the idea of taking my family to Washington. Alger Hiss was also on the move. He had rented a furnished house on P Street in Georgetown. He planned to move there at once. His lease on the 28th Street apartment still had two months to run. He proposed that, since he could leave most of his furniture in the apartment, we should go there to live until the lease expired. It was a voluntary, generous gesture, of a kind not unusual among Communists. There was no question of my renting or leasing the apartment, and, if I offered to pay rent for it, as I must certainly have done, Alger refused it.

My wife and I gave what furniture we had to the woman who ran the St. Paul Street house for the W.C.T.U. We took no furniture to Washington. Then Alger and I packed a few personal belongings, chiefly the baby's collapsible tub and dismantled crib, into the trunk and back of Alger's Ford. He and I then drove them to Washington. My wife had already left with the baby by train. We probably spent the night at the P Street house. Then we moved into the 28th Street apartment.

We lived there about two months. During that time I was often at the P Street house. I am not sure that Alger was ever at the 28th Street apartment, though Priscilla Hiss visited my wife there at least once and had lunch. I was not at home and I have no independent recollection of the visit. During the day, my wife and I sometimes took our daughter to the Washington zoo, which was a few blocks away. We always sat in front of the eagles' cage so that Priscilla could find us, for she sometimes joined us there.

Alger Hiss has testified that I lived at 28th Street under the name of George Crosley. It is possible, though I have no recollection of it, and I believe that I have recalled all the other names I used in the underground without effort.

At the P Street house I first met Timothy Hobson, Priscilla Hiss's son by a former marriage. Timmie was then about eight or nine years old, a high-strung, rather pathetic little boy, who was strikingly like his mother in features and nervous temperament. Alger was extremely kind and considerate in his treatment of Timmie. No one could have been more so. But my wife and I sometimes commented on the lack of warmth in their relationship.

Timmie knew me only as Carl. The fact that his eyes were always observing us together, and he was a quiet, watchful little boy, disturbed me. I was afraid that, if there should ever be any threat to the apparatus, Timmie would be a dangerous witness. I discussed it with Alger. He felt that Timmie was too young to constitute any danger. There was really nothing I could do about it, but Timmie always made me uneasy.

Sooner or later in this book, I must unavoidably take note of the slanders which at one time or another, as best suited their purposes, the Hiss forces have spread about my relations with every member of the Hiss household. Perhaps this is as good a point as any, when I was becoming what I was to continue to be until I broke with the Communist Party, a constant visitor at the Hiss homes.

Those slanders were part of an international whispering campaign, probably originated and spread by the Communist Party and made deafening by certain commentators and public figures. Its purpose was to confuse the public mind about the case by making Alger Hiss appear a martyr who would suffer any unjust punishment in silence rather than clear himself of my charges by revealing painful facts about members of his family. Alger Hiss is no martyr. So far as concerns me, there are no painful facts. No act or thought of mine toward Hiss or any member of his family or household was ever blemished by evil or even unkindness. Unqualifiedly, the slanders are lies.

Let me add only this, without any pride at all. So long as it was humanly possible, I shielded Alger Hiss and the others—for motives which I hope presently to make clear—from the consequences of their past acts. In his failure publicly to deny those lies, Alger Hiss is shielding no one but himself. In lending them the force of his silence, he is adding to his offenses, an offense against the human spirit.

XV

In October, 1948, during my pre-trial examination by Alger Hiss's lawyers, in the libel suit which he had filed against me in Baltimore, there was one significant moment. It was only a moment, but it should have warned some of Hiss's counsel that there were certain areas of his conduct better left unexplored. All day, William L. Marbury, Hiss's attorney, had been baiting me by snide innuendo and sneering skepticism. From the beginning, I took it quietly as something to be borne. So far I had not uttered a word about the espionage facts concerning Alger Hiss. But at last the knowledge that I sat there, covering up for him, while his lawyer viciously assailed me, became too much for me. There was one question too many as to how I could dare to suggest that Alger Hiss had ever been a Communist. Anger made me unable to answer. I paused—a long pause that does not show, of course, in the transcript.

Instead of responding, I asked (quoting from memory): "Did your client never tell you that while he was with the munitions investigating committee, he was able to secure documents from the State Department?" Mr. Marbury graciously replied that he was asking the questions and I was answering them. By then, I had got hold of myself again, and the dangerous subject was dropped.

I had reference to an episode that occurred while Alger was living at P Street. His position with the munitions investigation had become so strong that he himself proposed to me that he could use the authority of the Senate Committee to secure confidential documents from the State Department, which I could then photograph and turn over to the Communist Party.

I discussed the problem with Peters. He was again excited by the possibility of selling material to Bill. I told Alger to go ahead. In the name of the Senate munitions investigating committee, he requested certain documents from the State Department. The State Department was reluctant, but in view of the popular excitement about the Committee's investigation, no doubt thought it advisable to release a few documents. These Alger brought home. I photographed them in his P Street house.

But, Alger told me, the State Department had become anxious. Officially or unofficially there was a ban against further releases of confidential documents.

Peters fared poorly. Bill showed a complete lack of interest in the documents.

XVI

By the time that Alger Hiss's lease on the 28th Street apartment was up, I had decided to move my family back to New York. Probably the question of the English apparatus had become urgent again. My old college friend, Meyer Schapiro, now a professor of Fine Arts at Columbia University, was going to the country for the summer and offered to rent me his house in Greenwich Village.

Once more we loaded the Hiss Ford with our few personal belongings—all that we had ever taken to the 28th Street apartment—and the Hisses drove them to the Schapiro house in New York. My family and I went by train.

The summer was very hot and Greenwich Village very noisy. At that point, Maxim Lieber decided to move to the country for the summer (he kept his New York apartment), and we decided to give up the Schapiro house and move in with Lieber. This served a practical purpose: we could use the David Breen name and establish a record that Lieber had spent a summer in the country with the future manager of his London office.

We found a furnished cottage facing the Delaware River at Smithtown, on the Pennsylvania shore, a few miles below Frenchtown, N.J. We lived there during the late summer and probably the early fall of 1935.

At Smithtown, Priscilla Hiss visited us. My wife had given up her painting when our daughter was born so that she could devote her full time to the child. To Priscilla Hiss, who was stirred from time to time by a vestigial feminism, this seemed a penalization of talent by maternity. Very generously, she volunteered to come up to Smithtown and spend a week or ten days with us. She would keep an eye on the child and my wife would be free to go painting again. My daughter was used to Priscilla and fond of her. Everything went very nicely and my wife painted several pictures.

Priscilla had driven up in the Hisses' Ford roadster. For some reason, I drove the roadster back to Washington alone. There was a mist over the Delaware Valley. The windshield kept clouding and I had some difficulty in keeping it clear with the hand-operated windshield wipers. I did not realize as I struggled with them how important that recollection was to become years later. In my absence, Alger drove to Smithtown and took Priscilla back to Washington in the Plymouth car he had bought a short time before.

It was from this visit to Smithtown that Alger Hiss knew the name David Breen and learned about my English plans so that the Hiss defense was able to demand the Breen passport at Hiss's second trial. It is his knowledge of that visit that could have made Maxim Lieber an important witness in the Hiss case. Though he was available, and probably in New York during both Hiss trials, the Hiss defense never called him to the stand.*

XVII

The Plymouth, which, like the Ford roadster, was to roll importantly into the Hiss case, had been a floor model, and, because of that, Alger had got something taken off the purchase price when he bought the car two or three months *after* we left the 28th Street apartment. (The *after* is a matter of record.)

In those days practically everybody parked his car on the street in Washington. The Ford roadster had stood out winter and summer in all weathers. Now and again, I would use it to drive around Washington. I always returned the key to Hiss. But with the purchase of the Plymouth, Alger decided to get rid of the roadster. It was in good mechanical condition, but somewhat beat up, and its cash value was small. Alger decided that he wanted to give the car to the open Communist Party for the use of some poor organizer in the South or West—a close approximation of his own words. Perhaps this was a harkback to the days of Harold Ware and his agrarian undergrounds.

I strongly opposed the idea. The transfer of the roadster must inevitably establish a documentary connection between the Soviet underground and the Communist Party. Alger was unusually persistent. I took the problem to J. Peters, who also strongly opposed the transfer of the car for the same reason. For once, Alger would not be dissuaded.

Either Peters or I could, of course, have said a flat no. But in the underground as everywhere else, the use of flat noes is to be avoided. The enforced inaction in which Hiss was now living made him very restless. (Priscilla would presently attempt to satisfy her need for activity by planning to take a nursing course at Mercy Hospital in Baltimore—a project that she denied in the Hiss trials until the Government introduced one of her own letters to the Hos-

* Not long before this book was published, Lieber suddenly gave up his literary agency and moved to the Southwest.

pital which established the fact.) Both Peters and I saw in the car episode a symptom of that restlessness.

Peters presently worked out a solution. I think, moreover, that he was tempted by the car. He told me, as nearly as I could remember in 1948, that there was a used-car lot and filling station in the District of Columbia, or just across the District Line in Maryland, which was owned by a Communist. (An employe, and not the owner, it developed in 1948, was Peters' contact.) Alger was to drive the Ford roadster there and leave it. The rest would be taken care of without trace or trouble. Either Peters met Alger and gave him the address of the car lot, or he gave me the address, which I passed on unread to Alger.

In any case, I was at the Hisses' when Alger drove the Ford away. I was still there when he came back after having turned it over to the party. He was very pleased with himself. I never asked him any further details about the transaction.

I would have been shocked if I had known that he had asked a colleague in the Department of Justice (the late W. Marvin Smith) to notarize the transfer of title. For Alger was now in the Department of Justice. He had left the munitions investigation and the Solicitor General of the United States, now Mr. Justice Reed, had appointed Alger Hiss his assistant. Stanley Reed would have been dismayed if he could have known that Alger Hiss raised the question of his going to the Department of Justice with the Communist Party in my person, knowing that I would confer about it with J. Peters. Presumably he would not have believed it at all, for he was to be a character witness for Hiss at his first trial.

Neither Peters nor the Soviet apparatus had any immediate purpose for Alger Hiss in the Justice Department. But the munitions investigation was winding up. The Justice Department was a forward step in his career and might lead to a widening of contacts and of the apparatus.

XVIII

Peters was more often in Washington now, for Harold Ware was dead. His fondness for driving at high speeds had closed the career of one of the most dangerous, because one of the ablest, of native American Communists. He had been driving in Pennsylvania. A truck had turned out of a blind lane. Ware could not stop.

The Ware Group was without a leader. But Ware must have a

successor. Peters came down especially from New York for an election meeting of the leading committee of the Group. There was a long discussion in the living room of Henry Collins' apartment. I was in the apartment at the time, but I took no part in the discussion. I sat alone in the dining room, reading.

At last Peters joined me. He was worried. A crisis, he said, had developed in the Group. Victor Perlo believed that he should succeed Ware as Group leader. He was being stubborn and surly about it. All the other members of the leadership believed that Nathan Witt was Ware's natural heir. A deadlock had resulted, for, though the rest might easily have outvoted Perlo, they did not wish to risk trouble in the Group by alienating him. Peters was also for Witt. So was I. But Peters did not wish to use his authority to act against any member of the Group in favor of another member. Peters asked me if I would come in and, since my personal authority was high with the Group, give my reasons why I was for Witt.

I went in. I said that we must first of all treat the problem that had arisen as Communists, without personalities, and bearing in mind the peculiar nature of underground work and its unusual requirements, especially in the personal character of leadership. I asked Perlo's pardon for observing that he was a tense and nervous man, and that his very belief in his own qualifications for leadership, while perhaps quite justified, would actually be a handicap so long as it was not shared by the rest of the Group. Of course, we Communists did not believe in any mystical rightness of majorities over minorities, but we did believe in practical solutions to practical problems. Witt was acknowledged to be quiet, firm and solid. He had the confidence of all the members of the Group except Perlo. Therefore, I was for Witt.

Perlo, of course, was unconvinced, but he agreed to abide by discipline. Thereafter, he would scarcely speak to me. Later, according to Elizabeth Bentley, he rose to the leadership he coveted in her espionage group.

I had no organizational authority whatever to act as I had done in the Witt election. The episode reflects the unclassified position I had acquired among the Washington Communists.

XIX

When Alger bought the Plymouth car, there was some talk of ways and means between the Hisses. I noted it, but I supposed that it was the common practice of well-to-do people who like to "talk poor." Compared with us, the Hisses seemed affluent. I knew that Alger's party dues were high, and, that, unlike some others, George Silverman, for example, he paid them scrupulously. I did not realize at any time I knew them how closely they must have had to contrive sometimes.

But while Alger was in the Department of Justice, there was a real retrenchment campaign. The Hisses moved from the P Street house, a three-story brick house with a basement dining room, to a little box on 30th Street a few blocks away. The 30th Street house was much smaller and part of a row of similar frame houses so that in the living room we could sometimes hear the murmur of voices through the walls from the houses on either side. To make sure that our own voices did not carry, we took to foregathering downstairs. For like P Street, the 30th Street house also had a basement dining room. But, at P Street, the dining room was at the front of the house and, at 30th Street, it was at the back; a small kitchen and closet storeroom were at the front.

Alger Hiss had scarcely settled in as Assistant Solicitor General of the United States when he again had an opportunity to change jobs. Francis Sayre, then an Assistant Secretary of State, asked Alger to become his assistant. Hiss had been in the Justice Department so short a time that the question of propriety was involved. But the opportunity to go to the State Department could not be passed up. We discussed the question at length and decided that at whatever cost in the Solicitor General's good will, Alger Hiss must go to the State Department.

There was not a question of direct espionage at that time. But Hiss and I sensed that that was what we were heading for, and we discussed it. But the first result that we foresaw from Alger's new job was the possibility of widening the apparatus in the State Department. That soon became Alger's underground activity and took the form of a regular campaign. Alger described several liberals in the Department whom he thought might make possible recruits. He began to invite them to the 30th Street house. It was slow work and the approach had to be cautious. In the end nothing came of any of those contacts.

But two other contacts, who at first were unwittingly part of the same campaign, yielded surprising results, though not those intended. From my first day in Washington, I had heard the name of Laurence Duggan as a likely underground recruit. I also heard constant rumors about Duggan's great friend, Noel Field, a Harvard man and Quaker of good family who was in what was then the West European Division of the State Department. The Fields and the Duggans lived in the same apartment house.

Hiss began an intensive campaign to recruit Field and Duggan. He reached the point of talking very openly to Noel Field. I was afraid to ask just how openly they were talking, for I might have been tempted to urge caution, and in such delicate negotiations much must be left to the tact of the negotiator, in this case Alger Hiss. Too much supervision or advice may lead to disaster, or at least to an awkward situation.

I was soon to learn just how far the two young State Department men had gone. One night Alger reported to me that Noel Field claimed to be connected with "another apparatus." "Is it possible?" Alger asked me in surprise. "Can there be another apparatus working in Washington?" I told him that it was quite possible, that it was probably a parallel apparatus. I asked Peters what he knew about it. "It is probably the apparatus of Hede Gumperz [Hede Massing]," he said. I had never heard of Hede Gumperz. I asked who she was. "Oh, you know," said Peters—a stock answer when no more will be said. Peters urged me to let Noel Field alone. But Alger's spirit was up. He was determined to recruit Noel Field.

At the second Hiss trial, Hede Massing testified how Noel Field arranged a supper at his house, where Alger Hiss and she could meet and discuss which of them was to enlist him. Noel Field went to Hede Massing. But the Hisses continued to see Noel Field socially until he left the State Department to accept a position with the League of Nations at Geneva, Switzerland—a post that served him as a "cover" for his underground work until he found an even better one as dispenser of Unitarian relief abroad.

At the time, I had wondered why the parallel apparatus would let Noel Field leave the State Department. It was General Walter Krivitsky who first told me that Noel Field had left the State Department on orders from his apparatus to work for Krivitsky, who was then chief of Soviet Military Intelligence in Western Europe.

During the Hiss Case, Noel Field, his wife, his adopted daughter and his brother all disappeared into Soviet-controlled Europe. From that, I infer that they had knowledge about Alger Hiss and others that made it inadvisable to leave the Fields in any part of Europe or the United States where American officials or subpoenas could reach them.

In 1939 I gave to the security officer of the State Department, A. A. Berle, the name of Laurence Duggan as someone whom I believed, though I was not certain, to be connected with a Soviet apparatus. Duggan was then, or shortly afterwards, the chief of the Latin American Division of the State Department.

My belief was based upon two incidents. When Noel Field left for Europe, Alger Hiss asked him if he would not use his great influence with Duggan to recruit him into the special apparatus. Noel Field replied that, since he was going away, "Duggan would take his place." Hiss and I both assumed, therefore, that Duggan was working with the Massing apparatus. Hede Massing has told the facts, in so far as she knows them, in *This Deception.*

In 1937, Colonel Boris Bykov decided that we should again make an attempt to recruit Duggan. From Peters I had learned that Frederick Vanderbilt Field (recently in and out of court and jail in New York in connection with bail for some of the convicted Communist leaders) was also a great friend of Duggan. For the express purpose of recruiting Duggan, J. Peters introduced me to Fred Field in New York. The great-grandson of Commodore Vanderbilt took me to lunch, appropriately at the Vanderbilt Hotel, and I watched with some amusement the casual way in which my millionaire comrade signed the chit.

He went to Washington the next day and met Laurence Duggan. When he returned to New York, Fred Field told me that he had asked Duggan perfectly openly to work for the special apparatus, and Duggan had replied that he was "connected with another apparatus."

Duggan's fatal fall from his New York office window during the Hiss Case troubled me deeply. I had a strange sense of knowing the Duggans, whom I had never seen. For the Hisses talked frequently about Helen Duggan, Laurence Duggan's wife. Later on, by a curious chance, I was to meet her father and brother.

X X

Expansion went on in other directions also. From time to time, Peters would mention Harry Dexter White as a candidate for the special apparatus. I still refused to have anything to do with Wilton Rugg, whom Peters always mentioned as his best contact with White. One day Peters admitted that he had a better one. The better contact was Abraham George Silverman, the research director of the Railroad Retirement Board. I suspect that Peters was moved less by any sense of urgency about Harry Dexter White than by a desire to get George Silverman off his hands. Silverman, said Peters, was a whiner. Worse, he complained about the heavy party dues he had to pay (nothing could have outraged Peters more). He said frankly that he could do nothing with Silverman without hours of wrangling. He wanted to see what I could do with him.

I got along with Silverman easily and pleasantly by the simple method of recognizing that he was a highly intelligent child, and by letting him, in so far as possible, do whatever he wanted in his own way. Then I would say no firmly or tell him why I thought that he was mistaken. I also listened patiently and sympathetically to his personal and financial woes. One of his griefs was that, on advice from Lauchlin Currie, he was occasionally playing the stock market. Currie's advice did not always turn out well. Treated with consideration, Silverman co-operated readily, for he was a convinced Communist. He soon introduced me to White, delaying, as he explained to me, only until he was satisfied that I could handle that odd character.

Harry Dexter White, then the chief monetary expert of the Treasury Department, had been in touch with the Communist Party for a long time, not only through his close friend, George Silverman, but through other party members whom he had banked around him in the Treasury Department. He was perfectly willing to meet me secretly; I sometimes had the impression that he enjoyed the secrecy for its own sake. But his sense of inconvenience was greater than his sense of precaution, and he usually insisted on meeting me near his Connecticut Avenue apartment. Since White was not a party member, but a fellow traveler, I could only suggest or urge, not give orders. This distinction White understood very well, and he thoroughly enjoyed the sense of being in touch with the party, but not in it, courted by it, but yielding only so much as he chose.

He talked endlessly about the "Secretary" (Henry Morgenthau Jr.) whose moods were a fair barometer of White's. If White's spirits were up, I knew that the Secretary was smiling. If he was depressed, I knew that the Secretary had had a bad day. For some time, White seemed extremely casual in his manner toward me. I sometimes found myself wondering why I troubled to see him. But when once, quite by chance, I kept away from him for two or three weeks, I discovered that he was plaintive and felt neglected by the party, was very friendly and co-operative. I never really worried about White. For he and Silverman were almost fraternally close. Of the two, White was the more successful bureaucrat, and, in his special field, perhaps, had the better mind. But in all other fields, Silverman was much more intelligent and knew it. Their relationship seemed to have hinged for years on Silverman's willingness to let himself be patronized by White to whom his sympathy was indispensable whenever, for example, the Secretary was snappish and White had one of his crises of office nerves. Each, in fact, was a tower of weakness—a leaning tower. But, as they leaned together, they held each other upright.

XXI

Peters pushed expansion outside the circles of the Ware Group. He brought me in touch with still another Communist underground, having no discoverable connections (except through him) with the Ware Group. The new group also included Government employes, but of a somewhat less exalted order.

This second underground Peters introduced me to in the person of David Carpenter, a Baltimore Communist, a graduate of the University of Virginia and a paint chemist. Carpenter was a literal translation of his real name, which was Zimmerman. He had worked with Peters in an underground in Baltimore.

There was only one thing that Carpenter and I ever agreed on—we disliked each other at sight. I never doubted that he was a devoted Communist. My instinctive distrust of him was based on questions of personal character, judgment and general ambiguity. He was a slight little man who was a good deal older than he looked. His complexion was leaden so that he seemed chronically unhealthy. There were lines in his face that looked like lines of dissipation, but were not. I was always expecting him to sidle up to me and whisper: "Feelthy pictures?"

But I always knew that there was another side to Carpenter. He was bookish, and, with other people, liked to discuss philosophy. I suspected that he wrote poetry and was ashamed to admit it. He had grown up in one of Baltimore's poorer neighborhoods. No doubt, his college education had been a grim struggle. It is probable that in his whole life nothing very good, joyous or uplifting had ever happened to him, and that, moreover, he was incapable of enjoying it if it had.

For Carpenter was envious, and I know no way to deal with envy except to run away from it. Much worse, he was afraid of me, and there is almost no way to deal with that. He was afraid of me in general. Specifically, he was afraid that I had come to take over his kingdom. Working in some kind of loose relationship with J. Peters, he had established a number of connections among Government people in Washington. Most of them were Communists. Some were fellow travelers. They were all members or connections of Peters' second underground apparatus, and Carpenter had met most, if not all of them, through the head of the apparatus, the girl he was living with. They knew him as "Harold," and he had a curiously possessive feeling about them. They were his personal underground property.

The difficulty of his position was twofold. First, Peters had connected Carpenter with me for the specific purpose of having him turn over to me several of his connections. Carpenter was torn by the possible loss of his contacts. But he was tempted by his connection with me, for he greatly wished to become a paid functionary in the special apparatus, and his contacts were his price.

This I saw quickly. I tried to tranquilize and reassure him by keeping myself as much as possible out of his affairs and letting him handle relations with these people, with whom he soon connected me, as much as possible by himself.

There were three connections. One of them worked at the Bureau of Standards. In college, he had been a member of the Communist-controlled National Students League. Let me call him Abel Gross. He was, Carpenter gave me to understand, a member of the Communist Party.

Carpenter also gave me to understand that the third member of his trio was a Communist. He was a young employe of the Department of Agriculture named Henry Julian Wadleigh, whom I always called Julian. It was not until Wadleigh began to testify before the Grand Jury, in 1948, that I discovered that he had never been a Communist, but a very close fellow traveler.

Carpenter was profuse in his promise of more contacts. But he was elusive about them. The contours of his netherworld always remained shadowy to me. But I now know that he had some kind of contact, apparently through Abel Gross, with an underground cell at least one of whose members worked in the War Department. For that unfortunate man killed himself in the course of the investigations in the Hiss Case.

Due to Carpenter's special feelings, I never knew any of his three contacts in the way in which I knew Alger Hiss or Harry White. I met them from time to time, especially at first, chiefly to give them a sense of belonging to a new apparatus. One was never at any time more than a superfluous connection. The other, Abel Gross, was a much more mature character, quiet, observant, taciturn and solid. He was a chemist or a physicist.

Wadleigh seemed to me one of the oddest people I ever knew. He was an Oxford man. He always went bareheaded on principle and he affected a careful disorder in his dress. After some argument, Carpenter finally prevailed upon him to buy a hat, but he seldom wore it. My recollection of him is as very youthful-looking, with distracted hair and thick-lensed glasses. He was both highly sensitive and informed and, as time was to show, courageous. As sometimes happens with rather owlish young men, there was a puckish streak in him too. I think that nothing sums up that side of Wadleigh quite so well as a name he took during the second Hiss trial. To avoid the press, Wadleigh registered at his hotel as Jasper Q. Sprigg.

Shortly after I met him, Wadleigh was able to transfer from the Agriculture Department to the Trade Agreements Division of the State Department. He soon brought out several small batches of documents to be photographed. For Peters had had his usual motive in arranging these new connections, and he was once more stirred to photography. Abel Gross also brought out some documents from the Bureau of Standards. I must have photographed them, probably at Alger Hiss's, for at that time the apparatus had no independent facilities for such work in Washington.

Once more Bill showed no interest in the film. What his reasons were, he never told me. But I presently drew my own conclusions about them which I shall presently give. That was the fifth and last attempt at sporadic espionage while Bill headed the apparatus.

XXII

In 1935, the French police traced a post card which had been sent from Finland to Lydia Chekalova Stahl in Paris. The sender of the post card was a woman, who had recently been arrested together with the rest of a Soviet espionage apparatus, which also included Arvid Jacobson, the young Finnish-American with the missing fingers to whom I had introduced Ulrich in New York.

Lydia Stahl, known simply as "Lydia" while she worked for a Soviet espionage group in the United States *circa* 1930 and perfected her knowledge of Chinese at Columbia University, was the photographer of another Soviet espionage group in Paris. In that group was Paula Levine, the tenant of The Gallery, one of the first underground meeting places I knew in New York. She escaped when the French police swooped down and arrested, among others, Robert Gordon Switz, the young American who, unknown to me, had run the photographic workshop in the apartment of Joshua Tamer's mother, a floor or two above The Office in Brooklyn. Many paths crossed and some ended in Paris.

The head of the Soviet apparatus in Paris had been a neurotic Rumanian Communist. The group was filled with dissension and was on the point of inner collapse when the French police pounced. One of the most disaffected members was Robert Gordon Switz. He and his wife were placed in French prisons. For some time Switz refused to talk. Then he began to tell the French police everything that he knew.

I assumed that Switz would henceforth be an outcast from the Communist Party. To my surprise, Bill one day instructed me to get in touch with The Bank at once and arrange to meet a relative of Switz. For Robert Gordon Switz was not the only member of his family close to the Communist Party. Then Bill gave me five hundred dollars to turn over to the relative for any legal, or other expenses that might result from Switz's arrest.

Since the members of the Switz family in the United States might well be under surveillance, the meeting with the relative was carefully organized. A second surprise was in store for me. To guide me to my rendezvous, Peters brought along one of the witnesses of my marriage, Comrade Grace Hutchins.

Miss Hutchins led me to the West Side of New York, somewhere in the twenties, I believe. There, in a small park, we found Switz's relative. I turned over the money and hastily left him.

The Switz Case was not the only backlash of collapsing apparatuses abroad that I was to experience. Bill met me one day in great agitation. "There has been a *Durchfall* [an arrest]," he said. "Don has been arrested in Tokyo." Bill instructed me to liquidate the American Feature Writers Syndicate as quickly as possible, to get everybody in the office out of town and in every way to "make it nothing." We arranged to meet again the next day.

Bill was unfamiliar with American tempo. I set to work at once. By the next morning, the American Feature Writers Syndicate no longer existed. The name had been removed from the office door. The stationery was hidden somewhere by Lieber, who had declared a holiday and left town.

I was ready to report to Bill. When we met he seemed a little sheepish. "There has been a mistake in decoding," he said. "Don was not arrested." I asked Bill if I should put the pieces together again. He said no, that Don was about to be recalled from Tokyo in any case. There was great dissatisfaction with him.

Don arrived in the United States a month or so later. He was a saddened man. Everything had gone wrong with the Japanese apparatus. He had had difficulty establishing contact with Hideo Noda. When they did meet, it was on the Ginza, Tokyo's main street, and the day was the Emperor's birthday. The city was jammed with police. As nearly as I could learn, the Japanese apparatus, which must have cost thousands of dollars to organize and maintain, had produced exactly nothing. Don had just one success to report. He had won the handball championship of Japan at the Tokyo Y.M.C.A.

That would scarcely help him much in Moscow, where he was ordered to report at once. Again, I procured him a birth certificate from Peters, and Don secured a second passport in his new name. Then he left for Russia. He was to proceed to London where the Soviet embassy was alerted to give him a special visa for the Soviet Union. It would not show on his passport because, unlike the visas of other governments, it was not stamped there. It was stamped on a separate piece of paper.

I never expected to see Don again alive. I do not think that he expected to see me.

The second survivor of the Japanese debacle presently arrived in the United States, too. Hideo Noda appeared and made contact with me through a mutual friend. Bill gave me instructions and money for Noda. He was to go to France and in a hotel at Nice or Antibes simply wait until someone got in touch with him.

I met Noda in New York at night. I felt extremely sorry for him. For the talented young Japanese seemed to me to be destroying his great gifts. I thought that he was already showing signs of disillusionment as a result of his experience in Japan. I walked with him up Fifth Avenue along the east wall of Central Park. I wanted to say something to him, but I could not risk being too explicit. We sat down on a bench.

"Look, Ned," I said, "Russians are a very remarkable, but a very strange people. They have great virtues, but order is not one of them. You may sit in the hotel in France for weeks and no one will come near you. You will think that you are completely forgotten. You will get desperate. Instead of doing that, why don't you use the time you are waiting to go back to painting? That is what you were meant to do."

The next day Hideo Noda denounced me to the American Communist Party as a Trotskyist wrecker. Peters laughed when he told me. But I have sometimes wondered whether, before he died, Noda remembered the "Trotskyist wrecker" and his warning—if at the end, as I suspect, he knew moments of final terror not revealed in his public obituary. For Noda, though he still had many thousand miles to travel on three continents, was all the while traveling to his death.

XXIII

The underground worker at my level never knows where the impulses come from that shift him from one task to another. He can only guess that someone in Moscow or Paris or London has had an idea, or made a contact, or heard something that sets in motion a score of people in more than one country working at tasks whose real meaning and purpose they will probably never know.

Bill asked me one day what I knew about Ludwig Lore. I had been hearing the name for years. Lore had been the editor of the *Volkszeitung,* the very literate German Communist paper that had helped to swing me into Communism. He had been expelled from the Communist Party in 1925, a few months after I had joined it. For years, the whisper had run around the party that Lore was an enemy agent. At the time Bill spoke to me about him, Lore wrote a column called "Behind the Cables" for the New York *Evening Post.* It purported to give the news behind the news.

"He can have valuable contacts," said Bill. I knew what that meant. That meant that Bill had had instructions from "home" to get in touch with Lore. "You must meet him and talk with him," said Bill. He added that Lore had once been connected with an apparatus, but that "something stupid" had happened. I asked how I was to get in touch with Lore. Bill screwed up his face and said, "Your problem."

I had never seen Lore. I did not know anyone who knew him. I asked J. Peters about arranging a contact for me with Lore. His reaction was violent. He absolutely refused to have anything to do with contacting Lore in any way. "You people know what you are doing," he said, "but the party will not deal with Lore." I decided that the simplest approach was the best one. I relied on Lore's past underground experience and my own improvisation to carry me through.

Lore was an old Bolshevik. He had been a Socialist before the Russian Revolution. In those pre-revolutionary days, he had been the friend of Trotsky, then a New York Socialist journalist. After the Revolution, Lore had managed an American speaking trip for Alexandra Kollontai, the author of *Red Love,* later the Soviet ambassador to Sweden. Bukharin, in his New York days, had eaten and slept in the apartment on 55th Street in Brooklyn, where Lore, his outspokenly anti-Communist wife and three wholly American sons still lived. When he was ejected from the editorship of the *Volkszeitung*, Lore had been brutally slandered. His wife never forgave that ordeal. But in his heart, Lore, I believe, never quite freed himself from the spell of the party, even though he was divided in his feeling about it, even though in 1938, he was afraid, with good reason, that the G.P.U. meant to take his life.

I went to Brooklyn and rang Lore's doorbell. On the second floor of the apartment house, a short, stout man, in his upper fifties, came into the hall to meet me. With his thick moustache and shrewd eyes, he looked like a genial Stalin. He spoke with a heavy German accent. I said: "My name is Carl. I would like to talk to you." He led me into his office. I sat down beside his desk, which was cluttered with newspaper clippings. Lore's eldest son, Karl, was sitting at another desk. Big aquariums, filled with all kinds of tropical fish, stood around the walls. There was a constant gurgle from the pumps aerating the water in the tanks. A gray African parrot was loose in the room and he swooped down from time to time, using his beak, to climb over Lore's shirt and perch on his shoulder.

"Comrade Lore," I said, "I have come to mend a broken rope." As I expected, Lore had seen so many of my kind. He had spent thirty years of his life in the revolutionary movement. To such a man a great many things do not have to be said. "Such strange birds as you," says Ivanov to Rubashov in Koestler's *Darkness at Noon,* "are found only in the trees of the revolution." Lore and I understood one another at once with a birdlike intuition in which common experience took the place of explanation. An old revolutionist, especially a foiled revolutionist, if he is not embittered, is usually stirred by the sight of a younger man in whom he sees embodied his revolutionary self of years ago. In part, that is what I had counted on in going without credentials to Lore.

Lore asked me what nationality I was. I told him that I was an American. He laughed at me. "You are not an American," he said. He asked me whom I knew in the apparatuses, if I knew someone whom he called "Jim"—a short, dark, rough man who seemed to be a Turk. I did not know Jim. Then Lore asked me if I had known a Russian called Oskar, who spoke very fluent German and who had been killed. I suddenly realized that Lore had also worked with Herman. We talked about him for a long time. Herman-Oskar had been a constant guest in Lore's house. As much as I disliked Herman, Lore had liked him. Our common knowledge of the murdered man was like a password. Lore accepted me as an emissary from the underground.

He asked me to stay for lunch. I was introduced to those massive German meals. I was introduced to Lillian Lore, Ludwig's remarkable wife, who in large part provided those meals, and, by some economic miracle, had kept that amazing household together during the long, lean years, had fed the endless procession of guests. "*Die unvergessliche* Lores—the unforgettable Lores," a German friend had called them. (German was the household language.) I have seldom seen a happy family life so explicit in the characters of all who shared it. I have never known another in which hospitality was less a rite than a reflex. Nor have I often known one where family and hospitality seemed so much the achievement of a strong, devoted woman.

I soon came to regard the Lores' house as a kind of second home. For Ludwig I developed an almost filial feeling as of a younger for an older revolutionist. The kindness of all the Lores to me was personal, and in spite of politics, for all the other members of the family, except Ludwig, were outspoken in their detestation of the Communist Party.

I used to watch very carefully to see if I was followed when I visited Lore. For I could not entirely disregard the rumors about him. I did not know that at the very time I was visiting him most frequently, Lore was under surveillance. He was being watched, not by the American authorities, but by the Russian secret police. Eyes must have seen me come and go to that apartment house a number of times without knowing who I was or that I was going there to meet Lore, for there were other tenants in the house.

One pair of those eyes had already seen Alger Hiss as a Communist in Washington. They belonged to Hede Massing, who, under instructions of her apparatus, and with the help of a telescope, was watching Lore day and night from a room that the G.P.U. had rented across the street from his apartment.

Hede Massing could not imagine why the Russian secret police kept that watch upon Lore. I can. My first slight distrust of him passed through my mind when, after months of promising, he failed to make a single contact for me. But I explained his failure as that of a busy man who did not want to be bothered. I did not really care, for I had come to like the Lores entirely for themselves.

It was not until much later that I became openly suspicious of Lore's role. I discovered that he was afraid to walk alone with me on the street at night and that he was terrified to get into an automobile alone with me. Then I knew that there was something seriously amiss. But I had been out of the Communist Party six or seven years, and Lore was dead, before I discovered that the old Bolshevik, in whom, as a younger man, I respected the older revolutionist, had denounced me (around 1941) to the F.B.I. I learned it not from the F.B.I., but from another security agency of the Government.

I respected Lore all the more for that act. My feeling for him and for all the Lores remained unchanged.

XXIV

My family and I lived in a kind of organized flight. For all through 1934 and 1935, regardless of what else was happening, the English apparatus was still held, theoretically, to be the first order of business, and my instructions were to keep myself in instant readiness to leave for London. That led to our housing improvisations. One of them involved the Hisses.

During her stay at our Delaware River cottage, Priscilla Hiss and my wife worked out a new change of address for us and presented it for my consideration. The plan was that we should move into the third floor of the Hisses' P Street house. Organizationally, it was not a good arrangement, and I have seldom heard of two families living happily under one roof. But Priscilla was generously insistent. We no longer had any furniture of our own and, in view of England, there seemed to be no point in buying any. But the English project also made the organizational question less important. With some tacit reservations, I agreed. The Hisses made the third floor of the P Street house ready for us. When we left the Delaware River cottage, we moved in with them.

I have been asked how it was possible for us to live with the Hisses without meeting their friends at their house. At that time the Hisses had almost no visitors. They lived almost entirely to themselves. Alger was cut off from the Ware Group, which had formerly provided much of his social life. It was not until they moved to the 30th Street house that the Hisses really began to entertain.

We did not remain long at P Street. There was never any unpleasantness. The Hisses were the kindest of hosts. But from the first my wife felt in the way. Our daughter required a special food which my wife prepared. She felt that that upset the routine of the kitchen and annoyed the maid. Organizationally, the arrangement seemed worse in practice than in prospect. I was relieved when my wife insisted that we find a place of our own.

We went to Baltimore together and, in a day of searching, found an inexpensive apartment on Eutaw Place. A narrow park separated the uptown and downtown traffic on the street. My wife could sun the baby in front of our house. We rented the apartment under the name we had used before in Baltimore—Lloyd Cantwell. But we had no furniture. We bought some necessities, a bureau, a bed, a few chairs. The Hisses contributed some odd pieces—an old table that they had started to scrape, but never finished, a patched rug, a worn wing chair, a painted chest of drawers that had been Timmie Hobson's. Some of these things they brought by car from Washington. Some they brought from Alger's mother's house, which was a few blocks away. I knocked together some bookcases. But J. Peters who dropped into the Eutaw Place apartment during one of his Washington trips, shook his head and said that it was too conspicuously unfurnished for an underground worker.

One day, as my wife was walking down Eutaw Place, she met Edith, the bright young colored girl who had worked for her on St. Paul Street. That chance meeting was to have fateful meaning during the Hiss Case. Edith was delighted to be with us again. She loved our daughter and was loved by her in turn. We trusted her absolutely with the child, whom she called P.G. (for Pretty Girl). P.G. presently became Peachie, Peegee and at last Puggie, which has remained my daughter's name in the family ever since. Edith Murray was as sensible, shrewd and fun-loving as ever. I, who cannot bear to have people other than my family in the house, loved to have Edith with us. She was part of the family.

Those were the days when we probably saw the Hisses most frequently. Sometimes Priscilla would drive over from Washington and we would meet her downtown for lunch. Often Alger would drive over to see his mother and finish the evening at Eutaw Place. In general, the Hisses arrived after Edith had gone home. But once or twice they came while she was there. We never told her their names. But from hearing us talk with them, Edith, who missed very little, took to calling Priscilla, "Miss Priscilla" or "the lady from Washington."

On one occasion, Priscilla Hiss and Edith spent some time alone together in the apartment. My wife was carrying our second child. She wished to go and see the same doctor in New York who had delivered our daughter. For some reason, I was away and Edith could not stay all night. We arranged with Priscilla to spend the night with our child while my wife was in New York.

Edith was alone with the child when "Miss Priscilla" arrived and stayed until the baby was bathed and put to bed. It was while they were bathing the child together that "the lady from Washington" told Edith that she had a little boy of her own.

One of the incidental results of our summer on the Delaware had been Maxim Lieber's discovery of Bucks County. Near Ferndale, in upper Bucks, he had bought a farm. He was alone in an empty house on some hundred acres. He begged us to come and share the house with him. In the spring of 1936, we moved to Lieber's. Once more we used the Breen name, since it was under that name that I expected soon to represent Lieber in England. But just before we arrived at Ferndale, Lieber suddenly married for the second time. It was not a happy marriage and it did not last long. But it caused us quickly to look for another house of our own.

Again, the Hisses were involved. Since we expected to be at Ferndale, they had decided to rent a summer place in Bucks County. Priscilla would spend most of her time there. Alger would drive up for week-ends, holidays and spend his vacation there. They went house hunting and discovered a "charming little stone house" near

New Hope. It stood on the property of Tom Marshall at the foot of his apple orchards.

By prearrangement, we met the Hisses at New Hope one day. We told them about our new plans to move and they suggested that the stone house, which rented for something like thirty dollars a month, would be just the thing for us. They would rent another (actually, they never did). They were so enthusiastic that we all went up to look at the stone house. We were as enthusiastic as the Hisses and rented the house out of hand. When we went back alone to take another look at our new home, the Marshalls were somewhat disturbed that the real-estate agent had rented the place to us without first consulting them, for they knew nothing about us and their own house stood just below ours. A short conversation reassured them, and it was not until 1948 that they realized that the Soviet underground had operated from their orchards.

The stone house had been an old loom house. It was just big enough for the three of us. Its long, small-paned windows were set deep in the stone walls. There was a pleasant irregularity about the ground floor, with the little kitchen set below the one big downstairs room with its wide floor boards. The walls were cold-water-painted in a neutral cream color set off with white trim. As in many country farmhouses, there were black shields painted around the door handles so that small hands could not soil the door. The effect was a Quaker tranquillity, a basic tone style of such simplicity and dignity that since then we have used it exclusively wherever we have lived.

The front windows of the stone house looked out to big maples and a woods beyond which the orchards swept up the hill. The back windows looked out across a long garden of bee balm and sweet william to sloping farm lands. The seclusion was deep. It touched us all, even the child. My daughter always made a great din in the early morning, shaking the bars of her crib, like a young orang-utan, and shouting: "Ya! Ya! Ya!" One morning she was so quiet that my wife and I went to investigate. The child did not hear us even when we entered the room. She was standing upright in her crib, motionless and completely silent. She was watching a hen pheasant pick its fastidious way across the lawn.

The Marshalls were completely friendly. They were an old county family. They read the latest books and had something to do with a summer theater north of New Hope. But Tom Marshall was an outdoor man who spent most of his time in work clothes in his orchards. Mary Marshall was a big, forthright, sensible, wonderfully relaxed woman. We took a great liking to them, which lasted in memory through all the years that we have not seen them. Similarly my daughter remembers Charlie Marshall, their very self-reliant son, a boy about her own age. The two children played happily through many summer days.

While we were living at the stone house, our second child was born. For that event, I again rented my friend Meyer Schapiro's Greenwich Village house for two weeks. I took my daughter there and left her in Grace Lumpkin's care while I got my wife to the Booth Memorial Hospital. It was another long and terrible birth.

Through her fog of anaesthetic, sickness and pain, my wife managed to whisper to me in the morning how happy she was that she had given me a son. But this time she did not urge me to look at the baby, who had been taken with instruments. She warned me not to be shocked. John Chambers, when I finally saw him, was completely unlike his sister at the same age. He was wrinkled and red and hideous. The instruments had sloped in one side of his head. The nurse assured me that it would grow back to the usual shape, and so it did, very quickly. But I did not venture to look at my son again until I was driving my wife back to New Hope. Then I parked in a quiet spot and gingerly lifted the blanket from the basket in which my son was sleeping on the back seat of the car. I hastily dropped it again. Nature has compensated John Chambers for his initial rough handling by man. Together with a very satisfactory set of features he has inherited his mother's character, gentle, generous, courageous.

Our family was once more knit together at the stone house. At Christmas, 1936, the Communist Party first relaxed the bans against the Christmas spirit. "Father Frost," the Soviet Santa Claus, made his appearance on the streets of Moscow. Christmas had always been our one great holiday when I was a boy, and I determined to take advantage of the new Communist attitude. I drove up to Lynbrook and brought my mother down to spend the holiday with us at the stone house. She loved and was loved by my wife. With her grandchildren around her, the grief of the past began to thaw away, and all of us felt the continuity of the generations. Thereafter, my mother and I grew closer and closer together, despite her hatred of Communism and all its works.

In retrospect, it is clear that our life in the stone house had influences on us which, at the time, and even much later, we did not realize. I suspect that in that simple, beautiful and tranquil haven, and from the warm neighborliness of the Marshalls, a subtle chemistry began its work, which if it were possible to trace it, would be found to have played an invisible part in my break with Communism. The long ordeal of that break was to begin not many months after the early spring of 1937, when with real grief, we left the little stone house forever, and, with the snow still on the ground, I headed my family once more for Baltimore. I had rented a house on Auchentoroly Terrace, opposite that Druid Hill Park, where, as he once told me, Alger Hiss, when he was a boy, had bottled spring water to sell to the neighbors.

XXV

The last debris of Don's Japanese apparatus drifted into New York. Keith arrived, trailing two or three others until then unknown to me. One of them was a former Italian naval officer, a Communist who had been training himself as a short-wave radio operator with the idea of joining Don in Tokyo. His wife had been studying photography so that she could also serve with Don. Vaguely I remember meeting the Italian, though I cannot recall his face or his wife's. I should never have recollected him but for Keith's testimony about him. It was Keith, too, who recollected that he had brought back the money belt which I had given him in San Francisco. In it was still two thousand dollars. He had counted it out, he said, in my presence in the apartment of an underground worker named Paul, a literary agent. The apartment was between Broadway and Fifth Avenue in the forties. Obviously, the literary agent was Maxim Lieber. But until then, I had no recollection of the return of the money and had even forgotten that Lieber's underground pseudonym was Paul, though I recognized it as soon as I heard it.

I do not remember whether or not Bill was still in New York when Keith returned from the West Coast. In any case, he must have left soon after. Nor do I recollect the details of our parting, except that he assured me that we would soon meet again in London. I never saw Bill again.

It was the summer of 1936. Dr. Philip Rosenbliett left about the same time as Bill. His daughter had at last died of her lingering illness. In a few weeks, I saw The Doctor change from a robust man to a grief-stricken, gray-faced, almost voiceless, doddering skeleton from whom his clothes now hung in loose folds. The Doctor's office equipment, including the chair where so many curious patients had sat without benefit of dentistry, was shipped to the Soviet Union.

A period began in which I was left alone, in touch chiefly with Peters and Keith, who remained in New York. My only instructions were to hold together the Washington group and wait for orders to proceed to England. By then, I had begun to suspect that the English apparatus would never be organized.

During that period of waiting, I brushed another man's disaster.

XXVI

Bill had not been gone long when Peters brought me word that Richard wanted to see me. Richard was the head of a Soviet passport apparatus with which Peters did a prosperous business. Peters brought Richard and me together at the Rockefeller Plaza, just below what would later be my office at *Time* magazine.

Richard was a cat-faced Lett with an appropriately purring voice. He had a message for me about "the tomato-juice people." The message concerned my old acquaintance, Joshua Tamer, the proprietor of The Office and former employe of a big steel company, then a fugitive in the Soviet Union. He had had difficulty in getting his furniture shipped to Russia. Richard wanted me to report something about the status of the furniture (I believe that it was then in the hands of the Amtorg) to one of Tamer's relatives.

The Tamers were known as "the tomato-juice people" because of an unfortunate remark of Rose Tamer's. After her husband's flight to Russia, she and their baby had followed by another route. She had hesitated to go because, she said, she was afraid that in Moscow she could not get tomato juice for her little girl. That thought, in the moment of flight, struck the comrades as hilariously funny and soon spread through the international underground.

I met Richard once or twice afterwards, simply because Peters had business with him and I was seeing a good deal of Peters. Richard, Peters explained to me, was not a happy man. The chief of his international apparatus was known as "Starik" (Russian for Old Man). Starik was also a Lett and Richard's protector. Starik had just been removed and Richard was afraid that he had been liquidated (the purge was on). I did not know that Starik was really

General Berzin, and that he was not only Richard's international chief, but mine. Nor did I guess that Starik's removal might have had something to do with the strange, delayed history of the English apparatus. Least of all did I realize that Starik's removal was a stride in Stalin's consolidation of power and that it meant that the G.P.U. had moved in on the Military Intelligence, most of whose chiefs were about to be secretly shot, together with much of its personnel, including Richard.

One day, Peters reported that Richard was much cheered up. The rumors were false. Starik had not been removed. Richard had received a friendly message from him, pointing out that Richard had been away from "home" a long time, that he deserved a rest and inviting him back for the celebration (Russians are epicures of a grim irony) of the October Revolution. The letter was genuine, for Richard had recognized Starik's signature. With Peters' help, Richard began to prepare to return to Moscow.

First, Richard and his American wife procured two sets of fraudulent passports. The first set was actually taken out for an unknown young man and woman in the name of Robinson. The second set was taken out for Richard and his American wife in the name of Rubens. Both sets of passports were applied for the same day, but not, as is customary, at the passport bureau in downtown New York. Until late in 1937, the County Clerk's office of New York had the right to receive passport applications. Richard applied for both passports through the County Clerk's office where three contacts of J. Peters' underground apparatus were employed. After Richard received the passport in the Robinson name, he had the Robinson pictures replaced by pictures of himself and his wife. But the application filed in the State Department still bore the Robinson pictures. Hence the first confusion about the identity of the users when in the fall of 1936 Richard's return to Russia became the international mystery known as the Robinson-Rubens case.

With the Robinson passports, Richard and his wife set sail for Naples on an Italian steamship. Peters told me when Richard left. After that there was silence.

Then, one autumn day, there walked into Spasso House, the American embassy in Moscow, a frightened woman, who claimed that she was an American citizen whose name was Rubens. She said that she had a small daughter in the United States. Her husband had disappeared and she wanted help in locating him. She was, of course, Richard's American wife. The embassy officials took her address and she left.

She had not been gone long before the embassy people began to think that perhaps it had been imprudent to let Mrs. Rubens return to her hotel. Two or three of them went after her. At the hotel, they asked for Mrs. Rubens. The manager had never heard the name. She had never lived there. "But we know she is here," said the embassy officials, "we know her room number." "You are mistaken," said the manager. The Americans insisted on going to her room. There was no one in it. In fact, there was *nothing* in it. For, as they climbed the stairs, the embassy officials had met porters carrying down the furniture (possibly in case Mrs. Rubens had concealed a message in it).

It was some time before the American embassy located Mrs. Rubens. She was in the Butirki prison. An interview was arranged with her in the presence of a G.P.U. officer. Mrs. Rubens thanked the embassy officials for their interest and said that she was happy in prison and did not wish them to make any efforts on her behalf. The Soviet Government presently announced that Mrs. Rubens had decided to remain in Russia and become a Soviet citizen.

In West Palm Beach, Mrs. Rubens' mother received an unexpected visitor. He was a rather well-known American theologian, who is even better known as a fellow traveler of the Communist Party. He urged Mrs. Rubens' mother not to make any shrill outcries about her daughter. He was, he said, about to visit the Soviet Union and would personally intercede for Mrs. Rubens with Stalin.

Little more was ever heard again of Richard Robinson-Rubens, except for that State Department message in Alger Hiss's handwriting, which was one of the exhibits at the Hiss trials. But neither Peters nor I had any doubt as to what had happened to Peters' former passport purchaser. As Colonel Boris Bykov, whom I would soon meet, was to say to me in another connection: "You are right. You can be absolutely sure that our Bukharin is dead."

"Starik has been removed," Peters said to me one day. "Yes," I said, "Starik's signature was a forgery or was written under pressure. And Richard knew it." From the first, I had been puzzled as to why an underground worker of Richard's experience would make two passport applications in one day, in an unusual way in an unusual place. I also wondered why he would take his American wife to Moscow during the Purge. I decided presently that he had taken her on purpose so that she might intercede for him if necessary. And he had left that curiously open trail (there were other easily followed clues also) so that it would be discovered. How desperate he must have been! And, in returning to Moscow, what a razor's edge he elected to walk on.

I had never liked Richard. Yet it is all but impossible to have any man whom you have talked with, walked with, lunched with, shot down beside you, without feeling a small, very definite jolt.

XXVII

Between Bill's departure in the summer and Colonel Bykov's arrival in the fall of 1936, only two things of any moment happened.

Following Bill's last instructions, I secured an American passport in the name of David Breen which was mailed to Lieber's New York office. Later, Lieber accompanied me to the British consul general's office in New York, where he introduced me as his future representative in London and requested a visa for me.

Then one day, by way of Richard through Peters, I received a tiny penciled note. It was from Bill. Where it came from I could not tell, but I supposed that it came from Moscow. Underground workers were strictly forbidden to carry on personal correspondence, especially about apparatus affairs. I burned the note at once. As nearly as I can recall it, it said: "You will meet a man. You will do what he tells you to do. You will treat him as if he was my friend."

I knew that it was a warning and that only a sense of great urgency could have led Bill to send it. I knew that Bill meant me to read between the lines. That kind of double-talking letter, almost incredible to the rest of the world, is commonplace to underground Communists.

Clearly, Bill was trying to tell me that his successor was a bad character. He could not risk saying so openly in case the note fell into the wrong hands. But there would have been no reason, of course, to warn me to "do what he tells you to do" unless Bill expected the new man to behave in such a way that I could not do what he told me to do. "You will treat him as if he was my friend." What could that "as if" mean except that he was not Bill's friend? The implication was that he would be no friend of mine, either. It was the first hint I had of the character of Colonel Boris Bykov.

That little effort to warn me, passed along thousands of miles of devious route by unknown hands, was the last of Bill that I would ever know. It was like a final signature hurriedly scrawled in darkness with what generous desperation we can scarcely guess at. My instinct tells me that Bill was a man, by nature too kind, too human, to have survived the Purge, and that the note he sent me was his last effort to help someone else when he knew that he could no longer help himself.

COLONEL BORIS BYKOV

I

A "sleeper apparatus" is an underground group whose most important duty is to do nothing at all. Its first function is to exist without detection. Any kind of action exposes a secret apparatus to the risks of detection. Therefore, a "sleeper apparatus" exists not to act. It waits for the future. It is a reserve unit which will be brought into play only when those who control it see fit, when events dictate, or when it has matured. It takes time to mature a good apparatus. Any apparatus that includes an assistant to the Assistant Secretary of State and an assistant to the Secretary of the Treasury is a "good apparatus."

The special apparatus in Washington had been a "sleeper apparatus." That was why Bill had kept me for the better part of three years in the capital. That is why he had listened to my reports of the growth of the apparatus like a somnolent (but vigilant) cat. That is why he had curtly rejected Peters' premature attempts at photography.

There is no reason to assume that the special apparatus that included Alger Hiss and Harry Dexter White was the only "sleeper" in Washington even during those years. The device is standard practice. Colonel Boris Bykov, the Soviet agent whose activities I am about to report, informed me, in 1938, that I had been selected to head a second "sleeper apparatus" which would become active "only in event of war."

Ten years later, when I was testifying before the House Committee on Un-American Activities, a journalist whose integrity I know no reason to challenge described to me in considerable detail a Soviet "sleeper apparatus" which had been organized by a member of the United States Government (he has since left it) then so highly placed that, for fear of reprisals, I have never publicly uttered his name. Fortunately, I did not need to, since the existence of the "sleeper" and the names of its personnel were known to a security agency of the Government.

It is a conservative assumption that at least one "sleeper apparatus" exists in the United States at present. It is waiting for the time when orders reach it to pass from inactivity to active espionage.

For the special Washington apparatus that time came in 1936.

II

It came at the end of a weeping autumn day. J. Peters had walked me up Fifth Avenue. It was early evening. The rush-hour traffic was jamming Fifth Avenue and the rush-hour crowds were jamming the intersections. At 49th Street we were held up by the traffic and the crowd. Peters peered across in front of St. Patrick's cathedral and said: "There's our man." Neither of us then knew any name for him. Peters, who had already been connected with him in ways I never asked about, was there to connect me with him.

He was standing at the curb with his back to the traffic, staring steadily at the sidewalk. When we came up, he did not glance at me or greet me. He looked like a short, sturdy needle-trades worker who has been dressed by a tailor, instead of by a cut-rate clothing store. His hair was red and his reddish brown eyes peered resentfully from under ginger-colored eyelashes. He thanked Peters gruffly in German and, without moving, watched him distrustfully until he had disappeared in the crowd. Then he grasped my arm, and, dragging me with him, waded into the middle of the Fifth Avenue traffic, as if our safety lay in putting its plunging perils between us and pursuit.

We charged toward Sixth Avenue much too fast to waste breath on words. On Sixth Avenue, the stranger halted a cab practically by throwing himself in front of it. As the driver waited for directions, my companion growled in German: "Tell him, 'Drive on, drive on!' " After a block, my companion muttered: "Tell him, 'Stop! Stop!' " He swarmed out of the cab on the traffic side. As I paid the driver, I saw that he was on the point of asking me if his other passenger was a mental case.

We continued our flight for several blocks and plunged into a B.M.T. subway entrance. I was about to board the first train that drew in. With a murderous look, my companion dragged me back. After many furtive glances around us, we took the next train. Eventually we made our way to Columbus Circle.

I thought that our flight had gone far enough. "Tell me, just where do you want to go?" I asked in German.

"Na!" snapped my companion. "What is your name?"

I knew that he must know my name, but I answered that in the underground I was called Bob or Carl. I asked what his name was. He did not answer. Instead, he enveloped me in a sly stare and asked: "You know the Richard?" I said that I knew Richard (Robinson-Rubens).

"Too bad for you," he said dryly. It was meant to be menacing. But since he had used *"du,"* which in German is used only among members of a family or by extremely close friends, it was also ridiculous, and I smiled.

That was the beginning of my acquaintance with Colonel Boris Bykov, whose behavior baffled me beyond anything I had met with even in a Russian. It was only very slowly, as we continued to rush down streets and on and off conveyances, that I realized that Bykov was frightened.

At that time, I did not know that his real name was Boris Bykov or that he was a pathological coward—that under certain unexpected pressures, or in special situations, like his arrival in a strange country whose language he could not speak, his nerves came apart in rage, fear and suspicion. Those facts, and Bykov's name, I was to learn two years later from General Walter Krivitsky. Bykov had once been sent to assist Krivitsky in a Soviet espionage group in Fascist Italy. After a fortnight of the same kind of panic that I witnessed in New York, Bykov had to be sent back to Moscow because his flagrant terror endangered the whole apparatus.

Again, I asked Bykov what I should call him. Again, he snorted: "Na!" but added: "Call me Peter." I said that that might cause confusion with J. Peters. Bykov stared at me angrily. He intended the confusion.

We parted without my learning anything more from him than that I must meet him next day at the Rockefeller Plaza.

III

I met him the next morning. Soon we were tearing around the lower levels of the R.C.A. Building. Bykov was in flight again. As I watched him hunch his shoulders and thrust his head forward, while the sensitive tip of his nose seemed to twitch slightly, I nicknamed him (to myself): The Weasel.

On the lower level of the R.C.A. Building, the galleries are flanked by shops retailing curios, rugs, dolls and souvenirs of New York to the tourist trade. There is usually a drift of out-of-town window shoppers around the show windows. Bykov kept nervously eyeing them. At last he jerked his head toward them and asked in a tone of unfathomable cunning: "What are they?" I did not know a German word for window shoppers, but I tried to explain what they were doing. "*Nein,*" said Bykov triumphantly, "*Geheimpolizei*—secret police"

I saw that I had on my hands a new Herman, but one beside whom Herman no longer seemed an intermittently drunken barbarian whom the West had also taught to speak a mellow German and to play the piano. Herman at least had been fearless. Bykov was afraid, and he appeared to have no graces at all (his German was gritty and I always had difficulty in understanding it). Moreover, by almost every word he uttered, and the tone he uttered it in, he gave me pointedly to understand that he did not trust me. Underground work cannot exist without a basic mutual trust. For a man not to be trusted in the underground is the next step to being charged with disloyalty to it. And the fact that a man is suspect destroys in advance practically any chance that he might have to establish his innocence. The walls simply cave in and the ground drops out from under his feet, for he is absolutely at the mercy of his superior. But I was no longer the novice whom Herman had so nearly demoralized. I was used to dealing with many kinds of people and to making decisions about them.

Bykov's suspicion of me, it was soon evident, centered, at least in part, around my association with Richard. No doubt, he knew, what the world and I would shortly learn, that Moscow was about to lure Richard to Russia and execute him. In view of that fact, Bykov's hostility to me, and his panic in dealing with me, are more understandable.

I sensed at once that I was in for trouble, though I did not understand its cause. More trouble was not long in coming, and from a quarter where I least expected it.

IV

Maxim Lieber had moved from 47th Street to 52nd Street. His apartment was still my New York headquarters and I had a key to it. I walked in one night to find that Lieber was not alone. John Sherman was with him. I was overjoyed to see Don and asked him how he had managed to get out of Russia alive. He brushed off my questions in a way that made it clear that he wanted to be alone with me. We went out together.

We had no sooner reached the street than Sherman grasped both my arms, and, in a voice shaken with emotion, said: "I will not work one more *hour* for those murderers!" His story has become a fairly familiar pattern since then. As soon as he reached Russia, after his recall from Japan, his passport had been taken away from him. He was completely without identification, a situation made all the worse by the fact that he had been traveling on a fraudulent passport. In effect, he was a prisoner. He was filed away in a room somewhere in Moscow, and for weeks no one came near him. He tried daily to make some official contact. No one would see him. Despair engulfed him—the despair of a man who finds himself in a hermetic trap from which there is no apparent escape, who realizes that he has given the better years of his life to an activity that he suddenly perceives to be monstrous, and who remembers that, far away and beyond communication, a wife and small child are waiting for him, and that he may not see them again.

His despair was heightened by the discovery that he was not alone. He found that there were a score of other Americans in Moscow, hopeless, wretched derelicts of Communism, who, like him, had been used and cast away, but who were not permitted to leave Russia. But Don was a courageous man (he had served in the U. S. Navy in World War I). He induced the other Americans to sign with him a petition of grievances. He made contact with Herbert, to whom he had introduced me on my first night in the underground, and tried to enlist his support. Herbert was frightened and warned Don that he would destroy himself.

Don persisted. He presented his petition to some official. Interrogations about his loyalty began at once. Don was questioned for hours. At last he was called before Colonel Uritsky, one of the top apparatus leaders. Don thought that the end had come. But he is also a man of ruses. He pretended that he had a cold and wrapped his throat in some foul-smelling ointment. After a few moments of the smell, and Don's deliberately idiotic answers, Uritsky waved him out of the room.

There was another long official silence. Again Don demanded his passport and an exit visa. Then one day, he was summoned. His passport and visa were handed to him. He was given several thousand dollars and ordered back to the United States with instructions to organize an underground apparatus—in England. Why did the Russians let him go? I do not know the answer and neither did Don. Of course, he was an American citizen whose wife was not a hostage in Russia, but was free in the United States and capable of making protests. Perhaps the Russians put him down as a harmless crank who had years of underground work behind him and was still useful. Perhaps Herbert took his part. In almost every case where a foreign Communist has been trapped in Moscow and then set free there is some element of riddle.

Don had no intention of setting up an underground organization in England or anywhere else. He was through. He was determined at all costs to get out of the underground. But, curiously enough, his Communist faith was not impaired. Communism still seemed to him the only solution to the crisis of history. He blamed his troubles on the Russian temperament and the special evils inherent in the underground. His one desire was to return to the open Communist Party in California. He seemed to have forgotten that he had once been happy to escape from the open party into the underground.

He insisted that I cable Moscow at once, telling them of his decision and asking permission to keep the money he had in his possession. I explained that I had no way of communicating with Moscow, that I was not alone in the United States, as he seemed to suppose. There was someone else here, though I would not describe him to Don. In that case, said Don, I must take his case to the new man.

I saw that, through no act or will of mine, Don's crisis involved me in a crisis only a little less acute than his. The fact that I must be Don's negotiator, the very fact that I was in touch with a man who was trying to break, involved me in his defection, and the G.P.U., never noted for making fine distinctions, might very well lump us together and deal with us together. Whatever suspicions Bykov had about me, imaginary or complicated darkly by the fate of men unknown to me, must become acute, must become a certainty.

Bykov's reaction exceeded anything I had foreseen. He simply went insane. Volleys of vituperation aimed at Don, but inevitably shared by me, were followed by spasms of distrust and naked fear. How had the Don been able to reach me? Was the Lieber an agent of the American secret police? How could I prove that he was not ("You see, you can't prove it!")? Had Don already gone to the police? Clearly, Bykov believed himself trapped in a nest of counter-agents of whom I was certainly one—all the more so since I often smiled at his wilder charges. There was nothing else to do.

Bykov passed several dreadful days of tantrums alternating with despair, during which we outwitted a non-existent surveillance by dizzying chases through upper Manhattan, and, incidentally, considerably enriched all forms of rapid transit. At last, Bykov, who was clearly powerless to make any decision about Don himself, received his instructions, direct from Moscow or by way of the Soviet embassy in Washington. Through me he sent them on to Don. The apparatus granted Don's requests. He was permitted to leave the underground. He could keep whatever money he had. But he must return at once to the open Communist Party in Los Angeles. Before he left for the West Coast, he must meet with the Russian secret police in New York.

Don refused to meet with the secret police. "You must give me at least two days headway on them," he said. He had his wife and child with him. I agreed. I stalled off Bykov by telling him that Don had not made up his mind. Then, two days after Don and his family had boarded a train for the Coast, I fired the torpedo: "Don has already gone." There was another dramatic outburst, with Bykov stammering German in his furious, frightened voice.

At last, he insisted that I telephone a rooming house on upper Riverside Drive, where Don had been staying, to see if he had really left. I called the superintendent. There was a vaudeville scene with Bykov trying to crowd into the telephone booth with me to make sure that I asked the right questions and to try to catch the answers. I hung up and said: "Don is gone." "*Das wird auch abgerechnet*," said Bykov in the quietest tone of voice I had yet heard him use. "That account will also be settled later on."

Eventually, Don showed up in Los Angeles and Bykov reported to me almost gayly that he had returned to the open party where he could be "*eingekreist und beobachtet*—surrounded and watched." Until that time, I knew, whenever Bykov glanced at me that, if Don did not show up, among the accounts to be settled (and not much later on) would be my own. I would simply be, in one of Bykov's favorite words, *erledigt*—finished.

Thus I helped out of the Soviet underground the man who had helped me into it.

I never saw Don again. When he left, he begged me to break from the apparatus with him. He was too early by more than a year. But I never quite forgot that tone, of a man at the end of all his resources and part of his illusions, in which he had said to me: "I will not work one more *hour* for those murderers." Why murderers? I did not ask him. I took it for granted that Don had learned a number of things in Moscow that he did not tell me. So far he has steadfastly refused to tell them, or anything else, to anyone.

V

The Sherman incident, which was no fault of mine, was followed by another that was. Early in our acquaintance, Bykov made me recite a list of all my contacts with minute descriptions of their jobs, backgrounds, habits and a personal evaluation of each. When I reached the name of Ludwig Lore, Bykov had one of his tantrums. "How do you know the Lore?" he asked darkly. I told him. He ordered me never to see Lore again.

But, in the midst of my troubles with Bykov, the Lore household was a peaceful haven to me. I went there less often, and I always watched carefully to see if I were followed, but I still went there. In December of 1936, Lore pressed me to come to a big dinner that he was giving to celebrate the holidays. I pled that there would be too many guests. Lore insisted that they would all be "nonpolitical," just old friends of his; I need not worry about any of them. I still do not understand what antic mood moved him to invite me. Neither do I understand why I accepted. But in those days I was a troubled man.

I went to the Lores' early. The first guest to arrive was Max Nomad, the author, a militant anti-Communist, to whom Lore introduced me simply as Carl. Nomad looked me up and down, turned away and asked: "How long is it, Ludwig, since you entertain the G.P.U. in your house?" Worse was to follow. Alphonse Goldschmitt, the economist, arrived. Again, I was introduced as Carl. It was then that Dr. Goldschmitt fixed me sternly and asked: "Why do you call yourself 'Carl'? I knew you in Moscow in 1932. You are Colonel Dietrich of the General Staff." There was some natural stir among the guests, of whom there were several others, including a former editor of the *Berliner Tageblatt*, and a little round woman who played the harpsichord. After that, it was a somewhat strained evening, with everyone uncomfortably eyeing everybody else to try to guess what apparatus he belonged to—not without reason I was soon to learn.

I left before the rest. Lore accompanied me into the hall and apologized. "I am so sorry," he said. "It was impermissible of Dr. Goldschmitt to embarrass you by telling your name in front of everybody." I said that Dr. Goldschmitt certainly had a remarkable memory.

The next time I met Bykov, he greeted me by saying: "*Du bist bei dem Lore gewesen*—you've seen Lore." I said, yes, that I had seen Lore. Bykov was surprisingly relaxed. "He is a Trotskyist, isn't he?" he asked in a purring voice. I said that Lore was an old and tired revolutionist who had become some kind of liberal. "He is a Trotskyist," said Bykov flatly.

The Great Purge was on. Trotskyists were now held to be "diversionist mad dogs and counterrevolutionary wreckers." The implication was that, if Lore was a Trotskyist, and I had visited him, especially against orders, then I must also be a counterrevolutionist (like Don, Bykov was ahead of time). I saw that his gloating pleasure at having caught me was greater for once than his fear.

I never knew which of my fellow guests had been the other underground worker who reported to Bykov that I had sat with him at Lore's table.

VI

Bykov's friendly moods were much harder to bear than his routine rages. Their purposes were so transparent and their hypocrisy so painful. For he alternated calculated roughness with calculated chumminess, according to a pattern practiced by police the world over. But, like almost everything else, Bykov had simply memorized the rules. He applied them by formula without skill or intuition. When he had decided to be charming, he would veil his reddish eyes with his reddish lashes and, instead of glaring sullenly, would peer furtively from under them. In a burst of uncomfortable comradeship, he would grasp my arm in a grip that was as comradely as if he were marching me to a chopping block. He would soften his badgering voice to a mere banter or wheedle.

The first time that I experienced this startling transformation amidst the storms of our early acquaintanceship, Bykov hooked his arm in mine and said with alarming coziness: "Tell me about the *Quellen*." The image that always came into my mind when I heard that German word was a spring of water welling from the ground. "What *Quellen*?" I asked. "What *Quellen*!" Bykov echoed derisively, stopping and gesturing. "*Die Quellen, die Quellen*!" I turned the word into French to see if that would widen its meaning: *die Quellen—les sources*. Then I understood. We had never before called Alger Hiss and the others "sources."

V I I

I described the sources. Bykov put me through a long cross-examination about them. The main theme, repeated in endless variations, was always the same: "Are they secret police agents? How do you know they are not?" Obviously, if I knew, they could no longer be secret police agents. Therefore, the question was always unanswerable, and its pointlessness, iterated, sometimes for hours, exhausted me physically. But I sensed that cross-examination was one of Bykov's intellectual pleasures. In time, I came to think that it was his only one. I suspected that he was a former G.P.U. examiner.

From Bykov's questions, it was clear that he had already studied some report on the Washington sources and had memorized it minutely. He was most interested in Alger Hiss and Harry Dexter White, least interested in Wadleigh and Abel Gross. But whenever I suggested that we drop Wadleigh and Gross to make the apparatus more compact and more secure, he would not hear of it.

"What is Hiss's profession?" he asked me at one point. I said that Alger Hiss was a lawyer (in German, *Advokat*). "That is right," he said, as if checking it against his own information. "Henceforth, we will call Hiss 'Der *Advokat*.' "

The Christmas holidays were not far off. "What shall we give the sources?" Bykov asked. "Shall we give them a big sum of money?"

I was horrified. "Money!" I said. "They would be outraged. You don't understand. They are Communists on principle. If you offer them money, they will never trust you again. They will do nothing for you."

"All right, so they are Communists," he said, "but it is you, Bob, who do not understand." He spoke with a patient cynicism that pled with my stupidity, which baffled him. "*Siehst du,* Bob," he said, "*wer auszahlt ist der Meister, und wer Geld nimmt muss auch etwas geben*—who pays is boss, and who takes money must also give something." In those words, as if he stood beside me, I can still hear clearly the ring of Bykov's voice. He is saying: Communism has turned to corrupting itself.

Something in me more lucid than mind knew that I had reached the end of an experience, which was not only my experience. Out of that vision of Almighty Man that we call Communism and that agony of souls and bodies that we call the revolution of the 20th century was left that pinch of irreducible dust: "Who pays is boss, and who takes money must also give something." It might stand as the motto of every welfare philosophy. I sensed that those rags were truth because they were rags. They pretended nothing, for they had lost the knowledge that there is anything but rags. They concealed nothing, for they had lost the distinction between good and evil. The innocence of their shamelessness was its pathos. Henceforth, I knew that I was in the pit, though my mind would seek to elude the knowledge for many months.

I said to Bykov hopelessly: "You will lose every one of them."

He shrugged his shoulders. "Then we must give them some costly present," he said, "so that they will know that they are dealing with big, important people. You will buy four rugs, big, expensive rugs. You will give White, Silverman, Wadleigh and *Der Advokat* each one a rug. You will tell them that it is a gift from the Soviet people in gratitude for their help."

I said: "You know, these are good people, but they are not stupid people."

"Stupid!" he snapped. "Who's stupid? *Porca madonna!*" It was Bykov's invariable blasphemy, apparently the one thing that he had learned during his brief stay in Italy. I had insulted him. In time, I discovered that the only way to get along with him was to insult him. Every time he made me insult him, I disliked him more because he made me dislike myself more. On the other hand, he respected me more.

Before we separated, Bykov gave me a thousand dollars, or close to a thousand dollars, to buy the four rugs.

VIII

Eleven years later, during the Hiss Case, Bykov's "costly presents" became important in a way that he could never have foreseen. For they were tangible evidence. They still existed. They established a material link between me and the four members of the apparatus.

I did not buy the rugs myself. I knew nothing about Oriental rugs. I went to my old college friend, Meyer Schapiro. His knowledge was great and his taste flawless. Without telling him my purpose, I asked him if he would select and buy for me four Oriental rugs, and have them shipped to Washington. I gave him the money and George Silverman's address.

Schapiro did not ask me why I wanted the rugs. Nor did I ask him, when he presently told me that he had shipped them, where he had bought them. No experienced underground worker would want to know such a detail.

The rugs arrived in Washington. I had already carried out Bykov's instructions. I had given White, Silverman and Hiss Bykov's message from the grateful Soviet people. To my surprise, I saw that in the case of Silverman and White, Bykov had been right and I was wrong. They were clearly impressed. I was not quite sure what Alger Hiss thought. For the first time, I felt a riffle of disgust at my comrades, that is to say, at myself. I was one of them.

Silverman delivered Harry White's rug to him.

Years later, a member of Elizabeth Bentley's apparatus, with which Harry White was then working, visited his home. She noticed a handsome Oriental on the floor and said, "Why, that looks like one of those Soviet rugs" (presumably there had been other gifts from the grateful Soviet people). There was an awkward silence during which White became very nervous. When his friend next visited White, the rug was no longer on the floor.

The delivery of Alger Hiss's rug presented a special problem. I solved it by having Silverman drive his car with Alger's rug in it and park at night behind a restaurant on the Baltimore turnpike, called The Yacht, or some such nautical name, where Hiss and I sometimes had coffee. A few minutes later, I drove up with Alger in his car. The headlights were turned off in both cars, which were parked so that, in the dark, neither Hiss nor Silverman could see each other. I got out and carried the rug from Silverman's car to Hiss's, then he and I drove off.

All the other recipients were delighted with their "costly presents." But I never felt that Alger was. His was a very handsome red rug, but a little vivid. For a long time, he kept it roped up in a closet at the front of the basement dining room of the 30th Street house. In the Department of Justice Building in Washington, in 1949, I asked Claudia Catlett, one of Hiss's maids, who testified for him at both trials, if she remembered the rug in the closet. "Oh, yes," she said in the presence of several F.B.I. agents. Mrs. Hiss had once unrolled the rug and showed it to her, and Claudia Catlett had declared that it was a shame to keep such a handsome rug in a closet.

I believe that I had David Carpenter announce the coming of his rug to Julian Wadleigh. Probably Carpenter delivered it, for I have no recollection of how that was done. Indeed, for a long time, I remembered only three rugs and so testified. But since Meyer Schapiro was never at any time a Communist, and lacked the conspiratorial flair, he had kept the receipt for the rugs during all those years, so that there was documentary proof that there had been four of them.

Just before Alger Hiss was indicted, I have been told, George Silverman who, until then, had pled self-incrimination to practically all questions, suddenly admitted to the Grand Jury that he had had the rugs in his house. So far as I know, he never admitted anything else, and he invented a story, according to which, if I remember rightly, he and I had bought the rugs on speculation. But his sudden admission was startling enough in itself. In 1948, Julian Wadleigh still had his rug.

Alger Hiss had already testified that I once gave him a rug—at an earlier date and as "payment in kind" for "unpaid rent" on his 28th Street apartment. The value of the rug, incidentally, would have been more than the amount of the alleged rent. Hiss never produced the rug, though he admitted that it was still in his possession.

The date on Meyer Schapiro's receipt (late December 1936), together with the time it would have taken to ship the rugs to Washington, pretty well established the fact that Alger Hiss had known me in 1937, part of the period during which he had denied to the Grand Jury that he had seen me.

IX

On the four rugs we marched straight into active espionage. Early in 1937, Bykov began a personal inspection of the sources. He was, in general, so unimpressive, his manner was so rude and his cynicism so habitual, that I was afraid that his effect on a man like Alger Hiss, whom Bykov had chosen as the first subject to be interviewed, would be little short of disastrous. At first by indirection, and then quite openly, I began to prepare Alger for a disillusionment. I warned him not to expect too much, that Bykov was by no means the best that the underground had to show, but that in him we served the party and not the man.

Alger went to New York for the meeting. I met him by prearrangement in Manhattan, and took him to the Prospect movie theater on Ninth Avenue, in Brooklyn, where Bykov would meet us. Hiss and I were sitting on a bench in the mezzanine when Bykov came out of the audience. As they shook hands, Bykov smiled pleasantly, almost bashfully. Since Bykov did not trust himself to speak English, I interpreted for them.

We left the Prospect Theater together and presently made our way to the Port Arthur restaurant in Manhattan's Chinatown.

Bykov had himself well in hand. There was no rudeness, no cynicism, and he had stiffened his manner with a briskness that did duty for dignity. He had decided on the historical approach. The Socialist Fatherland (Russia) was threatened, he said, with encirclement by the Fascist powers—Germany and Italy in Europe, Japan in the East. The other imperialist powers, Britain, the United States, France—were secretly abetting this encirclement, hoping that the Fascists would destroy the Soviet Union for them. This was not news to Hiss.

But Bykov did it rather well, with flashbacks to the Allied attempts at intervention in the Russian civil war, so that the persistent character of the imperialist threat to Communism was stressed, while over the bodies of the "Fascist beasts" could be heard the thundering hoofs of the triumphant "*Konarmiya*"—Marshal Budenny's "horse army" which Bykov invoked.

Now the conflict had risen to a new plane, and the Soviet Union was threatened by a greater, more conscious coalition. It would not succeed, of course. For one thing, the Soviet Union could count on the help of the comrades abroad. There were many ways of helping. Alger Hiss could help, too, for one of the great needs was information about the Fascist plans. It was, for example, necessary to know what the American State Department knew about them. It was necessary to see the actual documents—especially those relating to Germany and the Far East.

"Ask him," said Bykov, "if he is prepared to help us in that way." I smiled and dutifully put Bykov's question to Alger Hiss, who also smiled. The question had been answered long ago. The preamble was superfluous. Later, I concluded that Bykov's method, which would have annoyed me, was effective with the others. Alger said that he was prepared to do whatever we wanted.

"Ask him," said Bykov eagerly, "if the brother will also bring out material?" By "the brother," Bykov meant Donald Hiss, Alger's younger brother, who was a legal adviser to the newly created Philippines Division of the State Department.

In his own way Alger answered: no. I translated his answer into German for Bykov: "Ask him," said Bykov, "if he can persuade the brother." For "persuade" Bykov used the word, "überreden," which in his special German, came out "ibber-edden." I could not understand him and Bykov had to repeat the word several times with growing irritation. I remember the exchange distinctly because I saw a curious expression in Alger's eyes. He was wondering why Carl, the good European, should have difficulty in interpreting.

I could have spared myself any concern about Bykov's impression on Alger Hiss. He said that he had found Bykov "impressive." I had underrated the transforming power of anything Russian.

X

The meeting with Alger Hiss was followed by a meeting with Henry Collins, the treasurer of the Ware Group, also in Brooklyn. Again I was the interpreter. Bykov believed that Collins should be able to enter the State Department or, failing that, that he could make valuable contacts there. Collins was just as impressed by Bykov as Alger Hiss had been.

David Carpenter followed Henry Collins in Bykov's inspection. That meeting also took place in New York. Julian Wadleigh followed Carpenter, this time in Washington. Their meeting is chiefly memorable for the fact that Wadleigh carried away from it, over the years, the fixed impression that Bykov, whom I had introduced to him as "Sasha," had only one arm. During the Hiss Case, that singular error of recollection to which Wadleigh testified (at that time, of course, without my knowledge), was to cause considerable perplexity to the Grand Jury and endless perplexity to me when they questioned me obliquely about it. Fortunately, Keith, who knew Bykov, if anything better than I did, soon testified that the Colonel had full use of both arms.

Next Bykov met George Silverman and Harry Dexter White, also in Washington. He never, to my knowledge, met Abel Gross.

Those meetings were important chiefly as they marked the beginning of intensive espionage. The water was already in the pipes. Bykov's function was simply to turn on the faucets. Only in the case of Harry White, I think, did he stimulate any enthusiasm that was lacking before. For, more than any of the others, White, the non-Communist, enjoyed the feeling that he was in direct touch with "big important people."

I have sometimes been asked at this point: What went on in the minds of those Americans, all highly educated men, that made it possible for them to betray their country? Did none of them suffer a crisis of conscience? The question presupposes that whoever asks it has still failed to grasp that Communists mean exactly what they have been saying for a hundred years: they regard any government that is not Communist, including their own, merely as the political machine of a class whose power they have organized expressly to overthrow by all means, including violence. Therefore, ultimately the problem of espionage never presents itself to them as a problem of conscience, but as a problem of operations. Making due allowance for the differences of intelligence, energy, background and political development among the individual men involved, and bearing in mind that two of them (White and Wadleigh) were not Communists, but fellow travelers, the answer to the question must still be: no problem of conscience was then involved. For the Communists, the problem of conscience had been settled long before, at the moment when they accepted the program and discipline of the Communist Party. For the fellow travelers, it had been settled at the moment when they decided to co-operate with the Communist Party. And of fellow travelers who co-operate to the point of espionage, it must be observed that in effect they have become Communists, whatever fictive differences they may maintain.

Faced with the opportunity of espionage, a Communist, though he may sometimes hesitate momentarily, will always, exactly to the degree that he is a Communist, engage in espionage. The act will not appear to him in terms of betrayal at all. It will, on the contrary, appear to him as a moral act, the more deserving the more it involves him in personal risk, committed in the name of a faith (Communism) on which, he believes, hinges the hope and future of mankind, and against a system (capitalism) which he believes to be historically bankrupt. At that point, conscience to the Communist, and conscience to the non-Communist, mean two things as opposed as the two sides of a battlefield. The failure to understand that fact is part of the total failure of the West to grasp the nature of its enemy, what he wants, what he means to do and how he will go about doing it. It is part of the failure of the West to understand that it is at grips with an enemy having no moral viewpoint in common with itself, that two irreconcilable viewpoints and standards of judgment, two irreconcilable moralities, proceeding from two irreconcilable readings of man's fate and future are involved, and, hence, their conflict is irrepressible.

The question of conscience can arise only when, for one reason or another, a Communist questions his faith, as I was about to do, or as, later on, in different ways Wadleigh and Keith would do. Then it rises terribly indeed.

X I

To take care of the flow of documents which the sources now began to produce, it became necessary to set up a photographic workshop. The first workshop was organized in Baltimore. Among David Carpenter's contacts were a man and wife who were Communist sympathizers. The husband was engaged in a small novelty business. His wife was a part-time teacher in the public schools. Carpenter arranged with them to rent the use of their apartment to the apparatus on whatever nights it was needed. I never told these people what their apartment was to be used for, and I doubt that Carpenter ever did. They always went out and left us alone on the nights when photography was done. But since photographic equipment was left in a suitcase or bag in their closet, they could scarcely have been in doubt that something rather odd was going on. (Incidentally, it was this man* who, in Grand Jury days, asked to listen to me speak because the man he knew as Carl spoke like a European.)

The existence of this Baltimore workshop has been established not only by my testimony, but by the testimony of the man and wife, and by Keith, who worked there briefly. It was the first workshop in which photography was done for Bykov, and it is Keith's recollection that there were large numbers of documents. For documents from all the sources were at first photographed at the Baltimore apartment, though not all on the same night.

The system of transmission was as follows. In the case of Alger Hiss, he would bring home a brief case containing documents from the State Department. I would go to his 30th Street house about the time of his arrival, that is about five o'clock in the evening, or a little later. We would transfer the documents from Hiss's brief case to one that I had brought (thus if the documents were found in my possession, Hiss could always claim that I had stolen them from him). I would then take the documents to Baltimore to be photographed, returning them to Alger Hiss late the same night, or, possibly, in a few instances, the next morning.

In the case of Harry Dexter White, George Silverman acted as the go-between. He would take a brief case of documents from White,

* In 1949, he testified before the Grand Jury about these matters. Therefore, I had not intended to divulge his name, for I could see no public advantage, and much private disadvantage, in doing so. But since this chapter was written, the House Committee on Un-American Activities has seen fit to call him before it, and it is now public knowledge that his name is William Spiegel.

which he would later give to me. They would be photographed in Baltimore and returned to Silverman the same night or the next morning. In the case of Wadleigh and Abel Gross, Carpenter was the go-between who received the brief cases of documents and turned them over to me.

My function was primarily that of contact with the sources and intermediaries, like Silverman and Carpenter. It was poor organization for me, as courier, to be connected directly with the photographic workshop. It established a direct personal circuit between all parts of the apparatus. Bykov solved that problem in two ways.

In New York, he introduced me to a young American "technical worker" whom he called "Felix." Felix, said Bykov, was an expert photographer. Bykov then instructed Felix to move to Baltimore and find himself a job as a "cover." That Felix promptly did, working for some downtown electrical or photographic concern. He also rented an apartment for himself and his wife on Callow Avenue, and set up a photographic workshop there. The original photographic workshop was presently abandoned, and I did not see its tenants again until we were all appearing before the Grand Jury in 1949.

In the first Baltimore workshop I had already taught Carpenter the rudiments of photographic copying. He then organized a second photographic workshop in Washington, again renting an apartment belonging to the Communist Party members or sympathizers. I must once have known the name of those people, but I have forgotten it. I was in the Washington workshop only once or twice, and neither I nor anybody else has yet been able to locate it. Probably its identification must wait until David Carpenter decides to testify about it. So far, he has pled self-incrimination on all material points.

The documents from the four active sources were now redistributed between the workshops. The material from Abel Gross and Wadleigh was photographed by Carpenter in the Washington apartment. Carpenter usually handled the whole transaction with the sources, receiving the documents from them, and returning them after they had been copied. He simply turned over to me the finished film for delivery to Bykov.

At first, Carpenter developed the films. Later, for greater security in transmission, Bykov ordered that film was to be turned over undeveloped. It would be developed elsewhere, probably in one of Bykov's New York workshops. Like me, Carpenter was a poor photographer, and his films, when developed, sometimes turned out to be botched. After one of those failures, which always aroused Bykov's suspicions ("Carpenter, that dirty boy, is he working against us?"), Carpenter would go back to developing his film before turning it in. Then Bykov would again decide to receive the film undeveloped until the next botched job. That seesaw pattern continued to the end, and it is the reason why, among the film that in 1948 I secreted in a pumpkin, there were three spools which had lain undeveloped for ten years.

The documents from Hiss and White were photographed by Felix in his Baltimore apartment. Felix would meet me in Washington in the early evening. I would turn over to him the brief case of documents that had been given me by Hiss or Silverman (for White). Felix would drive back to Baltimore with them in his car. After they were photographed, he would return them to me, usually later that same night in Washington, or, occasionally, in Baltimore. I would then return them to Hiss or Silverman late that same night. On nights when, for some reason, Felix was going to return the brief case to me in Baltimore, I would sometimes drive from Washington to Baltimore with him.

One night, as we returned to Baltimore, I asked Felix to drive me downtown. We decided that he should first drop the brief case of documents at his apartment. He parked the car near Callow Avenue in such a position that, from where I sat, I could see Felix go into an apartment house and come out again. I did not know the number of the house and I tried to put what I had seen out of my mind, for until then I had not known where Felix did his photography and I did not want to know. It was due to that slender chance that, eleven years later, I was able to point out to the F.B.I. the block of houses which I believed I had seen Felix enter. In a matter of hours, the F.B.I. discovered that, in 1937, a man named Felix Inslerman had rented an apartment in that block of Callow Avenue. A few more hours, and the F.B.I. had located Felix, who until then had been no more than a first name. He was living near Schenectady, N. Y., where he was employed by the General Electric Company (before that he had worked for the Glenn L. Martin airplane factory near Baltimore). Among other interesting oddments in Felix Inslerman's house, the agents found a Leica camera.

A camera leaves tiny, characteristic abrasions on film, just as a gun scratches a bullet that it has fired. Thus, it is possible to establish from those minute marks what camera was used in photographing a given strip of film. In the celebrated pumpkin were two strips of developed film on which Felix had photographed State Department documents given me by Alger Hiss. A Government expert certified that the minute marks on the film had been made by the same Leica camera which was found in Felix's possession in Schenectady. In both Hiss trials, the defense agreed to stipulate the point. That is the law's way of saying that the defense agreed to consider it as an established fact.

Felix pled self-incrimination.

XII

The Washington apparatus was not Bykov's only apparatus. He headed at least one other, based in New York City, with sources in Chicago, New England, Washington and elsewhere. Its function was industrial espionage, which, in an age of total war, means military espionage. I never had direct connection with that apparatus (though I was once introduced to one of its members). I knew of its existence and its personnel from hearsay. My testimony about it was later corroborated and amplified by Keith, who played in it roughly the same role that I played in the Washington apparatus. It is an important part of the Hiss Case that few people are aware of.

At the time I first testified about it, I knew only of two of its members and their names. One of them was important. He was the head of the experimental laboratory of a great steel company, himself a metallurgist of conspicuous ability, and a Communist. He was scarcely out of engineering college when he made certain useful inventions or improvements in metallurgical processes which he turned over at once to the Soviet consul in San Francisco. In 1937, he spent his week-ends, I had been told by Keith, flying from Chicago to New York to meet Bykov, presumably to transmit information to him. I considered the man so dangerous that (without mentioning Keith or Bykov) I turned over his name to United States security officers years before the Hiss Case began.

Another member of the second apparatus had been an expert in the War Department. He was a White Russian refugee in the United States. I believe that he had been a Tsarist officer before the Russian Revolution. His sister had not escaped from Russia. She was still living in Moscow. Keith once described to me how Bykov used to bring the unhappy expert to tears by threatening to have his sister turned out on the Moscow streets if he did not produce the material that Bykov demanded.

There were at least two other members of that apparatus whom I did not know about, but about whom Keith later testified. One was a man strategically placed with a nationally known munitions company. At the time of Keith's testimony, in 1949, this man had transferred to a nationally known aircraft company in California. Another member of the apparatus was a Russian engineer, also a refugee. I know only his surname and the fact that he was apparently useful to the Soviet apparatuses. Very likely, investigation has turned up other connections of this group, but of that I cannot speak.

I knew of the group at all only because, in 1937, Bykov decided to release Keith from the underground. "You look like a Russian," Bykov said to me in explaining his purpose, "but you are really an American; you get things done. Keith looks like an American, but he is really a Russian; he is a dreamer." Bykov planned to detach Keith gradually from the apparatus and therefore proposed to send him first to Washington to work with me. It was that tactic of Bykov's that enabled me to testify about the second apparatus. For, in Washington, Keith, who had always been friendly with me, gave me the facts about the second apparatus that I later gave the F.B.I.

Some time in the late summer of 1937, Keith, with Bykov's blessing, left the Soviet apparatus and returned to the open Communist Party in Los Angeles. There he once more met the man who had recruited both of us into the underground, John Sherman. When I shook hands with Keith in Washington (for the last time, I thought), I gave him as a stake all of my own money that I could spare. He did not know what lay behind my eyes as I wished him well or with what friendly envy I stood watching his car head for the West. For I already knew what I could not tell him—that I, too, must soon go out of the Communist Party by a road that could never be as simple as Keith's.

XIII

The volume of production by the Washington sources was high. Hiss's, Wadleigh's and Abel Gross's brief cases were well filled. But Bykov was continuously exasperated by their material and distrustful of them. In part, this was a deliberate policy of harassment. In part,

I think that at times Bykov convinced himself that he was being cheated. Usually, he would charge that the sources were purposely turning over worthless material and holding back more valuable information. In more charitable moods, he would merely sneer at the sources. Sometimes he would greet me, on my weekly arrival in New York from Washington, with a sullen stare and a favorite question: "How is our dear child today?" "What dear child?" I would ask, knowing perfectly well who was meant. *"Unser lieber Advokat,"* Bykov would answer derisively, "our dear lawyer." I would think of Alger Hiss and the others whose whole lives now turned on doing the apparatus' bidding.

Yet I was in the curious position of agreeing with Bykov about the value of the material, but for different reasons. In the early days, out of curiosity, I read Hiss's, White's and Wadleigh's documents. I quickly gave it up and seldom glanced at them afterwards. I concluded that political espionage was a magnificent waste of time and effort—not because the sources were holding back; they were pathetically eager to help—but because the secrets of foreign offices are notoriously overrated. There was little about political espionage, it seemed to me, that an intelligent man, who knew the forces, factors and general direction of history in our time, could not arrive at by using political imagination, backed by a careful study of the available legitimate facts.

I can remember only one specific assignment that Bykov gave. He once instructed me to request "our dear child" to steal the State Department's official seal—a request that Alger Hiss met with the same skeptical smile with which I delivered it. Otherwise, Bykov, in the Russian fashion, preferred the dragnet or volumetric production of documents. But he was obsessed by all information about the anti-Comintern Pact between Germany, Italy and Japan. I once asked him what he expected to find out that he did not already know about the Pact. The secret clauses, he said. He asked suspiciously why I was not curious about them. I answered that the secret clauses did not make the slightest difference. Whether or not there were secret clauses, it would always be necessary to assume that there were and that they must be directed against the Soviet Union. It was not necessary to read them because anybody who knew the world situation could write them sight unseen for himself. Bykov could write them. Documentary proof of them would not change by one iota the diplomatic or military dispositions of the Soviet Union. Reluctantly, Bykov agreed.

This is not said to minimize in any way the danger constituted by the Washington apparatus. It was formidable. No government can function with enemies dedicated to its destruction posted high and low in its foreign, or any other, service. Moreover, the Russians were able to use the Hiss (and possibly the Wadleigh) documents to break the State Department codes. Thus, in effect, they had a tap on the American diplomatic trunk lines. Of that fact I had no inkling until State Department officials testified to it in 1948. If Alger Hiss guessed it, and from his intimate knowledge of the State Department I do not see how he could have failed to, he did not mention it to me.

In the persons of Alger Hiss and Harry Dexter White, the Soviet Military Intelligence sat close to the heart of the United States Government. It was not yet in the Cabinet room, but it was not far outside the door. In the years following my break with the Communist Party, the apparatus became much more formidable. Then Hiss became Director of the State Department's Office of Special Political Affairs and White became an Assistant Secretary of the Treasury. In a situation with few parallels in history, the agents of an enemy power were in a position to do much more than purloin documents. They were in a position to influence the nation's foreign policy in the interests of the nation's chief enemy, and not only on exceptional occasions, like Yalta (where Hiss's role, while presumably important, is still ill-defined) or through the Morgenthau Plan for the destruction of Germany (which is generally credited to White), but in what must have been the staggering sum of day-to-day decisions. That power to influence policy had always been the ultimate purpose of the Communist Party's infiltration. It was much more dangerous, and, as events have proved, much more difficult to detect, than espionage, which beside it is trivial, though the two go hand in hand.

XIV

In Washington, the work lapsed into the monotony of a well-organized underground apparatus—meetings by day, meetings and transmission of materials by night. Two meetings, with the precaution of long advance rambles to throw off possible surveillance, would occupy an afternoon.

I had discovered at once that the meeting techniques used in New York were not suited to Washington. That big and beautiful village lacked the cover of teeming crowds. Its streets lay too open. People were too conscious of the proximity of government and, therefore, of security—at least the underground acted on the assumption that they were. Restaurants were too few, too small and too crowded, for in them crowds were a disadvantage. The man at the next table was almost certainly in some branch of the Government, and people in Government too often recognized one another. Movie houses, except at night, were too empty.

I quickly decided that the most anonymous places in Washington were drug stores. In summer, everybody crowded in for a quick soft drink, in winter for coffee. At first, I met almost everyone in drug stores. The first man at such a meeting would buy a Coke or a pack of cigarettes, idle around the novelties or leaf through a magazine from the rack. When the second man appeared, neither would greet the other. They would saunter out on the street and greet each other only when they were satisfied that there was no surveillance.

Later, I developed a system of meeting on the street which I believed to be almost surveillance-proof. Two men would prearrange a meeting. Both would agree to start walking toward one another at the same time from two different points some twenty blocks apart on the same street. One might walk east, one west. One would walk on one side of the street, one on the other. They would meet about midway. Usually, each would sight the other several blocks away. While they were walking, each would have a clear view for blocks behind the other. No one could follow either without being observed by the other. If either were suspicious, he would not greet the other. Each would continue walking until one turned and followed the other to catch up with him later in a side street. This method was only good in quiet residential neighborhoods where there were few people on the streets. These conspiratorial methods, while technically justified, were almost wholly unnecessary, for even a decade later the nation still could scarcely believe that such a thing as an underground existed.

Bykov, too, introduced an innovation into the Washington underground. It was Alger Hiss's custom to bring home documents from the State Department approximately once a week or once in ten days. He would bring out only the documents that happened to cross his desk on that day, and a few that on one pretext or another he had been able to retain on his desk. Bykov wanted more complete coverage. He proposed that the *Advokat* should bring home a brief case of documents every night. These would be typed in the Hiss household, either in full or in summary. Then, when I next visited him, Alger would turn over to me the typed copies, covering a week's documents, as well as the brief case of original documents that he had brought home that night. The original documents would be photographed and returned to Alger Hiss. The typed copies would be photographed and then returned to me by Felix. I would destroy them.

Sometimes important documents passed through Alger's hand, but he was able to keep them only for a short time, often only long enough to read them. He took to making penciled copies of such documents or notes of their main points, which he wrote down hastily on State Department memo pads. These he turned over to me also, usually tearing off the State Department letterhead lest I forget.

It was a number of these typed documents and penciled memos in Alger's certified handwriting that I secreted during the days when I was breaking with the Communist Party.

Harry Dexter White, in addition to giving original documents, also wrote a weekly or fortnightly longhand memo covering documents that he had seen, or information that had come to him, in the course of a week's work in the Treasury Department. One of those memos, running to four or five pages, I also secreted. It is now in the custody of the Justice Department and Senator Nixon read it into the Congressional Record shortly after the conviction of Alger Hiss.

Abel Gross and Wadleigh never turned over anything but original documents.

X V

Harry Dexter White was the least productive of the four original sources. Through George Silverman, he turned over material regularly, but not in great quantity. Bykov fumed, but there was little that he could do about it. As a fellow traveler, White was not subject to discipline. Bykov suspected, of course, that White was holding back material. *"Du musst ihn kontrollieren,"* said Bykov, "you must control him"—in the sense in which police "control" passports, by inspecting them.

I went to J. Peters, who was in Washington constantly in 1937, and whom I also saw regularly in New York. I explained the problem to him and asked for a Communist in the Treasury Department who could "control" White. Peters suggested Dr. Harold Glasser, who certainly seemed an ideal man for the purpose, since he was White's assistant, one of several Communists whom White himself had guided into the Treasury Department.

Peters released Dr. Glasser from the American Communist underground and lent him to the Soviet underground. Glasser soon convinced me that White was turning over everything of importance that came into his hands. Having established that fact, I simply broke off relations with Dr. Glasser. Later on, he was to establish a curious link between the underground apparatuses, current and past. Testifying before the McCarran Committee in 1952, Elizabeth Bentley told this story. In 1944, she was working with what she identified as "the Perlo Group" (after Victor Perlo of the former Ware Group). In the Perlo Group was Dr. Harold Glasser. At one point, Miss Bentley had made a routine check of the past activities of all the Group members. The check showed that Dr. Glasser had once worked with a man whom both Victor Perlo and Charles Kramer (also a member of the Group) at first refused to identify beyond saying that the unknown man was working with the Russians. When Miss Bentley insisted, Perlo and Kramer at last said that the unknown man was named Hiss. She had never heard the name before and checked with her Soviet superiors. "It is all right," they told her. "Lay off the Hiss thing. He is one of ours, but don't bother about it any more."

Early in our acquaintanceship, I had told White that I knew nothing whatever about monetary theory, finance or economics. Nevertheless, in our rambles, when he was not complaining that the Secretary was in a bad humor, or rejoicing that he was in a good humor, White engaged in long monologues on abstruse monetary problems.

One project that he kept urging was a plan of his own authorship for the reform of the Soviet monetary structure or currency. He offered it as a contribution to the Soviet Government. I sensed that the project was extremely important to White. I took the proposal to Bykov. He was lukewarm. But he informed Moscow, which reacted with enthusiasm to the idea of having its monetary affairs "controlled" gratis by an expert of the United States Treasury Department.

Bykov suddenly instructed me to get White's plan from him at once. Haste had now become all important. But by then, White had gone on his summer vacation at a country place near Peterborough, N. H. I saw that I would have to go after him. While I was wondering how I should manage it, I met Alger Hiss.

Hiss has testified that at that time, August, 1937, he and his wife were vacationing on the eastern shore of Maryland. Probably that is true. But, if so, Hiss must have returned to Washington or Baltimore on personal business or for the purpose of meeting me, for we met. Simply in the course of conversation, as an example of the underground problem of the week, I told him, without mentioning Harry White's name or my reason for seeing him, that I had to go to Peterborough.

Suddenly it was decided that we make an outing of it and all three drive to New Hampshire. Priscilla stipulated only that we should drive most of the way on Route 202, which avoids the cities and winds through the countryside. It was a favorite route of hers and we usually took it when we drove in Pennsylvania together. That trip, completely unimportant in itself, became important in the Hiss trials. It was one incident of our clandestine association that I thought must yield some evidence to support my story of our association. At first, it seemed that I was right. I had said that, near Peterborough, the Hisses and I had seen Goldsmith's *She Stoops to Conquer*. The F.B.I. soon established the fact that the Peterborough Players had presented *She Stoops to Conquer* just once, on the night of August 10, 1937, and never before or after. My careful description of White's summer house and its approaches tallied with photographs of it. The pond was where I said it was. But, after twelve years, I could not locate the tourist home in Thomaston. I located the tourist home in Peterborough, but its guest book showed no signature of Alger Hiss in 1937. Obviously, if I had been lying, I would have taken care to contrive a better story, since there was no need to invent any story at all.

White turned in his plan for monetary reform, though I recall no particular excitement about it. I had assumed that his eagerness was the evidence of a disinterested love for monetary theory and concern for the Soviet Union. But I sometimes found myself wondering curiously why he worked for the apparatus at all. His motives always baffled me, possibly, I now think, because I kept looking for them in the wrong place.

I believe that someone else understood him much better. One

day, when I was working at *Time* magazine, there passed over my desk a little news story. It said that in Washington, there lived a carpenter named Harry White. To his surprise, he received one day a container of caviar. Then a case of vodka arrived. Once the mail brought an engraved invitation to attend a social occasion at the Soviet embassy. Then Harry White, the carpenter, received a telephone call. It was from Harry Dexter White, the Assistant Secretary of the Treasury. He had traced his strayed presents. The Soviet embassy had made a mistake in the address because of the similar names. Generously, Harry Dexter White proposed that the other Harry White keep half the goods and return half.

"I was going to send them all back to him," the carpenter told a newsman, "but I thought: 'He's the kind of fellow, that if I send them all back, will still think that I kept half.' So I did."

The fellow traveler had met the proletarian mind.

X V I

David Carpenter worked incessantly to broaden his side of the apparatus, and so secretly that even I seldom knew just what he was doing. Toward the end of 1937, he proposed a new recruit for the apparatus. His name was Franklin Victor Reno, but Carpenter introduced him to me as "Vincent," and so I always called him.

Reno had been an organizer for the Communist Party or the Young Communist League in Montana. There he had used the name Lance Clark. When Carpenter first mentioned him to me, Reno had just taken some special examination and thought that he might get a job working on a bombsight at the Aberdeen Proving Ground in Maryland. It did not seem probable to me that he would. For, in addition to his Communist past, he was an immature-looking young man with somewhat timid, rabbitlike eyes and a nervous manner. I underrated him grossly. He was a very able mathematician who had no difficulty in passing his examination and securing a job at the Proving Ground.

The bombsight on which Reno went to work ceased to be a military secret when American planes equipped with it were shot down in Europe and Asia during World War II. But in 1937 it was a military secret, and considerable precautions were taken to keep it one. Once Reno had begun to work at the Proving Ground, it became almost impossible to maintain contact with him. Moreover, he was living at the house of the officer who supervised his project.

Contact was finally resumed through an employe of the Federal Government in Washington.

Reno was obviously a source of great potential importance, and Bykov at once proposed that we set up a photographic workshop in Aberdeen. I suggested that he set it up in the railroad station since it would scarcely be more conspicuous there than anywhere else in that small, security-conscious town. By the time I broke with the Communist Party, Reno had brought out material only two or three times. There was not much of it and none of it was on the bombsight. It was photographed by Felix in Baltimore.

When I came to testify about it, in 1948, I could not tell what material Reno had given. But Reno knew. My defection apparently loosened his ties with the Soviet underground, though after my break I never saw him again. He seems to have drifted away from the Communist Party. He corroborated my testimony about him.

XVII

Henry Collins, the treasurer of the Ware Group, made several attempts to find himself a post in the State Department. They always failed, although by background, education, experience and manner, Collins seemed to be a natural candidate. Moreover, he had at least one good personal connection in the State Department. I found myself wondering a little anxiously why Collins failed. But it was not until one day in 1951 that I thought I understood at last, when a State Department officer said to me: "I noticed Collins trying to get in and I distrusted him from the start."

But what he could not do himself, Collins found someone else to do. Late in 1937, or very early in 1938, he brought a new recruit to the apparatus. Let me call him Worthington Wiggens. He was a member of the Communist Party and a scion of a socialite family. At the time Collins first introduced him to me, Wiggens was employed in one of the New Deal agencies. He and Collins both believed that Wiggens would have little trouble entering the State Department. Given his social connections, I thought so too, but given his general air of apathy, it seemed unlikely. As in the case of Reno, I misjudged Worthington Wiggens. In a very short time, he had found himself a place in the State Department.

Wiggens entered the State Department for the express purpose of working for the Soviet apparatus. He, Collins and I discussed the matter in plain terms. But he never gave documents to the apparatus during my time. I broke very soon after he entered the State Department. He remained with it for another ten years, at least until 1948, about which time, after Loyalty Board hearings, Wiggens resigned.

XVIII

There was one other member of the Bykov apparatus. He was in the Government. He was never an active source. At no time did he ever turn over information. He knows the pertinent facts in the Hiss Case. We looked at each other in silence in the presence of the Grand Jury of the Southern District of New York. We are still looking at each other in silence.

It is not my intention to name him here or to write more about him. He must decide whether he can find the strength to speak out. There is a simple decency in men that the Communist experience cannot destroy. It is an instinct that must have justice, that yearns for right and hates wrong. If it must be a party to wrong, it will die. That is why I have insisted, from the beginning, that it is impossible that at least one among the former members of the Ware Group will not at some time come forward to corroborate my story.

It is to that man, that unnamed member of the apparatus, that I am speaking. I know what it will cost him, not for himself, but for others, to speak out. For myself, therefore, I may not ask it of him. But I will advance three presences to plead with him in silence for the truth—the nation, his honor, my children.

XX

Into the strange Hades of the underground, the Soviet Union now and again releases a ghost. Don was one such ghost. By a curious chance, I was to meet another.

In the course of one of Colonel Bykov's question and answer periods, I mentioned an explosives chemist, with whom Ulrich's apparatus had once had contact, and whom I had known. Bykov suggested that I try to get in touch with that once helpful friend and see what he was now doing.

I found the chemist at the Chemists' Club on East 41st Street, in New York. We had lunch together. I do not remember what he told me about himself; in fact, I was not to see him again until

1949, when he testified before the Grand Jury in the Hiss Case. What he had to tell me about someone else was more exciting. Dr. Philip Rosenbliett, said the chemist, was back in the United States and for weeks had been trying to make contact with me—without success, an indication of how far underground I then was. The Doctor was staying at the Hotel Albert in New York.

I went to see him at once. He looked more gaunt and lifeless than he had at the time of his daughter's death. It was in large part, he told me, to be able to visit his daughter's grave that he had undertaken his current mission to the United States. It was a mission of extreme importance. The Doctor had been assigned to it by Molotov himself. It had resulted from the fact that Stalin had personally inspected the Soviet munitions industry and discovered, to his wrath, that there was no automatic shell-loading machinery. Shells were still being loaded by hand by women. (I no longer believe this part of the story, which I now take to be The Doctor's way of misleading me about the real destination of the shell-loading machinery—Republican Spain.)

The Doctor was in the United States to purchase such machinery. It was not a simple deal. The Soviet Government wanted not only the machines at less than list price. It wanted a mass of technical information along with its order. Would I undertake the task? I explained to The Doctor that that was out of the question.

Then, said Dr. Rosenbliett, I must put him in touch with the smartest Communist lawyer I knew, preferably one who had some experience with patent work. I proposed Lee Pressman. He not only seemed to me the smartest Communist lawyer I know, but he had once told me that he had done some patent work for the Rust brothers, not on their cotton picker, but on some minor patents.

A few days later, I introduced Lee Pressman to Dr. Rosenbliett. The meeting took the form of a late breakfast at Sacher's restaurant on Madison Avenue near 42nd Street, in New York. I soon left Pressman and The Doctor together. I met Lee at least once afterwards. He told me that Dr. Rosenbliett had connected him with a Russian named "Mark." Later on, J. Peters told me that Pressman and Mark in the course of an airplane flight to Mexico City, in connection with arms purchases for Republican Spain, had been forced down near Brownsville, Texas. Mark had been worried that newsmen or security agents might pry into the passenger list.

I also saw Dr. Rosenbliett once or twice again. He was pleased with Pressman. But The Doctor was not destined to spend much time at his daughter's grave. One morning I met him at his hotel to find him gray and shaken. Something, he said, had happened. It was this.

His instructions for his American mission had expressly stated that Dr. Rosenbliett was to have no contact with former friends in the United States. Despite that, The Doctor had paid a visit to someone he knew (I suspect, his wife's sister, the wife of the Trotskyist leader, James Cannon). As he left the apartment house after his call, The Doctor found a loiterer in the lower hall. He recognized the man as a G.P.U. agent whom he knew. The man recognized him.* The next morning Dr. Rosenbliett received a cable from Moscow curtly ordering him to return to Russia at once—to be purged, I thought, and so, from the haggard look on his face, did he. But I know that Dr. Rosenbliett is very much alive.

Lee Pressman's recollection of these matters differs materially from mine. Testifying under oath before the House Committee on Un-American Activities, in 1951, he denied that he had ever known Dr. Rosenbliett. But, then in 1948, Lee had greeted my first testimony about his Communist membership in the Ware Group as "the stale and lurid mouthings of a Republican exhibitionist."

By 1951, he was prepared to concede that he had been a Communist, that the Ware Group had existed, that he had been a member of it. He named three other members whom I had named. He could not remember four other members whom I had also named, and he insisted that he had never known me in Washington. He had seen me, he testified, only once. That was when he said I had brought into his New York office for legal advice a man named Eckhart, for whom he subsequently did some business. Pressman's files on the subject were no longer extant and his recollection had dimmed. He placed the year of my visit with Eckhart as 1936. I had placed Pressman's meeting with Dr. Rosenbliett and me in 1937.

About the date Pressman may or may not be right. But about the other parts of his recollection Pressman is unqualifiedly mistaken.

First, the facts about our Washington association and Pressman's connection with Dr. Rosenbliett are substantially as I have reported them. Second, I have never at any time been in any office

* According to a security officer of the State Department, the loitering agent was Dr. Rosenbliett's old friend, Nicholas Dozenberg, arrested by the F.B.I. as the head of a Soviet apparatus in 1939, following his exposure by General Walter Krivitsky in the *Saturday Evening Post*.

of Pressman's in New York or anywhere else, though I once visited his Washington apartment. Third, I have never known anyone named Eckhart.

Nevertheless, an Eckhart exists. I have seen photographs of him, but I have never known him. Curiously enough, he resides, or resided until recently, in Mexico City.

I thought it odd that Pressman opened his testimony, in 1948 (he was then denying my testimony in full), by demanding to know if any witness before the House Committee on Un-American Activities had charged him with espionage. He was assured that no one had. Nor is any such charge implied in what I have written here. The purchase of arms for the Spanish Republicans, even under Soviet auspices, and on Dr. Rosenbliett's peculiar terms, does not constitute espionage. So brisk a lawyer as Pressman must know that, even if he does not, for example, know the present whereabouts of Dr. Rosenbliett.

XXI

The underground disgorged one other ghost. Some time in 1937 or 1938, Hideo Noda, the perpetual phantom from Don's dead Japanese apparatus, flitted through New York again.

Bykov instructed me to meet him and to send him to a candy store far out in Brooklyn where Noda would be met by a Russian who would direct his further destiny. I saw Ned only for a moment, to give him the address. I did not ask, of course, where he had been since I had sent him on to a hotel in Southern France. Before Noda had been alert, somewhat as birds are, as if in him mental and physical brightness were one. Now he seemed a little faded and tired. Our brief meeting was stiff. Perhaps he still considered me a "diversionist mad dog" and was disappointed to find that I had not, after his denunciation of me to the Party, been purged. But I suspect that Noda was so silent because, had he begun to speak, the words that came out would have been: "Oh, horror, horror, horror!" I stood and watched Ned as he walked away, something that I did not often do. I never saw him again.

In 1939, the New York *Times* published his rather impressive obituary. In Tokyo, the promising Japanese-American painter Hideo Noda had died suddenly, of a "cerebral tumor." He was in his twenties. I wondered whether, in Ulrich's words, Noda had "been shot by them or shot by us."

XXI

Almost until the very end, I felt that there must be something human about Colonel Bykov if I could only reach it. For without it he was a caricature. But no man is a caricature. At last I gave up, chiefly from lack of interest. I decided that in his case the caricature actually was most of the man. It was a special kind of caricature. It was one of the images in which Communism creates those who have never known anything else. Most of Bykov's life had been lived under Communism. He believed that he was constantly enveloped by the American secret police because he could not imagine a society in which the secret police were not everywhere. If he could have imagined anything so badly organized, he would have been revolted. He was an awed admirer of Nechayev, the 19th-century Russian who carried the logic of revolution to its limit, teaching (Lenin, among others) that murder, kidnapping, arson, robbery and blackmail, all crimes, are justified if they serve the socialist cause. From Bykov I first learned the name of Nechayev, who also served Dostoievsky as the terrible prototype of Pyotr Stepanovitch Veskhovensky in *The Possessed.*

Bykov did not belong to the generation that had made the Revolution, and they seemed as alien and preposterous to him as foreigners. They belonged to another species and he talked about them the way people talk about the beastly or amusing habits of cows or pigs. Most of the surviving revolutionary leaders were shot while Bykov and I knew each other. As each foredoomed man made his brief transit from the dark agony of prison and torture into the Klieg-lighted agony of public trial and back to the darkness of execution cellar and death, Bykov had an appropriate slur or sneer for each.

"Stalin will show them," he would say as if the thought gratified a kind of gluttony, "he's a tough boy, a tough boy. Put your hand in his mouth and he will bite it off."

When Karl Radek was on trial for his life, Bykov gleefully recalled a barracks prank involving the Old Bolshevik, who had been one of the outstanding minds and wits of Lenin's circle. Radek (in better days) had been asked to address the officers of the G.P.U. Two or three times he telephoned to make sure that a special G.P.U. car would call for him. "We sent him a car," said Bykov, spluttering with laughter. "We sent a tank. We invited him to get in. 'Please to get in, Comrade Radek,' we said politely. He was an old fox. At first he did not want to get in. Then he was ashamed. So he got in. We drove him through the roughest streets. We nearly beat his brains out against the top of the tank."

Leo Kamenev was almost the only man I ever heard Bykov mention without a malicious splutter. After the former commissar and Soviet ambassador to Italy was purged and shot, Bykov suddenly said: "I saw Kamenev once. We were in a Moscow streetcar. It was so crowded we could not move. He was just standing there. Nobody took any notice of him." There passed over Bykov's face the sheepish expression that replaced distrust or cynicism only in moments of embarrassment. "It gave me a queer feeling," he said. "An old man, like that, who had been a big, powerful man, who had been a commissar, and he was simply standing in a streetcar. Nobody looked at him and he did not look at anybody."

"What is the matter with him?" I thought. Then I realized what was distressing Bykov. Kamenev on the streetcar was the living evidence that careers have an end.

"Where is Juliet Poyntz?" Bykov once asked me when the press had reported her disappearance and it was as clear to Bykov as to me that the G.P.U. had murdered the defenseless woman. "Gone with the wind," he answered himself gayly. For he liked to collect topical tags.

Brutality stirred something in him that at its mere mention came loping to the surface like a dog to a whistle. It was as close to pleasure as I ever saw him come. Otherwise, instead of showing pleasure, he gloated. He was incapable of joy, but he had moments of mean exultation. He was just as incapable of sorrow, though he felt disappointment and chagrin. He was vengeful and malicious. He would bribe or bargain, but spontaneous kindness or generosity seemed never to cross his mind. They were beyond the range of his feeling. In others he despised them as weaknesses.

Bykov was Jewish, but he was a violent anti-Semite. His hatred of rabbis was pathological. If we passed a rabbi on the street, Bykov, who was otherwise so careful, would stop dead and stare while his face worked with anger. With one hand, he would grab my sleeve. With the other, he would point while he sneered in an audible voice: "Look! Look!" I would have to pull him away. Apparently, he could not control himself.

His sense of human relationships was also inhuman. Somewhere in the G.P.U. manual, there must be a passage which says that, when two underground workers meet, the senior is to inquire about the junior's family. As a sign of our improving relations, Bykov at one point took to inquiring about my family. He always asked as soon as we met, in the same way and the same order, like a military roll call: "How is your wife? How is your daughter? How is your son?" Then he would snap with relief from what was plainly a detested civility to the business at hand. At first that amused me. Later it annoyed me. At last I broke the rules one night to ask him if he had any children of his own. "No," he answered as if I had insulted him.

Unlike most Russians to whom children are quite literally the flower and fruit of life, to be celebrated always with a great outwelling of love and joy, Bykov showed no interest in children whatever. Sometimes if a child ran across his path, he would curse.

Once toward the end of our relationship, in the days of our personal cease-fire, Bykov announced that he meant to introduce me to his wife. I recognized this as the supreme gesture of good will. We met in a restaurant, instead of a movie house. Mrs. Bykov was several inches taller than her husband. She was a Russian woman in early middle age, plain but attractive, very blonde, very brainless, very shy, due in part to the fact that she spoke no English, in part, I felt, because she was afraid of her husband. Something made her appearance rather odd. At last, I discovered what it was. She was one of those women who wear glasses as if they are advertising them. Her pince nez did not blend with that most ordinary face.

It was an uncomfortable meal. I could not communicate with Mrs. Bykov. She was the only Russian I had ever met who could not speak German. She sat blankly, now and again moving forward in her chair and venturing a few Russian words. At such times, Bykov's eyes would glaze with their sullen look. He would answer glumly and she would slump back as if slapped. Bykov sometimes spoke English to me for practice. He was speaking English then. Suddenly, without any bearing on our conversation, Mrs. Bykov uttered a perfectly intelligible English sentence. "It's a gay farce," she said, clearly, but without any expression whatever. Then she lapsed into silence. It was exactly as if a parrot had suddenly spoken behind us.

The conversation continued. Mrs. Bykov suddenly spoke again. "It's a gay farce," she said, looking at me with a little, pleading smile. She said it three or four times in the course of the meal, always the same four words, always in the same expressionless tone.

I wondered in what Soviet book or play that one English line occurred, which she had memorized for special occasions in the same way that Stalin had memorized one line of English to surprise American visitors to the Kremlin: "This way to the water closet, gentlemen."

I gave up the human hunt in Bykov after a brief cultural exchange. With most Russians, music is an instinct. So when Bykov confided to me one night that music moved him deeply, I thought: "Of course. This is the missing piece. This is the side that I have overlooked."

I thought of Chicherin, in the commissariat of foreign affairs, going to the piano, after all-night diplomatic sessions, to humor his antagonist, the German ambassador, Count Brockdorff-Rantzau, by faultlessly playing Beethoven. I thought of Grigori Piatekov, the vice-commissar for heavy industry, playing Mozart between the massive sessions on hydroelectric projects. I thought of Lenin denying himself the right to hear any music at all because of the emotional turmoil it caused him.

I asked Colonel Bykov what music moved him. *"Devenatsi god,"* he said. He saw me struggling with the Russian words and turned them into German: *"Der zwölfte Jahr."* Then I understood: *der zwölfte Jahr*—the twelfth year—Tchaikowsky's *1812 Overture.*

XXII

The Washington espionage apparatus had been short-lived. It was about to end. My break with the Communist Party, which I had been quietly preparing, was about to end it. Its life had been crowded into the space of a year and a half, roughly from September, 1936, into April, 1938.

When I try to evoke what that life was like, it comes back to me as a succession of brief cases, of Washington streets at night, of a tight little world beyond the law, turning upon an axis of faith and fear. It was the only world that then mattered, composed of trusted, clandestine people, knit invisibly by a common historical conviction in whose name they performed the rites of a common crime, and by the fact that each carried the fate of the others in his hands. I see them now only as glimpses of people, standing, walking or talking in ways that are unimportant in themselves, but have become for me the residue of memory.

There is Alger Hiss, unlocking the door of the 30th Street house.

Priscilla and I have been waiting for him and turn at the sound of the key in the lock. It is a transmission night. Alger knows that he will find me sitting there. He smiles a smile that is sometimes a little tired and grave, but invariably gracious. On a chair, he conspicuously lays down his brief case. Then he peels off his long gray overcoat and the scarf he wears with it. When the cocker spaniel jumps on him, he says: "Down, Jenny, *down*!" with a trace of pettishness that I never hear him use except to the dog. In that tone is the only tension he ever shows.

There is Julian Wadleigh, waiting alone on a nighttime street. He is hatless. His short hair sticks up. He peers near-sightedly in an effort to make out whether the man walking toward him is really I. Above him the leaves of Norway maples hang limp in the streetlights where insects swoop.

There are Abel Gross and his wife, sitting in the soft light of a shaded lamp in their little house somewhere in suburban Washington. For some forgotten reason, David Carpenter has taken me there. Their baby has just been born and Mrs. Gross is quietly sewing while we talk.

There is George Silverman, driving me in his Ford, talking incessantly, so that there is one narrow shave after another with the swarming Washington traffic. He gnashes the gears whenever he shifts. At my protests, he advances a revealing argument. A car is a mechanical convenience. The sensible attitude toward it is to wear it out as fast as possible and trade it in on a new one. On principle, he never takes any care of his car. Then he switches to a subject much on his mind: he hopes that his son will become a violinist, but he is afraid that the boy will not.

There is Harry Dexter White. I see him sauntering down Connecticut Avenue at night, a slight, furtive figure. I am loitering near the Ordway Theater, where he has insisted (probably out of laziness) that I meet him for the third time in a row. Yet he is nervous at the contact, and idles along, constantly peeping behind him, too conspicuously watchful. He has a book under his arm. His wife has just written a book of Bible stories retold for children, for their two daughters, in fact. She wants Carl, whose reputation for literacy has reached her, to have a copy. In a dark shady side street beyond Connecticut Avenue, White slips the book under my arm. I still have it.

There is Felix, prematurely bulky in his overcoat, but with an immature face. He is lurking among the parked cars on a street behind the Union Station. He sees me, hesitates to recognize me until I smile that it is all right. We stroll off together. I have a brief case under the arm next to him. He suddenly draws it out and walks in the opposite direction.

There is Carpenter, who, as I walk toward him, I see in the distance, small and dingy, walking toward me. He scarcely greets me. He has microfilm in his pocket. He knows that he must not give it to me until I ask for it—a security measure. While we talk, we discuss his sources, his problems, our next meeting. Then I say: "All right!" His hand slips into his pocket. He passes me a little package. I slip it into my pocket. We walk in opposite directions.

There is Bykov. I am standing at the back of a movie house in New York or Brooklyn. I do not sit down. Bykov rises from the audience. I see him, silhouetted against the screen as he puts away the glasses through which he watches pictures. He slips up to me—sullen, piggish eyes forcing a hypocritic smile (these are the days of our great reconciliation). We go out and begin walking. Now and again, he glances back. Once he grips my sleeve. "Why is that man following us?" It is night. The street is absolutely deserted except for us and a stooped, very old Jewish man slowly making his way home. "Are you afraid the rabbi will catch you?" I ask in German. For a moment he is sheepish. Then he curses and laughs a nasty laugh. We walk for miles, through other dark deserted streets, through dark parks where other scarcely discernible figures drift past us. Like Carpenter, I must not turn over the film until Bykov asks me for it. "Give it to me," he says nervously after peering around. I give him the spools of film which I have carried in my tobacco pouch. He snatches them. We part.

I have another memory of a different kind. It is at our house on Auchentoroly Terrace in Baltimore. Alger and Priscilla arrive rather early in the morning. Priscilla looks downcast and we ask her why. "On our way over," she says, "we saw a sweet little field sparrow, and while we were looking at it, a sparrow hawk flew down and carried it away. It was screaming." Alger says something about nature's way of keeping life in balance.

Those are my dissolving impressions, after fourteen years, of people who believed that they were contributing to the future welfare of all mankind, finding in their effort the meaning of history and their own lives in the third decade of the twentieth century. Cocker spaniels and Bible stories retold for children. A man racking out his car and worrying about his son's future as a violinist. Another man quietly discussing underground work while his wife sews for their newborn child. A chief of military intelligence, cringing at the sight of an aged Jew on a lonely street, and a gentle girl close to tears because a hawk has snatched a sparrow.

In 1936, when my wife lay in the hospital ward after the difficult birth of our son, she asked me to bring her a book to help her over the painful days of recuperation. I brought her Aldous Huxley's *Eyeless in Gaza,* which had just been published. The title struck me in some hidden way and sent me back to reading Milton's *Samson Agonistes,* where Huxley had found it. Often and unaccountably in the winter of 1937, Samson's opening lines kept running through my mind:

Promise was that I
Should Israel from Philistian yoke deliver.
Ask for this great deliverer now, and find him
Eyeless in Gaza, at the mill with slaves.

XXIII

I have reached that point in my narrative at which this book began—the point at which I repudiated Communism and violently broke away from the slaves of the Communist mill. So great an effort, quite apart from its physical and practical hazards, cannot occur without a profound upheaval of the spirit. No man lightly reverses the faith of an adult lifetime, held implacably to the point of criminality. He reverses it only with a violence greater than the force of the faith he is repudiating. It is not a matter of leaving one house and occupying another—especially when the second is manifestly in collapse and the caretakers largely witless. That faith is not worth holding which a man is not willing to reach, if necessary, through violence, and to hold through suffering.

Julian Wadleigh has told, in a series of reminiscences that he published between the Hiss trials, how, in 1937, he was once complaining to me about his troubles and I answered that I had known trouble that kept me awake all night at my window. I remember that night well. It was the night when I faced the fact that, if Communism were evil, I could no longer serve it, and that that was true regardless of the fact that there might be nothing else to serve, that the alternative was a void. It was that void that I faced throughout the night until the alley below me again took form out of the opacity of a sultry dawn.

Nor did I mention that night to Wadleigh merely to relieve my feelings. I hoped to implant some dim sense of turmoil to him as the only way I knew of disturbing Wadleigh's faith, too. It was about as far as I dared go with anyone. For if they had known what my turmoil was about, my fellow slaves would gladly have tried to prevent my escape.

Therefore, I prepared my break carefully over the months, taking a series of practical precautions, which I have described earlier, and whose chief purpose was to deter my pursuers from killing me. Those were the days in which I bought a weapon, a car, induced the Communist Party to get me a job in the United States Government, organized a hiding place for my family and concealed the last consignments of copied documents, memos and film from the Washington sources. Those precautions have been called overprudent and crafty. Let anyone who sincerely thinks so, secure the safety of a woman and two small children, as well as his own, under the eyes of prudent, crafty, and conscienceless conspirators. I used against the Communist Party exactly the conspiratorial methods which it had taught me to use against others. In any case, God commands us to have courage; He does not command us to be fools.

How well-taken those precautions were, and how necessary, the Hiss Case proved ten years later. For had I not taken them in 1938, in 1948 Alger Hiss would have destroyed me without a second thought, as a party reprisal too long delayed. Had he succeeded, the fight against Communism would have suffered such a reverse that no second man would have dared for a long time to stand up against the secret Communist Party whose entrenched power would have been more untouchable than before. Or are there people who still believe that in 1948 Alger Hiss, impenitent and defiant to this hour, was not still an active Communist, working as such in close touch with some of the highest power centers in the country? Are there people who still do not see that in removing his power for evil in 1948, the secret apparatus that I had failed to smash singlehanded in 1938 was at least damaged?

In that sense, not only the safety of my family and myself, but the safety of many families, turned on the spin of my decision when I broke out of the Communist Party and fled from our house on Mount Royal Terrace, the last of the houses we had lived in in Baltimore. Had I acted by all that the world calls realistic and practical, or even prudent and crafty, I should never have broken.

I was just turned thirty-seven years old. The best years of my life were gone. I had no profession and no job, no usable experience, no standing in any community and the depression was still on. I had a wife and two small children to support. I was a fugitive from my own Government. I was a fugitive from the Soviet Government and its international apparatuses which I knew to be operating around me. I was a fugitive from the Communist Party whose people were more or less everywhere. The logical thing for the Soviet apparatuses and the Communist Party to do was to kill me. They must sometimes have thought bitterly since about their failure to do so.

My son was about two years old when I carried him to the car where his five-year-old sister was waiting for their mother to drive them out of those dangers that they had no inkling of toward a future that was blank to all of us.

Two things made that break and that flight possible. One was the devotion of my wife—devotion of a kind that asks only danger, trial and great hazard to prove its force. The other was a faith that, if I turned away from evil and sought good, I would not fail; but whether or not I failed, that was what I was meant to do, at all costs, without the measuring of consequences.

Of course, we do not simply step from evil to good, even recognizing that any human good and evil is seldom more than a choice between less evil and more good. In that transition we drag ourselves like cripples. We are cripples. In any such change as I was making, the soul itself is in flux. How hideous our transformations then are, wavering monstrously in their incompleteness as in a distorting mirror, until the commotion settles and the soul's new proportions are defined.

In that change, practicality and precaution are of no more help than prudence or craft. It is a transit that must be made upon the knees, or not at all. For it is not only to the graves of dead brothers that we find ourselves powerless at last to bring anything but prayer. We are equally powerless at the graves of ourselves, once we know that we live in shrouds.

At that end, all men simply pray, and prayer takes as many forms as there are men. Without exception we pray. We pray because there is nothing else to do, and because that is where God is—where there is nothing else.

THE DIVISION POINT

I

When I was a small boy on Long Island, sitting up in bed to listen in awe to the ocean pounding the beaches on winter nights, Rainer Maria Rilke stood one day on the tower of the castle of Duino near Trieste. There, while a storm hurled the Adriatic Sea, two hundred feet below him, at the tower's base, he heard a voice, partly within and partly without him, ask this question:

> *Wer, wenn ich schriee, hörte mich aus der Engel Ordnungen?*

> *Who, if I cried out, would hear me from among the orders Of the angels?*

It fills me with hope that, in my own lifetime, a few years before the war that would change the life and destiny of mankind, there was still left in the world a man who could hear such a question in a storm. The question is as changeless as the voice that asks it. The failure of an age or a man is not to hear it.

I have reached the division point of my life and of my book. Up to this point, I have been painfully sketching the personal sins and follies of a weak man. I have made no attempt to report them in full or in detail. Looked back upon once a man has left it behind, all sin seems childish, and, in my experience, most men feel childishly presumptuous about their sins. As if, were they to shout to their kind: "Ho, wayfarers!" the echo that answered them would not be the voice of humanity itself.

I have sought, too, to report, more painfully, how out of my weakness and folly (but also out of my strength), I committed the characteristic crimes of my century, which is unique in the history of men for two reasons. It is the first century since life began when a decisive part of the most articulate section of mankind has not merely ceased to believe in God, but has deliberately rejected God. And it is the century in which this religious rejection has taken a specifically political form, so that the characteristic experience of the mind in this age is a political experience. At every point, religion and politics interlace, and must do so more acutely as the conflict between the two great camps of men—those who reject and those who worship God—becomes irrepressible. Those camps are not only outside, but also within nations.

The most conspicuously menacing form of that rejection is Communism. But there are other forms of the same rejection, which in any case, Communism did not originate, but merely adopted and adapted.

Until 1937, I had been, in this respect, a typical modern man, living without God except for tremors of intuition. In 1938, there seemed no possibility that I would not continue to live out my life as such a man. Habit and self-interest both presumed it. I had been for thirteen years a Communist; and in Communism could be read, more clearly with each passing year, the future of mankind, as, with each passing year, the free world shrank in power and faith, including faith in itself, and sank deeper into intellectual and moral chaos. Yet, in 1938, I gave a different ending to that life.

Again, in 1948, exactly ten years later, I was leading a life prosperous beyond most men's and peaceful beyond my hopes. On its surface, this was the other typical life of my time—the life of career and success. Again, there seemed no possibility that I would not lead that second life to its close. I did not do so.

In the end, the only memorable stories, like the only memorable experiences, are religious and moral. They give men the heart to suffer the ordeal of a life that perpetually rends them between its beauty and its terror. If my story is worth telling, it is because I rejected in turn each of the characteristic endings of life in our time—the revolutionary ending and the success ending. I chose a third ending.

I am only incidentally a witness to a weak man's sins and misdeeds or even the crimes that are implicit in the practice of Communism. In so far as I am a true witness, it is because twice in my life I came, not alone, for I had my wife and children by the hand, to a dark tower, and, in a storm of the spirit, listened to that question that was both within and without me: Who, if I cried out, would hear me from among the orders of the angels? And because each time the question was answered.

The rest of this book is about what happened—translated into the raw, painful, ugly, crumpled, confused, tormented, pitiful acts of life—when I heard the first and the second cry.

10

THE TRANQUIL YEARS

I

I had had to hurry from my office at *Time* magazine to the airport to catch the six o'clock flight for Washington. I fastened my safety belt, chewed my gum, lay back and closed my eyes. The great plane took off into the serene evening sky of September 2, 1939.

On the plains of Poland, at the same moment, a new day was awakening the Polish nation to terror and insane distress as its cavalry tried to turn back, with lance and rifle, a new force in the history of war and men—the German panzer divisions.

In Moscow, a few days before, Stalin, with a tigerish smile, and a more reserved Ribbentrop, had signed the pact that made Nazism and Communism allies. By the same scratch of the pen, Stalin had unloosed upon mankind, for the second time in two decades, the horror of world war. Soon the Stukas would be screaming above the screaming babies, pushed or carried by long lines of frantic women, along roads jammed by the clutter of soldiers and civilians fleeing the collapse of armies, cities, nations, order, civilization. This was the war that, for as long as I had been a Communist, every Communist had foreseen and dedicated himself to struggle against. That a Communist had unloosed it upon mankind was a fact so monstrous that it absolved every man from the bonds of common humanity with that breed and made it a pious act to raise his hand in any way against them.

I was on the plane for that reason. Specifically, I was afraid that, with the Communist-Nazi Pact, the Soviet Government and the American Communist Party would at once put their underground apparatuses at the service of the Nazis against the United States. I had been told that in the past German and Russian intelligence groups had co-operated in the United States.

To prevent that, I had decided to do the only thing that I could do. I had decided to become an informer. I was flying to Washington to lay the facts about the underground apparatuses before Adolf A. Berle, the Assistant Secretary of State in charge of security.

II

To be an informer. . . .

Men shrink from that word and what it stands for as from something lurking and poisonous. Spy is a different breed of word. Espionage is a function of war whether it be waged between nations, classes or parties. Like the soldier, the spy stakes his freedom or his life on the chances of action. Like the soldier, his acts are largely impersonal. He seldom knows whom he cripples or kills. Spy as an epithet is a convention of morale; the enemy's spy is always monstrous; our spy is daring and brave. It must be so since all camps use spies and must while war lasts.

The informer is different,* particularly the ex-Communist informer. He risks little. He sits in security and uses his special knowledge to destroy others. He has that special information to give because he knows those others' faces, voices and lives, because he once lived within their confidence, in a shared faith, trusted by them as one of themselves, accepting their friendship, feeling their pleasures and griefs, sitting in their houses, eating at their tables, accepting their kindness, knowing their wives and children. If he had not done those things, he would have no use as an informer.

Because he has that use, the police protect him. He is their creature. When they whistle, he fetches a soiled bone of information. He and they share a common chore, which is a common complicity in the public interest. It cannot be the action of equals, and even the kindness that seeks to mask the fact merely exasperates and cannot change it. For what is the day's work of the police is the ex-Communist's necessity. They may choose what they will or will not do. He has no choice. He has surrendered his choice. To that extent, though he be free in every other way, the informer is a slave. He is no longer a man. He is free only to the degree in which he understands what he is doing and why he must do it.

Let every ex-Communist look unblinkingly at that image. It is himself. By the logic of his position in the struggles of this age, every ex-Communist is an informer from the moment he breaks with Communism, regardless of how long it takes him to reach the police station.

For Communism fixes the consequences of its evil not only on those who serve it, but also on those, who, once having served it, seek to serve against it. It has set the pattern of the warfare it wages and that defines the pattern of the warfare its deserters must wage against it. It cannot be otherwise. Communism exists to wage war. Its existence implies, even in peace or truce, a state of war

* I am not speaking of such people as the F.B.I. and other security agencies send into the Communist Party. In the true sense of the word, they are not informers but spies, working in exposed, and sometimes hazardous, positions.

that engages every man, woman and child alive, but, above all, the ex-Communist. For no man simply deserts *from* the Communist Party. He deserts *against* it. He deserts to struggle against Communism as an evil. There would otherwise be no reason for his desertion, however long it may take him to grasp the fact. Otherwise, he should have remained within the Communist Party, and his failure to act at all against it betrays the fact that he has not broken with it. He has broken only with its organization, or certain of its forms, practices, discomforts of action or political necessity. And this, despite the sound human and moral reasons that may also paralyze him—his reluctance to harm old friends, his horror at using their one-time trust in him to destroy them—reasons which are honorable and valid.

But if the ex-Communist truly believes that Communism is evil, if he truly means to struggle against it as an evil, and as the price of his once having accepted it, he must decide to become an informer. In that war which Communism insists on waging, and which therefore he cannot evade, he has one specific contribution to make—his special knowledge of the enemy. That is what all have to offer first of all. Because Communism is a conspiracy, that knowledge is indispensable for the active phase of the struggle against it. That every ex-Communist has to offer, regardless of what else he may have to offer, special skills or special talents or the factors that make one character different from another.

I hold that it is better, because in general clarity is more maturing than illusion, for the ex-Communist to make the offering in the full knowledge of what he is doing, the knowledge that henceforth he is no longer a free man but an informer. That penalty those who once firmly resolved to take upon themselves the penalties for the crimes of politics and history, in the belief that only at that cost could Man be free, must assume no less firmly as the price of their mistake. For, in the end, the choice for the ex-Communist is between shielding a small number of people who still actively further what he now sees to be evil, or of helping to shield millions from that evil which threatens even their souls. Those who do not inform are still conniving at that evil. That is the crux of the moral choice which an ex-Communist must make in recognizing that the logic of his position makes him an informer. Moreover, he must always make it amidst the deafening chatter and verbal droppings of those who sit above the battle, who lack the power to act for good or evil because they lack any power to act at all, and who, in the day when heaven was falling, were, in Dante's words, neither for God nor for Satan, but were for themselves.

On that road of the informer it is always night. I who have traveled it from end to end, and know its windings, switchbacks and sheer drops—I cannot say at what point, where or when, the ex-Communist must make his decision to take it. That depends on the individual man. Nor is it simply a matter of taking his horror in his hands and making his avowals. The ex-Communist is a man dealing with other men, men of many orders of intelligence, of many motives of self-interest or malice, men sometimes infiltrated or tainted by the enemy, in an immensely complex pattern of politics and history. If he means to be effective, if he does not wish his act merely to be wasted suffering for others and himself, how, when and where the ex-Communist informs are matters calling for the shrewdest judgment.

Some ex-Communists are so stricken by the evil they have freed themselves from that they inform exultantly against it. No consideration, however humane, no tie however tender, checks them. They understand, as few others do, the immensity of the danger, and experience soon teaches them the gulf fixed between the reality they must warn against and the ability of the world to grasp their warnings. Fear makes them strident. They are like breathless men who have outrun the lava flow of a volcano and must shout down the smiles of the villagers at its base who, regardless of their own peril, remember complacently that those who now try to warn them once offered their faith and their lives to the murderous mountain.

By temperament, I cannot share such exultation or stridency, though I understand both. I cannot ever inform against anyone without feeling something die within me. I inform without pleasure because it is necessary. Each time, relief lies only in the certainty that, when enough has died in a man, at last the man himself dies, as light fails.

Sometimes, by informing, the ex-Communist can claim immunity of one kind or another for acts committed before his change of heart or sides. He is right to claim it, for if he is to be effective, his first task is to preserve himself. Sometimes, he can even enjoy such immunity, if he is able to feel what is happening to him in the simplest terms, impersonally, as an experience of history and of war in which he at last has found his bearings and which he is helping to wage. By the rules of war, common sense and self-interest, the world can scarcely lose by allowing him his immunity. It does well, provided by acts he makes amends, to help him to forget his past, if only because in the crisis of the 20th century, not all the mistakes were committed by the ex-Communists.

I never asked for immunity. Nor did anyone at any time ever offer me immunity, even by a hint or a whisper. What immunity can the world offer a man against his thoughts?

And so I went to see Adolf Berle.

III

The meeting was arranged by Isaac Don Levine. Levine is the former editor of *Plain Talk*, one of the few magazines in the country that tried to tell some of the truth about the Amerasia Case while it was still happening. For years, he has carried on against Communism a kind of private war which is also a public service. He is a skillful professional journalist and a notable "ghost." It was Levine who led Jan Valtin out of the editorial night and he was working with General Krivitsky on *I Was in Stalin's Secret Service* when, sometime in 1938, I met both men.

I had gone to Levine in the first place with the idea of writing two or three pieces about the underground, notably the case of Robinson-Rubens. Nothing came of the project, about which, in any case, I was only half-hearted. But something much more important developed.

From the first, Levine had urged me to take my story to the proper authorities. I had said no. I was extremely wary of Levine. I knew little or nothing about him, and the ex-Communist is an outlaw, not only a fugitive from the Communist Party, but the natural prey of anyone who can turn his plight to his own purpose or profit. Levine gave me no cause for concern but I wished to be careful. When he proposed that he arrange a meeting at which I might tell my story directly to President Roosevelt, I was reassured. It seemed to me that in a matter so grave, touching the security of the country at top levels of the Government, the President was the man who should first hear the facts and decide where to go from there. I told Levine that, if he would arrange the meeting, I would co-operate.

Two factors chiefly moved me to agree. One was the force of history. The other was General Walter Krivitsky, who for me was to be fateful.

I V

History was moving torrentially. Seldom have such tensions been packed into one year as into the year 1939. For while I was struggling to begin life anew at the age of thirty-eight, in a world that I had given up as hopeless at the age of twenty-four, the historic crisis that had made me reject it reached a new crest.

The Spanish Civil War had ended. That is to say, the opening campaign of World War II had ended. The great interventionists in Spain—Fascism (in its German and Italian forms) and Fascism (in its Soviet guise)—were free to maneuver for new positions in other fields. Spain had disclosed the pattern of the war to come. Whatever the free nations meant to fight for, whatever the millions meant to die for, in reality, World War II, like the Spanish Civil War, would be fought to decide which of the great fascist systems—the Axis or Communism—was to survive and control Europe. In the end, the superiority of the Communist system was indicated by the fact that it was able to use the free nations to carry out its purposes, as indispensable allies in war, whose vital interests could easily be defeated in peace.

Godesberg was followed by Munich; the partition of Czechoslovakia by its occupation. My wife and I were among the invisible millions who haunted their radios in those days. We heard Jan Masaryk's voice break as he pled against the extinction of his country. Until the end, we heard, borne on the air waves across the ocean, the *Vltava,* Smetana's music, that describes the flowing of the Vltava River through Bohemia on its way to the sea. The motive forces of history conspire unknowably. Whoever, in that distracted studio in those distracted hours, kept playing that song, could not possibly have known that it would reach the ears of a defeated ex-Communist and his wife in Baltimore, or the impact it would have upon them.

As that childishly simple, descriptive music came over the air—a little peasant theme, repeated over and over like the hopeless crying of a child from whom everything has been taken—my wife wept. She wept for the Czech children and for all children. She wept for the night that was descending upon mankind. I had been a Communist in large part to keep that night from falling. I had failed. The force that I had hoped might save was abetting the disaster. That fact I had already learned, or was soon to learn, from

Walter Krivitsky. The knowledge made certain that what, as a Communist, I had tried and failed to do, I would now try to do as an ex-Communist, by other means, but, in fact, from much the same motives.

V

I met Krivitsky with extreme reluctance. Long after my break with the Communist Party, I could not think of Communists or Communism without revulsion. I did not wish to meet even ex-Communists. Toward Russians, especially, I felt an organic antipathy.

But one night, when I was at Levine's apartment in New York, Krivitsky telephoned that he was coming over. There presently walked into the room a tidy little man about five feet six with a somewhat lined gray face out of which peered pale blue eyes. They were professionally distrustful eyes, but oddly appealing and wistful, like a child whom life has forced to find out about the world, but who has never made his peace with it. By way of handshake, Krivitsky touched my hand. Then he sat down at the far end of the couch on which I also was sitting. His feet barely reached the floor. I turned to look at him. He did not look at me. He stared straight ahead. Then he asked in German (the only language that we ever spoke): *"Ist die Sowjetregierung eine faschistische Regierung?*—Is the Soviet Government a fascist government?"

Communists dearly love to begin a conversation with a key question the answer to which will also answer everything else of importance about the answerer. I recognized that this was one of those questions. On the political side, I had broken with the Communist Party in large part because I had become convinced that the Soviet Government was fascist. Yet when I had to give that answer out loud, instead of in the unspoken quiet of my own mind, all the emotions that had ever bound me to Communism rose in a final spasm to stop my mouth. I sat silent for some moments. Then I said: *"Ja, die Sowjetregierung ist eine faschistische Regierung*—the Soviet Government is a fascist government." Later on that night, Krivitsky told me that if I had answered yes at once, he would have distrusted me. Because I hesitated, and he felt the force of my struggle, he was convinced that I was sincere.

When I answered slowly, and a little somberly, as later on I sometimes answered questions during the Hiss Case, Krivitsky turned for the first time and looked at me directly. *"Du hast recht,"* he said, *"und Kronstadt war der Wendepunkt*—You are right, and Kronstadt was the turning point."

I knew what he meant. But who else for a thousand miles around could know what we were talking about? Here and there, some fugitive in a dingy room would know. But, as Krivitsky and I looked each other over, it seemed to me that we were like two survivors from another age of the earth, like two dated dinosaurs, the last relics of the revolutionary world that had vanished in the Purge. Even in that vanished world, we had been a special breed —the underground activists. There were not many of our kind left alive who still spoke the language that had also gone down in the submergence. I said, yes, Kronstadt had been the turning point.

Kronstadt is a naval base a few miles west of Leningrad in the Gulf of Finland. From Kronstadt during the Bolshevik Revolution in 1917, the sailors of the Baltic Fleet had steamed their cruisers to aid the Communists in capturing Petrograd. Their aid had been decisive. They were the sons of peasants. They embodied the primitive revolutionary upheaval of the Russian people. They were the symbol of its instinctive surge for freedom. And they were the first Communists to realize their mistake and the first to try to correct it. When they saw that Communism meant terror and tyranny, they called for the overthrow of the Communist Government and for a time imperiled it. They were bloodily destroyed or sent into Siberian slavery by Communist troops led in person by the Commissar of War, Leon Trotsky, and by Marshal Tukhachevsky, one of whom was later assassinated, the other executed, by the regime they then saved.

Krivitsky meant that by the decision to destroy the Kronstadt sailors, and by its cold-blooded action in doing so, Communism had made the choice that changed it from benevolent socialism to malignant fascism. Today, I could not answer, yes, to Krivitsky's challenge. The fascist character of Communism was inherent in it from the beginning. Kronstadt changed the fate of millions of Russians. It changed nothing about Communism. It merely disclosed its character.

Krivitsky and I began to talk quickly as if we were racing time. Levine first dozed in his chair, and then, around midnight, went to bed. About three o'clock in the morning, he came down in his bathrobe, found us still talking and went back to bed. Day dawned. Krivitsky and I went out to a cafeteria near the corner of 59th

Street and Lexington Avenue. We were still talking there at eleven o'clock that morning. We parted because we could no longer keep our eyes open.

We talked about Krivitsky's break with Communism and his flight with his wife and small son from Amsterdam to Paris. We talked about the attempts of the G.P.U. to trap or kill him in Europe and the fact that he had not been in the United States a week before the Russian secret police set a watch over his apartment. We talked about the murder of Ignatz Reiss, the Soviet agent whose break from the Communist Party in Switzerland had precipitated Krivitsky's. They had been friends. The G.P.U. had demanded that Krivitsky take advantage of his friendship to trap or kill Reiss.

That night, too, I learned the name of Boris Bykov and that Herman's real name had been Valentine Markin, and why he had been murdered and by whom.

But nothing else that we said was so important for the world, or for the course of action that it enjoined upon us both in our different ways, as what Krivitsky had to tell me about the designs of Soviet foreign policy. For it was then that I first learned that, for more than a year, Stalin had been desperately seeking to negotiate an alliance with Hitler. Attempts to negotiate the pact had been made throughout the period when Communism (through its agency, the Popular Front) was posing to the masses of mankind as the only inflexible enemy of fascism. As, in response to my first incredulity, Krivitsky developed the political logic that necessitated the alliance, I knew at once, as only an ex-Communist would, that he was speaking the truth. The alliance was, in fact, a political inevitability. I wondered only what blind spot had kept me from foreseeing it. For, by means of the pact, Communism could pit one sector of the West against the other, and use both to destroy what was left of the non-Communist world. As Communist strategy, the pact was thoroughly justified, and the Communist Party was right in denouncing all those who opposed it as Communism's enemies. From any human point of view, the pact was evil.

We passed naturally to the problem of the ex-Communist and what he could do against that evil. Krivitsky did not then, or at any later time, tell me what he himself had done or would do. It was from others that I learned the details of his co-operation with the British Government.

But Krivitsky said one or two things that were to take root in my mind and deeply to influence my conduct, for they seemed to correspond to the reality of my position. "*Konkret angegriffen,*" he said at one point, "*gibt es keine frühere Kommunisten. Es gibt nur Revolutionäre und Gegen-Revolutionäre.*—Looked at concretely, there are no ex-Communists. There are only revolutionists and counterrevolutionists." He meant that, in the 20th century, all politics, national and international, is the politics of revolution—that, in sum, the forces of history in our time can be grasped only as the interaction of revolution and counterrevolution. He meant that, in so far as a man ventures to think or act politically, or even if he tries not to think or act at all, history will, nevertheless, define what he is in the terms of those two mighty opposites. He is a revolutionist or he is a counterrevolutionist. In action there is no middle ground. Nor did Krivitsky suppose, as we discussed then (and later) in specific detail, that the revolution of our time is exclusively Communist, or that the counterrevolutionist is merely a conservative, resisting it out of habit and prejudice. He believed, as I believe, that fascism (whatever softening name the age of euphemism chooses to call it by) is inherent in every collectivist form, and that it can be fought only by the force of an intelligence, a faith, a courage, a self-sacrifice, which must equal the revolutionary spirit that, in coping with, it must in many ways come to resemble. No one knows so well as the ex-Communist the character of the conflict, and of the enemy, or shares so deeply the same power of faith and willingness to stake his life on his beliefs. For no other has seen so deeply into the total nature of the evil with which Communism threatens mankind. Counterrevolution and conservatism have little in common. In the struggle against Communism the conservative is all but helpless. For that struggle cannot be fought, much less won, or even understood, except in terms of total sacrifice. And the conservative is suspicious of sacrifice; he wishes first to conserve, above all what he is and what he has. You cannot fight against revolutions so.

In his own way, Krivitsky was saying what Ignazio Silone meant when he said to Palmiro Togliatti (echoing the words of the *Internationale*): "The final conflict will be between the Communists and the ex-Communists."*

* Ignazio Silone, the author of *Fontamara* and *The Seed Beneath the Snow,* was the head of the underground section of the Italian Communist Party until he broke with Communism in the 1930's. Togliatti, once Silone's close friend, is secretary of the Italian Communist Party.

In that all night conversation, Krivitsky also said: "In our time, informing is a duty." He added, like a sad afterthought: "*Man kommt nicht leicht von Stalin los*—one does not come away from Stalin easily."

I knew that, if the opportunity offered, I would inform.

VI

Unexpectedly, Levine provided the opportunity. Between the time that he proposed to arrange a conversation with the President, and the time I next saw Levine, some months had elapsed. I had gone to work for *Time* magazine. I was much too busy trying to learn my job to think of Levine, the President or anything else.

Then, on the morning of September 2, 1939, a few days after the Nazi-Communist Pact was signed, and the German armor had rushed on Warsaw, Isaac Don Levine appeared at my office at *Time*. He explained that he had been unable to arrange to see the President. But he had arranged a substitute meeting with Adolf Berle, the Assistant Secretary of State in charge of security. It was for eight o'clock that night. Would I go?

I hesitated. I did not like the way in which I was presented with an accomplished fact. But—"looked at concretely, there are no ex-Communists; there are only revolutionists and counter-revolutionists"; "in our time, informing is a duty." In fact, I was grateful to Levine for presenting me with a decision to which I had only to assent, but which involved an act so hateful that I should have hesitated to take the initiative myself.

I said that I would meet Levine in Washington that night.

VII

The plane was late. Levine was waiting for me nervously in front of the Hay-Adams House. No doubt, he thought that I might have changed my mind, leaving him with nothing to take to Adolf Berle but embarrassing explanations.

Berle was living in Secretary of War Stimson's house. It stood on Woodley Road near Connecticut Avenue. It stood deep in shaded grounds, somewhat junglelike at night. For some reason the cab driver let us out at the entrance to the drive and, as we straggled up to the house, I realized that we were only four or five blocks from the apartment on 28th Street where I had first talked to Alger

Hiss. With a wince, I thought of his remark when I told him that I had taken a job in the Government: "I suppose that you'll turn up next in the State Department."

The Berles were having cocktails. It was my first glimpse of that somewhat beetlelike man with the mild, intelligent eyes (at Harvard his phenomenal memory had made him a child prodigy). He asked the inevitable question: If I were responsible for the funny words in *Time*. I said no. Then he asked, with a touch of crossness, if I were responsible for *Time's* rough handling of him. I was not aware that *Time* had handled him roughly.

At supper, Mrs. Berle took swift stock of the two strange guests who had thus appeared so oddly at her board, and graciously bounced the conversational ball. She found that we shared a common interest in gardening. I learned that the Berles imported their flower seeds from England and that Mrs. Berle had even been able to grow the wild cardinal flower from seed. I glanced at my hosts and at Levine, thinking of the one cardinal flower that grew in the running brook in my boyhood. But I was also thinking that it would take more than modulated voices, graciousness and candlelight to save a world that prized those things.

After the coffee, Mrs. Berle left us. Berle, Levine and I went out on the lawn. Three anticipatory chairs were waiting for us, like a mushroom ring in a pasture. The trees laid down islands of shadow, and about us washed the ocean of warm, sweet, southern air whose basic scent is honeysuckle. From beyond, came the rumor of the city, the softened rumble of traffic on Connecticut Avenue.

We had scarcely sat down when a Negro serving man brought drinks. I was intensely grateful. I drank mine quickly. I knew that two or three glasses of Scotch and soda would give me a liberating exhilaration. For what I had to do, I welcomed any aid that would loosen my tongue.

Levine made some prefatory statement about my special information, which, of course, they had already discussed before. Berle was extremely agitated. "We may be in this war within forty-eight hours," he said, "and we cannot go into it without clean services." He said this not once, but several times. I was astonished to hear from an Assistant Secretary of State that the Government considered it possible that the United States might go into the war at once.

Gratefully, I felt the alcohol take hold. It was my turn to speak.

I remember only that I said that I was about to give very serious information touching certain people in the Government, but that I had no malice against those people. I believed that they constituted a danger to the country in this crisis. I begged, if possible, that they might merely be dismissed from their posts and not otherwise prosecuted. Even while I said it, I supposed that it was a waste of breath. But it was such a waste of breath as a man must make. I did not realize that it was also supremely ironic. "I am a lawyer, Mr. Chambers," said Mr. Berle, "not a policeman."

It was a rambling talk. I do not recall any special order in it. Nor do I recall many details. I recall chiefly the general picture I drew of Communist infiltration of the Government and one particular point. In view of the war danger, and the secrecy of the bombsight, I more than once stressed to Berle the importance of getting Reno as quickly as possible out of the Aberdeen Proving Ground. (When the F.B.I. looked for him in 1948, he was still employed there.)

We sat on the lawn for two or three hours. Almost all of that time I was talking. I supposed, later on, that I had given Berle the names of Bykov and the head of the steel experimental laboratory whom I have mentioned in Part 8 of this book. They do not appear in the typed notes. Levine remembers that we discussed microfilm. I have no independent recollection of that. But, while we must have covered a good deal of ground in two or three hours, it is scarcely strange that none of us should have remembered too clearly just what he said on the lawn, for most of the time we were holding glasses in our hands.

Around midnight, we went into the house. What we said there is not in question because Berle took it in the form of penciled notes. Just inside the front door, he sat at a little desk or table with a telephone on it and while I talked he wrote, abbreviating swiftly as he went along. These notes did not cover the entire conversation on the lawn. They were what we recapitulated quickly at a late hour after a good many drinks. I assumed that they were an exploratory skeleton on which further conversations and investigation would be based.

After midnight, Levine and I left. As we went out, I could see that Mrs. Berle had fallen asleep on a couch in a room to my right. Adolf Berle, in great excitement, was on the telephone even before we were out the door. I supposed that he was calling the White House.

In August, 1948, Adolf A. Berle testified before the House Committee on Un-American Activities not long after my original testimony about Alger Hiss and the Ware Group. The former Assistant Secretary of State could no longer clearly recall my conversation with him almost a decade before. His memory had grown dim on a number of points. He believed, for example, that I had described to him a Marxist study group whose members were not Communists. In any case, he had been unable to take seriously, in 1939, any "idea that the Hiss boys and Nat Witt were going to take over the Government."

At no time in our conversation can I remember anyone's mentioning the ugly word espionage. But how well we understood what we were talking about, Berle was to make a matter of record. For when, four years after that memorable conversation, his notes were finally taken out of a secret file and turned over to the F.B.I., it was found that Adolf Berle himself had headed them: *Underground Espionage Agent.*

VIII

Here are the notes that Adolf Berle jotted down as I talked in 1939—or a typed copy of them made for him later—as they were introduced into evidence in the second Hiss trial.

LONDON Underground Espionage Agent

(1) *Dr. Philip Rosenbliett*—Formerly of 41st B'way, NE).
Dr. Greenberg—MD (West 70th NY)
Brother-in-law
American leader of British Underground C.
Head in America Mack Moren (alias Philipovitch—allegedly Yugoslav)—real name—?

Rosenbliett—in U.S.
connected with Dr. Isador Miller—Chemist's Club—41st St. Chemist, Explosive Arsenal, Picatinny, N.J. war "front" behind Mack Moren existed—in Miller's employ
Knew Pressman—his alias was "Cole Philips"—
Introduced him to Mack Moren, buying arms for Spanish (Loyalist) Gov't.—
Pressman—as counsel—helped Moren—made a flight to Mexico with him; forced down at Brownsville, Tex. in late '36 or early '37—probably fall of '36.

Pressman

Underground organized by the late Harold Ware; Pressman was in his group—(1932-3??) Pressman then in the A.A.A.—

Nathan Witt—Secretary of the NLRB—head of the underground group after Harold Ware—

John Abt—followed Witt in that group—Tax Div'n—Dep't of Justice & now in CIO (M. Ware's widow—Jessica Smith Ed. Soviet Russia).

Mr. Abt—Sister: Marion Bacharach—Secretary—Communist from Minnesota.

(Jessica Smith: With Reuters in 1926—friend of Louis Fischer)

Meeting place: John Abt's house—15th St.

Charles Krivitsky—alias Charles Kramer—(CIO) worked in La Follette Committee—Physicist.

Vincent Reno—Now at Aberdeen Proving Grounds—Computer—Math. Assist. to Col. Zornig (Aerial bombsight Detectors) Formerly CP organizer under alias "Lance Clark."

Philip Reno—in Social Security (??)—was head of Underground Trade Union Group Political leader

Elinor Nelson, treasurer of Fed. Employees' union—(Fed. Workers' Union, CIO—headed by Jake Baker)

Reno connected with Baltimore Party

organizer—Benjamin (Bundey) Friedman alias Field—then California—then Russia—now organizer for Baltimore & Washington of Above-Ground Party—Underground connections—

STATE

Post—Editorship, *Foreign Service Journal.* Was in Alexandria Unit of CP—in "Underground Apparatus"—

Duggan—Laurence—(Member CP??)

(Wadleigh?) Wadley—Trade Agreement Section

Lovell—Trade Agreement Section

Communist Shop Group

Elinor Nelson—Laurence Duggan—Julien Wadleigh—

West European Div'n—*Field*—still in—

(Levine says he is out went into I.E.O.

Then in committee for Repatriation

His leader was Hedda Gompertz

Laughlin Currie: Was a "Fellow Traveler"—helped various Communists—never went the whole way.

S.E.C.

Philip Reno—used to be

TREASURY

Schlomer *Adler* (Sol Adler?)

Counsel's Office

Sends weekly reports to CP (Gen. Counsel's Office)

Frank Coe—now teacher at McGill.

There are two: brother—One of them in CP's "Foreign Bureau"—Bob Coe

---

Known from Peters—formerly in Bela Kun Govt. Agricultural Commissariat—called Gandosz (?) Then to Russia—then here, in Business Office of Communist paper "Uj Elori"—then, after 1929—head of CP Underground, lived in Hamilton Apts., Woodside, L.I.—under alias "Silver"—& lectured in Communist camps—Friend: "Blake" of "Freiheit"—real name—*Wiener*—American: Polish Jew.—

Peters was responsible for Washington Sector

Went to Moscow—where is he now?—

Wife—a Comintern courier—

West Coast—Head: "The Old Man"—Volkov is his real name—daughter a Comintern courier. He knows the West Coast underground—Residence: San Francisco or Oakland—

Alexander Trachtenberg—Politburo—

member of the Execu. Committee

Head of GPU in U.S.

Works with Peters—

Plans for two Super-battleships—

secured in 1937—who gave—

Karp—brother-in-law of Molotov—working with Scott Ferris, got this released—

Now: Naval Architect working on it, why??

Field was original contact

He introduced Duggan to Gompertz (Hedda)

Duggan's relationship was casual—

Shall excuse?—Where is Hedda Gompertz?—

Duggan & Field supposed to have been both members of party.—

Donald Hiss

(Philippine Adviser)

Member of CP with Pressman & Witt—

Labor Dep't.—Asst. to Frances Perkins—

Party wanted him there—to send him as arbitrator in Bridges trial—

Brought along by brother—

Alger Hiss

Ass't. to Sayre—CP—1937

Member of the Underground Com.—Active

Baltimore boys—

Wife—Priscilla Hiss—Socialist—

Early days of New Deal

NOTE—When Loy Henderson interviewed Mrs. Rubens his report immediately went back to Moscow. Who sent it? Such came from Washington.

These notes are obviously rambling and garbled. Even I can no longer remember what some of the references mean or how I came to know of them—for example, that the Russians had obtained the plans for two super-battleships in 1937. For while I have remembered a great deal, many facts that were fresh in my mind in 1939 have dropped out of it beyond recovery.

But if the notes are studied carefully, it will be seen that the essential framework of the conspiracy is here, even down to such details as the fact that Reno was working as Colonel Zornig's asssistant at the Aberdeen Proving Grounds. It is equally clear that I am describing not a Marxist study group, but a Communist conspiracy. The Communists are described as such. The reader has only to ask himself what he would have done, if he had been a security officer of the Government, and such information had come into his hands, or even if he had been told no more than the address for cables to the Soviet apparatuses, which is the meaning of one of the entries, or the fact that a Communist was working on the bombsight.

Two names I deliberately omitted from my conversation with Berle. They were those of George Silverman and Harry Dexter White. I still hoped that I had broken them away from the Communist Party. Perhaps it is worth observing, too, that the last name on the list, the one that I could not bring myself to mention until the very end, though I was repeating it for the second time that night, is the name of Alger Hiss.

IX

Isaac Don Levine went back to his hotel and sensibly wrote down at once as many names as he could remember from my conversation. It was fortunate that he did so. For when I was testifying before the House Committee on Un-American Activities in 1948, and I foresaw that I might have no choice but to go into the espionage story, I was disturbed by the fact that I could not remember the name of one of the sources in the State Department.

I telephoned Levine. The name I had forgotten, he was able to inform me by glancing at the jottings he had made in 1939, was Julian Wadleigh.

The same night that I had talked with Berle, I returned to New York. For the second time in two years, I had laid my life in ruins. I had only to wait for what would happen next. One of the things most likely to happen, it seemed to me, was my arrest.

X

But nothing at all happened. Weeks passed into months. I went about my work at *Time*. Then, one day, I am no longer certain just when, I met a dejected Levine. Adolf Berle, said Levine, had taken my information to the President at once. The President had laughed. When Berle was insistent, he had been told in words which it is necessary to paraphrase, to "go jump in a lake."

The thought crossed my mind that the story might have been put out to conceal the Government's real purpose. Surveillance and investigation were necessary. It might be some time before the Government was prepared to act. Meanwhile, it would watch and check.

I tried to believe that that was the fact. But I knew that it could not be, for if the Government were checking, it could not fail also to check with me.

XI

In going to Berle, I had keyed myself to the highest pitch of effort. When nothing came of it, I felt like a wire that has been stretched to the snapping point and let go slack. The effect on me was twofold.

On one hand, I felt a sense that causes beyond my grasp or control, causes not necessarily good in themselves, were working toward a beneficent purpose which I could obscurely feel, but not define. I believed that I had done what I should do; I had proved myself. But I had then come up against something unexpected with which I could not cope. One effect was to give me a reprieve, to give me time to prove myself in a larger way so that when my time came to speak out (and in my heart I never believed that the truth to which I was a witness could be indefinitely hidden), I would speak with an authority that I now lacked, an authority based upon accomplishment. Let no one suppose that this is wise hindsight. Those were my groping thoughts at the time. And I thought a great deal about the subject, for the failure of the mission to Adolf Berle filled me with astonishment.

And with astonishment I took my first hard look at the New Deal. This was the second effect of the Berle failure on me. It is surprising how little I knew about the New Deal, although it had been all around me during my years in Washington. But all the New Dealers I had known were Communists or near-Communists. None of them took the New Deal seriously as an end in itself. They regarded it as an instrument for gaining their own revolutionary ends. I myself thought of the New Deal as a reform movement that, in social and labor legislation, was belatedly bringing the United States abreast of Britain or Scandinavia.

I had noted its obvious features—its coalition of divergent interests, some of them diametrically opposed to the others, its divided counsels, its makeshift strategy, its permanently shifting executive personnel whose sole consistency seemed to be that the more it changed, the more it remained the most incongruously headed hybrid since the hydra. Now with a curiosity newborn of Berle, I saw how misleading those surface manifestations were, and tactically how advantageous, for they concealed the inner drift of this great movement. That drift was prevailingly toward socialism, though the mass of those who, in part directed, in part were carried along by it, sincerely supposed that they were liberals.

I saw that the New Deal was only superficially a reform movement. I had to acknowledge the truth of what its more forthright protagonists, sometimes unwarily, sometimes defiantly, averred: the New Deal was a genuine revolution, whose deepest purpose was not simply reform within existing traditions, but a basic change in the social, and, above all, the power relationships within the nation. It was not a revolution by violence. It was a revolution by bookkeeping and lawmaking. In so far as it was successful, the power of politics had replaced the power of business. This is the basic power shift of all the revolutions of our time. This shift *was* the revolution. It was only of incidental interest that the revolution was not complete, that it was made not by tanks and machine guns, but by acts of Congress and decisions of the Supreme Court, or that many of the revolutionists did not know what they were or denied it. But revolution is always an affair of force, whatever forms the force disguises itself in. Whether the revolutionists prefer to call themselves Fabians, who seek power by the inevitability of gradualism, or Bolsheviks, who seek power by the dictatorship of the proletariat, the struggle is for power.

Now I thought that I understood much better something that in the past had vaguely nibbled at my mind, but never nibbled to a conclusion—namely, how it happened that so many concealed Communists were clustered in Government, and how it was possible for them to operate so freely with so little fear of detection. For as between revolutionists who only half know what they are doing and revolutionists who know exactly what they are doing the latter are in a superb maneuvering position. At the basic point of the revolution—the shift of power from business to government—the two kinds of revolutionists were at one; and they shared many other views and hopes. Thus men who sincerely abhorred the word Communism, in the pursuit of common ends found that they were unable to distinguish Communists from themselves, except that it was just the Communists who were likely to be most forthright and most dedicated in the common cause. This political color blindness was all the more dogged because it was completely honest. For men who could not see that what they firmly believed was liberalism added up to socialism could scarcely be expected to see what added up to Communism. Any charge of Communism enraged them precisely because they could not grasp the differences between themselves and those against whom it was made. Conscious of their own political innocence, they suspected that it was merely mischievous, and was aimed, from motives of political malice, at themselves. But as the struggle was really for revolutionary power, which in our age is always a struggle for control of the masses, that was the point at which they always betrayed their real character, for they reacted not like liberals, but with the fierceness of revolutionists whenever that power was at issue.

I perceived that the Communists were much more firmly embedded in Government than I had supposed, and that any attempt to disclose or dislodge them was enormously complicated by the political situation in which they were parasitic. Every move against the Communists was felt by the liberals as a move against themselves. If only for the sake of their public health record, the liberals, to protect their power, must seek as long as possible to conceal from themselves and everybody else the fact that the Government had been Communist-penetrated. Unlike the liberals, the Communists were fully aware of their superior tactical position, and knew that they had only to shout their innocence and cry: "Witch hunt!" for the liberals to rally in all innocence to their defense. I felt, too, that a persistent effort by any man to expose the Communists in Government was much less likely to lead to their exposure than to reprisals against him. That fact must be borne constantly in mind in understanding what I did and did not do in the next nine years, and indeed throughout the Hiss Case, which was to prove on a vast scale how well-founded my fears had been.

One of my close friends, himself an ardent New Dealer, who knew my story in full detail, summed up the situation tersely. "I see," he said one day, "why it might not pay the Communists to kill you at this point. But I don't see how the Administration dares to leave you alive."

XII

One form of attack the Communist Party invariably makes upon all ex-Communists, big or little. It tries to make it impossible for them to live by preventing them from getting a job. If they succeed in getting one, the party tries to make it impossible for them to keep it. This is very easy to do. For unless an employer is acutely aware of the larger issues involved, and not always then, he does not want the orderly running of his business continually upset by an ex-Communist who is a constant focus of gossip or turmoil, as the Communists take care that he will be. I had not been at *Time* a fortnight before the Communists went to work on me. The fortnight's grace was due merely to the fact that the Communist Party had not yet discovered my presence at *Time* and warned its local members.

The first or second day that I was in my office, a researcher sidled up to me. A quiet, somewhat sheep-faced girl with slow, observant eyes, she was, as she later told me, a great friend of Vito Marcantonio's. "We are so glad you got the job," she confided in a whisper. "We were afraid that Rahv was going to get it." (Philip Rahv was a Trotskyite literatus of that era.)

A few days later, a *Time* writer stopped me in the hall and asked me to join the Newspaper Guild. At that time, and for a long time afterwards, the *Time* unit of the New York Newspaper Guild was tightly controlled by a small knot of Communists. I said that I did not believe that he would want me in the Guild. He thought I meant that I was so far underground that my politics were a secret from him. A great, knowing smile wreathed his rather striking face (one of *Time's* editors always referred to him as "The King of the Golden River"). "Oh *we* know," he said, "that you are a well-known revolutionist." I said: "You are mistaken. I have broken with the Communist Party." The sunlight faded from the mountaintop. He turned away, incredulous but cool. No doubt, he checked at once. A few days later, the smear campaign against me was in full swing.

This same journalist reappeared at *Time* (which had at last got shut of him) immediately after I began to testify about Alger Hiss, in 1948. He was canvassing my colleagues, asking them to make affidavits including "any dirt at all that you know about Whittaker Chambers."

XIII

During my first day's testimony before the Un-American Activities Committee, Congressman Rankin asked me if there were any Communists at *Time*. I answered that, like the United States Government, *Time* had had its troubles with Communists, but that, perhaps because it was a somewhat smaller enterprise, *Time* had been more successful in solving them.

I might as well have said: like every other publication, *Time* has had its troubles. There is probably no important magazine or newspaper in the country that is not Communist-penetrated to some degree. A staff member of one of the most persistently anti-Communist dailies in the country told me recently that the Communist Party book and registration number of its city editor, a man unsuspected and trusted for years, had just been discovered. So had the party book and registration number of another editor, of even longer standing and greater trust, while a switchboard operator, spotted by one of the paper's reporters who had been smuggled into a Communist rally, turned out to be a high official in the Communist Party's local bureaucracy. There is no defense against such infiltration except eternal editorial and personnel vigilance. *Time* was no more immune than any other publication, but, once it had reluctantly learned the facts of Communist infiltration, it acted with such tactful purpose that today there is not, so far as I know, a Communist writer on its staff.

Like the Government's, the great majority of *Time's* personnel was always overwhelmingly non-Communist. In fact, half the difficulty was that Communism was so remote from the experience of most *Time* people that they could not identify a Communist even when he was quoting Lenin. Their innocence sometimes made them almost perfect dupes. An instance stays in my mind.

I did presently join the Newspaper Guild, and I remember watching the Communists pop up here and there in the meetings to make their prearranged speeches about the points or people they wanted supported. The *Time* unit of the Guild was made up of a proletariat of file clerks, office boys, and other unskilled intellectuals whose interests the Communists were peculiarly solicitous of, for their numbers gave the Communists control. But the unit also included a sizable group of responsible writers and researchers, most of them college graduates, and, in the case of the writers, men who helped to shape the opinions of a million people every week. Yet there they sat, time and again dutifully voting what was wanted by the Communists whom most of them were completely incapable of recognizing for what they were. To them the Communists just looked like more impassioned liberals.

In those days, I had a horror of uttering half a dozen words in public. But one night the spectacle of so much passive stupidity among so many intelligent people brought me to my feet. "Can't you see," I stammered, "that these speakers are simply Communists and that, in voting their way, you are voting the Communist line?"

It was the first time that the hideous charge of Communism had ever been uttered in the *Time* unit of the New York Newspaper Guild. The meeting greeted it with murmurs of outrage from the non-Communists and a wave of pitying laughter from the Communists, some of whom just shook their heads at the hopelessness of my singular attitude. I saw that it was no use and soon after withdrew from the Guild, in spite of warnings that it was against the rules to do so.

But that night, as we left the meeting, one of the non-Communist girls, a young socialite of an old and good family, and an M.A. or a Ph.D., marched upon me. She was ultra smartly gowned and booted. But her studiedly cool and intelligent face was working in lines of most unintelligent anger. "How dare you," she asked with the voice of Bryn Mawr but the snarl of a fishwife, "how dare you call us Communists?" It was no use to explain to her that what I had said was, not that she and others like her were Communists, but that they were non-Communists who were letting the Communists lead them by the nose. She never spoke to me again from that night until she left *Time* to make one of the year's more brilliant marriages. Scores of her kind, just as impeccably pedigreed, socially and culturally poised, also staggering under M.A.'s and Ph.D.'s, and just exactly as witless, were to howl for my head in the Hiss Case.

The specific smear of me at *Time* was pitched in the same tone of pitying ridicule that greeted me from the Communists at the Guild meeting. No sooner had the Communists discovered that I was a deserter than word rippled through the *Time* staff that Chambers was a crank on the subject of Communism. Specifically, he suffered from a delusion that the Communists were after his life. At *Time,* which in those days was in effect a big fraternity where people either intangibly belonged or they didn't, such gossip was poison, not so much because of what it might imply about my past, but because it made me ridiculous. Even a year or two later, when I was working on a difficult cover story and holed up at a midtown hotel to write out of reach of the telephone and other office interruptions, I overheard my editor (no Communist at all) laughingly remark in good faith that I was writing outside the office because

I was hiding from the G.P.U. The Communists only have to start the smear; the others keep it going for them.

Actually, I was struggling desperately, with the thought of my wife and children haunting me, to make good at *Time.* I was having to learn from scratch how to write a wholly new (and to me) rather unnatural journalistic form. There were other difficulties. In my first or second month at *Time,* I had, for example, to write a readable cover story on James Joyce's *Finnegans Wake,* scarcely a line of which is intelligible to the average reader, and which few of my colleagues and, indeed, comparatively few people in the world then pretended to understand. My essay can be read in the back files of *Time,* together with the shorter, but much more sincerely felt obituary that I wrote during the war, when Joyce died.

The Communist whispers against me were abetted by other factors, as they always are; for the whole Communist smear strategy pivots on the knowledge that everybody is human, almost nobody can stand close scrutiny. For one thing, from the very first, I made no secret at *Time* of my Communist past (the Communists, of course, had the advantage of never admitting that they were Communists), and freely admitted that I had been underground. Over the years, a number of my colleagues knew what I had been doing in the past in considerable detail. Then, too, I never missed an opportunity to jab at Communism in my stories. That was completely out of line with *Time's* prevailingly liberal tone and made me at best a rather unmannerly fellow.

To complete my handicaps, I was deeply and organically different from most of the people at *Time.* It was not only a matter of appearance. One of my colleagues always wore low white sneakers to work and another affected plaid lumberjack shirts, corduroy suits with norfolk jackets and sported a beard. But those were recognizable carry-overs of campus individualism. My lack of clothes sense was a complete lack of ability to be interested in appearance at all. My years in the Communist Party and its underground had extraordinarily unfitted me for the conventions and relationships of ordinary life.

To me many of my colleagues at *Time,* basically kind and intensely well-meaning people, seemed to me as charming and as removed from reality as fish in a fish bowl. To me they seemed to know little about the forces that were shaping the history of our time. To me they seemed like little children, knowing and clever little children, but knowing and clever chiefly about trifling things while they were extremely resistant to finding out about anything else. There were, of course, mighty exceptions. *Time* was tops among the world's news-magazines, consistently able and sometimes brilliant, because of the work of a small group of men. The whole show was possible at all because, within the framework of his creation, Henry R. Luce is a publishing genius. T. S. Matthews' contribution to the humanity of *Time*, both in the intellectual and personal sense of the word, cannot be overstated. There were a few others. One thinks at once of James Agee, Robert Cantwell, Robert Fitzgerald, John K. Jessup, Louis Kronenberger, Winthrop Sargeant, Tom Hyland and the late Calvin Fixx among the writers.

If *Time* people seemed sometimes curiously truncated to me, I hesitate to think of how I must have appeared to them, though it is a happiness to remember the generosity with which they ultimately voted me into the club. Most of them were liberals, and I was incapable of being a liberal. Nor could my chronically equable and even fun-loving manner really deceive anyone. Mine was the gayety that has been retained in spite of life; their gayety was carefree. Experience had implanted at my core a somberness that I thought to conceal except in my writing, but whose mute shadow was stronger than I realized and sometimes made people uncomfortable. I was drinking one night with a group of my higher editorial colleagues. Among them was David Hulburd, then, I believe, the chief of *Time's* domestic correspondents, more recently the author of a best-seller about the Pasadena school situation. As the evening wore on, Dave suddenly shifted uncomfortably and said: "Look at Chambers. He just sits there, saying nothing, just watching us and thinking and thinking."

In my first months at *Time*, too, I inevitably went through the "*Time* curve" that most *Time* writers suffer and all experienced editors expect, dread and allow for. The curve graphs the rise and fall of a writer who begins by writing more or less naturally. Then he becomes conscious of something extra that *Time* requires. He tries to achieve it by writing "*Time* style," which he invariably succeeds only in parodying because his predicament proves that he has not yet grasped the fact that the style is a discipline of expression, and not a horseplay with queer words and elliptical phrases. The more he parodies, the worse he writes. The worse he writes, the more often his stories come back from the editor to be written over. The more he must rewrite, the more frantically insecure he feels, as writer and jobholder, and the worse he rewrites. Meanwhile, nobody comes near him to advise or guide. He is left strictly alone in his little bare *Time* office, which, if a writer is in form, is one of the best workshops ever devised, but if he is near disintegration becomes a setting for *Time's* special version of the pit and the pendulum.

There used to be a story at *Time* about a writer who went through the curve, month after month, with some of his stories accepted by the editor, but more of them rejected for rewrite, but with never a word of encouragement, advice or even criticism—in fact, no editorial contact of any kind. The monumental silence was driving the writer slowly mad when one day his heavy door swung open and his editor appeared holding the writer's latest story. "At last," thought the desperate man "now the axe—or he will tell me what's the matter."

The editor placed the copy on the writer's desk and laid his finger on the word "fourteen." "At *Time,*" he said, "we write all numbers above twelve as numerals." Then he walked out, and the door swung softly shut cushioned by compressed air.

Caught between a mounting sense of my failure as a writer and the intolerable atmosphere, due in part to my own behavior, but also to Communist whispers, I used to stand at my office window, stare across the Hudson and the blue Jersey Hills toward Maryland and my family, and long for release from my ordeal. "Will no one," I used to wonder, "have the simple mercy to fire me?" I could not quit. And each time I touched bottom, something drove me back to write and rewrite and rewrite my rewrites, all unconscious that a dozen eyes were watching the performance with great interest and understanding. I knew only that I must not fail. I must not fail because my family depended on me to succeed; but, above all, because the opportunity to succeed had been granted me by a kind of miracle, to prove whether or not there was in me something worth saving. If I succeeded in saving it, it would not be for myself primarily, but for something else.

I sat one night with a woman who became one of my closest friends at *Time.* "I don't know how you stand it," she said, "and I don't see how you've survived." "I stand it," I said, "for the same reason that I've survived. I cannot really be beaten because on my side is a Power."

XIV

From the first, I had wanted to write foreign news for *Time.* I was soon given a chance. The Foreign News staff was large. I was the last and least of its members. Moreover, I soon had reason to suspect that the writer who assigned and edited my copy was at least a close fellow traveler.

At first, I was given some Russian news to write. I wrote the stories with a tone clearly unfriendly to Communism. As stories, some of them turned out rather well. They clearly displeased my colleague. Soon I received no more Russian news to handle.

Instead, I got the stories that nobody else wanted, those that were least newsworthy and least likely to "make the book." Thus when the "marked copy" of the magazine reached the editor, with each writer's name indicated on the story he had written, my name would sometimes be missing altogether, or would appear only on a few lines of copy. In short, I was not worth my wages.

I did the best I could with the stories I had been given; my best was not very good. I particularly regretted the lack of background material and research that would give the stories body and color. For my stories there was seldom any research. One day, entirely by chance, I discovered why. I went to my senior colleague's office to ask him for something. He was not there, and while I was rummaging around for whatever I needed, to my astonishment, I found buried at the bottom of his basket, neatly clipped together in one lot, all the research for my week's stories.

A few days after that discovery, my editor called me into his office. He spoke frankly. My senior colleague, he said, had made an issue of me. He had announced that either I went or he went. *Time* valued my colleague highly, he said—and let his voice trail off. I expected him to say also that I was fired. Instead, I was put back to reviewing books. It was the spin of the coin for me at *Time.* To this day I know no practical reason why I was not fired. But for several years, it was the unwritten rule at *Time* that Chambers' treatment of Communism and Russia was so controversial that he was not to be permitted to write directly about either.

I was soon put to writing such comparatively uncontroversial departments as Art and Cinema. Even so, the forbidden subject sometimes crept in. My delighted review of the movie, *Ninotchka,* threw my fellow-traveling researcher into hideous gloom, while my review of *The Grapes of Wrath* (as smart cinema but mischievous propaganda) brought me my first invitation to a *Time* editorial lunch. At the head of a table, lined by my colleagues, sat Henry R. Luce, whom I had seen only distantly before, usually as the subject of awed whispers. He proved to be entirely human and thanked me briefly for my piece. It was almost the first kind word that I had ever received at *Time*.

Across the table from me was sitting John McManus, then *Time's* very fluent radio writer, later an American Labor Party candidate for Governor of New York. He stared at me balefully. "I should think your favorite movie," he said, "would be *The Informer*." A mighty armor is our innocence. Guilelessly, I agreed. The picturization of the novel by the brother of my old *Daily Worker* colleague, Tom O'Flaherty, was in fact one of my favorite movies. It was several minutes before I suddenly realized what McManus meant.

My tacit exclusion from writing Communist news at first exasperated me, for I saw no one around me (except the Communists, of course) who knew anything at all about the subject. But gradually I welcomed the ban. I began to see that the kind of sniping that I had been doing was shallow and largely profitless; anybody could do that. It seemed to me that I had a more important task to do, one that was peculiarly mine. It was not to attack Communism frontally. It was to clarify, on the basis of the news, the religious and moral position that made Communism evil. I had been trying to make a negative point. Now I had to state the positive position, and it was a much more formidable task than attack, for it meant explaining simply and readably for millions the reasons why the great secular faith of this age is wrong and the religious faith of the ages is right; why, in the words of the *Song of Roland*, the Christians are right and the heathen are wrong.

This change in my mood and my work reflected a deepening within myself.

X V

One of *Time's* top editors asked me one day what section of the magazine I would most like to write, if I had my choice. The implication was that, if possible, he would let me write it. I said: "Religion." He shot me a terrified glance. "I wouldn't dare," he said. He was thinking of my Communist past. A year later, by Henry Luce's personal order, I wrote the cover story on Pope Pius XII, and the Jesuits ordered several hundred copies of the essay to be used in their schools. I felt that I was beginning to carry out that command which I believed had been laid upon me in the hall at Mount Royal Terrace.

Men may seek God alone. They must worship him in common. The words of Miguel de Unamuno also express my own conviction: "A miserere sung in a cathedral by a multitude tormented by destiny is equal to a philosophy." The God it worships is what a nation is, and how he worships Him defines what a man is. I sought a congregation in which I could worship God as the expression of a common need. For I had not changed from secular to religious faith in order to tolerate a formless good will vaguely tinctured with rationalized theology and social uplift. I was not seeking ethics; I was seeking God. My need was to be a practicing Christian in the same sense that I had been a practicing Communist. I was seeking a community of worship in which a daily mysticism (for I hold that God cannot be known in any other way) would be disciplined and fortified by an orderly, and even practical, spirit and habit of life and the mind. Some instinctive sense of my need, abetted by a memory of a conversation with my grandmother Chambers, which I have written about earlier, drew me powerfully to the Religious Society of Friends, the Quakers.

Yet I hesitated. I hesitated because the Quaker rebuff to me in my youth, which I have also mentioned, lashing me at a moment of personal distress, and tender and naive submission to the Quaker spirit, had left an unhealing scar. But I hesitated even more because the traditional Quaker witness against war seemed to close the door of the meeting house against me, forever barring me from the peace within which it was my pathos to crave, but not my right to share. Friends refused to bear arms even in a righteous war because all war is, by its nature evil, and to bear arms even righteously can only perpetuate evil in the forms of hate and death. Few had reason to know better than I that the problem of evil is inseparable in our time from this century's inevitable struggle against it in its political form of Communism. For that very reason, I above all, could not refuse to struggle against it by all means, including arms. With a pang, I concluded that, for me, the Quakers were the friends to whom I had no natural right, and their peaceful meeting houses, the homes which were not destined to be mine.

But my need to be part of a community of worship was pressing. Chance threw me together at *Time* with Samuel Gardner Welles, who became my close friend and whose family became my friends. Welles was the son of a revered Episcopal clergyman and brother of a bishop. At the Cathedral of St. John the Divine, Welles introduced me to the Reverend William Dudley Foulke Hughes, who instructed and baptised me, and presently assisted at my confirmation by the late Bishop Manning. My sponsors were Welles and my old friend Robert Cantwell, who had returned to the church just before me. After the ceremony, the Bishop, then an old man, frail, but with an imperious and reverend fierceness, drew me aside and pledged me to the struggle for faith against secularism and evil.

Sunday is one of *Time's* two busiest days. Church attendance is all but impossible. On week days, I used to attend vespers, traveling for that purpose up to the Cathedral of St. John. There was a solemnity in the service at the altar. There was a solemnity of another kind in the great spaces of the unfinished church, in which huddled the little group with which I worshipped—old people mostly, who seemed in that vast nave less like the bearers of those great tidings that had once stirred and transformed men's souls than like the survivors of a spiritual catastrophe and an age that could not long survive them.

When Welles was urging me to become an Episcopalian, I had warned him that I felt myself really to be a Quaker, and that only Friends' witness against bearing arms in war kept me from becoming one of them. The need was stronger than I knew. The silence of Quaker worship continued to reach out and draw me irresistibly to it.

At that point, I opened the *Journal* of George Fox, the founder of Quakerism. It was the first Quaker book that I had ever read. Three hundred years after it was written, Fox's *Journal* is still less a book than a voice for those to whom it speaks. It was a voice that spoke peculiarly, as Quakers say, "to my condition." It summoned me to a direct daily experience of God and told me that His revelation is continuous to those who seek to hear His voice in the silence of all distractions of this world. It summoned me to know the Inward Light, that of God within myself, as within all other men without exception. It enjoined on me a simplicity of the spirit whose first commandment is compassion, which is expressly commanded not to judge, and whose answer to the surging enmity of the world must be yea yea and nay nay "because more than this cometh of evil." In short, it summoned me to the most difficult of vocations—to be a Christian as in the first century.

The saints are invariably violent. They know what the age has forgotten in its pews—that the spirit, if it truly stirs, never brings peace, but always brings a sword. Submission to the spirit may bring peace. But the spirit itself, aroused in man or nation, is a blade that exists to divide the truth from untruth, the living from the dead, the conformist from the Christian. George Fox, the man of peace, was also a man of force. "The man in the leather breeches" was a man of the people, of sheep herding and muddy fields, of lonely footpaths and hilltop vigils, of gross despairs and uncouth righteousness, of serene inspirations and dogged sufferings, of bloody beatings and stinking prisons. I knew him as if we had spoken face to face. Few who call themselves Quakers have added anything to what he had to say to me, though I have sometimes thought that they might profitably listen for what he might have to say to them.

In those days, the late Arthur Burke led a silent meeting on Wednesday nights at the 20th Street Meeting House in New York. I began to attend. The meetings were among the decisive experiences of my life. One in particular united the worshippers and what they worshipped in a stillness so intense that as, at its close, the spirit of the meeting seemed to ebb in great pulsations, Arthur Burke's voice broke the vibrant silence. "This meeting," he said, "has had a divine covering."

I was in fact, though not yet in name, a Quaker. An inward experience itself, beyond any power of the mind, had reached me. For what had happened to me, Robert Barclay has given the expression that all Quakers know because it is final for all who have suffered it: "Of which I myself, in a part, am a true witness; who not by strength of arguments or by a particular disquisition of each doctrine, and convincement of my understanding thereby, came to receive and bear witness to the Truth, but by being secretly reached by that life. For, when I came into the silent assemblies of God's people, I felt a secret power among them, which touched my heart; and, as I gave way unto it, I found the evil weakening in me and the good raised up. . . ."

There was a little Quaker meeting—Pipe Creek Monthly Meeting of Friends—near Union Bridge, about twelve miles from where we were living in Maryland. One summer Sunday, when for some reason I was not working, I drove over to it with my little daughter. The meeting house stood, screened by trees and bushes, on a windswept hill. Beyond, lay the Maryland farms. Behind, lay the meeting's burial ground. Within, my daughter and I sat in silence with a small group of Friends. The longest strand of spider web that I have ever seen looped from one wall of the meeting house to the other, and swayed gently in the breeze, for both doors were open, through which came the continual singing of birds in the burial ground behind. There is a beautiful 17th-century Quaker phrase: "in the silence of the creature." In that silence, I gave thanks to God that I had come home.

As we were driving back, I asked my daughter what she had been doing in the hour-long silence. "I was watching the spider web," she said, suddenly laughing like an illumination. Then she asked me, curiously, what the others had been doing. "They were listening for the voice of God," I said. "Did they hear it?" she asked, after considering the point for a while. "No," I said, "I am afraid not that time."

XVI

One night one of my close friends burst into my office at *Time*. He was holding a yellow tear-off that had just come over the teletype. "They have murdered the General," he said. "Krivitsky has been killed."

Krivitsky's body had been found in a room in a small Washington hotel a few blocks from the Capitol. He had a room permanently reserved at a large downtown hotel where he had always stayed when he was in Washington. He had never stayed at the small hotel before. Why had he gone there?

He had been shot through the head and there was evidence that he had shot himself. At whose command? He had left a letter in which he gave his wife and children the unlikely advice that the Soviet Government and people were their best friends. Previously, he had warned them that, if he were found dead, never under any circumstances to believe that he had committed suicide. Who had forced my friend to write the letter? I remembered the saying: "Any fool can commit a murder, but it takes an artist to commit a good natural death."

I had seen Walter Krivitsky in New York a few nights before he died. We had spent hours together, tramping the streets, taking circuitous routes and watching, as in the old underground days, to see if we were followed. I saw no sign of trackers. Much of our talk had been about religion. Like me, Krivitsky had become convinced that religious faith is a human necessity. But I sensed that with him that was a "position"—something that he had reasoned his way to, and not something that he had deeply felt. Nevertheless, he asked me if I would arrange for his instruction so that he could be baptized and confirmed in the Episcopal Church. My letter, conveying his request, was in Father Hughes's hands at the time Krivitsky was killed.

Krivitsky also told me something else that night. A few days before, he had taken off the revolver that he usually carried and placed it in a bureau drawer. His seven-year-old son watched him. "Why do you put away the revolver?" he asked. "In America," said Krivitsky, "nobody carries a revolver." "Papa," said the child, "carry the revolver."

XVII

The news of Krivitsky's death reached my wife through the newspapers before I could write to her. She and the children were spending the winter in a small, plain house in the plain and pleasant town of New Smyrna Beach, in Florida. She was overcome by panic and terror. She was unable to reach me at once at *Time,* and, knowing that I saw Krivitsky frequently, she was afraid that I also had been killed, or would be.

She took the children out of school, bundled everything portable into the car, and, when she finally got through to me, was in South Carolina. On the telephone, I told her to go back, first, because, if there were any danger, and the attack on Krivitsky was to be followed up by one on me, which I doubted, she and the children would be safer in Florida. Moreover, we were bound to help two others.

The day after Krivitsky's funeral, I met his widow and son during my lunch hour. I waited until just before train time to avoid observation. Then I hurried them aboard an Atlantic Coastline coach and sent them to join my family in New Smyrna Beach. The Krivitskys hid with us until spring. Then my wife drove them north.

For a while, we all lived together in that little house near Westminster which Alger Hiss had once intended to buy. We were crowded and our mutual discomfort had a consequence very important for my family and me. My wife and I had been discussing the question of settling permanently on a farm. The congestion caused us to act more quickly than we should otherwise have done. We bought the farm near Westminster where we have lived for the last eleven years.

But the Krivitskys did not remain with us long. Tonya Krivitsky, brave and independent, wanted to be on her own. The loneliness of our farm, and our secluded life, which we enjoyed, depressed her more sociable spirit. She and her son moved to a city, where she has ever since led an uncomplaining life of hard work, supporting herself and her son by the skill of her hands and the fortitude of her character.

XVIII

At last, I asked the Friends at Pipe Creek if my children might be admitted to the Meeting. I did not feel myself worthy of that fellowship. Instead, they proposed that my wife and I, together with the children, join the Meeting as a family.

I hesitated. I asked myself if so great a blessing could be meant for me. It seemed to me that it was indeed meant to be so, and that I would be doing no wrong to respond to the summons, for though Friends, as a society, still maintain their ancient witness for peace and against war, it is the sense of modern Quakerism that, for the individual, the decision in wartime is a matter for his own conscience. As a family, we were united to the Meeting.

Pipe Creek is an old and small Meeting. Some of the most peaceful hours of my life have been spent in the silence of its worship among its quiet and good Friends. In winter the meeting house is closed. Friends find it more convenient to worship in one another's homes. The tone of the meeting is one of peace, rather than a groping or a soaring of the spirit. Never have I known in it anything approaching the experience of the meetings on 20th Street, though I have known a similar experience in our neighbor meeting at Menallen, in Pennsylvania.

For that failure of the spirit, I look first of all into myself. I once heard a very old man complaining to our Friend, Eliza Rakestraw, that the meeting had been so dull that he fell asleep. "Thee brings thy meeting with thee, Henry," she said gently.

Others, I know, have felt what I have not. Sometimes, in one

Quaker house, I have gone upstairs at the close of the meeting to speak with Martha Englar, where she sits, year in year out, beside her window. She is a fragile woman with the pale, transparent flesh of the very old and the very good. "Is that thee, David (my favorite name)?" she will ask as she hears me, in the doorway. "Come here so that I may touch thee. I cannot see thee." She adds invariably, "I could not go downstairs. But I left my door open so that I could catch the vibrations of the meeting."

XIX

"Return Home to Within," wrote the 17th-century Quaker, Francis Howgill, "sweep your Houses all. The Goat is there, the little Leaven is there, the Grain of Mustard Seed you will see which the Kingdom of God is like. . . and there you will see your Teacher, not removed into a Corner, but present when you are upon your Beds and about your Labours, convincing, instructing, judging, and giving Peace to all that love and follow Him."

Most religious growth is slow, and so was mine. It was slow in the development of formal habits. (I have never developed satisfactory routines of worship.) I was slow in approaching the intellectual side of Christianity in which I am still a schoolboy. I tried to conform as closely as I could, without making myself singular, to the traditional habits of the sect I belonged to. I sought to discipline myself to say nothing unkind against any man and to curb gossip (an almost inhuman task in any human organization). I was surprised at how much I had been inadvertently guilty of in a day. I gave up swearing completely and I almost never drank even when heavy drinking was in swing. I did not believe in never drinking, for no one was ever able to tell me when drinking may not be as medicinal to the spirit as alcohol sometimes is to the body. I dressed as plainly as possible (my dark suit when I began to testify in the first Hiss trial was instantly a target for newsmen and I switched to grays because the darker suit had ceased to be a witness at that point and had become a provocation). Most Quakers have given up the witness of the "plain dress." I meant to keep to a form of it suitably modified. I believed with Job Scott: "The flesh saith, there is little in dress; religion does not consist in apparel; there is little in language, there is little in paying tythes etc. . . . . To which, I think, it may be safely added, there is little or nothing in people who plead as above hinted. . . ." For I hold, contrary to many Friends, that all the original Quaker witnesses were never more important, not because it is desirable that the world should be convinced by them, but that by means of them the Quaker should make his own person a living testimony against the world, should thereby protest mutely that those things which the modern world holds dear and indispensable are at the root of its despair.

Once I had been "secretly reached by that life" of Quakerism, I felt a human completion such as I had never known before—an adulthood, a maturity, that marked off the forty years of my life as a childhood. I knew then that, however it might be with others, I could never be a complete man without God. I suspected that the same fatal deficiency that I had known was at the root of all the troubles of modern man and must result inevitably, as I was to write later on in *Time*, "in intolerable shallowness of thought combined with incalculable mischief in action." Evidences of that mortal incompleteness I found in most of the minds around me.

As I acquired the power of overcoming myself and the habit of reaching beyond myself for help and guidance, I saw all men and women, no longer as creatures predominantly good or evil, kind or cruel, but as individual beings "tormented by destiny"—tormented more terribly because each was enclosed beyond the power to change in the ordeal of his individuality.

Like the Bishop of Digne, in *Les Misérables,* I inclined by nature "toward the distressed and the repentant." The "ferociously virtuous" always made me a little uncomfortable because they raised in the depth of my mind an unwanted question. For while I can grant at once the right of goodness to be ferocious, I suspect always that its ferocity, to ring clear, must be the ferocity of aroused compassion, which is rooted in the understanding of self-fallibility, not of self-righteousness.

Moreover, it is only the sins of the spirit that really appal me. The sins of the flesh affect me chiefly as unseemly and embarrassing, like the lapses of children, and for the same reason, because they betray the terrible immaturity of the spirit, at whatever age they occur. And who that is human will call himself safe from that mortal recurrence? This is not to condone sin. This is to mark a distinction between those sins of the spirit which are condign, in part perhaps because they always partake of the rebellious sin of Satan, and those sins that are ugly, wasteful, shameful, because, among other things, they impair that "dignity of the human substance" which the Mass explicitly celebrates (*Deus Qui humanae substantiae dignitatem mirabiliter condidisti*—God Who hast miraculously founded the dignity of the human substance).

Now a truly wonderful thing began to happen to me. I do not know what force moved the gravitation, but little by little people began to open my office door at *Time* which in my own need few had ever opened. They would sit down, and after a rambling preamble, suddenly confide to me some distress that was destroying their peace or their lives. Sometimes their trouble concerned the trifling and absurd relationships of the office, which, nevertheless, could be personally harrowing and even disastrous. Sometimes there were technical problems of writing that were bringing a writer to the brink of breakdown. Sometimes there were personal confessions of the most desperate kind. They came from people at all levels of the organization, from top to bottom. Men and women both have burst into tears in my office while I rose to snap the lock on the door.

I never spoke of religion to those sufferers unless I was specifically asked about it, and then reluctantly and little. I said very little at any time. For they did not often come to me, even though they might think that they did, for the comfort of words or practical guidance. They came for release from the cell in which they were locked alone with themselves. Why did they come to me? I think chiefly because, in ways that I do not understand, they sensed that I saw in each a subject to be consoled and not to be judged—the torment of destiny rules out judgment. From me they wanted not words, but the instinctive sense that I recognized what was peculiarly "that of God within them," and because I made them recognize it in themselves. And this was true even when they were godless. They felt, too, that I would not betray their confidence even to the point of never mentioning it again to them.

I never invited or even welcomed those confessions, which sometimes seriously hampered my work. But I could not ever turn anyone away, for, of course, they were not seeking me; they were seeking something that they felt through me. One of my favorite stories about the Bishop of Digne concerned the arrival of Jean Valjean in that town. Night was falling. He was hungry and needed lodging. Rough and menacing, he was thrown out of all the inns, turned away from all the houses and threatened with the police. He tried to crawl into a kennel. The dog attacked him. He drifted back to the main square and, in the dark, encountered a poor and pious woman. By then he was enraged by human inhumanity. He roughly asked for her money. She gave him what she had. She asked why he did not go to an inn. He told her. She asked why he did not seek lodging in a house. "Have you knocked at all the doors?" she asked. He said: "Yes." She pointed to the meanest door on the square. It was the Bishop's. "Have you knocked at that door?" she asked. He said: "No." "Knock there," she said.

That is why, when someone slipped into my office with that look I came to know, and, after carefully closing the door, said: "I want to tell you something," I sometimes nodded toward my door and said, in part to ease the tension, "Knock there." I never explained what I meant, which, indeed, was chiefly a reminder to myself.

Perhaps no part of my work at *Time* was so important, and perhaps it was less of a secret than I supposed. I suspected so one day after I had become an editor and my managing editor called me in and told me that I would have to take over a writer who was well on his way to a nervous breakdown. "I don't know whether you can save him," he said, "but nobody else can."

I came to feel that the problem of evil was the central problem of human life, and that it took as many forms as there were men and women. Through it, I thought I understood the meaning of that line of Charles Péguy's: "No one is so competent a witness to the substance of Christianity as the sinner; no one, except, perhaps, the saint."

In nothing did my preoccupation with the problem of evil affect me more acutely than in my thoughts about my former comrades in the underground and what my attitude should be toward them.

X X

Two years after I had talked with Adolf Berle, a special agent of the F.B.I. called me up at *Time* and asked to talk to me. I have forgotten his name. I shall call him Special Agent Smith. Half an hour later, he walked into my office accompanied by another special agent, whose name I have also forgotten, and whom I shall call Jones. They were the first F.B.I. agents I had ever seen.

Special Agent Jones took a seat to one side of me and just beyond my range of vision where he sat in complete silence throughout the interview. Special Agent Smith sat in front of my desk and began to ask me questions about underground activities in Washington.

I said that before I could answer his questions, I must first make a telephone call. The agent objected, but I insisted. I asked the *Time* operator to get me Adolf A. Berle at the State Department. The call went through at once. "Mr. Berle," I said, "there are two F.B.I. agents in my office. Have I your permission to tell them what I told you in 1939?" There was a moment's pause at the State Department end of the wire. "Of course," said Berle, "of course."

"Thank you," I said.

Special Agent Smith looked slightly puzzled. He did not tell me, of course, that neither he, nor anybody else in the F.B.I., had ever heard of the Berle notes (The Berle notes first passed into the hands of the Government after this interview). The F.B.I. had not come to me because of my conversation with Berle, but for an entirely different reason. My old friend, Ludwig Lore, had denounced me—a fact that I did not learn from the F.B.I., but from another security agency of the Government.

I no longer recall most of the details of that first conversation with the F.B.I., except that I told Special Agent Smith that in talking to Berle, I had omitted the names of Harry Dexter White and George Silverman.

Special Agent Smith seemed almost as excited as Assistant Secretary of State Berle had once been by what I had to tell him. He asked if I would agree to meet him somewhere else for a long conversation. He suggested a hotel room.

At once my suspicion was aroused. In those days I did not know what degree of control the Administration exercised over the F.B.I., about which, in fact, I knew almost nothing. But by then I was certain that the Administration was more interested in suppressing my story than in discovering the facts. From what I knew of history and politics, I did not doubt for a moment that it would resort to any feasible means to suppress them. Therefore, I told Special Agent Smith that I would meet him at any time in my office, but nowhere else.

As he was leaving, Special Agent Jones uttered his first remark. "You interest me greatly," he said. Special Agent Smith promised to be back in a few days. I never saw those special agents again. In fact, I did not see another agent of the F.B.I. for almost a year, and then only for a few moments. After that, I did not see another F.B.I. agent for almost two years.

Let that surprise no one. It should be pointed out that, in those days, the F.B.I. was gravely understaffed, and that, during the war, its chief assignment was German, not Soviet, espionage. Yet to me the inference then seemed inescapable that only a resolute lack of interest outside the F.B.I. in circles far above it could have checked for so long an investigation of my story which was slowly becoming an open secret known to Government officials and newsmen. Meanwhile my own feelings about informing underwent a decisive change.

In those years, too, unknown to me, most of the underground Communists were rapidly rising in the Government. For it should also be borne in mind that for nine years I had no communication of any kind with my former comrades, and, with one or two exceptions, almost never heard their names mentioned. Even about those one or two I knew practically nothing.

X X I

A few days after my first visit by the F.B.I., I was made a senior editor of *Time.* The appointment closed my third term as a Books writer, this time teamed with my friend, James Agee, probably the most gifted writer who ever worked for *Time.* A new insight had made the job very pleasant to me. I had perceived that *Time's* Books section, usually the last section in the magazine, and rather looked down on as something outside the main stream of the news, was, in fact, *Time's* editorial page. For no one could comment on books without at the same time commenting on the whole range of views and news. The Communists understood this just as well as I did, and, throughout my Books assignment, I wrote under a barrage from them and their unwitting friends. But it was no longer a massacre; it had become an artillery duel. "Every week," said one of my amused friends, "that mortar goes off in the last five pages of *Time.*"

I wrote with a new ease and authority. But I found *Time's* five-day week too short for my writing needs. I began the practice of working through a day, a night and the following day without sleep, that I was to follow (with one enforced interruption) throughout my years at *Time.*

Agee and I soon brought the Books section to the number one spot in the readers' polls, and Books began to be used as a text in

English classes in the schools. The section also caught the eye of the editor-in-chief of *Time, Life* and *Fortune,* Henry R. Luce, who asked me, in addition, to edit a series of philosophical essays for *Fortune.* That was my first association with Luce, with whom, over the years, I came to feel a bond of common editorial and journalistic intuition, and, more important, a common religious concern. For the world, which is accustomed to thinking of Luce as a publishing tycoon, does not know that he is also an intensely religious man.

As a senior editor, I first edited some seven sections in the Back-of-the-Book—Art, Books, Religion, Medicine, etc. One day Luce called me to his office, at the top of the Time and Life Building and asked me if I thought that one man could edit all the Back-of-the-Book. I said yes. He asked me if I would undertake to do it. I said yes. I was not taking anyone's job. One of *Time's* periodical changings of the guard was in full swing. While the former managing editor traveled around the world and his successor to be (still unannounced) ran *Time's* London bureau, Luce himself edited the magazine.

It was humanly possible for one man to edit the whole Back-of-the-Book, just as it is humanly possible for a man to lift a yearling heifer. It is harder to hold it aloft for five days on end. Henry Luce is a dynamic editor. Editing thirteen sections with Luce editing the whole book was an invaluable experience. But it was also somewhat like working directly behind a buzz saw, chewing metal faster than the eye can follow and throwing off an unremitting shower of sharp and shining filings.

As my immediate assistant, I had chosen my closest friend at *Time,* the late Calvin Fixx, a man who had curbed a naturally violent temper to become one of the wisest, gentlest and mellowest souls I will ever know. I have forgotten how long we worked together. Often we ended our week at four o'clock in the morning after having worked for thirty-six hours, almost without stopping and wholly without sleep. We kept up the pace by smoking five or six packs of cigarettes and drinking thirteen or fourteen cups of coffee a day.

One night, some of our colleagues found Fixx wandering dazedly on the street. His heart had given out. Though slowly, he recovered, and *Time* generously cared for him, then and afterwards, he was not destined to live many more years. He died while I was testifying during the Hiss Case. In him, and in the late Joseph L. Roesch, a New York attorney* who died about the same time, I lost two of the friends who had been closest to me in my middle years, and at the moment when I most needed them.

My turn came a few weeks after Fixx's. For some time, I had suffered intermittently from pains that began in my chest and shot down my left arm. Friends urged me to go to a doctor. I kept putting it off. But when at last pain forced me to go, the doctor diagnosed angina pectoris and ordered immediate, absolute rest.

I seemed to have reached another great divide. But if I must undergo a long convalescence, I was determined that it should not be at an expensive hospital. If I were going to die, I meant to die at home. I was much more concerned about my family's situation than my own. The farm was not paid for. It was bringing in no income. We were like people who have started across a shaky bridge and have been caught midway of it by disaster. Those were gray days. The children were worried and silent. As usual, my wife prepared without the slightest sign of dismay to carry on.

I had never rested in my life. I did not know how to rest. My mother had immediately come to be with my wife. One day I found her sanding a cabinet. I tried to help her. The slight exertion was a final touch. In half an hour, the problem of how to rest was settled for me. I went to bed. I did not get up again for several months.

My illness was memorable for one incident. I awoke one night about two o'clock in the morning. My heart seemed to be swelling out of my chest and I could scarcely breathe. I thought that that was probably the crisis. My first instinct was to call my family. Then I thought: "No. There is nothing that they can do for me. Why should their memory of me be one of fear and pain, instead of the peaceful good night that we have already said?" But I was deeply troubled by the thought of what would become of them. Then I realized that I had reached a point in experience where I could do nothing at all about them or about anything else in the world. They and all of life were completely beyond my

* By a curious chance, Joseph L. Roesch had been an unsuccessful aspirant to that judgeship to which President Truman appointed Samuel H. Kaufman, the judge in the first Hiss trial. As he waited to die, Joe somehow found strength to write that I was to have the good-luck pin which had belonged to his father, and which I carried, in memory of a brave and generous spirit, through the second Hiss trial.

help and therefore my concern. I said the simplest of prayers and felt complete peace in surrendering myself, my wife and children to God.

A very different kind of incident also took place during that illness. An F.B.I. agent called one morning. My doctor's orders were not to move my hands or arms even to shave. My third special agent found me propped up in bed with several months' growth of beard on my face. He stayed only a few moments. He had come for one purpose. He showed me a picture and asked me if I knew who it was. It was J. Peters.

A specialist later rejected the diagnosis of angina. I have no memory for symptoms which I always minimize, and I forget pain almost as soon as it has passed. For some time, I accepted the opinion that I had suffered a physical breakdown due to complete exhaustion. Later, it seemed impossible that I could have lived through the Hiss Case if my heart had been ailing. But of late, after a lapse of years, the paralyzing pains have returned again. Only, now, they have lost their power to make me anxious in any way.

This was the illness that the Hiss defense worked hard to build into a mental collapse. Unfortunately, the medical records are complete in great detail, and my doctor had attended me almost every day throughout my illness. There was no trace even of nervous breakdown, let alone mental collapse, so that it became impossible for the defense to use the story in court though it was fed out widely as a rumor. Perhaps the final flourish was given it by a nationally syndicated columnist who electrified his millions of readers on the eve of the first Hiss trial by asking: "Was that Whittaker Chambers who was seen leaving a Park Ave. psychiatrist's office?" At the time, I was in Maryland, a fact that could have been checked instantly by telephoning me.

XXII

I returned to *Time* seven or eight months after I had left it. At first, I edited only two or three departments of the magazine. My office had been furnished with a couch and my orders were to lie down at least two or three times a day. Sometimes I lay down oftener. For, though I told no one, I still suffered slight pains. But no company is geared to convalescence. Slowly, as my strength returned, I went back to editing seven sections. For, henceforth, the Back-of-the-Book was divided between two editors, one of them, at that time, a cousin of Priscilla Hiss's first husband.*

I had once told the managing editor of *Time,* who was also my friend, that the one section of *Time* I really felt equipped to edit was Foreign News. When the Foreign News editor elected to go abroad during the war, I was moved into his post to edit for two months. I remained for more than a year—one of the most strenuous years of my life. The tacit ban on Chambers' editing or writing of Soviet or Communist news had at last been broken. My assignment sent a shiver through most of *Time's* staff, where my views were well known and detested with a ferocity that I did not believe possible until I was at grips with it. With my first few Foreign News sections, the shiver turned into a shudder.

For I held certain facts to be self-evident on the basis of almost every scrap of significant foreign news: 1) the Soviet Union was not a "great ally"—it was a calculating enemy making use of World War II to prepare for World War III; 2) the Soviet Union was not a democracy; it was a monstrous dictatorship; 3) the Communist International had been dissolved in name only; in effect, it still functioned; 4) the Soviet Union was not a thin-skinned, underprivileged waif that must at any cost be wheedled into the family of free nations, but a toughly realistic world power whose primary purpose at that moment of history was conquest of the free world; 5) the indispensable first step in that conquest was the control of Central Europe and China; 6) the Chinese Communists were not "agrarian liberals," but Chinese Communists, after the Russian Communist Party, the Number One section of the Communist International.

History has proved that, in the main, these views were right—at least, I think, no soldier in Korea would seriously question them. But, in 1945, when it was most important to assert them because there was then still time to avert some of the catastrophe that would inevitably follow from a failure to grasp their reality, those views were anathema. They challenged an impassioned, powerful and all but universal official and unofficial pro-Soviet opinion. The nation can thank *Time,* and specifically Henry R. Luce, that week by week in that critical period, it pointed out, against a tide of foaming opinion, the true meaning of events. The files are there for those who have forgotten.

* Priscilla Hiss had also worked for *Time*; in the 1920's, when she had been head of researchers.

The effort that made this service possible cost a price. It is not my intention here to go into the details of that weekly struggle, which would make a most informative book in itself. But Foreign News was quickly nicknamed "bloody angle," and editing it turned into a kind of irrepressible conflict. Violently opposed to my interpretation of the news, on one side, were most of my colleagues on the editorial staff of *Time*. On the other side were half a dozen friends of varying degrees of like-mindedness, and myself. Fortunately, one or two of my friends were highly placed or I would not have edited Foreign News for a month.

I had scarcely edited it so long when most of *Time's* European correspondents joined in a round-robin protesting my editorial views and demanding my removal. They were seconded by a clap of thunder out of Asia, from the *Time* bureau in Chungking. Let me list the signers of the round-robin, or those among *Time's* foreign correspondents who supported it, and continued to feed out news written from the viewpoint that the Soviet Union is a benevolent democracy of unaggressive intent, or that the Chinese Communists are "agrarian liberals," for I think that they are enlightening. Foremost among them were: John Hersey, John Scott (son of my old teacher of the law of social revolution, Scott Nearing), Charles C. Wertenbaker, the late Richard Lauterbach, Theodore White. Those are the top names; there were others. Most of them are no longer with *Time*.

The fight in Foreign News was not a fight for control of a seven-page section of a newsmagazine. It was a struggle to decide whether a million Americans more or less were going to be given the facts about Soviet aggression, or whether those facts were going to be suppressed, distorted, sugared or perverted into the exact opposite of their true meaning. In retrospect, it can be seen that this critical struggle was, on a small scale, an opening round of the Hiss Case. The same basic issues, the same forces, the same fierce passions motivating the same people came into play.* Because of

* There is nothing strange in the fact that many of these same people were loud cheerers for Alger Hiss. The wife of one former *Time* employe—let me call her Mrs. Hinchingbrook—did more than cheer. One morning, during the Hiss Case, a *Time* bureau chief was reading in the library of a house where he had been an overnight guest. Suddenly, he became aware that there was a caller in the next room. He recognized Mrs. Hinchingbrook's voice, rising and falling in wrathful crescendo and decrescendo. She did not know that she was being overheard. My friend listened fascinated as the beautiful Mrs. Hinchingbrook proposed one rascally scheme after another for "framing" Whittaker Chambers. Her keening was due to the fact that, while ingenious, none of her schemes was really sound.

it, though most people had never heard my name, I was fairly widely known among liberal newsmen, who were itching to get at me. The Hiss Case gave them their chance. What made the Foreign News episode enlightening to me, and worth reporting in such detail, is the fact that the people who were implacably opposed to my editorial views on the Soviet Union and Communism were not Communists. Here and there, a concealed Communist may have been at work. But the overwhelming might of the opposition came from people who had never been Communists and never would be.

They were people who believed a number of things. Foremost among them was the belief that peace could be preserved, World War III could be averted only by conciliating the Soviet Union. For this no price was too high to pay, including the price of wilful historical self-delusion. Yet they had just fiercely supported a war in which one of their ululant outcries had been against appeasement; and they were much too intelligent really to believe that Russia was a democracy or most of the other upside-down things they said in defense of it. Hence like most people who have substituted the habit of delusion for reality, they became hysterical whenever the root of their delusion was touched, and reacted with a violence that completely belied the openness of mind which they prescribed for others. Let me call their peculiar condition which, sometimes had unconsciously deep, and sometimes very conscious, political motives that it would perhaps be unmannerly to pry into here—the Popular Front mind.

Nor can it be repeated too often that most of those who suffered from it were not Communists. Yet Communists, at a critical spin of history, had few more effective allies. The Popular Front mind dominated American life, at least from 1938 to 1948, and it is still grossly premature to count it out. Particularly, it dominated all avenues of communication between the intellectuals and the nation. It told the nation what it should believe; it made up the nation's mind for it. The Popular Fronters had made themselves the "experts." They controlled the narrows of news and opinion. And though, to a practiced ear, they never ceased to speak as the scribes, the nation heard in their fatal errors the voice of those having au-

She was much too intelligent not to know that, so that after each unfeasible suggestion, she would exclaim with a snap of vexation: "No, that won't work!" This barehanded rascality on the part precisely of the "nicest people" ran through the Hiss Case like rot through an apple.

thority. For the nation, too, wanted peace above all things, and it simply could not grasp or believe that a conspiracy on the scale of Communism was possible or that it had already made so deep a penetration into their lives.

Out of my experience on Foreign News, I began to suffer a feeling that would steadily grow stronger as the Soviet danger monthly grew greater and public apathy in contrast seemed to grow deeper. I began to sense that the struggle could never be won by words. It must also be fought by acts.

I was arguing desperately with my managing editor one day as to how to handle news about the Bretton Woods conference, where the Assistant Secretary of Treasury, Harry Dexter White, presided, and the World Bank was set up of which he subsequently became the head. At last I exclaimed: "But I *know* that Harry White is a Soviet agent." "Well, damn it," said my editor, "if that is true, why can't somebody prove it?" "Because nobody wants to prove it," I said hopelessly. But I thought: "*You* can."

XXIII

Threads of the future Hiss Case wound through the Foreign News experience in other ways. The climax of that experience was probably reached over Yalta. The week of that diplomatic disaster the extraordinary security regulations blacked out all news about the conference. Yet *Time* had to report something about it. What it would have reported had I then known that Alger Hiss was sitting not far behind Franklin Roosevelt, I cannot say.

At last, I decided to make the fantastic news blackout itself the take-off for a story. In the absence of firm news, I closed my office door for a day, and wrote a political fantasy in which I put into the mouths of the Muse of History and the ghosts of the late Tsar Nicholas and the Tsarina, foregathered on the roof of the Livadia Palace at Yalta, the hard facts about Soviet foreign aggression that I found it all but impossible to report in any other way. Shortly before I began to testify in the Hiss Case, *Time*, in an unusual gesture, reprinted *The Ghosts on the Roof*, to show how uncannily right it had been about foreign affairs at a time when so many had been wrong.

To get the piece into print, I had had to make a common journalistic compromise. I agreed to lop off the end which described the Soviet Union and the United States as two jet planes whose political destiny could be fulfilled only when one destroyed the other.

To most of my colleagues, *The Ghosts on the Roof* was a culminating shocker. Feeling ran so high against it, the general malevolence swelled into my office so fiercely, that again I closed my door, this time to edit in a semblance of peace. One of the writers who dropped in described the hubbub outside my closed door, as *The Ghosts on the Roof* went to press, as "like the night of a lynching bee." It took courage in those days for *Time* to run a piece like *The Ghosts on the Roof*.

XXIV

A Hiss Case ghost also brushed me at *Time* not long afterwards. Among *Time's* war correspondents was a young man named William Walton, who was once pointed out to me, but whom I do not recall ever having met. I knew only that he was personable and well thought of. Everyone spoke highly of his courage in parachuting into Normandy on or around D-Day.

After the collapse of Germany, Walton, for some reason, got to Prague. From there, he filed a ten or twelve-page cable describing how, under Soviet occupation, "a middle-class revolution" or a "white-collar revolution" had taken place in Czechoslovakia.

I read the long cable over several times with astonishment. I had no first-hand facts about the situation in Prague. But I knew something about how Communists could be expected to mask their control there. Above all, I knew that, in a country as intensely middle class as Czechoslovakia, a "middle-class revolution" is a contradiction in terms. Whatever Walton thought that he had seen, it could not be a "middle-class revolution." I concluded (quite correctly, we now know) that Walton's "middle-class revolution" meant that the Communists had moved into controlling positions in the Czech Government. If I ran the cable, as I was urged to do, a million Americans would gain a completely mistaken notion of the balance of political forces in the country of which Bismarck had said: "Who controls Bohemia controls Europe." I refused to run the cable or any part of it.

The ensuing storm swept from the editorial to the executive floors of *Time*. Clearly, I was behaving like a despot. Part of an editor's business, I pointed out, is to be a brute. But it was felt that I was questioning the integrity of a correspondent.

I was not questioning Walton's integrity at all, of course. I was questioning the political discernment of a war correspondent. I thought that Walton was an inexperienced young American who had been sold a bill of goods, and that is what I said. There was never any question of firing Walton. I believe it was two or three years later that he subsequently left *Time* entirely under his own steam.

Testifying in public session before the House Committee on Un-American Activities, on August 25, 1948, Alger Hiss said that a newspaperman had told him that a man on *Time* had told him that Whittaker Chambers was mentally unstable. Hiss was reluctant to name his ultimate *Time* source, but under pressure he did so. The source was William Walton.

Hiss also testified that he had heard a year or two before from someone that "a man at *Time*" was calling him a Communist. One wonders who that "someone" was, for he is nowhere identified. To me the conclusion is inescapable that Alger Hiss had long known that the "man at *Time*" was his old friend Carl; that, in fact, Hiss was able to keep a rather close check on me through friends and contacts at *Time,* and that he knew a great deal about me at a time when I knew almost nothing about him.*

X X V

It is all but impossible to convey briefly the special pressures that can be brought to bear upon a man who finds himself almost alone in a struggle for control of an important political department of the news. Those pressures are of many kinds, personal, social, corporative, editorial, political, disruptive, slanderous, and, above all, unremitting. A single man gets tired, craves respite, and wants especially to get on with his job and not to fight. The big battalion can rest its forces piecemeal; it is always refreshed and its whole job is fighting.

But perhaps the most potent pressure is the simple question, which is constantly buzzed about, and which a single man must constantly ask himself: "How can one man be right when so many say that he is wrong?" With it goes another morale sapper: "Is

* In this connection, another incident. In my first years at *Time,* the anti-Communist faction in the Newspaper Guild prevailed on me to attend one of the union's city-wide meetings. In the crowded hall, I became aware that someone was staring at me. I glanced into a face of undisguised hatred which at first I did not recognize. It was Nathan Witt.

the end worth the effort?" "It ought not to be so hard," one of my waggish anti-Communist colleagues once said in the days when *Time* cost less, "to get out a fifteen-cent magazine."

But in the end the most fatal pressure was simply the extra hard work that was a result of the situation. If writers wrote stories in which the interpretation of events or the general tone seemed to me only slightly wrong, I could wave such copy along, and, because of deadlines, often had to even against my better judgment. But if writers wrote stories about important situations in which the interpretation of news and the general tone seemed to me fantastically wrong, I could not then ask them to rewrite the news along lines which they did not believe in, even though in my opinion, those lines were right and theirs wrong. I could only do one of three things. I could ask another writer to write the same story over again. That was an invidious morale shaker that I tried to avoid. I could rewrite the story myself. Or, when I could plainly foresee controversy, I could assign myself the story in the first place and write it in the gasps of editing. Sometimes, I found myself writing or rewriting a fourth to a third of the Foreign News section. Every sound editor knows that is a ruinous way to edit anything—ruinous to the very concept of an editor and ruinous to the man who must shoulder the load. I had no choice. Once more, a working day without sleep became my standard practice.

One morning, coming to work, I blacked out on the train. I was unwise enough to admit it and ask for a week's rest. It was granted and I never went back to editing Foreign News (except on special occasions). *Time*, which had been through one long illness with me, firmly refused to let me work myself into another. At the time, I suspected that that was not the real reason for my removal from Foreign News. Now I am convinced that it was.

But, in any case, the civil war in "bloody angle" had to have an end. Almost no editor could have withstood indefinitely the pressures that played on me. No publication can endure indefinitely an editor who is a target twenty-four hours a day. But I had set an editorial course in Foreign News from which *Time* would never veer far again.

One point I must touch upon since others have publicly raised it. I think that I can say unqualifiedly that no other editor at *Time* would have stood for a week the insubordination, hostility and insulting behavior to which certain members of my staff treated me. I bore it as something to be borne. I tried to bear it as a Quaker should. I never lodged a complaint against any member of my staff (though some of them went to the managing editor about me). No man or woman ever lost his job because of me. Some would have lost their jobs had it not been for me. For I covered up many things even in cases when I knew that the individuals involved were my enemies.

All of the regular Foreign News writers subsequently became my good friends. All of them came to share my basic views on Soviet policy and Communism. But no report of my Foreign News experience would be complete without mention of two people. One was John Barkham (then a Foreign News writer, now editor of *Coronet*) whose unfailing loyalty, patience, evenness of temper, kindness and courage sometimes gave me about all the courage I had to go on. The other was Marjorie Smith, then a *Time* researcher, who fought the war beside me. Nor must I forget Yi Ying Sung, still a *Time* researcher. She too knew that the Chinese Communists were not "agrarian liberals."

XXVI

From Foreign News I fell down the whole flight of editorial steps. For the fourth time, I was set to writing Books. I was practically back where I began in 1939. Inevitably, I felt the bitterness of a man who has suffered defeat by doing a job whose merit was reflected in the steady upward climb of his salary (to use the crudest and least personal yardstick). But that only made matters worse, for I was no longer justifying the salary I had reached in Foreign News.

I did the only thing that a man can do who has fallen down a flight of steps. I lay perfectly quiet until my head had cleared a little and I could look around me more realistically. Occasionally, I uttered a yelp of pain and rage. But for the most part I lay still.

But we are probably never as friendless, or even as battered, at the foot of the stairs as we think we are. Presently, a new post was devised for me. It was called Special Projects. It was a new department of the magazine whose staff consisted of my friend, James Agee, and me. Its purpose was to provide *Time* chiefly with cover stories which, because of special difficulties of subject matter or writing, other sections of *Time* were thought to be less well equipped to handle. Thus, I became the only *Time* editor who both wrote and edited his own copy (subject to final editing by the managing editor). When I was not working on Special Projects, I edited any other section of the magazine that needed an editor for a week or a month.

At first, I regarded Special Projects with a deep distaste. Then I perceived that what I had taken for a final defeat was, in fact, my greatest opportunity. It gave me, on a scale impossible in Books, an opportunity to justify the ways of God to man that I had taken as my writing purpose. The brief Christmas cover of 1946, on the end of the war, was the first result of that discernment. It was followed by a cover on Albert Einstein and the atom bomb (a collaboration). The cover stories on Arnold Toynbee's philosophy of history, and the Christmas cover story of 1947 on Marian Anderson continued my purpose. Among many letters that reached *Time*, asking who wrote the Marian Anderson story, was one from Marjorie Kinnan Rawlings, who ventured a guess: "I believe that Whittaker Chambers wrote it." For the first time in its history, *Time* decided to break its precedent of never divulging the authorship of a story. In a publisher's letter it quoted the author of *The Yearling* and added: "Novelist Rawlings is right." Most writers are like little children in such matters; I was very much pleased.

For its twenty-fifth anniversary edition, *Time* asked me to write an essay on the theology of Reinhold Niebuhr of the Union Theological Seminary. I was asked by the same editor who had once said that he would not dare let me write *Time's* Religion section.

In many ways, the Niebuhr essay was a statement of my own religious faith at the time. And since, six months later almost to a day, I was to begin to testify publicly against the Communist conspiracy, I believe that it is relevant to quote what I then felt. I began by saying:

"With prayer, with humility of spirit tempering his temerity of mind, man has always sought to define the nature of the most important fact of his experience: God. To this unending effort to know God, man is driven by the noblest of his intuitions—the sense of his mortal incompleteness—and by hard experience. For man's occasional lapses from God-seeking end inevitably in intolerable shallowness of thought combined with incalculable mischief in action. Modern man knows almost nothing about the nature of God, almost never thinks about it, and is complacently unaware that there may be any reason to. . . ."

I tried to trace why this was so—what is in effect, and allowing for its gross simplifications, my indictment of the modern mind: "Under the bland influence of the idea of progress, man, supposing himself more and more to be the measure of all things, has achieved a singularly easy conscience and an almost hermetically smug optimism. The idea that man is sinful and needs redemption has been subtly changed into the idea that man is by nature good, and hence capable of indefinite perfectibility. This perfectibility is being achieved through technology, science, politics, social reform, education. Man is essentially good, says 20th-century liberalism, because he is rational, and his rationality is (if the speaker happens to be a liberal Protestant) divine, or (if he happens to be religiously unattached) at least benign. Thus the reason-defying paradoxes of Christian faith are happily by-passed.

"And yet, as 20th-century civilization reaches a climax, its own paradoxes grow catastrophic. The incomparable technological achievement is more and more dedicated to the task of destruction. Man's marvelous conquest of space has made total war a household experience, and, over vast reaches of the world, the commonest of childhood memories. The more abundance increases, the more resentment becomes the characteristic new look on 20th-century faces. The more production multiplies, the more scarcities become endemic. The faster science gains on disease (which, ultimately, seems always to elude it), the more the human race dies at the hands of living men. Men have never been so educated, but wisdom, even as an idea, has conspicuously vanished from the world.

"Yet liberal Protestants could do little more than chant with Lord Tennyson:

O, yet we hope that somehow good
Will be the final goal of ill,
To pangs of nature, sins of will,
Defects of doubt, and taints of blood. . . .

"It was a good deal easier to see that Tennyson was silly than to see that the attitude itself was silly. That was the blind impasse of optimistic liberalism."

Against that view, I set the findings of three men—the Danish theologian, Sören Kierkegaard, the Swiss theologian, Karl Barth and the Russian novelist, Feodor Dostoyevsky, whom I am not alone in holding to be one of the great religious voices of our time. I wrote: "Against liberalism's social optimism (progress by reform) and the social optimism of the revolutionary left (progress by force), Dostoyevsky asserted the eternal necessity of the soul to be itself. But he discerned that the moment man indulged this freedom to the point where he was also free from God, it led him into tragedy, evil, and often the exact opposite of what he intended." (I was thinking of myself.) Karl Barth had said: "Man cannot define God by talking about man, in however loud a voice. God is *ganz anders*—wholly different." (Religion is not ethics or social reform.) Kierkegaard had asserted that, between man's purposes in history and God's purposes in eternity, was "an infinite qualitative difference." That thought, in slightly different words, I was to repeat, a few months later, before the Grand Jury of the Southern District of New York, and I felt, despite the habit of intellectuals of ridiculing the minds of plain men, that the Jury knew exactly what I was talking about.

Then, in the Niebuhr piece, I sought to make what was at that time my most personal statement about religious faith: "Christian faith is a paradox which is the sum of paradoxes. Its passion mounts, like a surge of music, insubstantial and sustaining, between two great cries of the spirit—the paradoxic sadness of 'Lord, I believe; help Thou mine unbelief' and the paradoxic triumph of Tertullian's '*Credo quia impossibile*' (I believe because it is impossible). Religiously, its logic, human beyond rationality, is the expression of a need epitomized in the paradox of Solon weeping for his dead son. 'Why do you weep,' asked a friend, 'since it cannot help?' Said Solon: 'That is why I weep—because it cannot help.' "

If anyone seeks to know what the mind, the mood and character of Whittaker Chambers was like on the fore-eve of the Hiss Case, let him read the essay on Reinhold Niebuhr. Niebuhr himself wrote me about it, quoting his brother: "Only a man who has deeply suffered could have written it."

•

XXVII

In 1947, *Life*, looking for someone to write the text for its series on *The History of Western Civilization*, approached me. For it, I wrote the essays on the Middle Ages, the Venetian Republic, the Age of Exploration, the Enlightenment and the Edwardians. The published ending of that glorification of the gluttonous pursuit of pleasure, secular good works and progress was not the one that I originally wrote for it. I had sought for something that would say in the fewest and most searing words that there was another side to the age of the Edwardians—the age whose downfall we are living through.

For that purpose I went back to the book most of which I had translated just after my break with the Communist Party—*Dunant, The Story of the Red Cross.* At the height of his fame and wealth, Dunant had gone bankrupt. He had lost everything. He was attacked and vilified. He disappeared almost from the face of the earth. But, now and again, someone would glimpse him, wandering a voluntary outcast in one of the great European cities, living in the slums, wearing ragged clothes and broken shoes, shunning alike men's kindness and their blindness. At last, even the memory of him all but vanished. Dunant was reported to be dead.

Years later, an enterprising journalist found him still living, a white-bearded recluse, in a hospice in the Swiss mountains. A pang of conscience smote the world (in those days it was still possible to speak of a public conscience). A Dunant fad set in. Admirers sought him out. He fled them. The penniless old man was awarded the Nobel Prize for Peace. He gave it away.

One morning, in his whitewashed cell, Dunant was found dead. He had left a testament. It said: "I wish to be carried to my grave like a dog without a single one of your ceremonies which I do not recognize. . . . I am a disciple of Christ as in the first century, and nothing more."

That was the ferocious little parable with which I ended the Edwardians. *Life's* managing editor frowned. "It's like being slapped across the face with a wet towel," he said. That was what I had meant it to be. But since we were both professional journalists, we agreed that it must be killed.

My last effort for *Life,* written at the express request of Henry R. Luce, after several other writers had failed, was *The Devil,* a religious essay the response to which astonished *Life's* editors, who, like so many others, did not know that the American people is, above all, a religious people.

By New Year's, 1948, simply by trying to do what I believed needed to be done, I found myself again at the top of the stairs. I had become the joint property of *Time* and *Life,* and my salary was suddenly and startlingly upped to something close to that much-publicized figure of $30,000 a year. I am so constituted—so peculiarly constituted, the world would say—that I did not know (or care) exactly what I was earning until it became a matter of public concern.

XXVIII

Between man's purposes in time, and God's purpose in eternity, there is an infinite difference of quality. What should a man like me do about the Communist conspiracy and my former comrades in the underground? I was acutely aware of them as Communists. But, through the years, I was more and more aware of them as individual souls. I was more and more preoccupied with the wonder of the grace of strength which had enabled me to free myself from Communism, and of the grace of time, which had enabled me to restore myself to life. Why should those others be denied a similar grace by any act of mine? Who appointed me their judge or executioner? What right had I to complicate destinies that were inherently divine with a wholly human fatality? I had acted once and nothing had come of it. What sanction had I to act again?

There developed in my mind that conflict between my urgent sense that Communism must be fought and a concern to shield, from the worst consequences of their acts, the conspirators who to me were not simply enemies, or Communists or anything that can be neatly labeled, but living men and women whose souls, though they specifically denied them, pled with my compassion. It was a conflict that I would resolve only in the climax of the Hiss Case, and then only when their defiant evil had deprived me of any right to shield them further, and the failure of my final utmost effort to remove myself physically as a witness against them left me no choice but to go on to the end.

The problem was constantly with me. Early in the war, the agents of the Civil Service Commission flitted in and out of my office, seeking information about people who were entering Government service.

I was early in touch with an officer of the Naval Intelligence. I saw him rather frequently. He told me, years later, that the information I had given him was classified top secret by the Office of Naval Intelligence. In time we became personal friends. In 1950, I was having supper with him one night at the University Club, in New York, when he was called to the telephone. He told me that he had just been asked to become the minority counsel for the Tydings Committee, and asked what I thought he should do.

I urged him to accept. The country is more familiar with him now as Robert Morris, chief counsel to the sub-committee on internal security of the Senate Judiciary Committee (the McCarran Committee).

I had also had two visits from an officer of the State Department, one of the best-informed men on Communist matters whom I have ever known. On his second visit, I asked him if he thought that Alger Hiss was still a Communist. Tito (still at one with Stalin) had just shot down an American military plane and captured or killed its crew. "I can answer like this," my visitor said. "We're having Alger Hiss draft the note of protest: one, to put him on the spot; two, so he will tell the Russians secretly that we mean business." It was this man, too, who first told me that Alger Hiss had been at Yalta. "Imagine," he said, "what kind of a deal we got with Hiss sitting five feet from Stalin."

And yet, I was not convinced that Hiss was still a Communist. An irrational factor came into play which Hede Massing has put her finger on in *This Deception*. She remarks that she believed for a time that Noel Field had broken with the Communist Party. She believed it, not because of the evidence, but because we expect those who are our friends to do what we ourselves have thought it right to do. At that time, I had heard nothing at all for five or six years about my former friends in the underground. I found it almost unthinkable that Hiss and Collins, who had been my friends, could have remained Communists all that time. On the other hand, it would not have surprised me greatly to learn that Wadleigh, with whom I was not particularly friendly, was still in the Communist movement. Yet it was just he who had broken.

From 1946 through 1948, special agents of the F.B.I., too, were frequent visitors. Usually, they were seeking information about specific individuals. For some time they were much interested in Victor Perlo, Harry Dexter White, Dr. Harold Glasser, Charles Krivitsky, John Abt and others. At that time, I had no way of knowing that they were checking a story much more timely than mine—that of Elizabeth Bentley.

Most of these investigators went about their work in a kind of dogged frustration, overwhelmed by the vastness of the conspiracy, which they could see all around them, and depressed by the apathy of the country and the almost total absence in high places of any desire to root out Communism. I had heard constant rumors about the Grand Jury of the Southern District of New York which was reported to be looking into Soviet espionage. I would have been astonished had I known that, in February, 1948, Alger Hiss had appeared before it—six months before I began to testify—and had denied that he had ever been a Communist. This fact I first learned from William Marshall Bullitt, one of the trustees of the Carnegie Endowment, *after* Hiss was convicted. I would have been equally surprised to learn that the Assistant Secretary of the Treasury, Harry D. White, had also been questioned by the Grand Jury.

One day I asked someone who should have known about the Grand Jury rumors. He said that the Grand Jury was in session. "But take it from me," he added bitterly, "*nothing* will ever come of the Grand Jury of the Southern District of New York." Seldom has a man been so mistaken in an answer, especially in view of the man to whom he was making it. Some eight months later, the same Grand Jury indicted Alger Hiss.

To fight Communism while sparing my former friends, I had made a simple compromise. I informed about their Communist membership and their activities short of espionage. Those parts of the story that bore on the espionage angle, I suppressed. That still left the central core of Communists in the Government in full view. But there were individuals connected with espionage whom, because of the immediate danger they constituted, I felt obliged to name. One such was the head of the steel experimental laboratory whom I have mentioned earlier. Knowledge of the structure and membership of the Ware Group had been in the hands of the Government years before I began to testify publicly. The espionage implications were inescapable even to an inexperienced mind. The F.B.I. was chafing to develop them. The apathy, I concluded, lay elsewhere.

XXIX

During the decade from 1938 to 1948, the temper of my mind changed as completely as the cell structure of the body is said to change every few decades. It was deeply and continually preoccupied with the problem of writing—another of those problems that no one ever solves. To write or edit under pressure of deadlines almost every week for nine years is an exclusive experience that leaves little energy for anything that does not bear directly on it. At the same time, I was reintegrating myself in a new way of life with special ways of thought and conduct. I was constantly meeting new people and pushing out my intellectual horizon. And I was deeply engaged in developing a new way of life on the land, which I shall soon discuss.

Ten years is a short time in any man's middle age into which to crowd a new life. Perhaps it is not strange that in my haste I did not have to force the details of the past out of my mind. The pressure of my own transformation crowded them out. The main outlines of the past persisted as the plan of a structure can be traced in its ruins. But dates, time intervals, faces, places, names, happenings tended to run together or disappear. Two years of hard work, of excruciating effort of recollection, and corroboration wherever possible, were later necessary to reconstruct my picture of the past. Even so, some things have undoubtedly faded forever. Nor is it possible to say whether they may be important or not. For there seems to be no order of importance in what the mind retains and what it forgets. I may remember distinctly after years something completely trivial—a gesture, a wry remark, a shadow on a wall—and be incapable of recalling an important address, like the photographic workshop in Washington.

At what point in my years at *Time* did there fade from my mind the recollection of what I had given my wife's nephew to hide for me? I do not know. Probably very early, for I met him very occasionally in the ten years between the day, in 1938, when he took the envelope from me and the day, in November, 1948, when I took it back. This much is certain: if during the last six or seven years of that decade, anyone had asked me, "What is your wife's nephew hiding for you?" I should have answered, "Two or three scraps of Alger Hiss's handwriting and perhaps something of Harry White's." The heap of copied State Department documents, the spools of microfilm, had sunk from my memory as completely as the Russian regiments in World War I sank into the Masurian swamps.

It is extremely important to bear this failure of memory in mind. For no one who does not realize that it happened, or who cannot believe it possible, can rightly understand what happened in the Hiss Case. I believe that the notion is widespread that I began to testify against Alger Hiss knowing that I had the documents and films secreted as a weapon. That is completely untrue. I began to testify against Hiss, as it were, bare-handed. I had charged him over the air with having once been a Communist more than a month before his own attorneys demanded any specimens of Hiss's handwriting that I might have, and thus compelled me to look and to find the terrible evidence of the documents where I had had it secreted but forgotten it.

Nor can anyone who does not realize that understand the degree to which I find providential most of the happenings of the Hiss Case. And it is particularly the fact that I had forgotten the documents in which I feel this most clearly. For if I had remembered them, it is entirely within my character to have destroyed them, not as evidence, but so that I might never be tempted to use them, even if provoked, as I destroyed certain other things, and even today almost invariably destroy letters or communications which wound or arouse me, to deprive my mind of any reminder of human meanness.

XXX

Tuesday and Wednesday are the *Time* week-end. For eight years, more or less, I left *Time* every Monday night and took the train for Baltimore. There I changed to the train or bus for Westminster, Maryland. In Westminster, my family met me with the car or truck, or I found some other conveyance to take me the remaining six miles to our farm. Every Wednesday night I made the return trip to New York. For most of my term at *Time* magazine, I commuted to and from New York and our farm some four hundred miles a week. I tried all possible combinations of conveyance—train, bus, plane, car. I tried Pullman and day coach. I found that I slept no more (though more expensively) on a Pullman than on a day coach, and I finally settled for the latter. By trial and error, I found that I made my best connections by taking a 3:30 train on Tuesday morning from New York, which got me to Baltimore in time to make an early morning bus for Westminster.

It would have been more convenient for me to have my wife drive to Baltimore to meet me. She is an excellent driver, but I almost never let her meet me. Though it cost me much hardship, I felt a vague, but overpowering presentiment. I can account for it only by the play of that sixth sense that Robert Stripling was to note in me during the Hiss Case. For when, under the troubles of that Case, I did let my wife meet me in Baltimore, tragedy followed.

The hardest years of commutation were the war years. During the days of gas and tire rationing, I sometimes found myself tramping through the snow at five o'clock in the morning to make the last three miles to the farm. "How did we ever stand it?" my wife and I now sometimes ask each other. We stood it for the reason that people can stand almost anything: because it was necessary. "But is it worth it?" people used to ask me over the years. Some of them, when they visited the farm, answered their own question. "Yes," they would say, "I see why you do it and why you are able to do it. This is peace."

We call our farm Pipe Creek Farm. It takes its name from the Big Pipe Creek, which winds in mirroring meanders, or rushes over shallow rapids, through a quarter-mile of our back pasture, on its way to the Monocacy and the Potomac Rivers. The somewhat drab word "Pipe" comes from the clay banks along the creek. In Indian days, the creek and its flood plain were neutral ground. Various tribes came there to gather the clay for their pipes and perhaps for other uses. Hereabouts they later died. Not far off, the last of the Susquehannocks were massacred and the remnant of the Tuscaroras made their last camp grounds, fleeing from Carolina.

Pipe Creek Farm includes more than three hundred rolling acres. Some seventy-five acres are woodland, mostly rock oak and white oak, with some stands of white pine. Along the edges of the woodlands in the spring the dogwood and the shadblow bloom, interspersed with wilding peach and cherry (and we know where to find the arbutus, the lady ferns and yellow violets). The rest of the farm is cropland and pasture. Originally, it was three farms. Each has its dwelling house, barns and outbuildings. We bought the home place first. Later, we bought the Creek Farm. In 1947, we bought Medfield, a small farm that connected our two properties and made them a unit.

We needed so much acreage for two reasons. I hoped that both my children, after a necessary immersion in the outer world, would return to become farmers and marry farmers. I wished to leave each a workable farm. Moreover, I had always hoped to turn to farming before I died. But I am too old to farm with anything but power machines, and nothing less than three hundred acres justifies, in terms of investment and operating costs, the use of power machinery.

Pipe Creek Farm is a dairy farm. In the fall months, when the volume of milk a farmer ships is the volume for which he will receive a first-class milk price during the rest of the year, we ship around ninety gallons of whole milk a day. We keep about fifty head of registered Guernsey cattle, big and little, cows, bulls, heifers and calves, of which we milk about twenty-five head. Our herd sire is Langwater Truant that was reserve junior champion at the 1948 Western Maryland Field Day and whose get won top place at the Montgomery County fair this year. After a brief experience with hired help during the war, we vowed never to hire barn help again. We decided to do all the barn work ourselves as a family; otherwise, we would disperse the herd. We have done our own barn work since 1945. The milking and the barn work, when done properly, is an eight-hour job, four hours in the morning, beginning at half past five; four hours in the evening. We also have sundry other chores.

At Medfield, where I am writing these words, we run a half-dozen registered Angus cows and their calves, which we hope, slowly, over the years, to increase to a producing beef herd. We also use the barn as an overflow station for our dairy heifers.

At the Creek Farm, we have a first-rate hog barn, in addition to a big bank barn (where we sometimes winter our dry cows). We used to keep forty or fifty Hampshire hogs. We now keep only three brood sows. But we are on the point of considerably increasing our hog herd again. We keep the hogs at the far back of the farm because of the ease with which brucellosis (contagious abortion or Bang's disease) is transmitted from hogs to cattle. Our dairy herd is accredited Bang's negative.

Our Number Two venture is our flock of registered Shropshire sheep. It was the championship flock at the last Maryland State Fair. Our flock sire is one of the outstanding individuals of the breed. Our plans call for continual expansion of our sheep project, and, possibly, an eventual shift from dairy to sheep farming. For my wife and I feel too old and too tired, especially after the beating of the last few years, to know how much longer we can stand up under the drudgery of dairying; and the children will soon be away at college or in the armed services.

We grow most of our own feed and sell little but wheat off the farm. Our regular rotations include corn, wheat, barley, oats, soybeans, and, where we are too late in getting off the corn, sometimes rye (for hogs) in place of wheat. (We also use ground rye in place of corn or molasses in the silo.) We combine our small grains and pick our corn by machine. We put up from four to five thousand bales of hay a year. Most of this is alfalfa of which we make three cuttings a year. Thus, hay harvest is almost continuous.

When we went into sheep, I decided that we must learn to grow Korean lespedeza (a great lamb fattener). Lespedeza is broadcast in April in fall-seeded barley. Our first crop was a partial failure. But we found that by discarding Wong barley, which grows too rank, and going back to Tennessee barley, we could grow first-rate lespedeza, which now sometimes carries our hay harvest into the first week of October (lespedeza is cut late).

For these operations, we use a model A and model H John Deere tractor; a Case forager (for silage) and blower; a New Holland hay baler (a one-man rig); a two-bottom power-trol plough (for the big tractor); a single-bottom, hand-throw plough for the small tractor; and necessary supplementary machines. For milking, we use long-tube vacuum milkers (we hand strip after them). We shear our own sheep. We truck our own cattle (with the children showing at five or six fairs a season, that is quite a chore, apart from the incidental trucking to sales and the stockyards). We put up our own hay; each of the four to five thousand bales of hay is lifted by our arms into the mows of the three barns. We also bale and put up our own straw. For combining and corn picking we hire service. But by next harvest we hope to own our rig. We also work two kitchen gardens and a truck patch and freeze all our own meat and vegetables. But that is catch as catch can.

All these operations are carried on by one woman (my wife), one man, Mr. Pennington (about whom I shall presently have more to say), half a man (myself; for though I have done a surprising amount of work on this farm in view of the work I was doing elsewhere, I cannot rate my labors higher), and two children (my daughter Ellen, 17, and my son John, 15). I think I can hear a farmer say: it can't be done. It is done, though, and has been for years. But only a farmer will know what I mean when I say that a lot of things never get done.

Pipe Creek Farm is not a show place. It is a dirt farm, a working farm. It is a farm practically every foot of whose soil I know because at one season or another I have personally worked it. It is the farm that I labored at *Time*, like Jacob with Laban, to support until it could support itself, for a modern farm is a big investment. A visiting *Time* researcher, the urban Miss Essie Lee, once picked her way gingerly among the units of this enigmatic enterprise, seeking desperately to bridge the transition between it and the chrome and concrete simplifications of the Time and Life Building. At last she reached the cow barn and slid back the door of the milking stable. As eighteen munching Guernsey heads turned to look her over, she exclaimed: "What has Mr. Luce done!"

XXXI

Pipe Creek Farm is not simply a few hundred acres of dirt, some clusters of old barns and outbuildings, power machines, a herd of cattle, a few beeves and hogs or a flock of sheep.

Our farm is our home. It is our altar. To it each day we bring our faith, our love for one another as a family, our working hands, our prayers. In its soil and the care of its creatures, we bury each day a part of our lives in the form of labor. The yield of our daily dying, from which each night in part restores us, springs around us in the seasons of harvest, in the produce of animals, in incalculable content.

A farmer is not everyone who farms. A farmer is the man who, in a ploughed field, stoops without thinking to let its soil run through his fingers, to try its tilth. A farmer is always half buried in his soil. The farmer who is not is not a farmer; he is a businessman who farms. But the farmer who is completes the arc between the soil and God and joins their mighty impulses. We believe that *laborare est orare*—to labor is to pray.

In that sense, the farm is our witness. It is a witness against the world. By deliberately choosing this life of hardship and immense satisfaction, we say in effect: The modern world has nothing better than this to give us. Its vision of comfort without effort, pleasure without the pain of creation, life sterilized against even the thought of death, rationalized so that every intrusion of mystery is felt as a betrayal of the mind, life mechanized and standardized—that is not for us. We do not believe that it makes for happiness from day to day. We fear that it means catastrophe in the end. We fear it if only because standardization leads to regimentation, and because the regimentation that men distrust in their politics is a reflection of the regimentation that they welcome unwittingly in their daily living.

We make use of as much mechanization as we cannot escape, as suits our daily needs, but does not rule our lives. We are not going back to the grain cradle, the candle or the ox cart. We seek that life that will give us the greatest simplicity, freedom, fruitful work, closest to the earth and peaceful, slow-moving animals. We know that, at this hour of history, we cannot do this completely. We realize that we have undertaken this life late in our lives and under heavy handicaps of fixed habit and ignorance. But we were willing to offer our lives for the venture because it is a way of groping toward God and because we knew nothing better in life to give our children.

We bought this farm in my second year at *Time.* We knew something of the hardships we must expect. Soon we knew more of them. But we had decided that our children must grow up close to the soil, familiar with labor, embedded in the nation by attending its public schools and taking spontaneous part in its routine work and play. Above all, we wanted to place them beyond the smog of the great cities, seeing few newspapers, seldom hearing the radio, seldom seeing motion pictures, untouched by the excitements by which the modern world daily stimulates its nervous crisis. We wished them never to hear the word Communism until they had developed against it, and the modern mind from which it springs, the immunity of a full and good life.

The price was high. To a family as devoted as we are, it was doubly high. For years, it meant my separation from my family for five days a week. Five days a week I lived at my mother's house on Long Island while my wife and children remained on the farm. For years our weekly torment came when my wife and children stood beside the bus in Westminster, looking up miserably at me while I looked back miserably at them. There was no other way to buy the farm and set it in motion; and we always looked forward to the time when it would not be necessary to drive me to the bus on Wednesday night ever again.

Breathlessly we paid off our first mortgage by putting everything I earned into it, by depriving ourselves of whatever we could spare—even necessary clothes. When we bought the farm, it had no conveniences. It had not been lived in for five years. I could write a sizable book on what kind of farm not to buy. We put in heat, light, water. We remodeled the barn to meet the health requirements of the Baltimore milkshed. We began to assemble a registered herd. I could also write a book on whether registered cattle or grades make economic sense to the farmer of middling means—and many other things about that great game of chance, the cattle business. In all these things, and others, we made the usual mistakes, and some original ones of our own inspiration; and, of course, we paid for them, sometimes heavily, in money and lost time.

When we took over, there was scarcely a field on the farm that was not gashed with deep erosion gutters. One gutter at the back of the farm extended for half an acre, and, when I stood in it, rose like a canyon above me. Another man and I spent a day, filling it with brush, tangles of old fence wire, and other trash. Then we drove slowly round and round, ploughing in the edges while the tractors tried to slew into the crater. When we had filled it level, we sowed the scar to grass and grain. The next day a rain washed the whole fill across the road. That is farming. We ploughed the gutter shut again. Today there is not an open gutter on the farm.

I remember the first day I took a tractor to plough a field. I felt like a man alone against an enemy. I had never ploughed a field before. I thought: "Well, the way to plough is to plough." For my maiden effort, I had picked a field well out of sight of the road. But the discreetly smiling neighbor who appears universally on such occasions soon settled in to spend a fruitful (and for a long time perfectly silent) morning watching me. As I stopped at one furrow turn, he broke silence to observe, "You're doing all right." Then he added, "Do you always plough in low gear?"

During my two days at home, I worked most of the time—ploughing, disking, harrowing, haying, milking—whatever operation need called for. I can remember ploughing by headlight until a few minutes of the time when I had to rush for the *Time* office. In my last years at *Time,* when I could spend more days at home, I took a much greater part in the farm activities. I am perfectly happy at such work. I only regret that I did not come to it when my strength was at its peak and I had enough years left to live so that I could plan in terms of the decades that farming requires.

Two other people really made the farm possible. One was my wife. Without her, her faith, her vision and her hard work, we could never have succeeded. We could never even have begun. My wife was city bred. She was so much city bred that, when we were living in our barn at Glen Gardner, and young phoebes hatched in the nest over our door, she asked me one day, "Does the mother phoebe nurse the little ones?"

Today she runs Pipe Creek Farm. She holds it all together, with her mind and with her hands. When we bought our first cow, she used to ask anyone she met how to get the milk out of the teats. Today she is the best hand milker in the family. Twice a day, she strips twenty-five cows. To release me while I wrote this book, she took over the entire morning milking herself.

Her tenderness and patience with small animals and sick animals is extreme. The calves are like her children. The mention of blood makes her faint. But I have seen her release newborn pigs from cauls by ripping the membrane with her finger. When a cow recently suffered a breech birth, and, at two o'clock in the morning, the veterinary and I took turns sawing up the calf within the mother and removing it piecemeal, my wife quietly passed us the instruments. When we used our old Case baler, and the whole family had to man the rig, I have watched her sit through a sizzling afternoon, goggled against chaff, but defenseless against dust and raw fingers, tying the wires as the sticker pushed them through the bales. She is tireless, courageous, infinitely patient, devoted, loving and loyal to the family for which she would unhesitatingly give her life as she gives the days of it. How curious she seemed to the newsmen when she testified in the Hiss Case, how different from the women who watched her from the courtroom. And how different she really was. For she is of the stuff of the pioneers. There are not many like her left in the world.

The other force that made the farm possible was Stanley Pennington—"Mr." Pennington, as I have always called him, just as he has always called me "Mr." Chambers, even after years of ploughing together, tractor behind tractor, or sweating together on how many hay loads. For Mr. Pennington has an instinctive respect for the dignity of the human substance; he believes that that respect should be fixed by courtesy. "We of the common people," he has said to me once or twice; and we both knew that in the humble term, he was asserting a patent of nobility. I have known few men in whom tact was so instinctive, or a sense of rank based upon a sense of worth so real or so unassuming. I esteem him beyond most men whom I have known.

The world would call Mr. Pennington a rough man. He went to work at the age of fifteen. He has worked ever since. He has worked at almost any job there is to do, and there is almost nothing that he cannot do well. Mechanically, he is ingenious; and though he is wiry, his strength is brutal. He begins work before dawn. He ends work after dark. He believes, as he has sometimes told me, that work is the highest human good, the source of all other goods. The rest of his philosophy is kindness. Who hesitates to call him at the peak of harvest to start a machine hopelessly stalled in a field? Who hesitates to wake him in the middle of the night to drive a sick man to the doctor? Who in need has not borrowed from him, and very often failed to repay?

I no longer remember how this good man came to us, and I do not want to know; he is one of ourselves. He lives on a small farm two or three miles up the valley. But almost from the first month we were on this farm, most of his waking hours have been spent here. Throughout that time, in part the period of war wages, Mr. Pennington could have made over and over again somewhere else what I am able to pay him. No money can buy, just as no money can pay, the Penningtons of this world. Ours is a human relationship.

My son and his son have played together almost since they could walk. They have worked together since they could drive a tractor and both could drive tractors like men by the time they were nine. Before their legs were long enough to reach the controls, they used to collaborate on driving a truck. One would handle the wheel, while the other on the floor would work the clutch and brake. When fair time rolls around, they are alone together, for days at a time, thirty, forty, fifty miles from home, fitting and showing cattle and sheep. Young Donald Pennington always addresses me respectfully as "Mr. Chambers." But it amuses (and greatly pleases) me that when I am out of earshot, both boys always call me "Papa." During the Hiss Case, when it seemed as if my enemies must destroy me by mass of power and weight of numbers, I overheard Donald comforting my son. "They'll never get Papa," he said. "He's too smart for them." Somehow the faith of this child was like the faith of the race itself to me.

My daughter, who is almost eighteen, has a hazy recollection of an earlier life. My son, John, who is fifteen, can remember nothing but this farm. It is their realm. When they step off the school bus at the end of our long lane, they are home in the oldest, primal meaning of that word. They are among the things they intimately love and know, and which fill the whole horizon and fiber of their lives. They have literally grown up with their calves, and there are cows in the milking herd that they can remember as fresh-dropped masses of wet leg and bulging eye—and do remember tenderly, feeling in this living form the touch of time. Their acres have no secrets from them; nothing escapes them.

Even I do not know how they check and report on all that is sprouting and hiding—from mushrooms on the round-top to the pheasant hen brooding squat and invisible against the fallow field known as lower Legonier.

There was a night in one crowded harvest when John raked hay long after dark, and in the beam of the tractor headlights, a fox appeared, then its mate, and as he drove, they ran circles around the machine. Small wonder that his face was transfigured when he told me. The next day, disking, he saw a doe lead its fawn along the edge of an alfalfa field. So a boy is born into the creation.

The children take part in all the operations of the farm, and have since they could work. I have told them that no man owns land. Land belongs to the man who has worked it until he knows it so well that he can cross it in the blackest night and his feet will instinctively find anywhere on it where the little hollow lies and the rise begins.

In summer, they are often away. For the focus of their interest is 4-H club work and showing their cattle and sheep at the state and county fairs. They suffered some very dashing defeats before they began to make headway on the show circuit. Now they have their share, and perhaps more than their share, of purple (championship) and blue (first place) ribbons. There is scarcely anyone in the cattle or sheep business for miles around who does not know Ellen and Johnnie Chambers. Last year Ellen made the Maryland State cattle judging team.

I sat at the ringside at the Maryland State Fair at Timonium one day during the Hiss Case. A big class of Guernsey junior yearling heifer calves was being shown. It was an open class, and most of those showing were men about my own age. But among them trudged a stubby little boy about twelve years old, his white duck show suit a good deal rumpled by then. He was John Chambers, showing his prize heifer with an awful seriousness. ("Him and that heifer," the head of the Maryland 4-H said to me one day.) The ring of calves and men circled slowly round and round. At last the judge motioned the boy out of the moving circle, which one by one, as the judge placed the calves, fell in below him, until the little boy headed the line of towering men. I remembered what my own life had been like at his age. I felt what men feel when they know that some prayers are granted.

To give such life to children no sacrifice is too great. But we did not mean only to root our children in the soil. Above all, we meant to root them in the nation—that part of the nation each of whose days is a great creative labor. That is the part of the nation to which by choice I belong. The farm is the soil, in which, like my children, I spread my roots.

XXXII

In an age of crisis, the farm has been our way of trying to give our children what peace and security is left in the world. We have censored the world's influences as much as we thought good. We have never supposed that we could shut them out. We have never supposed that our children could escape their age or its history. We have hoped that from the life we have given them, they would draw the inner strength to face the years ahead.

Today I walked across the ridge from our home place to this house where I write. I climbed the first rise and the second, from which, in clear weather, we can see, far off, the dark blue wall of the Allegheny Front. As I passed the crest of the ridge, below me on the field in the hollow, my fifteen-year-old son was windrowing hay. He sat, small and brown, on the big green tractor while the side-delivery rake click-clicked behind. When I came down the slope in the sunlight, he waved to me—a wave that meant smiling pride in what he was doing and pleasure at seeing his father unexpectedly.

I thought: "Surely, this is a moment in a man's life, when he can stand in his fields and see such a son, to whom he has given life, and a tranquil, orderly way of living, wave his gratitude for that life and for that way of living it."

With that thought, there came between us, like a cloud shadow, the memory of the thousands of other children who have been crippled, body and soul, by the wars and revolutions of this distracted century, and still will be.

I thought: "In three years time, he and his generation will take their places in the most terrible of children's crusades. By every minute that he rakes this sunlit field, by every turn of the tractor wheels, he is a little less my son, and a little more a soldier of the inevitable war. That wave of his is, in fact, the saddest of farewells."

XXXIII

Shortly before Christmas, 1947, *Time* asked me to write a cover story about Rebecca West and her new book, *The Meaning of Treason.*

I began the piece by saying: "When, in 1936, General Emilio Mola announced that he would capture Madrid because he had four columns outside the city and a fifth column of sympathizers within, the world pounced on the phrase with the eagerness of a man who has been groping for an important word. The world might better have been stunned as by a tocsin of calamity. For what Mola had done was to indicate the dimension of treason in our time.

"Other ages have had their individual traitors—men who from faint-heartedness or hope of gain sold out their causes. But in the 20th century, for the first time, men banded together by millions, in movements like Fascism and Communism, dedicated to the purpose of betraying the institutions they lived under. In the 20th century, treason became a vocation whose modern form was specifically the treason of ideas."

I also wrote: "The horror of treason is its sin against the spirit. And for him who violates this truth there rises inevitably Bukharin's 'absolutely black vacuity,' which is in reality a circle of absolute loneliness into which neither father, wife, child nor friend, however compassionate, can bring the grace of absolution. For this loneliness is a penalty inflicted by a justice that transcends the merely summary justice of men. It is the retributive meaning of treason because it is also one of the meanings of Hell."

A million people more or less read the words. No one, presumably, heard in them a tocsin of calamity. No one, presumably, asked himself: "What manner of man could think such thoughts?" No one sensed that, in those words, he was hearing the presentiment of an event that would shock the nation, that he was listening to a man, sitting at his desk in a bare office, twenty-nine floors above the Rockefeller Plaza, talking to himself on paper. Nor did anyone know that that curious conversation was part of a decade-long conversation and that, not long afterwards, the man who held it with himself would rise from his desk because, under the impact of history, he had reached a sad conclusion.

That conclusion was that the time for the witness of words was over and the time for the witness of acts had begun—that the force of words alone was not enough against the treason of ideas. Acts were also required of a man if there was something in him that enabled him to act. It was hard because it is always peculiarly hard for a man who has once saved himself from a burning building to force himself to go back for any reason into the flames. But nothing less was required, if a man did not mean smugly to rot in peace and plenty, if, instead, against the dimension of treason in our time, he meant to raise at least a hand to help save what was left of human freedom, and, specifically, that nation on which the fate of all else hinged.

11

THE HISS CASE

I

On Sunday, August 1, 1948, I was sitting in my office on the 29th floor of the Time and Life Building when the telephone rang. Washington was calling and I was told that David Sentner of Hearst's Washington Bureau wanted to speak with me. I had not heard that name in some thirty-seven years. But I remembered Sentner. When I had been a student at Columbia University, trying to write poetry, I had once been introduced to him.

To me the introduction had been awesome. Sentner was then a student in the School of Journalism. He was a veteran of the First World War. He not only wrote poetry; he got it published in the campus magazines. He was a symbol of worldly experience and literary success. He, of course, knew nothing of my thoughts—we so seldom know what is passing behind the eyes that rest on us.

This flash-back, which took only an instant, was the first wrench, though I did not then know it, in an excruciating process of recollection that was to last the better part of two years and to amount almost to a total recall of my whole life.

Sentner did not remember me. "Are you the *Time* editor," he asked, "who has just been subpoenaed by the House Committee on Un-American Activities?" I said that I did not know. From the sudden silence, I realized that Sentner thought that I did know. It was the first flick of that universal disbelief that was to envelop me for more than two years.

Later, the New York *Journal-American* called and asked the same question. I still did not know the answer.

Karl Marx wrote that the great scenes of history are always enacted twice—the first time as tragedy, the second time as comedy. The Hiss Case reversed the Marxian order. The tragedy to come was prefigured by no sound of Fate knocking at the door, which, when opened, would reveal that the enemy was within the citadel, and had been for at least a decade. The Great Case began with a flourish of that showmanship which had dogged the Committee all its days, and which had been played up and exaggerated by countless enemies in the press and public life. Yet showmanship was almost the only weapon the Committee possessed. Without that flair for showmanship, which was the peculiar talent of the Committee's Chief Investigator, Robert Stripling, the extremely important work which the Committee had done in exposing the Communist conspiracy would have been smothered in silence and reduced to nullity.

The comedy with Sentner and the press occurred because the

Committee, without notifying me that a subpoena was coming, had already released the news to the press in Washington. "Is Chambers a Communist?" one newsman had asked Stripling. Stripling hemmed and said that he did not know. Possibly he did not. It is incredible, but it seems to be quite true that, at that time, few members of the Committee had more than a vague inkling of what I might testify, or even if they could get me to testify at all.

But Stripling's answer exasperated my friend, Frank McNaughton, who then covered the Capitol for *Time*. "I've known Whit Chambers for ten years," he snapped, "and you know damned well that he's no more a Communist than you are." His was the first voice raised in my behalf.

I do not mean to give the impression that I did not know that I might some time be subpoenaed. Several months before, a young newsman, also an ex-Communist, had dropped in at my office and told me a curious story. A young woman who had formerly worked in a Soviet underground apparatus in Washington had broken with the Communist Party. Knowing that Communists have their people posted pretty nearly everywhere, especially in cities like New York and Washington, she had first gone to the F.B.I. in Connecticut. There, she thought, the danger of eavesdropping would be less. She had told her story in great detail. "The F.B.I. asked her," said the newsman, "if she had ever known you. She had never heard your name. But she had heard mention once or twice of 'the man who went sour.'" I did not then learn the defected Communist's name.

On pleasant mornings, after the barn work is done, my wife and I sometimes stroll together down our long lane to get the daily mail. This little walk is one of our brief breathers, when we relax and look around us, note the growth of things that we have planted and the dozens of jobs to be done. It is our quiet time in the sun.

One July morning, I drew the local paper out of the mail box and saw that Elizabeth Bentley was to testify in Washington. I guessed that she was the former underground worker. I showed the story to my wife. I said: "I think that I may be called to testify too." "What will you do?" she asked. I said: "I shall testify."

We walked along in silence. On one side, the pasture sloped down steeply past the little brook and up to the state road—a green sweep. We had planted it. On the other side, was the third field that I had ever ploughed. When I first turned it under, the wild lettuce was so high that it reached up to the tractor seat; the rocks were so embedded that they kept breaking the plough point. Now it was a rolling field of alfalfa.

"What about the children?" my wife asked. I said: "We must be grateful that we have brought them along so far in happiness and peace." We did not mention the subject again. My wife said nothing at all about the fact that there was a $7,500 mortgage on the farm and that, as a result of my testifying, there was a distinct possibility that we might lose our farm and all of our lives that we had put into it. (This mortgage is still on the farm.)

I thought about those things a moment that August evening after the telephone call from Washington, sitting quietly in the gathering dark. Then I snapped on the light and wrote my managing editor and understanding friend a brief memo. I told him that I expected to be subpoenaed. I told him that any act a man performs, even the simplest and best, may set up reverberations of evil whose consequences it is beyond our power to trace; that my action might cause great suffering. But one man must always be willing to take upon himself the onus of evil that other men may be spared greater evil. For the sake of his children and my own, that all children might be spared the evil of Communism, I was going to testify.

The next morning I had coffee with Henry R. Luce, the editor-in-chief of *Time, Life* and *Fortune.* He had not heard of the expected subpoena. I said: "It seems to me that you will not want me around here any longer." "Nonsense," he said. "Testifying is a simple patriotic duty."

A reporter and a photographer arrived. I refused any comment or pictures until I should be subpoenaed. About noon the server arrived. I accepted the subpoena. A colleague suggested that I write a brief statement to give the Committee some background about me. I wrote one quickly. My colleague read it and approved. Then I took the train for Washington.

I was to spend the night with Frank McNaughton, who then lived far out in a northwest suburb of Washington. As we drove along, my cab driver began to talk about his chief interest in life. It was bees. He told me that he spent most of the time, when he was not hacking, among his beehives. He told me, slowing down to prolong his pleasure, about his troubles with swarms, winter killing, weak hives, robber bees. His tone of voice and language were somewhat less than Harvard. But I was impressed by his loving knowledge of the complex life and care of his insects. I thought of him driving all kinds of irrelevant people (including witnesses before Congressional Committees) through night-time Washington, while his mind lingered in his bee-yard. When I got out, he showed me frames and bottles of honey that he kept in the back of his cab—to give away, he said, but also, I suspect, to keep beside him a token of the things he really cared for. By this odd chance, I felt comforted as I took my first step into the inferno. I thought: the things I love too are still near me if only I can keep a grip on them.

Of my midnight talk with Frank McNaughton, I remember only a scrap. "There is one man on the Committee who asks shrewd questions," he said, "Richard Nixon of California."

II

It was late. I did not have many hours to sleep, and I did not sleep much. I felt something that was not only fear, though I felt fear, too. What I felt was what we see in the eye of a bird or an animal that we are about to kill, which knows that it is about to be killed, and whose torment is not the certainty of death or pain, but the horror of the interval before death comes in which it knows that it has lost light and freedom forever. It is not yet dead. But it is no longer alive.

This sense of having become the still live prey of forces that were impersonal to me in every way but that of destruction, began with the beginning of the Hiss Case, and never lifted from me until its end, and perhaps not wholly then. One of the torments of the Case for me would be the days when I was reprieved to return to my family and for a few hours became once more a man, a beloved husband and father, before I must return to that public dock where I was simply living prey existing to be rent.

Like any creature that knows it is meant to die, I simply went inert in an animal sense. I deliberately numbed and blacked out the soul so that only the body could be torn; for the body can endure any agony up to death. But the soul cannot endure the violation I have described, which is probably the most terrible in life, without dissolving in a liquefaction of panic.

Thus, when I look back upon my part in the Hiss Case, I see not myself, but someone who is not I, wandering under impersonal pressures in mazes where I am performing acts to which I submit only because they are imposed upon me, like an animal that is loaded on a truck to be carried off to the horror of stockyards, to be run into pens with other resistless animals, goaded into a public ring where shouting voices are heard, but scarcely felt, and staring eyes are felt, but scarcely seen. In the end, in ways it cannot comprehend, the creature may sometimes find itself beyond that horror, not dead, but not wholly alive because life has become little more than a recurring disbelief that it is not death. Something like that was my mood throughout the two years of the Hiss Case. This weakness did not imply an infirmity of will.

I did not wish to testify before the House Committee. I prayed that, if it were God's will, I might be spared that ordeal. I knew that I could simply keep silent about any names that I was not directly questioned about, with a good chance that I would not be asked about any that Elizabeth Bentley had not already mentioned. I could minimize whatever I had to say, in any case, so that it amounted to little. I knew that I was simply back-stopping Miss Bentley, that hers was the current testimony. The things that I had to tell were ten years old and I had only to let the shadows, dust and cobwebs conspicuously drape them to leave the stand unscathed.

I could not do it. I believed that I was not meant to be spared from testifying. I sensed, with a force greater than any fear or revulsion, that it was for this that my whole life had been lived. For this I had been a Communist, for this I had ceased to be a Communist. For this the tranquil strengthening years had been granted to me. This challenge was the terrible meaning of my whole life, of all that I had done that was evil, of all that I had sought that was good, of my weakness and my strength. Everything that made me peculiarly myself, and different from all others, qualified me to testify. My failure to do so, any attempt to evade that necessity, would be a betrayal that would measure nothing less than the destruction of my own soul. I felt this beyond any possibility of avoiding it.

For the moment had arrived when some man must be a witness, and so had the man. They had come together. The danger to the nation from Communism had now grown acute, both within its own house and abroad. Its existence was threatened. And the nation did not know it. For the first time, the Committee's subpoena gave me an opportunity to tell what I knew about that danger, not for the special information and purposes of this or that security agency, however important its work. I knew that the F.B.I., for example, could not initiate action against Communism. By law it could only gather information which the Justice Department might, or might not act on, as it saw fit. I felt at the time that the Amerasia case had been smothered. I believed that the Arthur Adams case had been smothered.* I knew that the Berle notes were not acted on seven years after I had given the information. I now know a little more about what I was then completely ignorant of—the problems of prosecution, the nature of evidence, the difficulties of proof, the long labors of investigation. Then I only felt, like many others, that the Communist danger was being concealed from the nation. The Committee in effect challenged me to spell out that danger where all men could hear it.

I, unfortunately, was the man who could speak. The necessity seemed clear to me. My intention was clear, too. I did not wish to harm, more than was unavoidable, those whom I must testify against, of whose lives in the years since I had left them I knew next to nothing, many of whom might no longer be Communists. I would not, therefore, testify to espionage against them.

But I must testify that they had been concealed Communists and that an underground had existed in the Government. That was the one indispensable fact. They and I must stand up in face of the nation and confess what we had been that it might take alarm, throw off its apathy and skepticism, see that the enemy really was embedded in its midst, and be given time to act and save itself. That was the least that we could do in atonement. That we must do. That my testimony would force the others to do, but that was all that it would force them to do. Moreover, I believed that most of them would do it, and that when the alarm had been sounded, and people had passed on to more pressing things, most of the witnesses would lapse back into their routine lives.

I did not believe that I would. From the moment when I had heard Sentner's voice on the telephone, I felt, with a certainty that I could neither explain nor shake off, that I was doomed.

* I did not know that there existed a sealed indictment of the Soviet agent, Arthur Adams. This fact, I am told, has never before been published. I am also informed that it was the intervention of the State Department that prevented the Justice Department from prosecuting that case.

III

The offices and hearing room of the House Committee on Un-American Activities are in the old House Office Building, just south of the Capitol. They are at the end of a long marble hall, rather dark, with many heavy oak official doors shutting out the light. Behind those doors are the hushed offices of congressmen.

About nine o'clock on the morning of August 3, 1948, Frank McNaughton led me into this impressive tunnel. We had come early to avoid the press. But a cluster of newsmen and sightseers had come earlier still, and were already clumped outside the Committee's door. For the first time, I heard, as a spatter of voices, what was soon to become a familiar cry: "Here comes Chambers." For the first time in my life, too, I felt, with an inward wince, the stare of a crowd. I winced not so much because the stare was inquisitive, but because it was impersonal. It came from eyes only. It was impossible to tell whether they were the eyes of friends or enemies.

I forced myself to go inert under that staring impact, an effort that I tried to cover with an impassive smile. Thus, at the door of the House Committee, I ceased to be a person; I became the target that I was to continue to be for two years. "The impassive Chambers," "the smiling Chambers" became catch-phrases which were turned against me by those whose self-interest it was to see in my effort at composure only heartlessness—as if a man had ever found any other refuge than impassivity when roped to a public stake.

We slipped into the Committee's outer office, where it was light (from many windows) and quiet (from a thick carpet), though many anonymous secretaries were moving about, and men were talking in discreet little groups. All were strangers to me. Frank McNaughton presently guided me into a side office and introduced me to a man who rose rather wearily from behind an impressive desk. This was Robert Stripling, the Committee's chief investigator. He issued me an indifferent hand to shake. His professionally impervious dark blue eyes made a leisurely trip from my face to my midriff to my shoes and back to Frank McNaughton. They betrayed neither the slight uneasiness nor the surprise that he was feeling—uneasiness at subpoenaing an editor of *Time,* surprise, which he had just expressed privately to McNaughton, that I had not dodged the subpoena. In a Texas drawl, he said: "McNaughton says you have a statement you want to read." I did not then know that, after its experiences with hostile witnesses, the Committee viewed any statement with loathing. I gave Stripling my statement which he promptly pocketed, feeling with relief, I sensed, that the witness could not be very bright or he would not have surrendered the document.

At that time, I knew even less about the Committee than it knew about me. I knew personally just one member of its staff—Ben Mandel, its able chief researcher. But I had met the former business manager of the *Daily Worker* perhaps twice, briefly, in the last ten years.

I knew by name only four of the Committee's members: Congressmen Mundt, Nixon, Thomas and Rankin. I had no impression at all of the first two and only the vaguest impression of the last two. In fact, I had only the vaguest impression of the Committee as a whole. I never read the reports it issued from time to time, and which occasionally reached my desk at *Time*. I almost never read a news story about it. I am a selective reader of the press, and among news I seldom read was crimes, disasters, scandals, the U.N., and news about the House Committee on Un-American Activities. I had had enough Communism in my life.

But, working at *Time*, it was impossible not to hear some characterization of the Committee, a characterization which I could have summed up in one word: outrageous. In greater detail, the notion was this: The Committee's members were the least intelligent in Congress because no decent man wanted to serve on it. They were uncouth, undignified and ungrammatical. They were rude and ruthless. They smeared innocent people on insufficient evidence or no evidence at all. They bullied witnesses and made sensational statements unfounded in fact. When, occasionally, they did seem to strike a fresh scent, they promptly lost it by all shouting at once or by making some ridiculous fumble.

I must confess that these charges did not particularly predispose me against the Committee. Uncouthness and rudeness, when unconscious, do not especially disturb me. I have lived at practically all levels of life, and I early observed that, while education and manners vary isothermically, native intelligence is about the same everywhere. One of the acutest political minds I ever knew was a workingman who had mastered political manipulation and motive, but never quite mastered his knife and fork. I was even less impressed by such shrieks of outraged innocence uttered by some of the Committee's witnesses as sometimes reached my ears. Experience had taught me that innocence seldom utters outraged shrieks. Guilt does. Innocence is a mighty shield, and the man or woman covered by it, is much more likely to answer calmly: "My life is blameless. Look into it, if you like, for you will find nothing." That is the tone of innocence. Nor did the Committee's fumbles cause in me the same boundless mirth that they caused some of my enlightened colleagues. Fumbles can be expected whenever any agency undertakes to investigate a conspiracy which is organized for the precise purpose of causing fumbles. What I had filed away in my mind was that the Committee was a force that was fiercely, albeit clumsily, fighting Communism.

Actually, in my prolonged experience with the Committee, none of those charges proved to be true. There was one Committee member so variable that he seemed consistent only in whirling on the pin of one or two fixed ideas. Even so, I thought that I could understand how a man of his time and place came to be impaled on those ideas. With that exception, the Committee acted, at least in the Hiss Case, with intelligence and shrewd force, despite great pressures not to act at all.

I watched the Committee's members behave with conspicuous patience and composure in the face of repeated, insolent provocation that no body of men in civil life would have endured. My own treatment by the Committee was uniformly courteous and deeply understanding. One of its members, Congressman (now Senator) Richard M. Nixon, and his family became my valued friends. With two others, Congressman (now Senator) Karl E. Mundt and Congressman John McDowell, a most cordial feeling developed. For Congressman F. Edward Hébert (of Louisiana), the most unsparing of interrogators, I developed a respect based upon what I felt to be his firm grasp of the human factors in the Hiss Case, and his equally firm grasp of reality that made him at last extremely skeptical of the antics of Alger Hiss.

In general, the Committee's treatment of Alger Hiss, in the face of his blistering sarcasm and repeated charges against it of double-dealing, was so exquisitely correct that I was sometimes moved to wonder with Hamlet: "Why do we wrap the gentleman in our more rawer breath?"

But, on the morning of August 3rd, that experience was all ahead of me.

I V

A little knot of Committee members soon gathered in Stripling's office. I was introduced, among others, to Congressman Karl E. Mundt of South Dakota, who, in the absence of Chairman J. Parnell Thomas, was the Committee's acting chairman. He informed me that he and I must step into the hall for news photos. I had never before witnessed this ordeal of 20th-century public life. Congressman Mundt and I stood side by side, looking a little uneasily at each other. The photographers scrambled, crouched for angle shots, focused, flashed, thrust burnt-out flash bulbs into their pockets. There were short cries, between a command and a plea: "Let 'em read something!" "Make out he's showing you something, Congressman!" "Just one more!" "Just one more!" "Just one more!"

Fully photographed, Congressman Mundt and I joined the rest of the Committee in the Committee's hearing room. It was a long, narrow, rather bare room. Across the front, and around one corner, ran a raised platform and desk, at which sat the Committee and its staff. I sat below in the first of a number of witness chairs I was to occupy—durable wooden chairs designed to cause whoever sits in them the maximum discomfort.

An executive session began. A Committee member, probably the acting chairman, questioned me about my knowledge of Communists in the United States Government. As nearly as I can remember, I sketched the organization of the Ware Group. Congressman Rankin broke in to ask darkly if there were any other ex-Communists at Time, Inc. I assured him that there were (of the two I had in mind, one has since died and the other has resigned).

Robert Stripling remarked that he had a statement that I wanted to read, that it was a good statement and that he thought I should be permitted to read it. Somebody said: "This witness seems to answer questions in a conservative way. I move that we go into open session." With the horror of a man whom the sea is closing over, I heard the Committee agree. The executive session had lasted only a few minutes.

There was a buzzing surge toward the Ways and Means Committee room. Congressmen were engulfed in the pushing crowd in the corridor. In tow to Donald T. Appell, a Committee investigator, I was propelled along with the rest. Above the crowd rose the informative cries of scrambling newsmen: "The Ways and Means room. Open session. They're going into open session."

I found myself face to face with Congressman Rankin. To me that day, the mutable member from Mississippi was friendly and gracious. To put me at ease, he asked: "Were you born in the state of Maryland, sir?" I said that I was born in Philadelphia. I thought that I heard the Mason and Dixon line drop between us with a clank.

The Ways and Means Committee room seemed to me enormous. I was never to see it except when I was under great tension and so perhaps I exaggerate its size. On either side of a central aisle, there were banks of seats, somewhat like a spacious funeral chapel. The seats were beginning to fill up with a shuffle of spectators. In this vast auditorium, before the company in those seats, I realized, in the dull way a man realizes that it is his turn to be shot next, that I must in a few moments give my testimony. I wondered how I could do it. I wondered how, with my low-pitched voice, I could even make myself heard.

Appell had steered me to an inconspicuous seat at the back of the hall. He was a brisk, pleasant young man who had served with the Navy in the Pacific. He was to play a more important role in my life than either of us could foresee. It was to Appell, late one night several months later, that I was to hand the historic contents of a hollowed pumpkin. Now he tried to raise my spirits by pointing out the technological triumphs of the preparations going on at the front of the room. It was hot. But I was sweating chiefly from nervousness. And what Appell pointed out only made me sweat more. Across the front of the Ways and Means Committee room ran a platform where the Committee members sat. Each member's name, on a brass plate, stood in front of him. A great public circus was being rigged of which I was clearly to be the speaking center. On the window side of the room, to the left of the witness chair, batteries of newsreel cameras and lights were being installed. Microphones were set up (though there was none for me). More and more people crowded into the seats. The press was filling the sections to the right and left of the witness chair.

Presently, Appell was leading me down the center aisle of the room to that chair—the same witness chair in which Elizabeth Bentley had sat three days before. The crowd's anonymous stare locked on me. The cameras whirred. I was sworn in. The room and the people in it sank into a blur. A dead man could scarcely have been more divided from the living world than I felt. But, unlike a dead man, I must speak. In a voice that barely carried to the straining ears in the room, I began the testimony which must continue in effect until I die.

Robert Stripling put the routine first questions. "Will you state your full name?"

"My name is David Whittaker Chambers."

"Mr. Chambers, will you raise your voice a little, please?"

"Where and when were you born?"

"I was born, April 1, 1901, in Philadelphia."

"How long have you been associated with *Time* magazine?"

"Nine years."

"Prior to that time, what was your occupation?"

"I was a member of the Communist Party and a paid functionary of the party."

* * *

"Mr. Chambers, people at the press table still feel they can't hear you. Will you please speak a little louder?"

My naturally quiet voice, further constricted by the effort of a public appearance, was soon to become a common point of attack against me. Among people who felt instinctively that I was maligning Alger Hiss, my voice seemed guilty evidence that I could not bear to utter my own falsehoods. I suppose that, if my voice were naturally resonant, the charge would have been bluster. It was not until the second Hiss trial that I overcame that handicap, and received an accolade. I was waiting in the corridor behind the courtroom during the first recess, when the court reporter appeared. "Man," he said with deep approval, "you should open a school to teach people how to testify." In time, a man becomes almost anything.

V

I asked if I might read my statement. I read:

"Almost exactly nine years ago—that is, two days after Hitler and Stalin signed their pact—I went to Washington and reported to the authorities what I knew about the infiltration of the United States Government by Communists. For years, international Communism, of which the United States Communist Party is an integral part, had been in a state of undeclared war with this Republic. With the Hitler-Stalin pact that war reached a new stage. I regarded my action in going to the Government as a simple act of war, like the shooting of an armed enemy in combat.

"At that moment in history, I was one of the few men on this side of the battle who could perform this service. I had joined the Communist Party in 1924. No one recruited me. I had become convinced that the society in which we live, Western civilization, had reached a crisis, of which the First World War was the military expression, and that it was doomed to collapse or revert to barbarism. I did not understand the causes of the crisis or know what to do about it. But I felt that, as an intelligent man, I must do something. In the writings of Karl Marx, I thought that I had found the explanation of the historical and economic causes [of the crisis]. In the writings of Lenin, I thought I had found the answer to the question: what to do?

"In 1937, I repudiated Marx's doctrines and Lenin's tactics. Experience and the record had convinced me that Communism is a form of totalitarianism, that its triumph means slavery to men wherever they fall under its sway and spiritual night to the human mind and soul. I resolved to break with the Communist Party at whatever risk to my life or other tragedy to myself or my family. Yet, so strong is the hold which the insidious evil of Communism secures upon its disciples, that I could still say to someone at that time: 'I know that I am leaving the winning side for the losing side, but it is better to die on the losing side than to live under Communism.'"

The someone to whom I referred was, of course, my wife, though, in that public place I could not have brought myself to mention her. Now, as I relived, in that tense hearing before those strange faces and intently listening ears, that moment of fateful decision, and retraced the path that had brought me from it to this witness chair, there flooded back on me the days of flight, the nights of fear, my wife's drawn face, and for an instant, my voice broke.

I continued:

"For a year I lived in hiding, sleeping by day and watching through the night with gun or revolver within easy reach. That was what underground Communism could do to one man in the peaceful United States in the year 1938.

"I had sound reasons for supposing that the Communists might try to kill me. For a number of years, I had myself served in the underground, chiefly in Washington, D.C. The heart of my report to the United States Government consisted of a description of the apparatus to which I was attached. It was an underground organization of the United States Communist Party developed, to the best of my knowledge, by Harold Ware, one of the sons of the Communist leader known as Mother Bloor. I knew it at its top level, a group of seven or so men, from among whom in later years certain members of Miss Bentley's organization were apparently recruited. The head of the underground group at the time I knew it was Nathan Witt, an attorney for the National Labor Relations Board. Later, John Abt became the leader. Lee Pressman was also a member of this group, as was Alger Hiss, who, as a member of the State Department, later organized the conferences at Dumbarton Oaks, San Francisco and the United States side of the Yalta Conference.

"The purpose of this group at that time was not primarily espionage. Its original purpose was the Communist infiltration of the American Government. But espionage was certainly one of its eventual objectives. Let no one be surprised at this statement. Disloyalty is a matter of principle with every member of the Communist Party. The Communist Party exists for the specific purpose of overthrowing the Government, at the opportune time, by any and all means; and each of its members, by the fact that he is a member, is dedicated to this purpose.

"It is ten years since I broke away from the Communist Party. During that decade, I have sought to live an industrious and God-fearing life. At the same time, I have fought Communism constantly by act and written word. I am proud to appear before this Committee. The publicity, inseparable from such testimony, has darkened and no doubt will continue to darken my effort to integrate myself in the community of free men. But that is a small price to pay if my testimony helps to make Americans recognize at last that they are at grips with a secret, sinister and enormously powerful force whose tireless purpose is their enslavement.

"At the same time, I should like, thus publicly, to call upon all ex-Communists who have not yet disclosed themselves, and all men within the Communist Party whose better instincts have not yet been corrupted and crushed by it, to aid in the struggle while there is still time."

With those irrevocable words, a segment of the greatest conspiracy in the nation's history heaved through the slick of public indifference, at the moment in history and the place where its disclosure was most relevant—in the shadow of the Capitol it threatened.

VI

As my statement listed the recognizable public names, newsmen bounded for the telephones like rabbits for their burrows.

The questioning in detail began, which would cement the public record.

STRIPLING: Who comprised the cell or apparatus to which you referred?

CHAMBERS: The apparatus was organized with a leading group of seven men, each of whom was the leader of a cell.

STRIPLING: Could you name the seven individuals?

CHAMBERS: The head of the group, as I have said, was at first Nathan Witt. Other members of the group were Lee Pressman, Alger Hiss, Donald Hiss, Victor Perlo, Charles Kramer. . . .

MUNDT: What was Charles Kramer's correct name?

CHAMBERS: I think his original name was Krivitsky. And John Abt—I don't know if I mentioned him before or not—and Henry Collins.

RANKIN: How about Harold Ware?

CHAMBERS: Harold Ware was, of course, the organizer.

I was asked who was the guiding spirit of this apparatus. I answered: "J. Peters." With that there emerged into public view the short, swart figure of that former Hungarian soldier, former official of the Hungarian Soviet under Bela Kun, close friend of Gerhardt Eisler and head of the entire underground section of the American Communist Party. Until then, most Americans had never even heard the name of that quiet, soft-spoken little man who, nevertheless, had so deeply influenced their lives.

Stripling broke into the testimony to say for the record that the Committee had in its possession a false passport in the name of Isidore Boorstein on which Peters had once traveled abroad. Obviously, Peters was a most important witness for the Committee, which had issued a subpoena for him in 1947. It had never been served. "We have never," said Stripling, "been able to locate him, and we have asked for assistance from the Department of Justice and Immigration authorities, but still we have been unable to serve the subpoena upon this individual." Said Congressman Mundt: "The presumption is that the top direction of these espionage activities carried on throughout our Government departments was conducted by a man who was not an American citizen." Nobody questioned the word espionage.

I was trying to restrict my testimony to the years 1934 and 1935. But one question threw a loop beyond the directory of the Ware Group which I had been describing to the Bykov apparatus and a later period of time. It concerned the late Harry Dexter White, who until shortly before that time had been an Assistant Secretary of the Treasury. I was asked if White was a Communist. I answered: "I can't say positively that he was a registered member of the Communist Party, but he certainly was a fellow traveler so far within the fold that his not being a Communist would be a mistake on both sides."

If the Committee had expected my testimony merely to provide some depth of background for Elizabeth Bentley's, it must by then have realized uneasily that the background was more startling than the foreground. About the most sensational of the names I mentioned there had been rumors for years. Now, for the first time, a man had stood up and said: "I was there, I knew them. The rumors are facts."

But in the hearing room, the impact of my testimony was somewhat dribbled off by the Committee's method of questioning. This is inevitable whenever the members of a large, diverse group of men, like the Committee, each has a question he wishes to ask. The result is to interrupt important lines of inquiry, which are not later followed up. Members go romping down irrelevant bypaths in which they have some personal interest. A crisp focus is lost in the effort to crowd everything into the picture. Though the Committee struggled against this diffusion, it never quite overcame it. As anyone who reads the transcript of his testimony can see, Alger Hiss was a master at sidetracking unwelcome questions by this means.

But if, on August 3rd, the full effect of what had been said was somewhat blurred, the main fact was clear enough: after ten years the conspiracy had been brought to light. No one can take the credit for that success from the Committee. I, too, had done what I set out to do. I had disclosed a conspiracy and named the conspirators as Communists. I had tried to shield those who were most deeply involved from the darker charge of espionage. Alger Hiss's name received scarcely more emphasis than Nathan Witt's or Lee Pressman's. "Would you say the purpose was, on the part of the Communists," Robert Stripling asked me, "to establish a beachhead or base from which they could move farther into the Government and obtain positions of power, influence and possible espionage?" "I would say power and influence were the paramount objectives." "At that time?" "Yes, at that time."

Just as I began to feel a little less tense, it was over. With a courtesy and an understanding of my personal position wholly at variance with the popular view of the Committee, Congressman Mundt thanked me. Congressman Rankin added: "Speaking for the minority, I want to say that the gentleman has made a splendid witness, and I only regret that every patriotic American could not be here to hear his testimony." A few days later, under the spell of Alger Hiss, he would change his mind.

I walked over to Frank McNaughton. "You behaved with dignity and nobility," he said, and, though I knew that it was not true, I welcomed the charitable words as an exhausted man welcomes a sip of raw spirits. Then Frank did something of great human tact. He said that it was his custom to spend one afternoon a month in the National Gallery and asked if I would go there with him that day. I realized that he was summoning me to a sanctuary he had found for his own trials. In that quiet and cool haven, among the paintings where other souls had permanently fixed their vision of the human condition, we passed the afternoon of my first day's testimony before the House Committee on Un-American Activities.

VII

There were a number of unintentional errors in my testimony at that first public hearing. A few were due to the strain of testifying publicly. More were due to the fact that I was reviewing the past in detail for the first time in years. Thus, I then supposed that I had joined the Communist Party in 1924. It was not until the second Hiss trial that the Hiss defense corrected me. I had joined in 1925, as they knew from one of two letters from me which my old faculty adviser at Columbia College, Mark Van Doren, had, without informing me, turned over to A. J. Liebling, then of the *New Yorker,* who, in turn, had obligingly handed them over to Hiss's lawyers.

I also supposed that I had first gone to Washington in 1935 and broken with the Communist Party in 1937. I soon realized that the latter date was wrong, and corrected it before the Committee. It was much later when, in untangling the sequence of past events, I realized that I had first gone to Washington in 1934.

In this way, Elizabeth Bentley had a great advantage in testifying. Her recollections were more current, and she had had the inestimable advantage of clarifying step by step in advance in her statement to the F.B.I. and her testimony before the Grand Jury. Quite apart from my effort to shield my former friends, I began to testify "cold." Even today, after exhaustive recollection, I sometimes remember fresh details that had slipped my mind.

Actually, none of the errors that I made in my first day's testimony, and subsequently, was serious. They did not greatly perturb me, for I assumed that most people are sensible enough to know that few men could testify without some error to details of ten, or even fourteen years, ago. I knew what the main outlines of the conspiracy had been, but I testified to details with much less reflection than was necessary. For I was completely unfamiliar with legal practice, and only gradually did I become aware of the necessity for absolutely exact statement in testifying.

I was slow, too, in becoming aware of something else. I had just disclosed a shocking conspiracy which had the further effect of corroborating some of Elizabeth Bentley's disclosures. Yet, when I rose from the witness chair, only one newsman of the many who stared at me (I thought) with a curious unfriendliness, asked me an amplifying question. He asked me how to spell a German word I had used. At the time, my reaction was merely professional. I thought: "If I had been covering this story, I would certainly have talked with the witness." It took me some time to realize that a part of the press itself, the fact gatherers, was to play a role of active hostility to me.

I had had a slight forewarning. While I was testifying, I had been conscious of only one person near me. He was a rather owlish newsman who, now and again, turned to stare at me so fixedly that I found myself turning involuntarily toward him. As Frank McNaughton and I left the Senate Press Room, I saw this owlish man whispering with another in a corner. I asked McNaughton who he was. "That's the Tass man," he said. (Tass is the Soviet Government's official news service.) "The other is from the Federated Press"—(the Communist-controlled news service of my *Daily Worker* days). The two men stopped whispering as we passed. Out of the tail of my eye, I saw them staring at us.

Congressman Nixon also had a curious encounter at about the same time. As he was leaving the hearing room, a young woman stepped up to him. He supposed that she was a newswoman. "Don't you know," she asked, "that Whittaker Chambers is an incurable drunkard?" Before he could question her, she had disappeared in the crowd.

The smear had begun.

VIII

I did not go home at once. I spent the night of my first day's testimony at the farm of friends at Olney, near Washington. I was most deeply concerned about the effect which the news of my testimony would have on my wife and children. Though I was outwardly calm, my nerves were spun tight. I wanted to give myself a cooling-off period before I met my family. I thought that my neighbors, too, needed some time to think things over before I appeared again among them.

A great weakness also contributed to my postponement of the train trip from Washington to Baltimore—my almost physical antipathy to being stared at publicly. I have learned to control it, but I have never mastered it. To avoid some of that, I telephoned my wife and asked her to drive to Baltimore to meet me.

When we met, the children flung their arms around me and my wife smiled courage. In the main, the news from home was reassuring. The first radio broadcasts about my testimony had electrified the countryside, but friends, including Quakers from our Meeting, had come at once to be with my wife. Farmers are pretty levelheaded people, and although there was no doubt a great hubbub among them, those who lived closest to us had watched us working among them for years; they stood by us. They never changed. I have an impression that the first news was more incredible than anything else. Perhaps, the initial surprise was summed up by our family doctor, who, on hearing that I had testified that I had once been a Communist, snorted: "I don't believe it."

The principal of my son's school immediately wrote me, saying that he understood why I was testifying, thanking me for doing so and offering to help in any possible way. Both my son's and my daughter's school quietly took all possible measures to protect the children from any schoolyard harassment, of which there were only two examples, so minor as to be meaningless.

But the day I came home, I could not foresee that. I thought that it might be necessary to sell the cattle and send the children away from the farm to another part of the country, where they would be separated for a while from their too public father. We discussed the problem as we drove from Baltimore to Westminister.

"What about Mr. Pennington?" I asked my wife. "He went away," she said, "when the first news broke, and he hasn't come back." Almost nothing could have struck me harder, for he was a man on whom, like Duncan, I built an absolute trust. His disappearance more than anything else darkened our trip home.

When we arrived, Stanley Pennington met me at the barn. He had done his thinking and come back. He wrung my hand and said something about men's courage. I had to walk away.

The next day he would draw my wife aside and say that we must not think of paying him during our troubles. Several times, afterwards, when he knew that the going was hard, he would offer to work for us as long as he could possibly do so without wages.

There was one other man and his family whose friendship meant a great deal to me. He was Paul Morelock, and his family was his wife, Ruth, and her sisters, Miss Agnes and Miss Margaret Reese. Paul Morelock is a breeder of Percheron horses and purebred Angus cattle; a grower of hybrid seed corn and acres of gladioli and pyrethrum. He and his family, now in their vigorous sixties, work their hereditary farm near ours.

I had not been home long before the Morelocks and Reeses drove up. As usual, the women were loaded down with flowers. While they chatted with my wife, Paul drew me aside. He wanted to get something straight at once. "I don't know anything about Communism," he said. "I'd rather be dead than be a Communist. But what I say is this: when a man is down, that's when he needs friends to stand by him. Yes, sir, when a man is down, that's when he needs friends to stand by him. So me and the women came over."

So me and the women came over—words to be written rather high, I think, on that monument which is headed: ". . . and thy neighbor as thyself."

I had hoped that the nation might come to understand what I

was trying to do. I had thought that it might take twenty or thirty years, perhaps late in my children's lives. Now I thought: "It is wonderful. It is past belief. But the nation is going to understand. For Paul Morelock and the Reese women are America."

IX

I went back to my office at *Time,* shut the door and continued my reading for the last of *Life's* essays on the *History of Western Civilization*—that on the revolutionary year, 1848, the year of the *Communist Manifesto.**

From the beginning, I had resolved not to read any news stories about my testimony, or to listen to radio broadcasts. I needed all the strength I could command for my purpose. The press and radio din could only deflect and diffuse it. My news quarantine was strictly kept. I seldom broke it until well into the second Hiss trial. I never broke it without regretting it. In this way, I was spared much of the harassment that I must have suffered had I read the press or listened to the radio. Only one or two of the most egregious attacks by great public figures reached me, and then softened at second hand. Some of the most shocking slanders did not come to my ears until comparatively late in the Hiss Case when the whole world was abuzz with them.

This censorship was as necessary to my morale as any censorship in wartime. But it often resulted in my knowing less about current developments in the Hiss Case than almost anybody else knew. Thus, it happened that, on August 5, 1948, I did not know that Alger Hiss was testifying before the House Committee on Un-American Activities.

The first inkling I had of it came while I was working at my desk. The telephone rang. Louis J. Russell, then the Committee's assistant chief (now its chief) investigator, was at the other end of the wire. "Are you sure," he asked me in a voice in which I caught the unmistakable note of desperation, "are you sure you are right

* Events decided that I was never to write it. Someone else wrote the published piece. But the lawyer of a well-known biographer, who knew that I had written other pieces in the series and assumed that I had written *1848,* threatened suit for plagiarism (and some $50,000) at that moment of supreme nuisance value. The suit never came off, of course. But, together with the Hiss libel suit and the damage claim for my wife's automobile accident in December 1948, it made me at one point liable for some $150,000 damages. The sum was so far beyond my capacity to pay that it reduced all the claims to a welcome absurdity.

about Alger Hiss?" I said: "Yes, of course." "Are you sure," he persisted, "you couldn't have mistaken him for somebody else?" I said: "Of course, I haven't mistaken him." "Well," said Russell, "Alger Hiss testified just now that he does not know you and never set eyes on you." I said: "If necessary, I will go down to Washington and testify all over again." I could probably have said nothing more frightening at the moment.

What stunned me as I stared at my desk, and was to puzzle me for some time to come, was a simple question: "How did Alger Hiss, in face of the facts that we both knew, and under the eyes of some 150 million people, suppose that he could possibly get away with it?"

I did not know a number of things. I did not know that Hiss had already denied that he was a Communist to the former Secretary of State, James F. Byrnes, to John Foster Dulles, his sponsor at the Carnegie Endowment for World Peace, and to the F.B.I. I did not know that, six months before, he had denied the same fact under oath to the Grand Jury of the Southern District of New York (the Grand Jury that later indicted him). I did not know, I could not have dreamed, of the immense scope and power of Hiss's political alliances and his social connections, which cut across all party lines and ran from the Supreme Court to the Religious Society of Friends, from governors of states and instructors in college faculties to the staff members of liberal magazines. In the decade since I had last seen him, he had used his career, and, in particular, his identification with the cause of peace through his part in organizing the United Nations, to put down roots that made him one with the matted forest floor of American upper class, enlightened middle class, liberal and official life. His roots could not be disturbed without disturbing all the roots on all sides of him.

Perhaps it was providential, too, that I did not know those facts at that time, for knowledge of them could only have defeated me in advance. The discrepancy between our strength was too staggering. I stood almost alone. Soon I seemed to stand even more alone than I could have believed possible. For my most powerful friends, and those who might naturally be expected to help me, in the day of decision were distinguished chiefly by the virtue of prudence. It was some time before I knew who my real friends were.

X

My puny plight was as nothing compared to that of the House Committee on Un-American Activities. Hiss's testimony had been sweepingly convincing. The crowd in the Ways and Means Committee room, including many newsmen, had attended with rapt sympathy. Hiss was a voluntary witness before the Committee and his manner combined, in very tactful proportions, well-bred outrage and well-phrased bafflement. His candor was disarming. Even his occasional sarcastic barbs did not transgress the limits of patience of an innocent man unjustly accused.

Under questioning, Hiss's impeccable career had unfolded. It began with a popular touch: "I was educated in the public schools of Baltimore." Then came high school, Baltimore City College. A soaring set in: preparatory school in Massachusetts, Johns Hopkins University, Harvard Law School. "My first employment in the Federal Government was immediately after my graduation from law school when I served as a secretary to one of the Associate Justices of the United States Supreme Court." "The Justice was Oliver Wendell Holmes." "I then went into private practice in Boston and New York . . . and came to Washington at the request of Government officials . . . as an assistant general counsel to the Agricultural Adjustment Administration." "A Senate Committee, known as the Committee Investigating the Munitions Industry . . . formally requested the Department of Agriculture to lend my services to that committee in its investigations as their counsel." "When I left the Senate Committee, I was next employed in the office of the Solicitor General of the United States, at my request, Mr. Nixon." "While I was still in the Solicitor General's office . . . Mr. Francis B. Sayre, then the Assistant Secretary of State in charge of Trade Agreements, asked me to come to his office as his assistant to supervise the preparation within the Department of State of the constitutional arguments on the Trade Agreement Acts. I did so. . . . " "I am the president of the Carnegie Endowment for World Peace."

There was the culmination of Yalta. Mr. Mundt: Did you draft, or participate in drafting, parts of the Yalta Agreement? Mr. Hiss: I think it is accurate and not an immodest statement to say that I did to some extent, yes.

It was history speaking through one of its personifications. Mr. Hiss: My best recollection, without consulting the actual records is that the text of what is now article 27 of the Charter was drafted in the Department of State in the early winter of 1944, before the Yalta Conference, (and) was dispatched by the President of the United States to the Prime Minister of Great Britain and to Marshal Stalin for their agreement, and represented the proposal made by the United States at the Yalta Conference, and was accepted by the other two after some discussion. I did participate in the Department of State in the drafting of the messages I have referred to that President Roosevelt sent in, I think, December, 1944, prior to the Yalta Conference."

Nevertheless, it had also been necessary to put certain questions about Whittaker Chambers.

MR. MUNDT: I want to say, for one member of the committee, that it is extremely puzzling that a man who is senior editor of *Time* magazine, by the name of Whittaker Chambers, whom I had never seen until a day or two ago, and whom you say you have never seen—

MR. HISS: As far as I know, I have never seen him.

MR. MUNDT: —should come before this committee and discuss the Communist apparatus working in Washington, which he says is transmitting secrets to the Russian Government,* and he lists a group of seven people—Nathan Witt, Lee Pressman, Victor Perlo, Charles Kramer, John Abt, Harold Ware, Alger Hiss and Donald Hiss—

MR. HISS: That is eight.

MR. MUNDT: There seems to be no question about the subversive connections of the six others than the Hiss brothers, and I wonder what possible motive a man who edits *Time* magazine would have for mentioning Donald Hiss and Alger Hiss in connection with those other six.

MR. HISS: So do I, Mr. Chairman. I have no possible understanding of what could have motivated him. There are many possible motives I assume, but I am unable to understand it.

"You say," Mr. Stripling presently asked, "you have never seen Mr. Chambers?"

* I had not said that. I assume that Congressman Mundt said it because a newsman had procured, in ways reminiscent of underground methods, a copy of the Berle notes (presumably shortened and garbled), which had then been seen by, or were in the hands of, certain members of the Committee.

MR. HISS: The name means absolutely nothing to me, Mr. Stripling.

The witness was then shown a photograph of Whittaker Chambers taken in 1934 or 1935, and asked if he had ever known "an individual who resembles this picture." Hiss did not answer directly.

MR. HISS: I would much rather see the individual. I have looked at all the pictures I was able to get hold of in, I think it was, yesterday's paper which had the pictures. If this is a picture of Mr. Chambers, he is not particularly unusual-looking. He looks like a lot of people. I might even mistake him for the chairman of this committee. (Laughter)

MR. MUNDT: I hope you are wrong in that.

MR. HISS: I didn't mean to be facetious, but very seriously, I would not want to take oath that I had never seen that man. I would like to see him and then I think that I would be better able to tell whether I had ever seen him. Is he here today?

MR. MUNDT: Not to my knowledge.

MR. HISS: I hoped he would be.

(It should be observed, parenthetically, that Alger Hiss was one of the only four people in the Hiss Case who ever failed to recognize me. Even Lee Pressman, who claimed to have seen me only once, briefly, in his office in 1936, had no difficulty in recognizing me. The reason was, of course, that I did not look markedly different in 1948 from what I had looked like in 1938.)

It had also been necessary to ask questions about Hiss's connections with the other members of the Ware Group. It turned out that, in one way or another, he had known all of them, with one exception, though he had scarcely seen them, he said, in recent years. The exception was Victor Perlo, who was deeply embedded in Elizabeth Bentley's testimony. With Witt, Pressman and Collins, Hiss had gone to Harvard. Collins he had known since boyhood. With Witt, Pressman, Abt, Kramer and even Harold Ware Hiss had worked in the Government. But he could not remember that Henry Collins had ever lived in St. Matthews Court ("Can anyone locate the place?" he was presently to ask), and he could not remember when he had last seen Charles Kramer (also deeply embedded in Miss Bentley's testimony).

MR. STRIPLING: When did you last see Charles Kramer?

MR. HISS: I couldn't be sure. I have probably seen him on the street. He is a rather distinctive-looking person. Do you know him?

MR. STRIPLING: I know him.

MR. HISS: He has reddish hair, very distinctive. . . .

Hiss also knew Lauchlin Currie, Harold Glasser ("officially, and I think only officially") and Harry Dexter White.

It developed, though no one seemed to take much note of the fact at the time, that the witness had been asked about his Communist sympathies before. That had been in 1946, "shortly after I came back from London where I had been at the first meeting of the General Assembly of the United Nations." Secretary of State Byrnes had called Alger Hiss into his office. "He said that several members of Congress were preparing to make statements on the floor of Congress that I was a Communist. He asked me if I were, and I said I was not. He said, 'This is a very serious matter. I think all the stories center from the F.B.I. . . . I think you would be well advised to go directly to the F.B.I. and offer yourself for a very full inquiry and investigation.' He also said he thought it would be sensible for me to go to the top man, and I agreed."

But J. Edgar Hoover was not in town. Hiss was "courteously received by his second in command. I think it was Mr. Tamm in those days." He had offered himself "for any inquiry." "They said did I have any statement to make? I said I was glad to make any statement upon any subject they suggested, and they had no specific one initially."

In 1947 agents of the F.B.I. had again called upon Alger Hiss. This time they asked him if he was a Communist. They asked him a number of questions "not unlike the points Mr. Chambers testified to." Among other names they asked him about was that of Whittaker Chambers. "I remember very distinctly because I had never heard the name Whittaker Chambers."

Then the public hearing swung around to Yalta. Again, the gulf between Alger Hiss, the privy counselor of the great President, and Alger Hiss, the gratuitously injured witness before the unpopular Committee, yawned embarrassingly vast.

Amidst the thanks of his inquisitors, the witness stepped down. Friendly newsmen crowded around him.

As spectacle, it had been superb. It might have succeeded, too, but for one fact—the fact that is never foreseen. One of the Committee members was a man with one of those direct minds which has an inner ear for the ring of truth. As Richard Nixon, a lawyer and a birthright Quaker, listened to the looping sentences and the rich vocables, marshaled like troops for an assault, the thought passed through his mind: "It is a little too mouthy." He noticed, too, that Alger Hiss never said that he did not know me; he always said that he did not know a man named Whittaker Chambers. And at the very beginning of the hearing, the Congressman had had a puzzling fencing bout with the witness—puzzling because Hiss's evasiveness was so obstinate and, apparently, so unmotivated.

Hiss had testified that "Government officials" had "requested" him to come to Washington in 1933. What officials? Nixon asked—his first question in the Hiss Case. Judge Jerome Frank, said Hiss.

MR. NIXON: You said it in the plural? Was he the only one then?

MR. HISS: There were some others. Is it necessary? There are so many witnesses who use names rather loosely before your committee, and I would rather limit myself.

MR. NIXON: You made the statement—

MR. HISS: The statement is correct.

MR. NIXON: I don't question its correctness, but you indicated that several Government officials requested you to come here and you have issued a categorical denial to certain statements that were made by Mr. Chambers concerning people that you were associated with in Government. I think it would make your case much stronger if you would indicate what Government officials.

MR. HISS: Mr. Nixon, regardless of whether it strengthens my case or not, I would prefer, unless you insist, not to mention any names in my testimony that I don't feel are absolutely necessary. If you insist on a direct answer to your question, I will comply.

MR. NIXON: I would like to have a direct answer to the question.

MR. HISS: Another official of the Government of the United States who strongly urged me to come to Washington after I had told Judge Frank I did not think I could financially afford to do so—and I am answering this only because you ask it—was Justice Felix Frankfurter.

Why the long struggle to elicit that name?

X I

When Alger Hiss stepped down from the witness stand on August 5th, after his flat denial that he had been a Communist, one of two conclusions seemed certain: 1) from unfathomable motives, I had committed perjury in making the charge; 2) it was a case of mistaken identity; I had mistaken Alger Hiss for someone else.

Hiss had also left a definite impression on the public mind (which much of the press and most of the radio did little to diminish) that he had never set eyes on me in his life; that the photographs of me that were showed him were those of a complete stranger. Actually, as Nixon's ear had caught, Hiss had been extremely careful not to make any definite statement at all on that point. He had used his practiced legal sinuousness to avoid a firm yes or no when asked to identify me.

Within a fortnight, Hiss would begin to feel his way along the lines of a reverse tactic which would lead him to identify me positively, in a snap of the fingers, as someone he knew quite well —though under another name.

But on August 5th, by flat denials and by drawing the toga of his official career about him, Hiss had made the Committee look like the gullible victim of a vulgar impostor—myself.

Gladly, the Committee turned its back on Alger Hiss and filed into its chambers. It severally stood or sat for a moment in attitudes of mute gloom. Then a member said: "We're ruined." It was one of history's moments of high irony. For a decade, the Committee (first as the Dies Committee and then as the House Committee on Un-American Activities) had been trying to hack off the Gorgon head of Communist conspiracy, which it had never quite succeeded in locating. Now, almost casually, the snaky mass had been set down on the congressmen's collective desk. It was terrifying. It petrified most of them.

Their terror was justified. It was an election year, and the seat of every member of the Committee was at stake. Moreover, the hostile clamor in the press and from public personages, together with other pressures, had battered the Committee into a state bordering on anxiety neurosis. The Committee's instinctive reaction was to get away as fast as possible from the monstrous challenge that had been set down before it. Someone proposed that the Committee drop the Hiss-Chambers controversy at once and switch to some subject sensational enough to distract public attention from its unnerving blunder.

That was the first decisive moment of the Hiss Case. If that small group of harassed congressmen had then acted out of their fears and dropped the Case, it is probable that the forces which for years had kept the Communist conspiracy in Government from public knowledge would have continued to be successful in concealing it. Alger Hiss would have remained at the head of the Carnegie Endowment, exerting great influence in public affairs through his position and ramified connections. With him, the whole secret Communist front would have stood more unassailable than ever because the shattered sally against it had ended in ridicule and rout. Elizabeth Bentley's charges would almost certainly have been buried in the debris.

That the Committee did not act on its fears is a fact of history that no one can take from it. Its stand was greatly strengthened by one man. Richard Nixon argued quietly but firmly against a switch from the Hiss investigation to any other subject. He pled the necessity of reaching truth in the Hiss-Chambers deadlock. By his action, then and later, he became the man of decision of the first phase of the Hiss Case, as Thomas F. Murphy (now Judge Murphy) was to be the man of decision of the second phase of the Hiss Case.* Richard Nixon made the Hiss Case possible. Thomas F. Murphy made it possible for the nation to win the Case. Without either man, the Case would, in my opinion, have been lost. Let any rational fellow who likes explain to the nation how, in that crisis, those two men, and just those two men, one a Quaker and one a Catholic, one a Republican and one a Democrat, each utterly unlike the other in mind and character, came to be where each, in indispensable succession, was needed.

The Committee never faltered again. Around Nixon rallied Congressmen Mundt, Hébert, McDowell, and the Committee's chief investigator, Robert Stripling, who persistently fought through the Case to the close of the Committee's phase. That was the first team, together with the investigators and researchers who backstopped it, that made the Hiss Case. At the time, I sometimes thought that it behaved clumsily, crudely, without intelligence, in-

* Nor must the services of Tom Donegan, a special assistant to the Attorney General, be overlooked. His conduct of the Grand Jury proceedings later on contributed greatly to the indictment of Alger Hiss.

tuition, or even order. Looking back on its conduct, with fuller knowledge of its handicaps and with much greater personal experience of such matters than I then had, I am astonished at the skill and pertinacity with which it made head against great obstacles.

If the Committee were to press the Case, the first point to establish was: who is lying? That could be got at most readily by finding out whether or not I had, in fact, ever personally known Alger Hiss. Nixon, acting on a suggestion of Ben Mandel's, proposed a simple procedure. The Committee would question me in executive session with a view to discovering what hard facts I knew about Hiss, his family, his life, the houses he had lived in, etc. Then it would separately question Hiss on the same points, and compare the two witnesses' answers.

Richard Nixon was appointed chairman of a sub-committee for that purpose. Its other members were Congressmen F. Edward Hébert of Louisiana and John McDowell of Pennsylvania. The sub-committee left for New York and summoned me for questioning at 10:30 on the morning of August 7, 1948, in Room 101 of the United States Courthouse (the Federal Building). Nine days later, it summoned Alger Hiss to a similar session in the Committee's hearing room in the Old House Office Building in Washington.

XII

I had to ask my way to the Federal Building where I was soon to spend some months of the most important waking hours of my life. I found the sub-committee waiting for me in one of those official rooms where no one lives but which bears the stale traces of many people passing through. With the sub-committee was a contingent of the Committee's staff. Most of them were standing or shuffling around nervously. Everyone was overtly polite under an air of fret. Ben Mandel hovered around me with disquieting solicitude.

The three members of the sub-committee sat down, facing me across a long table. Congressman Nixon sat directly opposite me; Hébert to his right, McDowell to his left. We were not more than four to six feet apart. The congressmen seldom took their eyes off my face. A drumfire of questions began which continued almost without pause until the end of the hearing. Nixon, as chairman of the sub-committee, opened fire.

NIXON: Mr. Hiss in his testimony was asked on several occasions whether or not he had ever known, or knew, a man by the name of Whittaker Chambers. In each instance he categorically said "No." At what period did you know Mr. Hiss? What time?

CHAMBERS: I knew Mr. Hiss, roughly, between the years 1935 to 1937.

NIXON: Do you know him as Mr. Alger Hiss?

CHAMBERS: Yes.

NIXON: Did you happen to see Mr. Hiss's pictures in the newspapers as a result of these recent hearings?

CHAMBERS: Yes, I did.

NIXON: Was that the man you knew as Alger Hiss?

CHAMBERS: Yes, that is the man.

NIXON: You are certain of that?

CHAMBERS: I am completely certain.

NIXON: During the time that you knew Mr. Hiss, did he know you as Whittaker Chambers?

CHAMBERS: No, he did not.

NIXON: By what name did he know you?

CHAMBERS: He knew me by the Party name of Carl.

NIXON: Did he ever question the fact that he did not know your last name?

CHAMBERS: Not to me.

NIXON: Why not?

CHAMBERS: Because in the underground Communist Party the principle of organization is that functionaries, and heads of the group in other words, shall not be known by their right names but by pseudonyms or party names.

NIXON: Were you a party functionary?

CHAMBERS: I was a functionary.

NIXON: This entire group with which you worked in Washington did not know you by your real name?

CHAMBERS: No member of that group knew me by my real name.

NIXON: All knew you as Carl?

CHAMBERS: That is right.

NIXON: No member of that group ever inquired of you as to your real name?

CHAMBERS: To have questioned me would have been a breach of party discipline, Communist Party discipline.

NIXON: I understood you to say that Mr. Hiss was a member of the party.

CHAMBERS: Mr. Hiss was a member of the Communist Party.

NIXON: Is there any other circumstance which would substantiate your allegation that he was a member of the party. . . . ?

CHAMBERS: I must also interpolate there that all Communists in the group in which I originally knew him accepted him as a member of the Communist Party.

NIXON: Referred to him as a member of the party?

CHAMBERS: That doesn't come up in conversation, but this was a Communist group.

NIXON: Could this have possibly been an intellectual study group?

CHAMBERS: It was in no wise an intellectual study group. Its primary function was not that of an intellectual study group . . . its primary function was to infiltrate the Government in the interest of the Communist Party. (Before the month was out Adolf A. Berle was to do me (and everybody else) a serious disservice by (in effect) contradicting this testimony.)

NIXON: At that time, incidentally, Mr. Hiss and the other members of this group who were Government employees did not have party cards?

CHAMBERS: No members of that group to my knowledge ever had party cards, nor do I think members of any such group have party cards.

NIXON: The reason is—

CHAMBERS: The reason is security, concealment.

NIXON: In other words, people who are in the Communist underground are in fact instructed to deny the fact that they are members of the Communist Party?

CHAMBERS: I was told by Peters (J. Peters) that party registration was kept in Moscow and in some secret file in the United States.

There then followed a point-blank fusillade, chiefly aimed at testing my factual, intimate knowledge of Alger Hiss, his household and his habits, which was the purpose of the hearing. Deliberately, the questions were fired so quickly as to give me as little time as possible to reflect on the answers. As in the first hearing, I made a number of errors of recollection, none of them very serious, and all of them together greatly outweighed by the answers which Hiss himself would verify nine days later.

To understand in somewhat the same way the impact that my testimony made upon the Committee, and the reason why its members slowly began to feel that Hiss had known me, it is only necessary to compare my testimony taken on August 7th with his testimony on similar points taken on August 16th. In each case the testimony was taken in executive session. Perhaps it should be noted, too, that I testified without having discussed the past with my wife whose memory for what Hiss was later to call "these petty housekeeping details" proved to be more detailed and vivid than mine.

MR. NIXON: Did Mr. Hiss have any children?

MR. CHAMBERS: Mr. Hiss had no children of his own.

MR. NIXON: Were there any children living in his home?

MR. CHAMBERS: Mrs. Hiss had a son.

MR. NIXON: Do you know the son's name?

MR. CHAMBERS: Timothy Hobson.

MR. NIXON: Approximately how old was he at the time you knew him?

MR. CHAMBERS: It seems to me he was about 10 years old.

MR. NIXON: What did you call him?

MR. CHAMBERS: Timmie.

MR. NIXON: Did Mr. Hiss call him Timmie also?

MR. CHAMBERS: I think so.

MR. NIXON: Did he have any other nickname?

MR. CHAMBERS: Not that I recall. He is the son, to the best of my knowledge, of Thayer Hobson, who I think is a member of the publishing house of William Morrow here in New York.

MR. NIXON: What name did Mrs. Hiss use in addressing Mr. Hiss?

MR. CHAMBERS: Usually "Hilly."

MR. NIXON: "Hilly"?

MR. CHAMBERS: Yes.

MR. NIXON: Quite often?

MR. CHAMBERS: Yes.

MR. NIXON: In your presence?

MR. CHAMBERS: Yes.

MR. NIXON: Not "Alger"?

MR. CHAMBERS: Not "Alger."

MR. NIXON: What nickname, if any, did Mr. Hiss use in addressing his wife?

MR. CHAMBERS: More often "Dilly" and sometimes "Pross." Her name was Priscilla. They were commonly referred to as "Hilly" and "Dilly."

MR. NIXON: They were commonly referred to as "Hilly" and "Dilly"?

MR. CHAMBERS: By other members of the group.

* * *

MR. NIXON: Did you ever spend any time in Hiss' home?

MR. CHAMBERS: Yes.

MR. NIXON: Did you ever stay overnight?

MR. CHAMBERS: Yes; I stayed overnight for a number of days.

MR. NIXON: You mean from time to time?

MR. CHAMBERS: From time to time.

MR. NIXON: Did you ever stay longer than 1 day?

MR. CHAMBERS: I have stayed there as long as a week.

* * *

MR. NIXON: What arrangements were made for taking care of your lodging at that time? Were you there as a guest?

MR. CHAMBERS: I made that a kind of informal headquarters.

MR. NIXON: I understand that, but what was the financial arrangement?

MR. CHAMBERS: There was no financial arrangement.

MR. NIXON: You were a guest?

MR. CHAMBERS: Part of the Communist pattern.

MR. NIXON: Did the Hisses have a cook? Do you recall a maid?

MR. CHAMBERS: As nearly as I can remember, they had a maid who came in to clean, and a cook who came in to cook. I can't remember whether they had a maid there all the time or not. It seems to me in one or two of the houses they did. In one of the houses they had a rather elderly Negro maid whom Mr. Hiss used to drive home in the evening.

MR. NIXON: You don't recall the names of the maids?

MR. CHAMBERS: No; I don't.

MR. NIXON: Did the Hisses have any pets?

MR. CHAMBERS: They had, I believe, a cocker spaniel. I have

a bad memory for dogs, but as nearly as I can remember it was a cocker spaniel.

MR. NIXON: Do you remember the dog's name?

MR. CHAMBERS: No. I remember they used to take it up to some kennel. I think out Wisconsin Avenue.

MR. NIXON: They took it to board it there?

MR. CHAMBERS: Yes. They made one or two vacation trips to the Eastern Shore of Maryland.

MR. NIXON: They made some vacation trips to the Eastern Shore of Maryland?

MR. CHAMBERS: Yes, and at those times the dog was kept at the kennel.

MR. NIXON: You state the Hisses had several different houses when you knew them? Could you describe any one of those houses to us?

MR. CHAMBERS: I think so. It seems to me when I first knew him he was living on 28th Street in an apartment house. There were two almost identical apartment houses. It seems to me that is a dead-end street and this was right at the dead end and certainly it is on the right-hand side as you go up.

It also seems to me that apartment was on the top floor. Now, what was it like inside, the furniture? I can't remember.

MR. MANDEL: What was Mr. Hiss' library devoted to?

MR. CHAMBERS: Very nondescript, as I recall.

MR. NIXON: Do you recall what floor the apartment was on?

MR. CHAMBERS: I think it was on the top floor.

MR. NIXON: The fourth?

MR. CHAMBERS: It was a walk-up. I think the fourth.

MR. NIXON: It could have been the third, of course?

MR. CHAMBERS: It might have been.

MR. NIXON: But you think it was the top, as well as you can recall?

MR. CHAMBERS: I think it was the top.

MR. NIXON: Understand, I am not trying to hold you to absolute accuracy.

MR. CHAMBERS: I am trying to recall.

MR. NIXON: Was there any special dish they served?

MR. CHAMBERS: No. I think you get here into something else. Hiss is a man of great simplicity and a great gentleness and sweetness of character, and they lived with extreme simplicity. I had the impression that the furniture in that house was kind of pulled together from here or there, maybe got it from their mother or something like that, nothing lavish about it whatsoever, quite simple.

Their food was in the same pattern and they cared nothing about food. It was not a primary interest in their lives.

MR. MANDEL: Did Mr. Hiss have any hobbies?

MR. CHAMBERS: Yes; he did. They both had the same hobby—amateur ornithologists, bird observers. They used to get up early in the morning and go to Glen Echo, out the canal, to observe birds.

I recall once they saw, to their great excitement, a prothonotary warbler.

MR. MC DOWELL: A very rare specimen?

MR. CHAMBERS: I never saw one. I am also fond of birds.

MR. NIXON: Did they have a car?

MR. CHAMBERS: Yes; they did. When I first knew them they had a car. Again I am reasonably sure—I am almost certain—it was a Ford and that it was a roadster. It was black and it was very dilapidated. There is no question about that.

I remember very clearly that it had hand windshield wipers. I remember that because I drove it one rainy day and had to work those windshield wipers by hand.

MR. NIXON: Do you recall any other car?

MR. CHAMBERS: It seems to me in 1936, probably, he got a new Plymouth.

MR. NIXON: Do you recall its type?

MR. CHAMBERS: It was a sedan, a two-seated car.

MR. MANDEL: What did he do with the old car?

MR. CHAMBERS: The Communist Party had in Washington a service station—that is, the man in charge or owner of this station was a Communist—or it may have been a car lot.

MR. NIXON: But the owner was a Communist?

MR. CHAMBERS: The owner was a Communist. I never knew who this was or where it was. It was against all the rules of underground organization for Hiss to do anything with his old car but trade it in, and I think this investigation has proved how right the Communists are in such matters, but Hiss insisted that he wanted that car turned over to the open party so it could be of use to some poor organizer in the West or somewhere.

Much against my better judgment and much against Peters'

better judgment, he finally got us to permit him to do this thing. Peters knew where this lot was and he either took Hiss there, or he gave Hiss the address and Hiss went there, and to the best of my recollection of his description of that happening, he left the car there and simply went away and the man in charge of the station took care of the rest of it for him. I should think the records of that transfer would be traceable.

MR. NIXON: Where was that?

MR. CHAMBERS: In Washington, D.C., I believe; certainly somewhere in the District.

MR. NIXON: You don't know where?

MR. CHAMBERS: No; never asked.

MR. NIXON: Do you recall any other cars besides those two?

MR. CHAMBERS: No, I think he had the Plymouth when I broke with the whole business.

MR. NIXON: You don't recall any other hobbies he had?

MR. CHAMBERS: I don't think he had any other hobbies.

MR. NIXON: Did they have a piano?

MR. CHAMBERS: I don't believe so. I am reasonably sure they did not.

MR. NIXON: Do you recall any particular pieces of furniture that they had?

MR. CHAMBERS: The only thing I recall was a small leather cigarette box, leather-covered cigarette box, with gold tooling on it. It seems to me that box was red leather.

MR. NIXON: Red leather cigarette box with gold tooling?

MR. CHAMBERS: That is right.

MR. NIXON: Do you recall possibly what the silver pattern was, if any? Was it sterling?

MR. CHAMBERS: I don't recall.

MR. NIXON: Do you recall what kind of chinaware they used?

MR. CHAMBERS: No. I have been thinking over these things and none of that stands out.

MR. NIXON: What kind of cocktail glasses did they have?

MR. CHAMBERS: We never drank cocktails.

MR. NIXON: Did they drink?

MR. CHAMBERS: They did not drink. They didn't drink with me. For one thing, I was strictly forbidden by the Communist Party to taste liquor at any time.

MR. NIXON: And you didn't drink?

MR. CHAMBERS: I never drank.

MR. NIXON: As far as you know, they never drank, at least with you?

MR. CHAMBERS: He gave cocktail parties in Government service.

MR. NIXON: Could you describe Mr. Hiss' physical appearance for us?

MR. CHAMBERS: Mr. Hiss, I should think, is about 5 feet 8 or 9, slender. His eyes are wide apart and blue or gray.

MR. NIXON: Blue or gray?

MR. CHAMBERS: I think they change.

MR. NIXON: Sort of a blue-gray?

MR. CHAMBERS: Blueish-gray, you could say. In his walk, if you watch him from behind, there is a slight mince sometimes.

MR. NIXON: A slight mince?

MR. CHAMBERS: Mince. Anybody could observe.

MR. NIXON: Does Mrs. Hiss have any physical characteristics?

MR. CHAMBERS: Mrs. Hiss is a short, highly nervous, little woman. I don't, as a matter of fact, recall the color of her eyes, but she has a habit of blushing red when she is excited or angry, fiery red.

MR. MANDEL: A picture of Hiss shows his hand cupped to his ear.

MR. CHAMBERS: He is deaf in one ear.

MR. NIXON: Mr. Hiss is deaf in one ear?

MR. HÉBERT: Which ear?

MR. CHAMBERS: I don't know. My voice is pitched very low and it is difficult for me to talk and make myself understood.

MR. NIXON: Did he wear glasses at the time?

MR. CHAMBERS: I think he wore glasses only for reading.

MR. NIXON: Did he tell you how he became deaf in one ear?

MR. CHAMBERS: I don't recall that he did. The only thing I remember he told me was as a small boy he used to take a little wagon—he was a Baltimore boy—and walk up to Druid Hill Park, which was up that time way beyond the civilized center of the city, and fill up bottles with spring water and bring them back and sell it.

MR. NIXON: Do you remember any physical characteristics of the boy?

MR. CHAMBERS: Timmie?

MR. NIXON: Yes.

MR. CHAMBERS: Timmie was a puny little boy, also rather nervous.

MR. NIXON: This is Mrs. Hiss' son?

MR. CHAMBERS: Mrs. Hiss' son by Thayer Hobson, who I think is one of the Hobson cousins, a cousin of Thornton Wilder. It is possible I could be mistaken about that.

MR. NIXON: Do you recall anything else about the boy? Do you recall where he went to school?

MR. CHAMBERS: Yes; I do. I don't know the name of the school he was attending then, but they told me that Thayer Hobson was paying for his son's education, but they were diverting a large part of that money to the Communist Party.

MR. NIXON: Hiss told you that?

MR. CHAMBERS: Yes, sir.

MR. NIXON: Did he say how much he was paying?

MR. CHAMBERS: No; I don't know how much he was paying.

MR. NIXON: Did he name the Communist Party as the recipient?

MR. CHAMBERS: Certainly.

MR. NIXON: He might not have said simply "the party"? Could it have been the Democratic Party or Socialist Party?

MR. CHAMBERS: No.

MR. HÉBERT: Hobson was paying for the boy's education?

MR. CHAMBERS: Yes; and they took him out of a more expensive school and put him in a less expensive school expressly for that purpose. That is my recollection.

MR. NIXON: When would that have occurred?

MR. CHAMBERS: Probably about 1936.

MR. NIXON: Did they change in the middle of the year?

MR. CHAMBERS: I don't recall. . . .

MR. STRIPLING: Do you remember anything about his hands?

MR. CHAMBERS: Whose?

MR. STRIPLING: Alger Hiss'.

MR. CHAMBERS: He had rather long delicate fingers. I don't remember anything special.

MR. MANDEL: How is it he never wrote anything publicly?

MR. CHAMBERS: Well, he came into the underground like so many Communists did—this was a new stage in the history of American Communists.

MR. MANDEL: He was never in the open Communist Party?

MR. CHAMBERS: He was never in the open Communist Party, came in as an underground Communist.

MR. HÉBERT: Did he have any other brothers or sisters besides Donald?

MR. CHAMBERS: He had one sister, I believe, living with her mother in Baltimore.

MR. HÉBERT: Did he ever talk about her?

MR. CHAMBERS: Yes; once or twice, and mentioned his mother. He once drove me past their house, which as I recall, was on or near Linden Street.

MR. HÉBERT: What did the sister do?

MR. CHAMBERS: I don't think she did anything besides live with her mother. Whether he had any more than that I don't know.

MR. HÉBERT: You know he referred to at least one sister?

MR. CHAMBERS: He did.

MR. HÉBERT: Do you recall her name?

MR. CHAMBERS: No.

MR. HÉBERT: And you don't recall what the sister did?

MR. CHAMBERS: No; I don't think she did anything.

MR. HÉBERT: Did it ever come up in conversation that the sister was interested in athletics?

MR. CHAMBERS: No.

MR. HÉBERT: Was he interested in athletics?

MR. CHAMBERS: I think he played tennis, but I am not certain.

MR. HÉBERT: With the sister now—it is very important—you don't recall the sister?

MR. CHAMBERS: We merely brushed that subject.

MR. NIXON: You never met the sister?

MR. CHAMBERS: No; nor ever met the mother. My impression was his relations with his mother were affectionate but not too happy. She was, perhaps, domineering. I simply pulled this out of the air in the conversation.

MR. STRIPLING: Did he go to church?

MR. CHAMBERS: He was forbidden to go to church.

MR. STRIPLING: Do you know whether he was a member of a church?

MR. CHAMBERS: I don't know.

MR. STRIPLING: Do you know if his wife was a member of a church?

MR. CHAMBERS: She came from a Quaker family. Her maiden name was Priscilla Fansler before she was married. She came from the Great Valley near Paoli, Pa.

MR. NIXON: Did she tell you anything about her family?

MR. CHAMBERS: No; but she once showed me while we were driving beyond Paoli the road down which their farm lay.

MR. NIXON: You drove with them?

MR. CHAMBERS: Yes.

MR. NIXON: Did you ever go on a trip with them other than by automobile?

MR. CHAMBERS: No.

MR. NIXON: Did you stay overnight on any of these trips?

MR. CHAMBERS: No.

* * *

MR. NIXON: When did you meet Donald Hiss?

MR. CHAMBERS: Probably within the same week in which I met Alger Hiss.

MR. NIXON: Did you ever stay in Donald Hiss' home?

MR. CHAMBERS: No, my relation with Donald Hiss was much less close. I can make that point now, if you will permit. My relationship with Alger Hiss quickly transcended our formal relationship. We became close friends.

MR. NIXON: Donald Hiss—what relation did you have with him?

MR. CHAMBERS: A purely formal one.

MR. NIXON: He knew you as Carl?

MR. CHAMBERS: Yes.

MR. NIXON: Did you collect dues from him?

MR. CHAMBERS: Yes.

MR. NIXON: Did you meet his wife?

MR. CHAMBERS: I think I met her once, not very often.

MR. NIXON: Where did you collect the dues from him, at his home?

MR. CHAMBERS: Probably in Alger's house. He frequently came there.

MR. NIXON: He came there to see you?

MR. CHAMBERS: Yes.

MR. NIXON: Do you recall anything significant about Donald Hiss, as to personal characteristics, hobbies?

MR. CHAMBERS: No. Something else is involved there, too. Donald Hiss was married, I think, to a daughter of Mr. Cotton, who is in the State Department. She was not a Communist, and everybody was worried about her.

MR. NIXON: Getting back to Alger Hiss for the moment, do you recall any pictures on the wall that they might have owned at the time?

MR. CHAMBERS: No; I am afraid I don't.

MR. NIXON: Donald Hiss—do you know any other characteristics about him, can you recall any?

MR. CHAMBERS: Except I can give you the general impression. He was much less intelligent than Alger. Much less sensitive than his brother. I had the impression he was interested in the social climb and the Communist Party was interested in having him climb. At one point I believe he was fairly friendly with James Roosevelt.

MR. NIXON: Did you have any conversations with him you can recall that were out of the ordinary?

MR. CHAMBERS: Yes; one I think I can recall. He was working in the Labor Department, I believe in the Immigration Section, and it was the plan of the Communist Party to have him go to California, get himself sent by the Government to California, to work in the Bridges case.

At that moment he had an opportunity to go into the State Department as, I think, legal adviser to the Philippine Section, which had just been set up.

It was the opinion of the party that he should do that and not the Bridges matter. It was his opinion that he should continue in the Bridges matter and there was a fairly sharp exchange, but he submitted to discipline and went to the State Department.

MR. NIXON: Did you make an affidavit concerning Mr. Alger Hiss?

MR. CHAMBERS: I made a signed statement. I should think it was about 1945. Before that I had reported these facts at least 2 years before to the FBI and 9 years ago to Mr. Berle and mentioned Hiss' name.

MR. NIXON: Nine years ago, are you certain that you did mention Hiss' name to Berle?

MR. CHAMBERS: I certainly mentioned Hiss' name to Berle. I was there with Berle precisely because—may we go off the record?

MR. NIXON: Off the record.

(Discussion off the record.)

MR. NIXON: Have you seen Hiss since 1938?

MR. CHAMBERS: No; since the time I went to his house and tried to break him away, I have never seen him since.

* * *

MR. NIXON: Thank you. I have no further questions.

MR. HÉBERT: I am interested in the houses he lived in. You said several houses. How many houses? Start from the beginning.

MR. CHAMBERS: As well as I can remember, when I first knew him he was living on Twenty-eighth Street and when I went to see Mr. Berle it struck me as strange, because Mr. Berle was living in Stimson's house on Woodley Road near Twenty-eighth Street. From there I am not absolutely certain the order of the houses, but it seems to me he moved to a house in Georgetown—that I know; he moved to a house in Georgetown—but it seems it was on the corner of P Street, but again I can't be absolutely certain of the streets.

MR. HÉBERT: It was on a corner?

MR. CHAMBERS: Yes; and as I recall, you had to go up steps to get to it.

MR. MANDEL: How many rooms were there in that house?

MR. CHAMBERS: I don't know offhand, but I have the impression it was a three-story house. I also think it had a kind of a porch in back where people sat.

Then if I have got the order of the houses right, he moved to a house on an up-and-down street, a street that would cross the lettered streets, probably just around the corner from the other house and very near to his brother Donald.

MR. HÉBERT: Still in Georgetown?

MR. CHAMBERS: Still in Georgetown. I have forgotten the reason for his moving. That was a smaller house and, as I recall, the dining room was below the level of the ground, one of those basement dining rooms; that it had a small yard in back.

I think he was there when I broke with the Communist Party.

MR. HÉBERT: Three houses?

MR. CHAMBERS: But I went to see him in the house he later moved to, which was on the other side of Wisconsin Avenue.

MR. HÉBERT: Three houses in Georgetown?

MR. CHAMBERS: One on Twenty-eighth Street.

MR. HÉBERT: The last time you saw him when you attempted to persuade him to break away from the party—

MR. CHAMBERS: That was beyond Wisconsin Avenue.

MR. HÉBERT: Did you ever see their bedroom; the furniture?

MR. CHAMBERS: Yes; but I don't remember the furniture.

MR. HÉBERT: Did they have twin beds or single beds?

MR. CHAMBERS: I am almost certain they did not have twin beds.

MR. HÉBERT: In any of the four houses?

MR. CHAMBERS: I can't be sure about the last one, but I am reasonably sure they did not have twin beds before that.

MR. HÉBERT: This little boy, Timmie—can you recall the name of the school that he went to?

MR. CHAMBERS: No.

MR. HÉBERT: But you do recall that he changed schools?

MR. CHAMBERS: Yes; as nearly as I can remember, they told me they had shifted him from one school to another because there was a saving and they could contribute it to the party.

MR. HÉBERT: What year?

MR. CHAMBERS: Probably 1936.

MR. HÉBERT: Or 1937, but probably '36?

MR. CHAMBERS: It is possible.

MR. HÉBERT: We can check the year.

MR. CHAMBERS: The school was somewhere in Georgetown. He came back and forth every day.

MR. NIXON: Is there anything further? If not, thank you very much, Mr. Chambers.

(Whereupon, at 1:10 p.m., the sub-committee adjourned.)

The questioning had brought out two unforeseeable points, one of passing and one of lasting importance. The more important was the testimony about Hiss's 1929 Ford roadster, which was to be the focus of the great August 25th public hearing. Hiss's inability to explain the documentary evidence of that transaction was first to turn the tide against him.

The point of passing importance was that about the prothonotary warbler, a bird little bigger than a half-dollar whose name many people hesitate to pronounce, and which I have never seen. It was that beautiful bird, glimpsed in a moment of wonder, one summer morning some fourteen years before, that first clinched the Committee's conviction that I must have known Alger Hiss. A mind might figure out (and many minds were soon avidly figuring out) how I might have known the answers to the other questions. But not the prothonotary warbler. The man who volunteered that information (in almost the same tone that a few days later Hiss himself would use in responding to it)—the man who knew that fugitive detail must have known Alger Hiss. Congressman McDowell grasped the meaning of that testimony before I did, and I believe, before his colleagues. When I mentioned it, his eyes flew open. For he, too, was a bird watcher and he had seen a prothonotary warbler.

There was another question that was also to have psychological importance in the Case. Toward the end of the hearing in the Federal Building, Congressman Nixon suddenly asked me: "Would you be willing to submit to a lie detector test on this testimony?"

I answered: "Yes, if necessary."

NIXON: You are that confident?

CHAMBERS: I am telling the truth.

Hiss's answer (in part) to the same question asked him nine days later:

MR. HISS: Would it seem to you inappropriate for me to say that I would rather have a chance for further consultation before I gave you the answer? Actually, the people I have conferred with so far say that it all depends on who reads, that it shows emotion, not truth, and I am perfectly willing and prepared to say that I am not lacking in emotion about this business.

I have talked to people who have seen, I think, Dr. Keeler's own test and that the importance of a question registers more emotion than anything else. I certainly don't want to duck anything that has scientific or sound basis. I would like to consult further.

I would like to find out a little more about Dr. Keeler. As I told you, the people I have consulted said flatly there is no such thing, that it is not scientifically established. . . .

MR. NIXON: . . . I might say also that the matter of emotion, of course, as you pointed out, enters into the test. One thing the members of the committee both remarked about is that Mr. Chambers is also a very emotional man.

MR. HISS: Have you ever had any experience with it yourself when you were practicing, Mr. Nixon?

MR. NIXON: No; I have not.

MR. HISS: But you do have confidence in it?

MR. NIXON: Frankly, I have made a study of it in the last week before I put the question. In fact, for the last two weeks I have been studying it and have been in correspondence with Mr. Keeler.

MR. HISS: You do have confidence in it as a device?

In fairness, it should be noted that there is a difference of opinion about the accuracy of the lie detector test. I knew almost nothing about it and I am extremely skeptical of most scientific claims until they have been proved. Nevertheless, I did not believe it possible that a test which had been in use some time, could possibly be so far out that it would fail to show a preponderance of truth, when truth was spoken, over error. Therefore, I answered yes.

A few days later Alger Hiss submitted a written reply to the Committee on the lie detector question. Like his original response in the matter, it was inconclusive. But in effect he said no.

XIII

Between my executive hearing on August 7th and Hiss's similar hearing on August 16th, a number of things had happened which, in big or little ways, deeply affected the developing Case and the actors in it.

The most important was the most unexpected, and to me, the most stunning. In answer to a newsman's question at a White House press conference, President Truman replied that the Hiss Case was a "red herring" whose political purpose was to distract attention from the sins of the 80th Congress. For thousands of people, that automatically outlawed the Case. To me, it meant that I was not only deprived of official good will in testifying against Communism; I must expect active hostility among most powerful sections of the Administration.

At about the same time, Congressman Nixon informed me that the transcript of my secret testimony of August 7th had been requested by the Justice Department, and that someone in the Justice Department (someone whose name I first learned from Robert Stripling, and later from Nixon) had at once turned it over to Alger Hiss.*

* Had this been true, it is unlikely that Hiss would, point by point, confirm parts of my testimony about him as he was soon to do. But there was nothing improbable about the allegation in the climate of that time.

I had already been warned by other sources—and was soon to be warned by the Committee—that the Justice Department was preparing to move against me, that it was actively making plans to indict me, and not Alger Hiss, for perjury on the basis of my testimony before the House Committee. I felt that my testimony had offended the powers that for so long had kept from the nation the extent of the Communist infiltration of Government, and the official heights to which it had reached. Not Alger Hiss (for denying any of the truth), but I (for revealing part of the truth) was to be punished. I became convinced then, and the immense mass of power that was tilted against me right up to the end of the first Hiss trial clinched my conviction, that the facts in the Hiss Case had come to light in the only way, time and place that they could have come to light. The very pressures that had made for their long suppression, once the facts reached the surface, contributed to the force with which, like a gusher, they burst out and filled the national landscape with a blackness malodorous and crude. I myself was only a chip in the play of that torrent.

By what I have written I do not mean at all to say that the Justice Department stood as a malign unit against the truth or me. I am convinced that that was not so. I observed and met men in that Department who were sincerely interested in reaching the truth and in fighting for it. Thomas F. Murphy, the Government's prosecutor in the Hiss trials, is there to prove it, and he stood for others of like mind, for example, John F. X. McGohey, then United States Attorney, now a judge of the United States District Court, and James M. McInerney, now chief of the Criminal Division of the Department of Justice. Almost from the first moment I saw him, I never doubted that Raymond P. Whearty, a special assistant to the Attorney General, was interested in the truth, and the truth alone. I remember the sad words later spoken by Tom Donegan, a special assistant to the Attorney General with the Grand Jury that indicted Alger Hiss: "If you had only given me documentary proof in the first place." And there is no question that Alex Campbell, then an assistant Attorney General, with no initial bias in my favor, became sincerely convinced, on the basis of the evidence and testimony, that I was telling the truth. Nevertheless, I was consistently warned and saw no reason to doubt that there remained throughout the Government immensely powerful forces that were determined to save Alger Hiss and destroy me by any means.

I seemed absolutely alone. I was still a senior editor of *Time*, and there is usually a reluctance to move hastily against anyone connected with the press. But I did not suppose that that would weigh long or importantly. Otherwise, I was a defenseless man. The Committee was still frantically seeking to discover whether I was telling the truth, though slowly Alger Hiss was convincing it that I was. But the Committee could do little for me. I assumed that the F.B.I., which is merely the investigative arm of the Justice Department, would be used as a matter of routine against me, and that it could do little or nothing about that regardless of what its officials or its agents might themselves believe. This feeling was strengthened by the fact that during a period from the end of July until some time in November, I had no communication with the F.B.I. and saw only one of its agents who came to ask me something so irrelevant and inconsequential that I no longer remember what it was or who he was. Until then I had been seeing the F.B.I. frequently. I faced this situation with that inertia of spirit which I have mentioned earlier. It was well that I did so. For if I had sought to face it actively, even if I had admitted to my waking mind the array of power against me, I must have become desperate.

But something else tormented me. Under the cry of: "Who's a liar?" the nation was beginning to see the Hiss-Chambers Case as a personal duel between two men. This had the advantage of simplifying and dramatizing the Case. But it reduced it to the level of a baseball game and blurred the great issues involved. There were moments when I wondered with despair whether it would ever be possible to make those issues clear to a nation that insisted on seeing in terms of a sporting event a struggle that touched its very survival. Time, a very short time, was to prove that I was wrong.

XIV

In the same nine days between the second interrogation of Chambers and Alger Hiss, one brief piece of testimony was taken by the Committee, which in its consequences proved curiously important. On August 13th, Donald Hiss, Alger Hiss's younger brother, testified at a public hearing.

Donald Hiss categorically denied my testimony about him. In a statement, which he read to the Committee, he repeated another, which he had already given to the press. Among other things, he said: ". . . I flatly deny every statement made by Mr. Chambers with respect to me. I am not, and never have been, a member of the Communist Party or of any formal or informal organizations affiliated with, or fronting in any manner whatsoever for, the Communist Party. In fact, the only organizations and clubs to which I have belonged are the local Y.M.C.A., the Miles River Yacht Club of Maryland, the old Washington Racquet Club, the Harvard Law School Association, the American Society of International Law, and college fraternities and athletic clubs.

"I have no recollection of ever having met any person by the name of D. Whittaker Chambers, nor do I recognize his photograph which I have seen in the public press. I am not and never have been in sympathy with the principles of the Communist Party. Any interested person could easily have discovered these facts by inquiry of the distinguished, respected and unquestionably loyal Americans with whom I have been intimately associated."

Other categoric denials followed. "As I understand your statement," said Richard Nixon, "you have made an unqualified statement that you have never known a man by the name of Carl who resembled that man." Donald Hiss: "I have never known that man by the name of Chambers, Carl, or any other name, sir." Later on he was to add; "If I am lying, I should go to jail, and if Mr. Chambers is lying, he should go to jail." Mr. Mundt: "There is no question about that."

Donald Hiss's forthrightness had a powerful impact on the public. But almost at once, that forthrightness was to prove a handicap to Alger Hiss. Donald Hiss had said flatly under oath that he had never known me under any name. Hence it followed that, though, from 1935 to 1938, the Hiss brothers had lived not far from one another in Washington, and saw each other frequently, Donald Hiss had never known a man by the name of George Crosley, and was unable to bear out his brother's testimony in any way at any time upon that interesting character, who, it must be inferred, had never even been mentioned between them.

For it was as George Crosley that Alger Hiss, in his first big change of tactic, would cautiously, very cautiously, begin to recognize me three days later.

XV

On August 16th, the Committee met with Alger Hiss in executive session in the Old House Building in Washington, D.C. Under questioning, he independently verified most of the testimony I had given about details of his life and household. Samples (which I take at random, out of the order of the transcript):

NIXON: Do you have any children, Mr. Hiss?
HISS: I have two children.
NIXON: You have two children.* Could you give us their ages?
HISS: One will be 22—he is my stepson—will be 22 September 19 next. His name is Timothy Hobson. . . .
NIXON: Did you testify before what your wife's name was?
HISS: Her name was Priscilla Fansler, her maiden name. Her first marriage was to a Mr. Hobson, H-o-b-s-o-n.
NIXON: Where did she come from? What town?
HISS: She was born in Evanston, Ill., but spent most of her early life outside of Philadelphia.
NIXON: In Paoli?
HISS: Frazer.
NIXON: Is that near Paoli?
HISS: It is on the main line not far from there. . . .
NIXON: Frazer and Paoli are a few miles apart?
HISS: Yes.
NIXON: Did she live there on a farm?
HISS: Her father was in the insurance business, and he acquired a small place—I suppose it could be called a farm. . . .
NIXON: What were the nicknames you and your wife had?
HISS: My wife, I have always called her "Prossy."
NIXON: What does she call you?
HISS: Well, at one time, she called me quite frequently "Hill," H-i-l-l.
NIXON: What other name?
HISS: "Hilly," with a "y."
NIXON: What other name did you call her?
HISS: She called me "Hill" or "Hilly." I called her "Pross" or "Prossy" almost exclusively. . . .
NIXON: Did you ever call her Dilly?
HISS: No, never.

* When I began to testify, I was not aware that Alger and Priscilla Hiss had a son, born since I had known them—a fact rather dashing, I should think, to those who still hug the belief that my knowledge of the Hisses was not first-hand, but the result of some prolonged investigation of their private lives.

NIXON: What did you call your son?

HISS: "Timmy."

* * *

NIXON: Where did you spend your vacations during that period?

HISS: . . . My son went to a camp over on the Eastern Shore of Maryland. . . . When he was at camp, we spent two summers, I think, during this period in Chestertown, Md.

NIXON: On the Eastern Shore?

HISS: On the Eastern Shore of Maryland. . . .

NIXON: Did you have pets?

HISS: We had a brown cocker spaniel. . . .

NIXON: What did you do with the dog when you went on your vacations; do you recall?

HISS: I think we took Jenny over on the Eastern Shore. She did spend some time in the kennels when we were away. . . .

NIXON: That is where you would have left the dog, boarded the dog?

HISS: Yes; at that time I think we left her there.

* * *

NIXON: What hobby, if any, do you have, Mr. Hiss?

HISS: Tennis and amateur ornithology.

NIXON: Is your wife interested in ornithology?

HISS: . . . . My wife is interested in ornithology, as I am, through my interest. . . .

NIXON: . . . As a boy, Mr. Hiss, did you have any particular business that you engaged in?

HISS: Yes.

NIXON: What was your business?

HISS: I had two businesses. One of which I was most proud was the delivery of spring water in Baltimore. . . .

NIXON: You had the spring water on your own place?

HISS: We had to go out to the park.

NIXON: The park?

HISS: Druid Hill Park is a park in Baltimore where there were good springs, and some of us had water routes and we carried water and delivered it to customers.

HÉBERT: As a child?

HISS: Twelve or so.

* * *

STRIPLING: Is Druid Hill right in the middle of Baltimore?

HISS: It was at the edge of town then and from our house it was 10 or 15 blocks. I have always been very proud of that. . . .

Hiss, of course, continued to deny the charge of Communism and related charges. Nor did he verify every one of the intimate details that I had testified to. In some instances, his memory was better than mine as in the case of the name Dilly, which I presently realized he had not called his wife. On the other hand, I was right in testifying that the members of the Ware Group commonly referred to the Hisses as Hilly and Dilly.

But the clinching point of this part of the testimony came when Richard Nixon questioned Hiss about his interest in ornithology. At that point, Congressman McDowell quietly asked: "Did you ever see a prothonotary warbler?"

HISS: I have right here on the Potomac. Do you know that place? . . .

NIXON: Have you ever seen one?

HISS: Did you see it in the same place?

MC DOWELL: I saw one in Arlington.

HISS: They come back and nest in those swamps. Beautiful yellow head, a gorgeous bird. . . .

Hastily, Nixon asked another question to cover the silence that crept over his colleagues.

XVI

There were even more startling developments at the August 16th hearing. I mean to report them, and the developments in the two subsequent hearings, in some detail, using the record, which is official, editing its text only insofar as is necessary to throw into relief the high points of testimony as I see them. For the 1378 pages of the Committee's hearings on the Bentley and Hiss-Chambers cases are not only fascinating reading. They are literal. It is all there, irrevocably, as it happened. Had the transcript of the hearings (popular demand has made it practically a collector's item) been available on a mass scale to millions of Americans, it has seemed to me since I first read it that there could have been little room for doubt among honest men, as there was little doubt in the minds of the Committee, that I was telling the truth as far as I had disclosed it up to that point, and that Alger Hiss was not.

To understand his drama of maneuver behind the skeletal question and answer, it is well to bear in mind Hiss's plight at that moment. Even assuming that he had seen a transcript of my secret testimony to the sub-committee (and Senator Nixon is still emphatic that that had happened), Hiss could not have been sure, he must, indeed, have been sickeningly unsure, just how much more I had told the Committee—especially since the sub-committee had gone off the record, as the transcript shows, precisely in questioning me about what I had told Berle in 1939. In the transcript of his testimony, Hiss can be seen groping with extreme tact for that indispensable knowledge without which he might at any moment be trapped. At one point, he even ventures the suggestion that the Committee should make known to him whatever I had told it, or might tell it, while he covers this tactic by charging the Committee with turning over his secret testimony to me. At other times, he varies his careful probing with bursts of diversive indignation.

The knowledge of what I had told the Committee was indispensable to Hiss because on it hinged the question: whether he must identify me at all, or whether he could continue the simpler, less entangling tactic of failing to recognize me. The record of the hearing shows, in his own words, that, on August 16th, Hiss came prepared to use either tactic, and that it was not until the middle of the session that the weight of questioning made him decide that non-recognition would no longer work. Then he switched to his second prepared tactic of recognizing me, qualifiedly, as George Crosley—a switch which, made by almost anyone else, must have been a violent jolt, but which Hiss managed with masterly smoothness and timing.

Early in the hearing Hiss was again shown pictures of me.

MR. NIXON: I am now showing you two pictures of Mr. Whittaker Chambers, also known as Carl, who testified that he knew you between the years 1934-37, and that he saw you in 1938.

I ask you now, after looking at those pictures, if you can remember that person either as Whittaker Chambers or as Carl or as any other individual you have met.

MR. HISS: May I recall to the committee the testimony I gave in the public session when I was shown another photograph of Mr. Whittaker Chambers, and I had prior to taking the stand tried to get as many newspapers that had photographs of Mr. Chambers as I could. I testified then that I could not swear that I had never seen the man whose picture was shown me. Actually the face has a certain familiarity. I think I also testified to that.

It is not according to the photograph a very distinctive or unusual face. I would like very much to see the individual face to face. I had hoped that would happen before. I still hope it will happen today.

I am not prepared to say that I have never seen the man whose pictures are now shown me. I said that when I was on the stand when a different picture was shown me. I cannot recall any person with distinctness and definiteness whose picture this is, but it is not completely unfamiliar.

Whether I am imagining that or not I don't know, but I certainly wouldn't want to testify without seeing the man, hearing him talk, getting some much more tangible basis for judging the person and the personality.

MR. NIXON: Would your answer be any different if this individual were described to you as one who had stayed overnight in your house on several occasions?

MR. HISS: I think, Mr. Nixon, let me say this: In the course of my service in Government from 1933 to 1947 and the previous year 1929-30, and as a lawyer I have had a great many people who have visited in my house.

I have tried to recall in the last week or so anyone who would know my house whom I wouldn't know very well. There are many people that have come to my house on social occasions or on semibusiness occasions whom I probably wouldn't recall at all.

As far as staying overnight in my house is concerned—

MR. NIXON: On several occasions.

MR. HISS: On several occasions?

MR. NIXON: On several occasions.

MR. HISS: I can't believe, Mr. Nixon, that anyone could have stayed in my house when I was there—

MR. NIXON: When you were there.

MR. HISS: —Overnight on several occasions without my being able to recall the individual; and if this is a picture of anyone, I would find it very difficult to believe that that individual could have stayed in my house when I was there on several occasions overnight and his face not be more familiar than it is.

MR. NIXON: Yes.

MR. HISS: I don't want to suggest any innovations in your procedure, but I do want to say specifically that I do hope I will have an opportunity actually to see the individual.

MR. NIXON: It is going to be arranged. I might say that before arranging the meeting, we want to be certain that there is no question of mistaken identity, as well as possible, and also that we had a clear conflict on certain pieces of testimony that had been given by both sides, and that we are getting now.

MR. HISS: Yes, sir.

MR. NIXON: I might say this, too: That Mr. Chambers, as you may be aware of newspaper accounts, appeared in executive session before us on Saturday.

MR. HISS: Saturday a week ago, I think.

MR. NIXON: Just 2 days after you appeared.

MR. HISS: I saw newspaper accounts of that.

MR. NIXON: At that time we went into the situation with him, showed him pictures of you, and he declared without question you were the man. . . .

Now, you have never paid any money to Peters?

MR. HISS: No.

MR. NIXON: Never paid any money to Carl?

MR. HISS: Never paid any money to Carl.

MR. NIXON: Never paid any money to Henry Collins that you can recall?

MR. HISS: I can't recall it even on a personal basis.

MR. NIXON: Never paid dues to the Communist Party?

MR. HISS: No.

MR. NIXON: Your testimony now is that you are not a member of the Communist Party?

MR. HISS: That is correct.

MR. NIXON: Never been a member of the Communist Party?

MR. HISS: Never been a member of the Communist Party.

MR. NIXON: Or of any underground organization connected with the Communist Party?

MR. HISS: Not any underground organization connected with the Communist Party.

Always uppermost in Hiss's mind is the necessity of learning how much of the whole story I have told the Committee. Therefore, he maneuvers to find out, choosing the boldest tactic as the best ("I would request that I hear Mr. Chambers' story of his alleged knowledge of me."). At the same time, he seems to give his demand force by implying that the Committee in questioning him is providing me with information about Hiss's life, which I can then produce as testimony. Cautiously, he prepares to identify me ("I have been cudgeling my brains, particularly on the train coming down. . . . "), though he is still uncertain whether he must take the step.

MR. HISS: I have been angered and hurt by one thing in the course of this committee testimony, and that was by the attitude which I think Mr. Mundt took when I was testifying publicly and which, it seems to me, you have been taking today, that you have a conflict of testimony between two witnesses—I restrained myself with some difficulty from commenting on this at the public hearing, and I would like to say it on this occasion, which isn't a public hearing.

MR. NIXON: Say anything you like.

MR. HISS: It seems there is no impropriety in saying it. You today and the acting chairman publicly have taken the attitude when you have two witnesses, one of whom is a confessed former Communist, the other is me, that you simply have two witnesses saying contradictory things as between whom you find it most difficult to decide on credibility.

Mr. Nixon, I do not know what Mr. Whittaker Chambers testified to your committee last Saturday. It is necessarily my opinion of him from what he has already said that I do know that he is not capable of telling the truth or does not desire to, and I honestly have the feeling that details of my personal life which I give honestly can be used to my disadvantage by Chambers then ex post facto knowing those facts.

I would request that I hear Mr. Chambers' story of his alleged knowledge of me. I have seen newspaper accounts, Mr. Nixon, that you spent the week end—whether correct or not, I do not know—at Mr. Chambers' farm in New Jersey.

MR. NIXON: That is quite incorrect.

MR. HISS: It is incorrect.

MR. NIXON: Yes, sir. I can say, as you did a moment ago, that I have never spent the night with Mr. Chambers.

MR. HISS: Now, I have been cudgeling my brains, particularly on the train coming down this morning, and I had 3 or 4 hours on the train between New York and Washington, as to who could have various details about my family. Many people could.

Mr. Nixon, I do not wish to make it easier for anyone who, for whatever motive I cannot understand, is apparently endeavoring to destroy me, to make that man's endeavors any easier. I think in common fairness to my own self-protection and that of my family and my family's good name and my own, I should not be asked to give details which somehow he may hear and then may be able to use as if he knew them before. I would like him to say all he knows about me now. What I have done is public record, where I have lived is public record. Let him tell you all he knows, let that be made public, and then let my record be checked against those facts instead of my being asked, Mr. Nixon, to tell you personal facts about myself which, if they come to his ears, could sound very persuasive to other people that he had known me at some prior time. . . .

Once more Hiss is shown a photograph of me. Once more he hesitates to make the identification. Instead, he asserts that the identification is not the point at issue.

MR. STRIPLING: Here is a larger picture. Let the record show this larger picture taken by the Associated Press photo on August 3, 1948, of Mr. Mundt and Mr. Whittaker Chambers, and, as the record previously stated, Mr. Chambers is much heavier now than he was in 1937 or 1938. Does this picture refresh your memory in any way, Mr. Hiss?

MR. HISS: It looks like the very same man I had seen in the other pictures, and I see Mr. Mundt and him in the same picture. The face is definitely not an unfamiliar face. Whether I am imagining it, whether it is because he looks like a lot of other people, I don't know, but I have never known anyone who had the relationship with me that this man has testified to and that, I think, is the important thing here, gentlemen. This man may have known me, he may have been in my house. I have had literally hundreds of people in my house in the course of the time I lived in Washington.

The issue is not whether this man knew me and I don't remember him. The issue is whether he had a particular conversation that he has said he had with me and which I have denied and whether I am a member of the Communist Party or ever was, which he has said and which I have denied. . . .

THE CHAIRMAN: Mr. Hiss, would you be able to recall a person if that person positively had been in your house three or four times, we will say, in the last 10 years?

MR. HISS: I would say that if he had spent the night—

MR. STRIPLING: Ten years?

MR. NIXON: Fifteen years.

THE CHAIRMAN: All right.

MR. HISS: I would say if he had spent the night—how many times did you say?

MR. STRIPLING: He spent a week there.

MR. HISS: A whole week at a time continuously?

MR. STRIPLING: Yes.

MR. HISS: And I was there at the same time?

MR. STRIPLING: Yes.

MR. HISS: Mr. Chairman, I could not fail to recall such a man if he were now in my presence.

THE CHAIRMAN: Wait a minute. You are positive then that if Mr. X spent a week in your house in the past 15 years you would recognize him today, assuming that Mr. X looks today something like what he looked then?

MR. HISS: Exactly, if he hadn't had a face lifting.

THE CHAIRMAN: No doubt in your mind?

MR. HISS: I have no doubt whatsoever.

THE CHAIRMAN: Now, here is a man who says he spent a week in your house in the last 15 years. Do you recognize him?

MR. HISS: I do not recognize him from that picture.

MR. NIXON: Did that man spend a week in your house in the last 15 years?

MR. HISS: I cannot say that man did, but I would like to see him.

THE CHAIRMAN: You say you cannot believe, but I would like to have a little more definite answer if you could make it more definite. Would you say he did or did not spend a week in your house?

MR. HISS: Mr. Chairman, I hope you will not think I am being unreasonable when I say I am not prepared to testify on the basis of a photograph. On the train coming down this morning

I searched my recollection of any possible person that this man could be confused with or could have got information from about me.

THE CHAIRMAN: Then you are not prepared to testify on this subject from a photograph?

MR. HISS: I am not prepared to testify on the basis of a photograph. I would want to hear the man's voice. . . .

By now, the Committee's questions have convinced Hiss that he must go further in recognizing me. But he is still extremely cautious because, in the course of further questioning, he hopes to elicit further information about my testimony. He renews his charge more pointedly that the Committee is conniving with me.

MR. HISS: I have written a name on this pad in front of me of a person whom I knew in 1933 and 1934 who not only spent some time in my house but sublet my apartment. That man certainly spent more than a week, not while I was in the same apartment. I do not recognize the photographs as possibly being this man. If I hadn't seen the morning's papers with an account of statements that he knew the inside of my house, I don't think I would even have thought of this name. I want to see Chambers face to face and see if he can be this individual. I do not want and I don't think I ought to be asked to testify now that man's name and everything I can remember about him. I have written the name on this piece of paper. I have given the name to two friends of mine before I came to this hearing. I can only repeat, and perhaps I am being overanxious about the possibility of unauthorized disclosure of testimony, that I don't think in my present frame of mind that it is fair to my position, my own protection, that I be asked to put down here of record personal facts about myself which, if they came to the ears of someone who had for no reason I can understand a desire to injure me, would assist him in that endeavor.

MR. NIXON: This man who spent the time in 1933 and 1934 is still a man with whom you are acquainted?

MR. HISS: He is not.

MR. NIXON: And where were you living at that time?

MR. HISS: He was not named Carl and not Whittaker Chambers.

MR. NIXON: Where were you living at that time?

MR. HISS: I have again written down here to the best of my recollection because I have not checked down with leases—this is something I did on the train coming down and the leases are in my house in New York—where I believed I lived from June of 1933 until September 1943.

Again, Mr. Nixon, if I give the details of where I was, it is going to be very easy if this information gets out for someone to say then ex post facto, "I saw Hiss in such and such a house." Actually, all he has to do is look it up in the telephone directory and find where it is.

THE CHAIRMAN: The chairman wants to say this: Questions will be asked and the committee will expect to get very detailed answers to the questions. Let's not ramble all around the lot here. You go ahead and ask questions and I want the witness to answer.

MR. NIXON: Your testimony is that this man you knew in 1933 and 1934 was in one of the houses you lived in?

MR. HISS: I sublet my apartment to the man whose name I have written down.

MR. NIXON: But you were not there at the same time?

MR. HISS: I didn't spend a week in the same apartment with him. He did spend a day or two in my house when he moved in.

MR. NIXON: This was the apartment you lived in between 1933 and 1934?

MR. HISS: It is exactly that apartment—1934 and 1935.

MR. NIXON: Between 1934 and 1935?

MR. HISS: That is right.

MR. NIXON: When you sublet your apartment? There was no other apartment and you can't testify as to what apartment that was?

MR. HISS: I can testify to the best of my recollection. If this committee feels, in spite of what I have said—

THE CHAIRMAN: Never mind feelings. You let Mr. Nixon ask the questions and you go ahead and answer it.

MR. HISS: I want to be sure Mr. Nixon definitely wants me to answer responsively in spite of my plea that I don't think he should ask me. But if he does—Mr. Nixon also asked me some questions in the public hearing that I didn't want to answer, and I took the same position that if Mr. Nixon insisted on an answer after he knew my position, I will answer. I will give every fact of where I lived.

MR. STRIPLING: Let the record show, Mr. Hiss, you brought up this ex post facto business. Your testimony comes as ex post facto testimony to the testimony of Mr. Chambers. He is already on record, and I am not inferring that you might know what he testified to, but certainly the United States attorney's office has several copies.

MR. HISS: I do not and made no attempt to find out.

MR. NIXON: Not only does the United States attorney's office have copies of Mr. Chambers' testimony before us on the subject—and you can confirm that by calling Mr. Morris Fay of that office, because he has two copies; he requested and received, and he will receive this testimony today. He will receive this testimony today, because I will tell you that he asked for it just 30 minutes before you walked into this room, and he will get it just as soon as we have completed this case.

Now, quite obviously, I think that you can see that we are not attempting at this time to have you testify to facts with which we are going to brief Mr. Chambers. What we are trying to do is test the credibility of Mr. Chambers, and you are the man who can do it, and you can help us out by answering these questions and, frankly, I must insist.

MR. HISS: If you insist, I will, of course, answer. . . .

Congressman Hébert, a blunt man, could stand the shifts and thrusts no longer. He burst forth, and in his outburst can be heard the rumbling of the nation itself, a little entangled in its own language, a little foiled, but with a rough grip of reality, a bludgeoning instinct for truth. It is the sincere outburst of a man who knows that he is being tricked, but does not quite know how the trick works. This indignation, Hiss can only answer with high impertinence ("You have made your position clear").

MR. HÉBERT: Mr. Hiss, let me say this to you now—and this is removed of all technicalities, it is just a man-to-man impression of the whole situation. I think it is pertinent. I don't surrender my place on this committee to any individual who has an open mind, particularly regarding you and Mr. Chambers. I am not interested in who is lying except to the extent that it will only give us an insight to further the case and that we are about to find out whether espionage was in effect in this country to the detriment of the security of this country.

I do not take the stand and never have taken the stand in this committee that anything is involved other than to get to the facts. I have tried just as hard in the public hearings to impeach those witnesses who are assumed to be so-called committee witnesses as I have tried to impeach the other witnesses. I think the record will speak for that.

We did not know anything Mr. Chambers was going to say. I did not hear your name mentioned until it was mentioned in open hearing.

MR. HISS: I didn't know that.

MR. HÉBERT: As I say, I am not trying to be cagey or anything, but trying to put it on the line as certainly one member of this committee who has an open mind and up to this point don't know which one of the two is lying, but I will tell you right now and I will tell you exactly what I told Mr. Chambers so that will be a matter of record, too: Either you or Mr. Chambers is lying.

MR. HISS: That is certainly true.

MR. HÉBERT: And whichever one of you is lying is the greatest actor that America has ever produced. Now, I have not come to the conclusion yet which one of you is lying and I am trying to find the facts. Up to a few moments ago you have been very open, very cooperative. Now, you have hedged. You may be standing on what you consider your right and I am not objecting to that. I am not pressing you to identify a picture when you should be faced with the man. That is your right.

Now, as to this inquiry which you make much over, and not without cause, perhaps, we met Mr. Chambers 48 hours after you testified in open session. Mr. Chambers did not know or have any inclination of any indication as to the questions that we were going to ask him, and we probed him, as Mr. Stripling says, for hours and the committee, the three of us—Mr. Nixon, Mr. McDowell, Mr. Stripling, and myself—and we literally ran out of questions. There wasn't a thing that came to our minds that we didn't ask him about, these little details, to probe his own testimony or rather to test his own credibility.

There couldn't have been a possible inkling as to what we were going to say about minor details, and he could not have possibly by the farthest stretch of the imagination prepared himself to answer because he didn't know where the questions were coming from and neither did we because we questioned him progressively; so how he could have prepared himself to answer these details which we now, and Mr. Nixon has indicated, we are now checking and for the sake of corroboration—for my own part I can well appreciate the position you are in, but if I were in your position, I would do everything I humanly could to prove that Chambers is a liar instead of me.

MR. HISS: I intend to.

MR. HÉBERT: And that is all we are trying to do here. Further than that, I recognize the fact that this is not an inquisitorial body to the extent of determining where the crime lies. We are not setting forth to determine ourselves as to which one of you two has perjured yourself. That is the duty of the United States attorney for the District of Columbia. He is confronted with the fact that perjury has been committed before this congressional committee, which is a crime. It is up to the United States district attorney and the Department of Justice to prosecute that crime and that is all we are trying to do.

Now, if we can get the help from you and, as I say, if I were in your position I certainly would give all the help I could because it is the most fantastic story of unfounded—what motive would Chambers have or what motive—one of you has to have a motive. You say you are in a bad position, but don't you think that Chambers himself destroys himself if he is proven a liar? What motive would he have to pitch a $25,000 position as the respected senior editor of Time magazine out the window?

MR. HISS: Apparently for Chambers to be a confessed former Communist and traitor to his country did not seem to him to be a blot on his record. He got his present job after he had told various agencies exactly that. I am sorry but I cannot but feel to such an extent that it is difficult for me to control myself that you can sit there, Mr. Hébert, and say to me casually that you have heard that man and you have heard me, and you just have no basis for judging which one is telling the truth. I don't think a judge determines the credibility of witnesses on that basis.

MR. HÉBERT: I am trying to tell you that I absolutely have an open mind and am trying to give you as fair a hearing as I could possibly give Mr. Chambers or yourself. The fact that Mr. Chambers is a self-confessed traitor—and I admit he is—the fact that he is a self-confessed former member of the Communist Party—which I admit he is—has no bearing at all on whether the facts that he told—or, rather, the alleged facts that he told—

MR. HISS: Has no bearing on his credibility?

MR. HÉBERT: No; because, Mr. Hiss, I recognize the fact that maybe my background is a little different from yours, but I do know police methods and I know crime a great deal, and you show me a good police force and I will show you the stool pigeon who turned them in. Show me a police force with a poor record, and I will show you a police force without a stool pigeon. We have to have people like Chambers or Miss Bentley to come in and tell us. I am not giving Mr. Chambers any great credit for his previous life. I am trying to find out if he has reformed. Some of the greatest saints in history were pretty bad before they were saints. Are you going to take away their sainthood because of their previous lives? Are you not going to believe them after they have reformed?

I don't care who gives the facts to me, whether a confessed liar, thief, or murderer, if it is facts. That is all I am interested in.

MR. HISS: You have made your position clear. I would like to raise a separate point. Today as I came down on the train I read a statement—I think it was in the New York News—that a member of this committee, an unidentified member of this committee had told the press man who wrote the article that this committee believed or had reason to believe from talking to Chambers that Chambers had personally known Hiss, not that Chambers had had the conversation which is the issue here, that Chambers had been in Hiss' house. That is not the issue before this committee. You are asking me to tell you all the facts that I know of people who have been in my house or who had known me whom I would not feel absolutely confident are people I know all about, personal friends, people I feel I know through and through. I am not prepared to say on the basis of the photograph—

MR. HÉBERT: We understand.

MR. HISS: —That the man, that he is not the man whose name I have written down here. Were I to testify to that, what assurance have I that some member of this committee wouldn't say to the press that Hiss confessed knowing Chambers?

In the first place, I have testified and repeated that I have never known anybody by the name of Whittaker Chambers. I am not prepared to testify I have never seen that man.

MR. HÉBERT: You have said that.

MR. STRIPLING: Have you ever seen that one (indicating picture)?

THE CHAIRMAN: What is the question?

MR. STRIPLING: Have you ever seen the individual whose photograph appears there?

MR. HISS: So far as I know; no.

MR. STRIPLING: You have never seen that person?

MR. HISS: No.

Shortly after Hébert's outburst, the sub-committee took a brief recess and Alger Hiss was left alone for a few minutes. They must have been terrible minutes. For during them, he reached the decision he had wavered over so long—the decision to recognize the man he had just denied knowing, but to recognize him as George Crosley. In his second sentence before the resumed hearing, he volunteered the identification—which was still tentative, still contingent, but a far cry from non-recognition. It was to lead much farther quickly. It was to lead almost at once to the 1929 Ford car.

MR. HISS: The name of the man I brought in—and he may have no relation to this whole nightmare—is a man named George Crosley. I met him when I was working for the Nye committee. He was a writer. He hoped to sell articles to magazines about the munitions industry.

I saw him, as I say, in my office over in the Senate Office Building, dozens of representatives of the press, students, people writing books, research people. It was our job to give them appropriate information out of the record, show them what had been put in the record. This fellow was writing a series of articles, according to my best recollection, free lancing, which he hoped to sell to one of the magazines.

He was pretty obviously not successful in financial terms, but as far as I know, wasn't actually hard up.

MR. STRIPLING: What color was his hair?

MR. HISS: Rather blondish, blonder than any of us here.

MR. STRIPLING: Was he married?

MR. HISS: Yes, sir.

MR. STRIPLING: Any children?

MR. HISS: One little baby, as I remember it, and the way I know that was the subleasing point. After we had taken the house on P Street and had the apartment on our hands, he one day in the course of casual conversation said he was going to specialize all summer in getting his articles done here in Washington, didn't know what he was going to do, and was thinking of bringing his family.

I said, "You can have my apartment. It is not terribly cool, but it is up in the air near the Wardman Park." He said he had a wife and little baby. The apartment wasn't very expensive, and I think I let him have it at exact cost. My recollection is that he spent several nights in my house because his furniture van was delayed. We left several pieces of furniture behind.

The P Street house belonged to a naval officer overseas and was partly furnished, so we didn't need all our furniture, particularly during the summer months, and my recollection is that definitely, as one does with a tenant trying to make him agreeable and comfortable, we left several pieces of furniture behind until the fall, his van was delayed, wasn't going to bring all the furniture because he was going to be there just during the summer, and we put them up 2 or 3 nights in a row, his wife and little baby.

MR. NIXON: His wife and he and little baby did spend several nights in the house with you?

MR. HISS: This man Crosley; yes.

MR. NIXON: Can you describe his wife?

MR. HISS: Yes; she was a rather strikingly dark person, very strikingly dark. I don't know whether I would recognize her again because I didn't see very much of her.

MR. NIXON: How tall was this man, approximately?

MR. HISS: Shortish.

MR. NIXON: Heavy?

MR. HISS: Not noticeably. That is why I don't believe it has any direct, but it could have an indirect, bearing.

MR. NIXON: How about his teeth?

MR. HISS: Very bad teeth. That is one of the things I particularly want to see Chambers about. This man had very bad teeth, did not take care of his teeth.

MR. STRIPLING: Did he have most of his teeth or just weren't well cared for?

MR. HISS: I don't think he had gapped teeth, but they were badly taken care of. They were stained and I would say obviously not attended to.

MR. NIXON: Can you state again just when he first rented the apartment?

MR. HISS: I think it was about June of 1935. My recollection is —and again I have not checked the records—that is, I went with the Nye munitions committee in the early winter of 1934. I don't even remember now when the resolution was passed. In any event, I am confident I was living on Twenty-ninth Street from December 1934 to June 1935 and that coincided with my service with the Nye committee. I say that because one reason we took the apartment was to reduce our living costs, because after I had been on loan from the Department of Agriculture for some months, I thought it would only be a 2-month assignment or so, it became evident that I was to stay on longer if I should complete the job, and my deputy in the Department of Agriculture was doing all my work and not getting my salary and I did not feel it fair, so I resigned from the Department of Agriculture to go on with the Nye committee work at the Nye committee salary and contemplated that and talked it over with my deputy in the Department of Agriculture for some time before I did it. So I am sure, from my recollection, that the Twenty-ninth Street apartment is definitely linked in time with my service on the Nye committee.

MR. STRIPLING: What kind of automobile did that fellow have?

MR. HISS: No kind of automobile. I sold him an automobile. I had an old Ford that I threw in with the apartment and had been trying to trade it in and get rid of it. I had an old, old Ford we had kept for sentimental reasons. We got it just before we were married in 1929.

MR. STRIPLING: Was it a model A or model T?

MR. HISS: Early A model with a trunk on the back, a slightly collegiate model.

MR. STRIPLING: What color?

MR. HISS: Dark blue. It wasn't very fancy but it had a sassy little trunk on the back.

MR. NIXON: You sold that car?

MR. HISS: I threw it in. He wanted a way to get around, and I said, "Fine, I want to get rid of it. I have another car, and we kept it for sentimental reasons, not worth a damn." I let him have it along with the rent.

MR. NIXON: Where did you move from there?

MR. HISS: Again my best recollection is that we stayed on P Street only 1 year because the whole heating plant broke down in the middle of the winter when I was quite ill, and I think that we moved from 2905 P Street to 1241 Thirtieth Street about September 1936. I recall that quite specifically though we can check it from the records, because I remember Mr. Sayre, who was my chief in the State Department, who had been my professor at law school, saying he wanted to drive by and see where I was living. I remember the little house on Thirtieth Street which we had just got, a new development, was the little house I drove him by, and it must have been September or October 1936, just after starting to work in the State Department.

MR. NIXON: Going back to this man, do you know how many days approximately he stayed with you?

MR. HISS: I don't think more than a couple of times. He may have come back. I can't remember when it was I finally decided it wasn't any use expecting to collect from him, that I had been a sucker and he was a sort of deadbeat; not a bad character, but I think he just was using me for a soft touch.

MR. NIXON: You said before he moved in your apartment he stayed in your house with you and your wife about how many days?

MR. HISS: I would say a couple of nights. I don't think it was longer than that.

MR. NIXON: A couple of nights?

MR. HISS: During the delay of the van arriving.

MR. NIXON: Wouldn't that be longer than 2 nights?

MR. HISS: I don't think so. I wouldn't swear that he didn't come back again some later time after the lease and say, "I can't find a hotel. Put me up overnight," or something of that sort. I wouldn't swear Crosley wasn't in my house maybe a total of 3 or 4 nights altogether.

MR. NIXON: You don't recall any subjects of conversation during that period?

MR. HISS: We talked backwards and forwards about the Munitions Committee work. He told various stories that I recall of his escapades. He purported to be a cross between Jim Tully, the author, and Jack London. He had been everywhere. I remember he told me he had personally participated in laying down the tracks of the streetcars in Washington, D.C. He had done that for local color, or something. He had worked right with the road gang laying tracks in Washington, D.C.

MR. STRIPLING: Was his middle initial "L"?

MR. HISS: That I wouldn't know. . . .

MR. NIXON: You gave this Ford car to Crosley?

MR. HISS: Threw it in along with the apartment and charged the rent and threw the car in at the same time.

MR. NIXON: In other words, added a little to the rent to cover the car?

MR. HISS: No; I think I charged him exactly what I was paying for the rent and threw the car in in addition. I don't think I got any compensation.

MR. STRIPLING: You just gave him the car?

MR. HISS: I think the car just went right in with it. I don't remember whether we had settled on the terms of the rent before the car question came up, or whether it came up and then on the basis of the car and the apartment I said, "Well, you ought to pay the full rent." . . .

Then Hiss was asked about the second car he bought.

MR. STRIPLING: What kind of car did you get?

MR. HISS: A Plymouth.

MR. STRIPLING: A Plymouth?

MR. HISS: Plymouth sedan.

MR. STRIPLING: Four-door?

MR. HISS: I think I have always had only two-door.

MR. STRIPLING: What kind of a bill of sale did you give Crosley?

MR. HISS: I think I just turned over—in the District you get a certificate of title, I think it is. I think I just simply turned it over to him.

MR. STRIPLING: Handed it to him?

MR. HISS: Yes.

MR. STRIPLING: No evidence of any transfer. Did he record the title?

MR. HISS: That I haven't any idea. This is a car which had been sitting on the streets in snows for a year or two. I once got a parking fine because I forgot where it was parked. We were using the other car.

MR. STRIPLING: Do those model Fords have windshield wipers?

MR. HISS: You had to work them yourself.

MR. STRIPLING: Hand operated?

MR. HISS: I think that is the best I can recall.

The Committee had further questions about the car, which presently led to something destined to be almost as important—the fact that I had once presented Alger Hiss with a rug.

MR. STRIPLING: On this man George Crosley, you say you gave him this car?

MR. HISS: Yes, sir.

MR. STRIPLING: Did you ever go riding with Crosley in this automobile?

MR. HISS: I might very well have.

MR. STRIPLING: I mean did you go around with him quite a bit, take rides?

MR. HISS: You mean after I gave it to him did he ever give me a ride?

MR. STRIPLING: Before or after.

MR. HISS: I think I drove him from the Hill to the apartment.

MR. STRIPLING: Did you ever take any trips out of town with George Crosley?

MR. HISS: No; I don't think so.

MR. STRIPLING: Did you ever take him to Pennsylvania?

MR. HISS: No. I think I once drove him to New York City when I was going to make a trip to New York City anyway.

MR. NIXON: Was Mrs. Hiss along?

MR. HISS: That I wouldn't recall. She may have been. I think I may have given him a lift when I went to New York.

MR. STRIPLING: Did you go to Paoli?

MR. HISS: If Mrs. Hiss was along; yes.

THE CHAIRMAN: Route No. 202?

MR. HISS: Route 202 goes through that part of Pennsylvania, and that is the route we would take.

MR. NIXON: Did you ever drive to Baltimore with Crosley?

MR. HISS: I don't recall it. I think he moved to Baltimore from here, as a matter of fact, but I don't recall that I ever drove him.

MR. NIXON: How did you know that?

MR. HISS: I think he told me when he was pulling out. He was in my apartment until the lease expired in September.

MR. NIXON: What year?

MR. HISS: I think it was September 1935 and I think I saw him several times after that, and I think he had told me he moved from here to Baltimore.

MR. NIXON: Even though he didn't pay his rent you saw him several times?

MR. HISS: He was about to pay it and was going to sell his articles. He gave me a payment on account once. He brought a rug over which he said some wealthy patron gave him. I have still got the damned thing.

MR. NIXON: Did you ever give him anything?

MR. HISS: Never anything but a couple of loans; never got paid back.

MR. NIXON: Never gave him anything else?

MR. HISS: Not to my recollection.

MR. NIXON: Where is he now?

MR. HISS: I have no idea. I don't think I have seen him since 1935.

MR. NIXON: Have you ever heard of him since 1935?

MR. HISS: No; never thought of him again until this morning on the train.

MR. STRIPLING: You wouldn't say positively George Crosley and this person are the same?

MR. HISS: Not positively.

MR. STRIPLING: You would not say positively?

MR. HISS: I think they are not. That would be my best impression from the photographs.

It was at this point that Robert Stripling became convinced that the car and the rug were the keys to the Hiss Case—evidence so dangerous to Hiss that he had himself introduced them in an effort to fend off in advance their worst perils to him.

It was at that point, too, that the Committee as a whole began to suspect that Hiss was covering up.

XVII

At the time, I did not, of course, know that Alger Hiss was appearing before the Committee. In those days, I was like a man becalmed by life. I lived at the dead center of the storm that was howling around me and deliberately sealed my eyes and ears as much as possible to the turmoil. Sometimes, I worked at my office at *Time*, shutting my door and talking to few people. And people, feeling helpless to do anything for me, kept away. Sometimes, I stayed at home, listless and undecided as to what I must do. My first sense of purpose had crumbled under the impact of the public spectacle that had developed and the human wretchedness that my testimony had caused. I suffered a similar wretchedness with those I had had to testify against.

Every venture into public had become an ordeal for me. One morning, I forced myself to leave the farm to go to New York. But by the time I reached Baltimore, I felt a curious need to go and see the Committee, as if its members were the only people left in the world with whom I could communicate. I had no purpose with them. There was nothing that I meant to tell them. But the impulse was so strong that, after buying a ticket for New York, I took the train for Washington.

It was about noon when I started up the steps of the Old House Office Building. To avoid lurking newsmen, I made for an entrance that I had never used before. Out of the door, as I climbed the steps, crowded Ben Mandel, the Committee's chief researcher, Donald Appell, an investigator and other members of the Committee's staff. They were astonished to see me and greeted me with wild relief. They had been frantically trying to reach me at home, in New York and Washington. Stripling fixed me with a somewhat birdlike stare and said darkly, "I believe he must be psychic." I sensed that he felt that among so many complicating factors that was one too many.

No one would tell me why I was wanted. Instead, the subcommittee bundled me into a car crammed with its staff. As we rolled to the Union Station, Appell wrestled a newspaper out of his pocket and pointed to a headline: Harry Dexter White had died of a heart attack. He had appeared at a public hearing a few days before and sweepingly denied my charges. White's appearance had been gallant. He had skirmished brilliantly with the Committee, turning their questions with ridicule and high indignation. He had uttered a credo of a liberal, his personal credo, a statement of democratic faith so ringing, that *PM*, the New York leftist daily, had printed it verbatim as something that every American should memorize.

It is true that, at that time, Miss Bentley's charges against White, and not mine, were serious. I had testified (as she had also) that White was not a Communist. But his death completed my sense of the human disaster. As the crowded car sped toward the Union Station, I thought: "White is luckier than the rest of us. He at least is well out of it."

The Committee swept me through the station, out to the platforms and onto a Pullman. By then, I had learned that we were going to New York. I still did not know why. Most of that long train ride I sat alone in an almost empty car, smoking my pipe, watching the farms flash by and the hundreds of people about whom I felt that wonder, known to all men in trouble, that so many other lives should be so routine and uncomplicated.

At Pennsylvania Station in New York, the sub-committee members (Nixon and McDowell), Stripling and their staff waited until the train had emptied. Then they slipped off. They did not want the press to discover prematurely that they were in New York. Appell whisked me, separately, up a back staircase. We loitered around the streets before taking a taxi that let us out of the ramp entrance of the Hotel Commodore in midtown Manhattan. I remembered that I had been there only once before. It had been to meet Lincoln Steffens who had wanted me to write a biography of his great friend, William Filene, the Boston department-store owner. Most of the time Steffens had spent describing to me the street fighting during the Bolshevik revolution. But after I had left him, he opened the door and called to me halfway down such a red-carpeted corridor as Appell and I were now treading, "Keep a warm spot in your heart, Whittaker." I wondered at the time, and I wondered again now, what obscure presentiment had moved him to call after me.

Appell opened the door to Room 1400 and closed it behind us. We were in the big twin-bedded bedroom of a suite (the subcommittee I soon became aware was in session in the next room). Sitting alone in the somewhat silken surroundings was the man who had first served me with the Committee's subpoena. He was a Mr. Bermingham, who, I had been told, had once acted as a professional bodyguard—a solemn man in late middle age whose eyes sadly looked as if they had seen everything.

Through a side door, Congressman McDowell entered. He was a man of instinctive sympathy who did his best to put me at ease without, however, explaining the reason for my odd adventure. He sat telling me how the depression had found him a poor young man and he had decided to challenge the economic crisis by starting a newspaper on a shoestring.

I thought I heard the hall door to the next room open and close. The side door to our room opened just enough to admit a head which, in a low voice, summoned away McDowell. Bermingham was left alone with me. It was oppressively hot. The window was open. Once or twice I leaned out to see if I could catch a breeze. Each time I started to do so, I caught Mr. Bermingham's sad eyes measure my intention with a slow stare.

Then a Committee investigator opened the hall door to our room. He beckoned me to follow him. We walked into the next room. It was crowded. The sub-committee was in session with Congressman McDowell in the chair. As I entered they sat facing me. Robert Stripling was standing beside Congressman Nixon. Other staff members were standing around the left side of the room.

A man was sitting with his back to me. Someone motioned me to a couch on the right-hand side of the room. The man with his back to me was Alger Hiss, whom I was seeing for the first time since I had left him at his door in Georgetown just before Christmas of 1938.

When I entered the room, Alger Hiss did not turn to look at me. When I sat down, he did not glance at me.

XVIII

Any confrontation is a horror. My feeling for Hiss had remained unchanged through the years. I felt about Hiss and myself as of people whom chance has led to live in different continents, but who had only to be brought together again for their friendship, like an interrupted conversation, to be taken up where it was dropped.

But years have a disembodying effect. Until we faced each other in the hotel room, I had been testifying about Hiss as a memory and a name. Now I saw again the man himself. In the circumstances it was shocking.

Until then, I had wondered how he could be so arrogant or so stupid as to suppose that he could deceive the nation into believing that he had never known me. (I did not know that Hiss had already tentatively identified me, with infinite qualification, as George Crosley.)

But when I saw him in person, that feeling, too, fell away, and I was swept by a sense of pity for all trapped men of which the pathos of this man was the center. For the man I saw before me was a trapped man. Under the calculated malice of his behavior toward me, which I could not fail to resent, under his impudence and bravado to the congressmen, he was a trapped man—and I am a killer only by extreme necessity. Throughout the session, my mind was in a posture of supplication, silently imploring strength for him to disclose the truth that I had already testified to about him so that I might not be compelled to testify to worse about him and the others. In short, I felt what any humane man must feel when, pursuing an end that he is convinced is right, he finds himself the reluctant instrument of another man's disaster, even though that disaster is being invited by the man who suffers it.

That feeling did not change at all my determination to lay bare the Communist conspiracy short of espionage and the fact that Hiss had been a Communist. It merely complicated almost past endurance the effort to do so.

XIX

Hiss quickly made it clear that he was numbed by no such feelings. He had been summoned to the confrontation with no more forewarning than I had had. Though I did not then know what had passed between him and the Committee members before I entered the room, he had arrived in conspicuously bad humor. He had brought with him a Mr. Charles Dollard, whom Hiss introduced as "not a lawyer," a friend—"he is of the Carnegie Corporation." I have never heard Mr. Dollard characterized more fully. He hovers at the edge of the ensuing scene like the "first attendant, friend to the Duke" in a Shakespeare play. Most of the time he lurked in one corner of the room—I do not recall that he sat down—with a curiously fixed smile on his face, which Hiss's loftier jibes turned incandescent with amusement. Now and again, Hiss tossed him an aside about telephoning the Harvard Club.

I am not alone in supposing that this by-play was intended to convey the sense that these two beings were native to another atmosphere, were merely condescending, a little impatiently, to the summons of the earthlings in the room.

Congressman Nixon stated the purpose of the hearing.

MR. NIXON: . . . It is quite apparent at this state (stage?) in the testimony, as you indicated yesterday,* that the case is dependent upon the question of identity. We have attempted to establish the identity through photographs of Mr. Chambers and that has been inadequate for the purpose. Today, we thought that since you had in your testimony raised the possibility of a third party who might be involved in this case in some way, and had described him at some length to the committee, that it would be well to, at the earliest possible time, determine whether the third party is different from the two parties or the same one, and so consequently we have asked Mr. Chambers to be in New York at the same time so that you can have the opportunity to see him and make up your mind on that point.

MR. HISS: May I interrupt at this point, because I take it this will take more than 10 or 15 minutes. Would it be possible for one of the members of the committee to call the Harvard Club and leave word that I won't be there for a 6 o'clock appointment?

MR. MC DOWELL: I would suggest it won't take much more time than that, but you certainly may. . . . There is a telephone, I believe, in the room here. Any time you want to call, you may.

MR. DOLLARD: I can make the call.

MR. HISS: May I also make a statement before you begin?

MR. MC DOWELL: Certainly.

MR. HISS: I would like the record to show that on my way downtown from my uptown office, I learned from the press of the death of Harry White, which came as a great shock to me, and I am not sure that I feel in the best possible mood for testimony. I do not for a moment want to miss the opportunity of seeing Mr. Chambers. I merely wanted the record to show that.

There followed a haggle between Hiss and the Committee as to whether the congressmen had leaked news of the executive session to the press. When that had abated, I was brought in. A hearing began that was different in form and kind from any other in the Case. Other hearings had been diffuse and sprawling. The hearing in the Commodore Hotel room had a single point of unity—the question of Hiss's identification of me. The August 25th hearing was

* For the timing, it should be noted that this confrontation in New York came a day after Hiss's testimony in executive session in Washington, when he had first cautiously suggested that I might be "George Crosley."

to be more important. It first dramatized Hiss's equivocation to the nation. But the August 17th hearing was the climax of one phase of the Case. In it the characters and roles of the two witnesses were epitomized, and in it was foreshadowed the future of the conflict.

Not its least horrifying aspect was that it was great theater, too; not only because of its inherent drama, but in part because, I am convinced, Alger Hiss was acting from start to finish, never more so than when he pretended to be about to attack me physically. His performance was all but flawless, but what made it shocking, even in its moments of unintended comedy, was the fact that the terrible spur of Hiss's acting was fear.

Congressman Nixon opened the sad play as soon as I was brought into the room.

MR. NIXON: Mr. Chambers, will you please stand. And will you please stand, Mr. Hiss? Mr. Hiss, the man standing here is Mr. Whittaker Chambers. I ask you now if you have ever known that man before.

MR. HISS: May I ask him to speak? Will you ask him to say something?

MR. NIXON: Yes. Mr. Chambers, will you tell us your name and your business?

MR. CHAMBERS: My name is Whittaker Chambers.

At that point, says the official transcript, Mr. Hiss walked in the direction of Mr. Chambers. To grasp the full preposterousness of what followed, it is necessary to bear in mind that here are two men each of whom knows the other perfectly well, though one pretends not to. Hiss, rising from his chair and walking across the room, sets his face in an expression of grim exploration, searchingly peers at Chambers' mouth and listens absorbedly.

MR. HISS (to Chambers): Would you mind opening your mouth wider?

After my first wince of surprise, I grasped that Hiss was acting. I decided to let him act up to the hilt.

MR. CHAMBERS: My name is Whittaker Chambers.

MR. HISS: I said, would you open your mouth? (aside to Richard Nixon) You know what I am referring to, Mr. Nixon. (To me) Will you go on talking?

MR. CHAMBERS: I am (a) senior editor of *Time* magazine.
MR. HISS: May I ask whether his voice, when he testified before, was comparable to this?

"His voice?" echoed Nixon, who had been expecting teeth.

MR. HISS: Or did he talk a little more in a lower key?

"I would say," said Congressman McDowell who could not quite edit out an overtone of irony, "I would say it is about the same now as we have heard."
MR. HISS: Would you ask him to talk a little more?

By then, I felt somewhat like a broken-mouthed sheep whose jaws have been pried open and are being inspected by wary buyers at an auction. Everyone in the room was watching fascinated.

MR. NIXON: Read something, Mr. Chambers. I will let you read from—
MR. HISS: I think he is George Crosley, but I would like to hear him talk a little longer.
MR. MC DOWELL: Mr. Chambers, if you would be more comfortable, you may sit down.
MR. HISS: Are you George Crosley?
MR. CHAMBERS: Not to my knowledge. You are Alger Hiss, I believe?
MR. HISS: I certainly am.
MR. CHAMBERS: That was my recollection.

Congressman Nixon had passed me a copy of *Newsweek,* which belonged to him, and indicated a passage for me to read.

MR. CHAMBERS: (reading) *Since June—*
MR. NIXON: Just one moment. Since some repartee goes on between these two people, I think Mr. Chambers should be sworn.
MR. HISS: That is a good idea.

I was duly sworn.

MR. NIXON: Mr. Hiss, may I say something? I suggested that he be sworn, and when I say something like that, I want no interruptions from you.

MR. HISS: Mr. Nixon, in view of what happened yesterday, I think there is no occasion for you to use that tone of voice in speaking to me, and I hope the record will show what I have just said.

MR. NIXON: The record shows everything being said here today.

* * *

MR. CHAMBERS (reading from *Newsweek* magazine): Tobin for Labor. Since June, Harry S. Truman had been peddling the labor secretaryship left vacant by Lewis B. Schwellenbach's death in hope of gaining the maximum political advantage from the appointment. (During the first Hiss trial, Lloyd Paul Stryker was to make much of this passage as evidence that I was playing Republican politics in making charges against Hiss. At the time, I was aware of something quite different. I noticed sharply for the first time, because the occasion was public, that I had difficulty in reading; some of the letters blurred. My once excellent eyesight had been worn down by years of reading copy. That failing vision was to be a factor in saving my life a few months later.)

MR. HISS: May I interrupt?

MR. MC DOWELL: Yes.

MR. HISS: The voice sounds a little less resonant than the voice that I recall of the man I knew as George Crosley. The teeth look to me as though either they had been improved upon or that there has been considerable dental work done since I knew George Crosley, which was some years ago. I believe I am not prepared without further checking to take an absolute oath that he must be George Crosley.

That wholly unexpected conclusion, coming a few minutes after Hiss had volunteered: "I think he is George Crosley," caused a moment's silence. Congressman Nixon broke it.

MR. NIXON: May I ask Mr. Chambers a question?

MR. HISS: I would like to ask Mr. Chambers, if I may.

MR. NIXON: I will ask the questions at this time. Mr. Chambers, have you had any dental work since 1934 of a substantial nature?

MR. CHAMBERS: Yes, I have.

MR. NIXON: What type of dental work?

MR. CHAMBERS: I have had some extractions and a plate. . . .

MR. HISS: Could you ask him the name of the dentist that performed these things? Is that appropriate?

MR. NIXON: Yes. What is the name?

MR. CHAMBERS: Dr. Hitchcock, Westminster, Maryland.

MR. HISS: That testimony of Mr. Chambers, if it can be believed, would tend to substantiate my feeling that he represented himself to me in 1934 or 1935 or thereabout as George Crosley, a free-lance writer of articles for magazines. I would like to find out from Dr. Hitchcock if what he has just said is true because I am relying partly, one of my main recollections of Crosley was the poor condition of his teeth.

MR. NIXON: Can you describe the condition of your teeth in 1934?

MR. CHAMBERS: Yes. They were in very bad shape.

MR. NIXON: The front teeth were?

MR. CHAMBERS: Yes. I think so.

MR. HISS: Mr. Chairman.

MR. NIXON: Excuse me. Before we leave the teeth, Mr. Hiss, do you feel that you would have to have the dentist tell you just what he did to the teeth before you could tell anything about this man?

MR. HISS: I would like a few more questions asked. I didn't intend to say anything about this, because I feel very strongly that he is Crosley, but he looks very different in girth and in other appearances—hair, forehead, and so on, particularly the jowls.

Congressman Nixon then led Hiss through a recapitulation of his relations with George Crosley. Hiss testified again that he had met Crosley when that impecunious writer was covering the munitions investigation. He had, in fact, known Crosley five or six months before Crosley said one day that he was looking for an apartment in Washington for the summer. "I asked him," said Hiss, "if he would like to sublet my apartment during that period of time, that it was not too cool, but that it was up on a hill and had a very decent location as Washington goes, that I would let him have it for what it cost me. In the course of the negotiation," said Hiss, "he referred to the fact that he also wanted an automobile. I said, 'You come to just the right place, I would be very glad to throw a car in because I have been trying to get rid of an old car which we have kept solely for sentimental reasons which we couldn't get anything on for a trade-in sale. . . .' We had had it sitting on the city streets because we had a new one." (At the August 25th hearing, that discrepancy would plague Hiss badly.)

Crosley, said Hiss, had never paid any part of the rent, which amounted to about $225 (Hiss was not sure whether his lease on the 28th Street apartment had run until October). Crosley had also borrowed $20 or $40 from Hiss. But he once brought Hiss a rug as "part payment" (incidentally, the value of the Bykov rug, even in 1937, the date when Hiss really received it, was at least $225; and the unpaid rent, it finally developed, could not have been more than $150). "My recollection is Mr. Crosley said some wealthy patron had bestowed it upon him as a gift."

Hiss also testified that he had possibly put Crosley up overnight after he left the 28th Street apartment. He had probably driven Crosley to New York; Mrs. Hiss may have been along ("I rather think she was").

All this was fairly close to what had actually happened and showed that there was nothing seriously wrong with Hiss's memory. He had simply re-worked the facts. He had transformed Carl, the Communist, into Crosley, the dead beat. If the story had not been shot through with provable discrepancies, it might have succeeded. For very few people knew anything about Communists, but practically everybody knew about dead beats.

Robert Stripling took over the questioning.

MR. STRIPLING: . . . I certainly gathered the impression [when] Mr. Chambers walked in this room and you walked over and examined him and asked him to open his mouth, that you were basing your identification purely on what his upper teeth might have looked like. Now, here is a person that you knew for several months at least. You knew him so well that he was a guest in your home.

MR. HISS: Would you—

MR. STRIPLING: I would like to complete my statement—that he was a guest in your home, that you gave him an old Ford automobile, and permitted him to use, or you leased him your apartment and in this, a very important confrontation, the only thing that you have to check on is this denture; is that correct? There is nothing else about this man's features which you could definitely say, "This is the man I knew as George Crosley," that you have to rely entirely on this denture; is that your position?

MR. HISS: Is your preface through? My answer to the question you have asked is this:

From the time on Wednesday, August 4, 1948, when I was able to get hold of newspapers containing photographs of one Whittaker Chambers, I was struck by a certain familiarity in features. When I testified on August 5th and was shown a photograph by you, Mr. Stripling, there was again some familiarity [in] features. I could not be sure that I had never seen the person whose photograph you showed me. I said I would want to see the person.

The photographs are rather good photographs of Whittaker Chambers as I see Whittaker Chambers today. I am not given on important occasions to snap judgments or simple, easy statements. I am confident that George Crosley had notably bad teeth. I would not call George Crosley a guest in my house. I have explained the circumstances. If you choose to call him a guest, that is your affair.

MR. STRIPLING: I am willing to strike the word "guest." He was in your house.

MR. HISS: I saw him at the time I was seeing hundreds of people. Since then I have seen thousands of people. He meant nothing to me except as one I saw under the circumstances I have described.

My recollection of George Crosley, if this man had said he was George Crosley, I would have no difficulty in identification. He denied it right here. I would like and asked earlier in this hearing if I could ask some further questions to help in identification. I was denied that.

MR. STRIPLING: I think you should be permitted—

MR. HISS: I was denied that right. I am not, therefore, able to take an oath that this man is George Crosley. I have been testifying about George Crosley. Whether he and this man are the same or whether he has means of getting information from George Crosley about my house, I do not know. He may have had his face lifted.

I was asked if I had any objection to being cross-examined by Hiss. I said: "No."

MR. HISS: Did you ever go under the name of George Crosley?

MR. CHAMBERS: Not to my knowledge.

MR. HISS: Did you ever sublet an apartment on Twenty-ninth Street* from me?

MR. CHAMBERS: No; I did not. . . .

MR. HISS: Did you ever spend any time with your wife and child in an apartment on Twenty-ninth Street in Washington when I was not there because I and my family were living on P Street?

MR. CHAMBERS: I most certainly did.

MR. HISS: You did or did not?

MR. CHAMBERS: I did.

MR. HISS: Would you tell me how you reconcile your negative answers with this affirmative answer?

I answered very quietly, from the depth of my distress: "Very easily, Alger. I was a Communist and you were a Communist."

MR. HISS: Would you be responsive and continue with your answer?

MR. CHAMBERS: I do not think it is needed.

Nixon broke in. "I will help you with the answer, Mr. Hiss. The question, Mr. Chambers, is, as I understand it, that Mr. Hiss cannot understand how you could deny that you were George Crosley and yet admit that you spent time in his apartment. Now would you explain the circumstances. . . ?"

MR. CHAMBERS: As I have testified before, I came to Washington as a Communist functionary, a functionary of the American Communist Party. (I pronounced those words very slowly and distinctly, for through them I was telling Hiss that I had not testified about the Soviet apparatus.) I was connected with the underground group of which Mr. Hiss was a member. Mr. Hiss and I became friends to the best of my knowledge. Mr. Hiss himself suggested that I go there (to the apartment), and I gratefully accepted.

Hiss was shaken by a spasm of anger; this time I do not believe that he was acting. "Mr. Chairman," he said, "I don't need to ask

* Hiss should have said 28th Street.

Mr. Whittaker Chambers any more questions. I am now perfectly prepared to identify this man as George Crosley."

MR. NIXON: Would you spell that name?
MR. HISS: C-r-o-s-l-e-y.
MR. NIXON: You are sure of one "s"?
MR. HISS: That is my recollection. I have a rather good visual memory (to me, one of the staggering statements of the day), and my recollection of his spelling of his name is Cr-o-s-l-e-y. I don't think that would change as much as his appearance.
MR. STRIPLING: You will identify him positively now?
MR. HISS: I will on the basis of what he has just said positively identify him without further questioning as George Crosley.
MR. STRIPLING: Will you produce for the committee three people who will testify that they knew him as George Crosley?

Apparently, Hiss was unprepared for that one. For the first and only time in that hearing or any other, I saw him gag for a moment. "I will if it is possible," he said. "Why is that a question to ask me? I will see what is possible. This occurred in 1935. The only people that I can think of who would have known him as George Crosley with certainty would have been the people who were associated with me in the Nye Committee.

MR. STRIPLING: Can you name three people whom we can subpoena who can identify him as George Crosley?
MR. HISS: I am afraid I will have to confer with the individual members. The people, as I recall them, who were on the staff—and they were in and out of Washington constantly—were Mr. Raushenbush. I would like to consult Steve Raushenbush. I don't know whether Crosley ever called on him.
MR. NIXON: Where is he now, Mr. Hiss?
MR. HISS: I don't know.
MR. STRIPLING: He is in Washington.
MR. HISS: Robert Wohlford was one of the investigators.*
MR. NIXON: Do you know where he is?
MR. STRIPLING: Department of Justice.
MR. HISS: I don't remember the name of the very efficient secretary to Mr. Raushenbush. Miss Elsie Gullender, I think her

*Robert Wohlforth, author of *Tin Soldiers,* a fictional attack on West Point, popular in leftist circles during the 1930's.

name was. Do you know the whereabouts of Miss Elsie Gullender? . . .

It was unlikely that anyone in the room would know of Miss Gullender's whereabouts, the more so since she was dead. Neither Mr. Raushenbush nor Mr. Wohlforth, it soon developed, had ever heard of George Crosley, nor had any of the newsmen who swarmed about the munitions investigation and of whom Crosley was supposed to be one.

Hiss was asked if he had had any idea that George Crosley was a Communist or if we had ever discussed politics.

MR. HISS: . . . May I just state for the record that it was not the habit in Washington in those days, when particularly if a member of the press called on you, to ask him before you had further conversation whether or not he was a Communist. It was a quite different atmosphere in Washington then than today. I had no reason to suspect George Crosley of being a Communist. It never occurred to me that he might be or whether that was of any significance to me if he was. . . . I would like to say that to come here and discover that the ass under the lion's skin is Crosley. I don't know why your committee didn't pursue this careful method of interrogation at an earlier date before all the publicity. . . .

MC DOWELL: Well, now, Mr. Hiss, you positively identify—

MR. HISS: Positively on the basis of his own statement that he was in my apartment at the time when I say he was there. I have no further question at all. If he had lost both eyes and taken his nose off, I would be sure.

I was asked to identify Alger Hiss. I said: "Positive identification."

"At this point," says the official record, "Mr. Hiss arose and walked in the direction of Mr. Chambers." In fact, Mr. Hiss advanced with fists clenched upon Mr. Chambers, who, perfectly certain that this was another act (for even lawyers do not think of saying things for the record when they are overcome with rage), sat quietly where he was on the couch.

MR. HISS: May I say for the record at this point, that I would like to invite Mr. Whittaker Chambers to make those same statements out of the presence of this committee without their being privileged for suit for libel. I challenge you to do it, and I hope you will do it damned quickly.

Louis J. Russell, the committee's assistant chief investigator, laid a restraining hand very gently on Alger Hiss's arm. Hiss by then had paused. "I am not going to touch him," he said. "You are touching me."

MR. RUSSELL: Please sit down, Mr. Hiss.
MR. HISS: I will sit down when the chairman asks me. Mr. Russell, when the chairman asks me to sit down—
MR. RUSSELL: I want no disturbance.
MR. HISS: I don't—
MR. MC DOWELL: Sit down, please.
MR. HISS: You know who started this.

During the remainder of the hearing, Robert Stripling made the telling point. "I am concerned," he said to Hiss, "with the statement you made before the Committee of Congress in the presence of quite a few hundred people that you didn't even know this person. You led the public and the press to believe that you didn't know such a person." "You are fully aware," he added, "that the public was led to believe that you had never seen, heard, or laid eyes upon an individual who is this individual, and now you do know him."

MR. HISS: . . . I did not say that I have never seen this man. I said, so far as I know I have never seen Whittaker Chambers.
MR. STRIPLING: Never laid eyes on him.
MR. HISS: I wouldn't have been able to identify him for certain today without his own assistance.
MR. STRIPLING: You are willing to waive the dentures?

Thus, a fortnight after the Case began, Alger Hiss, by an operation itself a good deal like a dental extraction, was brought to admit that, indeed, he knew me perfectly well. The hearing closed with a decision to hold a public confrontation in Washington on August 25th. Subpoenas were issued to Hiss and me at once.

"Thank you," said Chairman McDowell to Hiss as he was leaving. Said Hiss: "I don't reciprocate." Mr. McDowell: "Italicize that in the record."

When Hiss and Dollard had finally stalked out of the room, everyone was silent for a moment. Stripling turned to me. Completely deadpan, but in his broadest Texas brogue, he drawled: "Ha-ya, Mistah Crawz-li?"

It was after reading the transcript of this hearing that Thomas F. Murphy, the Government's prosecutor in the Hiss trials, ceased to have any doubt at all that Hiss was lying.

"The jury might well have believed," says the decision in which, two years later, the judges of the appellate court denied Hiss's appeal to set aside his conviction, "that the appellant (Alger Hiss) had been less than frank in his belated recognition of Mr. Chambers. . . ."

XX

I am aware, as I recall three years later the scene that I have just described, how much my feeling has changed, not necessarily for the better, under the pressure of experience. It is what always happens to people, struggle against it as they will, in a prolonged war. Now, as I go over the details, the feeling uppermost in my mind is a resentment close to anger, though it is a detached and impersonal anger. Above all, it is a sense of chill amusement at the preposterousness of the scene as human behavior. I felt resentment and I was aware of the comic by-play at that time, too. But then both feelings were overweighed by my sense of the human disaster of which I was a part and an agent.

At the time, nothing in the hearing at the Commodore Hotel appalled me like the moment when Hiss was asked to produce three witnesses who had known George Crosley, and realized that he could not do so, while across his face for an instant flitted an expression that meant that he felt he was trapped. As a man, I prayed that he would not be trapped. But in a historical sense, I knew that he must be trapped. So I was rent.

A devout Catholic woman once asked me what was in my mind as I sat there while Hiss insulted me. I said that I would rather not answer then, but that some day I would tell her. Through my mind as I watched that moment of fleeting panic on Alger Hiss's face, passed two lines of Kipling's that my friend, James Agee, had once pointed out to me:

Father in Heaven, Who lovest all,
Oh, help Thy children when they call. . . .

XXI

After that confrontation, I returned to my office at *Time* and went through the motions of working. Everyone was kind. No one pressed me. One day Henry Luce called me up and asked me to come to supper.

There were three of us. The second guest was a nimble, witty European whom I shall call Smetana. At supper, most of the talk was between Luce and Smetana. I was a rather silent guest. I was too fresh from the shadows; bright conversation hurt my mind. In fact, I had left behind the world of *Time* and those who lived within it. It was only the friendliest of fictions that I still belonged to it.

No one mentioned Communism or the Hiss Case until we sat over our coffee in the living room. Mrs. Philip Jessup had just used her personal good offices to try to get me off *Time.* Luce was baffled by the implacable clamor of the most enlightened people against me. "By any Marxian pattern of how classes behave," he said, "the upper class should be for you and the lower classes should be against you. But it is the upper class that is most violent against you. How do you explain that?"

"You don't understand the class structure of American society," said Smetana, "or you would not ask such a question. In the United States, the working class are Democrats. The middle class are Republicans. The upper class are Communists."

Luce was puzzled, too, by a question that many people were asking: If Hiss was a Communist, how could he, constantly meeting and dealing with intelligent people, have managed not to betray his real views from day to day? I was too tired to explain how, in our revolutionary age, Hiss was seldom in danger of betraying his real views. He had only to refrain from pressing extreme views, or drawing ultimate conclusions from views very widespread among enlightened people, to find himself simply saying what all his set was saying, only, perhaps, saying it a little more valiantly, so that he drew a bonus of intense sincerity. I might have said, of course, that, in other quarters, Hiss had betrayed himself frequently. But in those early days I knew less about that than I know now. It was not until after Hiss's conviction that a security officer of the Government would call to thank me for my part in the Case and remark: "The name Hiss has been an undertone in our work for years."

Smetana saved me from saying anything. "The Communist conspiracy," he said, "is unlike any ever known before. In the past, conspiracy has always meant secrecy, concealment. The peculiarity of Communism is that everybody really knows who these people are and what the conspiracy is and how it works. But everybody connives at it because nobody wants to believe his own eyes. It is something new under the sun. It is conspiracy in the open."

When Smetana presently rose to go, I started to leave with him. Luce drew me back. Alone, we sat facing each other across a low table. Neither of us said anything. He studied my face for some time as if he were trying to read the limits of my strength. "The pity of it is," he said at last, "that two men, able men, are destroying each other in this way." I said: "That is what history does to men in periods like ours."

There was another heavy pause. I knew that there must be something that Luce wanted to tell me or ask me, but I was too weary to help him. Suddenly he said, "I've been reading about the young man born blind." Frequently Luce asks his editors about stories in *Time* which they should have read and realize guiltily that they have not read. I reacted with that old *Time* reflex. Apologetically, I said, "I haven't read *Time* for the last two weeks."

"No, no," Luce said impatiently, "I mean the young man born blind. It's in the eighth or ninth chapter of St. John. They brought Our Lord a young man who had been blind from birth and asked Him one of those catch questions: 'Whose is the sin, this man's or his parents', that he was born blind?' Our Lord took some clay and wet it with saliva and placed it on the blind man's eyes so that they opened and he could see. Then Our Lord gave an answer, not one of His clever answers, but a direct, simple answer. He said: 'Neither this man sinned nor his parents, but that the works of God should be made manifest in him.' "

Slowly, there sank into my mind the tremendous thing that Luce was saying to me, and the realization that he had brought me there so that he could say those words of understanding kindness. He was saying: "You are the young man born blind. All you had to offer God was your blindness that through the action of your recovered sight, His works might be made manifest."

In the depths of the Hiss Case, in grief, weakness and despair, the words that Luce had repeated to me came back to strengthen me.

XXII

It seemed to me in prospect that I could not go through another public hearing. Another public hearing, especially another confrontation with Hiss in front of hundreds of strange people, was more than I could endure. In two weeks I had been through three hearings. Another great circus under eager, avid eyes, under batteries of news cameras and the hard stares of a prevailingly hostile press was too much.

I asked Nixon why there had to be a public hearing at all now that Hiss had admitted that he knew me. But if another hearing had to be held, why must it be public, why could it not be held in executive session?

Patiently, he put me off with reasons that did not seem to me to make sense. When I became insistent, he said reluctantly, "It is for your own sake that the Committee is holding a public hearing. The Department of Justice is all set to move in on you in order to save Hiss. They are planning to indict you at once. The only way to head them off is to let the public judge for itself which one of you is telling the truth. That is your only chance. That is why the hearing must be public." *

"If there is anything else that you have not told us about Hiss," he added, "now is the time to tell us. Think hard about it. If there is anything else, for your own sake, tell us now."

I liked and trusted Nixon. Clearly, my choice lay between procuring my own safety and the agony of the others. I sensed, too, that if things continued as they were going, in the end I must involve the others. I could not do it yet. I shook my head.

I left Nixon, feeling, in addition to all else that I felt, like a very small creature, skirting the shadows of encircling powers that would not hesitate to crush me as impersonally as a steam roller crushes a bug.

XXIII

To understand the atmosphere in which the August 25th hearing took place, it must be remembered that, since August 1, 1948, Elizabeth Bentley's revelations had been shocking the country. They

* Regardless of whether or not Richard Nixon was mistaken—and there are many who would claim that he was—I believed him, and his words weighed heavily upon me.

had been closely followed by my allegations, most of which had been lost to sight in the hubbub over my charge that Alger Hiss had once been a Communist, though all the charges were connected. The din in the startled nation was deafening. It was to be stepped up as the Hiss partisans stepped up their campaign of vilification of me, which was a little slow in getting under way, presumably because they had not yet concerted a plan of attack. Before August 25th, the great cry on all sides was: Which one is lying? But the whispers were growing louder that Chambers was a psychiatric case.

In the midst of this uproar, the men and women named by Miss Bentley, most of them Government officials or former Government officials, passed in a three-week parade before the House Committee on Un-American Activities. Most of them denied Miss Bentley's allegations or refused to testify under their constitutional privilege. A number of those whom I had named also appeared. On August 11th, Henry H. Collins, Jr., the former treasurer of the Ware Group, went before the Committee. He is now the executive director of the American-Russian Institute (cited as subversive by the Attorney General). Prior to assuming that post he had served for some fifteen years in the Federal Government.

MR. COLLINS: My Federal employment started late in 1933 with the National Recovery Administration. In 1935 I went with the Soil Conservation Service; in 1938, I think, I went with the Department of Labor in the Wage and Hour Division. From there, I was loaned to the House Committee on the Interstate Migration of Destitute Citizens, and later to the Senate Committee on Small Business, and subsequently to the Kilgore committee, a subcommittee of the Military Affairs Committee on War Mobilization. From there, I received a commission and went into the School of Military Government at Charlottesville and was shortly sent overseas and spent 2 years in the European theater, in England, France and Germany.

He was currently, he said, a major in the Reserves.

MR. STRIPLING: Are you a member of the Communist Party?

MR. COLLINS: I decline to answer that question on the grounds that my answer might tend to incriminate me.

He was shown a newsphoto of Whittaker Chambers.

MR. COLLINS: I cannot recognize that man. (Collins later suffered an eleventh-hour recollection of having had George Crosley in for cocktails, but, though he was available, the Hiss defense never saw fit to call him to testify.)

MR. STRIPLING: You cannot recognize this man? Did you ever know anybody by the name of Whittaker Chambers?

MR. COLLINS: I never knew a man by the name of Whittaker Chambers.

MR. STRIPLING: Do you know an individual known to you as Carl in 1935?

MR. COLLINS: I refuse to answer that question on the grounds of possible self-incrimination. . . .

MR. STRIPLING: Mr. Collins, did you ever live at St. Matthews Court in Washington?

MR. COLLINS: I did.

MR. STRIPLING: Did you ever meet John Abt at this apartment?

MR. COLLINS: I decline to answer that question on the grounds of possible self-incrimination.

MR. STRIPLING: Did you ever meet Alger Hiss at that apartment?

MR. COLLINS: I decline to answer that question for the same reason. . . .

MR. STRIPLING: Did you ever meet in the apartment of Alger Hiss on P Street in Georgetown in 1935?

MR. COLLINS: I decline to answer that question on the grounds of possible self-incrimination. . . .

MR. HÉBERT: Mr. Collins, were you ever investigated by the FBI for loyalty?

MR. COLLINS: I do not know, sir. I was called down and interviewed by them about 6 years ago, I think.

MR. HÉBERT: You know what that interview was. What was it?

MR. COLLINS Well, it is in the record.

MR. HÉBERT: I am not asking for the record. I am asking you.

MR. COLLINS: Sir, I do not think I understand the question.

MR. HÉBERT: What was the interview about that you had with the FBI 6 years ago?

MR. COLLINS: Well, it was on the question of some section of the law that required them to interview Government employees at that time.

MR. HÉBERT: What section of the law?

MR. COLLINS: I do not know, sir.

MR. HÉBERT: What questions did they ask you?

MR. COLLINS: Well, I cannot remember. It was a long time ago, sir.

MR. HÉBERT: Did they ask you about your connection with certain organizations in Government—I mean outside of Government but certain organizations in the country?

MR. COLLINS: Yes, that is the kind of questions that they asked.

MR. HÉBERT: Did they ask you about any communistic activity?

MR. COLLINS: I do not remember, sir.

* * *

MR. HÉBERT: You made the statement that you did not want to answer questions because they may tend to incriminate you. You did not want to answer questions of the chairman relative to your organizations. Is that your same attitude relative to individuals?

MR. COLLINS: Yes.

MR. HÉBERT: Why then did you readily say you never knew a man named Whittaker Chambers?

MR. COLLINS: Because that was a name that was used in the accusations in the newspapers. I never knew a man named Whittaker Chambers, so I thought I was entitled to say so.

MR. HÉBERT: Well, it is in the record that you knew a man named Carl. Why do you not answer that question?

THE CHAIRMAN: Are you consulting with counsel now for advice?

MR. COLLINS: Not now, sir.

THE CHAIRMAN: But you just were?

MR. COLLINS: Yes.

THE CHAIRMAN: I want the record to show that he consulted with counsel.

MR. HÉBERT: Why won't you say whether you know Carl or not? That is in the record.

MR. COLLINS: For the same reason, sir, that I refuse to answer any questions about knowing any individuals at this time in connection with these accusations.

MR. HÉBERT: But you just said you did not know Whittaker Chambers. You are blowing hot and cold. Which way do you want to blow, hot or cold? We have had a lot of talking out of both sides of the mouth on this, so we may as well give you a chance to do it. It is a great acrobatic feat. How do you justify, then, saying you do not know Whittaker Chambers? You did answer that question.

MR. COLLINS: I just go back to my previous statements, sir, in connection with that.

MR. HÉBERT: . . . Now, why do you refuse to say whether you know Alger Hiss, or not? He has made no accusations against you?

MR. COLLINS: I refuse to answer that question, sir, on the grounds that my answer might tend to incriminate me.

X X I V

On August 20th, a trio of witnesses collectively more interesting than Collins appeared before the Committee. They were Lee Pressman, who had been a member of the Ware Group, Nathan Witt and John Abt, each of whom, in succession, had been its head. Witt and Abt were now law partners in New York City. Each was accompanied at his hearing by an attorney, Mr. Harold Cammer, a partner in the law firm of Nathan, Witt and Cammer.

Like Hiss, all three witnesses were Harvard men, and if the aura about them was a little less rarefied, the trio, nevertheless, had an impressive official record. Each had held highly important jobs in the Government or in close touch with it. Lee Pressman, after having been general counsel of the Works Progress Administration, had become general counsel of the C.I.O., a title that by no means defines his power. John Abt, after having been assistant general counsel of the Works Progress Administration, had become a special assistant to the Attorney General of the United States in the Department of Justice. Nathan Witt had been the secretary of the powerful National Labor Relations Board. Thus, in the persons of Pressman and Witt, there subsisted between the C.I.O. and the N.L.R.B. an intimate tie of fellowship. It is scarcely necessary to stress the critical importance to the C.I.O. of the decisions of the N.L.R.B. or the bearing of those matters upon national politics.

In addition to the usual refusal to answer questions on grounds of self-incrimination, this three-man interlocking directorate had worked out some new objections. As prefaced to John Abt's testimony by Mr. Cammer, they were substantially the same for all three. Robert Stripling had asked Abt: "Are you a member of the Communist Party?"

MR. CAMMER: . . . I object to the question on the ground, first, that Mr. Abt's associations, views, opinions, affiliations, and the like are outside the scope of any inquiry under the first amendment to the Constitution.

The second objection is that this investigation, or the subject matter of this investigation, as stated by Mr. Nixon, is outside the scope of any congressional inquiry, and is an intrusion upon the judicial function which is invested exclusively in the judiciary by Article III of the Constitution.

The third objection, or the third basis of objection, is that this committee, and the subcommittee conducting this hearing under the aegis of this committee, is unlawfully constituted by reason of the membership thereon of one John Rankin who holds an alleged seat in Congress unlawfully, and in violation of the provisions of the fourteenth amendment, so that this committee may not interrogate for that reason.

* * *

MR. STRIPLING (to John Abt): Have you ever been a member of the Communist Party?

MR. ABT: On the grounds of objection stated to the previous question by my counsel, and in the exercise of my constitutional privilege against self-incrimination under the fifth amendment, I decline to answer that question.

MR. STRIPLING: Mr. Abt, do you know an individual by the name of Whittaker Chambers?

MR. ABT: On the ground of objection, Mr. Stripling, stated at the outset of this hearing by my counsel and in the exercise of my privilege under the fifth amendment against self-incrimination, I decline to answer that question. . . .

MR. STRIPLING: Mr. Abt, are you acquainted with Alger Hiss?

MR. ABT: On the grounds of objection stated by my counsel on [under] the first amendment to the constitution, and by virtue of the prior objections that the subject matter of this inquiry is a matter of judicial rather than congressional investigation—

MR. CAMMER: Article III of the Constitution.

MR. ABT: Under Article III of the Constitution, and on the

ground of the unlawful and improper composition of this committee under the fourteenth amendment, and in the exercise of my privilege against self-incrimination under the fifth amendment, I decline to answer that question.

On the same grounds, John Abt declined to answer whether he had ever known George Crosley, Carl, Donald Hiss, J. Peters, Earl Browder, Gerhardt Eisler and a number of other people. He waived his objections to say that he had made a trip to the Soviet Union in 1945, that the year before he had contributed articles to *Soviet Russia Today,* and that he was, in fact, married to its editor, Jessica Smith. Asked if she were not formerly the wife of Harold Ware, Abt once more pled self-incrimination and his other objections.

Lee Pressman came next. It may be borne in mind that three years later, Pressman was to testify before the House Committee on Un-American Activities that he had been a member of the Communist Party and of the Ware Group, and that so had John Abt and Nathan Witt. Scarcely had his counsel stated the usual objections, when Pressman began his testimony by asking a curious question.

MR. PRESSMAN: Has there been any charge made by any witness that has appeared before this committee that I have participated in any espionage activity, either while a member—or rather an employee of the Federal Government or thereafter?

The Committee assured him that there had been no such charge. Pressman was asked the routine questions, among others those about Hiss and Chambers. He, too, pled routine self-incrimination. Nathan Witt declined to say, on the grounds of self-incrimination, whether he had ever worked in the same office with Alger Hiss at the Agricultural Adjustment Administration. Curiously, the Committee did not ask him whether he had been a member of the Communist Party. Perhaps by then its members were worn down by beating their collective head into the elastic folds of self-incrimination. Perhaps the oversight reflected a weariness summed up by the Committee's chairman when Henry Collins declined to say whether or not he was a member of the American Legion on the grounds that any answer he might give might tend to incriminate him.

THE CHAIRMAN: That would incriminate you? It is a hopeless situation.

XXV

The Committee's immediate purpose in holding the August 25th hearing was to bring the nation abreast of the developments in the Hiss-Chambers deadlock. Its secondary purpose was to let those developments inform public opinion so that it might act as a block against any attempt to indict me in order to save Alger Hiss. Its method in the hearing was to lead Hiss back over his testimony of the last three weeks and to confront him whenever possible, with documentary evidence bearing on it. The effect of this evidence was to show that his story included misrepresentations and discrepancies so glaring as to call into question all his testimony.

The Committee, therefore, centered its interrogation on Hiss's testimony about his 1929 Ford roadster, which he claimed, at one time, to have sold, and, at another time, to have given to me, and which I had testified that he had turned over to the Communist Party. The Committee also went in careful detail into Hiss's purchase of a Plymouth sedan (which he had testified that he owned at the same time as the Ford), and explored again circumstances of my occupation of Hiss's 28th Street apartment and other relevant matters. For hours, the hearing dealt with dull details of leases, gas and electric records, transfers of title, verification of signatures.

At first, this made the August 25th confrontation seem one of the dullest of hearings. In the end, it made it one of the most effective. The impact was all the more powerful because it was delayed. As Hiss dodged and evaded those factual questions, qualifying almost every important answer with a wary "to the best of my recollection," the traditional legal phrase whereby a witness bypasses the hook of perjury, the spectators were first incredulous and then shocked. Slowly, there dawned upon them what the Committee's investigation had already demonstrated to it: the weight of available evidence confirmed my story about my relationship with Alger Hiss, and destroyed his story.

One point documents placed beyond dispute. Hiss had not given or sold me his 1929 Ford roadster. He had transferred it, almost a year after he claimed to have given it to me, to one William Rosen. And William Rosen would refuse, on every subsequent occasion, to say whether or not he was a Communist or whether he had ever owned a 1929 Ford roadster, on the ground that his answers might incriminate him.

Another development made the August 25th hearing fateful. Alger Hiss succeeded in reading into the record ten questions, each of which called for a searching probe of some part of my past. The night before the hearing Hiss had released them to the press, in the form of an open letter to the Committee. It was his strategy on August 25th to try to seize the initiative in the hearing by asking the Committee publicly to put those questions to me. In that he failed at first, but later on he succeeded.

The questions went into my family life, my pseudonyms and addresses, possible crimes, etc. They were of the kind against which every ex-Communist, as Hiss well knew, is almost completely defenseless, because every Communist has, in the name of Communism, committed some of the sins and crimes involved. The only possible answer is the unmitigated truth; and there is always a strong probability that, faced with such a public exposure, most men will retreat, make peace at any price or kill themselves. Those alternatives were among the first purposes of Hiss's questions. They had other purposes: 1) to suggest by their very phrasing that Chambers was a character so unsavory that he could not conceivably bear witness against anyone; 2) to deflect the brunt of the investigation and the public stare from Hiss to Chambers.

This was the great swinging maneuver of the Hiss Case. Under the smoke screen of the questions, Hiss, at the very moment when he had been almost completely discredited, could retire once more into the all but impregnable citadel of his public record.

In effect, not Hiss, but I, henceforth became the defendant in a great public trial, in which, in a manner startlingly reminiscent of the mechanics of the great Soviet public trials, press, radio, public personages, organizations of all kinds and a section of the Government itself were mobilized against the chosen victim while public opinion was enveloped in a smog of smearing whispers that rolled across the nation and far beyond its frontiers.* Through almost every medium of communication, the personal assault upon me was kept at a peak of uproar. Meanwhile, in the course of the whole Hiss Case, not more than five journalists were sent to find out at first hand what I might really be like. Only two of them,

*Thus, in London, one of my good friends, incidentally, a Harvard man, to his astonishment found himself having to defend me to Lord Beaverbrook.

Bert Andrews, the chief of the New York *Herald-Tribune* Washington bureau, and Nicholas Blatchford, of the Washington *Daily News*, proved equal to the assignment.

This personal assault upon me was the only real defense that Alger Hiss and his supporters ever developed. Each month that passes makes it clearer that it was chiefly a deafening noise. But it is also clear that it was a remarkable tribute to the propaganda skill of the Hiss forces and their enormous hidden power within the national community and the Government—a power rooted in the special crisis of history in which the nation, like the rest of the world, finds itself.

As a result of Hiss's questions and the strategy they initiated on August 25, 1948, I was to remain the defendant in that great public trial for almost two years.

XXVI

I had had warning of what was coming. On the evening of August 24th, I sat in *Time's* Washington bureau. I had been told that Alger Hiss had released to the press a number of questions calling for a public investigation of me. *Time's* bureau chief was on the telephone. Over the wire came the dry, rasping voice of John F. Davis, Hiss's counsel at the hearing next day. Halfway across the room, I could hear him repeating the questions put by Hiss: "I would like to ask him where and under what names he has lived. . . . . I would like to ask him if he has ever been convicted of a crime. . . . I would like to ask him. . . ."

I saw at once that it was the counterattack, though I did not then foresee its massive development. But I sensed that in a nation conditioned by press, radio and movies to crime and scandal, while knowing almost nothing about Communists, their motives and methods, and, much less about ex-Communists, the tactic was shrewd and dangerous. It struck me a psychological blow before the hearing began.

My approach to the hearing was distressing. The plaza in front of the Capitol was alive with people. A newsboy was holding up a paper with a banner headline in mock *Time* style: *C (FOR CONFRONTATION)* DAY! I repeated to myself the words that Luce had repeated to me a few days before: "Neither this man's nor his parents' is the sin, but that the works of God might be made manifest."

As Ben Mandel shepherded me to the Ways and Means Committee room, people, trying to get into the hearing, stood two abreast in a long line down the corridor. Guards slipped us into the hearing room. I was shown to a light, straight-back chair, where I was to sit among the spectators, just below the Committee's rostrum, and just behind the press tables. As I took my place, a cold wave of aversion and hostility swelled out toward me from the spectators. When I stood up, a few minutes later, to identify Alger Hiss, there were titters among them. "Good people," I thought, "it is yourselves you are laughing at. For I stand here not for myself, but for you."

A little girl about seven years old was sitting next to me. She had come with her father, mother and a woman whom I took to be her grandmother. Evidently, they had come to spend the day, for they had brought their lunch in a pasteboard box. When I sat down, the father got up and changed places with his daughter so that the child would not have to sit beside me.

XXVII

I suspect that Hiss and I went into the August 25th hearing with the same thought: to endure. Our reasons were different. Hiss was not often master of the situation that day, but he was master of himself to the extent of knowing that he must somehow, at any cost, outlast the entrapping questions that were about to be put to him. He knew that they were entrapping, and that they would be put, because he, too, had tried to reach the records on which they were based, and found that the Committee's investigators had got there first. Nothing indicates to me more clearly how well Hiss understood the importance of those "petty housekeeping details" that he was presently to complain about. But Hiss also knew that, if he could somehow hold off the onslaught, his questions against me were a reserve tactic that would probably turn the tide for him.

I was master neither of the situation nor of anything else. My sole thought was to endure a situation that I felt in prospect, and much more acutely while it was going on, as pure horror. In face of that intensely hostile crowd and the ordeal of taking the stand publicly again, I scarcely cared whether or not the hearing was all that stood between me and powerful enemies. I had no great faith that it would help much in any case. Vaguely, I hoped that the Committee would at least be able to clinch the fact that Alger Hiss was lying about me. I was not optimistic. I merely wanted to get through that day, as a man wants to get through a prolonged sickness, not caring much in the end whether it is by surviving or dying.

I had heard rumors that I was to be the Committee's first witness. With a cowardly relief, I heard Hiss sworn in. He was accompanied, as always, by counsel, the lawyer whose rasping voice I had heard the night before, issuing from the telephone in the *Time** office. This was John F. Davis, who, like Hiss, and many of the other middle-aging men around him, somehow managed to look like a college boy.

Hiss moved at once to take the offensive.

MR. STRIPLING: Mr. Hiss, you are here this morning in response to a subpoena which was served upon you on August 17 at the Commodore Hotel in New York City; is that correct?

MR. HISS: Mr. Stripling, as I told the subcommittee on that day, there was no need to serve a subpoena on me. A subpoena was handed to me. I had already told the committee I would be very glad to be here on August 25.

MR. STRIPLING: You are here also in response to a subpoena, however?

MR. HISS: I received the subpoena; yes, Mr. Stripling.

MR. STRIPLING: You are here in response to it; is that correct?

MR. HISS: To the extent that my coming here quite voluntarily after having received the subpoena is in response to it; I would accept that statement.

At once, Hiss asked if he might read into the record the questions about me (with some amplifications) that he had already released to the press. The Committee decided to take the request under advisement.

Hiss and I were then asked to stand up—the first time that any

*At his first hearing, when he appeared as a voluntary witness before the Committee, Hiss had been accompanied by William L. Marbury, later his Baltimore lawyer, in the libel suit Hiss filed against me. Hiss was always accompanied by counsel, whenever he appeared publicly and whenever he testified before the Grand Jury. I was never accompanied by counsel anywhere. Indeed, I only once discussed with counsel any important step that I planned to take in the Hiss Case; and that was to insist that, regardless of consequences to myself, I intended to plead truth before the Grand Jury.

large group of people had seen us face to face.* Hiss was asked if he knew me.

MR. HISS: I identify him, Mr. Stripling.
MR. STRIPLING: As who?
MR. HISS: As George Crosley.

I was sworn in and asked if I knew Hiss.

MR. CHAMBERS: I do.
MR. STRIPLING: Who is he?
MR. CHAMBERS: Mr. Alger Hiss.

This was the hearing, about three weeks after my first testimony, when I put on record my realization that I had met Alger Hiss almost a year before I had at first supposed.

MR. STRIPLING: When did you first meet Mr. Hiss?
MR. CHAMBERS: I think about 1934.
MR. STRIPLING: When did you last see Mr. Hiss?
MR. CHAMBERS: About 1938.

Again, Hiss was questioned about his failure to identify me from photographs. He promptly used this question to try again to secure my secret testimony.

MR. STRIPLING: When you appeared before the committee in executive session in Washington on August 16, you were again shown a picture of Mr. Whittaker Chambers.

MR. HISS: I think I was shown two pictures that day, according to my recollection.

MR. STRIPLING: You also failed at that time to identify Mr. Chambers as Mr. Crosley.

MR. HISS: I said that the pictures were definitely of a face that was not unfamiliar to me. There was a certain familiarity about it. Incidentally, Mr. Stripling is referring to certain testimony of mine taken in executive session, Mr. Chairman. I wonder if there

*Actually, whoever could reach a television set could see us. That was why I had to sit just where I sat on the uncomfortable chair and why two red electric eyes, whose function I did not then understand, were trained on me. So far as I know, the August 25th hearing was the first use of TV to bring congressional hearings into the home that the Kefauver Committee later developed on a greater scale.

is any reason why all of the testimony thus far taken in this case should not be made public. A good deal of it has reached the press by one means or another. There is a considerable amount of distortion and misunderstanding. I have no reason to want any of that testimony—mine or Mr. Chambers', which I have never seen—to remain secret. . . .

MR. STRIPLING: Mr. Chairman, I suggest that the committee make all of the testimony public as of this moment.

MR. HISS: I think that would be a very good idea.

MR. MUNDT: Mr. Chairman, may I suggest that yesterday, in your absence, the members of the committee who were here decided that today we would make all the testimony available. . . .

MR. HISS: I am very gratified.

Hiss was asked about the circumstances under which he had first met George Crosley. He countered with a tactic that was to serve him throughout the morning—a charge, sometimes direct, sometimes implied, that he could not testify exactly because the Committee was depriving him of the pertinent records.

MR. STRIPLING: Mr. Hiss, would you relate to the committee the circumstances under which you first met the person you have identified that you knew as George Crosley?

MR. HISS: Mr. Stripling, I have already in an effort to be helpful to the committee when I came to the executive session on the 16th willingly in response to a request from the chairman given the best recollection that I have.

As I said then, I have no opportunity to consult records. The connection between Crosley and Chambers did not enter my mind until Monday morning, the 16th, while I was on the way by train to the afternoon session. According to my best recollection, without checking the records—and I do think it would be more helpful if the committee would go by records; I would like to know what the records say; some of the records I find are not available to me; I believe they are in the custody of the committee. I have attempted through counsel in the last few days to have access to the records.

MR. STRIPLING: Just a moment, Mr. Hiss. What records have you attempted to obtain which were in the custody of the committee?

MR. HISS: I have attempted to obtain records of leases of premises where I was resident during the period in question. I have attempted to get the records with respect to the Ford automobile that I owned. I am informed that the records with respect to the latter in particular are not in their normal, official location but are in the custody of the committee.

MR. STRIPLING: That is absolutely untrue. The committee has issued no subpoenas upon any realty company nor has it obtained any leases.

It has subpoenaed a photostatic copy of a document from the Department of Motor Vehicles of the District of Columbia. However, the original document is still in the files.

MR. HISS: I am told, Mr. Stripling, that the original document is no longer in the files. I tried to have my counsel have access to it.

MR. STRIPLING: When did you try to secure that document?

MR. HISS: I will have to rely on counsel to say just when they tried.

THE CHAIRMAN: It would be interesting to the committee to know from counsel when you tried to get this document.

MR. DAVIS: A representative of mine tried to get this document yesterday afternoon, I am informed by the representative. I did not myself go to the Motor Vehicle Bureau. He was told that it was photostated at some time prior to yesterday but the document itself had been taken from its normal place yesterday.*

MR. MUNDT: Who was that representative and who told him it was taken from the place and who took it from the place? Let's get down to specific facts. If you were not told yourself, who was your representative?

MR. DAVIS: I am sorry—I am not trying to be evasive—I do not know who the person was that went. I can ascertain who went to the Bureau to find out. I do not know.

MR. MUNDT: You do not know who it was who told you that?

MR. DAVIS: I do not know and I do not know that it was stated that the committee had taken the original. All I know is he was told the original had been removed from its normal place.

MR. MUNDT: But you don't know who told you that or who told the other man that. That is very vague from the standpoint of our committee, you understand.

*If the document had been removed, it was presumably in the custody of a Federal agency.

MR. DAVIS: I understand it is very vague. I do not know who it was. I can ascertain who it was during a recess.

MR. MUNDT: Was he a member of your firm?

MR. DAVIS: He was not a member of my firm.

MR. NIXON: How did you find it out, then?

MR. DAVIS: I was informed.

MR. NIXON: By whom?

MR. DAVIS: I was informed of this—

* * *

MR. NIXON: It would be helpful to the committee if counsel would tell us how he received the information that these records were missing from their normal place. Who told him?

MR. DAVIS: I would be very glad to.

MR. NIXON: Yes.

MR. DAVIS: I was told, as I recollect, by Mr. Fontaine Bradley, who is an attorney in Washington, and whom I had asked while I was in New York to make certain inquiries in Washington in respect to these matters.

MR. MUNDT: Would you please identify the firm of which Mr. Fontaine Bradley is a member?

MR. DAVIS: I believe that Mr. Bradley is a member of the Covington firm.*

MR. NIXON: When did he tell you this?

MR. DAVIS: He told me this last evening when I saw him when I finally got to Washington.

MR. NIXON: Then you know this is the man who told you that, don't you? You said "to the best of my recollection." I mean, if he told you last evening, you certainly know if it was he or somebody else, don't you?

MR. DAVIS: I believe it was he.

MR. NIXON: You believe. Did you have a conversation with him, Mr. Davis?

MR. MUNDT: Mr. Chairman.

THE CHAIRMAN: Mr. Mundt.

MR. MUNDT: I would just like to register a protest at this continuous evasion on the part of these witnesses. I am getting tired of flying halfway across the country to get evasive answers. If

* This is the Washington law firm, two of whose partners were then Donald Hiss and Dean Acheson.

the gentleman doesn't know who told him, let him say, "I don't know." If he knows, let him say "I do know." Let's not say "I believe" or "I think."

* * *

MR. NIXON: I want counsel to take plenty of time to answer the question. I think the question is quite simple.

Last evening somebody told him about these records. Now certainly you can remember who told you last night, Counsel.

MR. DAVIS: Mr. Nixon, there were three people present at this time. There was Mr. Bradley, there was a partner of Mr. Bradley, and there was Mr. Hiss and myself, four persons present, as I remember, at the time of this conversation.*

MR. NIXON: I see.

MR. DAVIS: I think it was Mr. Fontaine Bradley who gave me this information.

MR. NIXON: Who else could it have been?

MR. DAVIS: It is possible it was his partner who was there who gave me the information, but I do not believe that was so.

MR. NIXON: Then it definitely was Mr. Bradley or his partner who gave you the information?

MR. DAVIS: That is to the best of my recollection, and I shouldn't forget what happened last night.

MR. NIXON: Certainly. This conversation you had wasn't a telephone conversation?

MR. DAVIS: It was a person-to-person conversation.

MR. NIXON: Just what did he tell you?

MR. DAVIS: He told me, as I have just stated, that inquiries—and my memory is not certain whether he said the Commissioner of Motor Vehicles, or what the bureau is, the official bureau where you go with respect to getting the certificates of title—inquiry had been made, I think not by him, but by some agent that he sent, to see if we could examine that certificate, and that he ascertained that the certificate itself had been photostated by the committee, I believe, at some prior time, but that the certificate itself had been removed from its customary place and was not available for inspection by our agent at the time we were there.

MR. NIXON: Thank you very much, Counsel.

*This unidentified partner of the Covington firm is still unidentified.

This long exchange has bearing upon two points. From the beginning of the Case, Alger Hiss was surrounded by expert legal talent, sometimes acknowledged, sometimes unacknowledged. Soon his affairs were handled by a battery of counsel. Meanwhile, he posed as a poor young man without resources, presumably in contrast to the affluent editor of *Time*. That line was presently discarded, in part because it was soon common knowledge that Chambers was not affluent, but more importantly, because the Hiss war chest was presently swelled by tens of thousands of dollars from sources, sometimes identified and sometimes unidentified.

Both these points were about to be underlined by the sudden intrusion into the hearing of a hitherto unknown figure, whose permanent and important role in the Hiss Case has never been fully noted. Says the official transcript: "At this point, an unknown person confers with Mr. Davis." The "unknown person" was a short, dark man. As he whispered over Mr. Davis' shoulder, he kept his dull but watchful eyes fixed on the Committee, with somewhat the expression of a small boy who wonders if he is going to be caught with his hand in the cookie jar but decides to risk it. He was challenged.

THE CHAIRMAN: Mr. Counsel, will you please identify the man who came up?

MR. DAVIS: The man who came up is Mr. Harold Rosenwald.

MR. MUNDT: A little further identification, please. Is he counsel?

MR. DAVIS: He is a practicing lawyer in New York City.

MR. MUNDT: His address and the name of his firm?

MR. ROSENWALD: 55 Liberty Street, New York City. The firm is Oseas, Pepper & Segal, O-s-e-a-s, Pepper & Segal. I am employed by them.

MR. HISS: Mr. Chairman, since the committee seems to be very much interested in counsel for giving me any kind of assistance, may I just state that not being a man of considerable means, I have been much gratified by the volunteer assistance of friends, many of whom not unnaturally are lawyers.* Mr. Rosenwald,

*In the early 1930's, Hiss had been a member of the International Juridical Association, of which the late Carol King, a habitual attorney for Communists in trouble, was a moving spirit. The International Juridical Association has been cited as subversive by the Attorney General. Also among its members: Lee Pressman, Abraham Isserman (one of the attorneys for the eleven convicted Communist leaders), Max Loewenthal, author of a recent book attacking the F.B.I.

who has just been identified, is a graduate of the same law school that I am (Harvard Law School). I knew him also in practice in Boston, and have kept in touch with him since. He has been voluntarily assisting me in attempting to get records and similar materials. Mr. Davis, who is with me today, is also a personal friend of some standing, some long standing. I have had some difficulty with respect to continuity of counsel. The first adviser I had, Mr. William Marbury, an old friend in Baltimore, who accompanied me to the other hearing on August 5, was sent within a week or within 10 days, to London by the Government on important business. I have been doing the best I could to get such assistance of a voluntary nature as I possibly could. I think it may be appropriate to put that in, since the committee seems to be very much interested in who are helping. . . .

THE CHAIRMAN: I will say this for the committee. We are very much interested in hearing what you have to say.

This congressional appearance of Mr. Rosenwald was my first glimpse, and practically everybody else's, of that shyly enigmatic figure, who was next to turn up, just as unexpectedly, as a silent member of counsel in Hiss's libel suit against me, who was to be very busy at the defense table in both Hiss trials, and even busier questioning anybody at all who might know Whittaker Chambers. In fact, Rosenwald seemed to be the master spirit of the investigatory side of the Hiss defense. But no inquiry ever shed much light on Rosenwald. During the Hiss Case, one or two articles about him appeared in the press. He was described as a loyal and self-effacing friend who had generously resigned his job to devote his full time to Alger Hiss's cause.

It was the lot of this generous and unassuming friend to be possessed of a manner and a face at once thought-provoking and cryptic. It was, to echo Alger Hiss's phrase, "definitely not an unfamiliar face. There was a certain familiarity about it." I had seen dozens much like it in my time. Perhaps the clue to its familiar type must be sought among the only hard facts I ever heard mentioned about Harold Rosenwald. He had worked for the Department of Justice, where he had been the assistant to Mr. O. John Rogge, an assistant to the Attorney General. The peculiar vehemence of Mr. Rogge's leftist views finally caused him to leave the Justice Department. He is now the legal representative of the Tito Government.

XXVIII

The questions shifted to the leases of Hiss's 28th Street apartment and his P Street house in Georgetown. The importance of this line of questioning had little to do with the leases themselves or with the fact that they would prove that my recollection of the length of my stay at 28th Street was in error by a few weeks and Hiss's recollection was in error by several months. The questions about the leases bore importantly on the 1929 Ford roadster. Two points were involved: 1) if, as was soon clear, I had left the apartment at latest in July, 1935, and had seen Hiss only a few times thereafter, under what circumstances had the Ford, which Hiss had testified to giving me, come back into his possession? 2) did Hiss, as he had also testified, own two cars at the time I was in the apartment? No one could have realized better than Hiss how dangerous those two points were to him.

He did not improve his case by testifying that he had destroyed his leases due to "a certain contraction of possessions," meanwhile complaining that he had been unable to procure the pertinent information. The Committee promptly proved that it was readily available by reading it into the record. And this despite the fact that Hiss had already testified to the assistance of at least three partners of the powerful Covington firm, and the indefatigable Harold Rosenwald, and would soon apologize for not mentioning the names of others who were helping him in his unfruitful efforts. At the same time, the Committee had only three overworked investigators while its editorial and research staff were doubling in the investigation.

MR. NIXON: I understood you to say that you thought the committee should check the leases and also I thought I understood you to say that you had not yet checked the leases yourself. I wanted to be sure I heard you correctly.

MR. HISS: Mr. Nixon, I have not checked the leases myself. I thought I had the leases in my papers in New York.

MR. NIXON: You so testified.

MR. HISS: I said on the 16th I thought they were there. I have now looked in my apartment in New York, and I must have got rid of the leases when I moved from the house into an apartment which meant a certain contraction of possessions. I did get rid of a good many old papers at that time, and apparently the leases were among them. So it has meant going back, first, remembering the real-estate agents I dealt with, and, second, going back to the real-estate agents to find out from them what the actual terms and dates of the leases were. I was asked on the 16th and on the 17th a good many questions by members of the committee and I think by Mr. Stripling as to where I lived at various times. I was not even able to recall the street correctly. To the best of my recollection, I testified that I lived on Twenty-ninth Street. I have now ascertained that it was Twenty-eighth Street. My reference to the leases was that I could not after all these years be expected to remember with accuracy and to be really helpful to the committee in its presumed search for truth and the complete truth unless I did have the opportunity to consult records. But I also told the committee that I was not in any sense going to be evasive. I hope the acting chairman's reference to evasiveness was not in any remote sense an implied reference to me. I went forward, Mr. Nixon, and said, testifying simply on recollection of rather trivial housekeeping details of 14 years ago, I would tell you the best I could recall, and so I did.

MR. NIXON: Then, the point is that you have not checked the leases as of this morning?

MR. HISS: I still have not been able to get hold of all the leases. (Only two were in question.) Some of the leases have been consulted, there have been some telephone conversations with the real-estate people. I have asked counsel to prepare as rapidly as possible a collection of all the available record evidence—photostats, originals, or copies—of all the record evidence on these matters, which it is apparent the committee considers of importance. That has not been completed yet.

MR. NIXON: That is all.

MR. STRIPLING: Mr. Hiss, do you have the lease between you and Mr. Crosley?

MR. HISS: I have never testified that there was any lease between me and Mr. Crosley. I said that it was an oral arrangement; a sublease orally arranged.

MR. STRIPLING: Now, you gave the committee the circumstances under which you met Mr. Crosley. Could you give us the date, the approximate date?

MR. HISS: Again, my best recollection would be—and this is a reconstructed memory trying to recall when I did various things with the Nye committee. I have not even been able to get the list of all the staff of the Nye committee, for example. I would think it must have been either in the late winter of 1934 or the early winter of 1935.

MR. STRIPLING: At this point, I would like to read from your testimony which you gave on August 16.

He then read the particular part of Hiss's testimony as it appears in Chapter XVI of this section of this book.

MR. STRIPLING: Now, is that as you recall it, Mr. Hiss?

MR. HISS: That was the best recollection I had on the day I testified and that is why I so testified. I have since learned that my lease on the house began earlier than I thought and my lease on the apartment terminated somewhat earlier than I thought. The overlap which I remembered, and which was the main thing in my memory, was, according to the best records I have so far been able to check, accurate.

MR. STRIPLING: When did you first move into the P Street house?

MR. HISS: Mr. Stripling, I really think the best way for this committee to get full facts is to go to records, if possible. I have said that several times in these hearings.

THE CHAIRMAN: Mr. Witness.

MR. HISS: I have not been able yet to get—and I will furnish it to the committee as soon as I get it—the actual records of when I took the lease on the P Street house and when I moved into the P Street house.

THE CHAIRMAN: Mr. Hiss, we appreciate your suggestions as to how to conduct these hearings, but if you do not mind, and if the committee does not mind, we have certain questions we would like to proceed with.

MR. HISS: Certainly.

THE CHAIRMAN: Go ahead, Mr. Stripling.

MR. STRIPLING: Mr. Chairman, at this point I would like to read into the record a letter from Sandoz, Inc., real estate and insurance, dated August 20, 1948, from Teresa B. Mileham, who signed herself as a bookkeeper, addressed to Robert E. Stripling, Chief Investigator:

My Dear Mr. Stripling: This is to certify that our records show that we rented 2905 P Street NW., to Priscilla Hiss for 1 year from May 1, 1935, to June 15, 1936, at a monthly rental of $105.

Very truly yours."

Does that refresh your recollection on that at all, Mr. Hiss?

MR. HISS: Mr. Stripling, I would have thought in view of information I have received as to the date during which my tenancy of the apartment on Twenty-eighth Street lasted, that I must have moved into the P Street house a little earlier than the date just read, which I understood to be May 1.

(Mr. Stripling hands letter to Mr. Hiss.)

MR. HISS: (continuing): And again I would like to check all possible records to see whether I moved in before the date of the lease, according to their records, which is sometimes the custom, to be given a month or so in addition to your regular lease, earlier or later, at the beginning preceding the lease or after its termination; so that again I can't testify with any exactness without an opportunity to refresh my recollection by trying to refer to various records which are not easy to get hold of after all this lapse of time.

MR. STRIPLING: Now I believe you testified earlier, Mr. Hiss, that you sublet your apartment on Twenty-eighth Street—that was apartment 42, at 2831 Twenty-eighth NW.,—to George Crosley. Is that correct?

MR. HISS: I did so testify and I did so sublet.

MR. STRIPLING: When did you sublet this apartment to George Crosley?

MR. HISS: My recollection had been that it was at the beginning of the summer. Whether it was a little earlier or a little later than that I couldn't be sure—and again I would want to have access to all the records possible in order to be as accurate as possible.

THE CHAIRMAN: What year?

MR. HISS: What year did what happen?

THE CHAIRMAN: The summer of what year?

MR. STRIPLING: That you sublet the apartment.

MR. HISS: The summer of 1935.

MR. STRIPLING: What was the agreement regarding this apartment between you and Mr. Crosley?

MR. HISS: According to my best recollection, the agreement was that of a simple informal sublease at the cost to me, the privilege of his occupying the premises as long as I had disposition of them, and it has been my recollection from Monday, the 16th of this month, on that I did have the disposition of that apartment or could assure the disposition of that apartment over a period of several months after I moved into 2905 P Street.

MR. STRIPLING: Do you recall just when your lease for the apartment expired?

MR. HISS: No; I do not.

MR. STRIPLING: How long did Mr. Crosley remain in the apartment? Before you answer that, I believe you testified on August 16 on page 52, you were asked by Mr. Nixon: "Can you state again just when he first rented the apartment?" referring to Mr. Crosley. You say "I think it was about June of 1935." Do you recall whether or not it was June?

MR. HISS: My best recollection at the time I testified was it was about June. Whether it was a little earlier or a little later after 14 years or so, I am afraid I just am not able to recall.

MR. STRIPLING: Do you recall how long he remained at the apartment?

MR. HISS: I have no idea. My recollection is that he was entitled, as far as I was concerned, to remain for several months and that I was in a position to assure him that he could remain for several months. Whether he did or not would be no concern of mine.

MR. STRIPLING: At this point, then, Mr. Chairman, I should like to read into the record a letter from Randall H. Hagner & Co., real estate, 1321 Connecticut Avenue, Washington, D.C. The letter is addressed to Robert E. Stripling, chief investigator of the Committee on Un-American Activities, and signed by Mary Petherbridge. The letter reads:

"Dear Mr. Stripling: Our records show that Alger Hiss made application to us through the manager, Mrs. W. M. Jeffers, on May 29, 1934, for apartment 42, 2831 Twenty-eighth Street NW. His tenancy began on July 1, 1934, for 1 year. We assume from the application that a lease was made. However, our old leases have been destroyed. Mr. Hiss vacated on June 28, 1935. His previous address given at that time was 3411 O Street NW. The number of occupants was listed as two adults and one child. This apartment was vacant for the month of July. On August 1, 1935, it was rented to W. E. Isemann.

Very truly yours."

MR. HISS: May I say it is apparent that the committee has been better staffed with people to inquire into records than I have been. May I also say with reference to my earlier statement about the assistance of friends, that I did not mean to exclude any friends who have been helpful by not mentioning their names. . . .

MR. NIXON: I think that from the testimony Mr. Hiss has given and from the documents Mr. Stripling has presented that it is very clear as to what these terminal dates for this lease were. As I understand it, Mr. Hiss' lease on the house he moved to on P Street started on May 1; is that correct?

MR. STRIPLING: That is correct.

MR. NIXON: Mr. Hiss has suggested he might have moved into that house before, that as a courtesy he might have received a month or so free rent before he moved into the house, but the lease as far as the records show—he first had his rental contract on his new house on May 1. You have also indicated that the apartment which he sublet to Mr. Crosley was rerented to a new tenant, not Mr. Crosley, commencing August 1. Is that correct?

MR. STRIPLING: That is correct.

MR. NIXON: Now, when did Mr. Hiss' lease on the apartment run out? Have you put that matter into the record yet?

MR. STRIPLING: That is in the record. It expired on the 28th of June.

MR. NIXON: Mr. Hiss' lease on the apartment expired on the 28th of June?

MR. STRIPLING: That is right.

MR. NIXON: In other words, the amount of time for which his sublease could have run would be approximately from May 1 to June 28. That was the period at which Mr. Hiss had the disposal of the apartment and in which he could have been in the new house. Is that correct?

MR. STRIPLING: That is what it appears from the records.

MR. HISS: Is that a question to me or to Mr. Stripling?

MR. NIXON: I am making the statement. If you have objection to the statement, you are perfectly welcome to make it.

MR. HISS: The only thing I would like to say, Mr. Nixon, first, in general there seems to me to be relatively little disagreement as between the testimony of Mr. Chambers as he now calls himself and me with respect to the period and the circumstances of our acquaintance . . . The important issues, the important charges are not questions of leases, but questions of whether I was a

Communist, and it was to try to get the issues raised that are the real issues—it seems to be topsy-turvy to be talking only about leases, Mr. Nixon; in such a serious charge as this it seems to me we should be getting after the question of my record and what did people who worked closely and intimately with me think of me.

THE CHAIRMAN: Mr. Hiss, I would like to say again that the committee appreciates your suggestions as to how to conduct these hearings, but we do have certain questions to ask and, if you don't mind, Mr. Nixon will continue questioning if he has any more questions.

MR. NIXON: Yes; I have. I would like to comment upon Mr. Hiss' statement that the only issue in this hearing today is whether or not Mr. Hiss was a Communist. The issue in this hearing today is whether or not Mr. Hiss or Mr. Chambers has committed perjury before this committee, as well as whether Mr. Hiss is a Communist.

Now, as far as these what are termed housekeeping details by Mr. Hiss are concerned, it isn't the intention of the committee to hold Mr. Hiss to exact dates, it isn't the intention of the committee to hold him to exact details on matters that happened years ago, but it certainly is the intention of the committee to question both Mr. Hiss and Mr. Chambers very closely on the matter of their acquaintanceship, because it is on that issue that the truth or falsity of the statements made by Mr. Hiss and Mr. Chambers will stand or fall.

MR. HISS: May I say, Mr. Nixon, that that does not seem to me a very rational basis for determining credibility. Obviously, the committee may ask the questions it chooses.

MR. NIXON: Mr. Hiss, you are an attorney. I think you are aware probably of the standard instruction which is given to the jury on cases of credibility of witnesses. That instruction, as I recall it, is that if [in] any matter a witness is found to be telling an untruth on any question which is material and which is raised during the course of the court's proceedings, his credibility on other questions is also suspect. Now, as far as this matter is concerned, you, yourself, have made an issue of the fact as to (1) whether you knew Chambers at all—that issue has now been resolved; and (2) how well you knew Chambers and whether you knew him as a Communist. That is the purpose of this questioning now. Now, I would appreciate it if you would again comment upon the matter of this lease. Do I understand that May 1 to June 28 would be approximately the length of the rental agreement with Mr. Crosley?

MR. HISS: May I refer back to what I said earlier this morning, that my recollection in terms of an impression about these events is that I considered that I had the disposition or could assure the disposition of the Twenty-eighth Street apartment for a period of several months. Whether my lease overlapped—whether my legal lease overlapped my moving into the P Street apartment by several months, or whether it was somewhat less than that, and I was aware that anyone who wanted to get the apartment month to month or any other way after my lease expired during the summer, whether that was part of my thinking at the time I frankly can't tell in terms of details.

The significant thing in my memory is my recollection that I was in position to assure Crosley of several months' occupancy of the apartment which I had been living in on Twenty-eighth Street.

MR. NIXON: I think we can cut through it with these short questions: You did not lease the apartment to Crosley until you had moved into the other house; is that correct?

MR. HISS: That is my best recollection.

MR. NIXON: Your lease on the other house according to the records began on May 1. You will agree with that?

MR. HISS: That is what the records seem to show. I have not seen the records myself.

MR. NIXON: We have the letter which Mr. Stripling just handed you. If the records show that, you will agree that the records are correct on that point?

MR. HISS: I have no reason for questioning the records.

MR. NIXON: You suggested that we go to the records.

MR. HISS: I didn't hear you.

MR. NIXON: You suggested that we go to the records.

MR. HISS: I have, indeed.

MR. NIXON: That is what we have done, and it shows that lease began on May 1.

MR. HISS: I have been trying to go to them, too, Mr. Nixon.

MR. NIXON: Certainly. The records also show that your lease on the apartment ran out on June 28. It is quite apparent, then, that the time Mr. Crosley could have stayed in this apartment was a period of approximately 8 to 9 weeks from May 1 and June 28.

MR. HISS: Mr. Nixon, I doubt if this is the occasion for any argumentation as to what the facts mean.

MR. NIXON: I am not arguing.

MR. HISS: But I think I heard Mr. Stripling read that the apartment, according to Randall Hagner—were they the agents?

MR. STRIPLING: Yes.

MR. HISS: According to their records was not leased to anyone during the month of July; so there could be a third month when, if Mr. Crosley had wanted to stay on in that apartment, he could presumably have done so by arrangements with Randall Hagner.

MR. STRIPLING: Mr. Chairman, this might clarify that point. According to the records of the Potomac Electric Co., the electricity was turned off at the Twenty-eighth Street apartment on June 29, 1935.

MR. NIXON: When was the gas turned off in that apartment?

MR. STRIPLING: It was turned off on June 26, 1935.

MR. NIXON: June 26. If Mr. Crosley did stay in that apartment another month up to August 1, he stayed there without gas or electricity.

For a few moments, the questioning shifted to another point: had Hiss been able to discover anyone else who had ever known Whittaker Chambers as George Crosley?

MR. STRIPLING: Mr. Hiss, George Crosley, who you testified you first met in 1934—do you know of anyone here in Washington who knew him as George Crosley?

MR. HISS: In answer to that question, Mr. Stripling, I have naturally among the very many other things that I have been trying to check in the few days since Monday of last week, I have been trying to run down the list of staff members of the Senate Committee Investigating the Munitions Industry. As far as I can find out, there is no one single official list anywhere now available. I have recalled certain of the members of the staff. I recalled three names offhand of people that Crosley might have met in addition to me around the committee. I mentioned Mr. Raushenbush, the chief investigator. He is away on vacation. I have seen in the press that the press reached him and he doesn't have any recollection of Crosley. I want to talk personally to Mr. Raushenbush. I want to see if he can recall from my description of the circumstances under which I knew Crosley more than he has told the press. I recalled the name of Robert Wohlford.

MR. STRIPLING: You gave both of these names to the committee in New York?

MR. HISS: Yes; I did—who was also a member of the staff. I recalled my off-the-cuff recollection. He is now in New York, I understand. I have asked friends of mine to talk to Bob Wohlford. I remembered also the name of Miss Elsie Gullender, who was, as it were, the chief receptionist of the committee. She was Mr. Raushenbush's secretary and acted as sort of an over-all chief of the secretarial staff . . . I have been informed that Miss Elsie Gullender is now dead. I am not sure that is the fact. I want, if possible, to locate Miss Gullender.

* * *

MR. MUNDT: Mr. Hiss, is this a fair summary, then, of your position up to now? That as of today you have not found anybody other than your wife who ever knew this man over here under the name of George Crosley?

MR. HISS: I received a telephone call—rather, one of my counsel did—from someone, a woman, who said she had known George Crosley at this time, that she was fearful of getting her employer in Dutch or something by publicity. We were not able to trace the call. She may have been imagining. So far, the answer to your question is: I have not yet been able to find any witness other than my wife who remembers him as George Crosley.

MR. MUNDT: Let me ask this question. The possibility would seem very plausible to me that since Mr. Crosley, as you call him, lived in your home for awhile while he was getting his furniture transferred, that your brother Donald undoubtedly visited your home frequently. Have you ever conferred with Donald to see whether he knew this man as George Crosley?

MR. HISS: I have asked him and he has no recollection.

MR. MUNDT: He had no recollection?

MR. HISS: No. . . .

MR. STRIPLING: Now, Mr. Chairman, the three names the witness has mentioned—Elsie Gullender, Robert Wohlford, Stephen Raushenbush—were the three that he gave the committee in New York, and we asked him if he could furnish us the names of three people to corroborate his statement that Whittaker Chambers was known to him as George Crosley in 1934 and '35. The New York Herald Tribune carried a story which stated that they had communicated with Mr. Raushenbush and he had no recollection of it. As Mr. Hiss has stated, according to our investigation, Elsie Gullender died September 24, 1946. We have been endeavoring to locate Robert Wohlford. His office here at the Department of Justice had advised us that he was ill. We have sent numerous telegrams, all of which have been returned.

Now, because Mr. Hiss stated Mr. Crosley was a freelance writer for American magazine and other publications—

MR. HISS: May I interrupt? What I think Mr. Stripling has been stating in summary is exactly my recollection of my testimony. I did not testify as a fact that Mr. Crosley wrote for American magazine. I testified that my best recollection was that he had told me that American magazine was one of the magazines he hoped to sell his freelance articles about the Munitions Committee to.

MR. STRIPLING: Well, Mr. Chairman, we asked the Library of Congress, Director of Legislative Reference Service, to check their files for any articles by George Crosley.

The following letter was received from Ernest S. Griffith, Director, Legislative Reference Service, addressed to Mr. Benjamin Mandel, Director of Research: "Dear Mr. Mandel: In response to your request for any writings by George Crosley, the following sources have been examined with reference to George Crosley or Crossley. The results of the search are indicated.

"Readers Guide to Periodical Literature, January 29-June 1941—No reference. Public Catalogue—Two references, one to a book of poems written by G. Crosley in 1905, the other to a scientific pamphlet on ultra-violet light by G. E. Crosley, M.D., in 1936. Copyright Division—No additional references.

"Any further searching you may suggest, we shall be glad to undertake. Sincerely yours,

"Ernest S. Griffith,
Director, Legislative Reference Service."

I also have a letter here, Mr. Chairman, from the American magazine that states that they have never published any articles by George Crosley.

At this point, a folded note was passed back to me from the press table. It contained a penciled question from James Reston, the learned Washington correspondent of the New York *Times,* and one of the two newsmen* who, when John Foster Dulles asked them their opinion of Alger Hiss as a possible candidate for president of the Carnegie Endowment, both agreed that he would be a very good choice. Reston's note said, as nearly as I can recall it: "Are you the G. Crosley who wrote a book of poems in 1905?" Other than Bert Andrews' visit, it was practically the press's first communication with me since the Case began. I thought that it must be a wry joke. But a glance at Reston's face assured me that it was not. I sent back the note with what seemed to me the obvious answer written on it: "I was born in 1901. In 1905, I was four." Later, Reston was to accuse me of refusing to answer his question.

XXIX

While the questions and answers were droning on, guards, from time to time, cautiously opened the heavy door of the hearing room and admitted one or two people who somehow wedged themselves among the ranks of those who were standing around the sides and back of the packed hall. Each time the door opened, it disclosed a double line of others still doggedly waiting to get in.

In the hearing room, the spectators had at first been restless, puzzled by the long exchange about leases. But when the Committee snapped the renting and utilities evidence into the record, there was an answering snap of tension out front. From that moment, people began to sense that the questioning was not aimless. It was leading somewhere. Where it was leading they began to realize when Stripling suddenly shifted to the Ford roadster, which, nineteen days

* The other was Bert Andrews, chief of the New York *Herald Tribune's* Washington Bureau. Andrews, a Pulitzer prize winner and author of *Washington Witch Hunt,* a book highly critical of the House Committee on Un-American Activities, had paid a visit to my farm, together with Richard Nixon, shortly after I first appeared before the Committee. Distinctly skeptical of me to begin with, Bert Andrews soon became convinced, as a result of his probing talk with me, and a close scrutiny of the testimony and developments in the case, that Hiss was lying. It was Andrews who first suggested the use of the lie-detector test to the Committee, and he was to play a crucial role in bringing the vacationing Nixon back into action after I had produced the so-called "Baltimore papers" (the State Department documents). Both Bert and his wife were great morale stiffeners to my family and me. I can still hear Nadine Andrews' voice, exhorting me by long distance at the time when I was testifying at the first Hiss trial: "Drop that Quaker thee and thou stuff, and begin to fight back!"

before, I had testified that Hiss, against the wishes of the underground, had turned over to the open Communist Party. Now the zeal that had then moved him rose up to confound him—first in the guise of one of the glaring discrepancies in his story, his claim that he had given George Crosley the Ford because Hiss then owned two cars. Now Hiss's endless evasiveness, which had already surprised, then exasperated, the many who had come to see him demolish the Committee and his uncouth accuser with a few crisp sentences, led at last to dreadful laughter at his plight.

MR. STRIPLING: Now, Mr. Hiss, I should like to read now from your testimony before the committee on August 16, page 53: referring to Mr. Crosley.

"MR. STRIPLING: What kind of automobile did that fellow have?"

"MR. HISS: No kind of automobile. I sold him an automobile. I had an old Ford that I threw in with the apartment and had been trying to trade it in and get rid of it. I had an old, old Ford we had kept for sentimental reasons. We got it just before we were married in 1929.

"MR. STRIPLING: Was it a model A or model T?

"MR. HISS: Early A model with a trunk on the back, a slightly collegiate model.

"MR. STRIPLING: What color?

"MR. HISS: Dark blue. It wasn't very fancy, but it had a sassy little trunk on the back.

"MR. NIXON: You sold that car?

"MR. HISS: I threw it in. He wanted a way to get around, and I said, 'Fine; I want to get rid of it. I have another car, and we kept it for sentimental reasons, not worth a damn. I let him have it along with the rent.' "

MR. STRIPLING (continuing): Now, would you give the committee the arrangements of this lease again, Mr. Hiss.

MR. HISS: Of the lease of the apartment?

MR. STRIPLING: That is right. And the car, the manner in which you threw the car in.

MR. HISS: My best recollection is that at the time, or shortly after we first talked about Crosley's subletting my apartment, he said that he wished to get a car because his family would be with him while he was in Washington. I think he asked if you could rent a car, and my best recollection is that I told him that I had an old car which I would let him have, a car which had practically no financial value. That is the best recollection I have on the car transaction after all these years.

MR. MUNDT: Was the reason that that car had no value to you the fact that you had another automobile at the time?

MR. HISS: My best recollection is that at some time, Mr. Mundt, I had both a Plymouth and this old Ford. Whether that overlap occurred prior to my letting Crosley use the Ford, I cannot recall with positiveness. I do have a very definite, although general, recollection that I had both a Ford and a Plymouth for a period of time, with the Ford of no use, deteriorating, being left outdoors.

MR. STRIPLING: Now, Mr. Chairman, I should like to read from—

MR. HÉBERT: Mr. Stripling, may I interrupt there to sort of pursue this a little further, with regard to what Mr. Mundt has asked Mr. Hiss? Mr. Hiss, you would remember if you had two automobiles at one time; would you not?

MR. HISS: I say I do remember that I did have two automobiles at one time. That made quite an impression on me.

MR. HÉBERT: It made an impression on you that you owned two automobiles at one time?

MR. HISS: That is right. But, as to the particular time when I had the two automobiles, it was sometime during this general period. As to the particular time, without consulting the records, I am not able to testify with positiveness.

MR. HÉBERT: I want to get this clear. In other words, you would not have given up the mode of transporation if you did not have any transportation yourself.

MR. HISS: Unless I was not going to need automobile transportation for a period of time.

MR. HÉBERT: Then the logical assumption would be that you did have two automobiles at the same time that you gave this man Crosley your automobile.

MR. HISS: That is my best recollection. Whether it is accurate in detail I will know better when I get the records and can attempt to refresh my recollection, Mr. Hébert.

MR. STRIPLING: Now, Mr. Chairman, let me put the remainder of the testimony regarding the ownership of the automobile which is on page 56.

"MR. NIXON: You gave this Ford car to Crosley?

"MR. HISS: Threw it in along with the apartment and charged the rent and threw the car in at the same time.

"MR. NIXON: In other words, added a little to the rent to cover the car?

"MR. HISS: No; I think I charged him exactly what I was paying for the rent and threw the car in in addition. I don't think I got any compensation.

"MR. STRIPLING: You just gave him the car?

"MR. HISS: I think the car just went right in with it. I don't remember whether we had settled on the terms of the rent before the car question came up, or whether it came up and then on the basis of the car and the apartment I said, 'Well, you ought to pay the full rent.'"

On page 58 the record continues, referring to the car:

"MR. STRIPLING: What kind of a bill of sale did you give Crosley?

"MR. HISS: I think I just turned over—in the District you get a certificate of title, I think it is. I think I simply turned it over to him.

"MR. STRIPLING: Handed it to him?

"MR. HISS: Yes.

"MR. STRIPLING: No evidence of any transfer. Did he record the title?

"MR. HISS: That I haven't any idea. This is a car which has been sitting on the streets in snows for a year or two. I once got a parking fine because I forgot where it was parked. We were using the other car."

MR. STRIPLING: (continuing): Now, Mr. Hiss, is that the testimony, according to your best recollection?

MR. HISS: That testimony was according to my best recollection at the time I gave it, and that is why I gave it. I have not yet been able to get the record, as my counsel has testified. We have not been able to ascertain from the Motor Vehicle Bureau people what their records show with respect to that car.

MR. STRIPLING: What did Mr. Crosley do with this car, do you know?

MR. HISS: I frankly do not recall. It is possible that he used it; it is even possible that he returned it to me after using it. I really would not be sure of the details. My impression and recollection was that I got rid of it by giving it to him, but if the records show that it bounced back to me from him, that would not surprise me either.

Stripling drew the pin, counted carefully and tossed his atomizing question: "Well, as a matter of fact, Mr. Hiss, you sold the car a year later, did you not?" At the pit of my own stomach, I felt a stir of that nausea inevitable when a man sees any creature mortally trapped by another. It was intensified by Hiss's trapped answer.

MR. HISS: Not to my recollection. I have no definite recollection of it.

MR. STRIPLING: You do not recall selling the car?

MR. HISS: I have no definite recollection.

Stripling stalked the question from the other side: "Did you have a Plymouth during this period? Did you have another car?"

MR. HISS: My recollection is that I did have a Plymouth during part of the time that I had a Ford.

MR. STRIPLING: Now, Mr. Chairman, I have here an application for a certificate of title of the Motor Vehicles and Traffic Bureau of the District of Columbia, wherein it states that "Alger Hiss, 2905 P Street, NW, purchased or acquired the above-described car: Plymouth, new, model PJ; year 1935; body, sedan." It gives the serial number, engine number and states: "How secured: Conditional sale; date, September 7, 1935, purchased from the Smoot Motor Co., Inc."

Since the leases had already proved that I had been out of the 28th Street apartment at latest by the end of June, 1935, Hiss could not have given or sold me the Ford roadster as part of the apartment deal.

MR. NIXON: Mr. Hiss, your recollection is still that you gave the car to Crosley as part of the apartment deal; is that correct?

MR. HISS: My recollection is as definite as it can be after this lapse of time, Mr. Nixon, that as I was able to give him the use of the apartment, I also and simultaneously, I think, although it could possibly have been a little later, gave him the use of the model A 1929 old Ford. That is my best recollection.

MR. NIXON: That was in the spring of 1935?

MR. HISS: My best recollection is that the car and the apartment transactions were simultaneous. That I cannot be sure of without checking the records more thoroughly.

MR. NIXON: Well, there were facts, as I recall, just checking through the record, 18 occasions in which you were asked the specific question, specifically about this on Monday and Tuesday in the record, as to whether you had given him the car, sold him the car, threw it in, given him the title, and as to whether it was part of the apartment deal, and in each case you said, "Yes," and at that time, you did not qualify your answers with "to the best of my recollection."

MR. HISS: Mr. Nixon—excuse me.

MR. NIXON: Proceed; I am sorry.

MR. HISS: It is my recollection that on the 16th and on the 17th I informed the committee that I had not been able to check my records.

MR. NIXON: On the leases.

MR. HISS: At one point I said to the committee that for them to ask me questions about various personal details of long ago did not seem to me entirely fair to me, because of the various leaks that had been occurring with respect to supposed secret testimony. I said that in spite of those reservations, if the committee wanted me to testify as to the best of my recollection, unsupported by records, I would, of course, do so, and I remember Mr. Hébert particularly spoke up and said he did want me to, and so did you, and I said, on that understanding of what I had said, made no difference to the committee, they still wanted me to testify, and on the basis of recollection, after all these years, I was perfectly prepared to testify. I think the record would show that, Mr. Nixon, and I am glad the entire record is going to be made generally available to the public and not just excerpts, which, in the past, have somehow reached the press, and which today are being put in out of context by Mr. Stripling.

MR. NIXON: Mr. Hiss, in that connection, I think the record should show that you requested and have received, a full copy of your testimony that you have given before this committee, both in public and in executive session; is that correct?

MR. HISS: May I answer that question by saying it was a long, hard pull to get that testimony. . . .*

MR. NIXON: Well, the point is, Mr. Hiss, that you got the testimony, didn't you, and you have had it for 5 days?

MR. HISS: I have had the testimony since Friday afternoon.

MR. NIXON: All the testimony that you have given before the committee.

MR. HISS: That is correct.

MR. NIXON: That is correct. Now, returning to the automobile, did you give Crosley a car?

MR. HISS: I gave Crosley, according to my best recollection—

MR. NIXON: Well, now, just a moment on that point. I do not want to interrupt you on that "to the best of my recollection," but you certainly can testify, "Yes" or "No" as to whether you gave Crosley a car. How many cars have you given away in your life, Mr. Hiss? (Laughter.) That is a serious question.

MR. HISS: I have only had one old car of a financial value of $25 in my life. That is the car that I let Crosley have the use of.

MR. NIXON: This was a car that had a certain sentimental meaning to you, I think you said.

MR. HISS: And that is why I had not been prepared previously to accept merely $25 for it.

MR. NIXON: That is right.

MR. HISS: I was more interested in having it used than in merely getting $25 for it.

MR. NIXON: And this car, which had a sentimental value to you, was the only car you ever gave away in your life?

MR. HISS: It is not only the only car that I ever gave away in my life, it is the only car of that kind that I have described that I ever had.

MR. NIXON: I see. And you cannot recall whether or not you did give Crosley that car?

MR. HISS: Mr. Nixon, according to my best recollection I definitely gave Crosley the use of the car, as I was able to give him the use of my apartment.

MR. MUNDT: May I interrupt just a minute? On page 53 of these hearings which took place in New York, at which I was not

* I never at any time asked for, or received, a copy of my own testimony, reading it first, like everybody else, as a printed public document.

present, the last 2 days, I, too, have read all of the testimony in this whole case, and you were asked the question "What kind of automobile did that fellow have," the man you called Crosley, and you said, "No kind of automobile. I sold him an automobile."

Now, Mr. Hiss, I am trying to get at the truth of this, and I wish you would make a statement and stand by it. Once you say, "I sold him an automobile, period." Now, you come here and say "I gave him the use of the car," and then you say "I cannot tell whether or not after he had the car he gave it back to me or not."

Well, now, in 1934 and 1935 we were in a depression; automobiles were not so numerous and so plentiful that a Government employee would forget what happened to the cars that he had in his possession. You certainly know whether or not you gave Crosley an automobile; you know whether or not Crosley gave that car back, and we want the truth, that is all.

MR. HISS: Mr. Mundt, I am as interested in getting at the truth of this matter as any member of this committee can be, and I shall do all I possibly can, whatever it costs me, within my means, to get at the truth.

MR. MUNDT: Then, tell us the truth.

MR. HISS: Now, what is the nature of your question? Will you repeat it, please, because I paid more attention to the embellishments—

MR. MUNDT: Did you not testify in New York under oath to the effect that "I sold him—Crosley—an automobile?" I find it here in the printed testimony which we are now releasing to the public at the request of the committee, and it is your request. . . .

MR. HISS: What is the specific question? The embellishments to your question made more impression on me than the question.

MR. MUNDT: There are no embellishments, and I ask you: Did you testify under oath in New York—

MR. HISS: I certainly did.

MR. MUNDT: As follows: "What kind of automobile did that fellow have?" Pointing at Crosley. And you said, "No kind of automobile. I sold him an automobile." Did you say that or not?

MR. HISS: If the record says I said it—

MR. MUNDT: The record says that.

MR. HISS: I do not challenge the record.

MR. MUNDT: Your counsel can look at page 53; there it is, it is in the record.

MR. HISS: Mr. Mundt, there may be one or two inaccuracies in the record which we will have to correct.

MR. MUNDT: Is that an inaccuracy?

MR. HISS: That is not an inaccuracy in the record. I have complete confidence in Mr. Banister as a reporter.

MR. MUNDT: You also know whether or not Mr. Crosley gave you back the automobile you sold him. You said this car had a good sentimental value to you, you had kept it a long time. You certainly know, and we know that you know, whether you got that car back. We want you to tell us the truth, that is all.

MR. HISS: You know a great deal, Mr. Mundt.

MR. MUNDT: It is very hard to know very much about this evasive type of testimony, but I am trying to get at the truth.

Congressman Nixon then read into the record all of Hiss's past testimony with respect to turning the Ford roadster over to me, and summarized it.

MR. NIXON: Mr. Chairman, those are the references to the car, and there are these points that I think are significant:

In the first place, we note that Mr. Hiss not only once but at least twice used the word "sold" in referring to the car.

In the second place, we note that there was discussion concerning a title, a transfer of title. A transfer of title on a car is a matter which is discussed when you are selling a car to another person, and transferring it rather than a case where you are loaning the car to another person; and Mr. Hiss discussed the transfer of title along that line.

Mr. Hiss, throughout this testimony, used the words "get rid of" and he used the words "threw it in," and in answer to a question concerning the words "You gave him the car," his answers were as the record has been read.

Now, I have read those portions from the record because I think that Mr. Hiss is entitled to have the entire record on the car read in at this point, and I wanted the committee to know what the references were.

I will say for myself that I am amazed to hear Mr. Hiss say this morning that he can only now testify to the best of his recollection as to whether he ever gave Crosley a car at all, that he is not sure as to whether or not he transferred the car to Crosley, that he might have given it to him for his use only, and that he is not even sure when the transaction occurred, and I think Mr. Hiss should be given every opportunity to explain just what his recollection was as to this car at the present time, and if he wants to change his testimony, that he change it, and tell us exactly what did happen to that car.

MR. HISS: Mr. Nixon, I am surprised if not amazed that you said just now that I testified this morning that I could not remember whether I had ever let Mr. Crosley have the use of my car. I don't think I did so testify, Mr. Nixon.

MR. NIXON: Mr. Hiss, since you have raised that point, you will recall that when I asked you, did you give Crosley a car, you said: "Mr. Nixon, to the best of my recollection, I did."

MR. HISS: Right.

MR. NIXON: And I said:

"Mr. Hiss, certainly on this point, you need not qualify your answer with the words 'to the best of my recollection.' If you gave him a car, you gave him a car, and you should be able to give a categorical answer to the question."

Now, I ask you again, just so that the record will be clear, did you give Crosley a car? And if you can answer the question, "Yes" or "No," I think the committee would be glad to get the answer.

MR. HISS: Mr. Nixon, it is evident that the committee has had access to far more record information than I have had.

MR. NIXON: Mr. Hiss, do you have to have records in order to know whether or not you gave a car away, the only car you ever gave away in your life?

MR. HISS: No; Mr. Nixon, I have testified, and I repeat my testimony, that my best recollection—and to have an exact recollection of trivial housekeeping details of 14 years ago, when I was a very busy man, doing more important things than these matters you are asking me to testify to about this morning, and I have been a relatively busy man since, it does not seem to me, being as objective as I can about it, that it is unusual for a man to preface his statements about the details by which he gave the use of a car, under the circumstances I have described, to a man who meant nothing in particular to him by the words "to the best of my recollection." Now, I do think the committee has had access to more records. It has had a fuller staff than I . . . .

MR. NIXON: My point on the car is, is your testimony now that you gave Crosley a car, or is it that you did not give him a car?

MR. HISS: Mr. Nixon, my testimony, I believe from the beginning, based upon the best recollection I have, is that I gave Crosley the use of the car, as I gave him the use of the apartment. Now, whether I transferred title to him in a legal, formal sense, whether he returned the car to me in connection with my upbraiding him for not having repaid various small loans, and the loans stick in my memory as of more significance than the rental of the house itself, because that rental did not involve anything that I was going to get from any other source in any event, a couple of months left over, a couple of months in the summertime, for an apartment in Washington—that was not a very great financial asset in those days.

MR. NIXON: Well, now, is your testimony this morning then that you did not give Crosley the car, that you gave him the use of the car?

MR. HISS: Mr. Nixon, I have testified, and I repeat it, that my best recollection is that I gave Crosley the use of the car. Whether I gave him the car outright, whether the car came back, I don't know.

MR. NIXON: You do not know whether you had the possession of this car after Crosley left you?

MR. HISS: That, I am afraid, I cannot recall. I do recall having a Plymouth and a Ford at the same time for some months, not just a few days. I do recall the Ford sitting around because it was not being used, the tires going down because it was just sitting on the street.

MR. NIXON: In fact, you have testified that that is the reason you gave Crosley the car, because you did have the two cars.

MR. HISS: I testified that that was the reason, I believe, the car was of no financial consideration to me, Mr. Nixon, during the period we are talking about.

MR. NIXON: Yes, Mr. Hiss. You will recall I had just read the testimony where you said "I gave Crosley the car because I had a new one."

MR. HISS: That is my best recollection.

MR. NIXON: In other words, this transaction in which you gave this car to Crosley occurred after you got your new car, is that correct?

MR. HISS: That is my recollection, Mr. Nixon. Whether my recollection is accurate or not, I frankly do not know without consulting records which are not available to me.

MR. NIXON: Now, is your testimony then that you did give Crosley the use of the car?

MR. HISS: That is my testimony, Mr. Nixon.

MR. NIXON: On that point you are sure?

MR. HISS: As sure as I can be of any of these details of 14 years ago, Mr. Nixon.

MR. NIXON: Mr. Hiss—

MR. HISS: Have you ever had occasion to have people ask you continuously and over and over again what you did on the night of June 5, 1934 or 1935? It is a novel experience to me, Mr. Nixon.

MR. NIXON: Mr. Hiss, I will answer the question. I will tell you this: That if I had given anybody the use of a car for a period of 2 months, I would remember.

MR. HISS: Well, I have testified to you that I do recall that.

MR. NIXON: All right. Now, your testimony is that you did give Crosley the car for a period of 2 months. When did that occur?

MR. HISS: My best recollection is that it coincided with the sublease. I am not positive that it occurred then, rather than in the fall or some other time.

MR. NIXON: And you do not know whether it occurred at the time of the sublease or in connection with that transaction?

MR. HISS: My recollection is that it occurred because it is fixed in my memory in a rather vague way as connected with the lease. Whether it preceded or followed or was simultaneous, I am afraid I am not able to testify with exactness.

MR. STRIPLING: Mr. Chairman—

MR. NIXON: Just a moment. Mr. Hiss, it is not likely that you would have given the car to Crosley after he failed to pay the rent, is it?

MR. HISS: I do not recall the details of when I concluded he was a fourflusher.

MR. NIXON: Well, now, you have testified that he went—

MR. HISS: It was sometime—not after this.

MR. NIXON: Your testimony was that you had seen Mr. Crosley after he failed to pay the rent.

MR. HISS: Yes; I feel quite confident I saw him some time after the sublease transaction.

MR. NIXON: Now, do I understand you to say that you might have loaned Crosley a car for a couple of months after he failed to pay the rent?

MR. HISS: I might have, if I had considered that his reasons for not paying were as plausible as his reasons had been for not paying back small loans, because the rent was not a major consideration in my mind. Of that I feel quite confident.

MR. NIXON: When were the small loans made?

MR. HISS: Again, Mr. Nixon, I am testifying from the best of my recollection, which I have certainly in the course of the last few days done my very best to go over and over again. I think I loaned Crosley a total, in small amounts, of $25 or $30. Whether they were made prior to the sublease, some of them after the sublease, I just frankly do not recall with exactness. But at some stage I reached the conclusion that this had better be terminated, that I was being used, that my kindness was being abused.

MR. NIXON: And your testimony then is that the car—that you are not sure that the car was tied in to the rental transaction; you think it might not have been.

MR. HISS: It could have been tied in toward the end, it could have been tied in toward the beginning. My best recollection is that there is a connection between the two transactions.

MR. NIXON: Could it have taken place several months after the rental transaction?

MR. HISS: Mr. Nixon, it could have.

MR. NIXON: You mean several months after he had refused to pay the rent?

MR. HISS: After he failed to pay the rent.

MR. NIXON: Well, didn't you ask him for the rent?

MR. HISS: Mr. Nixon, I don't recall at any time his ever refusing, ever saying, "I just am not going to pay." Quite the contrary, he was always going to pay at some time.

MR. NIXON: How long after he moved out of his apartment did you decide he was a dead beat?

MR. HISS: Mr. Nixon, I am not able to testify with exactness on that.

MR. NIXON: But you think it is possible that you loaned him a car or gave him a car after he failed to pay the rent?

MR. HISS: I may very well have given him the use of the car even though he had not paid the rent at that particular time.

MR. NIXON: And your testimony is that this man was simply a casual acquaintance.

MR. HISS: This man was an acquaintance. Under the circumstances this man was an acquaintance, under the circumstances to which I have testified.

MR. NIXON: You said he was not a guest in your home. You objected when Mr. Stripling used that phrase.

MR. HISS: That is correct.

MR. NIXON: You objected when there was any suggestion that Mr. Crosley was a friend of yours, and you are now testifying that it is possible that you gave him a car after he failed to pay the rent.

MR. HISS: Yes, Mr. Nixon.

MR. NIXON: All right.

MR. MUNDT: Mr. Chairman, I think we can resolve this matter of a car by a very simple question, and I want to say, first of all, that it is certainly inconceivable, Mr. Hiss, that you would not know some of the details of this automobile in the manner in which you have described it. You have described it as a car that was purchased about the time of your marriage, that you had a sentimental value connected with it, that, I say, is understandable. You say that it had been around for a considerable period of time, and you no longer had a need for it because you had another automobile, and so you either sold or gave or loaned the automobile to the man that you identify as Mr. Crosley. Now, that is a correct summation, I believe, of your position up to now.

MR. HISS: It sounds to me quite correct.

MR. MUNDT: And I want to ask you this question, and on this one, Mr. Hiss, you will not have to consult the records, and I certainly hope that you will not have to use the phrase "to the best of my recollection," which you have used over 75 times thus far before this committee. This one you should be able to say yes or no to. Did you ever dispose of that 1929 automobile to anybody else in any way besides to Mr. George Crosley?

MR. HISS: Mr. Mundt, I would hate to disappoint you in any expectation.

MR. MUNDT: You have already done that, but answer the question.

MR. HISS: I am not able, without consulting the records, to testify with exactness or finality as to the way in which I ultimately completely disposed of my interest in that automobile.

MR. MUNDT: You have no memory at all of having disposed of the car in any other way except by this series of three possibilities by which you conveyed it to Mr. Crosley? Would you like to have this committee believe, Mr. Hiss, actually believe, that you cannot remember how you finally disposed of an automobile that had such a sentimental attachment to you, and which meant something to you?

MR. HISS: Mr. Mundt, I have already testified that my recollection is that I let Crosley have the use of it; I may have let him have complete disposition. He may be the person who disposed of it.

MR. MUNDT: Yes; just a moment; may I interrupt you? As a matter of fact, whether you gave it to him or loaned it to him or made it part of the—a material part of the lease—unless you had let him make final disposition of it, you certainly would know what you had done with the car after that.

MR. HISS: If the car came back to me, if he returned the car to me, and I later disposed of it—

MR. MUNDT: You would know of it.

MR. HISS: I do not have a recollection of what I did.

MR. MUNDT: But you would have a recollection of it, of having it back.

MR. HISS: I would like to have an opportunity to consult the records, and I have been attempting to consult the records, and they are not available to me, Mr. Mundt. . . .

MR. MUNDT: But you need no aids to your memory on a matter like that automobile. On your leases I can understand, and your address I can understand. From the standpoint of disposing of an automobile of that type you certainly would stretch the credulity of this committee if you would have us believe that you have no memory at all of what happened to this automobile.

MR. HISS: I am not an expert on the credulity of this committee.

Then Robert Stripling read into the record the clarifying point about the car questions—my original testimony as to what Hiss had done with the car, given prior to any of his own testimony covering the same points. Could my testimony have been read at the beginning of the hearing, the logic of the drama would have been easier to follow. But in the nature of such an interrogation, it could not precede, it had to follow the questions based on it. So ably had the Committee organized this hearing that my testimony was timed to touch off one of the climaxes of the hearing, a climax that was about to be reached through the words of Louis J. Russell.

MR. STRIPLING: . . . In the meantime, Mr. Chairman, I should like now to refer to the testimony of Whittaker Chambers, which he gave on August 7th in New York City in the Federal Building.

"MR. NIXON: Did they have a car?—" referring to Mr. and Mrs. Alger Hiss.

"MR. CHAMBERS: Yes; they did. When I first knew them they had a car. Again I am reasonably sure, I am almost certain it was a Ford, and that it was a roadster. It was black, and it was very dilapidated. There is no question about that. I remember very clearly that it had hand windshield wipers. I remember that because I drove it one rainy day and had to work those windshield wipers by hand.

"MR. NIXON: Do you recall any other car?

"MR. CHAMBERS: It seems to me in 1936 probably he got a new Plymouth.

"MR. NIXON: Do you recall its type?

"MR. CHAMBERS: It was a sedan, a two-seated car.

"MR. MANDEL: What did he do with the old car?

"MR. CHAMBERS: The Communist Party had in Washington a service station; that is the man in charge or owner of this station was a Communist, or it may have been a car lot.

"MR. NIXON: But the owner was a Communist?

"MR. CHAMBERS: The owner was a Communist. I never knew who he was or where he was. It was against all the rules of the underground organization for Hiss to do anything with his old car but trade it in, and I think this investigation has proved how right the Communists are in such matters, but Hiss insisted that he wanted that car turned over to the open party so it could be of use to some poor organizer in the West or somewhere. Much against my better judgment, and much against Peters' better judgment, he finally got us to permit him to do this thing. Peters knew where this lot was and he either took Hiss there or he gave Hiss the address, and Hiss went there, and to the best of my recollection of his description of that happening, he left the car there and simply went away, and the man in charge of the station took care of the rest of it for him. I should think the records of that transfer would be traceable.

"MR. NIXON: Where was that?

"MR. CHAMBERS: In Washington, D.C., I believe; certainly somewhere in the District."

Now, Mr. Chairman, I have here a certificate of title, a photostatic copy of a certificate of title, District of Columbia, Director of Vehicles and Traffic. It shows that on July 23, 1936, Alger Hiss assigned the title of this car to the Cherner Motor Co., and I now ask that Mr. Hiss step aside, and that Mr. Russell take the stand.

X X X

One fact should be made quite clear. The information that J. Peters had given me about Alger Hiss's car transaction with the open Communist Party had misled me on one point, as no doubt Peters had intended that it should. The owners of the Cherner Motor Company, Washington's big used car dealers, were not Communists or in any way privy to what occurred in their car lot on the night of July 23, 1936—a whole year after the period when, to the best of his recollection, Alger Hiss claimed to have given his Ford roadster to George Crosley. An employe, who was a Communist or a Communist sympathizer, was the agent in the procedure which the Committee's assistant chief investigator was about to describe—a transaction so extraordinary as to spell out for anybody with any experience of such matters the warning: Communists at work.

MR. STRIPLING: Mr. Russell, I hand you a photostatic copy of an assignment of title, as recorded in the District of Columbia, and ask you to give the committee details of your investigation regarding this sale and assignment of title (handing photostatic copy of document to witness).

MR. RUSSELL: The space on the back of the document called the certificate of title of a motor vehicle, as issued by the Director of Vehicles and Traffic for the District of Columbia, reflects that on July 23, 1936, one Alger Hiss sold to the Cherner Motor Co. of 1781 Florida Avenue, NW., a motor vehicle.

MR. STRIPLING: Mr. Russell, is there any evidence that he sold the motor vehicle, on the face of that?

MR. RUSSELL: On the face, under the section which reads as follows: "The motor vehicle described on the reverse side of this certificate, and the undersigned hereby warrants that the title to the said motor vehicle, and certifies that at the time of delivery the same is subject to the following liens or encumbrances and none other."

Under that, in typewriting, is the word "None." There is no indication as to the amount of money involved in the transaction.

MR. STRIPLING: Now, did you proceed to the Cherner Motor Co. with a subpoena, and examine their records and subpoena all of their sales records for this date?

MR. RUSSELL: I did.

MR. STRIPLING: Do you have those records with you?

MR. RUSSELL: Yes.

MR. STRIPLING: Is there any evidence of a sale on that date from the records that we have obtained?

MR. RUSSELL: In the records which we obtained, which were the only ones available, there is no evidence that a sale or the subsequent sale of a 1929 Ford roadster was made by the Cherner Motor Co. on that date.

MR. STRIPLING: Now, just a moment. Going back to the assignment of title, does the photostatic document reflect that the car was sold or assigned on the same date that Mr. Hiss turned it in to the Cherner Motor Co.?

MR. RUSSELL: Yes; the reassignment of title reflects that on July 23, 1936, which is the same date that the car was turned over to Cherner Motor Co., by Mr. Hiss, that one William Rosen, of 5405 Thirteenth Street, NW., was the purchaser of the same motor vehicle involved for the amount—the amount is not given. However, it states, or there is a statement on this document, that there was a chattel mortgage of $25.

MR. STRIPLING: Did you go to the address listed there, 5405 Thirteenth Street, NW.?

MR. RUSSELL: No; but investigators attached to my division did.

MR. STRIPLING: Who were the investigators?

MR. RUSSELL: Mr. William A. Wheeler and Mr. Benjamin Mandel and Mrs. Howard also visited that address.

MR. STRIPLING: Did any person by the name of William Rosen reside at that address during 1936?

MR. RUSSELL: No.

MR. STRIPLING: Was there any record of a William Rosen having resided at that address?

MR. RUSSELL: No.

MR. NIXON: Who was the—who resides at that address at the present time?

MR. RUSSELL: Mrs. Howard would have to mention that. I am not familiar with the persons presently residing there.

MR. NIXON: You do not have the information as to that?

MR. RUSSELL: No; Mrs. Howard has that.

MR. NIXON: But what your record shows, I understand, Mr. Russell, is that this car was transferred by Mr. Hiss on what date?

MR. RUSSELL: July 23, 1936.

MR. NIXON: That is a year after the transfer to Chambers is supposed to have taken place?

MR. RUSSELL: Yes.

MR. NIXON: Is that in the handwriting of Mr. Hiss?

MR. RUSSELL: According to an identification of certain handwriting specimens consisting of the known handwriting of Mr. Hiss on the questioned document which is this assignment of title, the handwriting experts have testified that the signature appearing on the back of this document, called assignment of title, was written by Alger Hiss.

MR. STRIPLING: Here is the report of the handwriting experts at this time.

MR. NIXON: Is it true also that the words "Cherner Motor Co.," had been written in by Mr. Hiss, or are in the same handwriting?

MR. RUSSELL: Whether the handwriting examination shows that, I do not know. I do not believe that it does.

MR. NIXON: Mr. Stripling, you have information on that fact?

MR. STRIPLING: We have not made a determination on that point. I want to ask Mr. Hiss.

MR. NIXON: I see. Do the files of the Committee on Un-American Activities or the files which you have consulted disclose any information concerning the William Rosen who gave this address?

MR. STRIPLING: There are two William Rosens. This committee is now checking. We find no William Rosen who ever resided at that address. There are two Rosens. We are checking one in California and the other in Detroit. We are not prepared at this time to state definitely concerning these two William Rosens.

Could I clear up one point, Mr. Nixon?

MR. NIXON: Yes.

MR. STRIPLING: Now, Mr. Russell, you have the sales slips of the

Cherner Motor Co. for the date on which this car was sold to William Rosen.

MR. RUSSELL: I have.

MR. STRIPLING: Do you have the slips for the day before?

MR. RUSSELL: Yes.

MR. STRIPLING: And the following day?

MR. RUSSELL: Yes.

MR. STRIPLING: Would you explain to the committee the numbering system of those sales slips, and tell them whether or not the sales slips, as contained there in the files which were subpoenaed, reflect that this car was sold to William Rosen.

MR. RUSSELL: These sales invoices are numbered in consecutive order. The last sales invoice for the date July 21, 1936, bore the number 7879.

The first sales invoice for the following day, which was the day before the transaction was recorded on the assignment of title, begins with the number 7880, and ends with the number 7897. There were no invoices missing on that day.

On the following day, July 23, 1936, the date of the transaction, the number was 7898. The last invoice on that date was 7908, and on the following day, July 24, 1936, the invoices begin with the number 7909, and end with number 7923.

If you follow the numbers in consecutive order from the last number of July 2 through July 24, 1936, you will find that there are no sales invoices missing, which indicates that no sales invoice for the sale of this automobile to William Rosen was made out by the Cherner Motor Co. on the day before the sale was recorded on the assignment of title, on the day that the sale was recorded, on the assignment of title, nor on the day following the assignment of title, which was July 24, 1936.

MR. STRIPLING: Now, Mr. Chairman, I think this point should be an occasion for Mr. Nixon, who is chairman of a subcommittee, to state clearly for the record the investigation to this point regarding the Cherner Motor Co.

Yesterday Mr. Cherner, who is head of the motor company, was before the committee, as well as the treasurer, and the vice president in charge of used cars, I believe—three officials of the Cherner Motor Co., who were before the committee. There is no evidence at this time that any of these three officials or that the Cherner Motor Co. might have been a party to any such transaction. It is very possible that a person who was with the Cherner

Motor Co. at that time is involved. We expect to have something on that later in the day.

MR. NIXON: Mr. Chairman, the subcommittee yesterday heard Mr. Cherner, of the Cherner Motor Co., and Mr. Mensh, who was the sales manager of the Cherner Motor Co., at the time this transaction occurred. Both witnesses testified at length. Their testimony will, of course, be made public, and I want to say for the record that, as far as both of them were concerned, they had no recollection whatever of this particular transaction, and that, as far as the investigation of the sub-committee is concerned, there is no implication at all that they were involved in the transaction from the basis of their testimony. I want that to be made absolutely clear, because the record of their testimony, which will be made public, will bear out what I have just said.

Do I understand, first of all, that you do have the records of the Cherner Motor Co. for the day of that particular transaction?

MR. RUSSELL: Yes, sir.

MR. NIXON: And you find nothing in those records at all bearing on this transaction?

MR. RUSSELL: Yes, sir.

MR. NIXON: You have searched the records carefully to see whether possibly the invoice might have been misplaced?

MR. RUSSELL: Yes, sir. The invoices are numbered in consecutive order; and if you take the day before the transaction occurred, and find that number and trace that through, and the following day, and then take the first invoice for the day after the transaction, you will find that those numbers are in consecutive order, so there could not be a sales invoice for that day missing.

MR. NIXON: I see. And as far as Mr. William Rosen is concerned, the investigations of your staff have shown that the address that he gave was an address which the occupants of the home at that time deny was his at that time?

MR. RUSSELL: Yes, sir; that is true.

MR. NIXON: That is all I have at this time.

MR. STRIPLING: I ask that Mr. Hiss be recalled.

THE CHAIRMAN: Mr. Hébert.

MR. HÉBERT: I just want to ask one clarifying question.

In other words, this transfer of title which the Cherner Motor Co. supposedly gave to the man Rosen does not appear officially at all in their files or in their invoices?

MR. RUSSELL: That is right.

MR. HÉBERT: Am I to understand also, then, that if such a transaction did take place as reflected by this document from which you read, that it was a cover-up sale?

MR. STRIPLING: No.

MR. HÉBERT: In other words, what I am trying to clarify, Mr. Stripling, is what connection has the fact—what does it establish, that these invoices are consecutively numbered, and then, you have a missing invoice of a sale which is supposed to have taken place, and that one missing invoice relates to the car sold.

MR. STRIPLING: There is not a missing invoice.

MR. HÉBERT: There is not a missing invoice?

MR. RUSSELL: No.

MR. STRIPLING: The point we are making is that Mr. Hiss, according to this document, delivered the Ford automobile to the Cherner Motor Co. on July 23, 1936. On that same date the car was sold or transferred to one William Rosen, but there is no evidence in the sales records of this particular transaction.

MR. HÉBERT: It was an unusual case.

MR. STRIPLING: I believe that the officials—one of the officials of the Cherner Motor Co.—testified yesterday that it was a very unusual case.

To make what happened perfectly clear to those unversed in techniques of conspiracy, perhaps it is best to bear in mind the purpose of the unusual transaction. Hiss's insistence on turning his old car over to the Communist Party had faced J. Peters with this problem: how to obliterate as far as possible the documentary link, which the transfer of title of an automobile must make between the underground Communist Party and the open Communist Party. He solved the problem in this way: he had Hiss assign title to the roadster, not directly to a Communist, but to a neutral and unsuspecting third party—the Cherner Motor Company. Peters was able to do this because he had a Communist Party member or sympathizer planted at Cherner's.

To this man, Hiss personally turned over the roadster. On the certificate of transfer Hiss himself wrote in as recipient: the Cherner Motor Company. That is without question: the handwriting and notarized signature with date are certified to be Alger Hiss's. Thus, on the face of the record, Hiss sold the car to the Cherner Motor Company, and in the ordinary course of events the deception would never have been discovered.

But the Communist go-between at Cherner's did not enter the sale in the Cherner records; Peters wanted no record of the transaction which could be avoided, in the official document. Instead, at once, the same night, the go-between transferred title to the car to one William Rosen, located at a Washington address where no William Rosen had ever lived. The go-between (or someone else) also wrote in Rosen's signature. For Rosen's signature on the transfer is not in Rosen's handwriting. Yet Rosen repeatedly refused to testify before the Committee, and again at the second Hiss trial, whether or not he is a member of the Communist Party, and whether he ever owned a 1929 Ford roadster. His ground was self-incrimination. It is the belief of the Committee that Rosen did not receive the Hiss roadster, but that he was shielding someone else who did. No trace of the car has ever been found after it left Alger Hiss's hands.

This was the evidence, second in importance perhaps only to the copied State Department documents and microfilm, that Judge Samuel H. Kaufman excluded from the first Hiss trial. That is why Thomas F. Murphy, in summing up before that jury, said, "And Judge Kaufman would not let me prove what happened after that."

XXXI

Alger Hiss was recalled to the stand.

MR. STRIPLING: Mr. Hiss, I show you this photostatic copy of assignment of title, title No. 245647, for a Ford used, model A, 1929 roadster, and the numbers are A-21888119-19-33—that was the date on which it was originally registered in the District of Columbia. The tag, I believe, was 245647, in the name of Alger Hiss, 3411 O Street NW, Washington, D.C.

Now, Mr. Hiss, is this your signature which appears on the reverse side of this assignment of title? (showing witness photostatic copy.)

MR. HISS: Mr. Stripling, it certainly looks like my signature to me. Do you have the original document?

MR. STRIPLING: No; I do not.

MR. HISS: This is a photostat. I would prefer to have the original. Do you have the original?

MR. STRIPLING: The original document, Mr. Chairman, cannot

be removed from the Department of Motor Vehicles. They keep it in their possession.

MR. HISS: They have it in their possession now?

MR. STRIPLING: I assume they do.

MR. DAVIS: Could it be subpoenaed?

MR. STRIPLING: It might be possible to subpoena it here if they bring it up themselves.

THE CHAIRMAN: Well, Mr. Hiss, can't you tell from the photostat what this signature is? Whether it is your signature or not?

MR. HISS: It looks like my signature to me, Mr. Chairman.

THE CHAIRMAN: Well, if that were the original, would it look any more like your signature? (Laughter.) So, it is just reasonable to believe that you can tell from that whether or not it is your signature.

MR. HISS: I think if I saw the original document I would be able to see whether this photostat is an exact reproduction of the original document. I would just rather deal with originals than with copies.

MR. HÉBERT: Mr. Stripling, may I interrupt? In other words, in order to give Mr. Hiss every opportunity—if we recall what he did with the photograph, that he did not recognise Mr. Chambers for some time, and he finally recognized him. I suggest that the committee issue a subpoena duces tecum to the motor-vehicle people and let them come in here with the original, and it will be just a matter of hours, and he will have to admit it is his signature.

MR. HISS: The reason I asked was that we had not been able to get access to the original. I just wondered what had happened to it.

THE CHAIRMAN: We will try, and Mr. Stripling, you try at noontime, if we ever reach noontime.

MR. STRIPLING: I think we can reach it this way. Do you recall ever signing the assignment, Mr. Hiss?

MR. HISS: I do not at the moment recall signing this.

MR. STRIPLING: Is this your handwriting? There is written here, "Cherner Motor Co., 1781 Florida Avenue NW." Did you write that?

MR. HISS: I could not be sure from the outline of the letters in this photostatic copy. That also looks not unlike my own handwriting.

MR. MUNDT: Could you be sure if you saw the original document?

MR. HISS: I could be surer. (Laughter.)

MR. STRIPLING: Now, Mr. Hiss and Mr. Chairman, yesterday the committee subpoenaed before it W. Marvin Smith, who was the notary public who notarized the signature of Mr. Hiss. Mr. Smith is an attorney in the Department of Justice in the Solicitor General's office. He has been employed there for 35 years. He testified that he knew Mr. Hiss; he does not recall notarizing this particular document, but he did testify that this was his signature.

MR. HISS: I know Mr. Marvin Smith.

THE CHAIRMAN: You know who?

MR. HISS: I say I know Mr. Marvin Smith.*

MR. STRIPLING: The man who notarized this.

MR. NIXON: Mr. Hiss, you knew Mr. Smith, the notary, who signed this in 1936, did you not?

MR. HISS: I did. . . .

MR. NIXON: On the basis—in other words, you would not want to say now that you question the fact that Mr. Smith might have violated his oath as a notary public in notarizing a forged signature?

MR. HISS: Definitely not.

MR. NIXON: Then, as far as you are concerned, this is your signature?

MR. HISS: As far as I am concerned, with the evidence that has been shown to me, it is.

MR. NIXON: All right; you are willing to testify now then that since Mr. Smith did notarize your signature as of that time, that it is your signature?

MR. HISS: On the basis of the assumptions you state, the answer is "Yes."

* * *

MR. HÉBERT: Mr. Hiss, now that your memory has been refreshed by the development of the last few minutes, do you recall the transaction whereby you disposed of that Ford that you could not remember this morning?

*A few weeks later, W. Marvin Smith committed suicide by plunging several floors into the stairwell of the Justice Department building in Washington. I have never seen any published explanation for his act. Justice Department officials have said in my hearing that his reasons were purely personal.

MR. HISS: No; I have no present recollection of the disposition of the Ford, Mr. Hébert.

MR. HÉBERT: In view of the refreshing of your memory that has been presented here this morning?

MR. HISS: In view of that, and in view of all the other developments.

MR. HÉBERT: You are a remarkable and agile young man, Mr. Hiss.

A few moments later, the hearing recessed for lunch. As Robert Stripling was gathering up his papers, Alger Hiss stepped up to him. "I don't suppose you will want me here this afternoon," he said. Stripling subdued his astonishment. "You had better stick around, Mr. Hiss," he said. "He never missed a trick," Stripling added in describing the incident to me some months later.

XXXII

The Ford car was the battle. It was a battle ably organized and executed by the Committee, with a large share of the credit going to Robert Stripling. It was a battle whose verdict, even in the full force of his two-year countercharge with the massed power of political and social allies behind it, Hiss was never again completely able to elude. And, indeed, how was it possible that any man of honest mind and plain intelligence, following Hiss's testimony and behavior closely, observing the tireless twists and turns of his calculated equivocation varied with flashes of calculated insolence—how could such a plain man fail to know, after the evidence about the Ford roadster, that Hiss had wittingly engaged in a surreptitious transaction with Communists in which I had no part? The fact that Hiss had turned over his car to an unknown intermediary in a clandestine way was beyond question, while his elaborate efforts to cover up called into question the whole tissue of his story. Not to know that, a man must not have heard or read the testimony, not have understood it, or not have wanted to understand it.

The Ford roadster was the battle. But the Committee was not finished mopping up. For two or three long hours of the afternoon session of the hearing, it kept Hiss on the stand, leading him point by point over his past testimony, leading him to dodge, bend and weave—a spectacle of agile and dogged indignity—through his discrepancies and contradictions, but never bringing him completely to lose his footing or to yield an inch in his denials.

At last, in a recapitulation that runs to almost four pages of the official transcript, Congressman Mundt summed up. His conclusion was in substance that of the official summation which the Committee released in closing that phase of the Hiss-Chambers Case: ". . . . on every point on which we have been able to verify, on which we have had verifiable evidence before us, the testimony of Mr. Chambers stands up. It stands unchallenged. . . . You (Hiss), on the other hand, have also supplied some verifiable data . . . but, in the matter of the car, your testimony is clearly refuted by the tangible evidence of the sales slips from the Cherner Motor Company, by the registration material. On some of the other items, your testimony is clouded by a strangely deficient memory. . . . We proceed on the conclusion that if either one of you is telling the truth on the verifiable data, that you are telling the truth on all of it. . . ."

And that, in so far as my testimony had then gone, and allowing for errors of recollection, was the fact.

XXXIII

Almost any other man but Hiss would have been exhausted simply by the ordeal of hours of questioning. At that point, Hiss attacked. This was the moment he had endured for. Into the record he was permitted to read the letter that he had already sent to the Committee's chairman. Its purpose was threefold. First, it sought to establish Hiss's innocence by association, merging him at the moment of his public disfigurement with a constellation of distinguished names in whose usurped light he purely shone. Then came the iterated challenge. Again, Hiss challenged me to repeat my charge that he had been a Communist in such a way that he could sue me for libel. No doubt it seemed to the counselers who put their heads together over it that that was the final routing tactic. Then came the fragmentation blast, the questions that were aimed at destroying my credibility by challenging my past while raising the smear to the level of a public charge, for one question amounted to the charge that I was insane.

But perhaps no item of the tactic was more effective in rallying support to Hiss than that he advanced first—the warning that my charge of Communism against him must lead to re-examination of

American foreign policy and, by implication, of those who had made it with Hiss and enabled him to make it—or, as he put it, "to discredit recent great achievements of this country in which I was privileged to participate." That touched the rallying nerve of a common fear that would soon fill the nation with uproar as Hiss's questions soon filled the hearing room with commotion (for there were ghosts on more roofs than that of the Livadia Palace at Yalta).

THE CHAIRMAN: Just go ahead, Mr. Hiss, and read your letter, and you wait, Mr. Counsel, until he gets through.

MR. HISS: We are doing this at your choice. I do not know what you prefer.

THE CHAIRMAN: You wanted to get started, and everybody was getting in your way. Go ahead.

MR. HISS: The letter which I sent to the chairman yesterday afternoon is as follows:

"Tomorrow—"

that is now today—

"will mark my fourth appearance before your committee. I urge, in advance of that hearing, that your committee delay no longer in penetrating to the bedrock of the facts relevant to the charge which you have publicized—that I am or have been a Communist.

"This charge goes beyond the personal. Attempts will be made to use it, and the resulting publicity, to discredit recent great achievements of this country in which I was privileged to participate.

"Certain members of your committee have already demonstrated that this use of your hearings and the ensuing publicity is not a mere possibility, it is a reality. Your acting chairman, Mr. Mundt, himself, was trigger quick to cast such discredit."

Although he now says that he was very favorably impressed with my testimony.

"Before I had a chance to testify, even before the press had a chance to reach me for comment—"

after Chambers' testimony—

"before you had—"

so far as I am aware—

"sought one single fact to support the charge made by a self-confessed liar, spy, and traitor, your acting chairman pronounced judgment that I am guilty as charged, by stating that the country should beware of the peace work with which I have been connected.

"I urge that these committee members—"

your committee members—

"abandon such verdict-first-and-testimony-later tactics, along with dramatic confrontations in secret sessions, and get down to business.

"First, my record should be explored. It is inconceivable that there could have been on my part, during 15 years or more in public office, serving all three branches of the Government, judicial, legislative, and executive, any departure from the highest rectitude without its being known. It is inconceivable that the men with whom I was intimately associated during those 15 years should not know my true character far better than this accuser. It is inconceivable that if I had not been of the highest character, this would not have manifested itself at some time or other, in at least one of the innumerable actions I took as a high official, actions publicly recorded in the greatest detail.

"During the period cited by this accuser, I was chief counsel to the Senate Committee Investigating the Munitions Industry, at a great many public hearings, fully reported in volumes to be found in libraries in every major American city. During my term of service under the Solicitor General of the United States, I participated in the preparation of briefs on a great many of the largest issues affecting the United States. Those briefs are on public file in the United States Supreme Court, in the Department of Justice, and in law libraries in various American cities.

"As an official of the Department of State, I was appointed secretary general, the top administrative officer, of the peace-building international assembly that created the United Nations. My actions in that post are a matter of detailed public record. The same is true of my actions at other peace-building and peace-strengthening international meetings in which I participated—at Dumbarton Oaks and elsewhere in this country, at Malta, at Yalta, at London, and in other foreign cities. All my actions in the executive branch of the Government, including my work in the Agricultural Adjustment Administration on farm problems, are fully recorded in the public records.

"In all this work I was frequently, and for extensive periods, under the eye of the American press and of the statesmen under whom or in association with whom I worked. They saw my every gesture, my every movement, my every facial expression. They heard the tones in which I spoke, the words I uttered, the words spoken by others in my presence. They knew my every act relating to official business, both in public and in executive conference.

"Here is a list of the living personages of recognized stature under whom or in association with whom I worked in the Government (there may be omissions which I should like to supply in a supplemental list):

"Men now in the United States Senate:

"Senator Tom Connally, one of the United States delegates to the San Francisco Conference which created the United Nations, and to the first meeting of the General Assembly of the United Nations in London—

where I was present.

"Senator Arthur Vandenberg, a member of the Senate Committee Investigating the Munitions Industry—

under whom I served—

"and a member of the San Francisco Conference and London General Assembly delegations."

Next—

"Men now in the House of Representatives:

"Representative Sol Bloom, a member of both the San Francisco and the London delegations.

"Representative Charles Eaton, also a member of both the San Francisco and the London delegations, although his health kept him from making the trip to London."

Next—

"Former Secretaries of State:

"Cordell Hull, Edward Stettinius, James Byrnes.

"Former Under Secretaries of State—"

under whom I served—

"Joseph Grew, also a member of the Dumbarton Oaks delegation, Dean Acheson, and William Clayton.

"United States judges:

"Stanley Reed, Associate Justice now of the United States Supreme Court, who as Solicitor General was my immediate superior during my service in the Department of Justice.

"Homer Bone, former Senator from Washington, who was also a member of the Munitions Committee.

"Bennett Clark, a former Senator who was a member of the Munitions Committee.

"Jerome Frank who as general counsel of the Agricultural Adjustment Administration was my immediate chief in the Department of Agriculture.

"Men formerly in Congress:

"Former United States Senator Gerald Nye, chairman of the Munitions Committee, who appointed me as the chief attorney of that committee.

"Former United States Senator James Pope, who was a member of the Munitions Committee, and who is now, I believe, a director of TVA.

"Former United States Senator John Townsend, a member of the London delegation.

"Others at international conferences where I assisted their labors to build the peace:

"Isaiah Bowman, member of Dumbarton Oaks delegation, president of Johns Hopkins University.

"John Foster Dulles, a chief adviser of the San Francisco delegation, and a member of each delegation to the meetings of the General Assembly.

"Lt. Gen. Stanley Embick, a member of the Dumbarton Oaks delegation.

"Charles Fahy, former legal adviser of the Department of State and member of the United States delegation to the General Assembly.

"Gen. Muir Fairchild of the Air Corps, a member of the Dumbarton Oaks delegation.

"Henry Fletcher, former Assistant Secretary of State, and member of the Dumbarton Oaks delegation.

"Green Hackworth, former legal adviser of the Department of

State and a member of the Dumbarton Oaks delegation, now a judge of the International Court of Justice at The Hague.

"Admiral Arthur Hepburn, member of the United States delegation at Dumbarton Oaks.

"Stanley Hornbeck, a member of the Dumbarton Oaks delegation, later our Ambassador to The Hague, and earlier, as chief far-eastern expert of the Department of State, my immediate superior from the fall of 1939 until the early winter of 1944.

"Breckenridge Long, former Assistant Secretary of State, and a member of the Dumbarton Oaks delegation.

"Mrs. Eleanor Roosevelt, a member of the San Francisco delegation and also of each United States Delegation to the meetings of the General Assembly."

I am not sure that my memory is correct as to Mrs. Roosevelt's participation in San Francisco.

The Chairman: I should imagine so.

Mr. Hiss (continuing):

"Harold Stassen, a member of the United States delegation to the San Francisco Conference.

"Rear Adm. Harold Train, member of the Dumbarton Oaks delegation.

"Frank Walker, former Postmaster General and member of the delegation to the London meeting of the General Assembly.

"Edwin Wilson, my predecessor as director of the office for United Nations Affairs and my last immediate superior in the Department of State who was also a member of the Dumbarton Oaks delegation, now our Ambassador at Ankara.

"Other superiors to whom I reported:

"Chester Davis, Administrator of the Agricultural Adjustment Administration when I was there, and now president of the Federal Reserve Bank of St. Louis.

"Francis Sayre, my first direct supervisor in the Department of State, former Assistant Secretary of State and United States High Commissioner to the Philippines, now United States representative to the Trusteeship Council of the United Nations and member of the United States delegation to the General Assembly.

"These are the men whom I was honored to help in carrying out the finest and deepest American traditions. That is my record. I, too, have had a not insignificant role in that magnificent achievement of our Nation in recent times.

"These men I have listed are the men with whom and under whom I worked intimately during my fifteen years in Government service—the men best able to testify concerning the loyalty with which I performed the duties assigned me. All are persons of unimpeachable character, in a position to know my work from day to day and hour to hour through many years. Ask them if they ever found in me anything except the highest adherence to duty and honor.

"Then the committee can judge, and the public can judge, whether to believe a self-discredited accuser whose names and aliases are as numerous and as casual as his accusations.

"The other side of this question is the reliability of the allegations before this committee, the undocumented statements of the man who now calls himself Whittaker Chambers.

"Is he a man of consistent reliability, truthfulness, and honor? Clearly not. He admits it, and the committee knows it. Indeed, is he a man of sanity?

"Getting the facts about Whittaker Chambers, if that is his name, will not be easy. My own counsel have made inquiries in the past few days and have learned that his career is not, like those of normal men, an open book. His operations have been furtive and concealed. Why? What does he have to hide?

"I am glad to help get the facts.

"At this point I should like to repeat suggestions made by me at preceding hearings with respect to the most effective method of getting facts so far as I can supply them. The suggestions I made, beginning with the very first time I appeared before your committee, were not then accepted, and the result has only been confusion and delay. Let me illustrate by recalling to your minds what I said when you asked me to identify the accuser, not by producing him under your subpoena power but by producing only a newspaper photograph taken many years after the time when, by his own statements, I had last seen him. I said to you on the occasion of my first appearance:

" 'I would much rather see the individual—I would not want to take oath that I have never seen that man. I would like to see him, and I would be better able to tell whether I had ever seen him. Is he here today—I hoped he would be.'

"Let me add one further example of how the procedures followed have caused confusion and delay. In your secret sessions you asked me housekeeping and minor details of years ago that few if any busy men would possibly retain in their memories with accuracy. I told you, and one of your own members acknowledged, that you or I should consult the records. I warned you that I had not checked them and that I doubted if I could be helpful under those circumstances.

"I am having a check made of the records, and will furnish the results to you.

"One personal word. My action in being kind to Crosley years ago was one of humaneness, with results which surely some members of the committee have experienced. You do a favor for a man, he comes for another, he gets a third favor from you. When you finally realize he is an inveterate repeater, you get rid of him. If your loss is only a loss of time and money, you are lucky. You may find yourself calumniated in a degree depending on whether the man is unbalanced or worse."

Now, I would like this committee to ask these questions on my behalf of the man who calls himself Whittaker Chambers, and I would like these to be part of the statement which the committee has authorized me to make.

MR. STRIPLING: Just a moment.

MR. HISS: Where does he reside now?

THE CHAIRMAN: Just a minute.

MR. STRIPLING: I noticed that counsel is passing out these questions to the press.

MR. DAVIS: I will let you have these.

MR. HISS: "Where do you reside?" I would like that question asked of Whittaker Chambers.

THE CHAIRMAN: All right, proceed. The meeting will come to order. Everyone will please take his seat.

MR. HISS: Before reading these questions, I would also like to repeat in public what I said on the occasion of the executive session in New York, where I—

THE CHAIRMAN: Just a minute. Will you please take your seats?

MR. HISS: I would like to repeat in public, and in public session, what I said in New York at the executive session, where Chambers was present, and I said it in his presence. I challenge him to make the statements about me with respect to communism in public that he has made under privilege to this committee.

The questions that I would like this committee on my behalf to ask him—many questions have been asked of me, and I do not know what questions have been asked of him—I would like you to ask him where he now resides and I would like to know the answer. I have not been able to find out even where he lives at the present time. Shall I go on with the questions?

MR. MUNDT: Oh, yes; go ahead.

THE CHAIRMAN: Proceed.

MR. HISS: I would ask that you ask him to list the various places where he has lived since 1930, indicating the length of time he has lived at each place, and the name he has used at each place. As far as I am concerned, that is all a matter of the record of the committee as to where I have lived, and the name I have used.

Next, what name was he given when he was born? What names has he used at any time since his birth for any purpose?

Ask him to give his complete employment record during his membership in the Communist Party, since his resignation from the Communist Party, stating the name of each employer, stating his occupation, and his compensation, also the name by which he was employed in each instance.

I would like him to give a complete bibliography of all his writings. He says that he was a writer. Give the writings under any and every name he has used.

I would like him to be asked whether he has ever been charged or convicted of any crime.

I would like him to give the full particulars, if so, as to where, when, and for what.

I would like him to be asked whether he has ever been treated for a mental illness.

MR. HÉBERT: Mr. Chairman, may I interrupt there to tell Mr. Hiss that at least one question has been asked Mr. Chambers, No. 7. I asked him in New York whether he had ever been treated for any mental illness, whether he was ever in a mental institution or not, and he replied in the negative, and added also he was not an alcoholic. So, you can strike that. That was asked already.

MR. HISS: Was that the extent of the committee's inquiry into that subject?

MR. HÉBERT: The committee's inquiry into that was because a typical Communist smear is: When a man gets up to testify, and particularly a former Communist, is to say he is insane or an alcoholic or something else is wrong with him.

Immediately after Mr. Chambers testified before this committee, the committee heard reverberations already of the fact that he was a mental case; in fact, it said it came from Time magazine by his own associates, so I have always believed the only way to find out anything to start off with is to ask the individual involved, and I asked Mr. Chambers a direct question. "Mr. Chambers, were you ever in a mental institution or treated for any mental disease?" I wanted to know, and I wanted to ask him, and then check back from there.

THE CHAIRMAN: I might say—

MR. HÉBERT: I asked him, and he denied it, and said, "No," and also added to that that he was not an alcoholic, which was another charge that was made against him.

I may say to you now, Mr. Hiss, that I do not accept Mr. Chambers' word on his own statement. I intend to check that, too.

MR. HISS: So do I.

THE CHAIRMAN: I might say, Mr. Hiss, and also to the members of the committee, that Mr. Chambers will take the stand directly after you finish on the stand today.

MR. NIXON: Mr. Hiss, excuse me, do you have any evidence that you would like to present at this time that Mr. Chambers has been in a mental institution? You made the charge that he has been.

MR. HISS: I have made no such charge.

MR. NIXON: The charge has appeared in the newspapers.

MR. HISS: Not from me. I have made no such charge.

MR. NIXON: Then, you do not mean that by your statement?

MR. HISS: I mean that I am making no charges. I am seeking information.

MR. NIXON: The charge appeared yesterday from your letter, as you recall—the suggestion of Mr. Chambers being a mental case. Now, do you have any evidence to present to the committee that he is?

MR. HISS: I have made no such charge. I just read the record here—the letter into the record. I asked the question, "Is he a man of sanity?"

MR. NIXON: Will you answer the question as to whether you

have any evidence of his having been in a mental institution?

MR. HISS: I have had various reports made to me to the effect that he has been.

MR. NIXON: What reports have you had?

MR. HISS: I have had reports made by individuals.

MR. NIXON: What individuals?

MR. HISS: They are so far only hearsay. The reports that came to me were from individuals, individual members of the press, so far, that they had heard rumors to that effect.

MR. NIXON: What members of the press?

MR. DAVIS: Mr. Mundt, can he finish his statement? I understood we were not to be interrupted. Let them take notes and then ask the questions after he finishes.

THE CHAIRMAN: All right, go ahead and finish the questions.

MR. HISS: I would like the committee to ask him if he has ever been treated for mental illness, where, and when, and by whom. I would like him to be asked where, when, and to whom he has been married. How many children he has; where does his wife now reside.

I would like him to be asked to describe the circumstances under which he came in contact with this committee and to make public all written memoranda which he may have handed to any representative of the committee.

I would like to know whether he is willing, as I said at the outset of these questions, to make before this committee, in a manner free from the protections of this committee, the statements so that I may test his veracity in a suit for slander or libel.

THE CHAIRMAN: Now, does any member of the committee have any questions to ask Mr. Hiss over the statement he made or in relation to these questions he wants the committee to ask?

MR. HÉBERT: I would like to, Mr. Chairman.

THE CHAIRMAN: Mr. Hébert.

* * *

MR. HÉBERT: Now, the question has been asked: "Do you recall certain individuals with whom you were friendly?" I will recall them from memory and ask you each question. Do you recall Henry Collins well?

MR. HISS: I have answered that I have known Henry Collins since we were boys together at a boys' camp in Maine.

MR. HÉBERT: Do you know that Henry Collins is a Communist?

MR. HISS: I do not know that Henry Collins is a Communist. I do not know that he is not a Communist.

MR. HÉBERT: You do not know whether he is or is not a Communist?

MR. HISS: No; that is not the kind of thing I would know.

MR. HÉBERT: Do you know John Abt?

MR. HISS: I do know John Abt, and I have testified as to the circumstances under which I know and have known John Abt.

MR. HÉBERT: Do you know John Abt as a Communist or not as a Communist?

MR. HISS: I have never known John Abt as a Communist. I do not know whether he is or not.

MR. HÉBERT: Do you know Lee Pressman?

MR. HISS: I know Lee Pressman, and I have testified as to how and when I knew Lee Pressman.

MR. HÉBERT: Do you know whether or not he is a Communist?

MR. HISS: I do not know whether or not Lee Pressman is a Communist.

MR. HÉBERT: Did you know Harold Ware?

MR. HISS: I knew Harold Ware only to the extent that I have testified to in my public testimony.

MR. HÉBERT: Well, I will say this, that it is an established fact that Harold Ware was a Communist when he was living.

MR. HISS: I knew Harold Ware to the extent I testified to in 1933 or 1945. It was not my practice then to ask people whom I met casually whether they were Communists.

MR. HÉBERT: But you do not know whether any of these people were Communists or not.

MR. HISS: I do not.

MR. HÉBERT: And particular reference with regard to Henry Collins, who refused to testify here that it might incriminate himself.

MR. HISS: I have no reason for knowing what counsel advised Mr. Collins to do with respect to his rights.

MR. HÉBERT: Now, the reason I ask those questions, Mr. Hiss, is to bring you up to date on your letter which you just read and recited a long list of persons who would know you and know what you were about, and know who you are and what you are.

MR. HISS: That is right.

MR. HÉBERT: And it was an imposing array of fine American people. How would they know whether you are a Communist or not, when you don't know about intimate people that you know, whether they are communists or not?

MR. HISS: Mr. Hébert, I did not cite their names on that issue. I cited their names on my record, because I think my record is relevant to this inquiry.

MR. HÉBERT: You cited that list of names to leave the impression that these people could testify that you are not a Communist?

MR. HISS: I said, and I say now, that those people can testify as to whether they noticed in my demeanor over sometimes prolonged periods any indication of any departure from the highest rectitude.

MR. HÉBERT: Well, none of these people could testify as to whether or not you are a Communist, could they?

MR. HISS: Have any of them testified?

MR. HÉBERT: I did not ask that.

MR. HISS: Whether I departed from rectitude, in their opinion?

MR. HÉBERT: I asked you a question: Can any of them testify whether or not you are or are not a Communist?

MR. HISS: That is for them to say.

MR. HÉBERT: Can they testify? You have injected their names in the hearing. I did not.

MR. HISS: I did not cite them for that purpose, to you, Mr. Hébert. If you wish to ask them that question, that is your privilege. If you do not wish to ask them, I shall attempt to obtain affidavits from them for the committee's information.

MR. HÉBERT: Well, their testimony would not be worth any more than your testimony will be against Ware, Collins, Abt, Pressman.

* * *

MR. NIXON: Now, what is the implication that is left from the testimony that because of that $150 loan, which Crosley owed you, that he has willfully circulated this charge that you are a Communist?

MR. HISS: I did not testify to your committee that I had any understanding of the motive which could have led him to make such a serious charge. I am not prepared to say that I understand or have any inkling as to what could have led him to make such a charge, Mr. Nixon. I would not want to say that the words we had over these relatively minor financial transactions could possibly motivate any normal person to make such a charge.

MR. NIXON: Well, now, of course, as you have indicated, the charge that you or anybody else is a Communist now is a serious charge. Also the inference which, of course, the statements regarding which you made before the committee, and your answers to questions which you have given to the committee that somebody has been treated for a mental illness today is also a serious charge. I would appreciate, in helping the committee, to find out what the motive could have been, to find out whether possibly there is a mental condition here, if you would tell the committee now what your sources are that you have for believing that Mr. Crosley has been treated for a mental illness.

MR. HISS: Mr. Nixon, the first reference to that which came to my attention was on the afternoon of the morning which occurred after I first testified before the committee. One of two friends, who came to the hearing with me, a lawyer who was at law school with me, and who came with me to the hearings, simply as a friend, was told by a representative of the press that there had been reports being received by the press ever since Chambers had testified that he had spent a considerable part of the last 4 or 5 years in mental institutions. That seemed to me to be a significant assertion, and I have attempted to run it down. I have not found any evidence as yet. I shall continue to search for evidence.

MR. NIXON: Can you tell us who that was?

MR. HISS: The friend who accompanied me?

MR. NIXON: Yes.

MR. HISS: He was Joseph Johnston, of Birmingham, Ala., who happened to be in Washington at that time. What press person spoke to him, I do not know. I have not asked him what press person it was. I think it was a member of the press who came up to him casually while he was sitting with me.

MR. NIXON: And, Mr. Johnston told you that a member of the press had told him—

MR. HISS: Just what I have told you.

MR. NIXON: What you have just told me?

MR. HISS: That is correct.

MR. NIXON: And on the basis of that statement, which is hearsay twice removed, you are leaving the implication that Mr. Crosley has been in a mental institution.

MR. HISS: Mr. Nixon, you say I am leaving an implication.

MR. NIXON: Well, I cannot gather anything else from your statement.

MR. HISS: There have been other reports made to me.

MR. NIXON: What other reports?

MR. HISS: That an individual who formerly worked on Time said that Chambers had been to a mental institution.

MR. NIXON: Who told you that?

MR. HISS: This also came to me from a second-hand source. The name of the individual who was supposed to have made the statement—I do not like to bring names in unnecessarily, however, if you insist—

MR. NIXON: I insist.

MR. HISS: The name is of a person named Walton, who, I understand, formerly worked on Time, and who, I do not know that Walton, he said definitely that Chambers had been to a mental institution in 1946. The statement was made that Walton understood that or thought that.

MR. NIXON: Now, who else?

MR. HISS: I do not recall any other specific information because I have not personally been attempting to go into it. I have asked counsel if they could check on it. It is not an easy thing to check. It is not easy to check on.

MR. NIXON: Well, the committee is interested in this information because we, too, have the obligation to check on it. As I understand, both of your statements are made on the basis of what other people told you—

MR. HISS: Entirely.

MR. NIXON: Concerning things which have been told them.

MR. HISS: Entirely, and I have not gone into it personally. I have asked counsel to see if there is any way they could find out about it.

MR. NIXON: That is all I have, Mr. Chairman.

THE CHAIRMAN: Mr. Counsel, you have something there that you wanted to bring up some time ago. What is that?

MR. DAVIS: Thank you, Mr. Chairman. Will you bear with me? It won't take but just a minute. It seems as if it is ancient history now, but after Mr. Mundt made his statements, I felt I wanted to refer the committee to a statement made by Mr. Mundt during the hearing, the first public hearing, at which Mr. Hiss' name came up, and I would like to just read the two paragraphs:

"Mr. Mundt: Mr. Chambers, I am very much interested in trying to check the career of Alger Hiss. I know nothing about Donald Hiss, but, as a member of the Foreign Affairs Committee, the personnel committee, I have had some occasion to check the activities of Alger Hiss while he was in the State Department. There is reason to believe that he organized within the Department one of the Communist cells, which endeavored to influence our Chinese policy, and bring about the condemnation of Chiang Kai-shek, which put Marzani* in an important position there and, I think, it is important to know what happened to these people after they leave the Government. Do you know where Alger Hiss is employed now?"

MR. MUNDT: I am glad you read that, Mr. Counsel, because I was just going to make that statement now, and I won't have to do it, in connection with a statement in the letter of Mr. Hiss in which he implied or gave the impression that my disagreement with American foreign policy was because he had been connected with it, and I would not want it to go out that my only disagreement with some of these policies is because of your connection with them.

As far as I am concerned, Mr. Hiss, our policy toward China, the political agreement at Yalta, which you said you helped write, and the Morgenthau plan, you mentioned three of them, are hopelessly bad, and I shall continue to consider them hopelessly bad even though you prove yourself to be the president of the American Daughters of the Revolution. The fact that you were connected with them may or may not, when these hearings have terminated, increase my skepticism about their wisdom.

It is true, as I said in my summation, that as a member of the House Foreign Affairs Committee I have had brought to my attention several times the mention of the name Alger Hiss in connection with our Chinese policy. It is also true that after listening to him testify the following day I said publicly, and I said in the record, that he had been a very persuasive and convincing wit-

* Aldo Marzani, alias: Tony Wales, State Department employe convicted of perjury *circa* 1946 for denying his membership in the Communist Party.

ness, and had very well convinced me of his reliability. In fact, I advised Mrs. Mundt at dinner that night, and she said I had been taken in by his suavity. Perhaps a woman's intuition is better than a man's, I do not know, but at all events, I am willing to again state that Mr. Hiss was a willing and persuasive witness as far as I am concerned.

I would like to say just one other thing with regard to that part of the letter, Mr. Chairman, which says it is inconceivable that he, Mr. Hiss, could have worked in the Government for these many years and still have been a member of the Communist Party or disloyal. That is not inconceivable to me without in any way attempting at this time to indict the credibility of Mr. Hiss. But I wish to point out that John Peurifoy, Assistant Secretary of State in charge of security, has notified Congress that 134 members of the State Department* had weasled their way into the State Department alone, and had been removed from the Department for disloyalty reasons.

So it is not at all inconceivable that the number could just as well have been 135 as 134.

That was the end of Alger Hiss's testimony on August 25th. There had been little gasps of astonishment and outrage in the hearing room when he made his unsupported charge that I had been in a mental institution.** But, as he well knew, Hiss had only to utter the charge to have the press publish it in millionfold repetition. That was all that he needed, for who was there to deny it authoritatively for me? There was no one. Henceforth, the charge of insanity, and the whispering campaign that was linked to it, was the heart of the Hiss defense.

XXXIV

It was early evening, and the lights had already been switched on, or soon would be, when I took the stand and was sworn in. This time a microphone had been placed in front of me—the first I had ever talked into. I was puzzled by a sound like muffled thunder that seemed to come from behind me in the hearing room. Stripling

*Congressman Mundt meant to say "members of the Communist Party."

** Lest there be any question at all, exhaustive investigation, both by the Government and the Hiss defense, has established, as definitely as any fact can be established on earth, that I have never been in a mental institution, that I have never consulted a psychiatrist or a psychoanalyst.

nodded toward my hands. It was my thumbs drumming nervously against the sides of the microphone.

In the official transcript, my testimony that day fills some thirty-two pages. I had the impression at the time, borne out by re-reading the record, that my testimony was the firmest and clearest I had yet given, in part because the Committee had a better grip of its questions, in part because I had become a little more used to the routine of questioning and to speaking before a crowd. Nevertheless, my voice at times was still sufficiently blurred or hurried so that, despite the microphone, there are a number of grammatical scrambles and other errors in the official record, when the reporter could not catch clearly what I was saying.

Once more I was led, chiefly by Nixon and Stripling, over most of my former testimony about Hiss and the Ware Group. My answers were unqualified and terse and hence in marked contrast to Hiss's elaborate weaving and bobbing. Congressman Nixon and (later on) Hébert also put to me the questions with which Alger Hiss had challenged my past and my sanity. I responded simply and factually. I have been married for some seventeen years and was living happily with my wife; we had two children. I had never been charged with, or convicted of, a crime. I promised to furnish the Committee with a list of my pseudonyms and past employment. I was unable to furnish a bibliography of my writings. I had never, I confessed, written a book.*

* * *

MR. NIXON: Now, Mr. Chambers, you heard the charge made here that you have been treated for mental illness. Do you have any comment on that?

* During the second Hiss trial, one of the defense psychiatrists, Dr. Henry A. Murray, head of Harvard's psychiatry department, was to pick up my literary lapse. He found a dark implication (never, so far as I know, illumined) in the fact that I had never written a book. It is worth pausing a moment over Dr. Murray, because he typifies one important aspect of the Hiss Case. At first Dr. Murray made an impressive witness. Repeatedly, he testified under oath that he had reached his psychiatric conclusions about me wholly and solely from a study of my writings in *Time, Life* and elsewhere (he had never met me). He named a date when his conclusions had crystallized. In cross-examination Prosecutor Murphy carefully led Dr. Murray to repeat these statements. Then Murphy asked these questions: Was it not true that well before the date on which Dr. Murray said he had made his diagnosis solely on the basis of my writing, he had in person visited a former *Time* writer to question him about me? Was it not true that he had himself then drawn such a picture of me as a drunken and unstable character that the *Time* writer had exclaimed: "But

MR. CHAMBERS: Yes; I have never been treated for a mental illness—period.

MR. NIXON: You have never been treated in a mental institution?

MR. CHAMBERS: Never.

MR. NIXON: Never. Have you been treated for a mental illness or been in a [mental] institution during the past four years, which was the charge made?

MR. CHAMBERS: Of course, not; and anyone at Time Magazine can tell you that.

And yet, I knew as I answered the questions, that the effect of my answers was little or nothing. It was the questions themselves that had force and would henceforth hang like a poisonous fog over the Case, distorting all motives, issues and relationships seen through their murk.

How effective the insanity charge was can be glimpsed from the immediate reaction of the Committee's Chairman. I had testified that my wife and I had at one time lived on a farm near Glen Gardner, N.J.—our converted barn near the valley of the robins. The Chairman pressed me to locate the farm exactly. If I had ever known the name of the little dirt road we lived on, I had forgotten it. The Chairman insisted. His insistence puzzled me since the point seemed of no particular relevance and could, in any case, easily be established from a map. It was not the exact location that was troubling him. "You know," he was quoted to me by a Committee staff member as saying to his colleagues after the hearing, "you know, there are a lot of booby-hatches around Glen Gardner." (J. Parnell Thomas was a member from the Garden State.)

Yet it was Chairman Thomas who asked me one of the more important questions of the hearing.

THE CHAIRMAN: What influenced you to join the Communist Party originally?

MR. CHAMBERS: It is a very difficult question. As a student, I went to Europe. It was then shortly after the First World War. I found Germany in chaos, and partly occupied; northern France, and parts of Belgium were smashed to pieces. It seemed to me that a crisis had been reached in western civilization which

Chambers is not like that at all"? Was it not true that Dr. Murray had then answered angrily: "Oh, you're just trying to whitewash Chambers"? The distinguished head of Harvard's psychiatry department admitted that it was all true.

society was not able to solve by the usual means. I then began to look around for the unusual means. I first studied for a considerable time British Fabian socialism, and rejected it as unworkable in practice. I was then very much influenced by a book called *Reflections on Violence,* by Georges Sorel, a syndicalist, and shortly thereafter I came to the writings of Marx and Lenin. They seemed to me to explain the nature of the crisis, and what to do about it.

THE CHAIRMAN: Well, I can understand how a young man might join the Communist Party, but will you explain to us how a person who has made a real living in this country, a person with a large income, some of the witnesses we have had before this committee, over a period of time, what, in your mind, would influence them to join the party here in this country?

MR. CHAMBERS: The making of a good living does not necessarily blind a man to a critical period which he is passing through. Such people, in fact, may feel a special insecurity and anxiety. They seek a moral solution in a world of moral confusion. Marxism, Leninism offers an oversimplified explanation of the causes and a program for action. The very vigor of the project particularly appeals to the more or less sheltered middle-class intellectuals, who feel that there the whole context of their lives has kept them away from the world of reality. I do not know whether I make this very clear, but I am trying to get at it. They feel a very natural concern, one might almost say a Christian concern, for underprivileged people. They feel a great intellectual concern at least, for recurring economic crises, the problem of war, which in our lifetime has assumed an atrocious proportion, and which always weights (weighs) on them. What shall I do? At that crossroads the evil thing, communism, lies in wait for (them with) a simple answer.

But nothing in my testimony that day approached in feeling or meaning a dozen lines elicited by a more or less casual question from Richard Nixon. It must be remembered that I was speaking after seven or eight hours of public hearing. All day long, the special pressures of such an ordeal had beat upon me. Most of the time Alger Hiss had been on the stand, and the spectacle of that man, hopelessly baited by questions, although in a trap of his own contriving, had tormented me as much, or more, than anything I felt about myself.

Even if Hiss had never been my friend, my reaction would have been merely less personal, scarcely less acute. Had I witnessed in a moving picture or a play such a spectacle as I was called upon to participate in, I would have walked out of the theater, for the same reason that the Greeks made it a law of their drama that acts of violence, suffering and death must take place off-stage. For they aroused in those who watched them emotions that were merely horrifying and ugly without being tragic, since tragedy lies not in the horror, but in the surmounting of horror. But I was an enforced spectator, held in that room under the same invisible compulsions as Hiss. And, as hour by hour, the agony mounted, died away and mounted again, point by damning point, I was more and more bowed under the sense of how much each of us was the prey, rather than an actor, in this historic experience to which what had been best in us had led us, from motives incomprehensible to most of those who watched or heard us, to this end.

The exchange with Nixon began almost off-handedly.

MR. NIXON: Mr. Hiss was your closest friend?

MR. CHAMBERS: Mr. Hiss was certainly the closest friend I ever had in the Communist Party.

Alger Hiss was now sitting behind me among the spectators, surrounded by a little group of friends. As I testified, I could hear Hiss making sotto-voce sallies, and the titters of the others.

MR. NIXON: Mr. Chambers, can you search your memory now to see what motive you can have for accusing Mr. Hiss of being a Communist at the present time?

MR. CHAMBERS: What motive I can have?

MR. NIXON: Yes. I mean, do you—is there any grudge that you have against Mr. Hiss over anything that he has done to you?

That single question slipped the cord on all the pent emotion that had been built up through the day. Until that moment, I had been testifying as a public witness, trying to answer questions carefully and briefly. Now I ceased to answer in that way. As I struggled to control my feeling, slowly and deliberately, I heard myself saying, rather than said: "The story has spread that in testifying against Mr. Hiss I am working out some old grudge, or motives or revenge or hatred. I do not hate Mr. Hiss. We were close friends, but we are caught in a tragedy of history. Mr. Hiss represents the concealed enemy against which we are all fighting, and I am fighting. I have testified against him with remorse and pity, but in a moment of history in which this Nation now stands, so help me God, I could not do otherwise."

In the completely silent room, I fought to control my voice.

XXXV

At eight o'clock at night, the long hearing ended. The men and women who had watched and listened to it surged out of the room in intently buzzing groups and on the dark street were soon engaged in a brisk competition for taxicabs.

When Alger Hiss left his first public hearing, people crowded around him. When he left the hearing room on August 25th, no one crowded around him. In the nine hours of the hearing, the tide of sentiment in the room, which had run deeply for him, had turned against him.

I left the room with the head of *Time*'s Washington bureau. As we walked in silence together down the curved hall of the House Office Building, I heard footsteps pounding after us on the marble floor. A young man caught up with us. He was apparently Jewish and could not have been more than seventeen. He was embarrassed at his rashness, but determined. "Mr. Chambers, Mr. Chambers," he fumbled, "I want to thank you. That part about the tragedy of history—you don't know what it means to young people like me."

I did not know, in fact, that there were young people like him, or that the tragedy of history could possibly mean anything to them. But he suddenly rekindled in me a flash of what I had felt at the beginning, and then lost, in the long grind of the hearing—that I spoke, not for myself, but for others; others whom I did not know and could not imagine. I was too tired and too surprised to do more than thank him lamely and walk on.

12

THE

BRIDGE

I

In the forty-eight hours after the August 25th hearing, the whole character of the Hiss Case changed for me. In those forty-eight hours I became a witness in a deeper sense. Until then, in the three weeks of congressional hearings, I had been a witness only in the sense that, given the opportunity, I had decided that a man should testify against the Communist conspiracy in the Government; and since I could, I must. I was most truly a witness to the degree in which I was reluctant. For a witness, if he is sincere, senses, though he cannot spell out even to himself, or does not wish to, what that commitment means. "It is a bridge I had hoped that I would never have to cross," I said to my friend, John Chamberlain,* as I prepared to go to Washington to testify, "but now I have to cross it."

Even then, I did not know just what that bridge was, where it led or what it spanned. I did not even know whether I should have to cross it all the way.

By August 25th, I knew where the bridge led. By then, I began to grasp the degree to which I was not merely a man testifying against something. I was first of all a witness for something. The turn the struggle had taken made it clear that what most of the world supposed it to be—a struggle between two men—was precisely what it was not. It was a struggle between the force of two irreconcilable faiths—Communism and Christianity—embodied in two men, who by a common experience in the past, knew as few others could know what the struggle was about, and who shared a common force of character, the force which had made each of them a Communist in the first place, and which I had not changed when I changed my faith. It was the power to hold convictions and to act upon them to the limit of life itself. The whole law of motion of the Case, and the ultimate fierceness of purpose of its principals, lies at that point where the struggle was a conflict of faiths, and the witness that each man must make step by step drove the other to exertions, such as men in a mere clash of interests and personalities could neither have conceived nor sustained. Yet it is precisely at that point where we were most fiercely engaged that I found it least possible to feel hatred for Alger Hiss, although it was precisely the tactics whereby Hiss sought to conceal his guilt which constitutes, as Ralph de Toledano has pointed out, his real "crime against the human spirit." That attitude of mine toward Hiss, which to many seemed incredible or baffling, had less and less to do with my former

* Then the chief editorial writer for *Life* magazine; now one of the editors of *The Freeman*.

friendship for him. It had more and more to do with my deepening understanding of the witness that he, too, was making, and what it cost him to make it. For I cannot hate even an enemy, as I said in a broadcast immediately after Hiss's second trial, who shares with me the conviction that that life is not worth living for which a man is not prepared to die at any moment.

By August 25th, I had begun to grasp, too, what soundless void lay beneath the bridge. For I had begun to understand that to be a witness, in the sense in which I am using the term, means, ultimately, just one thing. It means that a man is prepared to destroy himself, if necessary, to make his witness. A man does not wish to destroy himself. To the full degree in which he is strongest, that is to say, to the full degree of the force that makes it possible for him to bear witness at all, he desires not to destroy himself. To the degree that he is most human, that is to say, most weak, he shrinks from destroying himself. But to the degree that what he truly is and what he stands for are one, he must at some point tacitly consent in his own mind to destroy himself if that is necessary. And, in part, that tacit consent is a simple necessity of the struggle. It is the witness' margin of maneuver. In no other way can he strip his soul of that dragging humanity, that impeding love of life and its endearments which must otherwise entangle him at every step and distract him at last to failure. This is the point at which the witness is always most alone.

In those decisive forty-eight hours, I knew, too, that I would go all the way across the bridge. I knew it at the moment when I tried to stop midway. For then I knew that I could not go back without betraying that faith for which I had begun my witness. And there was something more. At the heart of the crisis of our times lies the cold belief of millions, avowed or unavowed, that the death of religious faith is seen in nothing so much as in the fact that it has lost its power to move anyone to die for it. I sensed that the deepest meaning of the Case, and the meaning of my life for myself and for all other men, was the degree to which I could be so moved to act.

I do not mean that, by taking thought, I suddenly decided to become a witness in the fullest sense or that I never again wavered. No man decides to become a witness. In the last push, no height is stormed merely by taking thought. It is taken by those who throw themselves against the outnumbering odds, not counting them, because to count would be to fail. The point about my witness in the Hiss Case is never that I was a man driven by a fixed, implacable purpose. The point is that I was a man constantly wavering, from human and other considerations, a man constantly seeking guidance, constantly uncertain that his understanding of what it was right for him to do was the right understanding, and finally brought to desperation by the fear that it was not. I did not reach the height of my purpose in the Hiss Case immediately or all at once. I reached it by stages corresponding to the practical developments in the Case. I reached it by stages equal to the strength that I had for each successive effort. The wonderful thing is that, as each required new strength, new strength was given to me.

Toward the end of August 1948, I finally found the strength to cross the bridge and enter that region of grief, fear and death beyond. There followed about one hundred days in which was largely determined the form that the Hiss Case would take, and even whether there would be a Hiss Case, as we know it, at all. No period of the Case, I think, is more perplexing to most people. That is not strange, for many unusual factors were present. And there was going on a struggle in the dark between the forces which sought to bring the Hiss Case to light and those which opposed them. It is still impossible to be explicit about that struggle, in part because the full facts about the forces that, until the end, favored Alger Hiss, cannot in the nature of their operation be known. I can describe that struggle only as I knew it—one single man, seeking to do what was right to the limit of his understanding and strength, upon whom beat a surf of pressures, rumors, warnings, so that to keep my footing in the inevitable backwash of doubts and fears was a daily feat. It is possible that not all of the forces that I was then led to believe were working against me were working in unison, or to the same degree or from the same motives that I supposed. It is possible that some of those whom I was led to deem enemies were not enemies, even if they were not friends, or that some whom I deemed friends were not mistaken in some part of what they warned me of. Therefore, I claim no infallibility for my views which freely stand subject to the light of clarifying facts—facts, not arguments. I can only describe that struggle as I experienced it in terms of what I then felt. The struggle imposed upon the acts which shaped it forms which seem strange, and to some, grotesque, for example, the incident of the pumpkin.

In that struggle, though scores of people, chiefly enemies, were swirling around me, few men could have been more alone. Then, toward the close of that hundred days, the affairs of the Hiss Case passed out of my uncertain hands into the hands where they belonged—the hands of two forces stemming directly from the body of the nation and having its interests primarily at heart—rather than the interests of any partisan group. Those forces were the Grand Jury of the Southern District of New York working with Tom Donegan, a special assistant to the Attorney General, and the Federal Bureau of Investigation.*

The events of those hundred days are the subject of most of what remains of this book. For me, it is almost as painful to remember as to have lived through them. About them in my mind there clings, and always must, an air of death. And that not only because death tacitly seals the vocation of a witness, but also because in those days I tried to die. By the necessities of narrative, I must write of myself at that time as making certain decisions and performing certain acts. But, in fact, I cannot recall those days without again slipping to my knees as I did then, bowed down in trouble, but also in awe, to the dust of which I then most truly knew myself to be a part.

* Three other forces and a man, also deeply rooted in the nation, were necessary before the nation could win its Case. The forces were the second Grand Jury (that which first indicted William Remington); the jury in the first Hiss trial, which stood eight to four for his conviction; the jury in the second Hiss trial, which was unanimous for his conviction. The man was the Government's Prosecutor, Thomas F. Murphy, without whose grasp of the legal strategy of the trials, but, above all, his grasp of the total moral and historical meaning of the Case, all might still have been for nothing.

13

THE HISS CASE II

I

The hundred days began, characteristically, with an act of indecision. On August 24th or 25th, I wired Lawrence Spivak in New York that I would not appear after all on his radio program, *Meet the Press.* Spivak was then, among other things, the publisher of the *American Mercury.* I had known him for several years. I knew that he was an anti-Communist. I considered him friendly. A few days before, he had asked me, as a favor to him, and a service to the Committee and myself, to go on the air.

I had never listened to *Meet the Press.* I knew only what Spivak told me: that the program consisted of a panel of newsmen, including Spivak and a moderator, who shot questions at some guest currently in the news. I had no fear of questions. I agreed to go on, in part to please Spivak, in part because *Meet the Press* seemed to give me a chance to let the nation hear my voice. On the most controversial issue of the hour, no other agency in the country had been enterprising or impartial enough to approach me.

I gathered from the concern of friends, and from the general buzz, that the press and radio had in general succeeded in dropping a distorting curtain between the nation and me. But I believed then, and I still believe, that if the mass of people can hear a man's voice, listen to what he has to say and his way of saying it, they will, not invariably, but as a rule, catch the ring of truth, and pretty unerringly sort out a sincere man from an impostor.

Alger Hiss's challenge to me to repeat my charge of Communism where he could sue me for libel made me hesitate. He had first challenged me at the Hotel Commodore confrontation. His challenge had been repeated in the press on August 24th and was repeated at the August 25th hearing. Clearly, one of the first questions that I would be asked on the air was whether or not I was prepared to repeat my charge. Hiss would then be free to sue me. I did not want to be sued—the very idea of a lawsuit was alien and repugnant. Nor did I believe that Hiss could want a suit. How could he possibly want one? Even should he win, so much must come out about him in the course of a lawsuit that any verdict must be disastrous to him.

But whether Hiss's challenge were a calculated tactic or a bluff, two possibilities were implicit in it. As a tactic, it would serve to change the focus of the Case, to divert the chief issue from his Communism to a public ventilation of my life, and would put me, legally, on the defensive. If it were a bluff, it was such a bluff as he might have to make good on. Circumstances beyond his control, if I spoke out, might then force him to file suit to save face. I did not wish to back him into that corner any more than I wished to be sued by him. Therefore, I had wired Spivak: no.

I I

A single day at the farm convinced me that I was wrong. There I found the peace to measure how far three weeks of congressional hearings had brought me. I saw in the hearings something different from what anybody else I knew saw in them. Part of the nation saw in them startling or harrowing revelations. Another part saw in them irresponsible or lying charges. Others saw in them an amusing or distracting side-show to the presidential election of 1948. Still others saw in them something akin to a sporting event (which one is lying?) with sinister overtones.*

I left the August 25th hearing with two convictions that events soon intensified: 1) Alger Hiss was still an active Communist; 2) through him, I was at war with the Communist Party in its fullest extent. In the hearings, I saw a period of armed reconnaissance in which the Communist Party, taken by surprise by my testimony, had been feeling out what I was up to, how far I had gone, and how far I was prepared to go.

When the Hotel Commodore confrontation was over, the party suspected that I had not told all the facts.** By August 25th, it was reasonably sure of this and had decided how to deal with me. In the hearing, it handed me its ultimatum. I had little doubt that Hiss's repeated challenge to sue him, and his public demand for an inquiry into my past, were the snake skin wrapped around the arrows. Through them, the Communist Party said to me in effect: "This is the showdown. Stop testifying. Stop it or we will destroy

* A few days after the August 25th hearing, one of my *Time* friends found herself in conversation with another mother at their daughters' progressive school. The Hiss Case came up. The second mother was well aware of Alger Hiss, but my name had left no impression on her. "Chambers?" she said. "Chambers? Oh, you mean the little man who came from behind!" Neither my friend nor I had ever heard this racetrack term, but it seemed the almost perfect expression for the attitude of millions of people toward the Hiss Case at that time.

** Judge Murphy has pointed out to me something that I had missed and that I believe most others have missed. Hiss's question to the Committee at the Commodore—"May I ask if his voice, when he testified before, was comparable to this?"—which at the time seemed merely pompous and silly, really had a purpose. For through it Hiss was probing to find out whether I had told the Committee that he had once taken me for a European because of my inflection. If I had done so, that was a clue to Hiss that I had told the Committee a great deal more.

you. This is how we will do it." It dared me to step across the line and accept the challenge. It felt safe in daring me because it read into the fact that I had indeed held back part of the facts a motive of dishonesty. The Party would have been better advised to remember me better. But at that point the nature of Communism itself was its fate. For the Party could not possibly grasp the motives of my silence, and if it could, would have regarded them as a sign of weakness, and would have treated them with exactly that contempt which kept Vishinsky laughing all one night in scorn at the peace proposals of the West.

Besides, the Communist Party had already totted up the balance of forces and knew that it could proceed against me without even showing its hand. Lacking its intelligence facilities, I could, nevertheless, tot them up in my own fashion. They were overwhelmingly against me.

Beyond the masked power of the Communist Party, working in a thousand secret ways, there stood the resources of the Soviet Government, working through its underground apparatuses and other agencies. The United States Government was explicitly on record against me (the red herring), and the President would soon be saying at his whistle stops across the land: "If you work for *Time*, you're a hero. If you work for the State Department, you're a heel." I had been warned repeatedly that the brunt of official wrath was directed, not against Alger Hiss as a danger, but against me for venturing to testify to the danger. Moreover, the most articulate section of public opinion was bitterly aroused against me and persistent in its attacks, none of which was ever checked in the whole course of the Hiss Case against even one intelligent effort to talk to me personally and arrive at a first-hand impression of what I might be like or what I might think that I was doing. The Communist Party did not need to move openly against me. It had only to sit back, to give a quiet turn here, to prompt my enemies there, to feed out information, some of it true and damaging, but most of it slanderous and false, to iterate that most potent of falsehoods: that nobody can believe an ex-Communist, and the powers hostile to me that the Hiss Case had set in motion would do the rest.

It was against that rally of force (whose full weight and worth I by no means clearly understood) that I reconsidered Hiss's challenge and the wire that I had sent to Spivak. The very fact that such massed force could exist narrowed my choice of action; in fact, determined it. Whatever Hiss chose to do, I had no choice.

I had no more right to spare myself the ordeal of a libel suit than I could spare Hiss the possibility of suing me. To do so would not merely betray all that I had tried to do until then. I had only to glance across my fields and watch my neighbors at their timeless labors to know what the human betrayal would be.

Therefore, when Spivak telephoned me a second time to explain how gravely I had embarrassed him by retracting my promise to appear on *Meet the Press,* I answered that I had reconsidered, that I would appear. The program was scheduled for the night of August 27th.

As I write about these things, in the fall of 1951, three years after they happened, I hear the clip-clip sound of a tractor, moving far off in low gear. Through the pane in the door, I see in the distance that my neighbor and his son are working up a field for winter wheat. When the wind shifts, I cannot hear the tractor at all. It moves, slowly and stately, like a little galleon, while the two ploughs roll back a brown wake behind it. The son rides the machine. The father, an old man, walks behind to supervise the operation.

These are the men whose habitual labors hold the crumbling world together. They stand for all fathers and sons, including mine, for whom in that moment of the past I sought to act. I think:

> *And the ploughs go round and round,*
> *As year on year goes by.*

The lines bring back the day, when, as a youth, I walked along a field path and first read the *Antigone.* When I reached that second chorus, I stopped walking without realizing it. As I read for the first time:

> *Much is there passing strange,*
> *Nothing surpassing mankind,*

it seemed to me as if a second sun had burst upon the world, which, when I finally raised my eyes to look at it, was created a second time in that new light.

III

Before I could appear on *Meet the Press* something happened which made it clear that the Hiss Case had developed a life and a momentum of its own that it would be extremely difficult for anyone involved in it to impede. The first of the lurking factors emerged. The Baltimore *News-Post*, a Hearst paper, startled its readers with an exclusive story that Hiss and Chambers had, at different times, owned the same piece of property near Westminster, Md.

The story was backed up with photostats of Hiss's correspondence with a Westminster real-estate agent, and his records of purchase and mine. That both the head of the Carnegie Endowment for World Peace and a senior editor of *Time* magazine should have owned the same isolated property, a photograph of which accompanied the text, raised thrilling (and groundless) speculations about underground Communist hideaways. A further note of mystery was injected by photostats of my signature, taken from the register of the local hotel. But that was a purely gratuitous touch. Perhaps ten times during my years at *Time*, I had arrived late in Westminster for my week-end, and spent the night at the hotel to spare my wife the hardship of meeting me in town at two or three o'clock in the morning. This and other puzzling matters I could have cleared up if anybody had asked me to before the story went to press.

The Committee telephoned me at once. I stopped by its offices on my way to the *Meet the Press* broadcast. My testimony as to how Hiss and I came to own the same property can be read in the official transcript of that executive hearing. But nothing that was asked me that day struck me as so acute as a carefully casual comment of Robert Stripling's after the hearing. "I have been reading over your testimony, Mr. Chambers," he said, "and one thing about it impresses me. You answer questions readily enough, but I notice that you never volunteer information."

IV

I had taken my son* to Washington with me. It seemed to me that since history had overtaken the boy in a way that I should gladly have spared him, it might be less frightening to him to see that the actors in it were not merely impersonal, dread names, but people; that the most sensational of human actions still take place in a routine setting of buildings, offices and elevators, or the chromium commonplaces of a broadcasting studio. Above all, I wanted to

* Congressman Nixon, somewhat upset by the Westminster development, was to introduce him to newsmen with the startling announcement: "This is Mr. Hiss's young son."

spare him that shadow of fear, the menace of the unknown, which is, therefore, too real. At the moment, there was very little else that I could do for him.

We had supper with the Spivaks and Martha Rountree, the co-producer of *Meet the Press.* "One of the questions you will almost certainly be asked," said Spivak, "is whether you are willing to say that Hiss was a Communist." I said I hoped that I would not be asked that question. "Well, I think you will be," said Spivak, "and I certainly hope that you will answer it." From the way that Spivak glanced at me sharply over his glasses, I had no further doubt that that question stood high on the list. I said I hoped that Spivak had picked me a balanced panel, that at least two of my four inquisitors would not be actively hostile so that I might have an occasional chance to catch my breath. That part of the panel which included himself, Spivak assured me, once more glancing sharply over his glasses, would not be hostile.

I have only heard *Meet the Press* once since that night. From that occasion, and from what others tell me, I gather that the tone of the program seldom varies and that it can be summed up as fun for the boys but death for the frogs. In that respect, the program in which I participated simply ran true to form. But I also believe that few of the thousands who listened to *Meet the Press* on August 27, 1948, would fail to agree that it was enlivened by an unprecedented personal venom; that it amounted to a savage verbal assault and battery on the guest, without pause, and with little restraint or decency.

I should have known, if I could possibly have imagined, what was in store, from the moment that I entered the studio. In a waiting room, I was introduced to two of my questioners, Edward T. Folliard of the Washington *Post,* the most implacable of the pro-Hiss newspapers, and a correspondent from some other paper whose name I never caught. I was unprepared for the chilling stiffness of my fellow journalists, in part because I had not yet had time to overcome the habit of regarding myself as a working journalist and a *Time* editor.

James Reston of the New York *Times* quietly joined us. His role and manner acutely puzzled me. I did not know that he was to be the moderator for the evening. Reston complained to his colleagues: "I sent him a note and he would not even answer my question." He referred to his note during the August 25th hearing, asking whether, at the age of four, I had published a book of poems under the name of G. Crosley.

In the broadcasting room, I sat at a small table, facing my inquisitors. They were Spivak, the unrecollected newsman, Folliard and Tom Reynolds of the Chicago *Sun*. The *Sun* was a half-sister to Marshall Field's *PM*, the New York daily, sometimes referred to as the uptown *Pravda* or *Daily Worker*.* At my right sat Reston, the moderator. Somewhere beyond him sat Martha Rountree, the only person whom I recall as trying to moderate anything during the broadcast. At my left, sat a small studio audience, including my son and Louis Banks of *Time*.

It was my first time on the air. I knew that every word I spoke, every inflection of my voice, was critically important not only to the Committee and me, but to the future of the Case. I was concentrated on answering simply and directly. I sought not to let myself be crowded, not to lose my temper during the baiting.

The question that we were met to ask and answer was put almost at once. Folliard put it: Are you willing to repeat your charge that Alger Hiss was a Communist? I paused for the shade of a second. Then I crossed the bridge. I answered: "Alger Hiss was a Communist and may still be one."

It was almost certainly the most important answer that I shall be called upon to give in my life—and not only for myself. Millions who heard, or heard of it, caught only its surface meaning: Whittaker Chambers had deliberately opened himself to a libel suit by Alger Hiss. But I like to believe that some who heard it, heard at the same instant, its inward meaning. That meaning was that God, Who is a God of Mercy, is also the God of Whom it is written:

Der Gott Der Eisen wachsen liess,
Er wollte keine Knechte.

The God Who made iron grow—
He wanted no slaves.

Of the mayhem that followed, only one question and answer seems worth remembering. It bears directly on the Hiss Case. I was asked something about the economic problem of Communism.

* By then, or shortly after, *PM* had suffered a corporate, but not an editorial change into the New York *Star*.

I answered, citing Dostoevsky: "The problem of Communism is not an economic problem. The problem of Communism is the problem of atheism."

Tom Reynolds was the most unsparing of my questioners. His manner and bias are fixed, I think in one question. "Do you find it easier," he asked me, "to make a living now than when you were in the Communist Party?" At the time, I was too busy answering to catch the inner animus of that and other sallies. Even after it was over, Reynolds could not let go. He blustered up and asked how, if I were not a follower of Professor Toynbee, I explained the fact that I had written so favorable a piece about him in *Time*. The implication was that the piece was dishonest. I said that I had not been interested in presenting my views about Toynbee, but Toynbee's views about history. "Well, that's the kind of piece I'm going to write about you," Reynolds said. "It won't be my views, it will just be the truth about you."

I left the studio with my son and Louis Banks. "You are a brave man," said Banks. It was meant sincerely, but I could not help thinking with amusement of the way a buyer for a packing house eyes a beef admiringly and observes: "He'll string up a nice carcass."

It was a hot and breathless night. As we walked down Connecticut Avenue, a studio messenger caught up with us and handed me a note on which was written a telephone number that I was to call at once. From the *Time* office, I called it. An angry Nixon answered the phone. "It was a damned outrage," said the Quaker Congressman.

My son had been extremely silent. But as soon as we were alone in the dark car, heading out of Washington toward Westminster, he asked me quietly: "Papa, why did those men hate you so?" "Does it worry you?" I said. "Don't let it worry you. It is a kind of a war. They are on one side, and I am on the other side. Later on, perhaps you will understand. Now you don't have to think about it. But I am glad that you saw it and I hope you will always remember it."

He fell asleep while I drove on.

V

Until then, our home had been our sanctuary. This was especially true of the children. Their acres were their peace, and the distresses of the world beyond, rumors of which sometimes reached them, might brush their fields; they had no power to enter.

The *News-Post's* story changed all that. Our address had never been more secret than the telephone book in which it was listed. But neither had it been of public interest. Now the nation knew it. Now anyone who wished was free to walk into our home, and first of all the press. My children watched round-eyed, then horrified, then with a saving disgust, as newsmen and news photographers swarmed in with an enthusiasm that, to us, could only seem like the delight of urchins in trampling a garden. What was most frightening to the children was their incredulous realization that their father and mother, the source of all security in their lives, were clearly powerless to halt the violation. We could only treat the invaders, and counsel the children to treat them, courteously and simply, in the hope that they would presently drift on to fields of fresher sensation.

Of course, many of the newsmen had no more stomach for their assignment than we had. They had their own homes and families where they would much rather have been. They were doing a job. Some of them exuded a hostility and distrust that they could not entirely curb. Nevertheless, even these stayed just within the limits of civility. Only one, so far as I can remember, was ever outstandingly rude. He was a representative of the Washington *Post* and a former *Life* employe. He appeared, for the first time, at the very end of the Hiss Case, a few hours after Alger Hiss had been convicted. "I'm going to give you hell in my story tomorrow," this gracious fellow assured me. To my wife, he promised: "We're going to give your husband what he used to give the writers at *Time*." He kept his word (as he understood it), overwrought, no doubt, by Hiss's conviction.

On the other hand, a reporter from another pro-Hiss newspaper, sent to ply me with a set of provocative questions presumably dreamed up by his editor, noticed an expression of fatigue pass over my face. Suddenly, he thrust his pencil in his pocket. "I guess you're sick to death of this," he said, and getting up, with the rest of his questions unasked, walked out of the house.

Certainly Pipe Creek Farm and those who lived on it were puzzling to the press. The first wave of assault had come apparently expecting to find its own dream of a *Time* editor's country place—the miles of white wooden fences, the acres of clipped turf, the monogrammed Cadillac station wagon, the mansion of reconditioned antiquity, made livable, however, by the addition of a cocktail bar. Instead, they found a dirt farm where there had never been enough hands to do all that needed doing and where the only liquor in the house was used to revive sick calves. The family that claimed former friendship with the urbane Hisses wore work clothes, milked cows, spread manure, cooked its own meals and commonly ate them in the kitchen beside the range. The discrepancy was staggering. How could a newsman, fighting a deadline, be expected to probe what special experience of life and history could lead to a situation so unfairly confusing? Why would an editor of *Time* and his wife prefer the drudgery of a dairy farm when Baltimore's night clubs were only thirty miles away? Clearly, most of the newsmen regarded any hard work as a form of insanity. Clearly they regarded any man who would earn $30,000 a year in order to live in primitive peace in the countryside as out of his mind, or a fraud. I think that most of them settled quickly for a fraud.

Their bafflement fed the deeper suspicion, which just peeped through their formal manner, that we were impostors, and that Alger Hiss was a wronged man. No answer we could give to anything that they could ask could be taken at face value, and that they quietly made us feel. Our strong instinct for privacy, and our natural reticence merely seemed to them secretive and furtive. To the press, our life on the farm was clearly an act, which we had rigged for the occasion, part of a greater act that included my charge against Hiss. This viewpoint, which I am convinced was largely unconscious, was so ingrained that, even today, newsmen ask me, with a knowing smirk, if I have given up farming yet. The same notion lies presumably at the root of the repeated stories that I have returned to *Time.*

For months, no newspaper in the country sent anyone to the farm (always with the exception of Bert Andrews) who was equipped to report what he might find there. Questioning seldom got beyond the current news except to count and recount the number of our cows, or to ask, again in the tone of catching us in a fraud, if we did not use milking machines.

Not until the end of the first Hiss trial, did any newsman ask me an intelligent question. Then Nicholas Blatchford of the Washington *Daily News,* disregarding cows, barns, house, or acres, asked me simply: "What do you think that you're doing?" We were sitting in the living room. At his question I turned to look out at the mists that were rising from the bottom below the house, filling the valley. I answered slowly: "I am a man who, reluctantly, grudgingly, step by step, is destroying himself that this country and the faith by which it lives may continue to exist."

That was all. A newsman had had the imagination to ask a troubled man one of the only two or three questions worth asking and, as a result, Blatchford's story was instantly picked up all over the country. The movie cameramen who, in marked contrast to the press, were consistently friendly and kindly, were soon making me repeat my answer to Blatchford behind piles of hay bales, in front of the barn or encircled by cows.

Yet the evening of the day of Blatchford's visit, my daughter came out to the barn where I was milking, to say that a Baltimore newsman had arrived with a report that the jury in the first Hiss trial was out in New York. He had taken up his post in the house where he was going to remain until the jury returned its verdict. When I had finished milking, I went in to see our visitor. I explained to him that there could be only two probabilities: the jury would reach a verdict at once (which clearly had not happened), or the jury would be out all night. "Do you really mean to stay here all night?" I asked him. He made some indistinct noise. Later, I pressed him again. "You see," he said, "it isn't just the jury. My city editor seems to think that you are going to skip to Canada tonight." He glanced at me darkly.

I think that his candid answer about sums up the state of mind of much of the press from the beginning to the end of the Hiss Case. It was seldom betrayed quite so honestly. Perhaps, in general, it reflected the temper of the city desks rather than the legmen. It was an attitude very hard to bear, taken together with everything else, because it was set like cement, beyond any possibility of rationally counteracting it. There was no defense against it. It walked into our home and challenged us with its watchful eye and its faintly skeptical smile, too discreet to be frankly rude.

It was only one aspect of the dehumanization of Whittaker Chambers that was then in full swing, incubated by the Hiss defense. Within a month, the last ten years, the richest and fullest of my life, had been stripped away from me and publicly treated as if they did not exist. The enemy could not allow them to exist, for there was scarcely anything in them that could possibly be turned against me. Though I was still an editor of *Time*, I was for all practical purposes publicly an untouchable. At best, my editorship was becoming something to beat *Time* over the masthead with. A skilful and tireless campaign was rapidly turning me into something scarcely recognizable as human.

Yet our relations with the press had one very human moment. During the day when the first Hiss jury was finding it impossible to agree,* newsmen and newsreel men sat in a great circle of lawn chairs under the trees behind our house. It was a little like a siege. At noon and in the evening, my wife and daughter fed the occupying forces and brought them iced tea and coffee while they kept in touch with the living world over their portable radios. Mr. Pennington, my son and I were haying. Now and again, the Baltimore *Sun*'s jeep, packed with sightseeing newsmen, would rip across the hills or try to reach us through the maze of the contours. But I think that those scenes of dismayingly simple industry finally shook the prejudice of some. For, when it was leaving, the press did a very gracious thing.

The newsmen who had wandered through the house had noted the albums of recorded music lying about—Haydn, Handel, Mozart, Bach, Beethoven. The newsmen put their heads together. All chipped in, and two of them quietly slipped away to buy us a present which they presented to us in the name of the whole group. It was Sibelius' First Symphony. Nothing could have touched us more.

V I

During the August 25th hearing, an official of the Immigration Service (of the Justice Department) had asked me to talk to its agents in New York with a view to my testifying in the deportation proceedings against J. Peters. The head of the underground section

* The spokesman of the four jurors who were against Hiss's conviction was the foreman of the jury. Shortly after the opening of the trial, his wife was in a hospital. She told the elderly woman in the next bed that her husband had already decided that Hiss was innocent. The elderly woman happened to be Tom Donegan's mother. Thus, the prosecution knew almost from the beginning that the foreman had already made up his mind. To have asked for a mistrial would have given Alger Hiss a perfect defense of double jeopardy in any subsequent trial. For the jurors had already been sworn and evidence taken. Therefore, the Government suggested to Judge Samuel H. Kaufman that he excuse the foreman and substitute one of the alternates. But Lloyd Paul Stryker, Hiss's trial lawyer, felt that the foreman made an excellent juror and should not be disturbed. Judge Kaufman concurred.

of the American Communist Party had clearly become one of the most dangerous possible witnesses against Alger Hiss, if by any means he could be induced to talk. He had long eluded the efforts of the House Committee on Un-American activities to locate him. Now, after years of surveillance (of which I had long known) he was suddenly picked up by the Justice Department and held for deportation.*

I had a slightly uneasy feeling about the Immigration Service. I knew that, only a short time before, one of its high officials in New York had severed his connections with it due to his persistent conformity to the Communist Party line.

The agents called on me at my office at *Time*. One was a mute man, who, if I remember rightly, said nothing at all in the course of the interview that followed. The other asked the questions. I described to them in a good deal of detail my activities in the first Soviet underground apparatus into which I had been recruited. I described my activities as contact man between the Soviet apparatus and the Communist Party, an operation in which I had worked closely with Peters. I presume that I also described Peters' connection with the Ware Group, though I no longer remember distinctly. But my information about Peters and the Soviet apparatus was obviously of great importance to the Government. My visitors presently left, asking me to remain in New York until I should be notified whether or not I would be called as a witness.

While I was pondering upon the reasons why anybody could possibly wish to deport J. Peters at the moment when he had become important in the Hiss controversy, and allied disclosures, Congressman Nixon volunteered to enlighten me.

Once more, he and other members of the sub-committee had come up to New York. They also were interested in questioning Peters. The public hearing was held in the Federal Building. For

* Peters obviously stood high on the list of those who would be of interest to me if Hiss filed a libel suit against me. Just before the first Hiss trial began, he was suddenly permitted to leave the United States. He made a quick departure in a Dutch plane. It has been pointed out to me that since Peters would plead self-incrimination and would refuse to answer questions, he was of no value to anyone as a witness. But perhaps it is not unduly strange that in those taut days, I should have drawn only the unhappiest inferences from the dispatch with which, after he had been under surveillance for years, he was suddenly hustled from the scene. Few knew so much about the Hiss Case as he. For Peters had been in charge of everything. He had known everybody. Everybody. . . .

the first time, the nation caught a glimpse of the dark, rather undistinguished little man who had long played so cryptic a part in its affairs.

I was called as a witness. I identified Peters. Peters was unwilling to identify me, on the ground that his answer might incriminate and, as he said, glaring at me and lingering lovingly over the word, degrade him. At this hearing, I first saw Carol Weiss King, who accompanied Peters as his counsel. With bobbed gray hair, bulging brief case clutched under her arm and a cigarette drooped from her lips she seemed to be trying to caricature the common notion of a Communist.*

After the hearing, Nixon asked me if I were going back to the farm at once. I explained that I was waiting to be called by the United States Immigration Service in the hearings against J. Peters. "In that case," said Nixon, "you can go home tonight. They will never call you." I asked why, since there were few men in the country who knew as much about Peters and his activities as I knew, and almost no one who would testify to them.

"Don't you understand," said Nixon, "that if the Government calls you to testify against J. Peters, it will have admitted that you are a credible witness? If you are a credible witness against J. Peters, you are also a credible witness against Alger Hiss. They will never call you."

Two days later, an official of the Immigration Service telephoned me at *Time*. He was sorry, he said, if he had inconvenienced me, but the Immigration Service found that it had so many excellent witnesses against J. Peters that it would not be necessary to call me.

VII

An interval, like a long silence, followed my radio charge against Alger Hiss. For weeks he took no public action. I went about my work, sometimes at *Time*, more often at the farm, with a curious

* Carol King (she has died since this was written) received her early legal training in the office of Max Loewenthal, close friend of Justice Felix Frankfurter, and author of a recent book attacking the F.B.I. At the death of Joseph Brodsky, she succeeded him as a veteran counsel for Communists in trouble with the law. She was the sister of Louis S. Weiss of the New York law firm of Paul, Weiss, Wharton and Garrison. Weiss has since died. This firm had other curious connections with the Hiss Case. Not only was Weiss the brother of Carol King. Garrison was the brother-in-law of Dr. Carl Binger, the defense psychiatrist in both Hiss trials. Like her friend, Priscilla Hiss, Mrs. Binger is a Bryn Mawr alumna.

sense of continuing something that has ended, as a man might feel who has been revived after his heart had stopped beating.

It was the fall of the year. For the first time in my life, I felt the simple force of the words, the fall—the literal fall to the earth of all the leaves, which stripped away the illusion that summer had made of the world, leaving only its bare forms and opening space.

My wife and I found ourselves walking out together to various vantage points on the farm, to feel the sun and to look into the new distances. In general, we are people who have cared little for beauty as spectacle. It takes a good deal of persuading to make us go to look at a sunset. One of our earliest and most lasting memories of the Hisses had been their insistence that we drive out with them to see the autumn foliage. At the time, we thought that it was an esthetic dutifulness, both charming and amusing. But it remained in our minds much more vividly than some more important things about the Hisses because it seemed to mark so sharp a difference in temper of mind between us.

We like our beauty to be inherent in our way of life, not something we must make a special trip for. Thus, I have been suddenly struck, when I have put down the last hay at night before going to the house, by all the cattle gently munching at once in the warm comfort of the winter barn. Or I have wiped the puckering sweat out of my eyes suddenly to see, from the top of a hay load, the distant mountains stand out blue and massive in an hour of perfect light. Once, after a morning of mixing and chopping feed, following an exhausting week at *Time*, I slumped down on a full grain sack, thinking: "I can't keep it up." Then, in the hush of my fatigue, I saw the long shafts of sunlight piercing the cracks between the barn planks, with the meal motes dancing in them. High in the comb of the barn, all the pigeons cooed at once, and I knew: for this I can stand anything. The beauty glimpsed between bursts of the labor that justified our joy in it was the beauty that we felt. The kind of looking at the earth that my wife and I now found ourselves doing was new and different. We knew, without ever saying so, that it was a leave taking. It was looking at something we felt that we were leaving, or that was leaving us.

Deeply emotional people, we had never been wordy (for that reason), about anything that deeply moved us. We understood each other's feelings about most things, instinctively, without talk. Now we were more than ever reticent, not because of things that we did not need to talk about, but because of what we did not want to talk about. Silence seemed to absorb us. On my wife's part, I think that this was due to the shock of finding herself abruptly cut off from the whole world. A number of friends, both in Westminster and elsewhere, remained doggedly loyal to us throughout the Hiss Case. But that could not change, that could only point up, the fact that beyond the borders of our farm, the world surged against us out of curiosity or hostility or lack of understanding. Only someone who has been alone against the world will know what that means.

On my part, the enveloping silence, which no doubt communicated itself to my wife from me, had another cause. Its root lay close to what I meant when I spoke about the tragedy of history. It had to do with the spirit of man on the rack of necessity. The nerve was torn whenever the problem of informing arose, and it had now become the central problem of my days. Alger Hiss's defiance had already forced me a long way down that road which anyone in my place could see must, as a necessity of action, lead to fuller testimony against him, and that in turn must unfailingly involve all the others. Hiss's complete disregard for the suffering which must be caused those others, and which he could see just as certainly as I could, stiffened my own resistance to involving them by testimony which I considered irrelevant to the purpose of my main witness. I wondered at his inhumanity even while I understood its causes. In Communism the individual is nothing. But I knew that if I were compelled to testify in full against Hiss and the others, if I, who wished harm to no man, were driven by necessity to bring ruin upon so many lives, then, afterwards, I would never again really be able to live myself.

There is in men a very deep-rooted instinct that they may not inform against those whose kindness and affection they have shared, at whose tables they have eaten and under whose roofs they have slept, whose wives and children they have known as friends—and that regardless of who those others are or what crimes they have committed. It is an absolute prohibition. It is written in no book, but it is more binding than any code that exists. If of necessity a man must violate that prohibition, and it is part of the tragedy of history that, for the greater good, men sometimes must, the man who violates it must do so in the full consciousness that there is a penalty. That penalty is a kind of death, most deadly if a man must go on living. It is not violent. It is not even a deepening shadow. It is a simple loss of something as when a filter removes all color from the light. I felt its foretouch. It was soon to be on me.

VIII

I do not know, of course, what Alger Hiss may have been thinking or doing during those same days. But the public pressures moving him to sue me were becoming irresistible. At the end of three or four weeks, his staunch friend, the Washington *Post*, deplored, editorially, the impression that must be caused by Hiss's failure to file suit. The New York *Daily News*, in its terser style, merely asked: "Well, Alger, where's that suit?"

I knew that Hiss was preparing to sue by signs that at first confused me. Our farm is bounded at one end by a state road, clearly visible from the barn and yard. Along another side runs a county road. Without actually making a practice of it, over the years I have always kept half an eye on any cars that slowed down or parked near the farm because, if the Communist Party sent its agents against us, they would almost certainly arrive by one or the other of those roads.

Now I became aware that there were at least two strange cars prowling around the edge of the farm. One bore New York license plates. The other car was a conspicuously light gray or yellow convertible. I sighted it once from the ridge, creeping out of the back of the farm, which is far from the house. There was nothing we could do about these prowlers and intruders unless we cornered them somewhere on the property, which might be dangerous. Most of the time, they kept to the public roads. We had no protection of any kind and never have had any but what we could provide for ourselves.

At that time, it made perfectly good sense to suppose that the Communist Party might decide to remove me as the one dangerous witness against the conspiracy. That was our first thought. As the simplest precaution, we distributed bullets for handy use in all the rooms, not knowing just how we might be surprised. Much greater was our fear for the children. We had always felt a special anxiety that the Communist Party or its agents might kidnap one of the children to hold as a hostage. Now we warned the schools not to permit either child to leave the grounds, and, above all, to let no one take either child away on any pretext whatever. Both schools co-operated to the full.

Soon strangers began to question the neighbors about us. A young man in the New York car represented himself as a newsman who was writing a series of articles about the Hiss Case. Then he would put his questions. He was always careful to say knowingly that the full facts in the Hiss Case had not come out yet, but when they did, it would be seen that Hiss was innocent. This system served the double purpose of collecting information and attempting to rouse the suspicions of our neighbors against us.

The other stranger asked chiefly factual questions. He inquired in great detail how many cattle we had, how many chickens, how much farm machinery, how much corn we planted, etc. He became exasperated with one neighbor who insisted that we had no hogs. "I've been told that they have ninety hogs," he insisted. Most of these activities were reported to us the same day or soon after.

I said to my wife, "Those are Hiss's paid investigators. He is getting ready to sue."

IX

One morning while my wife and I were still busy with our chores, a stranger, whom at first I took for one of my neighbors, came up to me at the calf barn. He asked if I were Whittaker Chambers. "I guess I have been expecting you," I said. He was a United States marshal and he handed me a summons and complaint to defend myself in the United States District Court in Baltimore in a suit for libel brought against me by Alger Hiss whose reputation, the complaint charged, I had wilfully and knowingly damaged to the amount of $50,000.

The Associated Press promptly asked me what I had to say. I said: "I welcome Alger Hiss's daring suit. I do not minimize the ferocity or the ingenuity of the forces that are working through him. But I do not believe that, ultimately, Alger Hiss, or anybody else, can use the means of justice to defeat the ends of justice." By the "forces that are working through him," I meant, of course, the Communist Party.

A day or so later, Alger Hiss's attorneys decided that my statement to the AP had further injured his reputation to the extent of $25,000.*

At the time that Alger Hiss filed suit, my wife and I had perhaps two or three thousand dollars in the bank. We had several out-

* The damages claimed by Hiss remained at this $75,000 figure until shortly after his conviction, when Judge W. Calvin Chestnut dismissed the libel suit with prejudice. That is the legal way of saying that Hiss could not again bring suit against me on the same grounds.

standing debts. Pipe Creek Farm was worth perhaps $30,000 and against it was a $7,500 mortgage held by the Westminster Savings Bank, which had first claim to its money. Not only was the sum of $75,000 fantastic as compared with any ability I had to pay it, even assuming that Hiss won the libel suit and that the jury would award him the full sum. But it was impossible for him to collect any judgment from me in any case. For any judgment would have been against me alone. But Pipe Creek Farm, like most property in Carroll County, is jointly owned by my wife and me, and could not be attached or sold to satisfy any judgment that was not against *both* of the co-owners.

In my future actions in the Hiss Case, the problem was never, though I am convinced that many people suppose so, a problem of saving myself from a judgment in the libel suit. No doubt, the Hiss defense intended to force me to ruin myself financially by the costs of defending such a suit. But that was soon taken care of in another way. The developments that resulted from the libel suit were as unforeseen by Hiss as by me. But the motives that made them possible had nothing to do with dollars and cents. On my part, they were the same motives that began the Case.

X

Almost immediately after Hiss filed suit, I was suddenly subpoenaed to appear before the Grand Jury of the Southern District of New York. This sudden development surprised and puzzled me. For the Grand Jury had been hearing testimony on Communist espionage for months—three-quarters of its term of service had, in fact, expired. It had heard both Alger Hiss and Harry Dexter White (though that fact I did not then know). But I did know that in all that time the Government had never seen fit to call me before the Grand Jury, although the F.B.I. was checking with me frequently about the very people whom the Grand Jury was investigating, or questioning.

The Grand Jury sat in the Federal Building in New York City. The day I went to testify, that building (officially, the United States Courthouse) was picketed by a chanting chain of Communists protesting the trial of their eleven leaders which was presently to begin before Judge Harold R. Medina. I hesitated for a moment and stood watching the bawling pickets. I wondered if they might recognize me and decide to extemporize an incident around me. Then I walked through the line. No one recognized me. I recognized none of them. A whole new generation of Communists was chanting in the streets.

I made my way to the witnesses' waiting room next door to the Grand Jury room. Tom Donegan, a special assistant to the Attorney General, greeted me pleasantly. "It won't take long," he said. "There's been so much in the papers, we thought we'd better have you in."

Soon, an attendant ushered me, for the first time, into that Grand Jury room, which I was to see so many times again. I sat at the far end of a long table. At my left sat the foreman and, perhaps, the assistant foreman or secretary of the Grand Jury. At my right sat the official reporter. At the other end of the table, which was in effect the other end of the long room, Tom Donegan sat on a slightly raised platform behind a table or desk. At my right, sat four or five long rows of grand jurors, one row raised slightly above the other. Those completely strange men and women gazed at me (and into my life) with an expression, which on that day, seemed to me faintly amused and skeptical. So this was Whittaker Chambers—this little round man!

I had never heard of Tom Donegan before (though I never knew him well, I thought that I came to appreciate him better as man and public servant during the long grind of the Hiss trials). To me, he was simply the representative of the Justice Department. At that time, I was convinced, however mistakenly, that no one of any power in the Government wanted to know the real truth about Communism in Government. I was convinced that, on the contrary, the official purpose was to bypass or stifle that truth wherever it threatened to emerge. I submit that few men in my place would have had much reason to think anything else.

I no longer remember much of my testimony on that day. I remember describing in some detail the operations of the first Soviet apparatus I had known. I talked about Dr. Rosenbliett and how the Soviet underground had come into possession of the Chrystie tank data. I believe that I was asked about the Ware Group.

Two questions I remember vividly. I was asked why I had broken with the Communist Party. No simple answer could convey the heart of that experience to anyone. I told the Grand Jury how I had read Professor Tchernavin's book (*I Speak for the Silent*), and that it had had an impact upon me. But about religious matters I could speak only to the most intimate of friends, and not often then. In so far as my break was a religious experience, I felt that it was personal to a degree that made it impossible for me to describe it to those unknown people in that public place, even had I then been able to find the words to make what I must tell them comprehensible. I could only say to them that I had suffered some kind of religious experience. Even while I said it, I felt that it was unconvincing.

It was not until months later, when I testified before the succeeding Grand Jury, that I spoke without reserve. Then it was no longer a question of overcoming my natural diffidence. By then, all the defenses and shelters which ordinarily give the soul sanctuary in life had been torn down. Shyness, reticence, had become as incongruous as the legal fiction that I was still a person in the common meaning of the word. I had ceased to be a person. By then I was a witness, to whom, as such, I was given to know, as men seldom are in life, the meaning of two lines that often ran through my mind:

Quidquid latet adparebit,
*Nil inultum remanebit.**

Then, when I was asked the same or a similar question, I spoke as a man speaks who, in the ordinary sense is no longer living. When I had finished, a grave juryman in one of the upper tiers first broke the silence. "I may be out of order," he said, "but after the soul-searing testimony we have just heard, I do not see how anyone can fail to believe this witness." "You are certainly out of order," said the foreman of the Grand Jury.

But the second question that I was asked on that first occasion was even more difficult for me to answer. A juror asked me if I had had direct knowledge of Soviet espionage. If I answered yes, there would be no choice but to tell the whole story, implicating all the others. I asked to be permitted to think about the question overnight. (I had been told that I would appear again the next day.) Then I was excused.

Why did I ask for time to consider? What was there to think about? Whether or not I would destroy with shame and suffering people most of whom would gleefully destroy me?** I did not be-

* The *Dies Irae*: Whatever is hidden, shall be brought out; nothing shall remain unpunished.

** History has proved that my concern was, above all, ironic. Most of the Communists in the Hiss Case, like most of those in the Bentley Case, are going about their affairs much as always. It is not the Communists, but the ex-Communists who have co-operated with the Government, who have chiefly suffered. All of the ex-Communists who co-operated with the Government had broken with the

lieve that the Government had the slightest intention of proceeding against any of them. Recent experience gave me sound reason to suppose that its special wrath was reserved for anyone who might raise the issue of Communism in Government. Why should I act against the Communists as individuals? I knew what my answer would be, though my true answer still lay, as far as I knew, in Adolf Berle's files.

The next morning, Donegan spoke to me again before I entered the Grand Jury room. "I'm just going to run through the names of about twenty people," he said, "and you answer yes or no as to whether you knew them or not." I knew personally only a few of the names that I was asked. Most of them, if I remember rightly, were members of Elizabeth Bentley's groups. On the first day I had been before the Grand Jury perhaps three-quarters of an hour. The second day, I was before it about twenty minutes. Then I was dismissed.

That second day the grand juror repeated his question about espionage. I knew that there was no other way than by answering no that I could possibly jeopardize myself before the law. I answered: no.

X I

My no to the Grand Jury stands for all men to condemn. I will say only this about it. No man can have watched his brother die a spiritual death by inches, or have dragged him, half-dead, across the frozen ground, or have heard his mother scream as she learned that her son was at last dead, or have listened to her tears choke her in sleep as she lay beside his corpse, or have stood at night beside his brother's grave and listened to a rioting world smash a flask against the cemetery wall—no man can have known these things without feeling for all humanity, in its good and evil, an absolving pity that becomes the central mood of his life. Not to add to the sum of suffering that even in the happiest lives is almost more than can be borne. . . . I have always seen all life first with pity. The necessity springs from something deeply ingrained and unchangeable in my nature. It is that which has always whispered to me that, if a man can perform a saving act for others, and feels within himself the

party entirely as a result of their own conscience years before the Hiss Case began. It is worth noting that not one Communist was moved to break with Communism under the pressures of the Hiss case. Let those who wonder about Communism and the power of its faith, ponder upon that fact.

strength to bear the penalty for that act, he must perform it. For it is the soul which must prevail, or life has no more meaning than a gutter full of scum and algae.

I would suggest, too, that the source of what at last made it possible for me to bear witness against Communism, as a power of evil, lay close to the source of what made it necessary for me to bear a witness of mercy for the Communists as men. I do not know why, but I sense that the witness of mercy unlocks the possibility of a cycle of redemption, and that any other locks upon men the old coils of hatred, multiplying new evil.

XII

I had no doubt that Hiss, with his close ties in Government, would quickly learn what I had testified about espionage, and would at once take advantage of it. I wondered how he would feel, taking advantage of a man who had sought to shield him. And I was human enough to resent the fact that he would feel nothing. For such a witness acts in no sudden or miraculous way. Its action is slow, but it is enduring. It remains a measure against which the base must scale themselves, never more so than in the act of defying or deriding it.

XIII

Once Hiss sued me, *Time*, with its usual generosity, came to my aid. The magazine took the position that in charging me with libel, Hiss had impugned my veracity, not merely as an individual man, but as an editor of *Time*. *Time*, therefore, had a direct concern in my vindication.

For one reason or another, which I did not seek to explore, I was never privy to the exact arrangements made by *Time*. But I was presently informed that the costs of the legal defense had been, in so far as possible, lifted from me. Some of the costs I must unavoidably bear. *Time's* interests in the Case were looked after by Harold Medina, Jr., son of the now celebrated judge who was soon to preside over the long trial of the Communist leaders. It was sometimes necessary for me to confer with young Medina. I learned that now I had investigators of my own.*

* Their business was not to pry into Hiss's family history or finances—matters that were never publicly touched upon by any member of my counsel, by the

The names of a number of other Baltimore attorneys were given me from which to make my choice of counsel. I listened to as many first-hand opinions as possible about all of them. Then I decided on the man whom I had decided on the first time that I read over the list—Richard F. Cleveland, the youngest son of the former President of the United States, Grover Cleveland, and a partner in the Baltimore law firm of Semmes, Bowen and Semmes.

It was another of those turns in the Case which have seemed to me providential. I knew nothing whatever about Richard Cleveland. Until his name was handed to me, I had never heard of him. Yet it is hard to imagine that any other man could conceivably have filled the role that was thrust upon this quiet, deliberate, shrewd, deeply devout and deeply understanding gentleman. From the first, he sensed that there was something missing in the Hiss Case. From the moment that I confirmed his intuition and told him what that missing factor was—espionage—he grasped the Case in its full meaning. He understood exactly what I had to do and why I was doing it.

Twice, at least, his words reaching me when he himself was not present, bore me up in critical moments. His letter, which was handed me by the F.B.I. a few moments before I went in to testify in the first Hiss trial, offering me the support of a shared understanding and the force of his prayers, was a powerful help to me during my public evisceration by Lloyd Paul Stryker.

The other occasion was of a kind that no man could ever forget. It occurred in December 1948, during my days before the Grand Jury, when the outcry against me was deafening. Richard Cleveland and his wife had driven from Baltimore to our farm. If any conscious factor had influenced my choice of Cleveland as my lawyer, it was my respect for his father. To my gentle wife for whom in her loneliness that dark moment was darker than for me, Cleveland said in his gentle way: "In many ways, Whittaker reminds me of my father." It was, of course, the measure of Richard Cleveland, not of me.

Government's prosecutor or by me, and that not because no startling facts came to light. My investigators worked almost wholly to locate witnesses who could corroborate my story about Hiss. Nearly always, they found that Hiss's investigators had been there first and that possible witnesses had sometimes suffered strange black-outs of recollection. My investigators soon passed out of the picture.

XIV

Semmes, Bowen and Semmes occupies the twenty-first floor of the Baltimore Trust Building, Baltimore's skyscraper, at No. 10 Light Street. There I now began to visit Richard Cleveland in his office, which looked westward across the roofs of the city to a corner of that Druid Hill Park, where, as a boy, Alger Hiss used to bottle spring water.

There I first met William Macmillan, Sr. Macmillan is Cleveland's partner, and would have been the trial lawyer had the libel suit ever taken place. This resolutely cheerful, bouncy, alert and very human man was second only to Cleveland in upholding my morale when there was almost no one else to uphold it. I felt extreme confidence in him as a lawyer. At that time, I was completely unfamiliar with the procedures of the law. I was, in fact, a blank. From William Macmillan I first caught a sense of courtroom, a rudimentary notion of what constitutes evidence, of what is material and admissible, together with a consciousness of the jury, and how a lawyer, drawing upon a lifetime of experience, feels that the minds of jurors work.

My first interview with Cleveland and Macmillan was chiefly to give them a chance to look me over and to listen to my story before they decided to accept me as a client. I found that I came as something of a relief. "To tell the truth," said Cleveland as we parted that first day, "Bill and I were a little worried. When we heard that you were an ex-Communist, we expected a wild-eyed man without a necktie. You are quite a surprise."

XV

My life now began to revolve around the law, which fixed its pattern. Day after day, I drove to Baltimore and went over the story of the Ware Group, sometimes with Cleveland and Macmillan together, sometimes with Cleveland alone. Macmillan lingered insistently over details: what Communist undergrounds were like, how they worked, what the Ware Group had been doing and why I had been known to them only by the name of Carl. I felt a sense of dismay that highly intelligent men, living constantly in the atmosphere of history, justice and government, should be as completely unfamiliar with the character and practices of the Communist power that threatened them as I was with the procedures of the law. But I saw, too, that out of the accumulated experience of years of legal practice, they were probing for something that they could not put their finger upon, but which they sensed should be there, and which was not there. My confidence in them grew daily. I realized, too, that complete truth was the only possible working relationship between lawyer and client.

I was sitting alone one day with Richard Cleveland. Once more he led me over parts of the story. After a time, he paused and gazed off toward Druid Hill Park.

"You feel, don't you, that there is something missing?" I asked.

"I was discussing the case with my wife last night," he said, "and we both agreed that there was something missing."

"There *is* something missing," I said. "I am shielding Hiss."

Cleveland glanced at me over his half-glasses as he sometimes did.

"Espionage," I said.

XVI

I had reasoned that, once Alger Hiss made the gesture of suing me, there was an outside possibility that he would postpone the action, on one pretext or another, until people lost interest. Instead, Hiss's lawyers summoned me almost at once to a pre-trial examination in Baltimore. I had no further doubt that the Communist Party had decided on a frontal attack and that the purpose of the libel suit was to destroy me.

Pre-trial examination is cross-examination under oath of witnesses in a legal action by the opposing lawyers. Its purpose is at least twofold. It clears out of the way masses of testimony that would otherwise clutter the trial which it prefaces. It also gives the opposing lawyers an opportunity to probe into the past of witnesses—a so-called "fishing expedition."

My pre-trial examination took place in the library of the Marbury firm in the Maryland Trust Building. The library was a large room, with windows at the far end and part way down the two long sides. In the middle was a conference table. I took my place at one end of this table. At my right sat Macmillan, and, next to him, Cleveland. Facing me at the opposite end of the table, sat William Marbury. At his right, sat another member of the Marbury firm. Next to him, sat a figure new to me in the Case—Edward McLean, a member of a Wall Street law firm and part of Hiss's New York defense battery.

McLean was to be a member of Hiss's counsel in both criminal trials. I had never seen any of these men before.

But there was another member of Hiss's counsel at the pre-trial examination whom I had seen. Sitting beside McLean, on these first days, but later sitting apart from the others on the opposite side of the table, was a short, dark man who seemed oddly different in kind from the rest of Hiss's team. He was Harold Rosenwald, the little man with the lingering, sullen glance whose whispered conversation with Hiss's counsel had caused a brief interruption in the August 25th hearing.

As the Committee had challenged him then, William Macmillan now asked in surprise who he was. Mr. Rosenwald was assisting counsel, said McLean. "A very good lawyer, too," he added with one of his Mona Lisa smiles. McLean's face to the world was invariably one of a fastidious urbanity, counterfeiting an affability that dissembled a sneer. Most good lawyers are of necessity part-time actors. How far, in McLean's case, the mask and the man were one, I did not learn.

I went into my first day of pre-trial examination, wondering if William Marbury might be a Communist. Richard Cleveland had called the suggestion preposterous. I felt, of course, that it was no more preposterous than the fact that Alger Hiss, Noel Field, Grace Hutchins or a score of others of the same general breed were Communists. Marbury conducted my questioning. After an hour or two, I was convinced that Marbury was not a Communist and I never had reason to change my mind.

But I used to wonder, as my testimony unfolded, and particularly after the documents and the memos in Hiss's handwriting had been introduced, how a man of Marbury's acute mind and long legal experience could possibly continue to believe sincerely in Hiss's innocence. Of course, he did not have to believe in it. From the first, Marbury *knew* that my charges could not be true because he himself was not a Communist and Communists simply could not occur in the social and professional worlds that were his own. Hiss could not be guilty because he was Marbury's friend and belonged to both those worlds. Similarly, no charges against me could be too fantastic to explain my motives and conduct.

Throughout the Case, therefore, Marbury's mind was closed to certain possibilities, and a part of its natural acuteness blunted—a condition that would seem to be almost as dangerous to a lawyer as to a general in the field. It led Marbury to a fatal step. It led him to ask me to turn over to him any letters or other communications from Alger Hiss that I might have in my possession—the question that was in effect Hiss's undoing, and which need never have been asked, and scarcely would have been asked if Marbury had believed that I had anything to produce.

Like any man's impression of another, particularly one whom he has seen so briefly in circumstances so unfavorable, mine may be unfair to Marbury. But, in the main, I do not believe that it is far out. I began to form it from the start. For, as his first act of the pre-trial examination, Marbury jumped up from his place at the other end of the room. Tripping the whole length of the table, he held under my nose, in a shaking hand, a copy of the statement that I had made to the press when Hiss filed his suit. Had I, he demanded, made that statement? A brief snort, I believe, was his principal comment on my answer that I had. He seemed choking with a self-righteousness that subsided only intermittently in the course of the pre-trial examination until that sobering moment when I laid upon his table the copies of the sixty-five pages of copied documents which Alger Hiss had purloined from the State Department.

XVII

In part, Marbury said at once with the only touch of gayety that I recall that the pre-trial examination was to be a fishing expedition.* Its purpose was to dip into my past.

In response to Hiss's libel action, my attorneys had formally pled truth. In other words, I pled that I had not libeled Hiss by calling him a Communist because he was, in fact, a Communist. Therefore, no special strategy was necessary on our part. Cleveland and Macmillan counseled me simply to answer all questions as directly and fully as possible. That was also my own initial feeling. Later, as I watched the Hiss attorneys cataloguing with gleeful malevolence facts about my life of which they had known little or nothing until I told them, facts which had nothing whatever to do with Alger Hiss and Communism, I was personally inclined to let the enemy do his own investigating. I could see no point in making matters easier

* One of the few amusing stories of the Hiss Case, told me by a man with a rich Maryland inflection, concerns this purpose. "Well," said a fellow diner of Marbury's at the Merchant's Club after Hiss's conviction, "Bill went on a fishing expedition, and, by God, he caught the whole damn sea bottom."

for Hiss in contriving a rascally and misleading action against me. Nevertheless, I followed counsel who, from a legal standpoint, were right beyond question if only because the probing of a defendant's life is of necessity a part of any libel action.

Yet a confession made under legal duress, when a man knows that every word he utters will, if possible, be turned against him, is a special kind of ordeal. Perhaps it was less an ordeal for me than for Cleveland and Macmillan who hour after hour had to sit silent while questions and answers droned on. I, at least, could speak. In part, I was spared in somewhat the same way that I had been spared on *Meet the Press*—I did not know, I could scarcely have guessed, the intent behind many of the questions, or the dark thoughts that were hiving in the minds of the men who were my legal enemies.

I could not avoid knowing that I was being treated, with a blistering condescension, as a kind of human filth. From the moment the examination began, I was aware of a tone of carefully modulated evil playing over me, without ever quite divulging itself. It reminded me of something creepy which at first I could not quite bring to mind. It always just eluded me. Then, one day, it came back. It was the three boys in the schoolyard of my childhood, who had wet on a lollypop and then offered it to a fourth boy. Only, now, the lollypop was being offered to me.

It was offered in many forms. I think that I was first most deeply aware of it in the questioning about my brother. No one who had lived through such an experience as my brother's slow destruction could have the memory pawed by hateful minds without a wince of pain and horror. What possible bearing could my brother's suicide have on the Hiss Case? Nor could I fathom the gratuitous relish with which Marbury, obviously a man of intelligence and some sensitivity, insisted on referring to my brother by his nickname, Dickie, instead of by his full name. How could I have understood? It was late in the Hiss Case before any friend summoned the courage to tell me the slander in which the Hiss partisans had involved me with my brother—a story so inconceivable that it seemed to me that only a mind deformed by something more than malevolence could have excreted it. I said only to the woman who told me: "What kind of beasts am I dealing with?" The fact that men and women could be found to credit and spread a lie so disgusting and so cruel remains the measure of the Hiss defense and the pro-Hiss psychosis.

There was one moment, however, in the pre-trial examination, which perhaps it is best to characterize simply as "amusing." I had been testifying to the facts about the first Soviet apparatus, describing in detail the house on Gay Street and the courier system on the German ships, the microfilm messages and the mirrors. Harold Rosenwald had taken to sitting by himself, apart from the rest of the Hiss counsel, on the same side of the table with my lawyers. As I developed the details of that interesting Communist underground, Marbury treated them with his usual airy incredulity. Not so Harold Rosenwald. While I spoke, I became aware that he had leaned slightly forward, and was staring at me with his eyes bugged in what seemed to me a stare of pure hatred. He seemed quite unconscious of what he was doing. But it was so conspicuous that at last William Macmillan leaned forward to intercept Rosenwald's gaze. "I was trying," Macmillan said to me later, "to save you from the evil eye."

Then, one afternoon, Marbury asked me his precipitating question: did I have in my possession any letters or other communications from Alger Hiss? If so, would I turn them over to him? His smile meant that the question was merely routine. And so it was, the perfectly proper routine question that any other attorney in Marbury's place might have put.

A recess occurred in the pre-trial examination at that point; perhaps only a week-end, perhaps several days. In any case, when the examination was resumed and Marbury reminded me of his request, I said that I had not looked yet. If there had been the slightest anxiety at the bottom of Marbury's mind, my delay, no doubt, removed it. He repeated his demand.

I had not gone to look for Hiss's memos for two simple reasons. I did not believe that they were of much importance, and I was overcome with a deep inhibiting lethargy. I had realized from the tone and the maneuvers of the pre-trial examination how successfully the Hiss forces had turned the tables with the libel suit. The issue had ceased almost completely to be whether Alger Hiss had been a Communist. The whole strategy of the Hiss defense consisted in making Chambers a defendant in a trial of his past, real or imaginary, which was already being conducted as a public trial in the press and on the radio.

It was at that moment that there occurred the incident which I have described in the Foreword to this book, and which I called "the death of the will." I saw that I might well lose the libel suit, though it was not in my nature to lose it without a fight. Nor did the thought of the loss of the libel suit ever appall me, as it did some of my friends. For I believed, with a faith beyond mere intellection, that ultimately the truth cannot be destroyed, and that the loss of the libel suit would, in fact, rally to my support people and a power of opinion that was then merely passive or quiescent, waiting to see the outcome of the suit, satisfied, as people are, naturally enough, to let somebody else make the fight.

The root of my lethargy, what filled me with despair, was the apparent hopelessness of making anything understandable to a nation that could so easily be misled into supposing that a struggle that involved its life and death was merely a grudge fight or a scandal involving two men. Of course, the nation did not feel that way to any such degree as I then supposed. But I was sundered from the nation. In those days, I felt incredibly alone. Richard Nixon was busy with his own affairs. Richard Cleveland was almost the only friend to whom I could talk, and, like me, but in a legal sense, much more than I, he lived within the shadow of the Case as a libel suit.

My sense of loneliness drove me to keep all the more to myself. My lethargy made any effort seem futile. The idea of making the long trip to New York City to reclaim some scraps of paper that I had left there ten years before, seemed an unendurable effort. I wanted only to be with my family and not to leave the sanctuary of the farm. And so Marbury had to ask me a second time.

XVIII

This time Cleveland warned me that if I did have anything of Hiss's I had better get it. What I might have had seemed to me of so little importance that we had scarcely touched on it.

I communicated with my wife's nephew, Nathan Levine,* merely telling him that I was going to New York and asking him if he would have "my things" ready for me. It took him some time to think back ten years and figure out what my things might be. He, of course, had never known what was in the envelope which I had asked him to hide in 1938.

I left the farm with deep reluctance. It was a Sunday. In New York the streets were empty. I went by subway to Levine's apartment in Brooklyn. It was crowded with relatives, none of whom I had seen for years. Though my relations with Levine were warm they were infrequent. "My things," he told me, were at his mother's

* No relative of Isaac Don Levine.

house—my wife's sister's. She was coming to call upon him shortly and he wanted to wait until she and his father had arrived before he drove over to their house, where he had been living when I gave him the envelope to hide for me, and where he had hidden it. He did not want his mother to ask embarrassing questions when he took it out of hiding. She was suffering from a weak heart, of which, not long afterwards, she died. Almost as soon as she had arrived, Levine and I drove the short distance to her house on Rochester Avenue.

Levine led me up to the second floor. By then he was laughing at what seemed to him a somewhat absurd business. He led me to a bathroom, where, over the tub, a small window opened into a dumbwaiter shaft that had long been out of use. Inside the shaft was some kind of small shelf or ledge. There Levine had laid "my things."

He climbed upon the tub, opened the little window and half disappeared into the shaft. When he reappeared, he handed me an envelope that was big, plump and densely covered with the clotted cobwebs and dust of a decade. As I took it from his hands, that accumulation slid to the floor.

In surprise, for I had supposed that the envelope was a small one, I carried it to the kitchen, which was at the end of the hall, and laid it on a white enamel table top. Levine's chief concern was for the mess that I had made on his mother's floor, for she was a somewhat implacable housekeeper. He took a broom and dustpan and went back to tidy up.

In his absence, I opened the envelope and drew part way out the thick batch of copied State Department documents. At a glance, I saw that, besides those documents, and Hiss's handwritten memos, there were three cylinders of microfilm and a little spool of developed film (actually two strips). By a reflex of amazement, I pushed the papers back into the envelope. Then I held on to the edge of the table, for I had the feeling that the floor was swinging around me and that I was going to fall to it. That passed in an instant. But I continued to grip the edge of the table in the kind of physical hush that a man feels to whom has happened an act of God.

I was still standing there—it had all taken only a few moments—when Levine came back with his broom and dustpan and asked me, as nearly as I remember, if I had found what I was looking for.

My answer was more to myself than to him. "Good God," I said, "I did not know that this still existed."

XIX

I telephoned my wife from New York and asked her to drive to meet me at the station in Baltimore. I asked her to be sure to meet me on time. I did not want to wait in the station. She asked me if something was wrong. I said simply: "I have found something."

My wife was waiting for me in Baltimore. The children had been asleep on the back seat of the car, and woke to greet me. I got behind the wheel and laid the envelope on the seat between my wife and me. At home my wife went at once to put the children to bed.

In our living room, I examined for the first time all the contents of the envelope. There were sixty-five typed pages, copies or summaries of confidential State Department documents. There were two strips of developed microfilm, one containing the first part of a long document from the Trade Agreements Division of the State Department. It ran over onto the second strip, which also included some short State Department cables. There were three cylinders of microfilm, undeveloped, as I knew, because, on two of the cylinders, the caps were taped with adhesive tape. The cap on the third cylinder had been jarred off or never properly fitted. There was also a long memo on yellow foolscap in the handwriting of Harry Dexter White.* There were one or two smaller items of no particular importance.

That stunned sense which had come over me when I first saw the contents of the envelope had never quite left me. I took the papers, the film and the envelope, which was covered on one side with a crust of grime that had cracked with age, and hid them upstairs in my bedroom.

How could I help but feel stunned? For I knew that the documents and the film meant much more than any part they might play in the libel suit. They challenged my life itself. They meant that there had been given into my hands the power to prove the existence of the Communist conspiracy. They meant that I must decide once for all whether to destroy that documentary proof and continue to spare those whom I had so far shielded, or to destroy the conspiracy with the means which seemed to have been put into my hands for that reason by the action of a purpose that reached far back into the past to the moment and the impulse that had first led me to secrete the film and papers. There was this one chance, and

* This was the memo that Richard Nixon read into the Congressional Record in his speech after Hiss's conviction.

only this one, which, if I destroyed the evidence, would never come again. I knew, too, that whatever else I destroyed, I could do what I had to do only if I was first of all willing to destroy myself.

X X

The next morning I told Richard Cleveland that I had found something. In his careful and deliberate way, Cleveland had kept a tight grip of his reaction. Presently, William Macmillan joined us. We sat discussing the decision I must make and what I must do in making it. Both men decided to drive me to Westminster to examine the papers.

I write "papers" because it was the copied State Department, Hiss's handwritten memos and Harry White's long memo that I showed to Cleveland and Macmillan in our living room at the farm. They examined the documents slowly and thoroughly. I had the impression that, to their law-conscious minds, the grimed and crackled envelope was more telling at that moment than the documents. I knew what the documents were. I could not, like a lawyer, know that verification of type face, paper, etc., would have to be made before the authenticity of the documents could be certified. I was depressed by my friends' deliberateness. I thought with a renewal of hopelessness: "Is it impossible to convince anyone of the plain fact, even with the evidence in front of us?" This feeling was, of course, quite mistaken. Both Cleveland and Macmillan grasped the enormity of the documents at once.

Some of my feeling lifted when Cleveland said that, clearly, the documents must be put in a secure place and that he would take them into custody and put them at once in his safety-deposit box at the Semmes firm. Photostats would also have to be made. (They were made a day or so later, with Macmillan standing by to supervise every step of the operation.)

I surrendered the documents into Cleveland's keeping and drove back with Macmillan and him to Baltimore. There were some long silences on that drive. I had the impression that almost the same kind of hush had touched my friends that had touched me when I first found the documents.

Cleveland had at once said emphatically that he hoped that it was my intention to introduce the documents into the pre-trial examination. I pointed out what such action on my part would inflict on all those involved in my disclosure. This had happened on a Monday. On Tuesday I still had not reached a decision and said that I must have a day in which to think things through. But the next day I was scheduled to testify at the pre-trial examination. The Hiss lawyers had already given notice that they intended to examine my wife. Cleveland and Macmillan arranged to have my wife examined Wednesday in my stead. During the day while she was testifying, I would reach my decision about the documents.

XXI

It will be asked: Why did you not turn the microfilm, also, over to Richard Cleveland?

At the level of conscious motive, I did not turn over the film because the contents of the three cylinders were not developed and I did not know whether or not they had any bearing on the Hiss libel suit. I planned to try to develop the film myself, to see what was on it before I surrendered all of the film to anyone. (There was also a possibility for the first day or so that I would destroy it and myself, but I will come to that in its place.) To understand the next developments in the Hiss Case, it is necessary to consider briefly how, in retrospect, the Case then seemed to me.

For me the Hiss Case did not begin in 1948. It began in 1939 when I talked to Adolf Berle. As a result of that incident and later observations, I concluded that there were powerful forces within the Government to whom such information as I had given Berle was extremely unwelcome. I believed that they had no intention of acting on it, and that, if I made myself troublesome, any action taken would be taken against me. From time to time, rumors and reports had reached me of what I could only regard as a fitful struggle going on out of sight, among those who sought to bring the facts behind the Hiss Case to light and those who strove to keep them hidden. Sometimes, the struggle reached a peak, as when, shocked by what Isaac Don Levine had told him of my story, Walter Winchell again took it to President Roosevelt. Again nothing happened. It reached another peak when Ambassador William Bullitt took the same story to the President. It reached another peak when a newsman procured, from sources unknown to me, at least the substance of what was in the Berle notes, and tried to force action on them in other ways.

This official apathy, it seemed to me, was the reason why, with allegations in the hands of the F.B.I. for years that Alger Hiss and the rest of the Ware Group were Communists, nothing had happened.

In the end, this was why, I held, the House Committee on Un-American Activities, and not some other agency of Government more directly concerned, had at last to force the indispensable disclosure. It was why, convinced that the Communist infiltration touched the heart of the nation's safety, I had to respond to the Committee's summons, and make the revelations where they could be heard.

Once I had begun that testimony, only the existence of that higher apathy seemed adequate to explain why the full weight of official disapproval was directed at first against me, and not into following up my charges, and why the Hiss Case was "a red herring." It explained why the violent resentment of public and official persons was concentrated on me, just as, later on, it explained how the spectacle of the first Hiss trial was possible, and the singular behavior of some of those engaged in it.

Now it is proper to point out the facts that we all know: once I had put documentary evidence in the Justice Department's hands, Hiss *was* promptly indicted; Thomas F. Murphy *was* chosen by the Government to try the case; Hiss *was* convicted and his appeal opposed and denied. He *was* imprisoned. But in November, 1948, those developments lay ahead, and in the light of the past or the climate of the present and near future, they were not developments that the kind of mind that the world calls "realistic" would have cared to give odds on. Quite the reverse.

The climate of 1948 was set by a report that forces within the Government were determined to stifle the Hiss Case by indicting me and thereby removing the one witness who could make the case possible. Congressman Nixon believed that the Government had already taken the preliminary steps necessary to indict me. A special night session of members of the House Committee on Un-American Activities was called to discuss ways to counteract the effort to indict me—not because the Committee felt any personal fondness for me or wished to save me from indictment as an individual man, but because my indictment must clearly smother the Hiss Case.

Thus, beset by the conflict in my own witness, I was also beset by a political conflict outside me, and largely beyond my knowledge, with which I had little or nothing to do, but which steadily played on me.

What powers within the Government wanted the Hiss Case stifled? I have never been in a position to map with authority the geography of power within the Government, or beyond it. But, like everybody else, I have witnessed certain public acts. There was the appearance of two Supreme Court Justices, Justice Felix Frankfurter and Justice Stanley Reed, as voluntary* character witnesses for Alger Hiss at his first trial. A justice of the Supreme Court has no personal character. He is a living symbol. The intervention of two Supreme Court Justices in a trial in which the implied charge was espionage was an event in this nation's history, and one whose implications are deep-going.

Nor can Secretary of State Acheson's remark after Hiss's conviction be reviewed merely in those terms of personal feeling that I of all men must be the first to understand, for I shared that feeling. For a Secretary of State to say, after the conviction of a man on an implied charge of espionage: "I will not turn my back on Alger Hiss," cannot possibly be dismissed simply as an upwelling of personal feeling. This would be true even if the State Department aide, waiting in an anteroom with a Bible so that newsmen could check the Secretary's scriptural reference, did not make it clear that this was no spontaneous outburst. You will look in vain in history for anything comparable to it.

These are facts. We witnessed them. They are indisputable. They were evoked by a single focus of infection—the Hiss Case. They are sometimes explained, along with much else, as manifestations of partisan politics. I believe that those who suppose so are merely influenced by the traditional pattern of American politics at a time when that traditional pattern no longer holds good. The factor of partisan politics may have been in play, but I do not believe that, in the sense of two-party politics, it was decisive. The explanation lies deeper.

The simple fact is that when I took up my little sling and aimed at Communism, I also hit something else. What I hit was the forces of that great socialist revolution, which, in the name of liberalism, spasmodically, incompletely, somewhat formlessly, but always in the same direction, has been inching its ice cap over the nation for two decades. This is not a charge. My opinion of that revolution is not at issue. It is a statement of fact that need startle no one who

* Mr. Justice Frankfurter was a voluntary witness; Mr. Justice Reed, who, as Solicitor General of the United States, had appointed Alger Hiss to be his assistant, testified in response to a subpoena.

has voted for that revolution in whole or in part, and, consciously or unconsciously, a majority of the nation has so voted for years. It was the forces of that revolution that I struck at the point of its struggle for power. And with that we come to the heart of the Hiss Case and all its strange manifestations. No one could have been more dismayed than I at what I had hit, for though I knew it existed, I still had no adequate idea of its extent, the depth of its penetration or the fierce vindictiveness of its revolutionary temper, which is a reflex of its struggle to keep and advance its political power.

It was the forces of this revolution that had smothered the Hiss Case (and much else) for a decade, and fought to smother it in 1948. These were the forces that made the phenomenon of Alger Hiss possible; had made it possible for him to rise steadily in Government and to reach the highest post *after* he was already under suspicion as a Communist in many quarters, including Congress, and under the scrutiny of the F.B.I. Alger Hiss is only one name that stands for the whole Communist penetration of Government. He could not be exposed without raising the question of the real political temper and purposes of those who had protected and advanced him, and with whom he was so closely identified that they could not tell his breed from their own.*

No act of mine was more effective in forcing into the open the long-smothered Hiss Case than my act in dividing the documentary evidence against Hiss, introducing the copied State Department documents into the pre-trial examination (which, in effect, meant turning them over to the Justice Department), and placing the microfilm, separately, in the pumpkin.** It was my decisive act in the Case. For when the second part of the divided evidence, the microfilm, fell into the hands of the Committee, it became impossible ever again to suppress the Hiss Case.

That is the meaning of the pumpkin—a meaning that has been widely missed, I feel, in laughter at the pumpkin itself. Yet without an understanding of that meaning, the heart meaning of the Case is blurred, the logic of the ferocious animus against me is lost, and the acts which preceded and followed my division of the evidence

* Were it not for a socialist cyst within it, mere political expediency would scarcely stop any party from cleaning house of its Communists, a project that, pushed with vigor and sincerity, could only redound to its credit.

** A journalistic passion for alliteration has transformed the contents of the pumpkin into the "pumpkin papers." There were no papers in the pumpkin; there was film.

seem merely like the goings on in a thriller. That, I am convinced, is how many people still view them. They never were that. They are the sign that great conflicting forces were at grips. And the special necessities of that struggle impressed upon the acts, in which it was fought out, their special forms.

It is certainly true that, on the level of consciousness, I divided the evidence in order to try to find out what was on the undeveloped film. Yet I like to wonder sometimes if the subconscious, which so constantly occupies the minds of our intellectuals, could conceivably have been at work here. To put it in my own way, I like to trust that the God of Battles has this Republic in His care. I like to trust that I was moved by an intuition, if only from my reading of military history, that, in general, battles are won by the reserves. The microfilm stands for the reserves.

XXII

I drove my wife to Baltimore for the pre-trial examination with a feeling that I was throwing her to the wild beasts in my stead. I had driven her there a few weeks earlier to talk with Richard Cleveland and William Macmillan. On that earlier drive to Baltimore, we discussed for the first time our memories of the Hisses. Until then, I had never asked my wife what she remembered. I had cut short all attempts on her part to tell me. I did not want her to be involved in any way in the Case, which was a man's fight, and one in which she had no real part. I could not bear to admit, even to the extent of conversation with her about it, that in reality she was involved.

The Hiss lawyers had made that clear by summoning her to testify. Now we had no choice but to discuss the past. To my surprise, I found that my wife's recollection of many things was clearer than my own. This was especially true of personal and physical details—the interiors, drapes, furniture, wallpaper of the Hiss houses, occasions when the Hisses had been at our house, occasions when we had been at theirs. Moreover, my wife had a simple way of determining relative dates and events. She related them to the birth of her children and their various stages of development. Furthermore, she was extremely emphatic, not to say stubborn, about what she remembered. But in almost every case, she proved to be right.

On the morning of the pre-trial examination, I parked near the station in Baltimore and guided my wife to a taxicab. She suddenly realized that I was going to leave her.

"Aren't you coming with me?" she asked, in a voice all the more terrible because, as always, she sought to subdue her real horror of facing alone what lay ahead, so that her voice was without reproach, like that of an abandoned but brave child.

"No," I said, "they will not let me be there. But Dick Cleveland and Bill Macmillan will take care of you." She did not cry. We took each other's hands because we do not like to embrace before strange people. I watched the cab pull away from the curb and stood watching it as it disappeared. I did not know whether I would see my wife again.

XXIII

I drove back to the farm. I drove by the longest route because I wanted time to think out what I would do that day. But I cannot say that I really thought while I was driving. I can only say that there was in my mind a motion which seethed and broke, like waves, against two alternatives. Either was a reef, and I cannot call thinking what was, in fact, the agony of indecision.

The agony resulted from the conflict between two forms of witness that I had to bear—the witness against Communism and the human witness. It was precipitated by my act in turning over to Cleveland the copied State Department documents. That act meant, in effect, that I had already turned over the documents to the Government—for it was a matter of indifference whether I myself formally introduced them into evidence, or whether, if I were no longer alive to do so, they passed into the Government's hands in other ways. When I placed them in Richard Cleveland's hands, I had completed that part of my witness. Men might add sequels to that fact after whatever flourishes they pleased. They could not change the fact. They might choose to understand the evidence. They might reject the evidence. The hard fact was that the evidence was in. What they did with it would be a shrewd measure, in the crisis of the time, of men's ability or inability to save themselves. If it is remembered what a drowning sea of hostility, public and secret opposition, skepticism, hatred and simple lack of understanding of my purpose then washed around me, it may not seem strange that I should feel, with a strong taint of bitterness in my despair, that I could do little more, one way or another, to help men to make up their minds. There are limits to strength, and in that direction I had then reached one of the limits.

The decision concerned my other witness. It was what I was going to do about those whom I had implicated by turning over the documents and those whom I must next implicate by turning over the microfilm. It took this form: Should I destroy the microfilm and destroy myself? I had less than a day in which to make up my mind, and to act.

By turning over the documents to Cleveland, I had implicated only Alger Hiss and Harry White, who was already dead. By turning over the film, which must be my next step, I would implicate others. Of these I was sure that Abel Gross must be one, and I supposed, too, then, that Reno and Wadleigh might be implicated. I had forgotten that Wadleigh was in Turkey on a diplomatic mission during the forepart of 1938 and could not have been back long when the films were made.

By destroying the film, I could spare these people completely. What was of immediate urgency, by destroying myself, I could remove the only living witness against Alger Hiss (for at that time no other witnesses had appeared). Yet my witness against the Communist conspiracy would not be changed by my act. The documents, what Thomas F. Murphy was later to call "the immutable evidence," were the immutable witness. They spoke in silence for me.

Whether I lived and bore a witness of justice, or killed myself and bore a witness of mercy, I would in either case destroy myself. That was the point at which the alternatives arose. Which form of destruction should I choose? They arose, too, at the point at which I raised the question of my own suffering. Was it God's purpose that I should live and by consciously inviting a suffering such as I could scarcely conceive, bear a witness to the end that those infidels might be crushed completely? Did not everything tend to that conclusion? Had not everything that had happened in this respect in the Case since my first testimony been forced upon me, grudgingly, reluctantly, step by step, against my will, by the action of the others, and not my own?

Or was it God's purpose that, having borne my witness against the conspiracy, I should bear a higher witness, by sparing all whom I had implicated or might implicate, in the only way left to me—by destroying myself? If so, I would suffer damnation, which was perhaps the meaning of it all. For then the question became simply this: Should a man accept damnation in the full consciousness that he was destroying himself eternally as the ransom of those with whom he had shared a common evil, and whom nothing less than such an act could reclaim? Was that the penalty exacted by the past at that point where justice and mercy are one?

XXIV

I was alone on the farm. The children were at school. Mr. Pennington was probably in one of the farther fields. During my drive I had reached no conclusion as to what I should do. I sat down at the kitchen table. With the evidences of my family around me, I tried to sum up the practical considerations. They were not many. *Time* had insured my life for $20,000. There was the farm and the producing herd. Mr. Pennington would help my family to work the farm until my son was big enough to take over.

My family would be better off without me, not simply because my act would liberate them from their only connection with the Case, which would, in fact, cease to exist. Living, I could be nothing to them but a dishonored man. Dead, I knew that I would be the binding point of a memory of mutual love that could have few equals.

My gun was upstairs. It had the merciful merit of being instantaneous. But I shrank from the physical aspects of using it, especially the horror that it must leave for my wife. There is a gas-producing substance of which a cyanide compound is one component. It is in common use on farms. We had a can of it which my wife had bought and which I had never looked at. I decided that, if I chose death, I would use that gas whose action I then supposed to be much quicker than is the case.

I got up and began walking across the farm, for the relief of doing something, and to try to reach a decision.

XXV

At the middle of our farm, there is a little woods of white pine and oak. It is along its edge that the arbutus grows. I had sometimes sat in it in the past to think and to observe. I found myself walking toward it.

If an intense seeking for guidance is prayer, then my experience in the woods was prayer. But it was prayer much of which must be called a stupor of distress. I sought to lay myself open to God, not to demand anything of Him, in a silence of the self that amounted to inertness. I do not know how long I was in the woods. Nor have I any clear recollection of my earlier thoughts, which had reached the point of turmoil. What I am aware of is the moment at which a clarification set in. There came to me at last, by what processes of association, from what depths of memory I cannot trace, an image. It was the image of that Russian revolutionist who, as the only protest he was able to make against the flogging of his fellow prisoners, drenched himself in kerosene, ignited himself and burned himself to death.

The witness.

That was the precipitating image. It linked the purposes of my past and present and made one the meaning of my life. I do not mean that I thought that. The image rose in my mind. I am not conscious of a reasoning or an ordering of my thoughts, but of a kind of gradual separation like that by which, in clouded water, we see the sediment settle of its own weight at last, and leave the liquid clear and free. More and more, there settled upon me like a burden for which I slowly stooped, a sense that the weight of God's purpose laid upon me was that I must not destroy myself. Therefore, I must not destroy the film. I must continue to bear a living witness, which would only mean my destruction by slower means. That was my penalty, but what happened to me was not the point at all.

And though I cannot retrace the stages by which I reached that certainty, I do know the thought which closed my experience in the woods, and which took form in words close to these: "If I, who am the least man in this nation, which is dying of self-satisfaction and indifference—if I do not find within myself the strength to do this, then, in the war between this world and Communism which is inevitably coming, any man will have the moral right to ask: 'Why should I give my life?' But if I do find this strength, nothing, ultimately, can destroy this nation, for it is the power of souls to move other souls."

XXVI

I drove back to Richard Cleveland's office to get my wife. The Hiss lawyers had given her a bad time. No doubt, pre-trial examinations must often be rough. But there is little doubt, either, that that one went far beyond any routine roughness. For there is no doubt that the Hiss lawyers recognized instantly that Esther Chambers was a most dangerous witness to them, not only because her memory for concrete detail was vivid, but because her sincerity is transparent and infectious. "You reek of sincerity," said Thomas F. Murphy, concluding his first interview with her.

Therefore, the Hiss lawyers had harried her to tears. The tone of their treatment of her is fixed, I think, in the one question of Marbury's that has stayed in my mind. My wife had testified, in response to a question, that when we were living on St. Paul Street after my break with Communism, we had owned only a few plates that we had bought at a dime store. "Well, you didn't eat off the floor, did you, Mrs. Chambers?" asked William Marbury.

There is a natural gentleness that even the basest men accord to a woman, not by reason of courtesy alone, but by an instinct rooted in all that makes them men. The instinct played no part in the pre-trial examination of my wife by Alger Hiss's lawyers. "And then that —— took it away from her," Tom Murphy exploded, referring to a point in William Marbury's interrogation of my wife. Let that epithet stand to Murphy's honor as long as memories last.

Before I left Richard Cleveland, I told him that I had decided to introduce the copied State Department documents into the pre-trial examination the next day.

XXVII

At one or two o'clock on November 17, 1948, Cleveland, Macmillan and I filed into the Marbury law library for my resumed hearing. Under my arm I carried an envelope, containing the sixty-five pages of copied State Department documents, the four memos in Alger Hiss's handwriting and the envelope in which they had lain hidden for a decade. Edward McLean was absent.

When the examination opened, I said that I should like to make a statement. I said, in substance, that until that time I had testified only to Alger Hiss's Communism. I had done so because I wished to shield him. I could not shield him completely, but I had hoped to shield him from the most shattering consequences of his acts as a Communist. I had tried to shield him because, in my own break with Communism, I had been given strength and a time in which to reshape my life. I did not wish to deprive Hiss and others of the same possibility that had been granted me. But now I must testify that Alger Hiss had also committed espionage. In response to William Marbury's request, I had brought evidence of that. Then I exposed the documents and the memos on the table in front of me.

William Macmillan moved in at once. "I think," he said, "that in the interest of order, the recorder should number and list each document. If there is no objection, I will just read off the first and last words of each in sequence." There began half an hour of stunning itemization. Macmillan read: "Paris: To the Secretary of State, Strictly Confidential, Signed Bullitt; Rome: To the Secretary of State, I learn in strictest confidence, Signed Phillips; Vienna: To the Secretary of State, Signed Messersmith. . . ." On and on it went.

At the far end of the room, Marbury sat, staring fixedly at the table. At his right, another member of the Marbury firm watched the listing and listened to the reading with an expression of bewildered anxiety. Harold Rosenwald had got up from his place almost at once and stood staring gloomily out of the window with his hands clasped behind him.

When Hiss's handwritten memos were introduced, Marbury asked to see one. At the same moment he was called to the telephone. Taking the memo with him, he went into his own office. If there had been a doubt in anybody's mind that Marbury had compared the handwriting in the memo with some specimen of Hiss's handwriting on his desk, Marbury's face left little doubt when he returned. It was, of course, the same handwriting.

After the introduction of the documents, my examination was resumed. But the old spirit had gone out of it. That afternoon concluded my pre-trial examination until after Hiss's indictment. Then, the alert Hiss defense, by an action entirely permissible in law, however it may seem in justice, reopened my examination in the libel suit. The chief purpose of this tactic was to elicit from me under oath, when I could not refuse to answer anything, any developments in the Government's case against Hiss, up to that time, which might be of use to them. "There is nothing," Thomas F. Murphy told the first Hiss jury, "that the Hiss lawyers did not know in advance about the Government's case." Now McLean conducted the examination. Marbury put in merely perfunctory appearances. A representative of the Department of Justice sat in, as an observer, not as a participant.

When I left the pre-trial examination on November 17th, I did not know just what would happen next.

XXVIII

I went back to the farm to wait. Marbury, after a flying trip to New York to show Hiss photostats of his handwritten memos, telephoned Richard Cleveland. Marbury proposed that the documents be turned over to the Government at once. Together the two lawyers went to Judge W. Calvin Chestnut who saw no necessity for turning over the papers to the Government but said that he would not object if counsel felt it to be necessary. Marbury at once telephoned the Justice Department. Up from Washington rushed Alex Campbell, the head of the Department's Criminal Division, and two assistants. Thus the documents passed into the hands of the Department of Justice.

Marbury had seized the initiative. This was the period when, with Alger Hiss, he was doing everything possible to aid the Justice Department and the Federal Bureau of Investigation.*

I did not learn immediately of these developments. For a time, I lived in almost complete isolation at the center of the storm.

An event had already shaped my view of what to expect. On Election Day, I had listened to the first returns come over the radio. They were small tallies from widely scattered sections of the country. They showed the President leading almost everywhere. Until then it had been widely assumed that Governor Dewey would win. I reasoned that, if Truman was leading in the rural districts, he was certain of election when the city vote came in. "I think President Truman has won," I told my wife. I went to bed and slept soundly.

But with the red herring in mind, I took it for granted that the election results automatically meant that some way would be found to punish me for having tried to expose Alger Hiss. Scarcely anybody I knew supposed anything else. A few days after the election, one of the officials of our bank drew my wife aside. "It looks black for the Chamberses," he said.

* Among other "helpful" things, Hiss informed the F.B.I. that he had sold his Woodstock typewriter (on which the State Department documents had been copied), while Mrs. Hiss informed them that her former maid, Claudia Catlett, was dead. Mrs. Catlett was, of course, very much alive (she appeared as a Hiss witness at both trials). It was to her sons that, in 1938, shortly after my break with the Communist Party, Hiss had given the Woodstock typewriter.

XXIX

About a fortnight passed. During that time I had no communication whatever with the Justice Department or the F.B.I. On the surface all was calm. The nation was getting ready for Christmas. On December 1st, a spokesman for the Justice Department made his well-known comment: "Unless further evidence is forthcoming," the Justice Department was not planning to take any action in the Hiss-Chambers Case.

On the same day, something else happened of which I did not know. In a column in the Washington *Post,* a pro-Hiss organ, had appeared a few lines of gossip. They said: there has been a startling development in the Hiss libel suit in Baltimore.

I first became aware of an electric disturbance when Bert Andrews of the *Herald Tribune* telephoned me. He had read the column in the Washington *Post.* He simply asked me if anything had happened in the libel suit. I answered that I could not discuss the libel suit. Judge Chestnut, Richard Cleveland and William Marbury had given Andrews similar answers. Andrews at once drew the proper journalistic inference that if nobody would talk about what had happened in the libel suit, something had happened. He got in touch with Robert Stripling.

Before I had finished milking that night, the chief investigator of the House Committee on Un-American Activities suddenly appeared in the cow barn. As we walked down to the house together, Stripling glanced across the yard. "Nice pumpkins you've got there," he said. A volunteer pumpkin had come up in the strawberry patch. We had let it remain, for my wife and I had always thought that the leaves, flowers and fruit of the calabashes and melons are among the most decorative growths in nature. Now the vine had taken over the strawberry bed. It was covered with pumpkins, which, because of a late start, were still green.

XXX

In the living room, Stripling took out of his pocket a crumpled scrap of newspaper and handed it to me. It was the Washington *Post* column of which until then I was not aware. "Does that mean anything to you?" he asked. I said that I was not free to discuss anything at all about the libel suit. "I hear that there has been a bombshell in the suit," said Stripling. "What kind of a bombshell?" I repeated that I could not discuss the suit.

Stripling gazed at me silently for a few seconds out of those impervious blue eyes. The conversation, as nearly as I can remember it went like this: "Is your position," Stripling asked, "that you would not be free to discuss this bombshell even if there had been one?" I said yes. "In other words," he said, "you are not free to say whether or not you have introduced any new evidence in the libel suit, is that right?" I said yes. He asked: "Is there any evidence that you still have that you have not yet presented in the libel suit?" I shook my head.

Stripling has been in the business of reading men's faces for many years. He never took his eyes off mine while he questioned me. He left shortly after.

XXXI

The next day I was scheduled to testify as a witness in a loyalty case at the State Department. The hearing was scheduled for the afternoon. I had decided to drive to Washington and planned to leave early in order to give myself plenty of time.

My overcoat was on when it occurred to me that, since I was going to be away from the farm, perhaps I should find a better hiding place than my bedroom for the microfilm. Rumors that Hiss investigators were prowling around the farm had reached us again. I believed that there was no length to which these people would not go, especially since my disclosure of the documents must have made the Hiss forces desperate. I thought that the investigators might well force my wife to let them ransack the house.* The problem was to hide the film so that experts could not find it. Hurriedly, I tried to think of any classic examples of concealment. All that I could remember was an old Soviet moving picture, *Transport Agon* (*Transport of Fire*), a picture that was little noticed, but parts of which seemed to me among the best that the Soviet cinema had done. In that picture, underground Communists had transported arms and ammunition inside a number of big papier maché human figures. There had been one close up of the Chinese god of

* My fears were not far out. Just before the second Hiss trial, two strangers, identifying themselves only as "friends of Alger Hiss," came to the house and demanded that my wife turn over to them a passport and related papers. They had no subpoena or warrant and offered no credentials of any kind.

Fate, a seated, pumpkin-shaped idol whose hands waved, and whose head nodded, up and down, up and down, in a motion of perpetual and blandly smiling incertitude.

While I was wondering what clue that recollection offered in the way of a hiding place, the telephone rang. It was Robert Stripling, calling from Washington. I had told him the night before that I was to testify before the State Department Loyalty Board. Stripling asked if I would drop in at his office while I was in Washington. The problem of hiding the film was at the back of my mind while I talked with him. As I hung up, two filaments of thought spun into a single thread: the pumpkin-shaped god of Fate with the firearms hidden inside, and Stripling's remark about pumpkins the night before. A hollow pumpkin was the perfect hiding place for the microfilm. Investigators might tear the house apart. They would never think to look for anything in a pumpkin lying in a pumpkin patch.

My wife was in the barn. I broke off a pumpkin, took it into the kitchen, cut out the top, scooped out the seeds. I wrapped the developed film in waxed paper to prevent damage by juices from the pumpkin. Then I laid the developed film and the cylinders of undeveloped film inside the hollowed pumpkin and replaced the top. It was all but impossible to see that the top had been plugged. I took the pumpkin out and laid it where I had found it at the farther edge of the patch. There was no geometric pattern of pumpkins, as Lloyd Paul Stryker worked hard to prove at the first Hiss trial, to guide me back to the hollow one. Stryker could not grasp that the whole art of the concealment lay in its complete naturalness and its complete unexpectedness. This was, in fact, a critical point of the Hiss Case in which I fought Communism precisely with those arts which Communism had taught me, and no other experience could.

I did not tell my wife what I had done. For Communism had also taught me, as a basic rule of conspiracy, that what someone does not know, he cannot tell, even under pressure. I drove to Washington with an easy mind, feeling certain that inside the pumpkin the film was perfectly secure.

XXXII

I reached Washington early enough to stop first at the Old House Office Building. When I walked into Stripling's office, he did not rise from his desk. In the hand, which he extended for me to shake, he held a paper. It was a subpoena duces tecum, summoning me to turn over to the House Committee on Un-American Activities any evidence whatever that I might possess which related in any way to the Hiss Case.

Stripling said that he would drive back to Westminster with me that evening to pick up whatever evidence I might have. He did not, so far as I remember, ask me what I might have or where it was. He did not need to. He had read my eyes correctly the night before.

XXXIII

I did not return to Stripling's office until about five o'clock. He had decided not to make the long drive to Westminster. Instead, Donald Appell, who had sat beside me at my first public hearing, and William Wheeler, another Committee investigator, went with me. They drove their own car.

We reached the farm about ten o'clock. I first went into the kitchen to reassure my wife. The investigators followed me in. They were a little puzzled when I turned on the yard lights and immediately went out again. Both followed me back into the yard. I had to grope a moment before I found the right pumpkin. I tossed away the top. With the hollowed pumpkin in one hand, and the microfilm in the other, I walked up to Appell, who had moved closer to try to make out what I was doing in the shadows. I handed him the developed film and the cylinders. "I think this is what you are looking for," I said.

XXXIV

Before I was out of bed the next morning, a news photographer was trying to decide which pumpkin to take a picture of. As soon as he had gone, I smashed to pieces the hollow pumpkin, which for a few hours had contained the microfilm, so that there could be no sensational pictures in the press. The photographer had arrived because, in Washington, the Committee had at once released the pumpkin story to newsmen.

The Committee also had the undeveloped microfilm developed. The uncapped cylinder proved worthless. But even after lying undeveloped for almost ten years, much of the film in the other containers was legible. The enlargements made a pile almost four feet high.

The guffaw that went up about the pumpkin was nationwide. The pumpkin was a handy caricature with which the pro-Hiss forces could deride all my charges. But in the shrillest derision, it seemed to me that I could detect an undertone of rage. For the point about the pumpkin was not that it was absurd, but that it worked; and, together with that shocking pile of enlargements, the pumpkin meant just one thing. It meant that the Hiss Case had been broken open beyond the power of any self-interested group ever to lock it shut again.

XXXV

The Justice Department swung into action at once. From Baltimore, Richard Cleveland telephoned me that the F.B.I. would like to meet me in his office from which they and I would then go to F.B.I. headquarters. There I would be questioned. In view of the fact that the F.B.I. had been in touch with me for years, though out of touch with me (with one trifling exception) from the moment I began to testify against Alger Hiss, I found the protocol of meeting in Cleveland's office ominously formal.

When I left for that meeting, my wife and I looked at each other in silence for a moment, like people between whom a river is widening. "I don't know just when I will see you again," I said. She tried to smile courage.

About five o'clock, three agents walked into Cleveland's office. One of them was Frank Johnstone, whom I had known before, and whom I have since come to regard as a friend. Another was Daniel Callahan whom I had met but whom I did not know well.* The third was a special agent whom I had never seen before. His name has also passed out of my mind, for I never saw him again. I shall call him Special Agent Black. He scarcely greeted me, was extremely morose and even surly. He was apparently the ranking agent.

For reasons that then mystified me (they became apparent later

* Callahan has a special claim to my gratitude for the quiet sympathy and helpfulness with which he took care of my wife after the public mayhem inflicted on her by Lloyd Paul Stryker during the first Hiss trial. Another agent who similarly won my gratitude at the same time was James Shinners, who, with a tact beyond any mere duty, found the restorative words to revive my wife after her ordeal.

on), nobody made a move to leave Cleveland's office. Nothing was said about questioning me. We simply sat, chatting. This was no hardship since William Macmillan, who was present, and Frank Johnstone are, each in his own way, masters of psychological relief. Macmillan knows a great many funny stories. Frank Johnstone's humor plays over human foible with a gift for knifelike phrase. But it was a little like clowning on top of a time bomb. Only Special Agent Black did not speak or smile. Whenever I glanced at his face, I thought: "This is it." I was not particularly distressed. There is a point at which situations are accepted.

We talked for an hour or two. The telephone rang. It was a Washington newsman. "Listen," he said, "the scuttlebutt here is that the Department of Justice has ordered the F.B.I. to pick you up tonight." I thanked him and asked him to inform my wife and tell her to keep absolutely calm. "I've already talked to her," he said, "that's how I knew where you were." I went back and sat down again while the jokes and laughter continued.

The phone rang again. Again it was for me. This time it was a man in the Government in Washington. "The F.B.I. has orders to pick you up tonight," he said. "We are sitting together now," I said.

Once, while we were driving together, I told this part of the story to my son in the hope that some memory of it might help him to act in some other situation in his own life. "When I walked back into Cleveland's office," I told him, "I wondered if I should tell the agents what I had just heard. Then I decided: no, they're only carrying out orders. It could only embarrass all of us. So I said nothing." "You did right, Papa," said my son.

It was dark before the three agents, after consulting their watches, left with me. We did not go directly to the Court Square Building (F.B.I. headquarters in Baltimore). Instead, we went to supper at a nearby cafeteria. It would scarcely be possible to imagine a more uneasy meal. Even Frank Johnstone seemed a little strained. Special Agent Black ate in surly silence. I had a definite impression that he had taken a strong personal dislike to me.

We went up to headquarters—a gaggle of strange figures—through a deserted office building, in the night elevator (it must have been about eight o'clock). I was seated, facing an official desk. On one side of me sat Frank Johnstone; on the other side, someone else. Special Agent Black, clearly my inquisitor, seated himself opposite me behind the desk at which for a moment he stared. Then he looked up and, in a voice of the simplest human concern, spoke almost for the first time since I had met him. "Mr. Chambers," he said, "believe me, this was nothing that the Bureau wanted to do."

For a moment my mind whirred like the works of an adding machine before it adds up the right total. Then I grasped that his surliness had never been at me. It was at the way things are, about which there are times when a good man can do nothing.

The questioning began. It centered around the Baltimore documents, the microfilm and the Bykov apparatus. One thing I remember clearly—my sense that we had reached the moment when there could no longer be any question of shielding anyone. Everybody, big and little, greatly guilty or scarcely guilty at all, who was in any way implicated in the underground past, must now be named. There was nothing further that I could do for them. Alger Hiss and the Communist Party were their fate, which had been taken out of my hands. Yet, I felt myself gag inwardly as I mentioned each name.

Suddenly, there was a stir. A United States marshal entered and handed me a subpoena to appear before the Grand Jury of the Southern District of New York. No doubt, it was to allow time for the arrangements connected with the subpoena that we had stayed chatting in Cleveland's office.

The questioning was resumed. In half an hour or so, the marshal reappeared. He took back the original subpoena and handed me another. The first subpoena had summoned me to appear before the Grand Jury in three or four days. The second subpoena summoned me to appear at once. Someone must suddenly have realized that before I responded to the first subpoena, the Committee might have served me with a subpoena of its own and called me to a public hearing. The second subpoena outmaneuvered the Committee and prevented it from questioning me.

The interrogation ended around midnight. I had parked my car near Pennsylvania Station. Callahan drove me uptown, parked his own car nearby and watched until he saw me head toward Westminster. I wondered why, as I was to wonder once or twice later on when he insisted on waiting in the station with me until I boarded a train for Washington or New York. It simply did not occur to me at the time that Callahan was seeing me safely off. It did not occur to me that the Bureau was concerned in any way for my safety. I knew that individual agents were friendly to me, and I felt friendly to them, but I thought of the Bureau itself simply as the investigatory arm of the Department of Justice. As such, I saw no reason to trust the Bureau. I assumed that, in the Hiss Case, it had no choice but to be my enemy. For a long time, I did not trust it. I came to trust it only very slowly.

I missed completely the fact that with Special Agent Black's opening words, a new moment had arrived in the Hiss Case. It was the moment at which we all like to laugh because it is so hackneyed and so obvious, and because it, nevertheless, has power to stir us. It is the great American moment called: The Marines Have Landed.

The F.B.I. had at last entered the Hiss Case and the expert forces of that great fact-finding agency were now turned loose to procure the data from which justice would presently establish what was true and what was not true in the Case. The Bureau was not my enemy —and that not because of any personal affection it bore me, or any interest that it had in my fate as an individual, but because the F.B.I. stood for right and truth, because it was the enemy of Communism, and it had reasons for supposing (reasons presently confirmed in one of the most intensive, dogged and ablest investigations in its history) that, in the fight against the Communist conspiracy, I was on the side of truth.

X X X V I

The Saturday before I had to go before the Grand Jury, I had met Harold Medina, Jr. in Richard Cleveland's office. He brought me word that I was wanted at *Time* for a conference the next morning. I went back to New York with him. It was not a very cheerful trip. Much of the time I was silent. As we were nearing the city, I said to Medina, "I think I must offer my resignation." "Of course not," he said. "In six weeks this whole thing will be forgotten and you will be back at work as usual."

On Sunday morning, we met in the office of Roy E. Larsen, the president of Time, Inc. Seven or eight top editors and executives were present. Most of the discussion was about the necessity of my issuing a statement in view of the new developments in the Hiss Case. I was to draft the statement that day. The others filed out. Larsen and I were left alone. Nothing whatever had been said about resignation.

There are few kinder or more sensitive gentlemen than Roy Larsen. From the beginning of the Hiss Case, his position had been unusually difficult. He was a Harvard man. He knew and respected Alger Hiss. But he also knew and respected Whittaker Chambers.

"Roy," I said, "I think that I should resign."

"Perhaps you should," he said. I believe that few answers have been harder for him to make.

No other answer was possible. Time, Inc. is a business, and, like any other business, it exists for the purpose of making and marketing a product. As a result of my actions, past and present, Time, Inc. was taking a beating of which I did not then have any true idea. Worried stockholders and furious subscribers were deluging the company with angry pleas to get rid of me. There was no reason why Time, Inc. should be penalized because of me. No other honorable or practical course was possible except for me to resign. No other course was possible but for Time, Inc. to accept my resignation. That did not make it any easier on either side. A man in my situation must always hope that his friends will stand beside him in his need, even though he recognizes that it is impossible for them to do so and that it is right for them not to do so.

Time, Inc. made upon me a settlement so generous that, with what I had accumulated over the years in its trust funds, I did not have to worry about money again during the Case.

XXXVII

I now wrote a brief public statement of resignation from *Time*. The disclosure of the espionage aspects of the Hiss Case, I said, made my resignation imperative. I thanked my colleagues for their loyalty to me. But "No one," I added, "can share with me this indispensable ordeal."

It was an immense relief to be able at last to free Time, Inc. from involvement in my affairs. I should have done so sooner. But I feared the public effect of my resignation. I feared that the nation would look upon my resignation as a withdrawal of confidence in me by *Time*, evidence that those who knew me best had no faith in me. Few turns in the Hiss Case surprised me more than the nation's reaction. Far from feeling that my resignation implied a lack of confidence, people seemed to feel that a man who would resign a $30,000 a year job to join a fight must have a case. I felt a sudden general surge of sympathy for me.

I think I can say with complete truth that the loss of $30,000 never played any real part in my own thoughts. Nothing disturbed my wife and me less than the thought that we were now poor and that, even if nothing worse happened to us, I was now practically unemployable.* We had lived in a barn before and had been very happy in it. Not the roof, but the minds and souls it covers matter. And so we reminded the children.

My real pang at leaving *Time* was quite different. I simply felt that I had had friends, and that, now, they were not there.

XXXVIII

My resignation was not released to the press until a day or two after I began to testify before the Grand Jury. But I knew that it would be released, and it was in that mood of human destitution that I returned to the Federal Building, and went up to the witness waiting room next to the grand jury room. It was a bare-floored room with a heavy oaken door. A big window at the back of the room gave on the rookeries along the Third Avenue elevated, twenty or more floors below. There was a rack for hats and coats, a bare table set at right angles to the wall, a heavy wooden chair and a lighter chair. Above the table, an electric clock clicked loudly whenever a portion of what was soon to be endless, aching time had elapsed.

Tom Donegan, special assistant to the Attorney General, soon bustled in with an armful of documents. He was businesslike but not unkind, and I was there to take my medicine. "If only you had given me documentary proof in the first place," said Donegan. "But that's water over the dam now." He bustled out.

I was grateful to Donegan personally. For it was in his power to make our second meeting much uglier, and he chose not to do so.

* Not entirely, however. No sooner had I resigned from *Time* than John William Eckenrode of Westminster, Md., wrote, offering me an excellent editorial job with his highly successful book-selling and publishing business, the Newman Bookshop and the Newman Press—a Catholic enterprise. At that time Eckenrode had never met me. He merely understood what the Hiss Case was about. I was in no position to accept his offer. I declined with the gratitude that a man feels toward someone who has taken thought of what so many never think of: how a man is to feed his family. As our capital streamed away through the chinks of the complete disorganization of our lives by the Hiss Case, I began to wonder. For two years I had earned nothing at all, and the farm was running at a loss. I cannot forget the pleasure I felt, when just after the second Hiss trial, Richard F. Lewis, Jr., the owner of Station WINC (Winchester, Va.), made it possible for me to earn my first money since I left *Time*.

XXXIX

The Grand Jury had been in recess. It had been suddenly and unexpectedly reconvened, and at a most unwelcome time. For Christmas, 1948, was just ahead with all its little personal concerns, cares and loving plans. The image that comes to my mind at once from those days is the street-corner Santa Clauses whom I used to pass on my way to and from the Federal Building, with their faces nipped above their false white whiskers which always seemed to be slipping from place. And the sound that dominates that time for me is the clang of their hand-bells, beating for alms against the ears of those who hurried by, deafened by their own troubles or indifference. In that strange overtone of Christmas, the Grand Jury had to reach its hard decision.

It had to reach it quickly. The Grand Jury had only about two weeks of official life left. If it was to act in the Hiss Case, it must do so before the midnight of December 15th, when its term of service would automatically expire. Therefore, every hour counted and the grand jurors not only spent unusually long hours in their big room during the day. They had at least one session at night.

My door was open that first morning. I watched the grand jurors file past, grave men and women, or smiling at some small exchange in a kind of human life that I had withdrawn from. As they passed, most of them glanced at me, where I sat behind my bare table, facing the open door.

I was the man who had told them that I had no direct knowledge of Communist espionage. Now I had produced evidence that I had such knowledge. I did not even hope that these men and women could grasp or disentangle the conflict of motives or the conflict of forces that had brought these things about. I could not imagine that anything in their experience could give them a clue to these complexities. I took it for granted, as did almost everyone I knew, that it was I, and not Alger Hiss, whom the Government wished to indict. I had given it ground for action against me.

XL

The relevant parts of my testimony before that Grand Jury will be found earlier in this book. But my testimony before those earnest and deeply concerned men and women was only the technical necessity of the situation. Beyond that, I was there to begin the new phase of my witness.

To make that witness, I had left the little woods alive. To make that witness, I had lived my whole life. All that most truly made me Whittaker Chambers, and no one else, made it possible and necessary for me to make that witness—all that was peculiarly myself, good and bad, by special character and experience.

It was a simple witness. It required only that a man testify to every crime, every sin, every evil, that he had committed or that had beset his life, without reserve. In terms of the political issue implicit in the Hiss Case, the struggle between Communism and this nation, only a witness so unreserved and absolute could counteract the witness made by Hiss for Communism. In terms of the moral issue involved, only a witness of that desperate integrity could counteract the equally desperate witness made by Hiss.

I must do this because only by first exposing the evil in himself could a man free himself to expose the evil that beset and secretly threatened other men. Only by showing them the evil in himself could a man make other men understand that the evil was real and immediate. Since the political form of that evil was Communism and its practices, testimony would take the form of testimony about Communism—underground apparatuses, pseudonyms, microfilm. But the testimony and the witness must not be confused. They were not the same. The testimony fixed specific, relevant crimes. The witness fixed the effort of the soul to rise above sin and crime, and not for its own sake first, but because of others' need, that the witness to sin and crime might be turned against both.

There was always the possibility that the world would see only the shocking facts of the testimony and not the meaning of the witness, that it would see in the testimony only an abhorrent man, making himself more abhorrent by every act that he confessed to. That was not the concern of the man who must make the witness. His concern must be only that out of his patient exposure of crime and sin, first and most mercilessly in himself, might rise the liberating truth for others.

To those for whom the intellect alone has force, such a witness has little or no force. It bewilders and exasperates them. It challenges them to suppose that there is something greater about man than his ability to add and subtract. It submits that that something is the soul. Plain men understood the witness easily. It speaks directly to their condition. For it is peculiarly the Christian witness.

They still hear in it, whenever it truly reaches their ears, the ring of those glad tidings that once stirred mankind with an immense hope. For it frees them from the trap of irreversible Fate at the point at which it whispers to them that each soul is individually responsible to God, that it has only to assert that responsibility, and out of man's weakness will come strength, out of his corruption incorruption, out of his evil good, and out of what is false invulnerable truth.

That is the witness that I sought to make, however feebly, before the first Grand Jury and the second Grand Jury, and which I continued in my public witness in the Hiss trials. A man can bear such witness only in shame and pain. Therefore, it is always a vivisection. No man who is capable of sin, crime and weakness can find the strength for such a vivisection within himself. That strength must come from elsewhere. That is why such witness completes a greater witness, and why, out of its ugliness and ordeal, rises the truth that fills men's souls with hope.

It is a curious fact that it was my effort to make that witness which I felt that both Grand Juries sensed. It was my testimony about the facts of the conspiracy that I despaired of making them understand because it was so alien to anything in their experience.

XLI

That failure on my part filled me with the desperation of a man trying to claw open a locked door with his fingernails. For I sensed that that same inability to grasp the character and reality of Communism and its techniques of operation had in part made it possible for the conspiracy to exist in the first place, had made it possible to thrive and reach such heights and power, had made the Hiss Case possible. It was an invincible ignorance, rooted in what was most generous in the American character, which because it was incapable of such conspiracy itself, could not believe that others practiced it. It was rooted, too, in what was most singular in the American experience, which because it had prospered so much apart from the rest of the world, could not really grasp that there was a crisis of history, and, therefore, could not grasp the nature of that crisis or why there were Communists and why they acted as they did.

If my testimony was incredible, if Americans insisted on seeing in it the reflexes of a grudge fight or a personal scandal, then the nation could not save itself (this was before Korea had taught its inexorable lessons, still not wholly understood), for there was very little time left.

I used to slip out for lunch at an Automat, in part because the Grand Jury, the press and the personnel of the Federal Building filled the nearby restaurants, but, above all, because in the anonymous Automat crowds, I was anonymous. In that scramble nobody ever glanced at me twice.

But one day a man in late middle age walked over to my table and asked if I were Whittaker Chambers. He was tall, with an austere dignity and evidently poor. He apologized twice for intruding, but, he said, he felt that he must thank me for what I was trying to do. I was embarrassed and said something to the effect that I hoped that my effort would at least be of some help to the American people. "Nothing," he said bitterly, "nothing can save the American people." Then he walked away.

XLII

I was exhausted in every way. At that point I suffered something that was less like despair than a spiritual dissolution. My unknown friend echoed the secret fear that I would not admit to my own mind. For if what he said was true, and the very fact that there could be a Hiss Case made it a thought that lurked and would not be dispelled, then any witness was for nothing, everything that I had tried to do, the suffering that I had brought upon my family, and the suffering that I had caused those against whom I had had to testify, had been for nothing. It was an absolutely pointless agony. It merely sold newspapers.

And if that was so, then the defiance of the others was actually more sensible and more humane, and their refusal to inform against one another was more honorable. They were Communists, in large part, because they believed that the other side was hopeless, incapable of understanding history, incapable of understanding its own danger, incapable of understanding the nature of the enemy while he smiled at them in contempt, incapable of understanding those who were stupid enough to try to help them. Every public failure to understand my purpose, every official effort to shut off my testimony or to penalize me for testifying, pled that the Communists were right and that I was wrong, pled that I was a fool not to know that it is a law of history that no one can save those who will not save themselves, whose plight is the proof that they have lost the instinct of self-preservation. In their defiance, the Communists were strong and free. I was not. They had not violated themselves by informing against anybody. I had.

In those days, the heavy door of the Grand Jury room was constantly opening and closing. I could hear it in my adjoining waiting room. Witnesses were constantly going in and out, in and out—Alger Hiss, Priscilla Hiss, Donald Hiss, Julian Wadleigh, and others.

In order not to see them, I had taken to closing my door all but a crack. Sometimes the F.B.I. would ask me to peer through the crack at passing witnesses to see if I could identify them. Sometimes I was summoned into the Grand Jury room while a witness was on the stand to let him look at me. I would stand just inside the door in silence. The eyes of part of the grand jurors would be fastened on my face. The eyes of the rest would be fastened on the other witness' face. No word, of course, was spoken. Then I would go out. It was like being wheeled into an operating amphitheater for a quick incision.

Each time that the door of the jury room swung shut, a single question formed in my mind: "Where is thy brother Abel?"

XLIII

All through the time when I was testifying before the Grand Juries, I lived at my mother's house on Long Island. It seemed to me a proper irony that I should have come back to pass in that tragic house what more and more certainly I felt was the last of my own life. The wonderful goodness of my mother to me through those troubled days, tactful, reticent, and unquestioning, brought us completely together again and healed that simple bond of affection that the disasters of our family had impaired.

Every night, I left the Federal Building and traveled to Pennsylvania Station by subway, riding the Long Island trains to Lynbrook, jammed in the rush-hour crowds now swollen by the Christmas shoppers. Every morning, I rose between six and seven to reach the Federal Building about half-past nine. I liked to arrive early, for in that way I avoided the press.

The press was always lurking in wait for me. When I went out to lunch, or when I left at night, the cry would go up: "Here comes Chambers!" At first I tried eluding the newsmen by going up or down staircases in areas of the Federal Building from which the press was banned. The cry changed to: "There goes Chambers!"

while the whole pack would be off to try to find my point of emergence. By dividing their forces, they soon had all exits covered, and I gave up the game. Since, in the nature of the Case, I was not free to talk about my testimony, and I soon discovered that almost anything that I said was twisted in some way by inadvertence or malice, my stock answer became: no comment. Presently, the press also grew rather tired of the game.

I never knew when I might be called before the Grand Jury. Sometimes hours passed while I waited. Sometimes I testified for only a short time; sometimes for an hour or more—or so it now seems to me. During the long hours of waiting, which the clock quartered with its loud click, I used to read. I reread the *Divine Comedy*, for the little volumes of the Dent edition, with English and Italian on the facing pages, fitted easily into my pocket, and the subject matter fitted easily into the context of my experience.

"It's very good that you're able to keep your mind on a book," said Tom Donegan, coming in on me one day. Donegan often said good morning to me, out of a natural decency, but also, I suspect, to make sure that I was really behind my closed door. We never, of course, discussed the Case in any way. But one morning, probably the day that my resignation from *Time* was announced, he told me that he kept back issues of *Time* and *Life* so that some day his son could read certain articles that had impressed him in them—*Life's* essays on the Middle Ages and the Venetian Republic and an essay in *Time* on Arnold Toynbee's philosophy of history. I smiled. I had written all of them.

Now and again, the bailiff happened in to say a few words about the weather or to offer me his newspaper. He was a man of about sixty who was more or less attendant on the Grand Jury. He sat on a straight chair in the hall beyond their door, which he locked in their absence. "Have they still got you here?" he would sometimes ask in a pleasant Irish voice that he tried to make sound sincerely incredulous. He would tell me about his wife's illness and his own rheumatism.

I wondered sometimes that no friend of the many I claimed ever penetrated to me. I wondered even more that in the whole nation, no priest, no minister, no fellow Quaker, grasped what I was trying to do and came to say: "I do not want to ask or to tell you anything. I simply wish to be with you." From the outer world, no one came.

But, from time to time, two F.B.I. agents would drop in, always two together like carabinieri. Sometimes they would ask about some point in the vast investigation by which they were checking my testimony beyond my sight and even beyond my realization. For I paid little attention to what the F.B.I. might be doing. I needed all my strength for what I had to do. Sometimes they wanted me to make a statement, covering some point in the current proceedings. Sometimes they wanted me to identify a photograph. Sometimes I felt that they had dropped in to try to read my morale from my face. Their manner toward me was always correctly neutral. But, now and again, there came from those plain, hard-working men, what no one else in the world had to give—cheering or joking words that are ropes to the soul in such a storm.

Otherwise, I was always alone. I came and went alone. I ate alone. I sat alone in the waiting room. No counsel sat with me to advise me about my testimony as was the case with other witnesses. I used to glimpse Alger Hiss, chatting, apparently calm and detached, with Edward McLean, in the waiting room at the far end of the hall. Once I suddenly came upon David Carpenter just outside the locked jury room, accompanied by bearded counsel who looked like a Montenegrin goatherd.*

The fact that I was always alone no doubt did me harm. It fed the notion, spread by the Hiss forces, that I was a weird, friendless, unknown creature who had seeped up from the lower depths, and whom nobody wanted to be seen with.

I was alone not only in the simple physical sense. More and more, I was beginning to feel like a man who is separated from the world by the fact that he is really dead although by the action of some odd torment, he still moves and talks.

A single incident spun all the nerves of that torment together and pushed me toward the brink.

XLIV

With my resignation, *Time's* concern in the libel suit had naturally ended and so had my connection with *Time's* lawyers. In Baltimore, Richard Cleveland and William Macmillan volunteered to continue

* One would-be witness whom I was not to see until the first Hiss trial was a tall, saturnine, bespectacled figure who might have been the psychiatrist in a Hollywood comedy. He was Dr. Carl Binger, who even in those early days, when, so far as I know, he had never set eyes on me, was urging Tom Donegan to let him testify to the Grand Jury that I was a psychopathic case and that my testimony was worthless. Donegan refused.

as my counsel.* But if I was to be indicted, I would need counsel in New York, if only to explain to me my rights under the law and in the end to arrange for bail. Therefore, one day when for some reason I was excused from the Federal Building I went down to Wall Street to ask the advice of Harold Medina, Jr.**

While we were talking, Medina's telephone rang. "He's here now," I heard him say. Then his voice began to rise in surprise, in an incredulous tone, and he began to make brief answers in a conversation that I could not follow. Then he handed me the telephone. "It's Nixon," he said. "The Eastman Kodak experts," said Congressman Nixon, "have just reported that the film in those undeveloped rolls was manufactured in 1945. If you got them in 1938, how do you explain that?" "It cannot be true," I said, "but I cannot explain it." "The sub-committee's going to New York tonight," said Nixon, "and we want to see you at the Commodore Hotel at nine o'clock. We're going to get to the bottom of this." "I will be there," I said. "You'd better be there," said Nixon. His voice was harsh with the just anger of a man who has placed his confidence in another man who turns out to be an impostor.

I had felt that Richard Nixon was one of the few friends who really understood what was going on. I put up the receiver slowly. As I did so, I saw Medina's eyes rest on me with a scrutinizing glance. He had learned from Nixon about the film. I knew what unpleasant thoughts must be hovering behind his eyes.

I walked out of the broadloom and heavy oak hush of his office into the teeming Wall Street crowds. "God is against me," I thought.

* Their customary fee would have been beyond my individual ability to pay at any time. Now they asked of me a fee so nominal as to be little more than a token. As my resources dwindled away in the course of two workless years, with the farm disorganized as a result of the pressures on us, Cleveland and Macmillan offered to defend the libel suit without fee, should it come to trial. In the last hours of the second Hiss trial, Richard Cleveland answered a question from the press: "If Alger Hiss is acquitted, I will spend the rest of my life vindicating Whittaker Chambers, for he is telling the truth."

** Medina advised me to get in touch with the New York law firm of Minton and McNulty. Both of these men helped me greatly through some very troubled hours. They were never called upon to act for me, and they never accompanied me while I was before the Grand Juries. But they counseled me, in my vast ignorance even of small matters of law and procedure; and my confidence in them, and simply the knowledge that they were standing by, was a great comfort.

X L V

"God is against me."

I knew that the film had not been manufactured in 1945. I knew that it had been manufactured some time prior to April, 1938. How could I dispute the opinion of an expert? If the expert said that the film had been manufactured in 1945, that was what the world would believe.

That was what the world wanted to believe, anyway. For, in fact, the world's instinctive feeling was against the little fat man who had stood up to testify for it, unasked. The world's instinctive sympathy was for the engaging man who meant to destroy it, was for Alger Hiss. He, and not I, personified the real values of a world that could not save itself; and it was he, and not I, that that world felt that it understood. "God is against me."

I toted my frozen core about the streets of the financial district. I was not going anywhere. Kierkegaard had, of course, been right: "Between man's purposes in time and God's purpose in eternity, there is an infinite qualitative difference." I had sought to bow to God's purpose with me to the point of my own destruction. By my acts in the world of time, I had succeeded only in transgressing God's purpose. By informing against the conspirators, I had misunderstood God's purpose, and God was making that clear to me in the one way that reduced my error to the limit of absurdity. He was doing so by a simple mistake on the part of the one authority that the modern mind held infallible—science. It was an irony too great for me. I felt it to be neither cruel nor unmerciful. For the quality of God's mercy in that juncture must be sensed as a function of His purposes, and, like them, could not be measured by the human mind. I knew absolute defeat.

But an irony so tremendous staggers the mind. It rocks it and will not let it rest. It clamored for an alternative reading. Suppose that I had not misunderstood God's purpose, but that God's purpose itself had changed. Suppose that it had been God's purpose to save this nation. Suppose that He had intended all that had happened until this time to be its trial and its test. Suppose, then, that He had seen in the general failure to understand what had happened a final failure of the will to live, a failure of the power of this dying world to survive, a failure of more than intelligence, a failure of the force of life itself. Suppose He meant at last to plough it in as a man might plough in a smutted crop. For there was that intuition that no life can be saved which has lost the vital power to save itself.

If that were so, and neither I nor anybody else could know whether it was or not, then I was merely a rejected instrument, lesser, but not less abject in my rejection, than Jonah before Nineveh:

The waters compassed me about even to the soul; the deep hath closed round about; the sea hath covered my head.

I went down to the lowest parts of the mountains; the bars of the earth have shut me up for ever. . . .

So I thought, walking in the Wall Street maze, a man who had nowhere to go in heaven or on earth, sometimes stepping off the narrow sidewalks, more by instinct than by sight, to avoid colliding with the busy people.

XLVI

For some reason, I had promised to call Medina back later in the afternoon. "Say," he said, "Nixon called again and wanted me to tell you that that was all a mistake. The expert was mistaken. They manufactured that kind of film in the 1930's and then discontinued it. In 1945, they began to make it again."

The relief I felt was wholly about the point of fact. I was relieved that the error had been corrected, that there need not be the ugliness of so disastrous a mistake. But my mood did not change. An error so burlesque, a comedy so gross in the midst of such catastrophe was a degradation of the spirit. It continued to shake the soul. All the suffering of which I had been the cause and witness, all the distortion and abuse of which I was the object and whose more pertinent meaning was a universal inability to distinguish true from false, right from wrong, because the false was cast in the image of the world's desire, and the true was nothing that the world could fathom, or wanted to—all that pointless pain continued to roll me under in a drowning wave.

I walked to the west side of the City, to the district around Cortlandt and Vesey Streets, where in spring rose bushes and shrubs and trays of hardware are set out to snare commuters from New Jersey. I went into a seed store and looked for a while at the seeds. Then I strolled among the sprays and insecticides. I did not find what I was looking for. I was looking for that poison one of whose ingredients is a cyanide compound. At last I asked a clerk if they stocked it. From some hiding place, he brought me the big round, tan-colored tin. I paid for it and went out.

I went to another seed house. Again the poison was not displayed. I had to ask for it. "Is there any danger in using it?" I asked. "Be very careful," said the clerk, "if you breathe enough of it, it will kill you." I thanked him.

I took my two wrapped tins to the Pennsylvania Station and put them in a lock box. Then I got ready to meet the Committee.

XLVII

The Committee was in the preposterous position of having the microfilm in its possession, but of not knowing what it was all about. The Justice Department had acted so swiftly in whisking me off under subpoena to the Grand Jury in New York that the Committee in Washington had had no chance to question me about the film. Moreover, the Committee was in a high state of disorganization at the moment. Some members had gone home to mend fences in an election year. Richard Nixon had just started on a Caribbean cruise. Warning wires from Bert Andrews and Robert Stripling caught up with his ship. By Coast Guard cutter and plane, Nixon raced back to Washington.

Now the Committee with Nixon in command was determined to question me. The Justice Department was quite as determined that the Committee should not question me.* Moreover, the Justice Department wanted custody of the film, or at least the right to examine it. The Committee was determined to hold onto it at least until it could talk to me. It feared that, if the film got out of its hands, the Hiss Case would suffer another partial or total eclipse.

Battle was joined in the train shed of the Pennsylvania Station in New York. When the congressmen and their staff debouched from their coaches, representatives of the Justice Department were waiting for them. A strident scene followed on the platform. It was adjourned to a hotel room. It grew so shrilly invective at last, the air was so blue with shouts of meddling and bad faith, that at last

* In fairness to the Justice Department, it should be noted that, with a highly controversial case before the Grand Jury, it had every reason to dread that ventilation of evidence in the press that almost invariably followed a Committee hearing. The press was one of the Committee's few tactical weapons.

Robert Stripling threw open a window. "We might as well let them hear all about it on Fifth Avenue," he said.

Some kind of compromise was eventually worked out whereby the Committee permitted the Justice Department to have photostatic enlargements of some of the microfilm and the Justice Department agreed to let the Committee interview me.

All this had been taking place while I was shopping in the seed stores. I must narrowly have missed the warring factions when I left my parcels in the lock box in Pennsylvania Station. I had no idea of the factional cross fire I was caught in. Yet, as I neared the Commodore Hotel that night, some sixth sense suddenly told me that I was under surveillance. I was brooding upon that discovery, heading for the main entrance of the hotel, when I was suddenly whisked into a taxi, and Appell at last brought me by a long detour, for the second time, to the ramp entrance of the Commodore. "Don't let them see you," said Appell as we stood together for a moment on the balcony, "but look down there." The hotel lobby was seething with newsmen.

I was hustled into an upper room, where I found Congressmen Nixon and McDowell, Robert Stripling and others. There for several hours, I testified in executive session as to the nature and history of the microfilm in the Committee's custody.

It was a rather ghostly session. The Committee was convinced that the Justice Department had it surrounded, that the hotel room was wired or that the session could be overheard by wireless devices. Conversation would begin in a low cautious key, then rise naturally to an ordinary tone, then, at a monitory glance or nod, drop down again. Certain comments were not spoken at all. They were scribbled on a scrap of paper and passed around the room. None of them was important or had any direct bearing on the testimony. The only one I remember was the first, which warned that the room was wired. They were chiefly manifestations of the incredible atmosphere in which one agency of the Government believed itself to be under siege by another, and members of the Committee's staff stood guard at the doors to challenge intruders and keep off the press. In this extraordinary form the deep conflict that had always beset the Hiss Case was made manifest.

This was my first lengthy testimony to the Committee about the espionage angles of the Case. The hearing lasted for several hours, but my testimony was necessarily far from complete. I left the session late at night with the tired knowledge that I had to be at the

Federal Building early the next morning. I took my two tins out of the lock box and carried them to my mother's house on Long Island. I placed them in my bureau drawer under some shirts. I did not unwrap them, for I did not want my mother to see what was in them, and I knew that, if she found them wrapped, she would assume that they were Christmas presents. The scene that I had witnessed that night merely made me happier to have them.

XLVIII

Even before the mistake about the microfilm, I had suffered a spiritual exhaustion (abetted, no doubt, by simple physical exhaustion, natural enough in the experience through which I was passing). With it came an acute sense of what I understand older Quakers to mean by "dryness," a drought of the soul, a sense of estrangement and of being discarded. I had felt this almost from the time that I had disclosed the copied State Department documents. With that act, and the events that resulted from it, it seemed to me as if the plane upon which I had begun my witness had been lost and that we were now on another plane, crisscrossed and violated by the tracks of worldly interests and their passions with which I had nothing to do, but in which I was caught. When I sought prayerful guidance, there was none. There was nothing. I was not only alone among men. I was alone in an absolute sense.

I could not separate the acts that I had felt that I must perform from my repugnance at having to perform them. What I had done I had done from a necessity that I could not evade, and I had done it most reluctantly. Yet I could not free my mind from an organic revulsion that I should have had to denounce those men and women, none of whom, as human beings, I would ever have raised a hand to injure. I sought only to end their power to injure others. Now my self-revulsion was whipped to torment under the mounting sense of the futility of everything that I had done. Everything cited that futility: the inability of the nation to understand the Case, the official animus against me, the struggle between the Justice Department and the Committee. It all spelled futility and added to my sense of total defeat, my sense that I had misunderstood my purpose with consequent disaster for all. I had, for a time, reached the limit of my strength.

I could not undo what I had done, nor did I wish to. But there was one act that I could perform which would still spare the others.

I could spare the others by removing myself as the only living witness against them. As men and women, they would then be free of my charges. But my witness against the conspiracy would remain. It would remain in the form of the documents and microfilm. Let men make the most of it after what instincts of survival were left them.

One night I went to my room. My mother had already retired. I wrote a number of letters. The first was to my wife. "I could not get back to you," it began. I wrote to each of my children. I urged them never to leave the Quaker meeting and never to leave the land. On that land, which I had loved and worked, my spirit must unfailingly be about them. I wrote to my mother, asking her forgiveness. I wrote to my friends, Joseph and Patricia Roesch, reminding them of their promise, given before the Hiss Case began, that, if ever anything should happen to me, they would act as guardians to my children. I begged them to take care of my wife.

Then I wrote a letter addressed simply: To All. In it I said that, of course, my testimony against Alger Hiss was the truth (time would certainly bear me out), but that the world was not ready for my testimony. I wrote that, in testifying, my purpose had always been to disclose the conspiracy, never to injure any individual man or woman. That I had been unable to do. But I could spare them the ultimate consequences of my actions and their own, by removing myself as a witness against them. My act was not suicide in the usual sense, for I had no desire to stop living. It was self-execution. I urged others to try to understand my testimony that they might be spared the day of disaster and a similar act.

It had taken me several hours to write the letters. I unwrapped the tins of chemical. It was a substance that liberated a lethal gas in the presence of moisture. The instructions for use were printed on the side of the cans in blocks of small black type. I had the same difficulty that I had had at the Commodore Hotel confrontation: I could not make out the type. The letters were blurred. But I thought that I understood the principles involved.

I poured some of the chemical in the cover of each tin. But I was afraid that the fumes might be diffused in the air of the room. I thought to concentrate them by rigging a receptacle for my head. I moistened the chemical. The fumes began to rise.

I prayed for my mother, my wife and my children. I felt that I had no right to pray for myself and did not do so. On my bureau, there was a small picture of each of my children. I took one picture in each hand to have them with me through the night. Then I lay down with my head inside the receptacle, which I closed with another damp towel draped across the front.

The fumes were somewhat sickening, but, perhaps because of them, and because I was very tired, I fell asleep almost at once. Some time during the night, I half-awoke, as if I had been stabbed in the chest and my body had jack-knifed against the pain. I suspect that at that moment the fumes had begun to take effect, that my body had bucked against them, and that when it did so, the towel fell from the front of the receptacle; the fumes poured out and air moved in.

XLIX

I awoke abruptly and painfully in the early morning. My first thought was sheer horror to find that I was still alive; my second, disgust that I had failed. The room was full of the sickening smell and haze of the heavy fumes. The towel was gone from the front of the receptacle. I dragged myself out of bed and tried to stand. I was weak and sick. I vomited and retched ten or twelve times. I was still retching, holding to the bed when my mother, hearing the sound, knocked, and, when I did not answer, opened the door. Perhaps with the memory of her other son in mind, this possibility had tormented her since the Hiss Case began.

"What is the matter? What has happened?" she asked. Because there was nothing else to do, I told her. "Oh, how could you, how could you?" she said. "The world hates a quitter. They would never forgive you." Her reaction was admirable in a way that I could not fail to respect, and yet among the nauseating fumes and the retching it had a saving humor.

I drank several cups of black coffee, somehow made my way to the train and eventually to the Federal Building. I was still weak, my head was splitting and now and again I thought that I was going to be sick. For hours, I sat alone, wondering how I could possibly testify that day. That day I was not called to testify.

L

The physical and chemical causes of my failure are simple. They involved a mistake in moistening the chemical. I do not care to go into the details. Had I been able to read the instructions, I should not have made the mistake.

Once I had made such an attempt, it was never possible to make it again. I could scarcely think of it again, or see such a can of chemical, or smell similar fumes, without a shudder of organic horror. That act had been the utmost limit of my powers with respect to those against whom I was testifying. My shudder of revulsion at my act also shook me free once for all from the conflict in my witness—the conflict between what I must do against the conspiracy and what that had forced me to do against the men and women involved. I never wavered again. I do not mean that I did not constantly feel self-loathing at having to testify against those I had known as friends or even as mere co-workers. Both my wife and I suffered that horror right through the first Hiss trial. By then, my own feeling had changed. I still had no desire to send Alger Hiss to jail. I never thought that that would serve any real purpose. The important point to me was to smash the conspiracy, not to jail Alger Hiss. But he and others had chosen the kind of war they meant to fight. They were implacable and I saw at last that there was no choice but to fight them just as implacably, though without their rancor, to the finish which their own impenitence made unavoidable.

Probably no act less extreme than mine that lonely night could have disciplined me for the public ordeal that I was to undergo in the two Hiss trials. For it disciplined me in a deeper sense. From it, I took away an indispensable certainty, the knowledge that all we ever have the right to pray to God for in the end is a strength equal to our necessity. I no longer felt absolutely alone. I no longer felt estranged. I felt a sense of gentlest solicitude playing around me, as if a father had pushed his son, for his own good, too far, as fathers will, as I have sometimes done with my own son, only to suffer at the first sign of his real weakness, self-reproach, taking form in a special tenderness.

Still, no one who has been through such an experience can be expected to be quite the same man again. He is both freer and stronger, because he is, ever after, less implicated in the world. For he has been, in his own mind at least, almost to the end of everything, and knows its worth.

L I

A few days later, the Grand Jury had summoned me in and put to me the question that it had perhaps been discussing from the first:

why had I said no when I was asked if I had direct knowledge of espionage?

I had almost the same experience that I had had during the August 25th hearing, when Nixon had put his question about my motives in accusing Alger Hiss of Communism. I paused for a moment. Then the words came effortlessly and I listened to them as if someone else were speaking. I said: "There are in general two kinds of men. One kind of man believes that God is a God of Justice. The other kind of man believes that God is a God of Mercy. I am so constituted that in any question I will always range myself upon the side of mercy." I said much more about my understanding of the difference of purpose of God and man in time and in eternity, but it is those words that I remembered so clearly that I had no difficulty in repeating them under questioning in the Hiss trials.

In that argument about God and man, spoken so strangely in that bare official room, under the presiding presence of the law, I never doubted that the jurors understood exactly what I was talking about.

LII

To the distress of this period belongs another dark, and, as it then seemed to me, completely gratuitous shadow, which dropped across us coldly ten days or so after the Grand Jury had expired, but which is an organic point of my memory of those days. My wife was to drive from the farm to meet me at the Pennsylvania Station in Baltimore. She was not there when I arrived. I telephoned the farm. No one answered. I waited an hour, and part of another hour. There was nothing to do but wait. The dread rose in me that something had happened to my wife.

When at last she appeared, she tried to smile and begged me to forgive her for coming late. Then, "dear heart," she said, "something has happened. I had an accident." "Bad?" I asked. "Yes," she said. I knew the answer before I asked the question: "You killed someone?" No, she said, but she had hit someone. A very old woman, who, it later turned out, was also deaf, had stepped from between two parked cars directly into the front of my wife's car. My wife had been driving slowly. But the woman had been knocked down, though apparently she was not fatally hurt so that the police had let my wife proceed to meet me. The woman had been taken to a hospital.

I felt the same direct horror for the victim's sake that my gentle wife was feeling, and a special horror that my wife now stood, like me, in jeopardy. I saw the children might at a stroke lose both their parents and their home. Then there was the backlash of this unhappy disaster on the Hiss Case.

The first human necessity was to see about the woman who had been hurt. I said: "We must go to the hospital at once." My wife went in first while I telephoned Richard Cleveland to tell him what had happened and to ask his advice. As I finished talking to him, my wife rejoined me. The doctors had told her that they could not really say much yet, but they did not think that there was reason to worry.

I should have known better. I should have recognized the professional rubric. But the report lifted the weight from my mind, chiefly because it was too crushing to bear. Even so, the drive home was a dark one, with my wife, from time to time, convulsively shuddering, as the memory of the moment of the accident crossed her mind. And yet, as we drove up to the barn, and I saw a state trooper standing at the end of the lane, my first thought was that the Hiss forces had prepared some new mischief for us. That, coming on top of everything else, filled me with a rush of outrageous anger.

"That woman your wife hit," said the state trooper to me, "she died." My wife's knees buckled and she began to slide against me to the ground. The trooper and I raised her. She beat her forehead with her hand. "Oh, God, why?" she said in the voice of a pleading child. "Why, God, why?"

"We don't know," said the trooper gently. "We don't know why."

We went into the house. The children stood tense, white-faced and silent, staring at their distracted mother. They already knew what had happened. The trooper telephoned his headquarters. "Both the parties are here," he said, "and we're starting back now." He explained that he would drive us to the state police barracks in Pikesville, just northwest of Baltimore. There a municipal police car would pick us up and take us to Baltimore's northwestern police station. I called Richard Cleveland and asked him to be there to post bond so that my wife would not have to spend the night in prison.

We got into the state trooper's car and started back to Baltimore. My wife and I sat absolutely silent on the back seat. From time to time, the short-wave radio would come in with a harsh crackle and a metallic voice would utter instructions. There had been a holdup and a pursuit was in progress. While my wife and I, each with his own thoughts listened, we heard something like this: "Cars 28, 29, 30, proceed to number 9999 Fullerton Avenue. This is a tobacco store. There has been a holdup. Suspect is proceeding west on Fullerton Avenue in a green Chevrolet sedan. He is armed. Cars 28, 29, 30 proceed to number 9999. . . ."

The radio would crackle and sputter as if space itself were crashing. The same metallic voice would repeat the orders; then add: "Here is a description of the suspect. Five feet four. Hair blonde. Eyes blue. Wearing gray fedora hat, gray suit, brown overcoat, belted. Five feet four. Hair blonde. Eyes blue. . . ."

The ensuing silence of space would be suddenly broken by a single indecipherable sentence uttered in a perfectly casual voice: "Jack, the man you were to meet will not be there. Jack, the man you were to meet will not be there." The night was filled invisibly with human anguish which the genius of the human mind made audible to our anguished ears. All the thirty miles to Pikesville, we listened at crackling intervals to the stages of the pursuit of the green Chevrolet sedan, until at last the suspect ("he is armed") deserted it somewhere beyond Baltimore as the pursuit grew hot. In the last broadcast we heard, he was at bay in a group of farm buildings. The police were closing in.

The Pikesville headquarters was silent except for a ticking clock. We waited in a bare room for the Baltimore police to come for us. I could only press my wife's hand which was cold with that bloodless coldness of someone who is suffering a heart attack.

The Baltimore policeman looked at us impersonally and seated us in the back of his car. I was shocked to learn that we were racing through the dark roads of suburban Baltimore, not to the northwestern police station but to the northern police station. Cleveland, therefore, would go to the wrong station.

Suddenly, we swung into the courtyard of the police station and drew up with other police cars. We walked into a room which seemed to me glaring with light. It was filled with police and unidentifiable people, whom I did not even clearly see. A magistrate was sitting at a high desk. The policeman led my wife up to it.

From the anonymous onlookers of the police court, Richard Cleveland and Mrs. Cleveland suddenly broke and hurried up to my wife. They stood on either side of her. A bondsman, who had already retired for the night, had got out of bed and come down to post bond for my wife. In a few seconds she was free.

Outside, photographers of the Baltimore *News-Post* and *Sun* were lying in wait. Before the *News-Post* cameraman could snap his picture, Mrs. Cleveland threw her coat over my wife's head. Cleveland, white with rage, charged the *Sun's* photographer exactly as a bull goes after a dog.* We drove my wife to the Clevelands' to spend the night (she had to appear in court the next morning). Cleveland drove me back to Westminster so that the children would not be alone.

My wife was quickly exonerated of any responsibility for the accident. We were fully covered by $15 or $20 thousand worth of liability insurance. But a Baltimore lawyer filed suit against my wife and me for $50 thousand damages in the name of the unfortunate woman's relatives. Our insurance company would not settle for more than the four or five thousand. The Baltimore lawyer prepared to go through with his suit. The possibility of this harassing court action was always over us until, a day or two after the first Hiss trial, the claim was settled.

To my wife and me, this tragic episode seemed proof that there was no depth of the abyss that we were not to sound.

LIII

In those days, came the first of a series of letters that I was to receive throughout the Hiss Case. They came almost weekly and, in the depths of the Case, sometimes twice a week. After Hiss's conviction, they came at longer intervals and at last stopped.

They were never signed. They were written in an angular hand and contained just three words: "The ninety-first Psalm."

LIV

Sitting alone in the witness waiting room, I did not know how the Government proposed to proceed against me, and I never then, or at any subsequent time, made the slightest effort to find out. I went through both Hiss trials without knowing. Like everybody else, I first learned from the press, some time after Alger Hiss's conviction, that the Justice Department had no plans to take action against me. That is all that I ever learned. Until then, I had heard, without brooding on them (for I needed all my strength to do what I had to do), reports to the exactly opposite effect.

But, in the Grand Jury days, whatever the Government's feelings

* All the press, it should be noted, handled this story with great restraint and propriety.

about me, it was hampered by a difficult legal situation, in the face of mounting evidence against Hiss. If it insisted on indicting me, it could not indict Alger Hiss, for one of the two indispensable witnesses against him* would then be destroyed. Justice, in the most technical meaning of the word, might be satisfied by my indictment. But common sense, the problems of the country's security, and perhaps something more, must be somewhat defeated by action against a man (myself) who, despite an acknowledged offense in seeking to shield those whom he pitied, had at last done everything in his power to disclose the Communist conspiracy; had begun to do so nine years in the past. Action against me must, in fact, raise the whole invidious question of why my original information, repeated to a President by other warning voices, had never been acted upon.

I did not then know how thoroughly and tirelessly the F.B.I. had been checking my testimony and other information or what progress it had made. I did not know that the weight of verifiable evidence, and the corroborative testimony and statements of witnesses, like Julian Wadleigh,** Franklin Victor Reno and "Keith," was becoming so overwhelming as to convince important figures in the Justice Department that Hiss was guilty and to leave them almost no choice but to seek his indictment.

I did not know then, either, that, at the end of the week of December 7th, with only a few days of its term left to go, the Grand Jury reported that it could not find an indictment against Hiss. The Grand Jury had examined the copied State Department documents and had heard the witnesses. But Hiss still coolly denied that he had ever given me any confidential documents or that he had any knowledge of how they were typed or that he had ever seen me after 1937. His Woodstock typewriter (on which the documents had been copied) was missing.† The jury knew that the documents had been

* The other was my wife.

** It is worth noting that the Hiss defense, which tried to work up a highly implausible and easily disprovable theory that Wadleigh, and not Hiss, was the source of the copied State Department documents and microfilm, never included David Carpenter in their effort to shift guilt. And that despite the fact that Carpenter had recruited Wadleigh into the Soviet apparatus and was much more constantly in contact with him than I was. But then, Wadleigh had broken with Communism, and was therefore its enemy, while Carpenter was still a Communist, employed at that time by the *Daily Worker*.

† It was not to make its appearance until early in the first Hiss trial when the defense produced it with a flourish in court. The motives of the defense in producing the typewriter have seemed cryptic to many people. Actually, Prose-

copied on a Woodstock. They had no evidence that the documents had been copied on Hiss's Woodstock.

The old Woodstock had been given to Priscilla Hiss by her father, Thomas Fansler, who had been an insurance broker in Philadelphia. Working under high pressure on that critical week-end, the F.B.I. in Philadelphia uncovered specimens of typing made on the Woodstock when it was in Mr. Fansler's possession, and, from elsewhere, a letter typed on the same machine by Priscilla Hiss while it was in the Hisses' possession. The type face on the newly discovered documents and the type face on the copied State Department documents was identical. Evidence could scarcely be more conclusive. It was a stroke in the great tradition of the F.B.I.

The commotion of these activities reached me in my waiting room only as the touch of tensions whose nature I could not trace or define.

Then, on the afternoon of December 14th, two special agents of the F.B.I. dropped in for a minute to see me. For the first time, they spoke in a vaguely different way. "Things seem to be clearing up in there, don't they?" said one of them, nodding toward the Grand Jury. I did not have the slightest idea of what he was talking about.

L V

All through the morning of December 15th, the heavy door of the Grand Jury room kept opening and closing. There was a constant coming and going in the corridor. It was the last day of that Grand Jury's term. Someone told me that Alex Campbell, the chief of the Criminal Division of the Department of Justice, was in the Grand Jury room. I had heard that Alex Campbell had taken his post just prior to the November election. When everyone had expected a Democratic defeat, and few others wanted to take the job, he had had faith in the President. With the red herring in mind, I thought only that the presence of Campbell before the Grand Jury boded little good for me.

The very reverse was true. The evidence had convinced Alex Campbell that Alger Hiss was guilty. He had spoken to Hiss in the presence of his counsel, Edward McLean. "Mr. Hiss," he

cutor Thomas F. Murphy left them almost no alternative. For in his opening address he made it clear that he knew the defense had the machine and Lloyd Paul Stryker could scarcely keep silent about it without causing the jurors to feel that he was concealing something.

said, "I am convinced that you committed espionage. You have seen Chambers and the others go in and talk. If you do so, too, it will be better for you."

"What you have to say, Mr. Campbell," said Hiss, "is not of the slightest interest to me."

"I am also convinced," said Alex Campbell quietly, "that you committed perjury."

Hiss was called into the Grand Jury room. Tom Donegan and Raymond P. Whearty, the special assistants to the Attorney General, were presenting the Government's data. "Mr. Hiss," said Donegan, "you have probably been asked this question before, but I'd like to ask the question again. At any time, did you, or Mrs. Hiss in your presence, turn any documents of the State Department, or of any other Government organization, over to Whittaker Chambers?"

"Never," said Hiss, "excepting, I assume, the title certificate to the Ford."

A juror asked a question. "To nobody else did you ever turn over documents? To any other person?"

"And to no other unauthorized person," said Hiss.

"Mr. Hiss," said Donegan, "Mr. Chambers has testified that he obtained typewritten copies of official State Department documents from you."

"I know that," said Hiss.

He was asked: "Did you ever see Mr. Chambers after you went into the State Department?"

HISS: I do not believe that I did. I cannot swear that I did not see him some time, say, in the fall of 1936. . . ."

MR. DONEGAN: Can you say definitely that you did not see him after January, 1937?

HISS: Yes, I think that I can definitely say that.

By his answers, Hiss had perjured himself on two counts.

Then Hiss was shown the specimens of typewriting from the files of Mrs. Hiss's father and the letter typewritten by Mrs. Hiss. It was pointed out to him that the documents had been written on his Woodstock typewriter. He was asked if he could explain how it happened that the fifty pages of copied State Department documents also came to be written on the same machine.

"I am amazed," Hiss answered coolly, "and until the day I die, I shall wonder how Whittaker Chambers got into my house to use my typewriter."

With a terrible sound the hundred days ended, as grand jurors laughed.

L V I

Tom Donegan brought a stranger into the waiting room. "Mr. Alex Campbell," he said briefly. Campbell looked past me and shook hands. Then he went out. "There doesn't seem to be any reason why you should stay around here," said Donegan. "Just go to the F.B.I. on the sixth floor at eleven o'clock tomorrow morning." The sixth floor was the criminal division of the F.B.I.

I telephoned William McNulty, my attorney. "I believe I've just been indicted," I said. "Will you be on hand with a bondsman at eleven o'clock tomorrow morning? I'll need your help in going through this business."

I dreaded the details, the mugging and fingerprinting, the press, the photographers. I knew that, in the struggle that must now presumably fill the rest of my life, an indictment set me far back, that all the ground lost by it would have to be regained before I could regain even the weak point in the Case where I had stood before. But one thing I did not believe. I did not believe that the truth could be permanently defeated. I believed that, in prison, a man like me would be far more dangerous to those powers that sought to preserve the conspiracy than he was when free. For there is in men a craving for justice that ultimately cannot endure wrong. In prison, I would be the rallying symbol for all those who sensed that justice had been outraged, and I had no doubt that there would be thousands of them. My task was patiently and firmly to endure.

When I opened the door, I could hear that my mother was playing the radio in her bedroom. I called to her so that, if she heard me moving about, she would not be frightened. The radio snapped off. I heard her running across the room. "Oh, I'm so thankful," I heard her say, "so thankful."

"About what?" I asked. Her words seemed to make it more difficult to break the news I had for her.

She was halfway down the stairs now and could see my face. "You mean," she asked incredulously, "you don't know that Alger Hiss has been indicted?"

She threw her arms around me. I said something about Alger's mother. "Oh, I do think of her," said my mother. "Poor woman! Oh, poor woman!"

14

1949

I

The years changed. 1948 passed into 1949. Among the years, 1949 is to me the dead year, a dreariness differentiated chiefly by spasms of a public pang. It opened with a new Grand Jury sitting in New York. It ended while for the second time a trial of Alger Hiss was dragging toward its close. It was the year in which I endured the ordeal of preparation and public testimony in the Hiss trial that was for me the probation, which must set the seal of integrity upon all my earlier acts.

In the first months of the new year, I continued my testimony before the new Grand Jury. I had already begun with the F.B.I. what amounted to a total recall of my life. It amassed all that I could remember about Communism and Communists in the United States and elsewhere. In report-form it made a fair-sized book.*

Two special agents of the F.B.I., usually Tom Spencer and Frank Plant, worked with me on this project. We worked together for several months, from about ten o'clock in the morning until five o'clock in the evening, sending out for our lunch of coffee and sandwiches, which we ate at our desk. Merely the effort of such a total recollection is wearing. The recollection itself is exhausting. The great intelligence, tact and understanding with which Spencer and Plant brought me through that difficult experience, more than anything else, first moved my respect for the methods of the F.B.I. and won my trust on the human level.

Meanwhile, the immense investigation that preceded and accompanied the Hiss trials was going on. In time, there was probably no field office of the F.B.I. in the country that was not somehow engaged in that investigation. I could not fail to be impressed by the energy with which the organization as a whole, and the agents individually, threw themselves into their work. Wadleigh and Reno had early confirmed those parts of my story that concerned them. Other witnesses confirmed more. On the slim chance that my vague recollection of his real name might be right, the F.B.I. began to look for "Keith." In a few hours they had found him. To the Grand Jury and the F.B.I., that highly important witness corroborated my testimony, adding some facts that I had forgotten or never known.

On the chance that I might be able to locate the former resi-

* When we finished, Tom Spencer asked me if there was anything that I wanted to add. I took his pen, and, at the end of the report, wrote: *E quindi uscimmo a riveder le stelle* (And so we emerged again to see the stars). This literary flourish may seem more understandable when the context of that experience is remembered, and when it is recalled that these words are the last line of Dante's *Inferno* and the last line of Marx's *Capital.*

dence of the underground photographer, known only as "Felix," two F.B.I. agents and I sloshed one night around the snowy streets of Baltimore. As I have written earlier, I had glimpsed the apartment house where Felix had lived only once, for a few minutes, ten years or more before. I reconstructed as well as I could where I had then sat in a parked automobile, and sighting a block of apartments, said to the agents: "Try there." Within twelve hours, the F.B.I. had located Felix' old apartment, had discovered that his full name was Felix Inslerman, and had found him near Schenectady, N. Y.

There was a man with whom Hiss and someone else had attempted espionage dealings. I believed that the man was dead and said so. The F.B.I., checking back on my lead, found him alive. To the Grand Jury and the F.B.I., he confirmed my account of his dealings with Alger Hiss and others.

There were no "breaks" in the Hiss Case such as are common in more routine cases. The Communist conspiracy was too effective. The events involved had happened too long before. Time had effaced or changed too much. The far-flung investigation was a matter of daily grind varied by flashes of great probative intelligence. It is not my intention to discuss the details even of that part of it which I could observe. Much of it was beyond my sight. I will merely note that I myself was an object of its most intensive probing. Everything that I had said or done, every scrap of information I gave, every charge or rumor against me had to be laboriously checked and rechecked. In time, I came to feel that the F.B.I. knew much more about me than I knew about myself.

In time, too, the scores of agents * whom I was constantly dealing with began to take form for me as human beings. I began to know about their gripes and special interests, their families, their troubles and their hopes. It is in those human terms that I mean to speak of the F.B.I. and its agents. For it is in those terms, which few ever think of, rather than its organizational expertness, which everybody knows about, that my memory of the F.B.I. is most personal and most grateful. It reached its pitch in the days of my testimony in the two Hiss trials.

In the morning before I went into court, at the lunch recess, in the evening, when I had finished testifying for the day and simply sat still for an hour or so to drain Lloyd Paul Stryker or Claude Cross out of my system, the agents, singly, or in twos and threes, would

* My contact with the F.B.I. has always been at the agent level. The one administrator I know is the assistant chief of a field office.

come to sit with me. By their comments and conjectures on the progress of the fight, by gossip, by banter or a few considerate words quietly dropped—the immemorial, simple ways by which men have always kept up one another's morale in trouble, they kept up mine. They were like sturdier brothers in those days. I could catalogue their names. They would be meaningless to others. They know who they were and what they did, and why, when I hear that someone, like Max Loewenthal, has been shaken by fears that the F.B.I. is a potentially dangerous secret police, I smile, suspecting that, in general, such fears measure the F.B.I.'s effectiveness in the nation's interest. For how can those men be dangerous to the nation who, as at present headed and organized, are, in fact, the nation itself, performing its self-protective function?

II

The tremendous investigation was paced by the tremendous public defamation of me. I do not believe that there is a scrap of real evidence to show that the Communist Party inspired and from time to time stepped up the voltage of that vilification. Those who insist plaintively on evidence against a force whose first concern is that there shall be no evidence against it, must draw what inferences they please. Few who know anything about Communists will doubt what cloaca fed that bilge across the land.

It was avidly blotted up by much more articulate, widespread and socially formidable circles. In accusing Hiss of Communism, I had attacked an architect of the U.N., and the partisans of peace* fell upon me like combat troops. I had attacked an intellectual and a "liberal." A whole generation felt itself to be on trial—with pretty good reason, too, for its fears probably did not far outrun its guilt. From their roosts in the great cities, and certain collegiate eyries, the left-wing intellectuals of almost every feather (and that was most of the vocal intellectuals in the country) swooped and hovered in flocks like fluttered sea fowl—puffins, skimmers, skuas and boobies—and gave vent to hoarse cries and defilements. I had also accused a "certified gentleman,"** and the "conspiracy of the gentlemen" closed

* Some of them had more personal ties to Hiss. "Imagine," said a U.N. administrator to a friend of mine, "the embarrassment of all the people here whom Alger Hiss recommended for their jobs."

** For this term, which I cannot better, and for the next, I am indebted to an anonymous writer in the *Freeman*, who was discussing, not the Hiss Case, but more current manifestations.

its retaliatory ranks against me. Hence that musk of snobbism that lay rank and discrepant over the pro-Hiss faction. Hence that morganatic bond between the forces of the left and the forces of the right (a director of a big steel company, the co-owner of a great department store, a figure high in the Republican organization, come quickly to mind) which made confusing common cause in exculpating Hiss by defaming Chambers.

There was another, less tangible bond between those circles which, together, accounted for a large part of the articulate American middle class. Both groups lived fairly constantly in the psychoanalyst's permanent shadow, and few articles of furniture were less dispensable to them than a couch. And they shared a common necessity. Since my charge against Alger Hiss was that he had been a Communist and a Soviet agent, and there was, besides the Grand Jury's perjury indictment, a good deal of clear and simple evidence that he had been, something, anything at all must be believed rather than the common-sense conclusion. The old masters—Freud and the author of the *Psychopathia Sexualis*—were conned again. No depravity was too bizarre to "explain" Chambers' motives for calling Hiss a Communist. No hypothesis was too preposterous, no speculation too fantastic, to "explain" how all those State Department documents came to be copied on Hiss's Woodstock typewriter. Only the truth became too preposterous to entertain. The great smear campaign was the real red herring in the Hiss Case.

Meanwhile, there sifted in on me warnings that the Hiss Case would never come to trial (repeated postponements made this seem all too probable), that the Government meant to throw the trial, that the Government's prosecutor would be fixed, and infinite variations. I crowded most of these warnings out of my mind, for a man has only so much strength, and I could not have gone on if I had given them active credence. Those that I could not quite ignore, I discounted. But even when I had discounted them to the limit of human mischief and imaginative folly, there still remained something that I could not discount. Neither could I be sure exactly what it was. Its contours became somewhat clearer in the antics of the first Hiss trial. But in the bleak spring of 1949, I did not believe that there was an outside chance for justice in the Hiss Case. It seemed to me that nothing short of a minor miracle could save the Hiss Case for the nation. And, in fact, something was in store that no action of my mind could have foreseen.

One day, Tom Spencer broke into our routine talks to say that the Government's prosecutor for the Hiss trial had been chosen. "Who?" I asked quietly, for I knew that almost everything hinged on that choice. "Tom Murphy," said Tom Spencer. The name meant nothing to me. "Is it good?" I asked. "It is good," said Spencer.

I did not see Thomas F. Murphy until shortly before the first Hiss trial. He had scarcely undertaken the case before he had to undergo an operation. Once he came down to the farm, together with a trio of F.B.I. agents, to talk to my wife for the first time, and to discuss, among other things, the simple mechanics of a trial of which my wife and I knew almost nothing—where the jury sat, what the judge did,* what the lawyers did. Later, I talked with Murphy briefly in the Federal Building. "Do you really believe that you can stand it," he asked me, "with all those people sitting there and the press writing down everything?" "I think you will find," I said, "that I am not in any way a coward." Murphy turned and stared sadly out of the window (he knew much more about trials than I did). "No," he said at last, "I don't believe you are." Among all the other doubts and pressures of that time, his words puzzled me and I left him in a deep depression.

During the first Hiss trial, Murphy and I had no direct communication. What I saw of him, I saw only in the seven days, more or less, when I was on the stand. The experience was too new to me, and I was kept too busy plucking harpoons out of my skin, to form any opinion about Murphy. In the whirling atmosphere of that courtroom,** with Lloyd Paul Stryker spinning and flailing like a dervish, and Judge Kaufman snapping "Denied" to most of the Government motions, the last thing I took much thought of was the Government's prosecutor. But his summation to the jury impressed me greatly. More important, it seems to have impressed the jury.

Then, between the Hiss trials, Murphy visited the farm again. To me he seemed almost another man. His grasp of the intricacies of the Hiss Case was now firm and supple. He was at ease with it with the relaxed authority of a man who has mastered an art and now wants to practice it. He understood the Case, not only as a problem in law. He understood it in its fullest religious, moral, human and historical meaning. I saw that he had in him one of the rarest of human seeds—the faculty for growth, combined with a faculty al-

* That was not to be of much help to me. After half an hour on the stand I thought of Judge Samuel H. Kaufman: Of course, I know nothing about judges, but do they *all* act like this?

** In the second Hiss trial Judge Henry W. Goddard presided over his orderly court with complete authority and dignity.

most as rare—a singular magnanimity of spirit. Into me, battered and gray of mood after a year of private struggle and public mauling, he infused new heart, not only because of what he was, but because he was the first man from the Government who said to me in effect: "I understand." I needed no more.

The whole nation now gratefully knows that six-foot-four, stalwart figure, with the mild but firm face, and the moustache. It knows what he has done. It watched him do it. I cannot add to that knowledge, except to point out this.

When Thomas Murphy decided, somewhat reluctantly, to take the Hiss Case, almost nobody had ever heard of him. Within the Justice Department he was known as a man who had never lost a case. Otherwise, he was a man who jostled no one, for he seemed without ambition beyond his immediate work. And he was so little caught in the enveloping atmosphere of politics that he was presently discovered not even to belong to a political club.* Yet when the historic moment came, Murphy was waiting there at the one point in time and place where he could bring all that he was and all that life had made him to bear with decisive effect for the nation.

It is inconceivable to me that any other man could have replaced him. That is why I can think of his role only in this way: "It pleased God to have in readiness a man."

III

Those were the forces—Thomas Murphy, Richard Nixon,** the men of the F.B.I.—who, together with the two grand juries and Tom

* Murphy's success in convicting Alger Hiss seemed for a time to have ended his career in Government. After the second Hiss trial, he was called to the White House and officially thanked. When the next appointment to a judgeship came up, Murphy was passed over. It was said that he did not have sufficient political backing. Murphy resigned from the Justice Department to become Police Commissioner of New York City. Then the appointment of Judge Medina to the Appellate bench left a vacancy in the United States District Court. Once more, it seemed as if Murphy would be passed over. The White House considered Lloyd Paul Stryker, Hiss's trial lawyer, for the new judgeship. Only when powerful Democratic forces pointed out the unhappy impression that such an appointment might leave on the nation, and that the Senate might refuse to confirm, did the White House yield and appoint Murphy a judge.

** Senator Nixon's role did not end with his dash back to the United States to rally the House Committee when the microfilm was in its hands. His testimony before the Grand Jury that indicted Alger Hiss is a significant part of the Hiss Case. Throughout the most trying phases of the Case, Nixon and his

Donegan and the two trial juries, finally won the Hiss Case for the nation. It is important to look hard at them for a moment, and this book would not be complete without such a glance. For the contrast between them and the glittering Hiss forces is about the same as between the glittering French chivalry and the somewhat tattered English bowmen who won at Agincourt. The inclusive fact about them is that, in contrast to the pro-Hiss rally, most of them, regardless of what they had made of themselves, came from the wrong side of the railroad tracks. I use the expression as the highest measure of praise, as Lincoln noted that God must love the common people; He made so many of them. For, in America, most of us begin on the wrong side of the railroad tracks. The meaning of America, what made it the wonder of history and the hope of mankind, was that we were free not to stay on the wrong side of the railroad tracks. If within us there was something that empowered us to grow, we were free to grow and go where we could. Only, we were not free ever to forget, ever to despise our origins. They were our roots. They made us a nation.

No feature of the Hiss Case is more obvious, or more troubling as history, than the jagged fissure, which it did not so much open as reveal, between the plain men and women of the nation, and those who affected to act, think and speak for them. It was, not invariably, but in general, the "best people" who were for Alger Hiss and who were prepared to go to almost any length to protect and defend him. It was the enlightened and the powerful, the clamorous proponents of the open mind and the common man, who snapped their minds shut in a pro-Hiss psychosis, of a kind which, in an individual patient, means the simple failure of the ability to distinguish between reality and unreality, and, in a nation, is a warning of the end.

It was the great body of the nation, which, not invariably, but in general, kept open its mind in the Hiss Case, waiting for the returns to come in. It was they who suspected what forces disastrous to the nation were at work in the Hiss Case, and had suspected that

family, and sometimes his parents, were at our farm, encouraging me and comforting my family. My children have caught him lovingly in a nickname. To them, he is always "Nixie," the kind and the good, about whom they will tolerate no nonsense. His somewhat martial Quakerism sometimes amused and always heartened me. I have a vivid picture of him, in the blackest hour of the Hiss Case, standing by the barn and saying in his quietly savage way (he is the kindest of men): "If the American people understood the real character of Alger Hiss, they would boil him in oil."

they were at work long before there was a Hiss Case, while most of the forces of enlightenment were poohpoohing the Communist danger and calling every allusion to it a witch hunt. It was they who, when the battle was over, first caught its real meaning.* It was they who almost unfailingly understood the nature of the witness that I was seeking to make, as I have tested beyond question whenever I have talked to any group of them. And it was they who, in the persons of the men I have cited, produced the forces that could win a struggle whose conspicuous feature is that it was almost without leadership. From the very outset, I was in touch with that enormous force, for which I was making the effort, and from which I drew strength. Often I lost touch with it or doubted it, cut off from it in the cities, or plunged in the depths of the struggle. But when I came back to it, it was always there. It reached me in letters and messages of encouragement and solicitude, understanding, stirring, sometimes wringing the heart. But even when they did not understand, my people were always about me. I had only to look around me to see them—on the farms, on the streets, in homes, in shops, in the day coaches of trains. My people, humble people, strong in common sense, in common goodness, in common forgiveness, because all felt bowed together under the common weight of life.

And at the very end of the Hiss Case, I heard their speaking voice, like themselves, anonymous, and speaking not to me as an individual, but to me in the name of all those who made the struggle.

On the afternoon of January 21, 1950, one of the wire services first telephoned me in Maryland to say that the jury in New York had found Alger Hiss guilty of perjury as charged on both counts. I had not turned away from the phone before it rang again. An excited voice, apparently that of an elderly man, asked if I were Whittaker Chambers. In turn, I asked who he was. "Nobody. It doesn't matter," said the voice. "But I know that your telephone will be ringing every minute now and I had to reach you first. I had to say: 'God bless you! God bless you! Oh, God bless you!'" He hung up.

"What is the matter?" my wife called, seeing me turn away from the people who were already filling the kitchen, and walk quickly into another room.

* Enormously helped by a book, *Seeds of Treason*, co-authored by Ralph de Toledano and Victor Lasky, which first enabled the nation to see the Hiss Case as a connected whole.

15

TOMORROW

AND TOMORROW

AND TOMORROW

I

I have been seeing a good deal of the stars of late because, several times, in the course of writing this book, I have changed my working hours in an effort to fix the schedule by which I could best concentrate for the longest continuous time. Through this late fall of 1951, I have been rising, as a rule, about four o'clock in the morning, leaving the house at five and returning to it about seven o'clock at night. Thus, I see both the evening and the morning stars.

In the evening, in the east, the Pleiades are glittering in their faint way in the shoulder of the Bull. But Orion has not yet cleared the horizon for his nightly hunting with the big and little Dogs. In the morning, when I leave the sleeping house, Jupiter hangs tremendous in the east, while, by the nightly turn of the earth, Orion has swung far to the west with what I take to be Venus not far off. For I am not even an amateur star-gazer and know the more conspicuous constellations chiefly as a countryman to whom they are a rough timepiece and a guide, telling him something about the hour of the night and his direction if he is unsure in the dark.

But what little I know of the stars I have passed on to my son over the years. When we go together to secure the ewes in the orchard—our last chore on late summer nights—we often stop to watch through the apple trees the great sky triangle tipped by the evening stars: Vega in Lyra, Altair in Aquila and Deneb, burning in the constellation of the Swan. Sometimes, I draw my son's eye to the constellation Hercules, especially to the great nebula dimly visible about the middle of the group. Now and again, I remind him that what we can just make out as a faint haze is another universe—the radiance of fifty thousand suns whose light had left its source thirty-four thousand years before it brushes the miracle of our straining sight.

Those are the only statistics that I shall ever trouble my son with. I trouble him with them at all because I know that he and all his generation may soon bear witness of a kind before which every other shrinks in humility; and I want him to have a standard as simple as stepping into the dark and raising his eyes whereby to measure what he is and what he is not against the order of reality.

I want him to see for himself upon the scale of the universes that God, the soul, faith, are not simple matters, and that no easy or ingenuous view of them is possible. I want him to remember that God Who is a God of Love is also the God of a world that includes the atom bomb and virus, the minds that contrived and use or those that suffer them; and that the problem of good and evil is not more simple than the immensity of worlds. I want him to understand that evil is not something that can be condescended to, waved aside or smiled away, for it is not merely an uninvited guest, but lies coiled *in foro interno* at home with good within ourselves. Evil can only be fought.

I want him to know, in that dark, continuous struggle, that it is by his soul, and his soul alone, that he may sometimes glimpse, if only roughly, the hour of the night and his direction in it. I want him to understand, when he lifts up his eyes, that against the range of space and cold his soul, and his soul alone, is life for which, in the morning and the evening, he gives thanks to God to Whom it ties him. I want him to know that it is his soul, and his soul alone, that makes it possible for him to bear, without dying of his own mortality, the faint light of Hercules' fifty thousand suns.

For myself, I now view the stars with the curiosity of any man who wonders in what form his soul may soon be venturing among them. For the Hiss Case has turned my wife and me into old people—not a disagreeable condition. But we who used to plan in terms of decades, now find a year, two years, the utmost span of time we can take in. Repeatedly, in this last autumn of unseasonable warmth, my wife has drawn me out to stand with her among our gardens, once so pleasant, now overgrown with weeds, because, as we say, neither of us really fooling the other, we no longer can find time to tend them. It is not time that we cannot find. Repeatedly, my wife has planned what we must do to bring them back to life. We do not do it. I do not think we shall unless time itself can lift from us the sense that we have lived our lives and the rest is a malingering.

This, which we both feel, we force ourselves seldom to entertain as a thought. For, with us, discipline must take the place of energy in that life to which it is our children, of course, who bind us. It is for them that we run through the routines of our days, outwardly cheerful, for we count among our blessings the fact that, a very few years more, and we shall be safely dispensable. Our trouble is that the smallest things now have power to disturb our precarious self-discipline—an unkindness, a meanness, or, on a greater scale, a sudden insight into the smugness of the world before its vast peril, or an occasional reminder that we are still beset by enemies that are powerful and vindictive. Then it becomes an effort to sustain those formal good spirits that are our hourly improvisation—the necessary grace notes to lead the ear away from the ground-bass which is our reality. For there are kinds of music that the world should not hear.

In the countryside, people are already beginning to plan for the spring which they can sense, like a thaw-wind, just beyond the drift of winter. It is three years since I have been able to plough a field on this farm. I have sometimes thought that, if, in this coming spring, my son and I could simply work and seed a field and watch it sprout, an absolute healing would follow. Or my wife and I have sometimes said that a year, or even six months, completely unharried by the world and its agencies, would refit us for struggle. For it is a season of peace that, like the world, we most crave, and, like the world, are most unlikely to get. Failing that, our spirits fall back upon an ultimate petition where our fears and hopes are one.

One of the tenderest of Greek fables tells how the gods decided to go down to the earth as beggars to try the charity of men. The god, Hermes, clad in rags, knocked at many prosperous doors and was driven from each. Toward evening, he came to the meanest door of all, a mere hut, where two old people, Philemon and Baucis, his wife, tended a few vines and milked their goats. Hermes knocked there. Because his need touched them, the old people took him in. They shared their meal with him, and, at night, let him sleep on the floor before their fire, trusting to their poverty and their age to prevent any harm that the beggar might intend.

In the morning, Hermes asked each of the old people to name his most secret wish, supposing that it would be for longer life, gold or great flocks. The dearest wish of each turned out to be the same—that both might die, as they had lived, together, that neither might die first, for neither could endure to face what remained of a life that would be unendurable without the other.

The god, now gleaming through his rags, raised his staff—the caduceus with the twined snakes, interlacing good and evil. Where Philemon and Baucis had stood, two trees rustled up whose branches met and touched when the wind blew.

In a world grown older and colder, my wife and I have no dearer wish for ourselves—when our time shall have come, when our children shall be grown, when the witness that was laid on us shall have lost its meaning because our whole world will have borne a more terrible witness or it will no longer exist.

INDEX

C

D

E

F

G

N

O

P

Q

R

S

T

U

V

W

Y

Z